MW00997994

THE MODERN CRUISING SAILBOAT

THE **MODERN CRUISING SAILBOAT**

A Complete Guide to Its Design, Construction, and Outfitting

CHARLES J. DOANE

INTERNATIONAL MARINE / McGRAW-HILL EDUCATION
Camden, Maine • New York • Chicago • San Francisco
Athens • London • Madrid • Mexico City • Milan
New Delhi • Singapore • Sydney • Toronto

1 2 3 4 5 6 7 8 9   QPD QPD   3 2 1 0 9

© 2010 text and illustrations by Charles J. Doane
All rights reserved. The publisher takes no responsibility
for the use of any of the materials or methods described in this book,
nor for the products thereof. The name "International Marine" and the
International Marine logo are trademarks of The McGraw-Hill Companies.
Printed in the United States of America. Except as permitted under the
United States Copyright Act of 1976, no part of this publication may be
reproduced or distributed in any form or by any means, or stored in a database
or retrieval system, without the prior written permission of the publisher.

ISBN 978-0-07-147810-6
MHID 0-07-147810-8

Library of Congress Cataloging-in-Publication Data
Doane, Charles J.
The modern cruising sailboat : a complete guide to its design,
construction, and outfitting / Charles J. Doane.
391 p. : ill. ; 29 cm.
Includes bibliographic references and index.
ISBN 0-07-147810-8
1. Sailboats—Design and construction.
2. Boats and boating equipment—Equipment and supplies.
VM151 .D63 2010
623.81223 22
2010277285

Questions regarding the content of this book should be addressed to
www.internationalmarine.com

Questions regarding the ordering of this book should be addressed to
McGraw-Hill Education
Customer Service Department
P.O. Box 547
Blacklick, OH 43004
Retail customers: 1-800-262-4729
Bookstores: 1-800-722-4726

for Clare and the Lunacy sisters

CONTENTS

A BOAT TO CRUISE IN

Before you can reasonably ask yourself what sort of boat you would like to cruise in, you must first ask, what is cruising? Not in the broadest sense, of course, but in the personal sense. We may agree on certain fundamental concepts—for example, that cruising is not racing and that it involves the pure enjoyment of being on the water for its own sake. We can also probably agree that cruising means living on a boat for a limited or perhaps unlimited period of time. Beyond that, however—just as there are as many ways to live life as there are people—there are as many kinds of cruising as there are cruisers. All racing sailors share the same purpose, which is to sail as fast as possible. Every cruising sailor, however, has a purpose that is unique to him or her.

I learned I was a cruiser rather than a racer early in my sailing career. The first stages of my sailing apprenticeship were conducted in 11-foot lateen-rigged boats known as Sea Snarks, which were manufactured out of Styrofoam and weighed only 30 pounds. The venue was an island at the mouth of the Kennebec River, in Maine, where my family spent summers when I was growing up. Sea Snarks were cheap (just $125 each in those days!), so the family could afford to buy several of them. We kids learned to sail them in a pine-studded cove that was shielded from the worst of the Kennebec's strong tidal currents. The concept of racing them against each other was imported by a friend who often raced Atlantic sloops with his father on Long Island Sound. We set up a short triangular course, the far corners of which were marked by a wrecked barge and a large rock in midriver that was covered with seals, and for a

season or two my two brothers and I and various friends had good fun competing against each other in a fairly orderly manner. As we gained confidence, however, our races devolved into furious bouts of bumper-boating wherein we intentionally tried to T-bone each other as hard as we could. My parents weren't too happy when this resulted in several of our boats being split in two.

As much as I liked racing Sea Snarks and breaking them into pieces, what I most enjoyed was taking one out on my own and exploring the world around our island. Sometimes I had a specific objective: to circumnavigate our island, for example, or the next one upriver, and return to our cove in time for dinner. Sometimes I had no objective at all. I sailed wherever tide and wind might take me, and when I saw some interesting cove or island, I landed my little boat and set out on foot to see what I could find. The discoveries I made during these idle explorations always seemed more thrilling than the raw brutality of competition. Now, another 30 years on, I still practice the fine art of exploring Maine islands. There seems no end to them. My boat is considerably larger and I have done much sailing in other watery parts of the world, including a fair share of bluewater voyaging, but for me this sort of casual exploration still embodies the essence of cruising under sail.

In answering the question, then, of what sort of boat they would like to cruise in, people inevitably refer to different parts of themselves. For a few lucky people, selecting a boat is a purely rational process, and the factors involved are empirical. Many, however, can't help but make this an acutely emotional

1

matter, mixed up with all the stuff of their dreams. Most of us wrestle with some mixture of the rational and emotional.

A small minority, in fact, define cruising by the boat they do it in. Fixed in their minds is an image of themselves aboard a certain sort of boat, and they will sail that boat on Lake St. Clair or across the Pacific, for an afternoon or a year. For such people this book will be of limited utility. The rest of us—a vast majority, I hope—find our personal definitions of cruising informed by a wide array of factors, and the process of selecting and equipping a boat becomes far more complicated.

I hope this book will provide you with the knowledge you need to assess those factors and identify the specific attributes of specific boats that will enhance your experience on the water. I will not presume to tell you which factors and attributes should matter most to you. Precisely because definitions of cruising are so personal, there is little point in doing so.

What I *will* do, however, is urge you to segregate as best you can the emotional components of your cruising dream from the process of selecting a boat. Your decision should be as empirical as you can make it. An old adage states that there is no such thing as a bad boat, only boats that are used for inappropriate purposes. This is not quite true; there are bad boats, and hopefully this book will teach you how to spot them. But it is true that using a boat for an inappropriate purpose is usually an aggravating experience. You can use this book to avoid choosing an inappropriate boat, but only if you are honest with yourself about the sort of cruising you will actually do in it. If you blindly let an exalted dream of cruising trump the cruising you will actually do, you may well end up doing very little cruising at all. If instead you try hard to coldly appraise the reality of your situation and choose a boat accordingly, you are far more likely to maximize your time afloat aboard a boat you enjoy using. In making this appraisal, there are a few critical factors to consider—the same factors you should have in mind as you digest the information in this book.

SIZE MATTERS

The first thing most would-be cruisers consider when choosing a boat is the size of their crew. The larger your crew (usually your immediate family), the larger the boat you will naturally be inclined to consider cruising aboard. And, of course, there are many other reasons for favoring larger boats over smaller ones. The more space you have aboard, the more comfortable you will be, because your living quarters will be less cramped and you will be able to carry more stuff

and install more systems. Thanks to certain laws of physics, you'll find, all other things being equal, that large boats go faster than small ones. Also, if your ultimate goal is to cruise offshore, you will definitely feel more secure in a larger boat when the waves start looking big and angry.

For all these reasons, cruising boats over the last half century have constantly been growing larger. Boatbuilders, of course, have encouraged the trend, as profit margins grow more generous as a boat grows in size. Just over 40 years ago, when the fiberglass-boat-building industry was still establishing itself, a 40-foot boat was considered large. When it was introduced in 1965, the Pearson Countess 44, a stout motorsailer designed by Carl Alberg, was the largest production sailboat built anywhere in the world. Most cruising boats in those days ranged from 25 to 35 feet long. These days a 35-foot boat is considered small, and the average American cruising sailboat is something on the order of 43 feet long. If you like, you can now buy fiberglass production boats as large as 100 feet. Indeed, it is not uncommon to meet retired couples in their fifties and sixties cruising doublehanded aboard boats 50 feet and longer. This trend is epitomized by Steve and Linda Dashew, who began cruising offshore during the 1970s with their children aboard a stock production boat, a Columbia 50 named *Intermezzo*. Subsequently, as the kids grew up, the Dashews designed and built for themselves an ever-larger series of sailboats aboard which they continued cruising on their own. The last was a 78-foot aluminum ketch named *Beowulf*.

More space may always mean more comfort, but the size of your boat, ultimately, should not be determined by the number of people (family or otherwise) that you have aboard or by any personal proclivities you may have for living large. Instead, the very first factor to consider is the number of truly competent crew aboard who can help work the boat. You have to be honest here, both about your own abilities and those of your crew. Few cruising sailors are as experienced (or as wealthy) as Steve and Linda Dashew. Of course, the abilities of a small working crew can be greatly augmented by modern technology. Power winches, roller-furling headsails and mainsails, bow thrusters, electronic autopilots, and such allow a crew of two—or even one person sailing singlehanded—to efficiently operate a very large sailing vessel. I have often sailed on boats equipped like this, and I can testify that it is an intoxicating experience. It is a wonderful thing to be able to shorten sail by yourself on a moment's notice just by touching a button with your fingertip.

If you can afford this sort of technology, you should by all means enjoy it, but bear in mind that you and your working crew, however small, should be able to operate your vessel, even in extreme conditions, without the benefit of hydraulic or electrical power. It is true that mechanical sail-handling systems are much more reliable than they used to be, but they are not absolutely reliable and never will be. The realization that you are more dependent on them than you should be can come suddenly and will always be unpleasant.

TIME AND SPACE

The nature of your cruising ground, obviously, should dictate many of your boat's features. If, for example, you like to cruise in shoal waters, such as the Florida Keys or the Chesapeake Bay, you clearly will have more fun sailing a shoal-draft boat, perhaps even one with a centerboard or lifting keel, than you will sailing a deep-draft vessel that prevents you from going places you'd like to go and is constantly running aground. If your cruising ground is open to ocean swells (or is, in fact, the ocean itself), you will probably prefer a vessel with a seakindly motion. If your cruising ground is cold much of the year, you will appreciate having a heating system aboard; if it is hot, you will worship your refrigerator and your bimini. If you spend many of your nights in marinas, you will need minimal fuel and water capacity and will get a lot of use from an AC shore-power system. If you anchor out frequently and rarely come to a dock, you'll want bigger tanks and an efficient DC system, including perhaps a high-output alternator and/or solar panels or a wind generator to help you keep your DC batteries charged.

But the most important factor to consider—and one that many people neglect—is the nature of your cruising ground relative to the time you have available to explore it. The faster your boat, the larger your potential cruising ground. Where harbors and anchorages are few and far between—particularly if most of your cruising will be confined to weekends—a slow, heavy boat will not prove much fun. Your cruising ground will seem very small, and visiting the same one or two spots again and again will quickly get old. If you have more time to cruise, or if you are lucky enough to cruise where varied anchorages are only a few miles apart, you can afford to sail at a more stately pace. And if you are that supremely fortunate creature—a bluewater liveaboard on a cruise of indefinite duration—the speed of your vessel may seem irrelevant. Most of us, though, aren't that lucky. Whether we're coastal cruisers trying to squeeze in time on the water over weekends and the occasional long holiday, or bluewater cruisers whose commitments ashore require us to make passages on

a schedule, we need to give careful thought to the effective ranges of our vessels.

In calculating your vessel's potential range, you must again be realistic. The average cruising speeds given in a brokerage listing or a builder's brochure are typically achieved only in ideal circumstances when the boat is nearly empty and the sea is flat. In the real world, aboard a heavier, fully loaded boat moving through choppy water, performance will be degraded, sometimes drastically.

COST AND COMPLEXITY

What it costs to obtain and maintain a boat is, of course, another important consideration. It is staggering both how little and how much you can pay for a boat these days. I once crewed on an aging but classic 96-foot wooden Alden schooner that had been recently purchased by owners for just $60,000. For that same price you can find, say, a 50-foot fiberglass boat badly in need of work or a 55-foot ferrocement boat in very good condition. Or, for just $30,000, you can get a 30-foot fiberglass boat in excellent condition. For $10,000 you can buy that same 30-footer in poor condition. These last four are all available, as I write this, on Yachtworld's excellent yacht-brokerage website. On the other hand, covering the new-boat market as a magazine writer, I've been aboard large production "daysailers" in the 40-foot range that have minimal accommodations and sell for upward of $700,000. I have also often met wealthy men who have spent a million dollars or more building custom cruising boats of that size. At this moment, on Yachtworld.com, a brand-new 28-foot Bristol Channel Cutter is listed for just over $300,000. The irony here is that this classic (and very beautiful) Lyle Hess design mimics that of *Serrafyn*, the 29-foot engineless cutter owned by Lin and Larry Pardey, who for decades have been urging cruisers to get out on the water in cheap and simple boats.

This principle of KISS (Keep It Simple, Stupid) has long been promulgated in books on cruising boats. It is a credo I have adhered to ever since I started cruising aboard boats of my own. It is also espoused by almost every cruising sailor I have ever met. My point is not that the principle is universal, but that it is extremely flexible. The last man who told me he prided himself on the simplicity of his boat had a new million-dollar custom job hanging on his mooring. His was a simple boat, he felt, because it had no watermaker and only one power winch aboard—never mind the generator, air-conditioning, custom granite countertops, exotic hardwood interior, and the faux wood-finish carbon-fiber rig.

What drives this ever-expanding concept of simplicity is the fact that over the years boat systems and boat construction have grown increasingly more sophisticated and complicated. This is also a major reason (though not the only reason) why boats can be so insanely expensive these days. Back in the good old days, when the Pearson Countess ruled the waves, a cruising boat was considered lavishly equipped if it had a freshwater pressure pump aboard. Much equipment we now take for granted, like radar and refrigeration, was considered too exotic and often too power hungry to serve reliably on board an auxiliary sailboat. These days such devices are much more energy efficient and are remarkably reliable.

As for construction, solid hand-laid fiberglass, with perhaps a balsa core in the deck, used to be the only game in town for production boatbuilding. Now modern production techniques routinely involve exotic (and much more expensive) materials such as Kevlar and carbon fiber, together with sophisticated processes such as vacuum bagging and oven curing.

How do you navigate such a bewildering array of possibilities? The answer, once again, is to get real and stay focused. The major reason there are insanely cheap boats available on the brokerage market is that fiberglass is practically indestructible. Fiberglass boats that are remarkably degraded will always stay afloat, but will also prove increasingly efficient at sopping up any excess cash and time you have if you try to upgrade and maintain them in a responsible manner. As for ferrocement and wood boats, they may not even succeed in staying afloat. The end of that story about my crewing on the deal-of-the-century Alden schooner is that after three years of do-it-yourself renovations and tens of thousands of dollars spent in emergency maintenance, the owners finally lost the boat in a river in Spain after she ran aground and couldn't stand up to her own weight when she dried out on an outgoing tide.

On the other hand, the brokerage market does offer some truly amazing bargains. If you keep your head and know what you want and are patient, you'll find you can buy a boat in very good condition for a very reasonable price, with a lot of equipment you'd like to have thrown in seemingly for free. Hopefully, this book will help you achieve this sublime result. The key, I have always felt, is to scale back your personal notion of simplicity as far as you can. If you create needs out of thin air before you start cruising, you may find you spend more time and money than necessary upgrading and maintaining your boat.

The acid test is just this: how long does it take you to get underway? Your boat should be simple enough (and small enough, if need be) that you can easily yield to random impulses to get away ASAP. This, of course, is a matter of perspective. If you are a liveaboard bluewater cruiser, you will feel you are sailing at the drop of a hat if it takes you a day or two to cast off and head out over the horizon. If you are a weekend warrior, you should be able to head out for an impromptu daysail or an overnighter within a matter of hours, or preferably minutes. If your boat is so complex that you spend more time fretting over keeping it in good operating condition than you do sailing, then clearly something is wrong. After all, whatever your definition of cruising is, spending time on the water should be what matters most.

ONE

THE EVOLUTION OF CRUISING SAILBOATS

In the beginning, what we now call "yachting," or sailing for pleasure, was practiced solely by a wealthy elite. Indeed, the first leisure craft were owned by monarchs and were profligate in their construction and appointments. Ptolemy IV of Egypt, we are told, lolled about the Nile aboard an immense 300-foot catamaran whose hull stood 60 feet high and was propelled by thousands of galley slaves. Cleopatra is said to have bewitched Mark Antony aboard a luxurious barge that had silver oars, purple sails, and a gold-encrusted hull. As Shakespeare described it in *Antony and Cleopatra*, "The barge she sat in, like a burnished throne / Burned on the water." Even centuries later, when the industrious and more egalitarian Dutch took up pleasure sailing in the shallow waters of the Netherlands aboard their sturdy all-purpose *jaght schips*, the ancestors of what we now properly call "yachts," they could not resist lavishing their vessels with ornamentation.

Appropriately, the Dutch concept of the *jaght* was transplanted to English waters (and thence into the English language) by a royal personage. When Charles II, in exile for many years after his father was executed by Parliament, returned to England and ascended to the throne in 1660, he brought with him a 52-foot jaght, which he called *Mary*, that had been presented to him by the burgomaster of Amsterdam. Charles loved sailing and the sea, and he loved luxury, and was nothing if not energetic. Before his death 25 years later he built another 26 or more lavishly appointed yachts. He also, with help from Samuel Pepys, greatly expanded the English navy and merchant marine, though Pepys routinely had to resist requests that Admiralty funds be used to man and furnish the ever-growing fleet of royal pleasure craft. Charles particularly enjoyed racing his yachts against those of his brother James, the Duke of York, who shared Charles's passion for the sea. What is described as the first recorded yacht race in history was conducted in May 1661 between the 49-foot *Catherine*, owned by Charles, and the 52-foot *Anne*, owned by James, to settle a wager of 100 pounds. Charles won. The Dutch, meanwhile, in addition to racing their jaghts informally, especially liked to sail large numbers of them (as many as 400 at a time) in formation and would often stage elaborate mock battles between opposing flotillas.

The first true American yacht was not built until 1816. What is significant about her for our purposes is that she was conceived and constructed expressly for cruising. Not that she was a humble vessel. Her name, tellingly, was *Cleopatra's Barge*, and her owner, George Crowninshield, Jr., the flamboyant eldest son of a wealthy merchant mariner from Salem, Massachusetts, seemed determined that she should live up to it. Her design and construction were not particularly unusual. A conventional hermaphrodite schooner of the era, carrying square sails on her foremast and a fore-and-aft gaff spanker on her aftermast, *Cleopatra's Barge* was 83 feet long on deck, just over 100 feet long overall (with bowsprit), and 23 feet wide. She drew 12 feet of water, displaced 192 tons, and—superficially at least—looked like many trading vessels that might be found in Salem Harbor at the time. Her shape was also ordinary, with bluff, full bow sections

5

Cleopatra's Barge, *launched in 1816 by George Crowinshield, Jr., was perhaps the world's first purpose-built cruising vessel. Though her design was ordinary, her furnishings were lavish and eccentric. (Courtesy of the Peabody Essex Museum)*

tapering to a narrow underwater run aft. This classic "cod's head and mackerel's tail" configuration represented the early 19th century's most current thinking in naval architecture. The theory, unsupported by any scientific evidence, was that a vessel's underbody must operate most efficiently when shaped like a fish.

What was unusual about *Cleopatra's Barge* was the garish and extravagant manner in which she was decorated and furnished. Down below she was the acme of sumptuousness. Her cabins featured exotic inlaid paneling and floors, gilded deck beams, velvet grab ropes, fireplaces, chandeliers, and sideboards and secret cupboards crammed full of the finest silver, porcelain, and glassware. Her furniture, inspired by Crowninshield's admiration of the recently deposed French emperor Napoleon Bonaparte, was in the Empire style, decorated with imperial eagles. The chairs had lyre-shaped backs and velvet tassels hanging from their seats. Her appearance topsides was deliberately eccentric. Her starboard side was painted with bright multicolored stripes, while her port side was painted in an elaborate herringbone pattern. Her deck, sporting 12 cannons that had no ostensible purpose, was laced with more velvet grab ropes and featured a life-size wooden Indian that was nailed in place and seemed to have silent command of the entire vessel.

Crowninshield reportedly paid $50,000 to have this great plaything built, then blew another $50,000 furnishing it, spending in all some $2 million in today's currency, or nearly ten times what a conventional vessel of similar size cost at the time. When he was done, he embarked on what one Salem newspaper described as a "voyage of amusement and travels." Departing Salem in March 1817, Crowninshield struck out across the North Atlantic, stopped in the Azores and Madeira, then carried on to the Mediterranean, where he engaged in a whirlwind tour of the North African, Spanish, French, and Italian coasts. In each port where she appeared, the public was invited aboard to inspect *Cleopatra's Barge*, which they did in great numbers. In Barcelona alone, where she stopped for five days, an estimated 20,000 people toured the vessel. Crowninshield returned to Salem in October of that year amid swirling rumors that the real purpose of his journey had been to organize a rescue of Napoleon Bonaparte from his lonely exile on the island of St. Helena in the South Atlantic. Sadly, Crowninshield died just six weeks after his return. His famous yacht was stripped of her finery and sold, serving for a time as a packet on the U.S. East Coast. Sold again in 1821, she was sent out to Hawaii, where, appropriately, she was purchased in turn by King Kamehameha II, who renamed her *Ha'aheo o Hawaii* (or *Pride of Hawaii*) and made her his royal flagship. Unfortunately, she was lost in April 1824—just eight years after she was launched—when her drunken crew ran her aground at Hanalei Bay on the island of Kauai.

Cleopatra's Barge is often touted as the first pleasure vessel to cross the Atlantic, but this is not strictly true. More than 30 years earlier, in 1784, an Englishman named Shuttleworth crossed the Atlantic in a "ten-gun" yacht called *Lively*, then cruised the East Coast from Florida into northernmost Canada. *Cleopatra's Barge* was not even, strictly speaking, the first American yacht, as there is strong evidence that some small vessels were sailed purely for pleasure in New York Harbor as early as 1717. But she was the first American vessel opulent enough to be described as a true yacht by the European standards that then prevailed. She may also have been the first vessel built anywhere expressly for an extended pleasure voyage. It does not seem too big a stretch to say that she was the world's first purpose-built cruising vessel, and that the evolution of cruising boat design can be reasonably measured and recounted from her conception onward.

EARLY TRENDS IN MAINSTREAM YACHT DESIGN

Throughout the 19th century, yachting continued to be the domain of the wealthy. As the century progressed, the vessels and the egos behind them only grew larger and more extravagant. Yachting was very much about social status, and this led to the formation of exclusive clubs. The two most prominent were the Royal Yacht Squadron (RYS), formed in England in 1815, and the New York Yacht Club (NYYC), founded in 1844. Neither, however, was the first of its kind in its respective continent. The Water Club, formed in Cork, Ireland, circa 1720, is believed to have been the first yacht club in Europe, while the Boston Boat Club, circa 1830, was the first in North America.

The activities of these clubs centered on racing and wagering, and the racing could be quite vicious. Competitors in early RYS events, for example, would effectively wage combat against each other, wielding weapons of various sorts in efforts to cut away their opponents' rigs. Like their Dutch predecessors, RYS members also staged mock naval reviews in which large groups of yachts sailed in formation. Cruising, it should be noted, was not unheard of. Members of the RYS often cruised in company across the English Channel on wine-buying expeditions along the French coast. Likewise, the first thing members of the NYYC did upon forming their club was to cruise in company up Long Island Sound to Newport, Rhode Island, staging various "trials of speed" along the way. To this day the NYYC Annual Cruise with its competitive squadron runs is religiously observed.

Over time, yacht racing became more formal and less violent, though the wagering continued unabated. The designing of yachts also became a specialized practice. Originally, as was the case with *Cleopatra's Barge*, a gentleman's "yacht" was essentially a working vessel dressed in finery. Its construction might be specially commissioned and executed, but its design was based on common working craft. As the 19th century progressed, however, yachts became unique vessels in every respect. Eventually it became possible for men to earn a living by specializing in the creation of these pleasure craft.

As yacht design evolved, two fundamental paradigms asserted themselves. In Great Britain, where racing handicaps were based on government tonnage rules for taxing commercial vessels that penalized beam, yachts tended to be narrow and deep. These so-called cutters—the term in those days referred to a vessel's hull form rather than its rig—depended for their stability on a great deal of ballast fixed as low in the keel as possible. In the United States, where beam was not penalized and there was a considerable amount of shoal water along the coast, yachts tended to be wide and shallow. Vessels like this, described as sloops (again, the reference is to the hull, not the rig) and sometimes as "skimming dishes," depended on their wide hulls for stability (though some ballast was carried loose in their bilges) and on centerboards to minimize leeway. The centerboard, an American innovation first patented in New Jersey in 1811, was directly descended from the leeboards used by the Dutch aboard their wide, shallow jaghts.

Inevitably, these divergent design paradigms were forced to converge. The first equalizing event came in 1851, when the famous yacht *America*, owned by John Cox Stevens, a founding member of the NYYC, crossed the Atlantic and trounced a fleet of British yachts in a race around the Isle of Wight. *America*'s hull was not radically shallow, nor did she carry a centerboard, as she had been designed expressly to cross the Atlantic and was based more on New York pilot schooners than on cutting-edge racing yachts. But she was wider than the British yachts she competed against and, more important, carried much of her beam aft and had a hollow bow with a fine entry forward. This was the exact opposite of the crude "cod's head and mackerel's tail" shape (a wide entry forward with a narrow run aft) that still prevailed in Britain. As a result of *America*'s success, though British yachts did not immediately become significantly wider overall, their proportions started shifting. Bows became more hollow and concave, and the point of maximum beam moved farther aft. This was exactly in keeping with the first scientific theory of naval

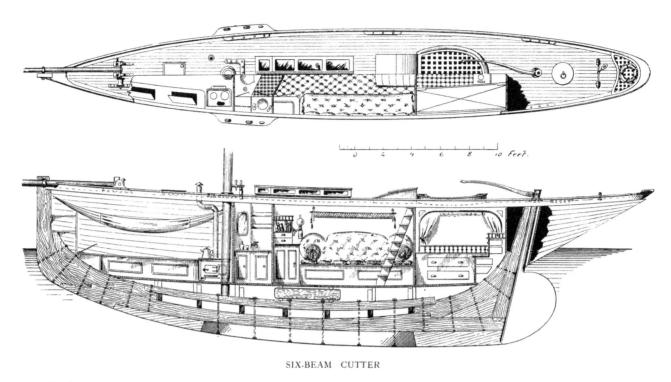

SIX-BEAM CUTTER

A radical example of a British cutter with a deep keel and a narrow hull.

architecture—called the wave line theory—which had been developed and promulgated by a Scotsman, John Scott Russell, nearly a quarter of a century earlier, but had until then been ignored in Britain.

The next significant equalizing event came in 1876, when the American centerboard schooner *Mohawk* capsized and sank in a sudden but relatively moderate squall off Staten Island in New York Harbor. The boat's owner, Will Garner, his wife, and a party of guests were killed in the incident. *Mohawk*, an extreme example of the skimming-dish type, was intended by Garner to be the largest, fastest, most opulent yacht in the NYYC fleet. She was 141 feet long, 30 feet wide, and had a draft of just 6 feet that increased to 30 feet when she dropped her massive 7-ton centerboard. She flew an amazing 32,000 square feet of sail. The fact that she could not stand up to all her sail in spite of her great beam helped

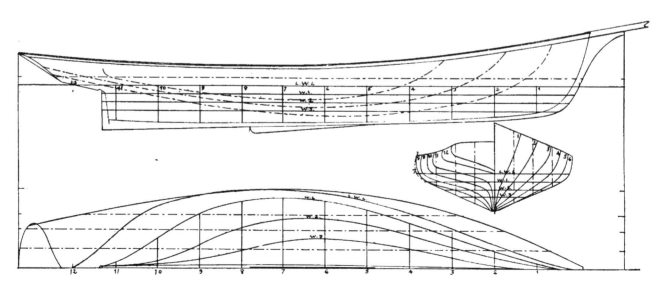

American centerboard sloops like Gracie, *shown here, were wide and shallow.*

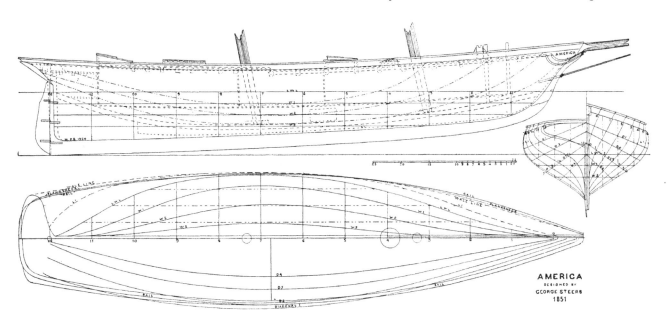

Besides winning her famous cup for the New York Yacht Club, the yacht America *was an early example of a scientifically designed sailboat.*

fuel arguments that the wide, shallow yachts favored in the United States were fundamentally unsafe. It did not help either, of course, that *Mohawk* was slower than Garner had hoped and proved a dud on the racecourse.

A narrow British cutter named *Madge* crossed the Atlantic and raced successfully against several U.S. yachts in 1881, and then another large centerboard schooner, *Grayling*, capsized on her maiden sail in 1883. As a result, a vociferous group of "cutter cranks," who called the skimming dishes "death traps" and favored British designs instead, became prominent in American yachting circles. This led to

the development of "compromise" designs pioneered by Edward Burgess of Boston, Massachusetts, an entomologist turned yacht designer who was heavily influenced by British cutters he had observed during a summer spent on the Isle of Wight. These compromise boats, like the British cutters, had heavy ballast keels, but they were not nearly as narrow or deep relative to their length. Also, like the American boats, they carried centerboards. The litmus test came in 1885, when the Burgess-designed *Puritan* defeated an American skimming dish, *Priscilla*, for the right to defend the America's Cup, then beat a British cutter, *Genesta*, in the Cup finals.

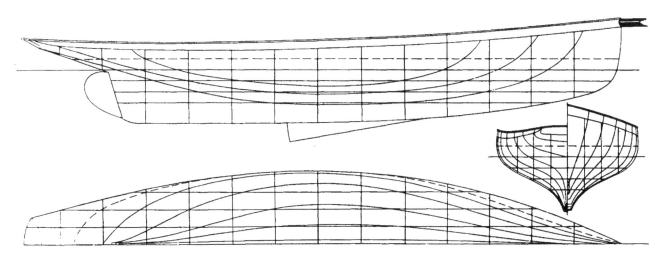

Puritan, designed by Edward Burgess, with her heavy ballast keel, bridged the gap between narrow British cutters *and wide American sloops.*

The final factor that helped unite the opposing camps of yacht design was the development of empirically based handicap rules for racing. As noted, handicaps originally were based on commercial measurements devised for tax purposes. Over time, however, it became clear that these formulas had little to do with a vessel's actual performance. Performance, it was noticed, depended most directly on waterline length—i.e., more waterline equals more speed. In 1883, the first handicap rule based on measurements of waterline length and sail area, the Seawanhaka Rule, developed by New York's Seawanhaka Corinthian Yacht Club, was adopted in the United States. Soon afterward, in 1888, a similar rule came into use in Great Britain. The result, ultimately, was a universal trend favoring boats with overhanging ends whose waterlines increased as they heeled to the wind.

One of the first yachts to exploit this little rule-beating trick was *Gloriana*, a 70-foot sloop designed and built by Nathanael Herreshoff for E. D. Morgan in 1891. *Gloriana*, thanks at least in part to her overhanging spoon-shaped bow, was undefeated the one season Morgan raced her and instantly secured Herreshoff's reputation as a yacht designer. Described by some as the first "scientifically contructed" yacht, she was also quite stable and could carry a great press of sail, as weight above her waterline was greatly reduced and was instead concentrated as ballast in her keel. In the decade that followed, the continued development of these features, plus a tendency to cut away as much keel as possible to reduce surface area below the water, produced increasingly radical boats. This evolution culminated in *Independence*, a 1901 design by Bowdoin B. Crowninshield (a descendant of the famous proto-cruiser George Crowninshield), that was lightly built with immensely long overhangs, a tiny keel, and a gigantic sail plan. *Independence* leaked badly, however, and handled, as her skipper put it, like "an ice wagon." Nat Herreshoff managed to perfect the concept in his equally radical *Reliance*, which defended the America's Cup in 1903. Termed a monster by many at the time, *Reliance* measured 144 feet long on deck (and a little over 200 feet overall if measured from the end of her boom to her bowsprit), and had a waterline length of just 90 feet, with over 16,000 square feet of sail area flying from a single mast that was 200 feet tall.

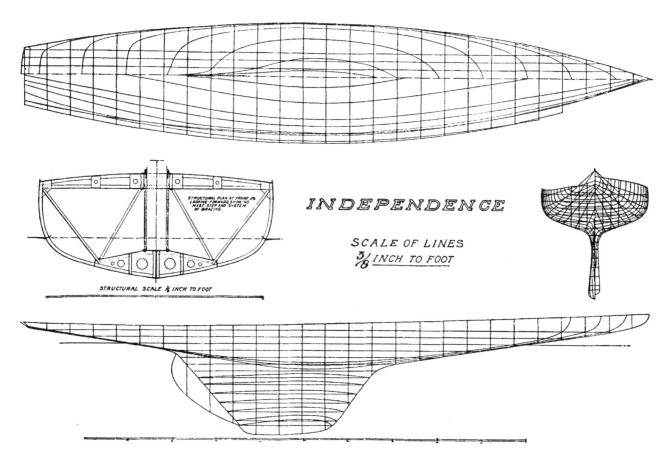

By the turn of the 20th century extreme designs like Independence, *by Bowdoin Crowninshield, came to dominate racing. With their small cutaway keels, long overhangs, and large sail plans these boats seemed monstrous to many observers.*

The general trend in yacht construction in the latter half of the 19th century was increasingly grandiose. This was particularly true in the United States, where the enormous expansion of the national economy in the years following the Civil War—the Gilded Age, as Mark Twain termed it—allowed for the accumulation of private wealth on a scale never before imagined. Picking up where George Crowninshield had left off with *Cleopatra's Barge*, the American "robber barons" competed with each other in creating ever more extravagant vessels. Originally, these 19th century superyachts could function both as cruising and racing vessels. Will Garner's *Mohawk*, for example, though intended to excel on the race course, also featured fabulous creature comforts, including gas lighting, hot and cold freshwater plumbing, and a steam-heat system, not to mention a grand piano and other lavish, heavy furnishings. Even America's Cup contenders were tricked out in this manner and were often cruised between campaigns. By the end of the century, however, super-wealthy yachtsmen tended not to cruise in the sailing vessels they raced, as these were becoming ever more extreme. Instead, they cruised for pleasure aboard enormous steam yachts that were even larger than their sailboats.

The trend toward profligacy, and toward steam, was reflected in the changing composition of the NYYC's squadron of members' vessels. In 1870 the squadron consisted of only 49 vessels, four of which were steam yachts. The largest vessel was a 145-foot schooner displacing 275 tons, owned by William Douglas. Within just 30 years, the squadron mushroomed to 402 vessels, 207 of which were steam yachts. The queen of the fleet was *Lysistrata*, a 314-foot steamer displacing 2,682 tons that belonged to newspaper magnate James Gordon Bennett. The nearly tenfold increase in the size of the squadron was not really a function of yachting's growing popularity as a sport. Instead it reflected yachting's growing importance as a venue for public displays of status and wealth—a fact, of course, that was also reflected in the growing size of the yachts themselves. Many of the "yachtsmen" who owned these vessels, unlike Crowninshield, who made his fortune at sea aboard trading vessels, had little interest in nautical matters. Even those who owned and campaigned racing yachts were often happy just to write checks (and make wagers) and never sailed their boats themselves.

As for cruising, the tycoons of the late 19th century did indeed wander far and wide in their floating palaces. One of these was an Englishman, Sir Thomas Brassey, who circled the globe in 1876–77 in his 170-foot steam auxiliary schooner *Sunbeam*. His wife, Lady Anna Brassey, published an account of the voyage (it was, in fact, the first circumnavigation ever made by a yacht) that became a bestseller both in Britain and the United States. The Brasseys were followed by many others, particularly Americans who, like Crowninshield before them, yearned to cruise the Mediterranean, where they could purchase art and perhaps hobnob with European royalty. J. P. Morgan, for example, bought his first yacht— *Corsair*, a 185-foot steamer—in 1881 and at once took off on an art-buying cruise to Palestine. His third *Corsair*, built in 1899, which he often cruised to Europe, was 304 feet long. James Gordon Bennett spent almost 20 years living aboard his steam yachts meandering back and forth across the North Atlantic. *Lysistrata*, his last and largest vessel, had more than 100 paid crew, a stable for a milking cow, and three separate owner's staterooms. Needless to say, cruising on this scale never trickled down to the lower strata of society.

THE EMERGENCE OF "ALTERNATIVE" CRUISING

The hoi polloi, however, were finding ways of their own to get afloat, as they, too, were determined to enjoy "messing about in boats." One pioneer was a stern British stockbroker named Richard Turrell (R. T.) McMullen, who, in 1850, at age 20, decided to teach himself sailing and commissioned the construction of a 20-foot half-decked cutter named *Leo*. Over the next 41 years he cruised throughout the British Isles and across the English Channel in a series of purpose-built vessels, the largest of which, a 42-footer named *Orion*, was a classic deep-draft, narrow-waisted British cutter.

McMullen's career as a yachtsman, described in meticulous detail in his book *Down Channel*, was significant both because he was not a wealthy tycoon or aristocrat and because he was acutely interested in sailing for its own sake. He cared nothing for racing or yachting society, but was instead fascinated by the minutiae of boats and boat handling and by the aquatic environment itself. He set strict standards and ultimately became competent enough to handle his vessels singlehanded. His first solo experience was aboard *Procyon*, an unusual 28-foot shoal-draft lugger with a cat-yawl rig and a short centerboard, or "drop-keel" as he termed it. McMullen also once sailed the much heavier *Orion* singlehanded from France to England after dismissing a crew he deemed incompetent. His last vessel, the 27-foot *Perseus*, was, like *Procyon*, a yawl-rigged lugger conceived specifically for singlehanded cruising, except that she carried a headsail and had more draft and no centerboard. In 1891 McMullen was found dead, alone, aboard *Perseus* in the middle of the English Channel, apparently a victim of heart failure.

Another important figure was a Scottish barrister, John MacGregor, who in 1865 embarked upon a tour of Europe in a 14-foot canoe called *Rob Roy*. The book he wrote about his adventure—*A Thousand Miles in the Rob Roy Canoe on the Rivers and Lakes of Europe*—was published the following year, and its success quickly led MacGregor to make more canoe voyages in Scandinavia (1866) and the Middle East (1869). These canoe trips were not really cruises in the proper sense of the term, since MacGregor hauled his boats by train or carriage from each river or lake he wished to explore and always found lodging for the night ashore. Nor were MacGregor's canoes much akin to what we now think of as proper cruising boats. They were, in fact, mere kayaks, or "double-paddle canoes" as some then called them, a design concept MacGregor freely admitted to having cribbed from the North American "Esquimeaux." But MacGregor's adventures did serve to open the public's eyes to the concept of recreation afloat and demonstrated in a very palpable way that the expense need not be prohibitive. MacGregor himself was, more than anything else, an indefatigable showman and expert propagandist with an unfailing instinct for garnering and exploiting publicity. His books and popular lectures were highly influential and led to the creation of "canoe clubs" throughout Britain and Europe.

In addition to his canoe trips, MacGregor also engaged in one "proper" cruise in 1867 aboard a 21-foot yawl (also called *Rob Roy*) that he designed himself. This was a more standard (albeit miniaturized) yacht with a ballast keel and a hull form roughly similar to that of larger British yachts of the era. It lacked a cabin (nights aboard were spent under a cockpit tent) but did feature such clever amenities as a

Besides cruising in canoes, John MacGregor also sailed to France in a 21-foot yawl that he lived aboard under a cockpit tent.

tiny galley that folded into a cockpit locker. The little yawl was seaworthy enough to take MacGregor across the English Channel from England to France, up the Seine River to Paris, and back again. The ostensible purpose of this voyage was to spread the gospel of canoeing (and the Protestant faith) at a French boating exhibition sanctioned by the Emperor Napoleon III, who, like many others, had been inspired by MacGregor's writing. MacGregor's book about the cruise, *The Voyage Alone in the Yawl Rob Roy*, led many who yearned to set sail on vessels more substantial than canoes to mimic his example.

MacGregor's American counterpart, Nathaniel H. Bishop, is no longer as well remembered but was also influential in his day. Inspired by MacGregor, Bishop first went cruising aboard a small paper canoe he called *Maria Theresa*. Subsequently, in 1875, he cruised down the Ohio and Mississippi rivers and along the Gulf Coast to Florida aboard *Centennial Republic*, a Barnegat Bay sneak-box he had built for $25. The sneak-box was a specialized centerboard spritsail skiff designed for use by duck hunters in the shoal waters of coastal New Jersey. Bishop's boat was 12 feet long with a beam of 4 feet and weighed just 200 pounds. The book he wrote about his experience, *Four Months in a Sneak-Box*, was well received, and in 1880, again following MacGregor's example, he helped form the American Canoe Association, of which he was the first commodore.

It is difficult to say how many would-be cruisers immediately followed in the wakes left by men like McMullen, MacGregor, and Bishop. This sort of unobtrusive sailing—small voyages for pleasure

Sailing for pleasure trickled down to the masses in the form of "canoe cruising," which was popularized by barrister John MacGregor and his canoe Rob Roy.

undertaken by ordinary people in modest craft—was not of immediate or compelling public interest. The high-profile exploits of the rich and famous, by comparison, whether conducted on shore or aboard their yachts, were always grist for the popular press. Unless they were willing to tell their stories themselves, common cruisers had to be, and were, content to do their sailing in obscurity. But something powerful was at work here—a seductive fantasy of autonomy and adventure that cruising under sail somehow promised to make real. MacGregor himself summed it up neatly in his account of his cruise to France. "Often as a boy," he wrote, "I had thought of the pleasure of being one's own master in one's own boat; but the reality far exceeded the imagination of it, and it was not a transient pleasure."

What we do know is that from the late 19th century onward, the number of middle- and upper-middle-class people engaged in cruising aboard their own small boats steadily increased, and gradually this aspect of the sport of yachting became just as significant as the nautical doings of the upper classes. By the early 20th century, there were enough London-based middle-class amateur yachtsmen cruising the coast of southern England that railway companies saw fit to offer them special fares. These open-ended round-trip tickets made it possible for sailors who were office-bound in London during the week to take a train south to one town on the English Channel on a Friday evening, spend the weekend aboard their boat sailing to some other town, and return to the city on Sunday night in time for work on Monday morning. In this manner, over a series of weekends, a persistent cruiser might hopscotch his way along a fair portion of the coast.

Small-boat cruisers, like their blue-blooded predecessors, also formed clubs. The first was the Cruising Club, which held its inaugural meeting in the office of a British barrister, Arthur Underhill, in 1880 and was officially ordained the Royal Cruising Club in 1902. There followed the Little Ship Club, another British club formed in 1926, and in the United States the Cruising Club of America, which first met in a Greenwich Village speakeasy called Beefsteak John's in 1922. These and several other cruising clubs that sprung up at the time focused on educating their membership in the intricacies of seamanship and navigation. In various ways—via newsletters, lectures, and lending libraries—members of these clubs sought not to assert their social status but to share information and expertise. This same impulse, leavened, of course, with pride of accomplishment, also led some to write and publish accounts of cruises they had made. This growing body of literature disseminated knowledge among those practicing the sport and attracted new sailors.

EARLY CRUISING BOATS

What most interests us here are the sorts of boats this new breed of yachtsman went cruising in. For many who wanted to venture forth in vessels that were substantial enough to survive a bit of weather and large enough to live aboard for limited periods of time in a modicum of comfort, the easiest and cheapest thing to do was simply to buy an old working boat and refurnish it. Some paint, some furniture tacked in down below, and perhaps some rig alterations could transform many such boats into perfectly serviceable cruisers. It helped, of course, that working sailboats everywhere were steadily being replaced by power vessels, and thus were available at reasonable prices in ever-growing numbers.

Fishing boats were the most popular candidates for conversion. Indeed, some types established reputations as cruising boats that ultimately eclipsed their previous identities. We tend to forget, for example, that two popular American craft now considered classic coastal cruising vessels—the Cape Cod catboat and the Friendship sloop—were both originally designed and used as inshore fishing boats. In Britain, lifeboats were also seen as ideal vessels to make over into cruising boats. This practice, which continues to this day, started at least as early as 1886, when E. F. Knight made a name for himself cruising from England to the Baltic and back aboard *Falcon*, a converted ship's lifeboat he purchased for just 20 pounds.

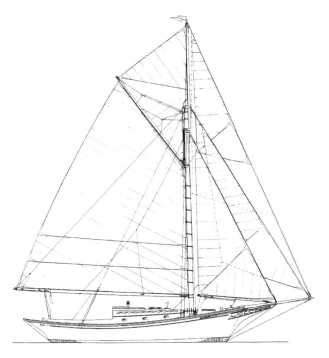

The Friendship sloop was a commercial fishing boat that found a second life as a popular coastal cruiser. (Courtesy of Good Old Boat *and Ted Brewer)*

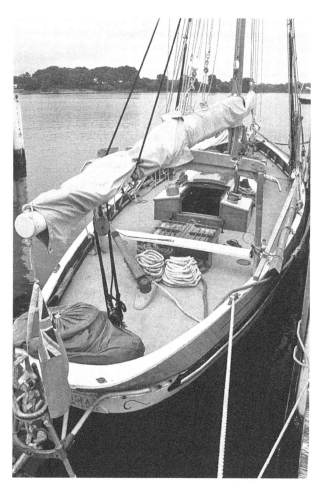

This 100-year-old fishing boat, a Morecombe Bay prawner, was rebuilt as a cruising boat in the late 1990s. Such conversions were common in the late 19th and early 20th centuries.

Old gaff-rigged pilot cutters that once worked for a living are still commonly used as cruising boats in Great Britain.

The most famous converted working boat, of course, was Joshua Slocum's *Spray*. Slocum does not at all fit the template of the amateur cruising yachtsman described here, but his influence on the sport was extraordinary. Ironically, he had something in common with George Crowninshield. Like Crowninshield, Slocum gained his nautical expertise as a professional merchant mariner. Unlike Crowninshield,

Colin Archer's Redningskoite ketch, originally conceived as a pilot/rescue boat, became a seminal cruising boat that still influences designers today.

Pilot boats were another logical choice, as they were usually designed to be fast (so they could compete with other pilot boats racing out of a harbor to do business with inbound vessels) and seaworthy enough to go out in any weather. Several types were pressed into service as yachts on both sides of the Atlantic. Bristol Channel pilot cutters became particularly popular as cruisers in Britain, but by far the most influential type was a beamy double-ended 47-foot pilot and offshore rescue boat designed by Colin Archer in 1893 for work along the coast of Norway. The simple symmetrical lines of these boats, known as Redningskoites, were explicitly copied by others seeking to create durable all-purpose cruising boats. The best-known example was *Eric*, a scaled-down 32-foot Redningskoite designed by William Atkin in 1925. Meanwhile, the design for another very influential double-ended cruising boat, the Tahiti ketch, conceived by John Hanna in 1923, was explictly based on boats sailed by Greek sponge fishermen.

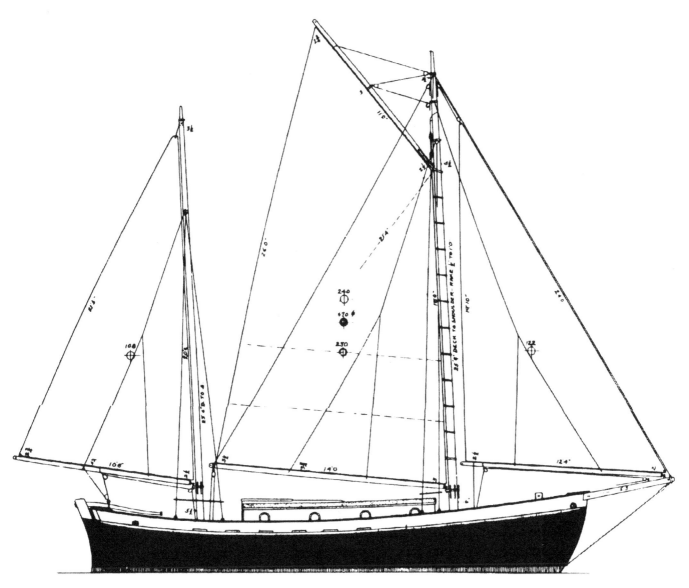

The famous Tahiti ketch, designed by John Hanna, was conceived as a cruiser, but was based on Greek sponge-fishing boats. (Courtesy of Good Old Boat*)*

he lived in the latter part of the 19th century, when commercial sail was being driven into extinction. Crowninshield took up cruising because it amused him, and he had been successful enough as a commercial mariner that he could indulge his fancy in a grandiose manner. Slocum, on the other hand, became a cruiser mostly in desperation. His professional life had been destroyed, and he was shorebound and down on his luck when, in 1892, a fellow ship captain, perhaps as a joke, gave him a decrepit 36-foot Delaware oyster smack that had been left in a field to rot. With characteristic tenacity Slocum rebuilt the boat and, after a brief attempt to earn a living fishing her, set out on a protracted singlehanded cruise around the world. This voyage and Slocum's book describing it, *Sailing Alone Around the World,* not

only helped legitimize "alternative" cruising, it also spread the seed of the cruising dream much farther than before. Indeed, Slocum's book is still in print today and still works its magic in the minds of cruising sailors.

What perhaps is most significant about *Spray* is how anachronistic she was. Even at the time of her circumnavigation, which Slocum completed in 1898, she was in many respects completely obsolete. She was, by Slocum's account, approximately 100 years old when he acquired her, and her hull form reflected this. Her shape tended toward the old "cod's head and mackerel's tail" school of naval architecture, with a fat entry, maximum beam at or a little forward of amidships, and a finer run aft on her waterline. She was wide (over 14 feet) with a

Spray, *a rebuilt Delaware oyster smack, took Joshua Slocum around the world and proved that cruisers in small boats could wander the oceans if they liked.*

relatively shoal draft (about 4 feet) and short ends—her waterline length (about 32 feet) was just 4 feet shy of her length overall. She was also immensely heavy for her size, displacing 24,000 pounds, and carried all her ballast in her bilges, with none at all in her keel. *Spray* had almost nothing in common with modern turn-of-the-century yachts (a fact in which Slocum seemed to take great pleasure), but she served well enough as a cruiser. Indeed, her performance, given her particulars and the fact that she was sailed singlehanded, was extraordinary. Slocum reported top speeds on the order of 8 knots, and he routinely averaged 150 miles a day on passage—numbers more typical of 36-foot yachts built in the mid-20th century that weigh half as much. He also boasted of the boat's ability to steer herself, but credit for this, and for the speeds achieved, must in fact go to Slocum himself. He was a master mariner who had the skill and nerve to drive a vessel hard and was an intuitive expert when it came to sail trim.

What is also significant about *Spray* is that, in spite of her putative obsolescence, her design is still considered viable today. Contemporary cruising boats that mimic her lines, most particularly steel hulls built to plans drawn by designer Bruce Roberts-Goodson, though not exactly common, are not hard to find. Some devotees, in fact, still insist that *Spray* represents the "ultimate" cruising boat. What this demonstrates is that—unlike a racing yacht, which succeeds only if it wins races—the worth of a cruising boat can be measured in any number of ways. One good reason, for example, why some (but certainly not all) traditional designs based on old workboats like *Spray* are still viable is that they yield lots of interior accommodations space, which is, for many cruisers, a key consideration. Other reasons for favoring such boats may include, as mentioned above, their affordability and availability, plus they are often extremely seaworthy. But perhaps their most powerful (and most subjective) attraction is their strong romantic appeal. Traditional boats tap directly into the zeitgeist of the cruising dream, and this unquestionably influenced the development of cruising boat design as cruising became more popular.

Of course, not all early small-boat cruisers were inclined to go sailing in old workboats. Many had the resources to commission the building of modest yachts to cruise in, and this led to a proliferation of specialized designs. As was the case with R. T. McMullen's 42-footer *Orion*, these were often unremarkable adaptations of mainstream yacht designs. It became common, however, for experienced amateur cruisers to commission idiosyncratic designs that reflected personal prejudices and preferences. Here again McMullen provides a useful example, as both *Procyon* and *Perseus*, his smaller purpose-built singlehanders, were unique vessels that must have seemed odd to mainstream yachtsmen of the time.

Some amateur cruisers acquired enough knowledge and expertise to become amateur designers as well. One of the first and most influential of these was Albert Strange, a British headmaster and art teacher

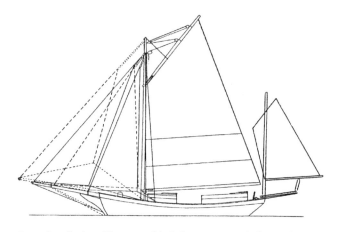

Spray's *sail plan. Slocum added the mizzen to balance the rig.*

In spite of the fact that Spray's *design was already obsolete at the time of her circumnavigation, some modern cruising designs, like this Bruce Roberts-Goodson ketch built in steel, are still based on her lines.*

born in 1855 who first started cruising the Thames estuary as a teenager in a converted workboat. As a member of the Humber Yawl Club, which was directly descended from one of John MacGregor's canoe clubs, Strange's design work followed a fascinating trajectory from small sailing canoes similar to those sailed by MacGregor to much larger double-ended deep-keel vessels known as "canoe yawls." Strange did not invent the canoe yawl, but he is credited with inventing the elegant overhanging pointed canoe stern that initially distinguished his boats from others and was later widely copied. Among the many amateur cruiser/designers who followed in his wake were T. Harrison Butler, W. Maxwell Blake, Fred Fenger, and Maurice Griffiths. Although the work of such men is unique and identifiable, their boats on the whole tended to be conservative, featuring moderate proportions, full ballast keels, narrow to moderate beam, and relatively short ends.

Yet another intriguing wrinkle was the advent of cruisers who sought to build their own boats. For a certain sort of fellow the notion of constructing a boat was just as alluring as the prospect of sailing it. Also, of course, for those with the time and skills backyard building was an economical way to get afloat.

The most adventurous build-it-yourself cruisers worked without plans and made things up as they went along. Remarkably, this was yet another trail

This elegant little yawl, Snickersee, *conceived by yachting author and historian W. P. Stephens, is an example of an amateur-designed cruising boat.*

blazed by Joshua Slocum. Some years prior to his voyage in *Spray*, Slocum had owned and commanded a 138-foot trading bark, *Aquidneck*, that he lost on a sandbar in Brazil in 1887. To get his family home to the United States, he and his oldest son, Victor, built themselves a bizarre 35-foot unballasted junk-rigged sampan (Slocum actually called it a canoe) that they christened *Liberdade*. Slocum and his wife and two children not only sailed this unlikely vessel more than 5,000 miles from Brazil to the United States, they then lived aboard the boat and cruised

it on the East Coast for nearly a year. A vessel as eccentric as *Liberdade* did not immediately inspire imitations, but Slocum's use of the Asian junk rig did anticipate such modern designers as Colonel H. G. "Blondie" Hasler, Tom Colvin, and Jay Benford, who installed junk rigs on both racing and cruising vessels. *Liberdade* also provided an important creative precedent, setting an example for future designers and sailors willing to think "outside the box."

The backyard builders who had the biggest impact on the development of cruising boats were those who

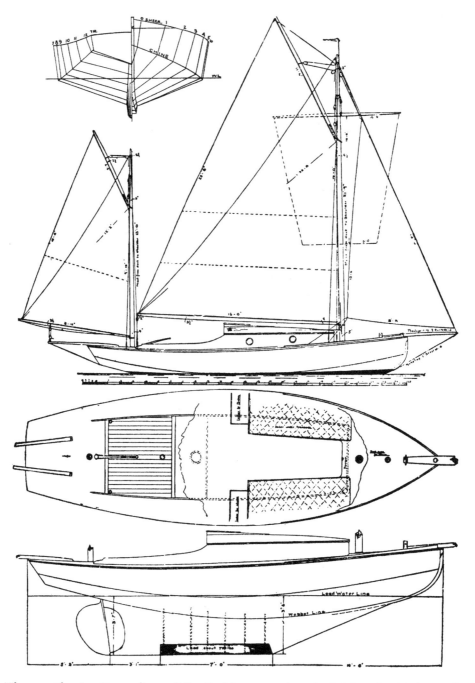

Popularized by Thomas Fleming Day, editor of The Rudder *magazine, the 26-foot* Sea Bird *was designed specifically to be built by amateurs. Day sailed across the Atlantic in her in 1911.*

wanted or needed plans to build to. To meet this demand, some designers started conceiving boats with simplified lines that were easy for amateurs to build. Often such designs were published and marketed through the several boating magazines that sprouted up on both sides of the Atlantic. One of the earliest and most significant was an American publication, *The Rudder*, founded in 1891 by a fiery small-boat evangelist named Thomas Fleming Day. Day believed strongly in the concept of backyard building—"No Boats, No Sport: All Hands Build Hulls" was a favorite slogan of his—and he published many build-it-yourself designs in his magazine. He also believed in practicing what he preached and in 1911 sailed one of these boats, a 26-foot yawl named *Sea Bird*, across the Atlantic from Rhode Island to Gibraltar with two companions as crew. *Sea Bird* was designed for ease of construction and had a simple V-bottomed hull with a single hard chine on either side. Her plans specified two underwater configurations: she could be built either with a centerboard or with a deep keel supporting 700 pounds of ballast. She also reportedly carried about 1,000 pounds of internal ballast. With her low freeboard, *Sea Bird* may not have looked particularly seaworthy, but Day's transatlantic voyage hushed many naysayers, while convincing others that Day himself was most likely a lunatic. Further support for the latter proposition came the following year when Day went transatlantic again, this time in a 36-foot powerboat carrying 1,200 gallons of gasoline.

Over the years, several hundred copies of *Sea Bird* were built by amateur cruisers. Among these was a larger sistership, a 34-foot boat named *Islander* built by Harry Pidgeon, a farm boy from Iowa, in a vacant lot in Los Angeles in 1917. Pidgeon, a self-taught sailor, completed a singlehanded circumnavigation in *Islander* in 1925, becoming only the second man (after Joshua Slocum) to perform this feat. He subsequently lived aboard for 16 years, made another circumnavigation, and was in the middle of a third (this time with his wife) when he finally lost *Islander* in a hurricane in the New Hebrides. Fortunately, Pidgeon and his wife escaped with their lives.

THE GOLDEN AGE OF THE CRUISER-RACER

By the early 20th century, the nexus of mainstream yachting was shifting away from the upper crust of society, most of whom viewed yachting primarily as a social activity, and toward more Corinthian middle- and upper-middle-class sailors, who practiced it as a sport. The boundaries were blurred, of course, and many upper-class yachtsmen were in fact hands-on sailors. A prime example was

E. D. Morgan, mentioned earlier, who was vitally interested in the boats he owned and actively participated in sailing them. Indeed, the Seawanhaka Corinthian Yacht Club, which Morgan joined before he joined the New York Yacht Club, was specifically conceived to accommodate aristocratic sportsmen who wanted to sail their boats themselves (the term "Corinthian" then, as now, referred to an amateur sailor). The primary difference between men like Morgan and their less affluent contemporaries was that they could afford to acquire yachts in bulk. As yachting historian William P. Stephens once put it: "'Alty' Morgan, as he was known to his intimates, thought no more of buying a yacht than the average man does of picking up a paper as he passes a newsstand." Likewise, of course, there were (and are to this day) many middle-class yachtsmen who were most interested in the social aspects of the sport.

But the general trend after the turn of the century was decidedly egalitarian and Corinthian. Interestingly, what helped precipitate this was a growing interest on the part of small-boat cruising sailors in the sport of ocean racing. This interest was fueled and perhaps created by Tom Day and his evangelist magazine *The Rudder*. Ocean racing between large "gold-plated" yachts dated back as far as 1866, when a group of flamboyant American tycoons—James Gordon Bennett, Pierre Lorillard, and brothers George and Franklin Osgood—pitted three vessels against each other in a spontaneous midwinter transatlantic gambit for an enormous wager of $90,000. Subsequent ocean races were occasionally held under similar circumstances, but Day managed to transform ocean racing into an organized sport featuring much smaller boats. The first such long-distance race, sponsored by *The Rudder* in 1904, was contested by six boats, none with a waterline longer than 30 feet, on a course from Brooklyn, New York, to Marblehead, Massachusetts. In 1905 Day organized another such race, this time from Brooklyn to Hampton Roads, Virginia, and attracted 12 participants. The following year he ran the first race to Bermuda, which was contested by just three boats. Day not only conceived these events, he also participated in them, first in his diminutive *Sea Bird*, then aboard a larger 38-foot yawl, *Tamerlane*, in which he won the first Bermuda race. He also, of course, vociferously promoted this sort of competition in his magazine, presenting it as an "in-your-face" challenge to members of the upper-class yachting establishment, whom he described as "a lot of grey-headed, rum-soaked piazza scows . . . who spend their days swigging booze on the front stoop of a clubhouse."

Day staged more Bermuda races from 1907 through 1910, then abandoned the effort in 1911 to take

Sea Bird transatlantic, as noted above. Competition of this sort died out for several years, due largely to the advent of World War I, but was revived in 1923 by members of the fledgling Cruising Club of America (CCA), which assumed stewardship of the Bermuda Race the following year and has maintained it ever since. In Britain, the first Fastnet Race was organized in 1925 by members of the Royal Cruising Club who wished to emulate their adventurous American counterparts. What became known as the Royal Ocean Racing Club (RORC) was formed during the awards dinner. In taking the torch from the controversial and incendiary Day, these more genteel organizations helped legitimize small-boat ocean racing in the eyes of the yachting establishment, yet did so without alienating less aristocratic enthusiasts—Day's core constituents—who were entering the sport in ever-growing numbers.

This blending of the ethos of cruising and racing led to some serendipitous boat designs. One of the most successful American ocean-racing designs immediately after World War I proved to be seamanlike schooners designed by men such as John Alden and William Hand. These boats were heavily constructed, moderately beamy, with moderate to deep draft, and carried ballast both in their bilges and low in their keels. They also featured short to moderate overhangs and full keels with forefoots that were gently cut away. Their hull form is still considered by many to be one of the most beautiful ever conceived. These "fisherman" schooners, as they were known, were nearly perfect dual-purpose vessels for their time—they had enough space below for comfortable accommodations, were heavy enough to feel safe and solid in a seaway, and were just fast enough to win races. They were the result of an interesting cross-pollination between yachts and working boats. The Grand Banks fishing schooners on which they were based had themselves been refined by yacht designers, including Bowdoin Crowninshield, who were commissioned to improve on older 19th-century fishing boat designs that had proved unseaworthy.

Competing with the fisherman schooners for dominance in early ocean races were a few New York 40 class boats. Designed and built by Nat Herreshoff as strict one-design racers pursuant to a commission from the NYYC, these boats were 59 feet long with 40-foot waterlines (see photo page 22). Because the New York 40s were intended for inshore use, many shivered at the thought of their competing offshore in distance races. They were narrower and deeper than the schooners, much more lightly constructed, with much longer overhangs, and carried all their ballast as low as possible. They also featured the new gaff-less "Marconi" rig, so-called because it

was the fruit of the same structural engineering that produced Marconi radio towers.

Compromises between the two types soon appeared. First came the 59-foot schooner *Nina*, designed by W. Starling Burgess, which made a splash in 1928 by winning a transatlantic race to Spain and the Fastnet Race later that same summer. *Nina* carried a huge Marconi mainsail aft and small staysails forward and was narrower, deeper, and lighter than the fisherman schooners, but less so than the New York 40s. She was followed soon after by the 52-foot yawl *Dorade*, designed by a 20-year-old upstart named Olin Stephens, which in 1931 repeated *Nina*'s feat of winning both a transatlantic race and the Fastnet in the same season. She and her immediate successor, another Stephens design called *Stormy Weather*, were the first truly modern ocean racers and featured inboard Marconi rigs with no bowsprits or long overhanging booms. These ultimately proved more efficient and safer than the old gaff rig. With their improved rigs, narrower beam, longer overhangs, lighter construction, and deeper ballast these new boats were consistently faster and more weatherly than the more traditional fisherman schooners.

Though the fisherman schooners were ultimately supplanted (by 1938 only 7 of the 38 boats starting the Bermuda Race were schooners), the ideal of a boat that could be both successfully raced and comfortably cruised was not forsaken. Indeed, the CCA's stated rationale for sponsoring ocean racing events (a practice some members strongly disavowed) was that it believed such races would stimulate the development of "suitable" cruising boats. And there was a great deal of logic in this. Unlike inshore racing boats that are manned by their crews for only hours at a time in protected water, offshore racing boats must be inhabited by their crews for days on end in the open ocean. Thus the factors of comfort and safety—always of great interest to cruisers—should (theoretically, at least) be carefully considered and treated in any successful offshore racing design.

For many years this was the case. Through roughly half of the 20th century, from about 1920 until 1970, American cruiser-racers flourished as a type and no new design ever became so extreme as to totally eclipse its predecessors. The tendencies of yacht designers and ambitious racing sailors to ignore comfort and safety in their pursuit of trophies were held in check by the CCA rating rule (adopted in the mid-1930s), which incorporated boundaries on dimensional proportions that prevented dramatic exaggerations of form in any given boat. The CCA rule, in effect, defined an ideal cruiser-racer and punished variations from the ideal that increased a boat's speed while rewarding those that decreased it.

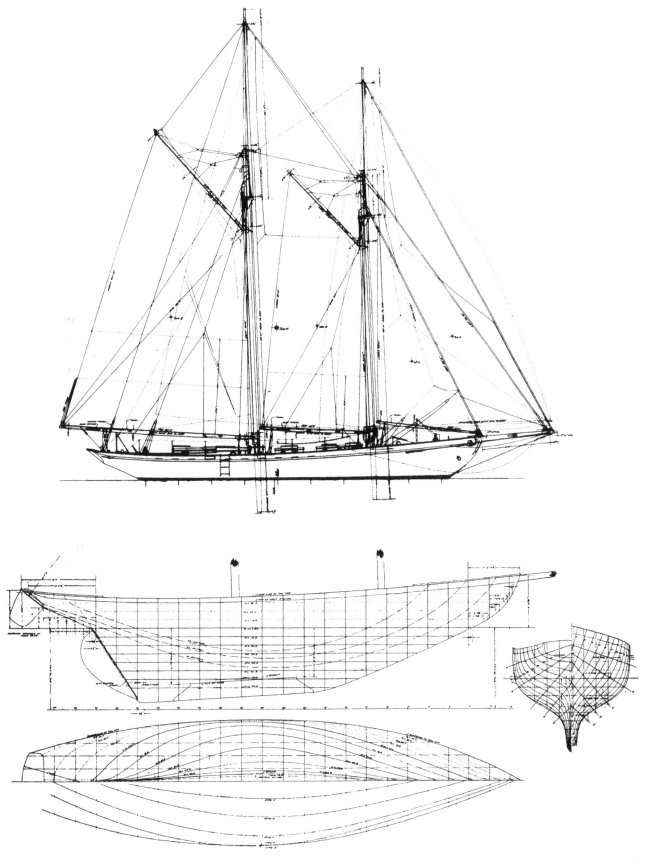

Fisherman schooners like Mohawk, *designed by John Alden, were great cruiser-racers in their day and dominated ocean racing in the years after World War I. Many sailors still covet them as cruising boats.*

The New York 40 Rugosa, *designed and built by Nat Herreshoff (and now owned by his grandson Halsey Herreshoff), showing her long overhangs: 59 feet on deck with a 40-foot waterline. (Courtesy of Stephen Mulhern Gross)*

This inhibited innovation to some extent, but the rule, often tweaked and amended, proved remarkably supple over time. It successfully accommodated a fundamental design advance—the advent of fin keels and separated rudders, which started becoming popular in 1963—and also accommodated a revolutionary change in the way boats were built—the advent of fiberglass construction in the late 1950s. Yet it was generous enough to older designs that boats from the 1920s and '30s could still occasionally place well in top races on corrected time as late as the 1960s. Two examples are the schooner *Nina*, mentioned above, which won the Bermuda Race in 1963, and a 1932 Alden fisherman schooner, *Constellation* (ex-*La Reine*), which twice took first place in Class A of the Transpac Race during the 1950s.

CCA cruiser-racers really came into their own in the years following World War II. One of the most successful boats of the era—a fat, heavy, 38-foot centerboard yawl called *Finisterre*—leaned markedly toward the cruiser side of the equation. *Finisterre* was designed by Olin Stephens in 1954 for Carleton Mitchell, an active sailor/author who wanted a relatively small shoal-draft boat packed with creature comforts, including heavy refrigeration and heating units and a large battery bank. The design's core concept,

that of a ballast keel with a centerboard descending from it, harkened back to the compromise designs that Edward Burgess had pioneered some 80 years earlier. With her board up, *Finisterre* drew just 3 feet, 11 inches (perfect for sailing the Bahamas, one of Mitchell's favorite cruising grounds), and her wide beam (over 11 feet) and heavy displacement (over 22,000 pounds, much of it arrayed in the bilge as either house systems or bronze structural members supporting the centerboard trunk) gave her a smooth, easy motion in a seaway.

Mitchell cruised *Finisterre* much more than he raced her (his own estimate was 10:1, mileage-wise, in favor of cruising), but when he did race her, he did extremely well. His crowning achievement was three straight wins in the Bermuda Race (1956, 1958, and 1960), one of the few records in all of sport that still seems truly unassailable. Some have argued that this success, at least initially, was a function of *Finisterre*'s very low rating under the CCA rule ("almost too good to be true," Olin Stephens once described it). Mitchell's ability as a sailor was also an important factor. He was known for preparing his boats meticulously prior to a race and for driving them without mercy once across a starting line. But several of the many keel/centerboard boats

The Pearson Invicta was one of many CCA keel/centerboard designs that followed in the wake of Carleton Mitchell's famous cruiser-racer Finisterre. *The example pictured here,* Burgoo, *was the first fiberglass boat to win the Bermuda Race (1964). (Courtesy of Dan Spurr; Photo by Norman Fortier.)*

that followed in *Finisterre*'s wake, including fiberglass boats, likewise did well on the racecourse, even after the CCA adjusted its method of quantifying a boat's ballast to eliminate the rating advantage that *Finisterre* had enjoyed early in her career.

Of course, many boats that raced successfully under the CCA rule in the postwar years were not as cruise oriented as *Finisterre*. Most had less beam, less weight, and deeper keels and were more evenly poised between their dual functions. Several heavily favored the racer side of the equation and featured spartan accommodations. For decades, however, all variations under the CCA rule, from *Finisterre* to the most race-oriented designs, shared a distinctive hull form featuring a full keel with a slightly cut-away forefoot, an attached raked rudder, and moderately long overhangs forward and aft. Dimensions could be tweaked and weight could be increased or decreased and spatially distributed to favor cruising or racing, but the range of variation was limited. On the whole, the form was oriented more toward cruising than racing.

All this changed in 1963 when C. William Lapworth designed the fin-keel Cal 40 for Jensen Marine, a

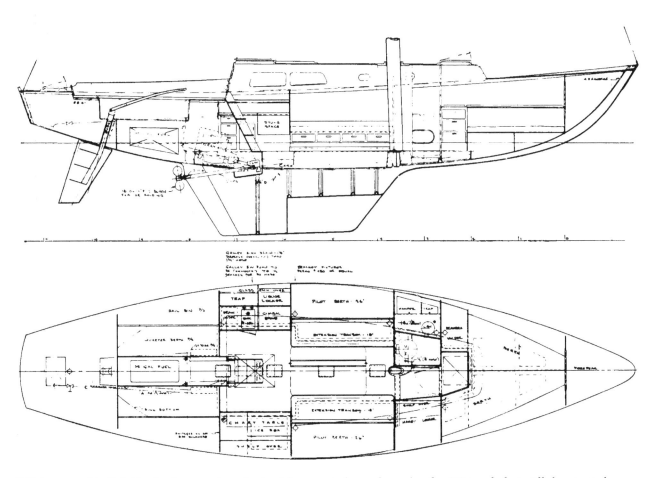

Bill Lapworth's Cal 40, the first modern fin-keel boat, rated poorly under the CCA rule but still dominated ocean racing in the mid-1960s. It spelled the beginning of the end for new full-keel designs.

California-based fiberglass production boatbuilder. The Cal 40 was not the first boat to sport a fin keel and a separated rudder. Nat Herreshoff had designed and built such a boat, *Dilemma*, in 1891, having borrowed the idea of a fin keel from a boat built in Michigan 10 years earlier. *Dilemma* and her sisters, precisely because they were radically fast, were banned by the rating rules then in effect, though the concept of the fin keel survived in much smaller boats, most notably the 22-foot one-design Star class skiff, which first appeared in 1911 and is still actively raced today. But the Cal 40 was the first boat of any size built in the 20th century to sport a fin keel, and it represented a significant breakthrough. With its relatively light displacement, short overhangs, flat bilges, and radically cut-away underbody, the Cal 40 had an unfavorable rating under the CCA rule (indeed, Lapworth more or less ignored the rule when conceiving the boat), but still it did well on the racecourse. It won the Transpac Race three years in a row (1965–67), the 1966 Southern Ocean Racing Circuit (SORC), and the 1966 Bermuda Race (in which 5 of the top 15 boats were Cal 40s). The Cal 40 did not kill the CCA rule (Bill Lapworth in fact later argued the rule should be retained), but it did put an end to any notion that a full-keel boat could be a cutting-edge racer.

EARLY FIBERGLASS CRUISERS

The CCA rule remained the primary rating rule in American racing until 1970, when it was supplanted by the International Offshore Rule (IOR), which was promulgated to encourage international competition by resolving differences between the CCA rule and the RORC's rating rule, which governed racing in Great Britain. Whereas the CCA rule had explicitly sought to encourage development of boats that could both cruise and race, the IOR, like the British RORC rule, sought more to promote performance. As a result, racing and cruising under sail once again diverged.

Early IOR boats were not radically different from boats conceived in the twilight years of the CCA rule. Indeed, some boats designed during the transition between the two rules, with rudders hung on skegs and swept-back fin keels that seemed like organic remnants of the full keels they supplanted, are among the most beautiful ever conceived. They were

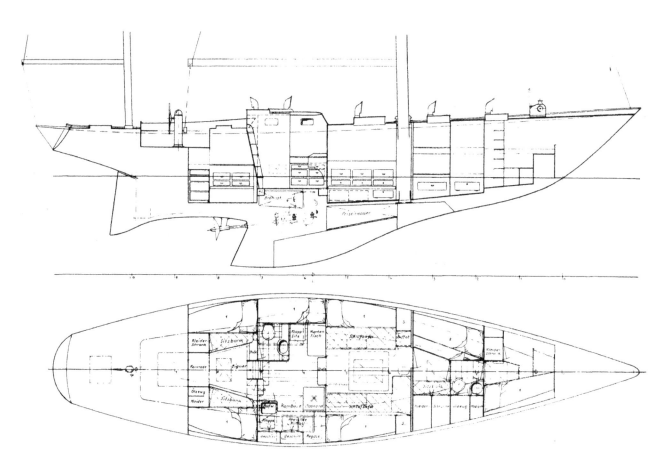

Several boats built during the transition between the CCA and IOR eras were just as graceful as the full-keel boats that preceded them, but also performed better. Boats like Gudrun, *designed by Abeking & Rasmussen, could succeed both as cruisers and racers.*

also capable, like the best CCA boats, of succeeding as both racers and cruisers. By the mid-1970s, however, everything had heated up. Fiberglass production was making boats more and more affordable, drawing larger numbers of people into the sport of sailing. Offshore racing was growing more popular and increasingly intense, with more events and more sailors competing in them.

Designers therefore were under more and more pressure to produce cutting-edge boats—not only so that keen racing sailors could win trophies with them, but also so that salespeople could tout winning records when marketing them. By the end of the decade, the typical IOR boat was a more specialized light-displacement racing machine with a narrow stub of a fin keel; a spade rudder situated perhaps a bit too far aft; flat bilges; a beamy midsection; narrow, pinched ends; a large sail plan; and a relatively high center of gravity that required lots of crew weight on the rail to keep the boat upright and sailing its best. Some of these features improved boat speed, but the intent of others was solely to exploit loopholes in the rating rule. The result, in any event, was a type of boat that was faster than old CCA cruiser-racers but not as comfortable or seaworthy, as was dramatically demonstrated during the Fastnet Race of 1979, during which a strong gale sank 5 boats, capsized dozens of others, and took the lives of 15 sailors.

But even as fiberglass race boats were becoming more specialized and more cranky, there also appeared a new generation of specialized fiberglass cruising boats. It is tempting to infer a cause-and-effect relationship here, but in fact the two trends emerged simultaneously. Again, it was the immense increase in the size of the sailing market that was driving events. The mature industrial economy of the late 20th century had created more wealth for middle- and working-class families even as it lowered the costs of boat ownership through the efficiencies of fiberglass production. The concomitant increase in active sailors fed the ranks of both cruisers and racers and allowed both types of boat to flourish side by side.

As the Fastnet tragedy demonstrated, racing sailors were perfectly willing to let modern technology, their greed for speed, and the perversities of rating rules drive them toward the edge of safety. Dedicated cruising sailors instinctively headed in the other direction. What most appealed to the prospective cruising boat buyer, production builders quickly learned, was the romance of cruising, and the best way to evoke this in a boat design, they also deduced, was to make it a traditional one. The "breakthrough" boat in this respect was the phenomenally successful California-built Westsail 32. Its design, cobbled together by Bill Crealock, was anything but innovative. Indeed, it was a direct rip-off of William Atkin's fat double-ender

Eric, which in turn had been directly based on Colin Archer's pilot and rescue boat, the Redningskoite, a concept that was nearly a century old.

In its first incarnation as the Kendall 32, the Westsail was a complete failure. But then its mold was purchased at a bankruptcy auction by a young couple, Snider and Lynne Vick, who knew little about sailing and nothing about boatbuilding but saw the cruising dream incarnate in the boat's design and had a vision of sharing that dream with the world. Their deft marketing of the boat, which they reintroduced as the Westsail 32 in 1972, strongly emphasized the romance of voyaging under sail (and the boat's heavyweight indestructibility) and thereby struck a major chord not only with sailors, but with the public at large. By 1974 the boat was featured in *Time* magazine as something akin to a lifestyle phenomenon. By the end of the decade the Vicks had sold more than 800 copies and had expanded their model line to include a 28-footer and a 42- and 43-footer.

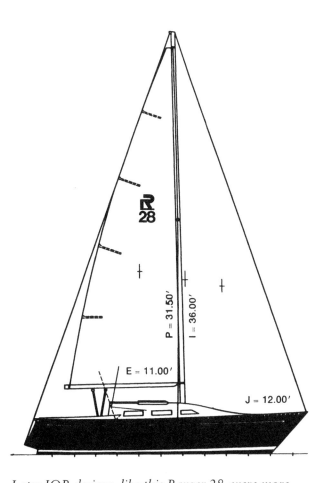

Later IOR designs, like this Ranger 28, were more focused on racing than cruising. They became more extreme, with pinched ends, fat midsections, spade rudders, and less substantial keels (see next page). They were also less seaworthy.

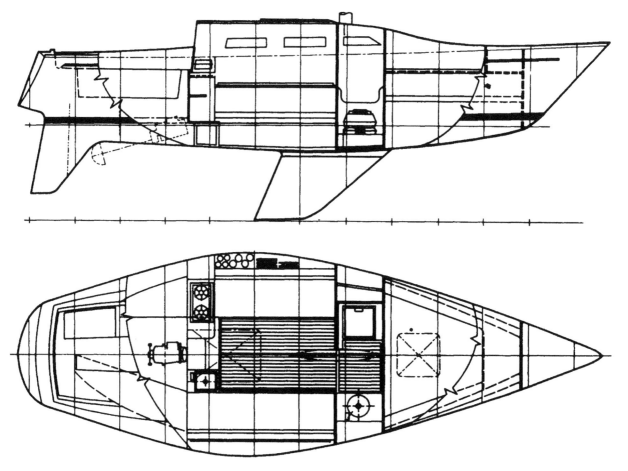

Ranger 28.

The Westsail's cult status had a profound effect on the design of fiberglass cruising boats. For years afterward, builders who wanted to be sure of tapping into the cruising zeitgeist felt compelled to produce heavyweight full-keel double-enders that mimicked the look and feel of this iconic boat. Some were direct variations, most notably the Ingrid and Alajuela 38 (circa 1973), which were also designed by William Atkin. Like the Westsail, such boats were heavy, carried simple outboard rudders controlled with large tillers, and featured hulls with full forefoots. Other designs were more derivative and slightly more sophisticated, with canoe sterns (to retain the double-ended look), inboard rudders controlled with wheels, and hulls with slightly cutaway forefoots. Many of these boats were built in Taiwan, where lavish teak joinery and deck work, which always helps evoke a traditional mood (and increase weight on board), could be economically executed. Examples of such designs, some of which are still in production today, include the Baba 30 (designed by Robert Perry circa 1978), the highly popular Tayana 37 (Robert Perry, circa 1979), and several models offered by builder Hans Christian.

Other builders, however, sought to significantly refine and modernize the Westsail template and soon produced much more sophisticated designs. These also sported canoe sterns, but were lighter and narrower and had taller sail plans, flatter bilges, and more cutaway underbodies with generously sized fin keels and separated rudders. Significant examples include the Valiant 40 (another Robert Perry design, circa 1973), the Fast Passage 39 (designed by William Garden, circa 1976), and several boats produced by Pacific Seacraft that were designed by the original perpetrator himself, Bill Crealock.

The old double-ended Redningskoite was not, however, the only archetype available to fiberglass builders who wanted to market traditional-looking cruising boats. Another significant type was seen in certain heavy full-keel designs, most with ketch rigs, with traditional features like clipper bows, bowsprits, wide wineglass transoms, and carved wooden taffrails and bow-boards. The first of these, the Cheoy Lee Clipper 36 (circa 1969), actually predated the Westsail by a few years. Imitators included the Hardin Sea Wolf 31 (circa 1973), the Fuji 35 (circa 1974), and the Vagabond 47 (circa 1978). Unlike the Westsail, which

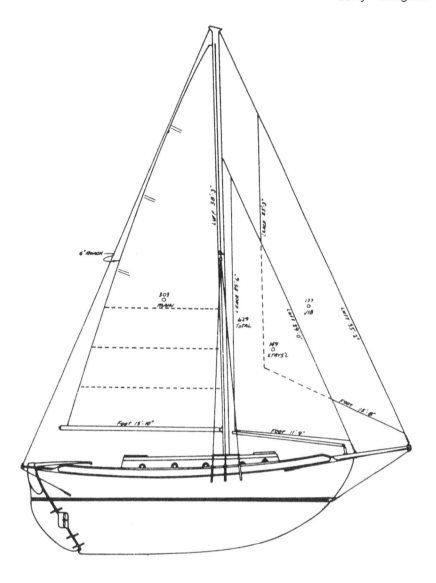

The traditional design and ambiance of the Westsail 32, coupled with deft marketing, touched a nerve and made cruising a cultural phenomenon. The boat is strong, but performs poorly and is derided as "the Wetsnail" by some critics. (Courtesy of Good Old Boat *and* SAIL *magazines; Photo by Malcolm White.)*

After the emergence of the Westsail 32 cruisers strongly favored double-ended hulls. This Tahitiana production cruiser, modeled after the old Tahiti ketch, was one of many boats introduced in the 1970s that sought to exploit this prejudice. (Courtesy of Good Old Boat)

introduced similar cruising ketches during the 1970s, the larger examples of which, again, tended to feature center cockpits. Some of these boats, including some of the faux-traditional models just mentioned, diverged from the tried-and-true full-keel hull form, but never too far. Larger Irwin ketches, for example, often carried centerboards and had slightly cutaway underbodies with separated rudders.

One builder, Garry Hoyt, founder of Freedom Yachts, was not at all afraid of trying new ideas. His Freedom 40, first introduced as a prototype in 1977, showed just how different a cruising boat could be. It featured a radical unstayed cat-ketch rig that had a self-tacking main and mizzen on wishbone booms with no headsails. The hull form, however, deliberately conceived by Hoyt as a "retro" challenge to the fad of fin-keel IOR hulls, featured a full shoal-draft keel with a long centerboard descending from it. The deck layout included a massive center cockpit. Originally the unstayed masts on the Freedom 40, and on other Freedom models introduced by Hoyt,

was in fact simply an old design recast in fiberglass, these were contemporary designs that were conservative in nature. The larger examples did feature a new concept—the center cockpit—that quickly became popular with cruising sailors because it opened up space belowdecks for an aft stateroom.

There were also several early fiberglass boats marketed strictly as cruisers that did not explicitly evoke or mimic traditional designs. One example was the Allied Seawind 30, a small ketch designed by Thomas Gillmer that was introduced in 1962. In its hull form and rig the Seawind had much in common with the more affected "clipper ketches" that followed in its wake. It was relatively heavy with a full keel, generous beam, and a conservatively sized sail plan.

Though not particularly fast, the Seawind was (and is) eminently seaworthy, as was demonstrated by an early enthusiast, Alan Eddy, who took one around the world singlehanded during the years 1963 through 1969 (thus earning the Seawind the distinction of being the first fiberglass boat to complete a circumnavigation). In its first iteration, the Seawind had a simple outboard rudder, but the Seawind II, introduced in 1975, had an inboard rudder and was lengthened by 2 feet to create more interior space. In 1972 the Allied Boat Company also introduced two larger ketch-rigged cruisers in the same vein—the Princess (36 feet) and the Mistress (39 feet). Other builders, notably Irwin, Morgan, and Gulfstar,

Romantic-looking ketches with clipper bows and stern windows were also very popular with cruisers during the 1970s. (Courtesy of SAIL *Magazine; Photo by Malcolm White.)*

were aluminum, but in 1980 he switched to carbon-fiber masts, a prescient innovation that anticipated by several years a shift to carbon spars in race boats. A few other builders later followed Hoyt's lead and marketed cruising boats with unstayed rigs, most notably Hinterhoeller, a Canadian company, whose Nonsuch boats featured one big sail on a single unstayed mast with a wishbone boom. The hulls of the several Nonsuch models combined a beamy footprint with relatively light displacement and a modern underbody that featured flat bilges, fin keels, and separated spade rudders.

MULTIHULLS AND OTHER ALTERNATIVES

Even as fiberglass production techniques were thrusting sailboats into the heart of the 20th-century consumer economy, some cruising enthusiasts were determined to stay outside the mainstream. One of these was James Wharram, who in 1954 designed and built for himself an extremely crude 24-foot plywood catamaran he called *Tangaroa*. In company with two young German women, he cruised this unlikely craft from his home in England across the Atlantic to the Caribbean. On a beach in Trinidad, Wharram designed and built yet another plywood cat, the 40-foot *Rongo*, to replace the disintegrating *Tangaroa*, then sailed this new boat with his all-women crew back to England via New York in 1959. Wharram documented his adventure in various magazine articles and later in a book, *Two Girls Two Catamarans* (featuring several photos of his bare-chested crew), and thus helped bring the concept of the catamaran to the attention of the 20th-century sailing public.

Wharram was hardly the first Westerner to build and sail a catamaran. Eighty years earlier, in 1876, Nat Herreshoff conceived and patented a unique design for *Amaryllis*, a twin-hulled sailboat that proved capable of outstanding speed and was soon banned from competition. Even earlier, in 1662, Sir William Petty designed and built for Charles II an innovative "double-bottomed" yacht that, appropriately, was named *The Experiment*. Wharram himself was aware of at least one Western predecessor, the Frenchman Eric de Bisschop, who in 1937 built a 38-foot "double canoe" on a beach in Hawaii and then sailed it to France via the Cape of Good Hope. Indeed, Wharram carefully studied de Bisschop's book, *The Voyage of the Kaimiloa*, when designing and building his first boat. But ultimately (like de Bisschop before him) he was much more influenced by the Polynesians, who first traversed the Pacific in double-hulled voyaging canoes thousands of years earlier. (Note that the English term "catamaran" is not Polynesian in origin, but in fact derives from the

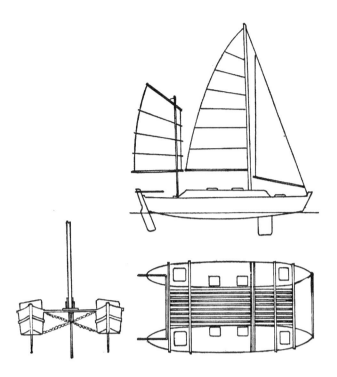

Jim Wharram's first catamaran, Tangaroa, *was crude and simple. He built the boat himself in a barn in England, sailed it across the Atlantic, and went on to become a successful designer of build-it-yourself cruising cats. (Courtesy of James Wharram)*

Tamil term *kattumaram*, for "bound wood," which describes a type of raft once used in southeast India.) There were also other more immediate predecessors, including Roland and Francis Prout in England, Francis "Skip" Creger in California, and Woody Brown in Hawaii, all of whom began experimenting with small beach cats in the mid-1940s.

Wharram was among the first to promote cruising not just as a mode of sailing that might challenge certain orthodoxies of the yachting establishment, but as an entire countercultural lifestyle that called into question the values of 20th-century industrial society. He was also one of the first Westerners to devote his attention exclusively to the creation of larger cruising catamarans. Since the early 1960s, Wharram has generated a large portfolio of build-it-yourself designs, from small beach cruisers to huge 63-foot "tribal" voyaging vessels, that to this day he sells to others who want to sail away from civilized life on the cheap. Having sold over 8,000 sets of plans to date—half of which, he estimates, have led to the creation of finished boats—he is perhaps the most successful and influential designer of build-it-yourself boats in history.

Another visionary who began creating larger multihulls around the same time was Arthur Piver, a retired pilot and trade-journal publisher from California. Piver designed and built a small 20-foot catamaran in 1954, but soon shifted his attention to trimarans. By 1957 he was selling build-it-yourself trimaran plans (his boats, like Wharram's, were plywood and thus simple to build). In 1960 he gained notoriety by sailing a 30-foot plywood trimaran he designed and built, *Nimble*, across the Atlantic from Massachusetts to England. Piver died at sea in 1968 while attempting to qualify for a singlehanded ocean race, but lived long enough to mentor other men—Norm Cross, Jim Brown,

and Dick Newick—who also began designing and building trimarans. Newick has focused more on performance designs, but most of the boats designed by Cross, Brown, and Piver himself were intended to function primarily as cruisers. All three of these men, though perhaps not to the same degree as Jim Wharram, saw cruising multihulls as catalysts for alternative lifestyles.

The old-school yachting establishment, unsurprisingly, was for many years disdainful of multihulls and the colorful men who created and promoted them. But by this time the yachting establishment had little to do with the mainstream of the sport, which was increasingly consumer oriented. As is so often the case, the market did not hesitate to wrap its arms around a product with a countercultural image, and by the late 1960s the first fiberglass multihulls were being offered for sale. The potentially greater speed of multihulls, their larger living spaces, unsinkability, and disinclination to heel under sail were all palpable advantages that were easy to promote to middle-class, family-oriented cruisers. The first mass-produced multihull in the United States was evidently a trimaran, the Corinthian 41 (circa 1967), designed by Ted Irwin for Symons-Sailing. Most other early fiberglass multihulls were catamarans built in Great Britain. These included the Buccaneer 24 (circa 1968), Iroquois 30 (circa 1969),

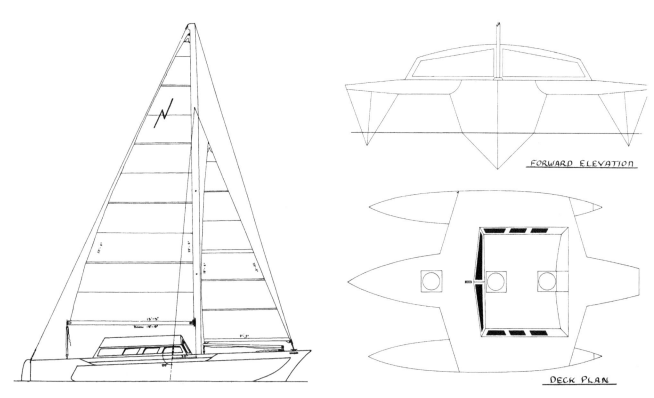

Arthur Piver's Nimble *was one of the first cruising trimarans. Like Jim Wharram's catamarans, Piver's plywood trimarans were simple to build.*

Hirondelle 24 (circa 1970), the Snow Goose 34 (circa 1971), and Solaris 42 (circa 1971).

Other alternative cruising boats began emerging during the 1960s and '70s. These included boats built of metal, most especially steel. The key evangelist was an iconoclastic French colonial, Bernard Moitessier, who first took to bluewater cruising in the mid-1950s as a way to escape his homeland, Vietnam, which had been engulfed in a bitter anticolonial civil war. Moitessier had wrecked two wooden boats early in his career, the second of which he designed and built himself, and was stranded in Trinidad when he first considered alternative construction materials. His initial idea for getting away from Trinidad was to build a composite boat of newspaper and pitch on a wood frame, but he set this scheme aside when offered passage to Europe as crew aboard an oil tanker. Working on the tanker, he spent a lot of time scraping and painting the ship's steel topsides and concluded, as he later put it, "that a properly built steel yacht could be maintained by a well-trained monkey." Moitessier, who had spent much time attending to rot aboard his wood boats, was greatly attracted to the seeming ease of maintenance and the indestructibility of steel as a building material.

With his next boat, *Joshua*, a crude 40-foot steel ketch designed by Jean Knocker and launched in 1961, Moitessier gained an international reputation by making record-breaking nonstop ocean passages. The first was from Tahiti to Spain via Cape Horn with his wife in 1965–66. The second, in 1968–69 during the the first nonstop solo around-the-world race, took him one-and-a-half times around the world singlehanded. These voyages, and the bestselling books Moitessier wrote about them, helped popularize steel yacht construction, which up to that time had been common only in Holland. This was particularly true in France, where Moitessier was (and still is) revered. Soon there appeared a variety of designs for steel cruising boats, many of them featuring hard-chine hulls that significantly simplified construction. Aluminum, which is much lighter than steel, was also recognized as a viable building material, and by the mid-1970s one-off aluminum racing and cruising yachts were likewise increasingly common.

Metal boatbuilding ultimately became mainstream in Europe, and this has been reflected in design trends there. The Europeans quickly moved away from the conservative precedent established

Metal cruising boats, like this steel pinky schooner designed by Tom Colvin, appeal strongly to certain sailors who favor strength and durability over performance. They first became popular in the early 1960s.

by *Joshua*, which had a double-ended full-keel hull form very similar to Redningskoites, and soon were building more modern hulls with fin keels and separated rudders. Some production metal boatbuilders, notably Garcia and Alubat in France, both of which remain successful to this day, also appeared. In the United States, metal boatbuilding has never been anything more than marginal. With the exception of those developed for aluminum racing boats, American metal sailboat designs have favored traditional forms and have been built on a one-off basis, by either custom builders or adventurous build-it-yourself types. Probably the most successful American designer of metal cruising boats has been Tom Colvin, whose work is based largely on working vessels such as pinky schooners, Chesapeake skipjacks, Chinese junks, and other types. His most popular design, the 42-foot Gazelle (of which over 700 have been built), blends the hull of a traditional working schooner with an Asian junk rig. Other American designers favoring metal boats include Ted Brewer, Charles Wittholz, and Jay Benford.

Ferrocement was yet another alternative building material that briefly attracted the attention of cruising sailors. This technique, similar to that proposed by Moitessier for paper, involved plastering concrete over a frame constructed of steel pipe and rod and wire mesh. Hailed at first as the ultimate do-it-yourself building method because it required no specialized skills, ferrocement was enthusiastically embraced for a short period starting in the late 1960s. Then it became clear that ferrocement construction in fact required a great deal of persistence and patience and that construction quality was extremely variable. Improperly built hulls soon exhibited a tendency to disintegrate, and by the end of the 1970s the ferro building craze was pretty much over. These boats were most often built to traditional full-keel designs, as this simple hull form was relatively easy to frame in wire mesh.

CONTEMPORARY DUAL-PURPOSE BOATS

Fortunately, the concept of the purpose-built fiberglass cruiser did not stay mired in the staid yet romantic realm of traditional boat design. Nor was the concept of a boat that could be both raced and cruised ever abandoned. Production builders have always sought to market as dual-purpose vessels many boats designed to modern rating rules (not only the IOR, but its various successors as well). And of course it is possible to cruise aboard modern racing boats

that have at least minimal accommodations—some berths, a galley, and a head. Many such boats from J-Boats, C&C, X-Yachts, Dehler, Farr, Grand Soleil, and other builders offer much more than minimal accommodations and are perfectly comfortable tied up to a dock or at anchor.

But these modern so-called dual-purpose boats, unlike those built to the old CCA rule, are more oriented toward the racing side of the equation. It is an incontrovertible fact of modern sailing that if you are truly interested in winning races with your boat, you need to think about speed first and comfort second. These boats are more accurately described as racer-cruisers rather than cruiser-racers. As expected, they feature fin-keel/spade-rudder underbodies, but these appendages have become increasingly narrow and deep. Weight is kept as low as possible in ballast bulbs attached to minimalist foil-like keels. Rudders, likewise, have as little surface area as possible. Construction has grown increasingly exotic (and more expensive) as lighter materials such as carbon fiber and Kevlar have replaced fiberglass in hull laminates. Carbon fiber is now the competitive standard in racing spars, and racing sails are also constructed of exotic laminates rather than simple polyester. Rigging, likewise, is made from increasingly exotic high-modulus fibers. All of this saves weight and increases speed but does not necessarily improve a boat's suitability for cruising.

In parallel with these racer-cruisers, however, there has also evolved a species of mass-produced dual-purpose boat that is more cruiser than racer. Superficially, at least, these boats are similar to racer-cruisers, featuring relatively short overhangs, shallow hulls with flat bilges, narrow fin keels, and separated spade rudders. Indeed, this is now the most common type of sailboat hull, for several reasons. The first, most obviously, has to do with performance. Even to those uninterested in racing, speed is seductive, and the fin-keel/spade-rudder underbody has effectively redefined acceptable average cruising speeds. In many situations, fin-keel boats also handle much better than boats with full keels and attached rudders. Because they can pivot on their keels, they are easier to steer, as it takes less effort to turn the boat. The helm of a fin-keel boat feels lighter, and steering is more crisp and precise. The difference is particularly dramatic when maneuvering under power in close quarters.

Probably the biggest reason fin-keel boats have become so popular has to do with simple economics. All other things being equal (i.e., assuming modern exotic construction materials are not involved), they are cheaper to build because relative hull volume is decreased and it takes less material to construct them. A lighter-displacement fiberglass hull typically requires less laminate and less resin on a per-square-inch basis. This adds to up to lower costs and lower prices.

The shift from relatively simple, low-volume fiberglass boat production to true mass production began in the 1970s. Significantly, it was contemporaneous not only with the emergence of fin keels, but also with the emergence of large-scale bareboat chartering fleets. The first fiberglass boats purpose-built to work in charter fleets were heavy center-cockpit cruising ketches similar to those discussed above. The CSY Carib 41 (circa 1969) and the Morgan Out Island 41 (circa 1971) both had beamy, shoal-draft, full-keel hulls. Subsequent iterations, such as the CSY 37 (circa 1978), an aft-cockpit cutter with an intriguing raised-deck configuration, had hulls with partially cutaway underbodies but were just as heavy and beamy and also tended to be shoal draft. Charter fleets grew larger and more numerous during the late 1970s and early '80s, thanks to lease-back ownership deals that allowed boat buyers to cover their financing costs by immediately putting their new boats into charter service. For a time this market continued to be dominated by purpose-built boats and by production cruising ketches from builders such as Irwin and Gulfstar. But by the end of the 1980s, most bareboat fleets were filled with relatively light-displacement mass-produced sloops with fin keels and spade rudders.

A unique sort of racing/cruising synergy has allowed mass-production builders such as Beneteau, Jeanneau, Dufour, Bavaria, and Catalina to market similar boats to the low-end racing market and the highest-volume portion of the cruising market. The template on which both types are built is a light-displacement, shallow-bilge hull with a long waterline, generous beam carried well aft, and a fin keel and spade rudder. Because the hull has lots of beam, it can satisfy the most basic requirement of a charter boat, which is that there should be lots of room for berths and toilets. Typically, on bareboats 35 feet and larger there are now no less than three private double-berth staterooms. The fin-keel configuration helps keep unit costs down and does not at all hamper the boat's basic function, which is to sail short distances (normally downwind) in relatively protected waters. These charter boats usually have slightly truncated rigs to ease sail-handling chores and shoal-draft keels to increase access to cruising grounds.

This same hull—tricked out with a taller rig, a deeper fin keel, and more sophisticated running

Many mass-production fiberglass sailboats are now designed to serve in large bareboat charter fleets like the one pictured here. Boats like this make serviceable coastal cruisers and are relatively inexpensive. (Courtesy of SAIL Magazine; Photo by Malcolm White.)

rigging—can also be sold as a racing boat. Here again, low prices help make the boat attractive to those racing on a budget, and the fin keel and relatively light displacement promise to make the boat reasonably competitive in local club races if not in the major regattas and grand prix events that tend to be dominated by more sophisticated boats. This convenient dual-purpose synergy has made it possible for mass-production builders to sell thousands, as opposed to merely hundreds, of boats from a single mold and design. Thus these boats have dominated the general sailboat market for the past 20 years and are, thanks largely to their prevalence in charter fleets, by far the most common type of cruising boat in use today.

Another type of boat embraced by charter fleets in the past 10 years or so is the catamaran. Cruising cats from such builders as Jeantot, Robertson and Caine, Jeanneau, Voyage, and Fountaine Pajot are increasingly popular with bareboat charterers. The increased living space (typically four or more private staterooms can be fit into a cruising cat's accommodations plan) and the fact that they do not heel under sail makes them ideal charter platforms. They are also increasingly popular in the cruising market at large. The typical modern fiberglass cruising cat is not at all performance oriented and, except in ideal conditions (reaching in a strong breeze), is not much faster than a fin-keel monohull. Its hulls are wide to maximize interior volume, it has shoal-draft keels rather than daggerboards (for simplicity's sake and, again, to maximize interior volume), and it has a low bridgedeck to increase the living space between the hulls.

Two boats from opposite ends of an era. The monohull in the foreground is typical of the most popular cruising boats built in the early days of fiberglass production. The catamaran in the background is one of the most popular contemporary fiberglass cruisers and is increasingly prevalent in bareboat charter fleets. (Courtesy of SAIL *Magazine; Photo by Malcolm White.)*

MODERN PERFORMANCE CRUISERS

The latest chapter in the evolution of the cruising sailboat involves the development of purpose-built boats that bend modern construction and design techniques to the discipline of cruising. This type of boat, commonly called the performance cruiser, appeared in embryonic form in the mid-1970s. Early examples include such double-ended designs as the Valiant 40 and Fast Passage 39, discussed earlier, which sought to improve on the Westsail 32 template by paring away underbodies and reducing displacement. Soon the conceit of the canoe stern was abandoned, and what became known as the modified fin keel was installed on most purpose-built cruising boats starting in the 1980s. The modified fin, a low-aspect foil normally longer than it is deep, was, in effect, a compromise between a cutaway full-keel hull and the conventional fin keel, which is normally deeper than it is long. Coupled with a separated rudder on a skeg, a modified fin offered cruisers an appealing blend of performance, strength, and directional stability. Today this is the basic configuration of many production fiberglass cruisers, including those from

such builders as Caliber, Oyster, Hylas, Taswell, Saga, Najad, and Tartan.

The concept of the performance cruiser was further refined in the 1990s, when two events combined to greatly popularize cruising as a lifestyle. The first was the advent of easily affordable satellite navigation systems in the early part of the decade, which freed prospective voyagers from having to master the esoteric art of celestial navigation. The second was a technology-driven boom in the U.S. and world economies that, starting in mid-decade, again favored the accumulation of large personal fortunes. This fueled not only a strong market in superyachts reminiscent of the enormous and sumptuous vessels of the Gilded Age, but also greatly increased spending on high-end yachts of all types, including purpose-built bluewater cruising boats.

Steve Dashew, an early pioneer here, developed his Deerfoot designs in the early 1980s and his Sundeer series in the 1990s. The Sundeer, in particular, became an archetype for performance cruising designs. It featured a long, narrow hull with no overhangs (lengths ranged from 56 to 66 feet),

The Valiant 40, designed by Bob Perry, was one of the first modern performance cruisers. Considered quite conservative today, it is still much sought after, and a slightly larger version, the Valiant 42, is still in production.

a small modified fin keel, a spade rudder, and a moderately sized sail plan with a big, full-roach, full-batten mainsail. The boat's freshwater tanks were situated on either side of the hull and were plumbed so water could be shifted from side to side as internal movable ballast. The general design concept was mimicked and refined in another production boat, Able Marine's Apogee 50 (later taken up by Morris Yachts), and in several custom one-off boats, many of them developed (as was the Apogee 50) by designer Chuck Paine.

Many other expensive one-off performance cruisers with various hull forms have been designed and built for wealthy owners since the late 1990s, some disguised as prototypes for limited high-end production boats. Many have made use of modern exotic construction materials, carbon-fiber rigs, laminated sails, water-ballast systems, and innovations such as large hydraulic lifting keels. Other owners have sought to employ modern construction and design principles to refashion and rethink more traditional designs. Such "retro" boats often seek to replicate the look and feel of classic cruiser-racers from the early 20th century that sported long overhanging ends and sweeping sheerlines. In some examples, performance is dramatically improved by coupling a modern fin-keel/spade-rudder underbody with classic lines above the water. In other instances the traditional full-keel underbody is retained, and performance is improved by reducing weight and lowering the boat's center of gravity with modern construction techniques and carbon-fiber spars.

A Chuck Paine Bermuda-series performance cruiser going through sea trials. Boats like this are fast and comfortable and, for a few lucky owners, the fruition of a lifelong dream. (Courtesy of Chuck Paine/Mark Fitzgerald)

Needless to say, boats like these are expensive. Prices have ranged from several hundred thousand to well over a million dollars even for relatively small boats less than 50 feet long. Though such boats are beyond the reach of the average cruising sailor, some of their features have trickled down into more affordable production boats. For example, water-ballasting systems, which were first used on singlehanded ocean racers in the late 1980s, are now often seen on basic trailer-sailer cruising boats. Likewise, lifting ballast keels similar to those seen on some high-end performance cruisers are now appearing on much smaller, less expensive cruising boats.

Today's high-end cruisers also give a dramatic sense of how far the concept of the cruising boat has evolved since the distant days of George Crowninshield and *Cleopatra's Barge*. Only a few can spend as lavishly as he did to create a vessel in which to escape the cares of life on shore. But many more, fortunately, have the means to pick and choose from an increasingly impressive array of more humble ships and can thus share Crowninshield's dream of embarking upon a "voyage of amusement and travels."

TWO

CRUISING SAILBOAT DESIGN

It is not my intention to inflict on you a full-fledged discourse on yacht design. A thorough understanding of the subject will certainly enhance your appreciation of sailing and sailboats, but you needn't be fully conversant in its mysteries to discern whether a specific boat will suit your purposes. My object here is to equip you with enough knowledge that you can look at drawings of a boat and its published specifications and extract from them a reasonable understanding of the boat's likely characteristics.

If you are interested in reading more about sailboat design, the two books I most recommend as a starting point are *Understanding Boat Design*, by Ted Brewer, and *Yacht Design Explained: A Sailor's Guide to the Principles and Practice of Design*, by Steve Killing and Douglas Hunter (see Books for Cruising Sailors on page 368). You should also take a close look at *The Nature of Boats: Insights and Esoterica for the Nautically Obsessed*, by Dave Gerr. Dave's book is not a straightforward explication of the subject, but rather a collection of short idiosyncratic essays that jump from topic to topic in an entertaining and informative fashion.

DEFINING A BOAT'S LENGTH

The first specification to consider when evaluating a boat is its length. This is the one dimension that immediately yields the most information about what a vessel is like. Equipped with this one number, you can at once make some general assumptions about how fast a boat will sail, how many people and how much gear it might carry, and how much it will cost

to acquire and maintain. This is why length is normally the primary characteristic used to organize and categorize a diverse group of vessels. Brokers' listings, for example, are useful and accessible when organized by boat length. They would be less so if organized by keel type, rig type, sail area, or even displacement.

When asking how long a boat is you must be careful to define your terms. The dimension most commonly referred to is *length overall* (LOA). Ask a yacht designer what it means, and he will probably say it refers to the horizontal distance from the forwardmost part of a boat's hull to its hindmost part, excluding rigging and horizontal hull appendages such as bowsprits, boomkins, and outboard rudders. Ask a yacht broker, marina dockmaster, or boastful boatowner, all of whom may be interested in exaggerating a boat's length, and they will say a vessel's LOA does include horizontal appendages. In truth, whatever designers may think, the latter is probably the more common usage, although the once boastful owner will, of course, be careful to use the former definition when negotiating fees with the marina dockmaster.

To help cut through the confusion, there is another term, *length on deck* (LOD), which means exactly what it says. It refers to the horizontal distance from the forwardmost part of a boat's deck to its hindmost part. On most boats LOA and LOD are synonymous and both accurately describe the length of a boat's hull. This is the number you should be most interested in if you want a general idea of a boat's interior volume and how much it can carry. If a boat's listed

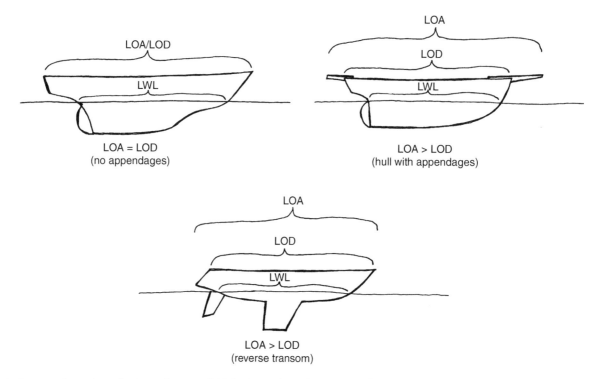

Variations on boat length. Length overall (LOA) is often the same as length on deck (LOD), but LOA will be greater if a boat has horizontal appendages or a reverse transom. The load waterline length (LWL) changes a small amount if the boat gets heavier or lighter.

LOA exceeds its LOD, the boat probably carries a bowsprit and/or boomkin. LOD in such cases is the more useful dimension. The LOA of a hull without appendages will only exceed its LOD if the hull has a reverse transom, in which case LOA more accurately reflects the boat's volume, though the extra interior space inside the transom may be small.

Another meaningful way to measure the length of a boat is along its waterline. This is normally the single most determinative factor in establishing how fast a boat can go. Again, however, waterline length can be measured in different ways. *Load waterline length* (LWL) refers to the length of a hull as measured at the water's surface when a boat is carrying a normal load. *Design waterline length* (DWL) refers to the length of a hull at the waterline anticipated by its designer. Some designers calculate DWL assuming a "light-ship" condition with no crew, stores, or gear on board. If they are good at what they do, the DWL and LWL will be identical when a boat is first launched. As the boat's load is increased, however, it will sink deeper into the water and its LWL will likely increase, assuming the boat has an overhanging bow and/or stern. Cruisers who live aboard their boats and accumulate lots of stuff are very familiar with this phenomenon. The day a liveaboard is compelled to scribe a new waterline for bottom-painting purposes is usually a significant one.

Waterline lengths published by builders on spec sheets are normally described as LWL. This is a little disingenuous, as a builder obviously has no way of knowing how much stuff an owner may put aboard a boat. In most cases the published LWL represents an estimate of how long a boat's waterline will be when it is loaded with its standard equipment and its fuel and water tanks are half full. In that water and fuel are usually the heaviest components of a boat's payload, this theoretical "half-load" waterline length is intended to stand as a reasonable average figure. Unless a boat has quite long, low overhangs its waterline length will in fact vary by relatively small amounts as it is loaded and unloaded. In most cases, therefore, a published LWL is reliable enough to use in estimating a boat's speed potential.

Why Longer Is Faster

As a general rule, the nominal maximum speed of a displacement hull—commonly called its *hull speed*—is governed by a simple formula: hull speed in knots equals 1.34 times the square root of the waterline length in feet: $HS = 1.34 \times \sqrt{LWL}$. Thus, for example, the hull speed of a 35-foot boat with a waterline length of 28 feet works out to be a little over 7 knots: $1.34 \times \sqrt{28} = 7.09$. To understand why this is and where this mysterious multiplier of 1.34

comes from, you first need to understand that the term *displacement hull* refers to a hull that travels *through* rather than *on top of* the water. Such a hull displaces large amounts of water as it moves along, creating two series of waves—one at the bow and another at the stern. We know from physics that the speed of any series of waves in knots equals 1.34 times the square root of their wavelength, which is the distance in <u>feet</u> between successive wave crests: $WS = 1.34 \times \sqrt{WL}$.

Pursuant to this formula, as wavelengths increase waves must move faster, and vice versa. The bow waves created by a boat necessarily travel at the same speed as the boat. At lower speeds the wavelengths are short enough that multiple bow waves can pass down the length of the hull before meeting the stern wave. As boat speed and wave speed increase, however, a point is reached at which the wavelength is equal to the boat's waterline length, and thus there is only room along the hull for one cycle of the bow wave before it meets the stern wave. At this point the boat has dug itself a hole. If it maintains this speed, its bow and stern will be supported by their respective wave crests, and the boat can continue moving forward efficiently. If it goes any faster, however, the stern wave will be pushed farther aft by the lengthening trough of the bow wave, and the back of the boat will fall into the hole. The boat is left trying to climb up the hill presented by its own bow wave, which by now is relatively large. From

this speed upward, disproportionately large increases of power are needed to achieve ever more minuscule increases in speed.

From a mathematical point of view it is easy to see what has happened. The two formulas cited above have become exactly the same; the values for waterline length and wavelength are now identical, as are the values for hull speed and wave speed. One interesting (though not particularly useful) corollary of this relationship is that it should be possible to measure a boat's speed by measuring the distance between the wave crests it generates. For example, if the distance between the wave crests is 15 feet, the boat generating them must be traveling almost 5.2 knots: $1.34 \times \sqrt{15} = 5.189$.

This all sounds logical and tidy, but in fact the concept of hull speed is viewed skeptically by many designers. In reality many boats, even those with honest-to-goodness displacement hulls, easily exceed their nominal hull speeds. One reason for this is that a boat's effective waterline length often increases as it goes faster, particularly if it has long overhangs, and its speed potential increases accordingly. Another reason is that a boat's stern can be designed to suppress its stern wave and increase buoyancy aft, both of which keep the stern from squatting too much as boat speed increases. A stern overhang exiting the water at a shallow angle, usually 15 degrees or less, helps suppress the stern wave, and wide stern sections carrying lots of volume aft increase buoyancy. If a

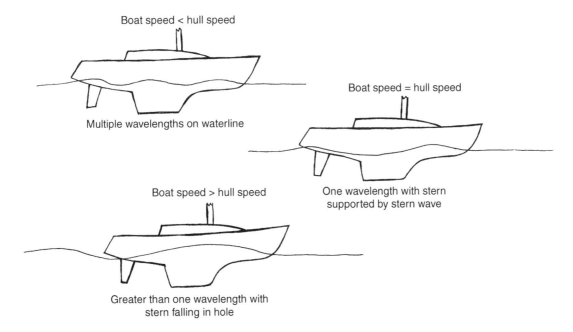

Theoretical hull-speed scenarios. When boat speed is less than a displacement boat's nominal hull speed, multiple waves move down the hull; the boat can easily go faster. When boat speed equals hull speed, there is one wavelength between the bow and stern waves; this is as fast the boat can comfortably go. When boat speeds exceeds hull speed, the stern is unsupported; speed increases require inordinate amounts of extra power.

You can tell this full-keel cruiser is moving at hull speed because there is but one large wave trough running the length of the hull between the bow and stern waves. (Courtesy of Chuck Paine/Mark Fitzgerald)

This sport boat is planing on top of the water and is way over its theoretical hull speed limit. (Peter McGowan)

boat with a stern like this is also light and has a shallow hull with a flat bottom, it will also be capable of getting on top of the water and planing when conditions are right. In this case it ceases—temporarily, at least—to have a displacement hull and may exceed its nominal hull speed by a large margin. Indeed, many light-displacement boats with flat bottoms are capable of planing to some extent, regardless of how their sterns are configured. Also, even heavy boats with narrow sterns and lots of deadrise in their hulls will often exceed hull speed when surging down large wave faces in a strong following wind.

The bottom line is that any boat's hull speed is not necessarily its actual maximum speed. Probably it is more accurate to say hull speed is a minimum maximum speed. Still, it provides a useful estimate of how fast you can expect a cruising boat of any given waterline length to go, particularly if you bear in mind that most cruising boats rarely travel at top

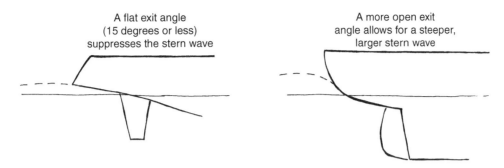

A flat exit angle
(15 degrees or less)
suppresses the stern wave

A more open exit
angle allows for a steeper,
larger stern wave

A stern with a flat exit angle suppresses the stern wave and makes it easier for a boat to exceed hull speed. A larger exit angle creates bigger stern waves and slows the boat down.

speed. Note, however, that this discussion applies only to monohulls. For a way to guesstimate the top potential speed of a multihull (and a more accurate way to do it for monohulls), see "A Better Way to Estimate Hull Speed" later in this chapter.

Longer Becomes Larger Faster Than You Think

It's not possible to precisely estimate a boat's interior space based solely on its length, as too many other variables are involved. Beam is the most important, but freeboard, hull shape, the dimensions of the cabinhouse (if any), and how (and of what) a boat is built all affect interior volume. Beyond stating the obvious, that boats generally get larger as they get longer, I can offer a warning, which is that the growth rate is exponential.

This is a function of simple geometry. Double the dimensions of any three-dimensional form and its surface area will increase by a factor of four. Its volume, meanwhile, will increase by a factor of eight. As far as boats go, this is helpful when it comes to sleeping guests and stowing gear and stores, but can be unhelpful in other ways. The weight of a boat dramatically increases as it grows longer—on average, from about 5,400 pounds for a 25-footer to about 12,000 pounds for a 35-footer, to about 24,000 pounds for a 45-footer. The sail area you have to handle also increases—from about 330 square feet to 600 square feet, to about 1,000 square feet, respectively. Likewise, the size of the boat's auxiliary engine will increase from roughly 15 horsepower to 30 horsepower, to 60 horsepower.

This adds up to a lot more money and effort. Loads on running rigging increase exponentially, which means bigger winches (not to mention *more* of them), bigger lines, stronger hardware, and heavier fasteners all around. It also means a much greater chance of injury should anything break or be mishandled. Acquisition costs also increase rapidly. A brand-new 25-footer, for example, may cost around $50,000, while a new 35-footer may go for around $125,000, and a 45-footer may cost over $250,000. Maintenance costs are subject to the same sort of diabolical multiplication.

DEFINING A BOAT'S WEIGHT

The next most significant characteristic of a boat after its length is its weight. This is known as its *displacement*, thanks to a fundamental law of physics said to have been discovered by Archimedes in the third century B.C. This states that the weight of an object is equal to the weight of the water it displaces when placed in water. The volume of water displaced is also equal to the object's immersed volume.

If we know a boat's displacement, we can therefore also calculate its underwater hull volume. This volume, however, will vary slightly depending on whether the boat is floating in salt or fresh water, because salt water is heavier (64 pounds per cubic foot) than fresh (62.4 pounds per cubic foot). A 12,000-pound boat, for example, has an underwater hull volume of 187.5 cubic feet when floating in salt water (12,000 ÷ 64 = 187.5) versus 192.3 cubic feet when floating in fresh water (12,000 ÷ 62.4 = 192.3). In both cases the boat weighs the same, as does the water it displaces, but the amount of water displaced is different. The end result is that the boat floats higher on its lines in salt water, as slightly less water is displaced.

A boat's displacement tells us more about the boat than just its underwater hull volume. Displacement influences speed (lighter boats are generally faster), load-carrying ability (heavier boats can carry bigger loads), and comfort (heavier boats normally have an easier motion). To get a realistic sense of these characteristics, however, you first need a realistic displacement number to work with—i.e., you need to know what your boat actually weighs when you are using it. In most cases, you can be certain that the displacement number published by the boat's builder

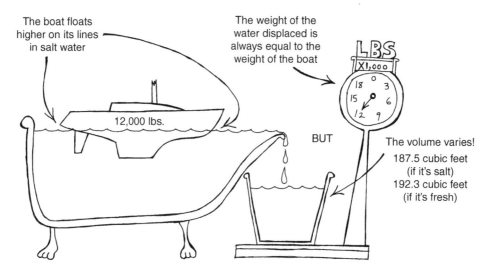

The boat floats higher on its lines in salt water

The weight of the water displaced is always equal to the weight of the boat

LBS
X1,000

BUT

The volume varies!
187.5 cubic feet (if it's salt)
192.3 cubic feet (if it's fresh)

12,000 lbs.

A boat and the amount of water it displaces always weigh the same, but less water is displaced when it floats in salt water, because salt water weighs more than fresh.

is a low-ball figure. Builders do this to make their boats look fast, and because they know other builders do the same thing—a classic case of the power of the lowest denominator.

Unfortunately, it is not a common denominator. Some builders are unscrupulous and publish lightship displacement numbers that don't include the weight of such essential equipment as sails, rigging, batteries, and ground tackle. Others may factor in basic working equipment but do not include the weight of crew, fuel, water, or any extra equipment. Because extra equipment on cruising boats may include generators, life rafts, enlarged battery banks, extra ground tackle, and other heavy items, this can be significant. Also, many builders base published displacement figures on the designer's estimated hull weight rather than the actual weight of the hull as built. In most instances, the actual weight exceeds the design weight to some extent.

Fortunately, some order is being imposed, and in the European Union there is now a displacement standard promulgated by the International Standards Organization (ISO), which establishes standards that are often used by the European Union for certifying goods (including boats) sold into the European market. Known as "light-craft condition," it includes the weight of basic gear but assumes empty fuel and water tanks. This is now the number most often published for new boats built on both sides of the Atlantic that are Conformité Européene (CE) and certified for sale in the European market.

The bottom line is that unless you have specific information to the contrary, you should assume any published displacement number needs to be adjusted upward, usually by a significant amount. The surest

way to get an accurate number is to load a boat with what you want to have aboard and weigh it yourself. This is rarely feasible, particularly if you are evaluating a boat you don't already own. But whenever you do happen to have your boat (or a boat you are subjecting to a prepurchase survey) hauled by a Travelift equipped with a load cell, be sure to note its actual weight.

Absent such a serendipitous opportunity, you can only estimate how much extra weight you will put aboard and add it to the published figure. In *Nigel Calder's Cruising Handbook*, Nigel Calder suggests the best average adjustments to make to arrive at a reasonable half-load displacement figure (i.e., for a boat loaded to cruise with tanks half full) are as follows: plus 2,500 pounds for a lightly used coastal cruiser; plus 3,750 pounds for a bluewater cruiser or a heavily equipped coastal boat; and plus 5,000 pounds for a long-term liveaboard bluewater boat. These estimated average corrections are as good as any I have seen. If you want to be fussy and make a detailed itemized estimate of the extra weight on your boat, you can use the handy worksheet that appears in Calder's book.

DISPLACEMENT/LENGTH RATIO

Considered separately, length and displacement yield only a general notion of what a boat is like. Considered together, however, they give us a much more concrete idea.

The *displacement/length ratio* (D/L) is what designers use to blend the two values for purposes of evaluation. This is found first by calculating a boat's displacement in long tons (DLT), with 1 long ton equaling 2,240 pounds. Then take the boat's load waterline length, multiply it by 0.01 and cube the result. Finally, take this result and divide it into DLT. The complete formula is: D/L = DLT ÷ (0.01 × LWL)³. For example, to find the D/L ratio of a 12,000-pound boat with a load waterline length of 28 feet, first divide 12,000 by 2,240 to find the boat's displacement in long tons: 12,000 ÷ 2,240 = 5.36 long tons. Then multiply 0.01 by 28 (0.01 × 28 = 0.28) and cube the result (0.28³ = 0.022). Then divide the DLT by this number to find the D/L ratio: 5.36 ÷ 0.022 = 243.6.

A boat with a D/L ratio below 100 is considered ultralight; a D/L value between 100 and 200 is light; 200 to 300 is moderate; 300 to 400 is heavy; and over 400, by modern standards, is very heavy. For a boat of a given length the lower the D/L ratio, the less power it takes to drive the boat to its nominal hull speed and the more likely it is the boat can exceed its hull speed. The 12,000-pound boat in our example above, with its D/L ratio of 244, falls almost exactly in the middle of the range; it needs a moderate amount of power to reach its nominal hull speed of 7.09 knots (1.34 × √28 = 7.09) and stands a reasonable chance of exceeding that speed in some situations.

The higher a boat's D/L ratio, the more easily it will carry a load and the more comfortable its motion will be. Depending on the sort of cruising you do, these factors may be more important than how fast you are going. Boats with moderate characteristics are generally best suited for cruising, but that a "moderate" coastal boat should be lighter than a "moderate" offshore boat. Coastal cruisers carry less gear and supplies and normally sail shorter distances in more protected water. They also benefit more from incremental increases in speed, as they are more likely to sail on a tight schedule and normally seek a safe harbor every night. For this type of sailing I recommend a D/L range of 150 to 300.

Conversely, bluewater cruisers carry more gear and supplies, are subject to extreme motion in open water, and are less likely to be sailing on a tight schedule. For this type of sailing I recommend D/L ratios between 250 and 400. You can fiddle these ranges upward or downward according to your own preferences.

When using D/L ratios to evaluate boats, bear in mind how much the ratio varies depending on the displacement value used to calculate it. This is precisely why you need reasonably realistic displacement numbers. Our hypothetical 12,000-pound boat, for example, with its moderate D/L ratio of 244, quickly becomes less moderate as we load it for a cruise. Add the minimum recommended correction

for light coastal cruising (12,000 + 2,500 = 14,500 lbs.) and the boat's D/L ratio becomes 294, which nearly qualifies it as a heavy boat. Up the ante even more by loading the boat for heavy coastal or moderate bluewater use (12,000 + 3,750 = 15,750 lbs.) and it moves well into the heavy range with a D/L ratio of 320.

These are not just theoretical increases. Many is the sailor (myself included) who has purchased an empty boat and has reveled in its sprightly performance, only to be demoralized upon discovering how much less sprightly it is when loaded for cruising. The lighter a boat is to begin with (particularly if it is a catamaran), the more dramatic (and demoralizing) this transformation will seem. Most cruisers soon forget how much better their boat sailed before they loaded it with stuff. If you are devoted to performance, however, you should be draconian when loading your boat and should closely monitor your D/L ratio.

SAIL-AREA/DISPLACEMENT RATIO

Evaluating a boat's speed potential is all well and good, but it tells us only half the story. A fast hull can't actually go fast unless there is enough power available to drive it at or near its potential. Aboard sailboats, of course, the source of this power is the boat's sail plan. The tool designers normally use to evaluate a boat's sail power is the *sail-area/displacement* (SA/D) *ratio*. Like the D/L ratio, this is a nondimensional value that facilitates comparisons among vessels of different types and sizes.

To calculate a boat's SA/D ratio we must first quantify its sail area in square feet. In that many boats carry sails of different sizes so sail area can be adjusted to suit conditions, it is important to use a uniform standard when making comparisons. The accepted convention is to add the mainsail area to 100% of the foretriangle area, with the foretriangle defined as the lateral plane reaching above the deck between the mast and forestay. If the boat is a ketch or a yawl, the most common practice is to add in half the area of the mizzen sail. For schooners, the accepted practice is to add the area of the main and foresail to 100% of the foretriangle.

Boatbuilders like to overstate sail area, just as they understate displacement, to make their boats look faster on paper. Some may include all the area of a large overlapping 130% or even 150% genoa in their calculations. Fortunately, it is easy to correct for these exaggerations.

To figure out the size of a boat's foretriangle, just collect the I and J dimensions of its sail plan. These are often published in detailed spec sheets;

A Better Way to Estimate Hull Speed

Having calculated a boat's D/L ratio, you can use this number to get a more refined estimate of a boat's maximum speed potential than that afforded by the classic hull-speed formula discussed earlier. This more accurate method, devised by designer Dave Gerr and published in his book *The Propeller Handbook* (see Books for Cruising Sailors on page 368), can also be used to estimate hull speeds for catamarans and trimarans. Gerr warns, however, that catamarans with very narrow hulls (for mysterious reasons no one really understands) will routinely exceed the speeds predicted by his method.

The classic hull-speed formula cannot be used on catamarans, which often have much higher potential top speeds than monohulls. This stern wave was generated by a cat sailing in excess of 15 knots on a transatlantic passage.

To comprehend Gerr's formula, we first need to comprehend that the multiplier (1.34) we used in the classic hull-speed formula (HS = 1.34 × $\sqrt{\text{LWL}}$) is itself a *speed/length* (S/L) *ratio* that quantifies the relationship between a boat's speed (BS) and its waterline length at any given point in time. Specifically, the S/L ratio equals a boat's speed in knots divided by the square root of the boat's load waterline length in feet: S/L ratio = BS ÷ $\sqrt{\text{LWL}}$. As you can see, this is simply the classic hull-speed formula run backward to solve for the speed/length ratio instead of speed.

The hull-speed formula assumes that 1.34 is the maximum S/L ratio that can ever be achieved (due to the characteristics of waves we discussed earlier). Gerr's formula instead estimates a boat's maximum S/L ratio based on its D/L ratio so as to more accurately reflect the fact that lighter boats can more easily exceed their nominal hull speeds. Once we've derived a new and more accurate S/L ratio for a given boat, we can then plug it into the classic hull-speed formula to derive a new, more accurate estimate of that boat's nominal hull speed.

Gerr's formula holds that a boat's maximum S/L ratio equals 8.26 divided by its D/L ratio raised to a power of 0.311: max S/L = 8.26 ÷ D/L $^{0.311}$. For our hypothetical 12,000-pound boat with a 28-foot waterline and a D/L ratio of 244, we get the following results: 244 to the 0.311 power equals 5.53 (you'll need a scientific calculator to figure that out), and 8.26 ÷ 5.53 equals a maximum S/L ratio of 1.49. Plug 1.49 into the hull-speed formula (1.49 × $\sqrt{\text{LWL}}$) and you get a new nominal hull speed of 7.9 knots (1.49 × 5.29 = 7.88), as compared to the boat's old nominal hull speed of 7.1 knots (1.34 × 5.29 = 7.09).

This is an appreciable difference, but it grows even larger as the boat grows lighter. If, for example, our 12,000-pound boat sheds 3,000 pounds and becomes a 9,000-pound boat with the same load waterline length, its D/L ratio drops to 183. Its old nominal hull speed, based solely on its LWL, remains 7.1 knots, but its new nominal hull speed, figured according to Gerr's method, becomes 8.6 knots!

Things get even more exciting if we bear in mind that this revised hull-speed estimate still does not account for a boat's potential to plane. That is, we're still only talking about the top potential speed that may be achieved by a hull in displacement mode. Dave Gerr does warn that the higher speeds predicted by his method require a lot of extra power to achieve, but he does believe it is more accurate than the old one.

if not, they are otherwise easy enough to come by. Sailmakers often keep sail plan dimensions for production boats on file, or you can measure them for yourself. The I dimension is the vertical height in feet of the foretriangle (from the deck, not the cabintop), and J is the horizontal distance in feet from the front of the mast to the bottom of the forestay. To find the area of the triangle in square feet, just multiply the two together and divide by 2: 100% foretriangle = (I × J) ÷ 2. Mainsail area is supposed to be calculated in the same way, using the P and E dimensions (P = mainsail luff length and E = mainsail foot length) to solve for the area of the main triangle: main triangle = (P × E) ÷ 2.

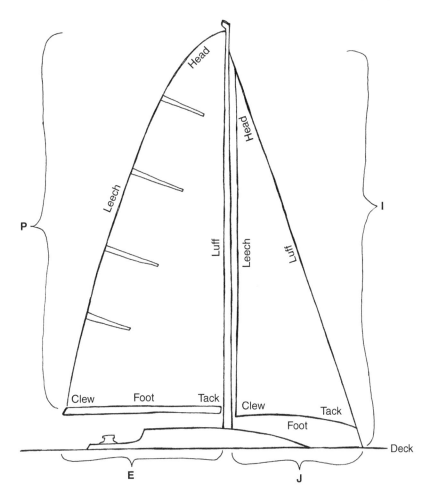

Sail plan dimensions. To find the area of the foretriangle multiply I by J and divide the result by 2. The area of the main triangle is P times E divided by 2, but this ignores the roach of the mainsail. Also shown are the proper names for different parts of the sails.

This, however, ignores the extra area carried outside the triangle in the roach of a battened mainsail. It also ignores the loss of area inside the triangle of a roller-furled mainsail with no battens and a hollow leech. Given that boats don't carry different size mainsails the way they do headsails, I think it is fair and more accurate to use the actual mainsail area when calculating an SA/D ratio.

Having found a boat's sail area, we next need to calculate its displacement in cubic feet (DCF). This is easy, as a boat's weight and the volume of water it displaces are directly related. The normal practice is to assume a boat will be used in salt water, which again weighs 64 pounds per cubic foot. To find displacement in cubic feet, we therefore divide a boat's displacement in pounds by 64: DCF = D ÷ 64.

To then find the boat's SA/D ratio, divide its sail area in square feet (SA) by its displacement in cubic feet raised to the two-thirds power: SA/D ratio = SA ÷ DCF$^{0.667}$. If our hypothetical 12,000-pound boat has a sail area of 650 square feet, we calculate its SA/D ratio by first dividing 12,000 by 64 to find its displacement in cubic feet: 12,000 ÷ 64 = 187.5. Raise that number to the two-thirds power (187.5$^{0.667}$ = 32.8) and divide the boat's sail area by the result to get an SA/D ratio of just under 20: 650 ÷ 32.8 = 19.8.

SA/D ratios below 16 indicate an underpowered boat; 16 to 19 suggests reasonably good performance; 20 to 22 indicates high performance; and anything over 22 implies super-high performance. Our hypothetical boat with an SA/D ratio of 20 is on the cusp between good and high performance and should do a better-than-average job of realizing its speed potential. Note again, however, how adjustments in the displacement value skew the final result. If we load our 12,000-pound boat for light coastal cruising and make it a 14,500-pound boat, its SA/D ratio becomes 17.4. Loaded for heavy coastal or moderate bluewater use at 15,750 pounds, its SA/D ratio is 16.5, which puts it decidedly on the low side of the good-performance range.

What sort of SA/D ratio you should look for depends largely on how much you like to sail your boat. I like to sail my boat as much as possible and use my engine only as a last resort. Unless pressed for time, I'm willing to cover less distance in a day and keep the sails up, so I prefer a large sail plan.

Subject only to the proviso that a boat should not carry more sail than it can stand up to, the only downside to a large sail plan, even aboard a heavy boat, is that you may spend more time than you otherwise would taking in reefs and letting them out again and/or changing sails as conditions fluctuate. The heavier your boat is, the more sail area you will want to drive it. A heavy boat driven hard can often sail nearly as fast, and sometimes even faster, than a lighter boat that is undercanvased or driven conservatively. And when the wind is light, a heavy boat will want to fly as much canvas as possible. Cruisers who really like to sail therefore want SA/D ratios as high as possible, normally 17 or better.

Many cruisers, however, while happy to sail when the wind is moderate or strong, prefer to motor when the wind goes light to keep moving at a good speed. Some almost always motor to windward, no matter how strong or light the wind, in order to save time or effort. And there are a few I've met who rarely hoist sail and always motor unless conditions are truly optimal. For cruisers like these, a high SA/D ratio is much less important.

Another key consideration is the type of cruising you will be doing. Coastal cruisers should generally favor faster boats with higher SA/D ratios, but a coastal cruiser sailing shorthanded may prefer a sail plan with a lower ratio that is easier to manage and doesn't need to be reefed as promptly. On the other hand, although most bluewater cruisers, particularly those with small crews, want ease of sail handling and thus should look for lower ratios, some prize performance and don't mind doing more work to achieve it. These should favor boats with higher ratios.

You must also consider a boat's SA/D ratio in relation to its D/L ratio. If you want the comfort and stowage capacity of a heavier hull but also want decent performance, you need a higher SA/D ratio to compensate for the weight. If you want decent performance without a lot of sail handling, look for a light boat with a relatively low SA/D ratio and be prepared to carry less stuff. If you want the best performance possible and are willing to sacrifice load-carrying ability, comfort, and ease of handling to get it, look for a light boat with a high SA/D ratio. If you want a comfortable heavy boat that's easy to manage, look for a lower SA/D ratio, but be prepared to go slow.

Light-Air Performance: How Wet Is Your Bottom?

If you're a cruiser who likes to keep sailing when the wind is weak, be aware that the SA/D ratio is *not* the best indicator of light-air performance. Neither is the D/L ratio, since it too involves displacement and relates to the amount of resistance a moving boat encounters due to its own wave-making ability. Because wavemaking resistance is insignificant when the wind is light, displacement-based performance ratios are not necessarily indicative of a boat's speed potential in low-power situations.

What most affects performance in light-air conditions is the friction between hull and water, which is directly related to the amount of *wetted surface area* the hull presents to the water. The larger the area, the more friction there is, and the more effort it takes to move the boat. The *sail-area/wetted-surface* (SA/WS) *ratio* quantifies this relationship and thus more accurately predicts performance in light air. Ironically, it is by far the easiest performance ratio to calculate: just divide a boat's sail area in square feet by its wetted surface area in square feet (SA/WS = SA ÷ WS), and you've got it. Unfortunately, this is of little use to laypeople. A boat's wetted surface area is never included in its published specifications, and you pretty much have to be a naval architect to figure it out.

This is not quite as tragic as it seems, since light boats normally have less wetted surface area than heavier boats. As we discussed in the last chapter, having less hull in the water is often a big part of what makes one boat lighter than another in the first place. In most cases you can therefore expect light boats to perform better in light air than heavy boats.

While you may not be able to calculate a boat's precise wetted surface area, you can get a sense of it simply by eyeballing the boat. Those few unusual boats that are light in spite of having a lot of underwater surface area should be readily apparent. The likeliest example would be a lightly constructed shallow-bilged boat with a long deep keel. Note, too, that between two boats of the same length, with the same wetted surface area, the heavier boat, once it is moving, will maintain more momentum in light air than the lighter one.

Regardless of whether you use displacement or wetted surface as your basis of comparison, the other half of the formula in both cases is sail area. Whether a boat is heavy or light, with lots of wetted surface or very little, more sail always means better light-air performance.

QUANTIFYING A BOAT'S MOTION

D/L and SA/D ratios are the most commonly used parameters for quantifying a sailboat's performance. They are often referred to in magazine articles and are often included by builders in a boat's published specifications. Because so much attention is paid to these two numbers, and because speed is normally perceived as such an attractive quality, builders, as mentioned, almost always tweak the numbers to make their boats seem faster. Besides correcting published numbers to get more accurate estimates of a boat's speed potential and sailpower, as a smart cruising sailor you should also expand your conception of performance to include another important parameter, which is the boat's motion while underway.

Racing sailors are famously unconcerned with this factor. Judging from some accounts of modern long-distance races, it seems they pride themselves on sailing aboard the most uncomfortable boats imaginable. On the most extreme boats the motion can become so violent crewmembers sometimes wear helmets while sleeping in case their heads are smashed into bulkheads or overheads as they lie in their berths. For many cruising sailors, however, the comfort of a boat's motion is of primary importance. While sailing fast is always good for morale, a lack of physical well-being on a cruising boat usually obliterates any sense of psychological well-being. No single parameter can quantify all aspects of a boat's motion, but the relatively simple *comfort ratio* developed by designer Ted Brewer does provide a reasonable indication of how comfortable a boat will be in certain conditions. Originally proffered by Brewer half in jest, it is now widely accepted as the best available tool for predicting motion comfort. The comfort ratio is rarely mentioned in magazine boat tests and is never publicized by boatbuilders, but you should use it when analyzing potential cruising boats, particularly bluewater cruising boats. It adds a much needed third dimension to the two-dimensional picture painted by the D/L and SA/D ratios.

Sailing in large seas always dramatically increases motion on a boat. Of the six crew on this rough passage, two were incapacitated by seasickness. When evaluating a boat, cruisers should always take motion into account.

The formula runs as follows: comfort ratio = $D \div [0.65 \times (0.7\ LWL + 0.3\ LOA) \times beam^{1.33}]$, where displacement is expressed in pounds and length is in feet. Turning again to our hypothetical 12,000-pound boat with a load waterline length of 28 feet, let us say that it is 35 feet long overall and has a beam of 11 feet. To find its comfort factor, we first multiply its LWL by 0.7 ($0.7 \times 28 = 19.6$) and its LOA by 0.3 ($0.3 \times 35 = 10.5$), then add these results together, which gives us 30.1: $19.6 + 10.5 = 30.1$. Next we take the boat's beam to the 1.33 power, which is 24.27 ($11^{1.33} = 24.27$) and multiply this result by the previous result and then by 0.65, which gives us 474.84: $0.65 \times 30.1 \times 24.27 = 474.84$. Finally, we divide this result into the boat's displacement, which yields a comfort ratio of 25.27: $12,000 \div 474.84 = 25.27$.

What the formula purports to assess is how quickly and abruptly a boat's hull reacts to waves in a large seaway, these being the elements of a boat's motion most likely to cause seasickness. The formula favors heavy boats over light ones, as more weight always helps dampen motion, and also favors boats with smaller *waterplanes*. This is the horizontal plane of a boat's shape at its waterline and is generally a function of length and beam. Boats with more waterplane and less weight tend to have a quicker motion because more waterplane means more area for waves to push up against, and less weight means there is less resistance to the pushing.

Longer boats have larger waterplanes than shorter boats, but the exponential increase in their displacement always counteracts this. As a result, the comfort-ratio formula also favors length, though it penalizes beam. Generally, then, it favors heavy boats with narrow beam, but longer boats may have considerably lower D/L ratios than shorter ones and still fare much better by comparison.

Use the following general guidelines to interpret comfort-ratio results: below 20 indicates a lightweight racing boat; 20 to 30 indicates a coastal cruiser; 30 to 40 indicates a moderate bluewater cruising boat; 50 to 60 indicates a heavy bluewater boat; and over 60 indicates an extremely heavy bluewater boat. If you are evaluating a larger boat, say 45 feet or longer, expect results to be skewed somewhat higher on this scale; if the boat is quite small, say 25 feet or less, results will be skewed slightly downward.

Once again, increasing displacement to account for loads carried seriously affects results. Our hypothetical 12,000-pound boat, with its comfort ratio of 25.27, becomes decidedly more comfortable as

Basic dimensions and performance ratios for the hypothetical 35-foot cruising sailboat discussed in this chapter. Create a similar list of numbers for any boat you are evaluating.

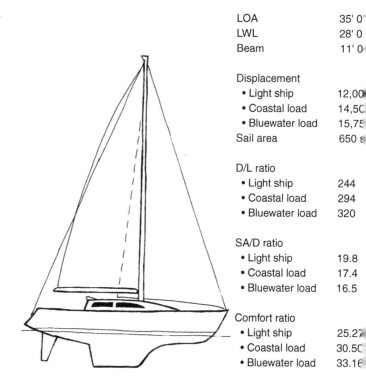

LOA	35' 0"
LWL	28' 0"
Beam	11' 0"
Displacement	
• Light ship	12,00
• Coastal load	14,50
• Bluewater load	15,75
Sail area	650 s
D/L ratio	
• Light ship	244
• Coastal load	294
• Bluewater load	320
SA/D ratio	
• Light ship	19.8
• Coastal load	17.4
• Bluewater load	16.5
Comfort ratio	
• Light ship	25.27
• Coastal load	30.50
• Bluewater load	33.16

we load it to cruise. Add another 2,500 pounds for light coastal cruising and the ratio rises to 30.5; make that an extra 3,750 pounds for bluewater cruising, and it becomes 33.16.

What the comfort ratio does not assess is how comfortable a boat seems in relatively smooth water. In these conditions it is normally a boat's heeling that creates discomfort onboard. The best way to make a boat stiffer and decrease heeling is to increase its beam, which ironically is one of the things that make it much less comfortable in a strong seaway. A narrow boat that heels easily may seem more comfortable in a seaway compared to a beamy boat, in spite of its heeling, but less comfortable when sailing well in flat water.

Comfort ratios should normally matter most to bluewater sailors and to coastal cruisers who often sail in open water. If you sail mostly in protected water, but are interested in keeping yourself and those onboard comfortable on those rare occasions when you do encounter angry waves, you should also pay attention to comfort ratios. If your desire to sail upright in normal conditions trumps your desire to avoid discomfort on the rare occasions you are caught in rough conditions, you should pay less attention to comfort ratios and more attention to beam and initial stability characteristics.

Another factor the comfort ratio does not account for is ballast location. This is not often remarked upon, but I have found the closer you are to a boat's ballast the more comfortable you tend to be. Presumably this is because ballast represents the greatest concentration of weight on a boat so has a dampening effect on motion. On most modern boats with ballast keels, this effect won't really come into play. It will be noticeable, however, on older wooden boats that carry some ballast in their bilges, and even more noticeable on certain modern centerboard boats that have no keels and carry all their ballast in their bilges. Such boats in my experience are much more comfortable in a seaway than their comfort ratios suggest.

The comfort ratio also does not pertain to multihulls. Because these boats carry no ballast at all and rely entirely on beam for stability, their motion is entirely different from monohulls. Many cruisers are attracted to catamarans for precisely this reason. Because cruising cats normally do not heel, they are perceived by many as being inherently more comfortable than monohulls.

This is true as far as it goes, but don't assume that a catamaran's motion in large seas is ever negligible. A monohull in a seaway may experience more motion than a catamaran, primarily because it rolls more from side to side. Like the cat it will also be heaving up and down. But the motion of the monohull will usually have a distinct rhythm. Unless the seas are absolutely confused, their pattern will be reflected in the motion of the boat. Those onboard can learn the pattern and anticipate it. The motion, because it is not random, is easier to adapt to.

This is not the case with a catamaran. Catamarans not only have two hulls in the water, each reacting to separate sets of waves, they also have a bridgedeck connecting the hulls, which is struck by the irregular waves that heap up between the hulls at irregular intervals. A catamaran thus may be receiving simultaneous input from three different sets of waves. Its aggregate motion, as a result, often has no rhythm that can be easily discerned. Because it has no ballast and is light for its size, a cat's motion is also fast and abrupt. The total effect in a seaway is quick, quirky, random, and harder to anticipate and adapt to. Some sailors aren't bothered by this motion and are happy to live with it in exchange for not heeling. Others, however, prefer to deal with the slower and more predictable, albeit somewhat more exaggerated, motion of a monohull, and take their heeling as they find it.

Wave action under a catamaran's bridgedeck is irregular and unpredictable; this helps to make a catamaran's motion more quirky and harder to adapt to than that of a monohull.

LATERAL HULL FORM

One of the most important choices to make when selecting a boat concerns its hull form. This one factor affects many of the boat's most critical characteristics: how heavy it is, how fast it is, how it handles, how much space it has inside, how it is hauled out of the water, what tactics can be employed in rough weather, and so on.

A hull's underwater profile is determined primarily by what sort of keel and rudder it has. In modern parlance these are referred to as a boat's underwater appendages or foils. The latter term reflects our increasingly sophisticated understanding of their function. Once it was assumed a keel must reduce leeway and resist sideways motion simply by presenting lateral surface area to the water. A rudder likewise seems to turn a boat by brute force, deflecting water beneath the hull and increasing resistance on one side more than the other. These ideas are not incorrect, and in some circumstances, particularly when a boat is moving slowly, this is exactly what a keel and rudder are doing. We now know, however, that once a boat is sailing at speed its keel and rudder develop hydrodynamic qualities. Knifing through the water, they generate lift that helps resist leeway and steer the boat much more efficiently.

The principle behind this effect, known as Bernoulli's principle (after Daniel Bernoulli, the Swiss physicist who discovered it in the 18th century), is the same as that which allows an airplane's wings to lift it into the air. To create lift, water (or air, in the case of a wing) must flow over a foil's two sides at different speeds, thus creating a pressure differential. The foil lifts toward the side with lower pressure, which is the side over which water or air is flowing faster. An airplane wing can do this due to its asymmetric shape. Air strikes the front of the wing head on and accelerates over the top of it, because that side is longer and more curved and air passing over it must cover more distance to reach the wing's trailing edge. Keels and rudders, however, have symmetric shapes. They create lift only when water strikes them at an angle, thus shortening the route the water must follow over one side of the foil

while lengthening it over the other. For a keel this *angle of attack* is created by leeway when a boat is sailing to windward, or has the wind on its beam, and the keel is pointed in a direction slightly different from the one in which it is moving. In other words, a keel actually *needs* leeway in order to create lift to resist it. For a rudder, an angle of attack can be created simply by moving the tiller or wheel that controls it, and the resulting lift moves the stern in one direction or the other.

Full Keel/Attached Rudder

The most venerable hull shape, the traditional full-keel configuration, does generate some lift but does little to amplify the effect. As we saw in the previous chapter, this simple hull form, in which a boat's keel runs the length of its hull from bow to stern with little or nothing in the way of overhangs, dominated yacht design until the late 19th century. It survives in certain boats still built today and, as recently as 35 years ago, when the Westsail 32 burst upon the scene, was believed by many to be the best shape for bluewater cruising boats.

There is no denying that full-keel boats don't perform well by modern standards. They are generally heavy and slow, often with D/L ratios of 400 or higher, and are not very close-winded. They also back down poorly under power, are slower to turn going forward because of the extra lateral resistance under their bows, and are harder to tack through the wind.

That said, full-keel boats do have certain advantages. Due to their long underbodies, they usually track well underway. Get them going in one direction, and they tend to keep going in that direction. This makes them easy to steer over long distances and makes it easy to trim their sails so they sail themselves. This in turn makes it easy for autopilots and

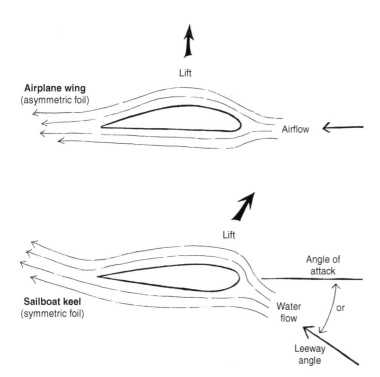

The Bernoulli effect works with both asymmetric foils, like an airplane wing, and symmetric foils, like a sailboat keel. The symmetric keel, however, needs leeway to create lift.

- Tracks well
- Heaves-to well
- Easy to balance sails
- Very strong

- Slow to turn
- Very heavy
- Backs down poorly
- Inefficient keel foil

A traditional full-keel underbody, though it does not perform well in many respects, does have other virtues making it attractive to cruisers.

wind vanes to steer them. Because they have a lot of lateral area underwater they also heave-to well. With the headsail aback and helm down, they lie quietly with their bows at a nice angle to the wind, making no headway and little leeway. This can be an invaluable tactic in heavy weather and is useful in many other situations.

Another big advantage of a traditional full-keel hull is its robust simplicity. Its rudder is mounted on the trailing edge of the keel and is thus well protected and supported. In many surviving examples the upper part of the rudder is mounted directly on the boat's transom, providing even more support to the structure. There is no need to pierce the hull to accommodate a rudderstock, and the rudder can, if necessary, be removed and remounted while the boat is afloat. The propeller is well protected in an aperture between keel and rudder. The propeller is less likely to be struck by jetsam or fouled by fishing gear, and its shaft is situated entirely within the boat. The ballast, assuming fiberglass (or even metal) construction, can be encapsulated in the bottom of the keel, which is itself an integral part of the hull. Even on boats where external ballast is bolted to the keel, the shape of the hull and keel are such that the ballast is unlikely to be displaced if the boat runs aground. Full-keel boats, thanks largely to their weight, but also to their unitary form, have a smooth motion in a seaway, with comfort ratios on the order of 60 or better. They are also great load carriers. Their cross-section form yields lots of storage space in their bilges, and because they are heavy to begin with, extra payload weight leads to smaller proportional increases in overall displacement compared to lighter boats.

An external ballast shoe for a traditional full-keel boat. A long, low shoe like this can easily survive a hard grounding.

Though not as common as they used to be, traditional full-keel boats are still often seen in boatyards. One big advantage is their simple shape makes them easy to haul. Note, too, how the rudder and prop on this boat are well protected and supported.

As discussed in the last chapter, the trend in modern yacht design has been to pare away the traditional full-keel hull. The trend really began with Nat Herreshoff's *Gloriana* in 1891, whose design showed a cutting away of portions of the keel, particularly its forefoot, and with the hull extended above the water to create bow and stern overhangs. Initially this was done not so much to improve hydrodynamic lift as to minimize wetted surface area, itself a worthy goal, and to take advantage of waterline-based rating rules. The end result was a longer boat atop a shorter keel with rudder still attached, and this remained the dominant hull form until the end of the CCA period in the late 1960s. These cutaway full-keel designs, because they were predominant when fiberglass production became popular, have been handed down in myriad seemingly indestructible older glass boats still widely available on the used-boat market.

Boats with cutaway full keels have many of the qualities of boats with traditional full keels, with

Not all boats with cutaway full keels have long overhangs. This British-built Nicholson 31 has short ends and a full keel aft supporting a transom-hung rudder, but its forefoot is cut way back.

some differences. They are a little faster, because they are lighter and have less wetted surface area. They point higher, because their keels are more foil-like and generate more lift, and they turn through the wind more easily, thanks to their cutaway forefoots. This improved performance is not, however, fully reflected in a comparison of D/L ratios. Because they have short waterlines relative to their weight, boats with cutaway full keels and long overhangs always get tagged with higher D/L ratios than they deserve. This, of course, is precisely why they rated well under waterline-based racing handicap systems.

One advantage of overhangs, apart from cheating defunct rating rules, is that the extra volume in the bow and stern above the waterline provides reserve buoyancy in the ends of the boat. This helps dampen pitching and keeps the boat drier as it rises to waves, though on lightly constructed boats long ends can instead lead to increased pitching in some situations. Disadvantages include poor performance when backing down in reverse. This occurs because the ends of the boat, with no keel in the water under them to resist crosswinds, are more easily blown off line when the boat moves slowly. This hampers all close-quarters maneuvering to some extent, but the problem is aggravated in reverse because the rudder, besides being attached to the keel, is well forward of the stern and thus has less influence on where it is going. Also, rudders on boats of this type often must be raked at an angle so the top of the rudderstock can reach the cockpit behind the short keel, and this compromises rudder performance generally. In later

years, designers learned to overcome this problem by putting more rudder area down low, near the bottom of the keel.

Otherwise, boats with overhangs and cutaway full keels share most of the advantages of traditional full-keel boats. Their shape is more complex, but their hulls and keels still form a unitary whole. They are therefore strong and take the ground well. They have good directional stability, and their motion in a seaway is smooth and even. Their comfort ratios, though not as high as those of traditional full-keel boats, are still significantly higher than those of most other boats. Their propellers and prop shafts are just as well protected, and their rudders are likewise well supported. An overhanging stern does, however, make it necessary to pierce the hull below the waterline to bring the top of the rudderstock into the cockpit. Also, the overhanging ends tend to blow off in a breeze, which makes it harder for boats like this to heave-to.

Though most performance sailors consider full-keel boats obsolete, both types have endured and are still reasonably popular, thanks mostly to their virtues as cruising boats. Both types are still built today, not only to old designs that have never fallen out of favor, but also to more sophisticated contemporary one-off designs. Full keels in these modern custom designs are shaped more efficiently to generate more lift. Rudder performance is improved by moving part of the rudder forward of its pivot axis into an oversize prop aperture. Modern construction techniques can also be used to increase speed and stability by reducing both hull and rig weight.

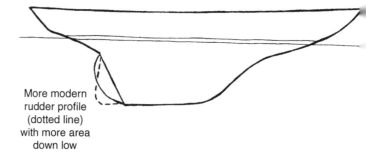

- Turns more easily
- Still tracks well
- Improved keel foil
- Buoyant ends

- Backs down very poorly
- Ends blow off in cross-br
- Less efficient rudder
- Still relatively heavy

More modern rudder profile (dotted line) with more area down low

A cutaway full keel generally offers better performance than a traditional full keel, but also has some unique disadvantages. The improved modern rudder profile (shown with a dotted line), though not as pretty, is more efficient.

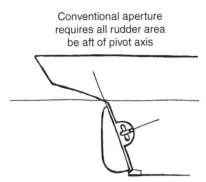 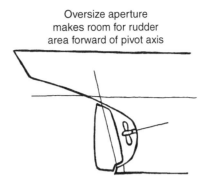

Conventional aperture requires all rudder area be aft of pivot axis

Oversize aperture makes room for rudder area forward of pivot axis

By enlarging the propeller aperture on a full-keel boat, room can be created for a portion of the rudder to fit forward of the rudderstock, thus easing helm loads.

Even if you can't afford a modern one-off boat, there are many older full-keel boats on the used-boat market that still make excellent cruising craft. Many coastal cruisers who want to cover more ground in less time will likely find traditional full-keel boats, with their great weight and generous underbodies, a bit too slow and unwieldy. But boats with cutaway full keels are often just fast enough to make the grade. Several fiberglass boats of this type, created by such legendary designers as Carl Alberg, Bill Tripp, Phil Rhodes, Bill Luders, Olin Stephens, and Ted Hood, are widely available and can be purchased for less than $30,000 fully equipped. The conservative nature of these boats—most particularly their ability to survive a hard grounding—has long made them a popular default choice for neophyte cruisers. Really their only significant disadvantage, which is important to keep in mind if you often maneuver around docks, is how poorly they handle in close quarters.

For bluewater sailors, a full-keel boat will seem even more attractive. Many conservative bluewater cruisers still default to traditional full-keel designs, and cutaway designs are also popular. One reason bluewater sailors favor these boats is because they can be hoisted from the water by most any method in ports with minimal facilities without undue risk of damage to rudders, propellers, or prop shafts. Other benefits include improved self-steering, a more comfortable motion in a seaway, and better handling in extreme weather.

Fin Keel/Separate Rudder

The development of modern keels and rudders has focused largely on improving their hydrodynamic qualities. This is why the fin keels and spade rudders on the most advanced contemporary racing sailboats often look much like airplane wings. They reach deep into the water at steep vertical angles and have short *chords* (the term refers to their fore-and-aft length). They also are precisely shaped according to principles promulgated by the U.S. National Advisory Committee for Aeronautics (hence the expression "NACA foil," which is sometimes bandied about in the yachting press). On hulls like this, wetted surface area is reduced to an absolute minimum. The keel has a small surface that creates relatively little lateral resistance and instead relies on hydrodynamic lift to combat leeway. The rudder, too, has a reduced area and relies mostly on lift to steer the boat.

Often these days there is a pronounced ballast bulb at the bottom of a racing fin keel. The bulb may be integrated into the shape of the keel tip or, in more extreme designs, attached to the tip as a large

This large modern full-keel cruiser, designed by Chuck Paine, is easily steered with a tiller thanks to its super-large prop aperture and semi-balanced rudder. (Courtesy of Chuck Paine/Mark Fitzgerald)

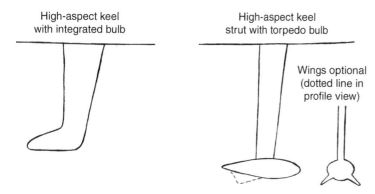

Two examples of modern high-aspect racing keels. They are fast, but fragile, and may not be suitable for cruising.

torpedo, with the keel serving as little more than a strut to support it. Sometimes a keel bulb or the tip of a straight keel will have wings, an innovation first seen on the famous America's Cup challenger (and winner) *Australia II* in 1983. The wings improve upwind performance by marginally increasing draft when a boat is heeled. A bulb and/or wings can also improve hydrodynamic efficiency by acting as an end plate that limits the amount of water flowing from the high-pressure side of the bottom of the keel to the low-pressure side, an effect that increases drag and creates tip vortices.

Boats with extreme hull forms like this are fast and very close-winded. For cruising sailors, however, they can be problematic. Their underbodies are quite fragile compared with the full-keel boats discussed above. High-aspect fin keels that are deep and narrow with short chords cannot be made a unitary part of a boat's hull, but instead must be fastened into place with keel bolts. If the keel strikes the bottom, much of the impact is transmitted to these bolts and the adjacent hull, which are then at risk of failing. Damage to the keel joint often creates leaks that must be promptly addressed by hauling the boat. The deeper and more vertical the keel, the greater the chance damage suffered in a grounding will be significant, as the longer lever arm and more perpendicular angle increases the force of the blow. Also, of course, a deeper keel restricts access to shoal water and makes grounding more likely in the first place. If the keel has wings these may dig into the ground and make it harder to refloat the boat.

The rudders on these boats are also vulnerable. Unlike the attached rudders on full-keel boats, spade rudders are supported only by their rudderstocks and dangle from hulls in a perfectly exposed position. Any blow received may bend the stock, perhaps jamming the rudder or, worse, breaking it in two, in which case all or part of the rudder will be lost. The propeller and aft end of the prop shaft, hanging in the open under the hull on a small strut, are likewise exposed to danger. Both may be damaged if struck by an object; they are also more likely to get entangled in fishing gear.

A Volvo Open 70 ocean racer with a deep ballast-bulb keel on the hard for inspection and repair during a port stop on the 2009 Volvo Ocean Race. Extreme keels like this pose all sorts of challenges. (Courtesy of Molly Mulhern)

Spade rudder variations. Swept-back rudders like the one on the left were common in the past, but most rudders these days are shaped more like the one on the right.

Yet another significant drawback to this sort of hull from a cruiser's perspective is a lack of directional stability, though this is mitigated if the hull is long and narrow. The greatly reduced lateral surface area below the water and the separation of the rudder from the keel makes steering quick and precise, but the downside is the helm needs much more minding. Because the boat so easily changes direction, steering requires careful attention and a light touch. Consequently, it is more difficult to balance the sails against the helm and get the boat to steer itself for any length of time, which means more work for an autopilot or a wind vane, not to mention a helmsperson. It is also difficult or impossible to get a boat like this to heave-to in heavy weather. Like the wings of an airplane, the underwater foils must be moving at speed to generate the lift needed to resist leeway. Once the boat slows to a near stop, the lack of lateral resistance causes it to blow off quickly to leeward, with its bow at a broad angle to the wind. Tactics in extreme weather must therefore be more active than on a full-keel boat. It is necessary either to run off downwind with crew on the helm (perhaps while towing a drogue) or to deploy a sea anchor off the bow to "park" the boat and keep it head to wind.

Dependence on lift can also make spade rudders less reliable in rough conditions even when a boat is moving at speed. When a boat with a high-aspect spade rudder is pressed so hard that a lot of helm is suddenly needed to maintain course, the rudder's angle of attack can become so large that the flow of water over it detaches and degenerates into turbulence, causing it to stall. When this happens, the rudder stops generating lift and ceases to function as a rudder. The boat then suddenly rounds up and broaches out of control, a nerve-racking event that has long been a staple of sailboat racing photography. Well-designed rudders normally don't stall even under a heavy press of canvas, and cruising sailors are unlikely to push a boat so hard in the first place, but still you occasionally meet boats with spade rudders that are much too temperamental. For example, I recall testing one European racer-cruiser with a spade rudder that repeatedly stalled in very moderate conditions.

From all I've said here you might think fin-keel boats with spade rudders are hardly ever used for cruising, but in fact they are by far the most popular type sailed by cruisers today, and for good reason. As discussed in the previous chapter, they are faster, easier to maneuver in close quarters, and generally cheaper to buy.

The owner of a typical 35-foot CCA-type full-keel cruiser-racer expects to average 4 to 6 knots while cruising and rarely tops 7 1/2 knots. A modest fin-keel boat of the same size, by comparison, can average 5 to 7 knots and might easily top 9 knots while surfing downwind. This is a significant advantage, even when applied over modest distances. For short-hop coastal cruising, it can easily mean a 20% increase in range or a 20% decrease in time underway between anchorages. For bluewater cruisers trying to cover longer distances, the absolute difference in ground covered and time saved is considerable. For the many sailors who keep boats in marinas, the superior close-quarters handling of fin-keel boats is an even greater advantage. A fin-keel boat with a spade rudder can, with practice, be driven long distances and maneuvered in reverse with great precision. Even those who keep their boats on moorings must occasionally land at fuel docks, or may like to put in at marinas while cruising, and thus can also appreciate these virtues.

While extreme racing hulls generally are unsuitable for cruising, there are plenty of other more moderate types of fin-keel hulls. The disadvantages described above can be mitigated or even eliminated, usually by increasing underwater lateral surface area and by decreasing the aspect ratio of the foils (that is, by increasing chord length and decreasing depth).

On the most conservative boats, the fin keel is so long that it has nearly as much surface area as a cutaway full keel, and the rudder, though still separated from the keel, is supported by a good-sized skeg with a propeller aperture. This configuration offers much of the security of a full-keel hull. The keel is large enough to be constructed as a unitary part of the hull and thus can take the ground well. The rudder, propeller, and prop shaft are well supported and

- Strong keel is part of hull
- Tracks well for a fin
- Lots of support for rudder
- Better performance than a full keel
- Prop is protected

- Not as efficient as a high-aspect foil
- Rudder is not balanced
- Does not back down well
- Still relatively heavy

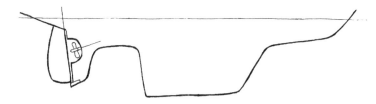

A conservative long fin-keel underbody with a full rudder skeg and a propeller aperture offers somewhat improved performance without sacrificing much security.

protected. The keel also has enough lateral surface to provide respectable directional stability, making the boat easier to heave-to and steer over long distances. To achieve this, however, means sacrificing performance. A hull like this generates more lift and is a bit faster and more close-winded than a full-keel hull, but it won't be nearly as fast, closewinded, or maneuverable as a boat with a spade rudder and a higher-aspect keel.

Between these extremes are a large variety of keel and rudder configurations and combinations. This allows a discerning sailor to establish a fairly specific hierarchy of personal preferences. Short of ordering a custom one-off design, it may be impossible to satisfy them all, but given the multiplicity of boats on the market, you should be able to find some satisfactory compromises.

As to rudders there are four basic options. The pure spade rudder is always a balanced foil with a significant portion of its surface area is forward of its pivot axis (i.e., the rudderstock). This greatly reduces helm loads, improves performance generally, and makes it possible to steer a boat in reverse with some precision. A semi-spade rudder mounted on a partial skeg enjoys similar advantages, though perhaps not to the same degree, and is better supported. But the joint between the bottom of the skeg and the rudder is prone to snagging fishing lines and nets.

Rudders supported by full skegs were probably the most popular configuration on fin-keel boats in the late 1960s and early '70s and are still fairly common. They do offer more precise steering than rudders attached to full keels, but unlike spade rudders cannot steer in reverse with great precision. They are, however, much more secure than spade rudders. As noted above a full skeg can include a propeller aperture, which also protects the propeller and its shaft, and this to my mind is a great configuration for a cruising boat. Unfortunately, however, most full-skeg boats instead have exposed props and shafts.

Keel variations are even more numerous. Fin keels once were usually simple straight-sided quadrilateral forms, but these days any number of bizarre shapes can be found dangling from a sailboat's hull. Designers offer all manner of esoteric theories in support of their preferences for certain shapes over others, but in my experience there is little to be gained in trying to sort these out. For the purpose of selecting a boat to cruise in, it is best to focus on more fundamental characteristics.

The first question to ask is how deep the water is in your favorite cruising ground. All things being equal, cruisers should favor shoal-draft keels, since less draft always means you can go more places. Because deeper keels usually perform much better to windward, cruisers who really enjoy sailing often break this rule, but you should be wary of doing so. Just a couple of extra feet of draft can greatly reduce available anchoring spots, even in areas where the water is relatively deep. If you want the best of both

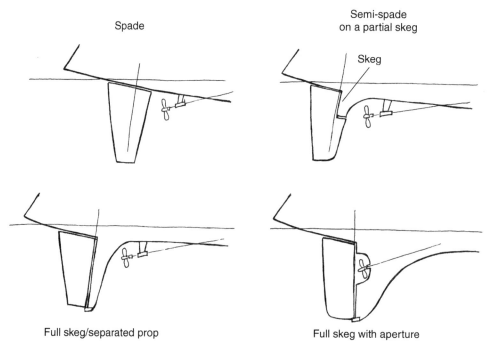

The four basic types of rudders that can be paired with a fin keel.

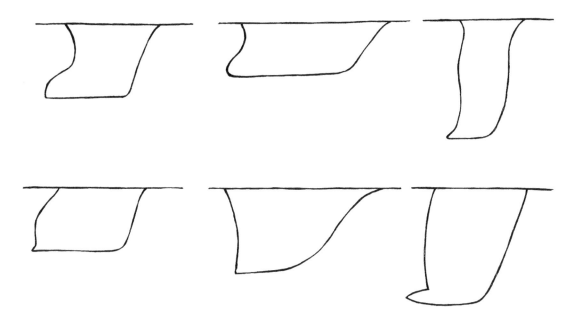

Modern fin keels come in a wide range of shapes and sizes. These are only a few of the many variations.

worlds in a boat with a fixed keel, look for a shoal keel with a ballast bulb on the bottom. These have become increasingly popular because the lower center of gravity recoups much of the performance advantage sacrificed by decreasing draft.

The next question to ask is what happens when you run aground. Fin keels are always more vulnerable than full keels in this respect, but certain fins are more vulnerable than others. The worst is the extremely deep, short, plumb racing keel described above. The perpendicular angle, the long lever arm,

and the small area of the keel joint all combine to make serious damage likely when this type of fin hits the bricks. The best is a keel that is integral to the hull and is not bolted into place. These normally have longer chords and thicker roots and unfortunately are not too common these days.

This interesting looking keel would probably not fare too well in a hard grounding. Its leading edge is nearly vertical and its root is considerably shorter than its bottom part, which can only increase loads in the area when the keel hits something. It also has wings at the bottom (hard to see in this photo) and these may make it a bit harder to get off afterward.

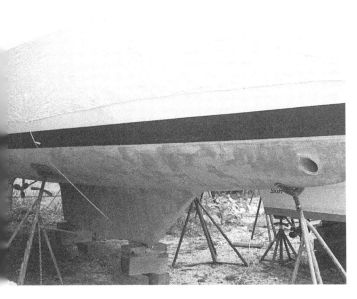

This boat's shoal fin keel would work better if it had a ballast bulb at the bottom.

The features that make a bolted-on keel more secure in a grounding are shoal draft, a swept-back (rather than vertical) leading edge, and a long keel joint. Less draft, of course, means that the shock to the hull and keel bolts is transmitted along a shorter lever arm. The shock is further minimized by a swept-back leading edge, and a longer keel joint spreads the shock load over a larger area of the boat's structure. It helps, too, if the root, or stub, to which the ballast keel is bolted slopes downward fore to aft, as this reduces shear loads on the keel bolts.

You'll note that the ideal grounding-resistant fin keel—one that is shallow and long—is not at all performance oriented. Likewise, a keel offering more directional stability—one with more lateral surface area—is not particularly fast or maneuverable. This is the conundrum around which any decision regarding a boat's underbody must bend itself, as performance and security are ultimately mutually exclusive. You can ameliorate this harsh truth to some extent by mixing and matching rudders and keels. Put a long shoal keel on a hull with a spade rudder, for example, and you'll have a boat with better directional stability that can take the ground and back down nicely in reverse, but it won't be as quick or close-winded as a boat with a high-aspect fin. Put a full rudder skeg with a prop aperture on a hull with a deep high-aspect fin and you'll have a boat that is fast and closewinded, with its rudder and running gear well protected, but it won't back down nearly as well (or be quite as fast and responsive) as a boat with a spade rudder. In sum, you can exchange some characteristics you care less about for those that matter more, but you can never have the best of all worlds.

Centerboards and Lifting Keels

Although the underwater foils of most sailboats are fixed in place, some have foils that can be shifted up and down, thus varying draft. This gives a cruising sailor a great deal of flexibility. Draft can be reduced to gain access to shoal areas, a feature that is often useful when anchoring or mooring a boat, or draft (and total wetted surface area) can be decreased for better performance sailing off the wind, when deep foils aren't needed to combat leeway. Conversely, draft can be increased when sailing to improve performance to windward.

By far the most common adjustable foil is the unballasted centerboard, which pivots on a pin at one end and swings down from a slot in the bottom of the boat. On larger boats centerboards are normally housed inside a shoal-draft ballast keel—either a full keel or a long fin keel. These keel-centerboard boats, as they are known, were often raced back in the days of the CCA rule but are now used solely for cruising.

Another variation is the bilge-centerboard boat, which has no keel. Instead, the centerboard is the major foil and is housed in a case in the boat's bilges. This configuration is commonly seen on small sailing skiffs and dinghies, on small trailerable cruising boats, and on some slightly heavier traditional cruising boats such as sharpies and Cape Cod catboats. It is also found on a few larger contemporary cruising boats, including several French designs built in aluminum or steel, as well as some fiberglass boats built by Lyman-Morse in the United States and by Southerly in Great Britain. (Southerly, it should be noted, refers to the centerboards on its boats as "swing keels" because they are ballasted.) On most

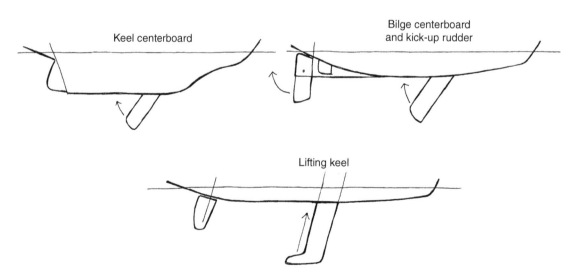

The three basic types of shifting foils. The keel-centerboard configuration is most common, though lifting keels have become increasingly popular. Bilge-centerboard configurations are seen primarily on French boats.

Here's a bilge-centerboard cruiser built by Alubat in France demonstrating one advantage of having no keel. Note the end plate on the kick-up rudder. (Courtesy of Alubat)

boats of this type, if crew weight alone cannot serve as adequate ballast, it is necessary to carry ballast in the bilge in order to keep the boat upright.

The advantage of a keel-centerboard boat is that it can sail even when its centerboard is not deployed, though with diminished windward performance. Indeed, I've met several owners of keel-centerboard boats who never use their boards (one had even glassed over the slot on the bottom of his boat) and are content to sail on the shoal keel alone. A bilge-centerboard boat, by comparison, cannot hope to sail to windward, or even on a reach, without its

board. The big advantage of such a boat is that it stays upright when not afloat and can dry out on the tide or even be driven onto a beach.

Another less common type of adjustable foil is the lifting keel. These carry ballast, normally in a bulb at the bottom of the foil, and rather than pivoting they slide straight up and down like daggerboards. There is no open slot in the bottom of the boat to create turbulence, as is often the case on centerboard boats, and when the keel is fully deployed, the boat's ballast is as low as possible, like on a fixed-keel boat. The great disadvantage is that it takes considerable

A high-aspect centerboard foil (left) leaves an open slot when lowered, which increases turbulence; a low-aspect centerboard foil (right) can be configured so its slot stays closed.

effort to raise a ballasted lifting keel, and on a boat of any size this requires a hydraulic or motorized lifting mechanism. A centerboard, by comparison, can normally be raised with a line on a winch.

Lifting keels are most often seen on big one-off performance cruisers. On most such boats the keel cannot be fully retracted, as the foil is long and the distance it can be hoisted within its casing is limited by the height of the boat's cabintop. Typically draft on these boats ranges from deep (say 14 feet or so) when the keel is down to only moderately deep (say 7 feet) when it is retracted.

There are at least two small lifting-keel cruising boats, the Seaward Eagle 26 and 32, on which the keel can be fully retracted (the draft on the 32 varies from 20 inches to 6 foot 6 inches) without any powered mechanical assistance. There are also larger boats with lifting keels that can be fully retracted, but these are rare and do not perform as well as their deeper-keel brethren.

On any cruising vessel with variable draft the rudder should never be the deepest foil, whether the keel or centerboard is raised or lowered. Otherwise the rudder is potentially vulnerable and could be destroyed should the boat run aground. On keel-centerboard boats this is not normally a problem, as the rudder can be shallower than the fixed keel and still reach deep enough to be effective. Likewise on large lifting-keel boats there is usually enough draft for an ample rudder, even when the keel is retracted. On boats with keels or centerboards that come all the way up, it is common to see shoal rudders with hinged end plates that swing down under sail to increase rudder draft, then kick up when the boat takes the ground. Alternatively, some boats have twin shoal-draft rudders instead of one deep one.

The biggest drawback of adjustable foils is their complexity. A hull with major moving parts is by nature more vulnerable and requires more maintenance than a hull with fixed appendages. Many owners of centerboard boats tell stories of stones getting jammed in centerboard slots, of boards whumping around in their cases in heavy weather, of boards bent or broken in a grounding, of broken pendant lines, and of badly corroded pivot pins that are almost impossible to access. Such travails are what lead some to never use their centerboards at all. Lifting keels are stronger than centerboards and can withstand more abuse, but still depend on whatever mechanism is used to raise and lower them. In most cases these are complex and need power to function.

Multiple Keels

Just as two shoal-draft rudders can do the work of one deep rudder, two (or more) shoal keels can do the

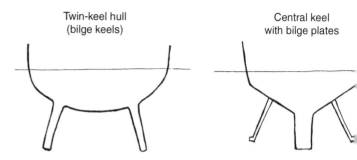

Two basic types of multiple-keel hulls. A twin-keeled hull (bilge keels) on left and a full-keel hull with bilge plates. Both will stand upright when aground.

job of one deep keel. This sort of hull—commonly referred to as a *twin-keel* or *bilge-keel* hull—in effect has multiple lateral planes. Usually there are two fin keels fixed side by side; less common is one long shoal-draft full keel on the centerline with two small fins, or bilge plates, fixed on either side of it. There is no performance advantage in arranging underwater foils like this. The foils are not deep enough to be hydrodynamically efficient, and their extra wetted surface area serves only to decrease boat speed, especially when conditions are light. Instead, the purpose of such a configuration is to improve access to shoal water and make it possible for a boat to stand upright when aground.

Bilge-keel boats are most common in Great Britain, though a few examples do sometimes appear in North America. For some British cruisers they make a great deal of sense, as tidal ranges in Britain are large and mooring space is often limited. Many must

The underbody of a small twin-keel boat. Note how the large skeg and rudder in effect form a third keel.

keep their boats in "mud berths" that dry out at low tide, which is less nerve-wracking if the boat remains upright. Mud berths are rarely seen in U.S. waters, but still there are distinct advantages to cruising in a shoal-draft boat that can take the ground standing up. Anchoring in a secluded gunkhole no one else would even think of entering, and then being able to wander forth on foot directly from your boat after the tide has gone out is a uniquely liberating experience. Bilge-keel boats also have a smooth motion in a seaway, as their multiple parallel keels act something like flopper-stoppers and help dampen rolling. They also have great directional stability due to the increased lateral surface area of the keels.

The downside of a hull that takes the ground so well is that it may not willingly let go of the bottom if you run aground accidentally. Parallel keels make it hard to twist a boat off a shoal bank, plus you can't heel the boat to reduce draft. Normally, the only option is to back straight off. Multiple keels are also more work to maintain. There is that much more surface area to prep and paint, and working between the keels is not pleasant (believe me, I speak from experience).

Multihulls

The primary underwater foils on catamarans and trimarans need not support any ballast and play no role in keeping the boat upright. Their sole purpose is to resist leeway and improve windward performance. As on monohulls, the foils that do this best have high-aspect shapes and reach deep into the water to generate lots of hydrodynamic lift. On all trimarans and racing catamarans, and on some performance cruising cats, the foils of choice are vertically retracting daggerboards. Cats with daggerboards normally carry two, one in each hull, with only the leeward board deployed at any given time. Trimarans carry a straight

daggerboard in their main hull, and the most radical tris also have curved daggerboards in their outriggers, or amas, that work as hydrofoils and almost lift the boat out of the water when it sails at high speeds.

The great advantage of a daggerboard, of course, is that it can be retracted when not needed, thus greatly reducing draft and, to a lesser extent, wetted surface area. The disadvantage is that daggerboards, because they don't swing up like centerboards when they hit something, are susceptible to damage in a grounding. Not only can the board itself be damaged, but large shock loads can be transmitted to the case containing the board as well. In a worst-case scenario, the case may rupture and the boat may take on water. To mitigate this threat, some builders install foam "crush boxes" in daggerboard cases abaft the board to help absorb impacts.

From a cruiser's perspective the biggest drawback of daggerboards is that their cases take up

The daggerboard case inside this performance cruising cat makes a narrow space seem even narrower. Though the space between the case and hull side can be used for storage, as seen here, you must also guard against putting too much extra weight on a cat.

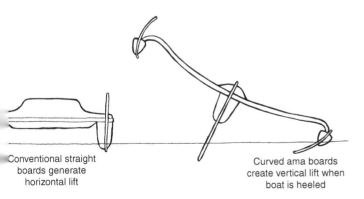

Conventional straight boards generate horizontal lift

Curved ama boards create vertical lift when boat is heeled

A performance cruising cat with daggerboards in each hull (left) and a racing trimaran (right) with one straight daggerboard in its main hull and curved boards in its amas.

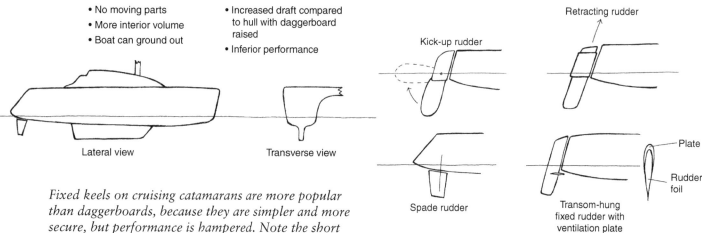

- No moving parts
- More interior volume
- Boat can ground out

- Increased draft compared to hull with daggerboard raised
- Inferior performance

Lateral view

Transverse view

Kick-up rudder

Retracting rudder

Spade rudder

Transom-hung fixed rudder with ventilation plate

Plate

Rudder foil

Fixed keels on cruising catamarans are more popular than daggerboards, because they are simpler and more secure, but performance is hampered. Note the short spade rudder.

If the rudder on a multihull is fixed, as with the spade and transom-hung rudders, it should draw less than the boat's keel to save it from being damaged in a grounding. Other multihull rudder variations include the kick-up and the retractable rudder.

valuable living space inside the boat. Hulls on cats and tris are relatively narrow to begin with, and space only gets tighter when large vertical structures are inserted into them. On larger cats, this problem can be relieved a bit by placing the daggerboards outboard of the centerline in each hull. On most cruising cats, however, builders leave off the boards and install long, fixed shoal-draft keels beneath each hull. These are not hydrodynamically efficient, and cats with keels never sail as well to windward as cats with boards. The fixed keels do free up interior space, they take the ground well, and they have no moving parts to worry about. They are also found on a few cruising trimarans, but this is increasingly rare.

Because multihulls are almost always shoal-draft creatures, their rudders must be carefully conceived. On cruising cats with keels, there is usually enough draft to accommodate a pair of short spade rudders, or rudders on skegs, that are deep enough to control the boat yet not so deep as to suffer when the boat is aground. On boats with retracting daggerboards, it is common to see retracting rudders as well. These may be rudders with hinged end plates or vertically retracting rudders that slide up and down in a sleeve or cassette like a daggerboard. The latter, like daggerboards, are more susceptible to damage, since they cannot kick up easily when striking the bottom.

Rudder ventilation is another issue. This can occur when an outboard transom-hung rudder is used on any boat (multihull or monohull) capable of high-speed sailing, as air can get sucked into the water along the low-pressure side of the foil, thus ruining its effectiveness. The problem can be mitigated by putting small horizontal ventilation plates on the rudder to block air from being drawn down from above, but the best solution is to keep the rudder fully immersed by locating it under the hull.

HULL SECTIONS

A hull's three dimensional shape obviously cannot be defined by referring solely to its lateral plane. Its transverse planes, or cross sections, play an equally important role in determining its characteristics. In the terminology of naval architects these are known simply as *sections*. When conceiving a design, a designer often draws the midship section first and works forward and aft from there. Curiously, however, published drawings of boats rarely include midship sections. Instead, this critical aspect of a boat's shape must be inferred from published data, photographs, or drawings from other sources.

The most useful number to consider is the boat's *beam,* or width, but again the information provided is usually incomplete. Published specifications always include a boat's beam on deck at its widest point, but rarely include its waterline beam. Only by considering both together can you start to get a useful idea of the shape of a boat's midship section.

You also want to know how a boat's beam is distributed forward and aft. Fortunately, a boat's accommodations plan, which is always published, shows the shape of the hull as viewed from above, and from this it is easy to see, for example, whether the boat has narrow ends but is fat in the middle, or is fat along its entire length, or is long and skinny. What you cannot see, however, is how beam is distributed along the waterline. Unfortunately, you often can't get a complete idea of how a boat's sections are shaped until you see the boat out of the water.

Interpreting a Lines Drawing

The best way to get a sense of a hull's three-dimensional shape without actually seeing the hull itself is to look at a *lines drawing*. This is the drawing a boat's designer creates when conceiving its hull. In the past these were often published in magazines, but this rarely happens now, as magazines have less space in their editorial pages and designers worry more about having their designs ripped off. Still, with a bit of research, you can sometimes get hold of one.

A lines drawing presents three views of a hull—from the side (the *profile view*); from the bottom (the *plan view*); and from ahead of and behind the boat (the *body plan*, which offers a split view of the sections as seen from both ends of the boat). Each view presents the hull's three-dimensional form in two dimensions using three or four sets of lines. The contours and orientation of these lines vary from view to view.

according to their distance from the DWL. WL+12, for example, describes a waterline 12 inches above the DWL; WL-6 describes a line 6 inches below the DWL. Waterlines appear as straight horizontal lines in the profile and body plan views and as curved oblong- or teardrop-shaped planes in the plan view.

The *buttock lines* cut the hull into vertical slices that run fore and aft parallel to the boat's *centerline* (CL), which cuts the hull into two equal halves. Buttock lines are placed at regular intervals on either side of the CL and are identified according to their distance from the CL. Because a hull is normally symmetrical on both sides of its CL, the same label identifies two identical buttock lines. Butt+24, for example, describes the pair of buttock lines located 24 inches either side of the CL. Buttocks, as they are often

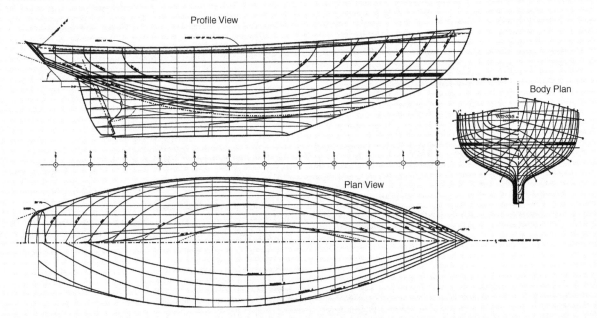

A lines drawing of a modern full-keel cruiser designed by Chuck Paine. (Courtesy of Chuck Paine/Mark Fitzgerald)

The first set of lines are called *stations*. They are transverse vertical slices of the hull (otherwise known as sections) placed at regular intervals along the length of the hull's waterline. Usually they divide the hull into twelve segments and are numbered 0 through 10, beginning at the forward end of the waterline. While the ten segments between stations 0 and 10 are equal in length, the two segments outboard of the waterline that define the overhangs (if any) can be different lengths. In the profile and plan views stations are straight vertical lines; in the body plan they are curved lines.

The *waterlines* are horizontal slices of the hull running fore and aft parallel to the design waterline on which the boat is expected to float. Waterlines are placed at different intervals above and below the DWL; shorter intervals are normally used below the DWL to describe the hull's more rapidly changing underwater shape. Waterlines are identified

called for short, appear as straight vertical lines in the body plan, as straight horizontal lines in the plan view, and as curved lines in the profile view.

The fourth set of lines used in many (but not all) lines drawings are called *diagonals*. These slice downward and outward from the boat's fore-and-aft centerline plane and help a designer define and fair the shape of a hull's bottom. They appear in the body plan as pairs of straight diagonal lines forming V-shaped chevrons along the CL. They are represented as curved lines in a split view of the plan view, in which one side of the drawing shows waterlines and the other shows where the diagonal planes intersect the hull's surface. Diagonals are usually identified alphabetically starting with Diag A, which often (but not always) lands at or near the DWL in the body plan and is always the outermost diagonal in a plan view.

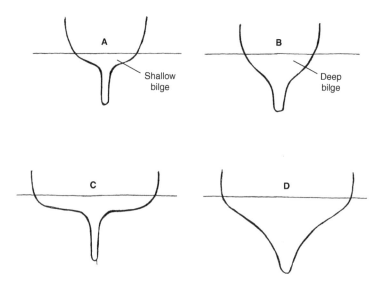

Basic section shapes: A) narrow section with low deadrise and shallow bilges; B) narrow section with high deadrise and deep bilges; C) wide section with low deadrise and shallow bilges; and D) wide section with high deadrise and deep bilges.

Monohull sailboats have four basic midship section shapes. These are defined by the hull's beam and its *deadrise*, which refers to the angle at which a hull section descends from the waterline to the bottom of the hull where it joins the keel. A hull with little or no deadrise generally has shallow bilges and a flat bottom; a hull with lots of deadrise has deeper bilges and more of a sloping or V-shaped bottom. Thus the four basic midship shapes are: narrow beam, low deadrise, shallow bilge (A); narrow beam, lots of deadrise, deep bilge (B); wide beam, low deadrise, shallow bilge (C); and wide beam, lots of deadrise, deep bilge (D).

One great advantage of a low-deadrise hull is that a flatter bottom helps a boat get on top of the water and plane if the boat is light enough and conditions are favorable. This and the fact that they are generally easier and cheaper to build are why low-deadrise hulls are the most common type today. Even contemporary boats with full keels or long fin keels are apt to have moderately low deadrise and relatively shallow bilges.

One significant disadvantage of a shallow bilge, particularly for cruisers, is that space under the cabin sole is greatly reduced. Heavy items such as fuel and water tanks and battery banks, which are easily situated under the sole on boats with deep bilges, often must be situated above the sole instead, under settees or other furniture, thus raising the boat's center of gravity and reducing the space available for storing other things. If the boat starts leaking, water will

rise above the sole more quickly. If the boat is well heeled when the leak develops, the water will pool up on the boat's lee side, where centerline bilge pumps cannot reach it. On boats with lots of deadrise and deep bilges a great deal of water can fit under the sole, even when the boat is heeling, and it stays closer to the centerline, which makes it much easier for a bilge pump to control any flooding.

Another characteristic of a flat-bottomed boat with low deadrise is that its hull slams against the water with great force when sailing to windward in choppy water. In rough conditions this creates an uncomfortable, abrupt, jarring motion. It also makes an awful racket that is unnerving. Pounding to windward in severe weather aboard boats like this I have often wondered how it is their hulls are not smashed into pieces. A hull with more deadrise and more wedge-shaped sections slams much less in heavy windward going and is more comfortable.

Section shapes are also important on multihulls. Early in the development of multihulled boats, V-shaped hulls with lots of deadrise were favored, first because they were easy to construct, but also because a V section creates enough lateral resistance to resist leeway. This inherent ability can be accentuated, at least on a catamaran, if its two hulls are asymmetrically shaped, with curved inboard surfaces and flatter outboard surfaces. This improves the hydrodynamic lift of the leeward hull and helps the boat point higher, but only if the windward hull is lifted clear of the water. If both hulls are in the water, the lift created by one hull will cancel the lift created by the other. For this reason, asymmetric V-shaped hulls are normally seen only on small beach cats (such as the Hobie 16) that can easily fly a hull when sailing at speed.

The drawback of a V-shaped hull that digs into the water and creates lateral resistance is that it is also more difficult to turn, especially when there is

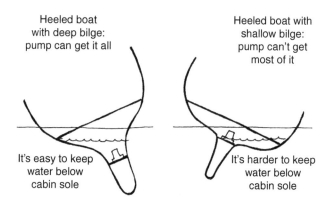

Heeled boat with deep bilge: pump can get it all

Heeled boat with shallow bilge: pump can't get most of it

It's easy to keep water below cabin sole

It's harder to keep water below cabin sole

There is a significant advantage to having a deeper bilge when taking on water.

V-shaped hull
- Easier to build
- Resists leeway
- More wetted surface

U-shaped hull
- Harder to build
- Needs foils to resist leeway
- Less wetted surface

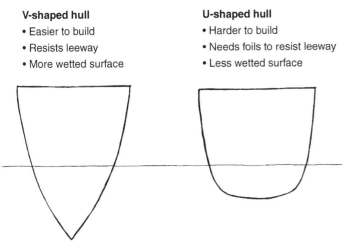

Basic catamaran hull sections.

more than one of them. Large cats or tris with V hulls are notoriously hard to tack, and except on a few anachronistic craft, such as those still being designed by James Wharram, most modern multihulls instead have hull sections with much less deadrise and flatter bottoms. If equipped with appropriate underwater foils, such U-shaped hulls are both faster and more weatherly than V-shaped hulls.

It is true of both multihulls and monohulls that a narrow hull, all things being equal, travels faster through the water than a wide one primarily because it has less wetted surface area. Any hull constructed solely for speed, with no other consideration taken into account, is invariably long and skinny. Think, for example, of rowing shells, which are so narrow they are entirely unstable without their oars deployed.

It is also true, however, that a narrow hull has less interior space than a wide one. This is exactly why so many contemporary cruising boats are so beamy. Their midship sections are much beamier than in the past, and that extra beam is carried much farther aft. This creates more living space, which increasingly is what cruisers are most interested in.

Aboard monohulls, fortunately, more beam does have some performance benefits. More beam aft increases buoyancy in the stern, which keeps it from digging into the water as the boat approaches hull speed. Assuming a hull with low deadrise and a flat bottom, it also helps the boat break free of the water and surf downwind in large seas. More beam also allows a boat to carry more sail, a matter we will soon discuss in more detail, and the extra power often more than makes up for the added resistance created by the extra wetted surface.

Aboard multihulls, however, increasing beam in the hulls does nothing but hurt performance.

Multihulls are hypersensitive to increases in wetted surface area and do not rely on the width of their hulls to increase stability. Instead the ability to carry sail is a function of the distance between the hulls. Also, multihulls are so light they need no extra buoyancy to get on top of the water. To create more accommodation space without increasing waterline beam, cruising multihulls therefore often have flared hulls or flanges above their waterlines that increase interior volume without increasing waterline beam.

Another conundrum concerns the bridgedeck connecting a cat's two hulls. On straight racing cats, this is little more than some crossbeams and netting, a configuration that minimizes both weight and the resistance the bridgedeck creates by quarreling with passing waves. It also, however, restricts available accommodation space to the interior of the two hulls, which are often narrow. Aboard most cruising cats the bridgedeck is a solid platform on which is perched the most palatial portion of the interior, a vast enclosed saloon with lots of windows offering wraparound views of the outside world.

The more cruising-oriented a boat is, the farther its bridgedeck will extend forward and aft so as to increase floor space in the saloon, and the closer it will reach to the water so as to increase headroom. But this can cripple a cat's performance. Bridgedeck accommodations not only add a lot of weight due to the extra structure involved, they also increase resistance. The larger the surface area of the bridgedeck's underbody, and the lower it is, the more time it will spend in contact with the water. The bridgedeck's superstructure may also add a great deal of windage, depending on how it is configured. As a result of these disadvantages, many cruising cats perform no better than moderately able monohulls. In some cases, particularly when going to windward, they may actually perform worse.

Racing cat
- Lots of clearance
- Narrow hulls
- No superstructure between hulls
- Daggerboards

Cruising cat
- Little clearance
- Wider hulls
- Lots of superstructure between hulls
- Fixed keels

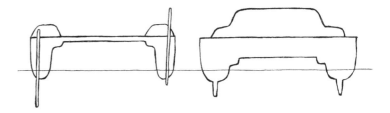

Catamaran bridgedecks.

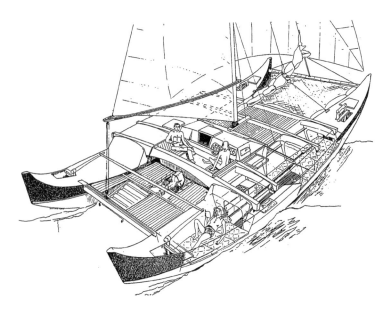

This Wharram Pahi 42 has a low-resistance bridge-deck, but the interior accommodations are mostly in the narrow hulls. (Courtesy James Wharram)

Compromises between the two extremes are seen in certain performance cruising catamarans. One popular variation retains the interior bridgedeck accommodations but limits their size. The bridgedeck does not extend far forward, and its underbody is kept well clear of the water. Another less popular variation eliminates the bridgedeck accommodations, but retains the solid bridgedeck, which serves as a large open cockpit and lounging area with a hard or soft bimini that provides shelter from sun and rain. This configuration, seen on boats such as the Maine Cat, eliminates a great deal of superstructure and weight and allows the bridgedeck to be elevated high above the water. The downside is that interior accommodations are confined to the two narrow hulls.

Form Stability

Stability, fundamentally, is what prevents a boat from being turned over and capsized. Whether you are a cruiser or a racer, it is a desirable characteristic. A boat's shape, particularly its transverse hull form, has an enormous impact on how stable it is. This *form stability* is one of the primary reasons you should be interested in the shape of a boat's hull.

The basic principle is self-evident: an object that is wide and flat is harder to turn over than one that is narrow and round. With this in mind, we can see at a glance which midsection shapes in the illustration on page 64 have the greatest form stability. Section C, with its wide flat bottom, is inherently

more stable than any of the others; section B, which is narrow with lots of deadrise and a deep bilge, is the least stable. Whether section A, the narrow hull with little deadrise, will have more or less form stability than D, the wide hull with lots of deadrise, will depend on each hull's precise dimensions and shape. Between two hulls of equal width, however, the one with less deadrise and a flatter bottom will have greater form stability.

As far as form stability is concerned, the controlling dimension is always waterline beam. You therefore should not jump to conclusions based on a boat's published maximum beam, as boats with the same maximum beam may have very different waterline beams. Another important factor is how a boat's beam is distributed along the length of its hull. A hull that carries more waterline beam into its bow and stern sections—that is, a hull with a larger waterplane—has more form stability than a hull with a wide midsection and narrow ends. The classic example of the latter are the IOR boats that dominated racing during the 1970s. Because the IOR rating rule favored beamy boats but measured beam only in the midsection, designers thought they could have their cake and eat it, too. By making their boats fat in the middle they could gain a rating advantage; by pinching the ends they could reduce displacement and wetted surface area. Such hulls, however, as demonstrated during the 1979 Fastnet Race, are often not very stable.

Form stability is an important component of what is termed *initial stability*, which refers to a boat's ability to immediately resist heeling when pressure is applied to its sails. A boat with lots of initial stability is said to be *stiff*; one with little initial stability is *tender*. Stiffness is a desirable feature, as a boat never sails as well when heeled way over on its ear. The keel's effective area and draft and its capacity for generating lift are reduced, as are the effective height and area of the sail plan (by about 10%, for

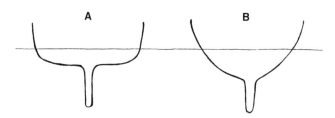

It's not beam on deck but beam on the waterline that counts most when it comes to form stability. Both hulls here have the same maximum beam on deck, the same draft, and the same area underwater. Hull B, however, has much less waterline beam and thus less form stability.

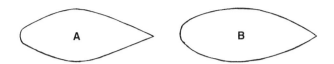

Waterplane area. The distance beam is carried forward and aft also affects form stability. Both hulls have the same waterline length and beam, but hull B has fuller ends and more waterplane area and thus more form stability.

example, when a boat is heeled to an angle of 25 degrees). A stiff boat that stays more upright not only retains more keel and rig efficiency, it can also stand up to a larger sail plan in the first place. In many cases, particularly if a boat is light, this negates any loss of performance caused by an increase in beam and wetted surface area.

Stiff boats with good form stability in one sense are more comfortable, especially for novice sailors, than boats that heel easily. In another sense, however, they can be very uncomfortable. Though they are rolled to less severe angles, they snap back from those lesser angles more quickly and abruptly than boats with less form stability that are rolled to greater angles. The resulting motion can seem jerky and violent, as is reflected in the motion-comfort ratio discussed earlier. This, combined with the tendency of a flat-bottomed boat to pound in a steep head sea, may lead some to conclude that there is such a thing as too much form stability.

The most important thing to remember about form stability is that it does not translate into ultimate stability. A sailboat's hull form can help it resist heeling up to a point, but past that point all bets are off. The classic example is *Mohawk*, the enormous American "skimming dish" schooner described in Chapter 1. Here was a boat that depended far too much on form stability. It had a broad, flat hull capable of supporting an enormous sail plan in moderate conditions, but when caught by a sudden squall with all its sail up, it was laid over and capsized quickly.

In a worst-case scenario, after a hull like this has capsized, its form stability may even help keep it inverted. Fans of singlehanded ocean racing will recall a dramatic series of Open 60 capsizes in the mid- to late-1990s. These extremely wide, flat monohulls, designed to surf at high speeds off the wind in the Southern Ocean, stayed upside down after being flipped over in spite of the very deep (or tall, as the case may be) ballast keels attached to their bottoms.

Multihulls, of course, rely entirely on form stability to stay upright. They are extremely stiff, and it takes an enormous amount of energy to heel them to any appreciable degree. Once pushed to the limit,

however, they must flip over and must remain flipped over until an even greater amount of energy arrives to right them. Monohull cruisers, of course, point to this as the Achilles heel of the multihull. Multihull cruisers respond by noting that in a worst-case scenario their boats at least will still be floating (albeit upside down) while the monohull sailor's craft will be sitting (albeit somewhat upright) at the bottom of the sea.

Ballast Stability

And what is it that will drag the poor monohull cruiser's stalwart craft to the bottom when worse comes to worst? The answer, of course, is its ballast. Ballast is weight added to a boat to help it stay upright. As with form stability, the principle is obvious: an object is harder to up-end if a heavy weight is placed at the bottom of it. Witness the iconic inflatable punching clown. With the majority of its weight concentrated at floor level, the clown pops back upright every time you knock it down. This, of course, is exactly what we want our sailboats to do.

Besides helping boats sink, however, ballast is counterproductive in another way: it makes a boat heavier and increases displacement, thus increasing resistance and decreasing speed. But this sad fact can be mitigated. The amount of ballast needed to counteract the capsizing forces of wind and wave decreases dramatically the lower it is placed in the boat. Unlike the clown, which must always have its feet on the ground, the bottom of a sailboat can reach as far down as there is water for it to float in. This is yet another reason why racing sailors prefer very deep keels and why gunkholing cruisers must

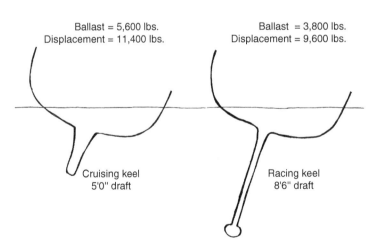

Ballast and draft. "How low can you go?" is always an important question when ballasting a boat. Two identical hulls with shoal and deep ballast keels require different amounts of ballast to achieve the same amount of stability.

agonize over draft. On a stock 40-foot boat, for example, the weight differential between a shoal-draft cruising keel and a deep racing keel installed on otherwise identical hulls can amount to 20% or more of the boat's total displacement. For many, this will seem a heavy price to pay (pun intended) for shoal-draft capability.

Just as weight down low increases stability, weight up high—generally, any weight added at or above deck level—decreases it. It is important, therefore, not to think of ballast as a discrete feature. Think instead of a boat's total weight and how it is distributed. For example, adding one pound of weight at the masthead of a 35- to 40-foot cruising boat effectively subtracts 7 to 10 pounds of ballast from its keel. Conversely, subtracting that pound adds 7 to 10 pounds of ballast. The effects are less dramatic but are still significant when weight is redistributed closer to the boat's center of gravity.

Aboard most cruising boats, the center of gravity is more or less about 6 inches above the waterline. Any weight subtracted above or added below this point increases the boat's effective ballast and lowers its center of gravity. Such increases are multiplied according to the weight's vertical distance from the center of gravity. For example, subtracting 1 pound of weight 35 feet above the center of gravity is equivalent to subtracting 35 pounds 1 foot above it. Adding 1 pound 7 feet below the center gravity is equivalent to adding 7 pounds 1 foot below it.

The bottom line (another intended pun) is that you should always strive to keep weight as low as possible, whether or not it is officially designated "ballast." This is why racing sailors eagerly embrace technologies that dramatically reduce weight aloft, such as carbon-fiber spars and fiber rigging. It is also why cruising sailors should be more circumspect when adding weight to their rigs. Roller-furling headsails, in-mast furling mainsails, extra-heavy wire rigging, mast-mounted radomes, mast steps, and other such gear may increase a boat's "cruise-ability," but their cumulative weight also significantly decreases its stability.

Boats that rely primarily on ballast for stability tend to be narrow and deep. In the past they also often had a great deal of deadrise in their hulls, though this is less true now. Narrow, heavily ballasted boats, particularly those with lots of deadrise, usually are tender and quickly heel to significant angles when pressed by even a moderate breeze. But this does not make them "unstable." When pressed to extremes, they are usually more stable than stiffer boats that rely more on form stability to stay upright. Unlike form stability, which increases a boat's initial stability, ballast stability increases *ultimate*, or *reserve*,

Cruisers often store lots of gear on deck, but extra weight above a boat's center of gravity (usually about 6 inches above the waterline) decreases stability.

stability, which is what helps a boat recover and roll upright again—just like the punching clown—after it has been knocked flat or even capsized.

Tender boats, like stiff boats, can be both comfortable and uncomfortable. Their tendency to heel a lot can be unnerving, and even for experienced sailors, working at severe angles for extended periods of time is taxing. But when the sea gets rough a tender boat has a smoother motion than a stiff one. It rolls to greater angles, but rolls more slowly, without the vicious snapping and jerking that characterizes the motion of a stiff boat. Sailing to weather in a strong breeze a tender boat's lee rail will be buried much of the time, and the crew on deck will get wet, but the boat will not pound as violently.

For cruising sailors, the question of which sort of stability to favor when selecting a boat is a serious one. Many designs available today, of course, are relatively moderate and compromise between extremes. As a general rule, however, popular modern designs tend to be relatively light and wide with shallow bilges, and thus are more stiff than tender. Older designs from the CCA era are usually heavier, narrower, and more tender. Again, as a general rule, coastal cruisers who expect to sail primarily in moderate conditions can, if they like, favor faster, more modern, stiffer designs. Bluewater cruisers who are more likely to encounter extreme conditions should think more seriously about whether to favor slower, more tender designs with more ultimate stability.

Shifting Ballast

The most effective way to increase initial stability aboard a boat that may or may not have good form stability is to shift significant amounts of ballast to windward while it is sailing. This creates a lever arm that operates at a right angle to the sail plan, increasing the ballast's effectiveness and allowing a boat to carry significantly more sail.

This principle is seen at work on any unballasted sailing dinghy that depends primarily on crew

The author and friends demonstrate how shifting crew weight outboard helps to keep this otherwise unballasted Bahamian racing sloop upright.

weight to stay upright. To prevent the boat from toppling over to leeward, the crew hikes out on the windward rail. The farther to windward they can get, the more sail the boat can carry, as the crew's effective weight is increased by the longer lever arm. On modern dinghies you often see devices such as trapezes and/or hiking rails that allow crew to get as far outboard as possible. On such traditional boats as Bahamian sloops and Chesapeake log canoes the crew sits out over the water on long planks that protrude from the windward rail. When the boat is tacked, the planks are moved from one side to the other, and there is a mad scramble as the crew repositions itself.

These days ballast on larger boats can be shifted in more sophisticated ways. In one method known as water ballasting, large quantities of seawater are moved from one side of the boat to the other as it tacks. The water is shifted between dedicated tanks on the outboard edges of the hull's interior either with a pump or by letting the water run downhill from the windward tank to the leeward tank before tacking. Water ballast augments a conventional ballast keel and is released overboard when it is not needed. Another way to shift ballast is with a canting keel. These are struts with heavy ballast bulbs that can swing from a vertical position under a boat's hull out to angles of up to 55 degrees. Large canting-keel monohulls 70 feet and longer have hit top speeds in excess of 30 knots, which is comparable to speeds routinely achieved by large racing catamarans. Several canting-keel boats have sailed 500 miles or more in open water in a single 24-hour period, maintaining average speeds of over 20 knots. What makes canting keels so powerful is that they shift all of a boat's ballast to windward while keeping it well below the hull, thus greatly increasing its effectiveness. A keel capable of canting 55 degrees requires 25 to more than 60 percent less ballast than a fixed keel to support the same hull and sail plan. The result is a much lighter boat with a much higher SA/D ratio and a much lower D/L ratio.

Canting keels do have their complications. When canted well to windward, a keel ceases to function as a hydrodynamic foil and other foils must therefore take its place. These can be significantly smaller than the keel itself, due to the high speeds at which the boat travels. Often these auxiliary foils are daggerboards in the boat's midsection, one on each side, with only the leeward board deployed at any given time. Or there may be a second rudder forward of the keel, often called a *canard*, that works in conjunction with the primary rudder to both resist leeway and steer the boat. This configuration, referred to as the Canting Ballast Twin Foil (CBTF) system, is a

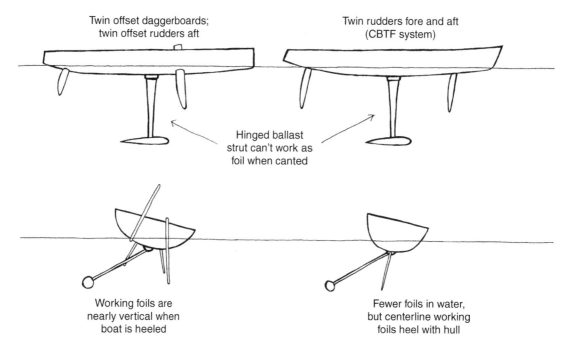

Twin offset daggerboards;
twin offset rudders aft

Twin rudders fore and aft
(CBTF system)

Hinged ballast
strut can't work as
foil when canted

Working foils are
nearly vertical when
boat is heeled

Fewer foils in water,
but centerline working
foils heel with hull

Canting-keel variations. Systems like these have appeared on some large high-end performance cruisers.

patented technology seen on large maxi yachts such as Roy Disney's last *Pyewacket*. Centerboards and centerline daggerboards have also been used.

Another major complication is the mechanism that swings the keel back and forth. This mechanism is somewhat simpler on smaller boats, as the top of the keel, which protrudes several feet into the boat's interior, can be pulled to either side with nothing more than a hefty tackle. On larger boats, however, the weight that must be shifted can be enormous (the 140-foot super-maxi *Mari Cha IV*, for example, has a 10-ton bulb at the end of its canting keel) and mechanical assistance is required. This is normally provided by large hydraulic rams and pumps powered by the boat's main engine or a donkey engine, which must be running when the keel is moving. In all cases the pivoting keel joint in the bottom of the hull must be properly sealed and protected against flooding. Not surprisingly, there have been some dramatic failures. Though canting-keel technology has been in use since the mid-1990s, it is still in its developmental stage.

Canting keels have been installed on a few large, expensive, custom performance cruisers. Examples include the Baltic 78, certain luxury performance cruisers built by Wally Yachts, and a sleek 65-foot one-off boat, *Spirit of Adventure*, designed by Owen Clarke Design of New Zealand for a private client (see page 364). The canting keel on *Spirit* is also a lifting keel, as is the canting keel on the 100-foot super-maxi *Maximus*, a no-holds-barred racer

launched in 2005. It is unlikely that canting keels, lifting or otherwise, will trickle down any further into the cruising-boat market in the near future. The systems are too complex, too expensive, and potentially unreliable.

Water-ballast systems, on the other hand, have proven more popular. Indeed, several small trailerable cruising boats use static water ballast as their primary ballast. On these boats the ballast tanks are low in the bilge on the boat's centerline and are filled after the boat is launched to increase its displacement and stability. When the boat is hauled from the water, the ballast tank is emptied to reduce trailering weight. Since the ballast is never shifted, these are more appropriately termed static variable-ballast systems. Dynamic shifting-ballast systems are less common but have appeared on several performance cruising designs over the past 15 years. These include at least one production boat, Hunter Marine's HC-50, which was designed to be sailed by a couple. On some other production performance cruisers it is possible to shift water stored in the freshwater tanks from one side of the boat to the other.

Like canting keels, water-ballast systems make a boat much more complex. The ballast tanks take up interior space that could otherwise be devoted to accommodations, and they require a great deal of extra plumbing for picking up and discharging raw water and for moving it from tank to tank. Because water is not particularly dense, because ballast tanks

Canting keels have appeared on a few high-performance cruising boats. The keel on this custom cruiser, Spirit of Adventure, *designed by Owen Clarke Design, both cants side-to-side and shifts up and down. (Courtesy of Owen Clarke Design; Photo by Paul Todd.)*

must be located inside rather than below the main hull, and because the water ballast represents only a portion of the boat's total ballast, water-ballast systems also do not have nearly as dramatic an effect upon performance as do canting keels.

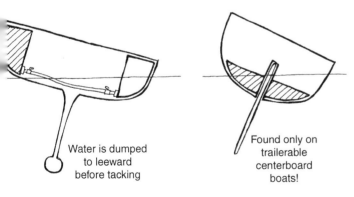

Water is dumped
to leeward
before tacking

Found only on
trailerable
centerboard
boats!

Two variations on water-ballast systems. On a boat with dynamic shifting ballast (left), the ballast tanks are outboard and the water is moved between them to shift weight to windward. On boats with static variable ballast (right), the ballast tank is in the bilge and is filled with water when sailing to lower the overall center of gravity. The tank is emptied when the boat is trailered.

QUANTIFYING STABILITY

It is unfortunately impossible to thoroughly analyze the stability of a given sailboat using commonly published specifications. Indeed, stability is so complex and is influenced by so many factors that even professional designers find it hard to quantify. Until the advent of computers, the calculations involved were so overwhelming that certain aspects of stability were only estimated rather than precisely determined. Even today, with computers doing the number crunching, stability calculations remain the most tedious part of a naval architect's job.

You can, however, always make certain intuitive deductions as to whether or not a given boat is more or less stable, and in what sense, using the general information provided above. Or, if you are willing to do a little digging, there are some resources available that allow you to make more sophisticated appraisals.

Stability Curves and Ratios

The most common tool used to assess a boat's form and ballast stability is the *stability curve*. This is a graphic representation of a boat's self-righting ability as it is rotated from right side up to upside down. Stability curves are sometimes published or otherwise made available by designers and builders, but to interpret them correctly you first need to understand the physics of a heeling sailboat.

When perfectly upright, a boat's *center of gravity* (CG)—which is a function of its total weight distribution (i.e., its ballast stability)—and its *center of buoyancy* (CB)—which is a function of its hull shape (i.e., its form stability)—are vertically aligned on the boat's centerline. CG presses downward on the boat's hull while CB presses upward with equal force. The two are in perfect equilibrium, and the boat is motionless. If some force heels the boat, however, CB shifts outboard of CG and the equilibrium is disturbed. The horizontal distance created between CG and CB as the boat heels is called the *righting arm* (GZ). This is a lever arm, with CG pushing down on one end and CB pushing up on the other, and their combined force, known as the *righting moment* (RM), works to rotate the hull back to an upright position. The point around which the hull rotates is known as the *metacenter* (M) and is always directly above CB.

The longer the righting arm (i.e., the larger the value for GZ), the greater the righting moment and the harder the hull is trying to swing upright again.

Up to a point, as a hull heels more, its righting arm just gets longer. The righting moment, consequently, gets larger and larger. This is initial stability. A wider hull has greater initial stability simply because its greater beam allows CB to move farther away from CG as it heels. Shifting ballast to windward also moves CG farther away from CB, and this too lengthens the righting arm and increases initial stability. The *angle of maximum stability* (AMS) is the angle at which the righting arm for any given hull is as long as it can be. This is where a hull is trying its hardest to turn upright again and is most resistant to further heeling.

Once a hull is pushed past its AMS, its righting arm gets progressively shorter and its ability to resist further heeling decreases. Now we are moving into the realm of ultimate, or reserve, stability. Eventually, if the hull is pushed over far enough, the righting arm disappears and CG and CB are again vertically aligned. Now, however, the metacenter and CG are in the same place, and the hull is *metastable*, meanings it is in a state of anti-equilibrium. Its fate hangs in the balance, and the least disturbance will cause it to turn one way or the other. This point of no return is the *angle of vanishing stability* (AVS). If the hull fails to right itself at this point, it must capsize. Any greater angle of heel will cause CG and CB to

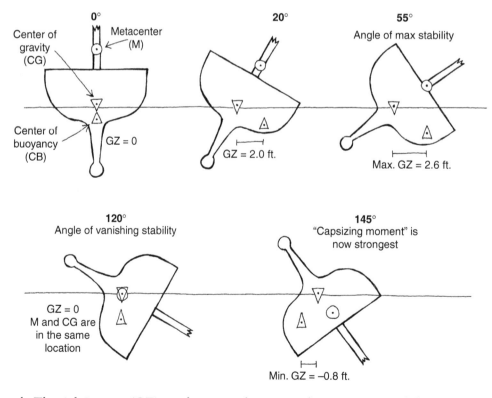

Stability at work. The righting arm (GZ) gets longer as the center of gravity (CG) and the center of buoyancy (CB) get farther apart, and the boat works harder to right itself. Past the angle of vanishing stability, however, the righting arm is negative and CG and CB are working to capsize the boat.

separate again, except now the horizontal distance between them will be a capsizing arm, not a righting arm. Gravity and buoyancy will be working together to invert the hull.

A stability curve is simply a plot of GZ—including both the positive righting arm and the negative capsizing arm—as it relates to angle of heel from 0 to 180 degrees. Alternatively, RM (that is, both the positive righting moment and the negative capsizing moment) can be the basis of the plot, as it derives directly from GZ. (To find RM in foot-pounds, simply multiply GZ in feet by the boat's displacement in pounds.) In either case, an S-curve plot is typical, with one hump in positive territory and another hopefully smaller hump (assuming the boat in question is a monohull) in negative territory.

The AMS is the highest point on the positive side of the curve; the AVS is the point at which the curve moves from positive to negative territory. The area under the positive hump represents all the energy that must be expended by wind and waves to capsize the boat; the area under the negative hump is the energy (usually only waves come into play here) required to right the boat again. To put it another way: the larger the positive hump, the more likely a boat is to remain right side up; the smaller the negative hump, the less likely it is to remain upside down.

The relationship between the sizes of the two humps is known as the *stability ratio*. If you have a stability curve to work from, there are some simple calculations developed by Dave Gerr that allow you to estimate the area under each portion of the curve. To calculate the positive energy area (PEA), simply multiply the AVS by the maximum righting arm and then by 0.63: PEA = AVS × max. GZ × 0.63. To calculate the negative energy area (NEA), first subtract the AVS from 180, then multiply the result by the maximum capsizing arm (i.e., the minimum GZ) and then by 0.66: NEA = (180 – AVS) × min. GZ × 0.66. To find the stability ratio divide the positive area by the negative area.

Working from the curve shown in the accompanying graph for a typical 35-foot cruising boat, we get the following values to plug into our equations: AVS = 120 degrees; max. GZ = 2.6 feet; min. GZ = –0.8 feet. The boat's PEA therefore is 196.56 degree-feet: 120 × 2.6 × 0.63 = 196.56. Its NEA is 31.68 degree-feet: (180 – 120) × –0.8 × 0.66 = 31.68. Its stability ratio is thus 6.2: 196.56 ÷ 31.68 = 6.2. As a general rule, a stability ratio of at least 3 is considered adequate for coastal cruising boats; 4 or greater is considered adequate for a bluewater boat. The boat in our example has a very healthy ratio, though some boats exhibit ratios as high as 10 or greater.

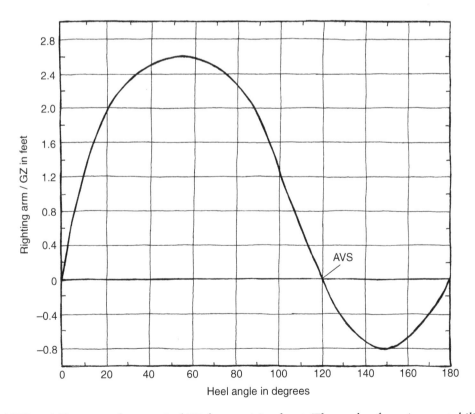

Righting arm (GZ) stability curve for a typical 35-foot cruising boat. The angle of maximum stability (AMS) in this case is 55 degrees with a maximum GZ of 2.6 feet; the angle of vanishing stability (AVS) is 120 degrees; the minimum GZ is –0.8 feet.

You can run these same equations regardless of whether you are working from a curve keyed to the righting arm or the righting moment. The curve in our example is a GZ curve, but if it were an RM curve, we only have to substitute the values for maximum and minimum RM for maximum and minimum GZ. Otherwise the equations run exactly the same way. The results for positive and negative area, assuming RM is expressed in foot-pounds, will be in degree-foot-pounds rather than degree-feet, but the final ratio will be unaffected.

GZ and RM curves are not, however, interchangeable in all respects. When evaluating just one boat it makes little difference which you use, but when comparing different boats you should always use an RM curve. Because righting moment is a function of both a boat's displacement and the length of its righting arm, RM is the appropriate standard for comparing boats of different displacements. It is possible for such boats to have the same righting arm at any angle of heel, but they will not have the same stability characteristics. It always takes more energy to capsize a larger, heavier boat, which is why bigger boats are inherently more stable than smaller ones.

Another thing to bear in mind when comparing boats is that not all stability curves are created equal. There are various methods for constructing the curves, each based on different assumptions.

The two most commonly used methodologies are based on standards promulgated by the International Measurement System (IMS), a once popular rating rule used in international yacht racing, and by the ISO. Many yacht designers have developed their own methods. When comparing boats, you must therefore be sure their curves were constructed according to the same method.

Perfect Curves and Vanishing Angles

To get a better idea of how form and ballast relate to each another, it is useful to compare curves for hypothetical ideal vessels that depend exclusively on one type of stability or the other. A vessel with perfect form stability, for example, would be shaped very much like a wide, flat board, and its stability curve would be perfectly symmetrical. Its AVS would be 90 degrees, and it would be just as stable upside down as right side up. A vessel with perfect ballast stability, on the other hand, would be much like a ballasted buoy—that is, a round, nearly weightless flotation ball with a long stick on one side to which a heavy weight is attached, like a pickup buoy for a mooring or a man-overboard pole. The curve for this vessel would have no AVS at all; there would be just one perfectly symmetric hump with an angle of maximum stability of 90 degrees. The vessel will

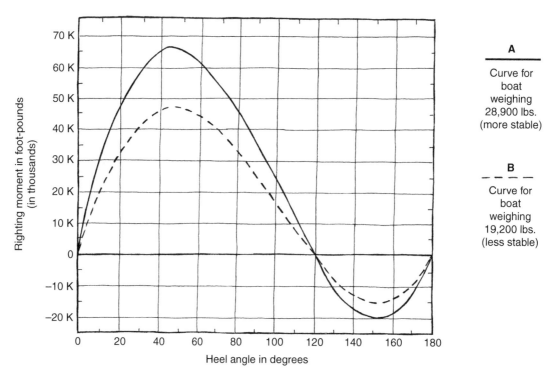

Righting moment (RM) stability curves for a 19,200-pound boat and a 28,900-pound boat with identical GZ values. Because heavier boats are inherently more stable, RM is the standard to use when comparing different boats. (Courtesy of Dave Gerr)

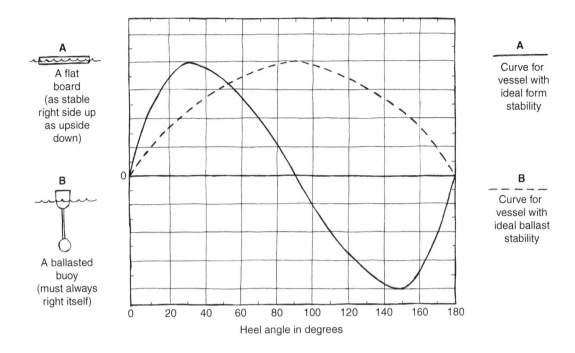

A
A flat board (as stable right side up as upside down)

B
A ballasted buoy (must always right itself)

A
Curve for vessel with ideal form stability

B
Curve for vessel with ideal ballast stability

Heel angle in degrees

Ideal righting arm (GZ) stability curves: vessel A, a flat board, is as stable upside down as it is right side up; vessel B, a ballasted buoy, must right itself if turned upside down. (Courtesy of Danny Greene)

not become metastable until it reaches the ultimate heeling angle of 180 degrees, and no matter which way it turns at this point, it must right itself.

Beyond the fact that one curve has no AVS at all and the other has a very poor one, the most obvious difference between the two is that the board (vessel A) reaches its point of no return at precisely the point that the buoy (vessel B) achieves maximum stability. A subtler but critical difference is seen in the shape of the two curves between 0 and 30 degrees of heel, which is the range within which sailboats routinely operate. Vessel A achieves its maximum stability precisely at 30 degrees, and the climb of its curve to that point is extremely steep, indicating high initial stability. Vessel B, on the other hand, exhibits poor initial stability, as the trajectory of its curve to 30 degrees is gentle. Indeed, heeling A to just 30 degrees requires as much energy as is needed to knock B down flat to 90 degrees.

To translate this into real-world terms, we need only compare the curves for two real-life vessels at opposite extremes of the stability spectrum. The curve for a typical catamaran, for example, looks similar to that of our board since its two humps are symmetrical. If anything, however, it is even more exaggerated (see graph page 76). The initial portion of the curve is extremely steep, and maximum stability is achieved at just 10 degrees of heel. The AVS is actually less than 90 degrees, meaning that the cat,

due to the weight of its superstructure and rig, will reach its point of no return even before it is knocked down to a horizontal position. The curve for a narrow, deep-draft, heavily ballasted monohull, by comparison, is similar to that of the ballasted buoy. The only significant difference is that the monohull has an AVS, though it is quite high (about 150 degrees), and its range of instability (that is, the angles at which it is trying to capsize rather than right itself) is very small, especially compared to the catamaran.

The catamaran, due to its light displacement and great initial stability, will likely perform well in moderate conditions and will heel very little, but it has essentially no reserve stability to rely on when conditions get extreme. The monohull, because of its heavy displacement (much of it ballast) and great reserve stability, will perform less well in moderate conditions but will be nearly impossible to overturn in severe weather.

Other Factors to Consider

Stability curves may look dynamic and sophisticated, but in fact they are based on relatively simple formulas that can't account for everything that might make a particular boat more or less stable in the real world. For one thing, as with the performance ratios we discussed earlier, the displacement values used in calculating stability curves are normally light-ship

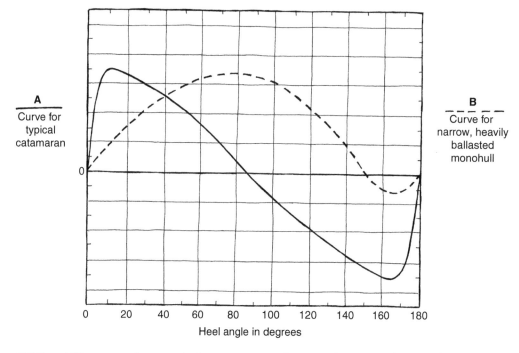

A ___
Curve for
typical
catamaran

B _ _ _
Curve for
narrow, heavily
ballasted
monohull

Heel angle in degrees

Righting arm (GZ) stability curves for a typical catamaran and a typical narrow, deep-draft, heavily ballasted monohull. Note similarities to the ideal curves in the last figure.

figures and do not include the weight that is inevitably added when a boat is equipped and loaded for cruising. Even worse, much of this extra weight—in the form of roller-furling units, mast-mounted radomes, and other heavy gear—will be well above the waterline and thus will erode a boat's inherent stability. The effect can be quite large. For example, installing an in-mast furling system may reduce your boat's

AVS by as much as 20 degrees. In most cases, you should assume that a loaded cruising boat will have an AVS at least 10 degrees lower than that indicated on a stability curve calculated with a light-ship displacement number.

Another important factor to consider is downflooding. Stability curves normally assume that a boat will take on no water when knocked down

An Adequate AVS: How Long Can You Hold Your Breath?

If you plan to content yourself with coastal cruising in protected waters, you should theoretically be perfectly safe in a boat with an AVS of just 90 degrees. Assuming you never encounter huge waves, the worst that could happen is you will be knocked flat by the wind; so as long as you can recover from a 90-degree knockdown, you should be fine. It's nice to have a safety margin, however, so most experts advise that average-size coastal cruising boats should have an AVS of at least 110 degrees. Some believe the minimum should be 115 degrees.

For offshore sailing you want a larger margin of safety and should consider your boat's AVS more seriously. Recovering from a knockdown in high winds is one thing, but in a survival storm, with both high winds and large breaking waves, there will be large amounts of extra energy available to help roll your boat past horizontal. There is near-universal consensus that bluewater boats less than 75 feet

long should have an AVS of at least 120 degrees. Because larger boats are inherently more stable, the standard for boats longer than 75 feet is 110 degrees.

The reason 120 degrees is considered the minimum AVS standard for most bluewater boats is quite simple. Naval architects figure that any sea state rough enough to roll a boat past 120 degrees and totally invert it will also be rough enough to right it again in no more than 2 minutes. This, it is assumed, is the longest time most people can hold their breath while waiting for their boat to right itself. If you don't ever want to hold your breath that long, you want to sail offshore in a boat with a higher AVS. As the accompanying illustration shows, an AVS of 150 degrees is pretty much the Holy Grail. A boat with this much reserve stability can expect to meet a wave large enough to turn it right side up again almost the instant it's turned over.

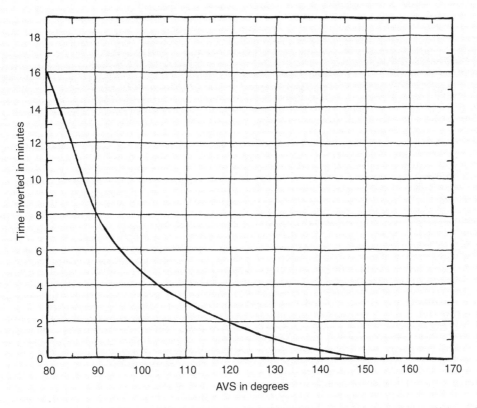

Estimated times of inversion for different AVS values. An AVS of 120 is recommended for offshore boats, assuming you can hold your breath for as long as 2 minutes. (Courtesy Dave Gerr)

past 90 degrees, but this is unlikely in the real world. The companionway hatch will probably be at least partway open, and if the knockdown is unexpected, other hatches may be open as well. Water entering a boat that is heeled to an extreme angle will further destabilize the boat by shifting weight to its low side. If the water sloshes about, as is likely, this free-surface effect will make it even harder for the boat to come upright again.

This may seem irrelevant if you are a coastal cruiser, but if you are a bluewater cruiser you should be aware of the location of your companionway. A centerline companionway will rarely start down-flooding until a boat is heeled to 110 degrees or more. An offset companionway, however, if it is on the low side of the boat as it heels, may yield down-flood angles of 100 degrees or lower. A super AVS of 150 degrees won't do much good if your boat starts flooding well before that. To my knowledge, no commonly published stability curve accounts for this factor.

Another issue is the cockpit. An open-transom cockpit, or a relatively small one with large, effective drains, will drain quickly if flooded in a knock-down. A large cockpit that drains poorly, however, may retain water for several minutes, and this, too, can destabilize a boat that is struggling to right itself.

Fortunately, not all unaccounted for stability factors are negative. IMS-based stability curves, for example, assume that all boats have flush decks and ignore the potentially positive effect of a cabinhouse. This is important, as a raised house, particularly one with a rounded top, provides a lot of extra buoyancy as it is submerged and can significantly increase a boat's stability at severe heel angles. Lifeboats and other self-righting vessels have high round cabintops for precisely this reason.

ISO-based stability curves do account for a raised cabinhouse, but not all designers believe this is a good thing. A cabinhouse only increases reserve stability if it is impervious to flooding when submerged. If it has open hatches or has large windows and apertures that may break under pressure, it will only help a boat capsize and sink that much faster. The ISO formulas fail to take this into account and instead may award high stability ratings to motorsailers and deck-saloon boats with large houses and windows that may be vulnerable in extreme conditions.

Other Measures of Stability

In addition to developing stability curves, which are fairly complex, designers and rating and regulatory authorities have worked to quantify a boat's stability with a single number. The simplest of these, the *capsize screening value* (CSV), was developed in the aftermath of the 1979 Fastnet Race. Over a third of the more than 300 boats entered in that race, most of them beamy, lightweight IOR designs, were capsized (rolled to 180 degrees) by large breaking waves, and this prompted a great deal of research on yacht stability. The capsize screening value, which relies only on published specifications and was intended to be accessible to laypeople, indicates whether a given boat might be too wide and light to readily right itself after being overturned in extreme conditions.

To figure out a boat's CSV divide the cube root of its displacement in cubic feet into its maximum beam in feet: CSV = beam ÷ $\sqrt[3]{DCF}$. You'll recall that a boat's weight and the volume of water it displaces are directly related, and that displacement in cubic feet is simply displacement in pounds divided by 64 (which is the weight in pounds of a cubic foot of salt water). Returning once more to our hypothetical 35-footer, you'll also recall that its beam is 11 feet and its displacement is 12,000 pounds. To find its CSV, first calculate DCF (12,000 ÷ 64 = 187.5), then find the cube root of that result: $\sqrt[3]{187.5}$ = 5.72; note that if your calculator cannot do cube roots, you can instead take 187.5 to the 1/3 power and get the same result. Divide that result into 11, and you get a CSV of 1.92: 11 ÷ 5.72 = 1.92.

Interpreting the number is also simple. Any result of 2 or less indicates a boat that is sufficiently self-righting to go offshore. The further below 2 you go, the more self-righting the boat is; extremely stable boats have values on the order of 1.7. Results above 2 indicate a boat may be prone to remain inverted when capsized and that a more detailed analysis is needed to determine its suitability for offshore sailing.

As handy as it is, the CSV has limited utility. It accounts for only two factors—displacement and beam—and fails to consider how weight is distributed aboard a boat. For example, if we load our hypothetical 12,000-pound boat with an extra 2,500 pounds for light coastal cruising (per Nigel Calder's formula), its CSV declines to 1.8. Load it with an extra 3,750 pounds for heavy coastal or moderate bluewater use, and the CSV declines still further, to 1.71. This suggests that the boat is becoming more stable, when in fact it may become less stable if much of the extra weight is distributed high in the boat.

Note too that a boat with unusually high ballast—including, most obviously, a boat with ballast in its bilges rather than its keel—will also earn a deceptively low screening value. Two empty boats of identical displacement and beam will have identical screening values even though the boat with deeper ballast will necessarily be more resistant to capsize.

Another single-value stability rating still frequently encountered is the *IMS stability index number*. This was developed under the IMS rating system to compare stability characteristics of race boats of various sizes. The formula essentially restates a boat's AVS so as to account for its overall size, awarding higher values to longer boats, which are inherently more stable. IMS index numbers normally range from a little below 100 to over 140. For what are termed Category 0 races, which are transoceanic events, 120 is usually the required minimum. In Category 1 events, which are long-distances races sailed "well offshore," 115 is the common minimum standard, and for Category 2 events, races of extended duration not far from shore, 110 is normally the minimum standard. Conservative designers and pundits often posit 120 as the acceptable minimum for an offshore cruising boat.

Since many popular cruising boats were never measured or rated under the IMS rule, you shouldn't be surprised if you cannot find an IMS-based stability curve or stability index number for a cruising boat you are interested in. You may find one if the boat in question is a cruiser-racer, as IMS was once a prevalent rating system. Bear in mind, though, that the IMS index number does not take into account cabin structures (or cockpits, for that matter), and assumes a flush deck from gunwale to gunwale. Neither does it account for downflooding.

Another single-value stability rating that casts itself as an "index" is promulgated by the ISO. This is known as STIX, which is simply a trendy acronym for stability index. Because STIX values must be calculated for any new boat sold inside the European Union (EU), and because STIX is, in fact, the only government-imposed stability standard in use anywhere in the world, it is likely to become the predominant standard in years to come.

A STIX number is the result of many complex calculations accounting for a boat's length, displacement, beam, ability to shed water after a knockdown, angle of vanishing stability, downflooding, cabin superstructure, and freeboard in breaking seas, among others. STIX values range from the low single digits to about 50. A minimum of 38 is required by the European Union for Category A boats that are certified for use on extended passages more than 500 miles offshore where waves with a maximum height of 46 feet may be encountered. A value of at least 23 is required for Category B boats that are certified for coastal use within 500 miles of shore where maximum wave heights of 26 feet may be encountered, and the minimum values for categories C and D (inshore and sheltered waters, respectively) are 14 and 5. These standards do not restrict an owner's use of his boat, but merely dictate how boats may be marketed to the public.

The STIX standard has many critics, including yacht designers who do not enjoy having to make the many calculations involved, but the STIX number is the most comprehensive single measure of stability now available. As such, it can hardly be ignored. Many critics assert that the standards are too low and that a number of 40 or greater is more appropriate for Category A boats and 30 or more is best for Category B boats. Others believe that in trying to account for and quantify so many factors in a single value, the STIX number oversimplifies a complex subject. To properly evaluate stability, they suggest, it is necessary to evaluate the various factors independently and make an informed judgment leavened by a good dose of common sense.

As useful as they may or may not be, STIX numbers are generally unavailable for boats that predate the EU's adoption of the STIX standard in 1998. Even if you can find a number for a boat you are interested in, bear in mind that STIX numbers do not account for large, potentially vulnerable windows and ports in cabin superstructures, nor do they take into account a boat's negative stability. In other words, boats that are nearly as stable upside down as right side up may still receive high STIX numbers.

The bottom line when evaluating stability is that no single factor or rating should be considered to the exclusion of all others. It is probably best, as the STIX critics suggest, to gather as much information from as many sources as you can, and to bear in mind all we have discussed here when pondering it.

THREE

HULL AND DECK CONSTRUCTION

I was not far along in my career as a liveaboard blue-water cruiser before I started meeting more rarefied members of the species who had themselves built the boats they were cruising on. I found they had a strange habit of asking if I, too, had built my boat. In that my boat was obviously an elderly fiberglass production boat, I was at first taken aback by this. I assumed the question was being asked in jest and was intended to put me in my place. I always answered truthfully and somewhat sheepishly, "No, I bought the boat used. All I do now is try to keep it afloat." Only later did it occur to me that the question might be sincere, inspired not by any sense of superiority, but by a naive assumption that anyone living on a boat must, of course, have also created it.

For our purposes I will assume that you, like me, intend only to purchase a cruising boat, or have already purchased one, and do not have the time, energy, or expertise to construct one from scratch. Still, you will find that anyone who owns a sailboat for very long in some sense becomes a co-creator of it. While maintaining and upgrading your boat you will place an indelible stamp upon it. In doing so, you must become familiar with how your boat was put together in the first place.

No matter how your boat was built, and whatever it is made of, you need a working knowledge of its construction in order to preserve it over time. The sea is an aggressive and unforgiving environment, and if you harbor delusions of somehow finding and obtaining one of those mythical creatures, the maintenance-free boat, you should strike them from your mind. Maintenance is inescapable when it comes to boats, particularly sailboats. Some sailboats may

be less trouble to maintain than others, but there is always a significant amount of work involved. If you understand how a boat is built before you acquire it, you will have a much clearer idea of what sort of maintenance and repair regimen you are getting yourself into.

How you use your boat is also relevant. Racing sailors want boats constructed as lightly as possible and are willing to flirt with the limits of structural integrity. The only restraining factors are technological feasibility and the size of their bank accounts. Cruising sailors, however, usually want a reasonable degree of performance, plus they want to feel reasonably certain their boats can withstand some abuse. Bluewater cruisers are usually the ones most focused on boat strength. If anything, they have traditionally favored boats that are overbuilt, though this has changed in recent years. Coastal cruisers, because they spend more time sailing close to shore, are, if anything, more likely to pile up on the rocks somewhere. The smart ones, therefore, will try to balance weight and strength, as well as financial and technical feasibility, in evaluating a boat. In both cases an understanding of basic construction techniques is extremely useful.

FIBERGLASS BOATBUILDING

Over the millennia humans have built boats from many different materials. In Chapter 1 we saw how Bernard Moitessier, when stranded on a beach in Trinidad, developed a plan to build a boat of newspaper and tar. He got the idea from junks he'd seen as a boy in Indochina that were constructed of bamboo wickerwork covered with cow dung, oil, and resin. Long before Moitessier thought of it, the ancient Egyptians built "paper" boats out of papyrus reeds. Irish seafarers built boats known as *coracles* that were made from animal hides stretched over tree branches. Polynesian mariners built boats of palm fronds and other plant fibers before mastering the art of hollowing out tree trunks. These days boats are built not only of wood, which at least floats, but also of heavy materials, such as metal and concrete, that do not.

But by far the most popular contemporary boatbuilding material is a strange substance known as fiberglass. Originally described by traditionalists as "frozen snot," it now dominates recreational boatbuilding. The term *fiberglass* is somewhat misleading, as it describes just one component of a composite material. The other component is a plastic resin, usually polyester, although vinylester and sometimes epoxy are increasingly used these days. Thus the more accurate term is *fiberglass-reinforced plastic* (FRP) or *glass-reinforced plastic* (GRP).

The principle behind any composite building material is simple. A binding medium that is not structurally sound can be stiffened and made stronger by adding another more fibrous material. You cannot, for example, build a solid house of just mud or straw, but if you mix mud and straw together, you can build a very fine house indeed. It is the same with concrete and rebar, plaster and lath, or even papier-mâché. In all cases, the sum is much stronger than its parts. In this case, the medium is the resin, and the stiffening fibers are spun glass filaments ten times thinner than a single human hair. These fine glass fibers are in one sense quite fragile, but when held in column by plastic resin they are also stiff and strong.

The resin begins as a liquid and becomes solid after a catalyst or hardener is added to it. This is a chemical reaction that cannot be undone. Unlike thermoforming plastics like polythene and PVC that can be melted after they set and recast like metal, thermosetting plastics like polyester, vinylester, and epoxy become permanently solid after setting. Applying heat softens them a bit and greatly weakens them (indeed, they have very low heat resistance compared to most metals), and they may be set on fire, but they cannot melt and become fluid again.

The glass fibers come in rolls of fabric. The most common sort is electrical-grade glass, known as E-glass, which was originally developed for use in electrical circuit boards. The alternative is structural-grade glass, called S-glass, which was developed for use in airplane construction. S-glass is a much better structural material and is nearly half again as stiff as E-glass and has much better impact resistance. Unfortunately, it also

The stuff from which boats are made. Rolls of different types of fiberglass fabrics in a modern boatbuilding facility.

costs three times as much, which is why most boats are built of inferior E-glass. Quality builders often use limited amounts of S-glass to reinforce certain heavily loaded areas of a hull or deck, but only rarely will you see an entire boat built out of it.

To make something as large as a boat out of liquid resin and floppy fabric, you need a mold to shape and support the materials until they solidify. When building with a male mold, fiberglass fabric is laid over the mold's exterior surface and is then saturated, or *wet out*, with liquid resin that has just been catalyzed. Working with a female mold, the fabric is laid out in the mold's interior before being wet out. In both cases, multiple layers of fabric are built up into a laminate, and after the resin in all the layers has set up hard and cured, the now solid part can be separated from the mold. For this to be possible, the mold's working surface must first be coated with a waxy separating agent before the laminating begins.

When working with a male mold you are building up laminate from the inside out; the outermost layer goes on last, and if you want the outside of your boat to look nice and shiny you must fair and polish the exterior surface afterward. With a female mold, the outermost layer goes on first. If you take the trouble to carefully fair and polish the mold's working surface, your boat emerges from the mold with a shiny exterior finish already in place. Either way you must take the trouble to fair and polish the entire surface at least once. But with a female mold you need do it only once (though some intermediate cleaning and polishing is required) and can then pop multiple fair-skinned boats from the mold thereafter. This is why production builders always use female molds. They also use *gelcoat*, a thin coat

A typical female fiberglass sailboat mold. The interior surface is faired and polished so the outside of the hull is already finished when it is removed from the mold.

of resin thickened with colored pigment, as the very first layer in the laminate so boats emerge from their molds prepainted as well as prefaired.

One advantage of fiberglass construction is that it facilitates the creation of complex hull shapes. But some shapes are easier to form than others. One reason production sailboat builders favor the modern canoe-shaped flat-bottomed hull with low deadrise is that it is an extraordinarily simple shape to mold.

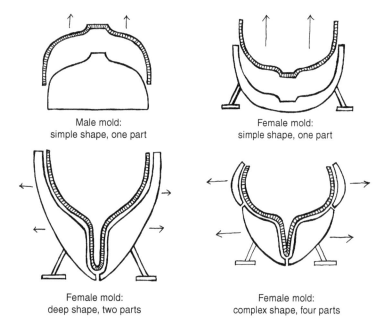

Male mold:
simple shape, one part

Female mold:
simple shape, one part

Female mold:
deep shape, two parts

Female mold:
complex shape, four parts

Fiberglass boat molds. Complex or deep shapes may require multipart molds.

You do have to bolt on a keel afterward, but that is a relatively simple matter of drilling holes and installing fasteners. A classic full-keel shape with lots of deadrise and deep bilges, by comparison, is more problematic since it is often impossible to extract a deep, narrow keel from a one-part mold, no matter how carefully the mold is waxed beforehand. To ensure success a two-piece mold is often used, so the molded part can be more easily released by separating the halves of the mold. It is also difficult to properly lay up and wet out fiberglass fabric in a deep mold with hard-to-access spaces. In other cases, with tumblehome hulls for example (i.e., the beam on deck is less than the hull's maximum beam), it may be necessary to use a four- or even five-part mold to release the molded part after it sets up solid.

Molds themselves, of course, must also be created. To build one fiberglass boat, it is often said, you must in fact build two boats: the finished product and the mold from which it springs. With a female mold, you normally build three boats to get one—first a male plug on which the female mold is formed, then the mold, and finally the boat itself. Capital costs, therefore, are quite high, which is why truly custom one-off fiberglass boats are quite rare. It is possible to build fiberglass boats cost-effectively, but only if many boats are born of the same mold.

This is what is unique about fiberglass construction. As late as the middle of the 20th century, boats were always built one at a time. Since the advent of fiberglass, however, boatbuilding has increasingly become an industrial process as opposed to a craft. The biggest builders these days can churn out hundreds—or even thousands—of boats a year on massive assembly lines studded with computer-controlled robots that do everything from spraying gelcoat into molds, to cutting hatches and drilling holes for fasteners in decks, to cutting, trimming, and even varnishing interior woodwork. But even on the most automated production line, a lot of manual labor is still needed for a boat to be built properly. Given the relatively small market for new sailboats, there is also a surprisingly large number of small builders who still build only limited numbers of boats using little automated machinery.

For many in the industry boatbuilding is primarily a labor of love; to them boatbuilding will always be an avocation and never just a business. Generally, however, the companies with the best long-term chances of survival are those that focus on economic reality and production efficiency. One thing builders have come to realize is that their biggest competition is not other builders of new boats, but the ever-growing number of older glass boats that are still on the water. It is now 60 years or so since the first glass boats appeared on the market, and there is still no evidence of any inherent limit to their useful life spans. As far as we know, a well-built, carefully maintained glass boat can last virtually indefinitely. This, unfortunately, only encourages builders to produce boats that are less than durable. Buyers who expect to trade in or sell a new boat within a few years need not worry about this, as serious maintenance issues are unlikely to arise in the first few years of ownership. But for those buying used glass boats, particularly those built in the last 10 or 15 years, the guiding principle should be "buyer beware." Many corners can be cut when building a boat, particularly a fiberglass one, and the consequences may not manifest themselves for several years.

Solid Laminates

To understand fiberglass lamination, it is best to focus first on simple solid laminates in which multiple layers of fiberglass fabric are built up to the thickness necessary to make a part strong enough to do its job. Solid hulls were the rule in the early days of fiberglass boatbuilding, and many are still found in both older boats and new boats. There is a popular myth that early glass hulls were built as thick as wood hulls because builders didn't know how strong glass was and wanted to play it safe. This is not true, and you'll often find solid laminates in older boats are a bit thinner than their owners like to believe. Still, early solid hulls were built robustly, and many show little sign of deterioration even 40 or 50 years after they were first created.

Types of Fiberglass Fabric

As mentioned, the major ingredients in any solid laminate are resin and fiberglass fabric. Various types of fabric have different properties, and different types are usually used together in the same laminate. The crudest fabric is *chopped-strand mat*, or *mat*, which consists of fibers chopped into strands up to 2 inches

long that are laid down in a random pattern and pressed into a spongy, felt-like material. The fibers are held together by a light binding adhesive, usually a polyester powder or polyvinyl acetate emulsion that dissolves when exposed to resin.

Mat is easy to work with because it wets out quickly and is bulky. This makes it possible to build up thickness in a laminate with minimal effort. Mat also bonds well with other layers in a laminate, particularly other layers of mat that are still wet with resin, as the fibers from each layer can then intermesh with each other. Because it becomes quite malleable after its binding agent dissolves, mat is particularly good for working into crevices and corners in a mold. Because the fibers in mat are randomly oriented it is equally strong in all directions, but because the fibers are also very short, it is not as strong as fabrics with longer continuous fibers.

Chopped fiber can also be laid down in (or on) a mold with a chopper gun. This device cuts continuous bundles of fiber called *rovings* into short strands and spits them out into the air while simultaneously expectorating streams of resin and catalyst. Pull a trigger and a gooey mass of catalyzed resin mixed with chopped fiber spews forth from the gun. Though messy to work with, chopper guns make it easy to build up laminate quickly.

In the early days it was common to see entire boats built of mat, and after the advent of the chopper gun in the mid-1960s it became even easier to build hulls of nothing but chopped fiber. Such hulls are perfectly sound if built thick enough to compensate for the short fibers they contain. However, because they are thick and contain a lot of resin, they are quite heavy and have poor strength-to-weight ratios.

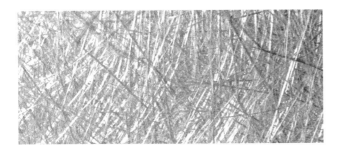

Chopped-strand mat is the crudest fiberglass fabric. It wets out easily and bonds well with other layers in a laminate, but its short fibers limit its strength. (Courtesy of Glen-L Marine)

A chopper gun at work. It sprays out a stream of chopped fiber and catalyzed resin. Once used to build whole hulls, they are still used by many builders to quickly lay up smaller parts.

The next coarsest type of fabric is *woven roving*. Here bundles of fiber—those rovings just mentioned above—are woven together at right angles into a loose, bulky cloth. Though the fibers are crimped by the weave of the cloth and so lose some unidirectional strength, they are long and continuous and thus much stronger than the short fibers found in chopped-strand mat *if* they are oriented in more or less the same direction as the load being imposed on them. If the load path, however, runs at an angle to the fibers, their strength decreases proportionally. Any woven fabric with fibers oriented at 0 and 90 degrees is weakest when resisting loads imposed at a 45 degree angle. In such instances, woven roving is in fact weaker than chopped-strand mat. Because of the thick, bulky weave of the cloth, woven roving is also harder to wet out with resin than is mat. Its knubbly surface, once the resin has set, also bonds poorly with other layers in a laminate.

One good way to build up a laminate is to alternate layers of woven roving and mat, as the two fabrics complement each other very well. This was the best practice in the early days of fiberglass boatbuilding and is still viable today. Because they are often used together, there is also a popular composite fabric, known as *combi-mat*, which consists of a layer of mat pre-stitched to a layer of woven roving. Like mat, woven roving is bulky; it quickly builds thickness in a laminate, but also takes a lot of resin to wet out. A traditional woven-roving/mat laminate, though it has many virtues, is therefore still heavy compared to other more sophisticated laminates.

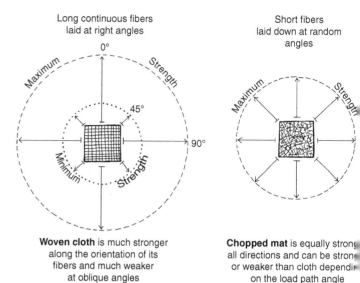

Strength characteristics of woven roving cloth versus chopped-strand mat.

The finest sort of fiberglass fabric is *cloth*, in which individual fibers, rather than bundles of fibers, are tightly woven together. A wide range of weights and weave patterns are available, including numerous sophisticated satin weaves and knitted cloths that minimize the crimping of the fibers, thus enhancing their strength. Because it is a finer fabric than mat or woven roving, cloth takes less resin to wet out, which reduces laminate weight and increases strength-to-weight ratios. Because it is woven, however, its strength still varies depending on the angle of the load path imposed upon it.

Fiberglass cloth is both expensive and quite thin, and thus is not a cost-effective material for building up bulk in a laminate. Normally it is used in the body of a laminate only in small boats or in race boats and high-end performance cruisers where saving weight is a priority. It is sometimes used as an outer finish layer in laminates in larger general-purpose boats, as it does not "print through" a surface coating of

Woven roving is the next crudest fiberglass fabric after chopped-strand mat. It doesn't wet out as easily as mat, but its long, continuous fibers make it much stronger in certain directions. (Courtesy of Fiber Glass Industries)

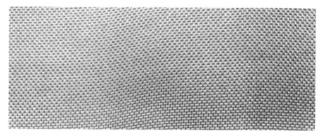

Fiberglass cloth is thinner and finer than chopped-strand mat and woven roving. Less resin is needed to wet it out, which saves weight, but it is expensive and not always cost-effective. (Courtesy of Glen-L Marine)

gelcoat as easily as woven roving. Most builders, however, prefer to put chopped-strand mat under gelcoat because it is much cheaper. Some quality builders not only use cloth under gelcoat, but also to sheathe a hull's inner surface to further improve finish quality and increase overall strength. Cloth also may be used to reinforce heavily loaded areas of a hull and is commonly used to sheathe wooden hulls and/or decks.

Yet another even more sophisticated sort of material is known as *unidirectional fabric*. In a "uni-di" fabric the glass fibers are laid out parallel to each other in bundles that are lightly stitched together or held in some binding or seizing. Because the fibers are not kinked or bent by weaving and all run in the same direction, unidirectional strength is maximized. Because they are packed close together and are neatly aligned, much less resin is needed to wet them out. By carefully aligning uni-di fabric along anticipated load paths, builders can thus greatly increase a laminate's strength-to-weight ratio. By orienting layers of uni-di at specific opposing angles, multidirectional loads can be supported as efficiently as possible. As with combi-mat, multiple layers of uni-di can be pre-stitched together to create a *biaxial fabric* (two

This stitch-mat fabric consists of a biaxial fabric (the plies are biased at 45 degrees) combined with a layer of chopped mat. (Courtesy of Fiber Glass Industries)

layers of uni-di oriented in two different directions), or even or a *tri-* or *quadra-axial fabric*. Uni-di or biaxial fabric is also often pre-stitched to chopped-strand mat (this is called a "stitch-mat" fabric) as the mat, again, improves the bond between layers in a laminate.

Exotic Fabrics

Not all fabric used these days to build laminate boats is made of fiberglass. Over the past 15 years both Kevlar and carbon fiber, which are much stiffer and lighter than glass, have appeared in more and more race boats and high-end performance cruisers. Kevlar is extremely impact resistant, and thus is often used as a reinforcing material, particularly around the bow, which is most likely to be involved in collisions. It can also, however, be difficult to work with in a laminate because it does not like to bend and is hard to wet out. As far as I know, no one has ever built a sailboat of any size entirely out of Kevlar. It is common, however, to see large boat hulls reinforced with Twaron, an aramid fiber similar to Kevlar, or with glass-Twaron hybrid fabrics.

Carbon fiber, meanwhile, has become the most popular material for building the lightest, fastest, most cutting-edge race boats. Not only are entire hulls now built of carbon fiber, but also masts, booms, rudders, spinnaker poles, steering wheels, and all manner of small components. Carbon fiber, in a word, is trendy. Its sleek, black finish personifies all that is cool and hip in modern-day yachting, and there is a tendency now to assume that anything must be better if it's made of carbon fiber.

But carbon does have an Achilles heel. It is stiff and light, but it is also brittle, has low impact resistance, and is not resilient. Unlike a fiberglass laminate, which bends and

flexes quite a bit before breaking, a carbon-fiber laminate hardly flexes at all when subjected to severe loads. Up to a point this is good, but when it does reach its breaking point, carbon fails suddenly and catastrophically. It also fares poorly in collisions and other sudden point-loading situations.

The fragility of carbon fiber has been amply demonstrated. In the past several years, three different all-carbon America's Cup boats have sunk after experiencing critical structural failures. At least two large carbon racing cats have had their bows suddenly break away. And the list goes on. For a cutting-edge race boat, where small advantages are important, building in carbon is a no-brainer. For a cruising boat, however, even a serious performance cruiser, it makes little sense. Other sophisticated materials—most notably S-glass—work much better. An S-glass laminate is just 2% heavier than an equivalent carbon laminate and is three times as resilient.

Carbon fiber, like Kevlar and Twaron, is also sometimes used as a reinforcing material within a fiberglass laminate. This makes good sense in theory, because carbon is good at resisting compressive loads, but it must be done carefully. Because carbon is so much stiffer than glass, a local carbon reinforcement must be properly engineered and installed or it can actually increase stress under certain loading conditions.

Like regular fiberglass cloth, these directional fabrics are quite expensive. Mass-production builders therefore use them sparingly, if at all, and only in specific high-load areas, such as around frames and stiffeners, chainplates, mast steps and partners, and keel stubs. Those building race boats or high-end performance cruisers are much more likely to use these fabrics to reduce weight and maximize strength.

Properties of Different Resins

The resin in which a fiberglass fabric is encapsulated is just as important as the fabric itself in determining the qualities of a laminate. The cheapest, most common types are polyester resins. These were used exclusively in the early days of fiberglass boatbuilding and are still the most popular today. Polyester resin begins to harden the moment it is created; to stop this and keep the resin in a liquid state, an inhibitor must be added. The function of the catalyst (usually methyl ethyl ketone and peroxide, or MEKP) is to destroy the inhibitor, thus reinitiating the curing process. The inhibitor breaks down eventually anyway, which means polyester resin has a limited shelf life. Polyester resin also will not cure at room temperature unless an accelerator (usually purple cobalt naphthenate) is added to it. Normally this is added when the resin is manufactured; otherwise it must be added separately or the resin must be cured in an oven.

Common polyester resins are based on either orthophthalic or isophthalic acids. Ortho-polyester resins are the weakest and most brittle of all resins used in boatbuilding. If used with unidirectional or multiaxial glass fabrics or more exotic fabrics like Kevlar or carbon fiber, they will crack before the fabric's full strength is utilized. They are also the most vulnerable to chemical attack and are the least water resistant. This last feature is particularly important, as the more easily water can pass through a resin into a laminate, the more likely it is the laminate will develop osmotic blisters over time (see the Blisters sidebar on page 89).

Iso-polyester resins are slightly less brittle and are considerably more chemical and water resistant. They are also, of course, more expensive. Builders therefore commonly use iso-polyesters in the gelcoat and external layers of a laminate and cheaper ortho-polyesters in the internal layers. Iso-polyester resins are just strong enough to support most sophisticated glass fabrics, though they are probably not quite strong enough to be used effectively with exotic fabrics.

Vinylester resins are the next step up in quality and cost. They are similar to polyester resins and utilize the same catalysts, but are markedly stronger.

For example, where a good iso-polyester resin may elongate by as much as 2.5% along its length before failing and fracturing and has a tensile strength of about 9,400 pounds per square inch, a vinylester resin can elongate up to 5% of its length before fracturing and has a tensile strength of about 11,800 pounds per square inch. This makes vinylester the resin of choice when laminating with more sophisticated fabrics. Vinylester is also much more water resistant than both ortho- and iso-polyester resins, thus is less prone to blistering.

Because they are chemically similar and bond to each other well in both a cured and uncured state, vinylester and polyester can be used interchangeably in a laminate, which gives builders great flexibility. As boat buyers have become ever more wary of blisters, it has become common for even mass-production builders to use vinylester resin in the exterior layers of a laminate to reduce water permeability. They then switch to polyester to finish the bulk of the laminate and so keep costs under control. Vinylester is now also commonly used throughout a laminate in racing and high-quality cruising boats.

The best, most expensive boatbuilding resin is epoxy, which is stronger than both polyester and vinylester. Its elongation before failure is usually more than 5%, and its tensile strength is about 12,500 pounds per square inch. Epoxy is also more adhesive, forms better bonds (particularly post-cure bonds), and is even more water resistant (and thus more blister resistant) than vinylester resin. It is, however, a fundamentally different substance. Its secondary component is not a catalyst that enables a chemical reaction, but a hardener that is integral to the reaction that causes epoxy to set and solidify. To achieve full structural strength, it is best to post-cure epoxy at elevated temperatures. It is incompatible with most chopped-strand mat, as it does not properly dissolve the binder in the fabric. Plus, it is only semi-compatible with vinylester and polyester; it may be laid down on top of cured polyester and vinylester, but they may not be laid down on it, whether it has cured or not.

Epoxy is often used when making repairs to fiberglass boats and may be used in the secondary phase of construction when structural parts are being attached to an already cured hull. Epoxy is also often applied below the waterline as a barrier coat to prevent blistering. But because it is so very expensive, it is rarely used as the primary resin in a laminate, except in the most cutting-edge boats.

Laminating Techniques

The easiest way of laying up a fiberglass hull is by hand in an open mold. The resin itself can be applied in different ways. The crudest method is to simply slap it on with brushes from buckets of catalyzed resin. Now, however, it is more common to see workers wetting out fabric with airless spray guns or special resin-fed rollers. With spray guns the resin and catalyst are mixed as they are sprayed onto the fabric. With rollers the resin is catalyzed before being pumped to the roller head.

Spray guns and rollers obviate the need to constantly mix small batches of resin, which remains perfectly fluid for only a few minutes after it is catalyzed. Though it takes a long time to cure completely (unless post-cured at higher than room temperatures), resin only remains "wet" in any meaningful sense for a few hours. This is important because for one layer of a laminate to form a chemical bond and cross-link with another on a molecular level they must be laid on each other "wet on wet." If the receiving layer is too dry, the bond with the next layer is only adhesive and is not nearly as strong.

Each step in creating an open-mold laminate is therefore a race to get the next layer of fabric laid down and wet out before the previous one sets up too hard. One advantage of using polyester and vinylester resins is that the time it takes for the resin to kick can be controlled to some extent by varying the amount of catalyst used. But this buys only so much time. The maximum recommended time between the application of layers is normally about 16 hours, but the shorter the interval the better. This is less daunting if the hull being laid up is a small one, but if the hull is large it can be problematic. In many cases, an ideal chemical bond is not always achieved and some areas of an open-mold laminate can thus be inherently weaker than others.

Voids are another problem. These are small pockets of air that get trapped in a laminate as it is laid up. They not only undermine the laminate's solidity, they also promote blistering by providing a place for moisture that penetrates the laminate to pool up and mix with chemicals in the resin.

The simplest way to drive air out of a laminate so it sets up solid is to compress the layers of wet-out fabric together with handheld ribbed rollers. The ribs on these rollers crush air bubbles and spread resin more evenly through the fabric. This increases the fabric-to-resin ratio, thus increasing the laminate's strength relative to its weight. Using rollers, however, is labor intensive, and the extra time spent squishing down each layer of wet fabric only decreases the chances of a chemical bond being formed with the next layer.

There is a more sophisticated technique for pressing air out of a laminate called *vacuum bagging*, which in fact has been around since the earliest days

Ribbed rollers can be used to squeeze air out of a laminate and spread resin through it more evenly. This is slow and labor-intensive, however, and works best when fabricating small parts, as shown here.

of fiberglass boatbuilding. Here a plastic skin is taped over a layer of laminate after it is laid down and wet out, then air is pumped out from beneath the plastic. The vacuum applies a large amount of pressure evenly over the entire surface of the laminate; the end result is a denser, more void-free layup than can be achieved working by hand.

An even more sophisticated technique for both efficiently saturating fabric with resin and squeezing the whole layer to ensure no air is trapped involves a process known generically as *resin infusion*. Though there are numerous variations, the best known is a proprietary procedure called the Seemann Composites Resin Infusion Molding Process, or SCRIMP. Here all the laminate layers are laid down dry in a mold and tacked in place with spray adhesive. The entire dry laminate is then covered with a plastic vacuum bag plumbed with a network of tubes connected to vats of resin. Air is pumped out of the bag and resin is sucked through the tubes into the laminate. Once the laminate is fully saturated, the flow of resin is shut off and the laminate is then allowed to set up under pressure. There are several advantages to this. The layers of the laminate are sure to form chemical bonds with one another because they are saturated simultaneously. Only the minimum amount of resin needed to wet out the fabric is used, so the laminate's fabric-to-resin and strength-to-weight ratios are maximized. Finally, as with regular vacuum bagging, the resulting laminate is dense, with a minimum number of voids.

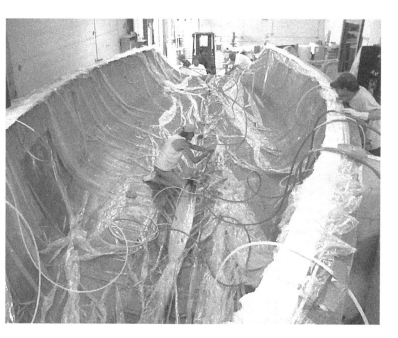

Workers prepare a hull laminate for resin infusion. A vacuum pump sucks air out from the plastic vacuum bag covering the laminate. Resin is sucked into and through the laminate through the feeder tubes. (Courtesy of Alcan Baltek)

Resin infusion is also a much cleaner process. Both polyester and vinylester resins contain significant amounts of styrene, the vapors of which are classified as a hazardous air pollutant by the U.S. Environmental Protection Agency. It is styrene that gives fresh fiberglass its strong sweet chemical odor and makes it necessary for workers handling resin to wear protective clothing and respirators. Unlike open-mold layups, where the resin fumes all escape into the atmosphere, resin infusion allows for emissions containment. As boatbuilders come under increasing regulatory pressure to limit styrene emissions, they will likely be forced to abandon open-mold building methods and rely exclusively on resin infusion instead. This will drive up the cost of fiberglass boat production and may force some builders out of business. It may instead be possible to use new low-styrene resins, but so far these set up too quickly to allow chemical bonds to form between layers in a laminate.

The challenge of resin infusion, other than the extra expense, is that it must be done carefully. Any tiny leaks in the vacuum bag or resin tubes leads to air getting sucked into the laminate. The distribution of resin through the laminate must also be carefully monitored. If resin is unevenly distributed or is cut off prematurely, the result can be a resin-starved laminate with patches of dry fabric buried within it. Builders must play a fine game here—if they use too much resin, a boat will be heavier (and weaker) than

necessary; if they use too little, it may delaminate in short order. In recent years there have been some dramatic failures of this sort where large expensive boats with resin-infused hulls have required extensive postproduction repairs shortly after being delivered to their new owners.

Quality control is important no matter how a lamination is performed and at all stages in the creation of a laminate. Resin can be significantly degraded if not stored and handled properly. Shelf life must be closely monitored, drums must be kept carefully sealed in a dark climate-controlled environment, the resin itself must be carefully stirred before being removed from a drum, and must also be carefully mixed with proper amounts of catalyst. Climate, too, must be closely monitored. If a workspace is too hot, too cold, or too humid, the quality of a laminate can be seriously compromised.

Unfortunately, there is no way a buyer of a boat can ensure that a builder has produced a sound laminate. Buyers of new high-end semicustom fiberglass boats with resin-infused hulls now sometimes insist on clear gelcoat so the hull can be visually inspected for voids and resin-starvation prior to painting. Surveyors inspecting both used and new boats carefully sound a hull with a hammer, listening for dead spots that indicate lamination problems, and also scan the hull with a moisture meter, searching for water-saturated areas. Such precautions are helpful, but certain issues—such as poor climate control, poor bonding within a laminate, mishandling of resins and/or catalysts, etc.—may never come to light until a laminate fails.

Cored Laminates

The most effective way to decrease weight in a laminate while increasing its strength is to install a lightweight core in the middle of it. Cored decks have been standard since the earliest days of fiberglass boat production; they help decrease weight well above the waterline and also eliminate the need for beams to help support the deck from below, thus increasing accommodations space. Cored hulls, meanwhile, are also increasingly common, particularly on performance-oriented cruising boats and serious race boats.

The principle is similar to that of an I-beam girder (see illustration on page 92). Two sections oriented in one direction are separated by a third, lighter section oriented at a right angle to the first two. In theory, this is the ideal way to dramatically increase thickness and stiffness while not increasing weight. Except here, unlike an I-beam, which is 100% steel, we are (again) creating a composite structure, as the internal core is made of a different substance than

Blisters: Whence the Dreaded Pox?

The subject of blisters is immensely complicated, and I cannot treat it completely here. If your boat already has blisters, I urge you to learn all you can so you don't waste time or money on unnecessary or ineffective repairs and treatments. There are numerous so-called experts (many equipped with gelcoat-peeling machines) who will be happy to fill your ears with self-serving advice. The best references I know of are *Fiberglass Boats* by Hugo du Plessis; *Osmosis & Glassfibre Yacht Construction* by Tony Staton-Bevan; and *Blisters*, a collection of articles published by *Professional Boatbuilder* magazine, most of them written by Bruce Pfund. (See Books for Cruising Sailors on page 368.)

There are literally hundreds of causes of blistering, but the primary cause is the presence of water-soluble molecules in a laminate. These impurities come from innumerable sources, including glycols in improperly cured resin, any dust, sweat, or snot that falls into a mold during lamination, trace chemicals left over from a catalyst or mat binder, as well as certain agents used to treat fiberglass fabrics. It's impossible to ensure that none of these pollutants will ever find their way into a laminate, but the likelihood is greatly decreased if a builder is truly fastidious in his practices. The other major factor is the presence of voids in a laminate. Again, these can never be absolutely eliminated—there is always some air in a laminate somewhere—but, as discussed, steps can be taken to keep voids to a minimum.

What precipitates blistering is the migration of water through a laminate. Though once upon a time we all believed fiberglass is absolutely waterproof, now we know better. Compared to wood, for example, fiberglass absorbs little water (no more than about 3% of its total weight in a healthy laminate), but there is no way to prevent some water from coming in. As it moves through a laminate, water dissolves any water-soluble molecules it finds, creating an acid solution that can pool up in voids. These acidic pools are eventually pressurized, either through osmosis, wherein the laminate around the pool continues to allow water to pass through but traps the accumulating acids inside; or when the pools are heated, as may happen when a boat is hauled out and left to bake in the sun. At a certain point the pressure is sufficient to raise a visible blister in the laminate's surface.

Most blisters are merely cosmetic. These occur directly under the exterior gelcoat and are relatively easy to repair as they crop up. If they are prevalent, however, the gelcoat must be removed and replaced. The most serious blisters occur deep within a laminate and form larger bulges on its surface. The pressure in these blisters is sufficient to cause delamination, and repairs will involve relaminating affected portions of the hull. Within these two basic categories of blisters, there are many subvariations exhibiting different characteristics and surface patterns. To ensure the most effective and least intrusive repair, it is best to study these closely and figure out if possible what caused them.

Gelcoat blister	Interlaminar blister
• The most common type	• Not so common
• Easy to repair	• Harder to repair
• Cosmetic damage only	• Damage is structural

The two most basic types of blisters—but there are many other lesser variations. Learn as much as you can about what caused your blisters before trying to cure them.

As mentioned, the best way to deter blistering is to maintain scrupulous construction standards and minimize laminate voids and impurities. Most builders, however, focus more on improving water resistance in a laminate's surface layers and brag in their literature about such things as epoxy barrier coats, special gelcoats, and vinylester resin. These certainly do help retard blister formation. Bear in mind, however, that builders are most concerned about keeping a boat blister-free until its warranty expires. Even an epoxy barrier coat is somewhat permeable, and in the end, no matter what is on the outside, water will enter the laminate, in which case only the quality of the laminate will save it.

Geography and how a boat is used are also significant factors. Warm water and fresh water migrate through a laminate more easily, thus boats kept in southern and/or inland waters are generally more blister-prone than saltwater craft kept in colder climates. Continual immersion also accelerates water absorption. If you're looking for a boat to buy, the ones with the fewest blister problems are usually found in northern coastal areas where boats spend much of the year sitting on shore. Boats from the south that are in the water year-round, especially those kept in fresh water, have many more problems.

the external skins. This is often referred to as a sandwich construction, for obvious reasons.

Depending on how thick the core of the sandwich is, the outer skins can be quite thin indeed. On a boat, however, there are practical limits, as the skins must at least be thick enough to resist ordinary impacts. As a general rule, as the lightweight core gets thicker, the relatively heavy skins can get thinner, and the whole structure gets stiffer and lighter. The larger the structure, the greater the weight savings relative to a solid structure of similar size and strength. For boat hulls the practical minimum limit is about 30 feet. On any boat shorter than this, the skin thickness needed to resist impacts is so great relative to the core's thickness that there is no appreciable weight savings.

Another great benefit of cored hull laminate is that it provides great insulation. If you have ever cruised in cooler climates aboard a solid glass boat in the early spring or late fall and have awoken to rivers of condensation pouring off the overhead, you will appreciate the importance of this. A cored hull is always drier than a solid hull and is less likely to become a mildew farm. It is also warmer when it's cold outside, cooler when it's warm outside, and quieter as well.

Cored laminates do have some disadvantages and are in certain ways more fragile than solid laminates. There is no way to create a chemical bond between a core and its skins; instead the bond must be primarily adhesive. The best methods are either to lay up the core between two resin-rich layers of chopped-strand mat or to glue the core in place with a resin-based adhesive putty. But even when a cored laminate is laid down with scrupulous care, it is more likely to delaminate than a solid one, particularly after suffering impact damage, whether the outer skin is punctured or not. In such cases, though there may be only a small area where damage is visible, the

core will likely have separated from its exterior skin over a much larger area. Furthermore, the extent of delamination, however it occurs, can be difficult to ascertain if the core remains in close contact with its skin, as is often the case.

Cored laminates are also more susceptible to water damage. Any underwater core will eventually be invaded by some small amount of moisture migrating through its exterior laminar skin. Any puncture in the outer skin, no matter how small, will also readily admit moisture. If the puncture is underwater, even the speediest repair cannot prevent some saturation from taking place. This is why some builders insist on building only solid hulls and others will core a hull above the waterline, but never below it. Many cruisers believe no serious cruising boat should ever have cored laminate below its waterline; others believe a lighter hull is worth the risk of having to make more expensive repairs after a collision.

In addition to the threat of impact damage, cored decks are susceptible to water intrusion anywhere a fastener pierces their surface. On most boats there are dozens (or even hundreds) of such penetrations, and it is rare to find an elderly deck on a glass boat that is not a bit soggy somewhere, if not completely saturated. It is therefore common for older fiberglass boats to have had all or part of their decks recored at some point. This is a difficult, expensive job, and you do not want to be the owner of the boat in question when it needs doing.

When water does penetrate a core, it theoretically should not travel far, as any reasonable core material will be a closed-cell substance that does not allow water to migrate through it. In practice, however, water in a core often migrates long distances.

Laying out a balsa core in an open-hull mold by hand in the early days of fiberglass boatbuilding. (Courtesy of Alcan Baltek)

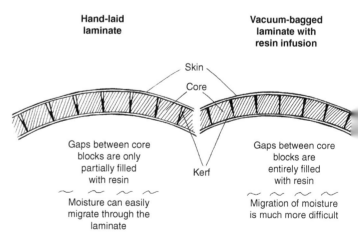

Kerf saturation in cored laminates. Resin infusion and vacuum-bagging ensure that kerfs are filled with resin, which minimizes the migration of moisture in a laminate's core.

The primary culprits here are small grooves or notches called *kerfs* that are scored into the body of a core in a grid pattern and enable it to conform itself to curved surfaces. Anywhere the core meets a curve its kerfs must spread open to accommodate it and so create an easy channel for water to travel through. Even in areas where the kerfs are closed tight, the tiny slits they present are much more permeable than the core material itself. As a result, even if water enters a core at only a few discrete locations, the entire core may become thoroughly saturated. Drill a hole in a hull like this, and the water literally comes shooting out.

The only way to prevent this is to make sure kerfs are filled with resin or putty during lamination. When laminating by hand this can be difficult to achieve. Prior to layup, the core can be draped over some appropriately shaped object section by section, and resin can be sprayed into the opened-up kerfs (this is known as *hot-coating* a core), but this is labor intensive. Many builders do it only in a cursory manner, if they bother at all. It is also necessary to apply pressure to the core after it is set in place so as to drive resin or putty as far up into the kerfs as possible. In a hand layup, this is usually done by laying weights all over the core—an inexact method at best. No matter how carefully the work is performed, there will still likely be some areas where the kerfs are not completely filled.

In the end, the only truly effective method of laying up a core is with resin infusion and a vacuum bag. This way pressure is evenly applied over the entire core and resin is sucked up into all the kerfs. The strength of the bond between the core and skins is also maximized. It is an overstatement to say that cores laid up by hand must be deficient, but you should consider them to be somewhat suspect. This is less true of deck cores, as decks are normally pretty flat and core can be laid down straight, without any kerfs, thus reducing the potential for moisture migration. With hand-laid hull core, however, it is best to be skeptical.

Core Materials

Balsa wood has long been the most commonly used core material. It is light, inexpensive, and stiff when loads are imposed along its grain (though it is soft and weak, as any model airplane buff will tell you, when loaded across its grain). Oriented in end-grain fashion, with its grain perpendicular to its laminar skins, a balsa core is structurally very efficient. Balsa also has the highest shear strength of any core material, meaning it most strongly resists being separated from its skins. It is heat resistant as well, much more so than any resin it is apt to be paired with in a fiberglass laminate.

End-grain balsa is technically a closed-cell material, but in my experience it does seem to have a tendency to spread moisture through itself. It is also supposedly just as strong wet as it is dry, but if you have ever opened up an old soggy balsa-core deck, you will not believe this. Also, though balsa is reasonably impact resistant (if an impact is received in the direction of its grain), it will not regain its shape once it is crushed.

Before it is laid down in a laminate a balsa core must first be wet out with resin—otherwise the balsa wood, which is absorbent, will suck resin out of the laminate surrounding it. Any resin-starved patches created as a result are likely to delaminate in short order. In the early days, there were several dramatic failures of this sort, and balsa core consequently for many years had a bad reputation it did not deserve.

Another type of wood that was sometimes used as deck core in older glass boats is plywood. As a rule, it is best to avoid these. Because it is a laminar material with much of its strength oriented laterally, like the laminate around it, plywood is not structurally efficient. Plywood does resist compression well, but is also heavy compared to other core materials. Worst of all, because of its laminar structure, moisture spreads through it quickly.

After balsa wood, plastic foam is the next most commonly used core material. There are different varieties, but they are all *isotropic*, meaning they are strong in all directions, rather than in just one direction. Some of foam's strength is therefore wasted in a laminate. Though not as structurally efficient, it is lighter than balsa, but is not nearly as heat resistant. It is more likely to regain its shape after being crushed and is also more nearly

The sheets of balsa core on the right have been scored with kerfs. Balsa is an excellent lightweight core material—structurally efficient with great shear strength. (Courtesy of Alcan Baltek)

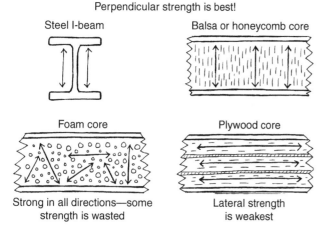

Perpendicular strength is best!

Steel I-beam

Balsa or honeycomb core

Foam core

Strong in all directions—some
strength is wasted

Plywood core

Lateral strength
is weakest

Different core materials have different strength orientations.

Honeycomb core, like this plastic NidaCore, is light and stiff. It is increasingly used in furniture and interior bulkheads on performance cruising boats; it only appears in the hulls of exotic race boats.

a 100% closed-cell substance and so better resists water migration. It is generally more expensive than balsa, too.

Most foam cores are made of polyvinyl chloride (PVC). These include Airex, a linear PVC foam that is resilient and easily springs back into shape after being crushed. Divinycell and Klegecell, which are cross-linked PVC foams, are less expensive and lighter, but are more likely to crack when crushed. The most expensive commonly used foam is Core-Cell, which is a styrene acrylonitrile (SAN) foam, and is reputed to be more impact resistant than its competitors.

The most exotic lightweight cores have a honeycomb structure and are made of various materials, including paper, aluminum, and plastic. Honeycomb cores are extremely stiff for their weight and, like balsa wood, are structurally efficient. The big problem with such cores is that their exterior lateral surface area is severely reduced. There is minimal contact between the body of the core and its laminar skins, which makes it difficult to achieve a strong bond. Vacuum bagging with epoxy resin is practically mandatory; as a result, this sort of construction is very expensive.

Honeycomb cores are increasingly used in interior bulkheads and furniture installations in both race boats and high-end cruising boats. The weight savings are tremendous: a honeycomb bulkhead weighs as little as 2 pounds per square foot, compared to a conventional plywood bulkhead, which weighs nearly 5 pounds per square foot. And when finished with thin hardwood veneers, honeycomb components can look very traditional. The material most commonly used is paper, though plastic is popular as well.

Honeycomb hull core, meanwhile, is found only on the most cutting-edge race boats. Usually the skins are carbon fiber rather than fiberglass. The core material is most often aluminum and sometimes plastic. Hulls like this are incredibly light and stiff and represent the state of the art in modern yacht construction, but they are engineered to fine tolerances and are prone to delamination and other dramatic failures. Such construction therefore is not normally appropriate for a cruising boat.

Internal Structures within the Hull

The molded fiberglass hull of any boat much larger than a dinghy is not normally rigid enough to withstand much abuse. To stiffen a glass hull without overbuilding its laminate, it is necessary to add some structure to its interior. The most basic sort of reinforcements are floors and stringers. *Floors* are transverse sills in the bottom of a hull on which cabin soles are traditionally installed. Besides stiffening the bottom of the hull, floors provide critical support to the root of a sailboat's keel where it meets the hull. *Stringers*, meanwhile, are lateral beams installed along the bottom of a hull. Instead of floors and stringers many modern shallow-bilged boats have a grid structure, sometimes called an *egg crate*, consisting of structural beams running both laterally and transversely across the bottom of the hull. Bulkheads, partitions, and other structural components of a boat's interior accommodations also play an important role in stiffening a hull. Bulkheads are particularly critical, as they can simultaneously provide support to the deck overhead, the bilges below, and the sides of the hull as well.

Much of a modern boat's interior is constructed before the deck is installed. Furniture components and bulkheads help stiffen the hull.

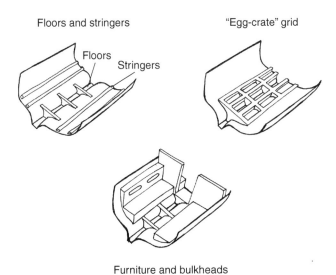

Methods of hull reinforcement found in today's fiberglass boats.

A primary concern with internal structural components is how they are attached to the hull. On some modern vacuum-bagged or resin-infused boats an egg-crate grid is molded into the bilge as part of the primary hull layup, which is an excellent practice. The traditional procedure, however, is to bond, or *tab*, internal components in place with strips of fiberglass tape after the hull has been molded. These secondary adhesive bonds are weaker than primary chemical bonds. To create a superior secondary bond the surfaces involved must be properly prepared. In many cases the component being tabbed to the hull is made of wood (often it is plywood), in which case the wood grain must be sealed beforehand or it will suck resin out of the tabbed joint when the fiberglass tape is laid down and wet out. Surfaces on both the structural part and the hull itself should be scratched with sandpaper or a grinding disk to give the resin texture to bite onto; they should also be wiped down with solvent before any glass or resin is applied.

The area of the bonded surfaces must also be large enough to absorb loads on the joint. The rule of thumb is there should be at least a 2-inch margin of tabbing either side of any joint, though a minimum of 3 inches is better, particularly on bulkhead joints. Discrete parts such as grids, floors, and stringers located in the bilges of a boat should be completely glassed over so they don't absorb any oil or water. Limber holes should also be cut through structures in the bilge so water can flow freely and easily to the lowest point in the hull, where a bilge pump can evacuate it. It may also be necessary to cut access holes through these parts to accommodate wiring or plumbing. The interior surfaces of all such holes must be carefully sealed so they don't absorb any water or oil passing through them.

Particular care should be taken with any bonded joint that forms a sharp right angle. The danger here, especially with parts like bulkheads or lateral partitions that transfer loads all the way from the deck to the hull, is that *hard spots* will be created. These are areas where abruptly imposed structural support within a hull amplifies the total amount of stress created when the area is subject to load. Even where hard spots are created by isolated minor structures such as interior cabinetry, significant stress can result if there is an abrupt impact or collision in the area. The best analogy is that of a stick broken over a knee. The narrow fulcrum of the knee focuses stress in a single area and greatly decreases the load required to break the stick. Bend that same stick over a wider surface—a barrel, say—and there is much less stress. A greater load can be imposed without the stick breaking.

To avoid hard spots it is best if any perpendicular structure bonded to a hull does not actually meet it. Instead, there should be a small gap filled with a softer material like foam, balsa wood, or putty. The joint should also be nicely radiused with a wide fillet. This serves both to reduce stress in the area and to strengthen the bond generally, as the transition from one bonded surface to the other is more gradual. The wider the radiused angle, the stronger the bond will be and the less stress it will experience.

As you may have gathered by now, properly installing an interior hull structure is labor intensive. Any economy of scale realized by popping multiple bare hulls from the same mold can be quickly negated by the attention to detail required to properly finish a hull's interior. This is probably the one phase of boat construction where builders have tried hardest to streamline their procedures. Their key weapon here is the molded hull liner, which is simply

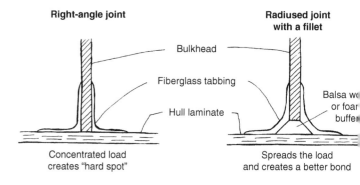

Bulkhead bonds are more impact-resistant if radiused with a fillet, which spreads the load.

another large fiberglass part incorporating elements of a boat's interior that is inserted into a hull. The larger the part, the bigger the savings in terms of work and effort. A truly comprehensive one-piece hull liner can include not only a structural bilge grid, but also all major furniture components from the bow to the stern. Bulkheads and partitions in these cases are not bonded directly to the hull, but are fitted and glued into premolded slots in the hull liner and overhead deck liner or, alternatively, are bolted to special flanges in the liner.

A liner can't provide much structural support unless it is firmly bonded to its hull in as many places as possible. The usual practice is to lay down beds of adhesive putty or thickened resin in appropriate spots, then set the liner down on top of these. This relatively light bond should then be improved by tabbing the liner to the hull with glass tape anywhere there is access to contact points between the two parts. Such access, however, is always limited, and work spaces are often

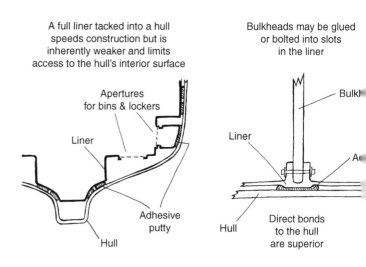

Hull liners greatly simplify the fleshing out of a boat's interior, but can compromise structural integrity.

cramped and awkwardly situated. In the end, it is never possible to create as strong a structure as is formed when all individual components are bonded piece by piece directly to the hull. If the hull is unduly stressed, the liner may break free in some areas. I have heard more than one tale of mass-produced boats failing like this in strong weather. Such damage can be difficult to detect and is always difficult to repair. It may involve cutting away and then rebuilding large portions of the liner in situ, which may prompt an underwriter to declare the boat a total loss.

The best practice is to create the hull liner in small sections and install the parts separately. Ideally, support for the bottom of the hull, usually a grid of some kind, is laid in first. One-piece grid pans are often used, but it is best if the grid is built up in place with each part bonded directly to the hull. Bulkheads and hopefully partitions should also be bonded directly to the hull. Separate interior liner sections can then be laid in place around the bulkheads and on top of the grid. It is easier to create strong bonds between the hull and these smaller, more discrete parts; both the bulkheads and bilge structure will also offer more support to the hull than would otherwise be the case.

A small liner section with furniture components waiting to be installed in a hull. With discrete sections like this it is easier to create strong bonds between the liner and the hull.

Another disadvantage to a hull liner, no matter how it is installed, is that it limits or precludes access to the hull once it is in place. This makes it hard or impossible to repair damage to the hull from within the boat without first cutting away the liner. If the hull is breached while underway, a liner makes it harder to both find and stanch any leak, which is why some cautious cruisers always carry a heavy tool such as an ax or a crowbar for quickly tearing away a liner in an emergency.

Hull-Deck Joints

Almost all builders first install a boat's interior and then close up the hull by placing the deck, another large fiberglass part, on top of it. Large pieces of equipment, such as engines, electrical generators, and water and fuel tanks, are also installed while the deck is off. Sometimes owners later discover they cannot remove such equipment from inside the boat, as there is no deck aperture large enough to accommodate it. A few builders install all mechanical equipment after decks are installed to make sure this never happens.

The bond between a deck and hull is critical. Ideally, it includes all interior bulkheads and partitions. The best practice is to tab these separately to both the deck and hull so that the finished boat is a solid unitary structure. Often, however, these important vertical structures are merely tacked to the deck (or worse, to a deck liner) with adhesive putty. In all cases the exterior perimeter of the hull and deck must be directly joined to each other. This primary hull-deck joint is usually the area most likely to leak when you are actually using a boat. Normally you only learn about such leaks sailing close-hauled into a fresh breeze with the boat well heeled.

There are many different ways to engineer a hull-deck joint, particularly if you consider the myriad methods for installing caprails, toe rails, and rubrails on top of them. Their basic architecture, however, falls into three categories. The most common method on sailboats is an inward horizontal hull flange mated to an outward-facing flange or margin on the deck. Another option is the so-called shoe-box joint, where a downward-facing vertical deck flange fits like a shoebox lid over a vertical lip on the hull. In the third variant both the deck and hull have outward-facing horizontal flanges that are joined together.

However a hull-deck joint is formed, what's most important is how the two surfaces are joined together. Most high-quality joints these days are bedded with a tenacious adhesive sealant (usually 3M 5200 compound) and are through-bolted at regular short intervals ($\frac{1}{4}$-inch bolts on 6- or 8-inch centers

A deck hangs poised, waiting to be installed on a hull. Both parts are normally finished as completely as possible with all wiring and systems already in place before being joined.

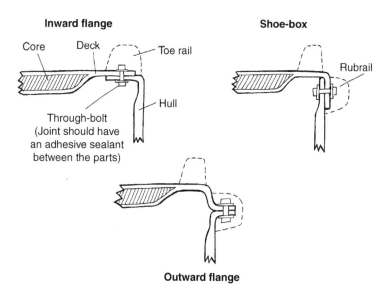

These basic types of deck joints are all through-bolted, which is normally the best practice; some lesser-quality joints are merely screwed or riveted together.

are highly recommended). An acceptable alternative is to glass over a bedded joint with fiberglass tape so that the hull and deck effectively become one part. The most bulletproof method is do all three: bed the joint, through-bolt it, then glass it over.

Unfortunately, many hull-deck joints are of poor quality. The most common practice, especially on mass-produced boats, is to bed the joint with an adhesive sealant and fasten it with self-tapping screws rather than bolts. Screws can be installed much more quickly than bolts, but they make poor fasteners when threaded into fiberglass laminate. An even worse practice—and you will find this on some boats—is to fasten the joint with lightweight aluminum pop rivets.

Otherwise the difference in terms of quality between the basic types of joints is open to debate. Some prefer the double outward-facing flange because the joint is outside of the boat. It is much easier to install through-bolts on a joint like this; it's also easy to ensure a good fit and trim away excess material.

Prepping an inward-facing hull flange prior to installing a deck. Roughing up the surface makes it easier for an adhesive sealant to grab onto it. The hull-deck joint on this Sabre 38 will also be through-bolted at short intervals.

Others dislike these joints because they are more likely to be damaged in collisions. The flip side of this argument is that repairs can also be made more easily. The other types of joints, by comparison, are better protected but are also harder to install and repair, as the working surfaces are hard to reach. Probably the most problematic type is the shoe-box joint, as the tolerances between the hull and deck are quite fine and a close fit is hard to achieve.

Installing Deck Hardware

This is another area where builders often try to streamline their methods to save time and money, particularly when it comes to installing deck hardware such as winches, cleats, genoa tracks, travelers, stanchion bases, and the like. As mentioned, almost all fiberglass decks are cored these days, which presents two problems any time a deck is penetrated to receive a fastener. First, the core must not be crushed; second, it must not be exposed to any moisture. Given the enormous number of fasteners

needed to secure deck hardware and the enormous loads some hardware carries, it should come as no surprise that proper hardware installation is both critical and troublesome.

The traditional practice is to treat the fasteners individually. This can be done by drilling out an oversize hole for each fastener, filling it with a plug of epoxy paste, waiting for the epoxy to cure, then redrilling a proper-size hole through the plug. The plug both seals the core, protecting its internal face against moisture intrusion, and acts as a compression post that prevents the deck skins from being squashed together. Another alternative is to drill a proper-size hole for the fastener, ream out the core around the perimeter of the hole with a bent nail or router, then fill the cavity with thickened epoxy filler. Again, the epoxy both seals the core and resists compression as the fastener is tightened down. Yet another alternative, rarely seen, is to drill a slightly oversize hole, seal the core perimeter with epoxy resin, then insert a metal compression tube to bear the load of the tightened fastener.

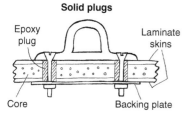

Solid plugs

Epoxy plug · Laminate skins · Core · Backing plate

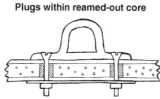

Plugs within reamed-out core

Solid laminate

Core · Solid laminate

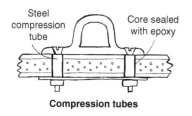

Steel compression tube · Core sealed with epoxy

Compression tubes

Worst case!
• Core is not sealed
• No compression protection
• No backing plate

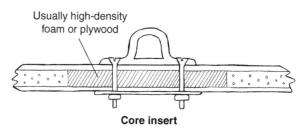

Usually high-density foam or plywood

Core insert

When sealing individual fastener holes in decks, the object is to protect the core both from water intrusion (and subsequent saturation) and from compression when fasteners are tightened.

Laminate alternatives under deck hardware: rather than focusing on individual fastener holes, the entire area is laminated with a solid laminate or with a core insert of high-density foam or plywood.

Few, if any, builders took such obsessive precautions in the early days of fiberglass boat production. Older boats often have deck hardware installed with fasteners piercing unsealed balsa-cored decks with no compression fittings of any kind. The assumption then was that the core would not be crushed if nuts on bolts were not overtightened, nor would it get wet if the hardware's footprint was well bedded with sealant. But heavily loaded hardware may in fact crush a core even if its fasteners are only finger-tight, and even the best sealant, liberally applied, will eventually break down over time and allow moisture to creep in. In the end, it is often some poor boatowner many years later (or a yard crew hired at great expense) who must properly seal and secure the fastener holes.

The best and most efficient way to install deck hardware on a production basis is to properly prepare the areas in question when the deck is molded in the first place. For example, the deck can be molded with only solid laminate in areas receiving hardware. If this is done, transitions from cored to uncored laminate within the deck should be made gradually, with the core gently tapering down in thickness so hard spots are not created. Another more common method is to replace compressible core material under hardware with another firmer material. Plywood is often used for such inserts because it is cheap and is not easily compressed. Plywood does, however, readily absorb moisture, so each fastener hole, again, should be sealed with epoxy. Another alternative core material is high-density plastic foam, which is lighter and less

absorbent than plywood, but also more expensive. Yet another sensible alternative, which hopefully will become more popular over time, is StarBoard, a lightweight solid plastic faux wood that cannot be compressed and is entirely waterproof.

All fasteners should be threaded through-bolts with nuts on the end, as illustrated. This is the only reasonable option, unless the hardware in question is never subject to any load, in which case self-tapping screws may be used if they are well bedded with sealant.

Besides being through-bolted, all loaded hardware should be supported underneath the deck by substantial backing plates with generous margins extending beyond the hardware's footprint above-deck. This spreads loads over a much larger area of the deck. It is best if these plates are metal—either

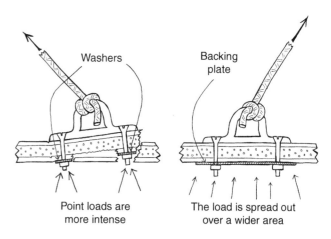

Washers · Backing plate

Point loads are more intense · The load is spread out over a wider area

Washers vs. metal backing plates. When mounting hardware, what's under the deck is also important!

stainless steel or aluminum—although plywood is commonly used and is usually acceptable *if* large fender washers are also installed. Sheets of StarBoard are another excellent alternative. Builders, unfortunately, often omit backing plates and instead install fender washers that may not spread loads sufficiently. I myself have seen cleats secured with fender washers torn clean out of decks by docklines strained by passing boat wakes.

There is another method for installing deck hardware without washers or backing plates that is now popular with many builders. First, during the deck layup, aluminum plates are glassed into areas where hardware will be installed. Then holes are drilled and tapped into the embedded plate (this can even be done by computerized robots), and hardware is fastened in place with stainless-steel machine screws. The great advantage is the entire installation can be made from above the deck, which simplifies deck design, as no allowance need be made for access under the deck. It also saves manpower, as a second worker is not needed belowdeck to install washers or backing plates and thread nuts on bolts.

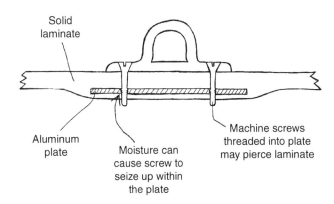

Hardware mounting plate embedded within a deck laminate. This increasingly common method simplifies the initial installation, but may create problems later.

The long-term viability of such installations is suspect. The embedded aluminum plate, if appropriately sized, can act like a backing plate and help spread loads, but the load may be carried by only a portion of the laminate. Moisture may also cause problems. With through-bolted hardware, if moisture gets into fastener holes it eventually emerges in

Coping with Deck Liners (or Not)

Comprehensive one-piece deck liners that cover all the overhead in a cabin interior are now common on production sailboats. Such liners may restrict access to fasteners under the deck, making it impossible to remove hardware without cutting away part of the liner. The best practice when a liner is fitted is for the builder to cut small access hatches with removable covers so fasteners can be reached easily. Often this is done after the fact by owners seeking to remove old hardware or install new hardware in new locations.

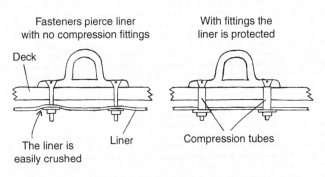

Compression tubes protect the liner from being crushed or distorted by fasteners.

Alternatively, fasteners may pierce the liner, spanning the gap between the liner and deck. In this case, some sort of compression fitting should be installed so the liner is not warped or crushed by the fasteners. It is best, too, if a backing plate is also installed, though this is rarely done.

Ultimately, it is best if there is no deck liner. On well-built boats you'll find instead a series of removable overhead panels in open areas of the cabin. These are often held in place with Velcro strips, which makes it easy to access under-deck fasteners, though the Velcro eventually wears out and needs replacing. Overhead panels can also be secured with trim strips and/or small screws, which are more permanent and reliable, but take much more time to unfasten if panels must be removed.

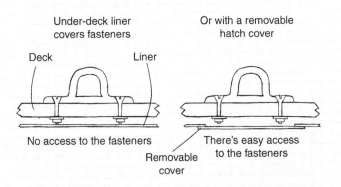

Accessing fasteners under deck liners can be a challenge. On the boat at left there is no access to the fasteners from below; in the example on the right a removable cover allows access to them.

the interior of the boat, having done no significant damage as long as there is no unsealed deck core to absorb it. The resulting leak can be discovered and redressed by rebedding the hardware with fresh sealant. But with an embedded aluminum plate, moisture may be trapped in the laminate, eventually causing a problem. It will certainly cause corrosion where the aluminum plate and stainless-steel screw are threaded together. Expanding powdery waste from the corroding aluminum (you often see this on aluminum masts and booms where stainless-steel fasteners are installed) may someday cause significant delamination.

This can be prevented by removing the hardware and rebedding it on a regular basis, before the sealant fails. Removing hardware will be hard, however, if the aluminum plate and stainless-steel screws have seized together, as often happens. Then it will be necessary to drill out the screws. To replace the hardware, the holes will have to be re-tapped to receive a slightly larger screw. This can probably be done only once or twice before the screws are too large to fit the hardware's fastener holes. All of which only discourages an owner from trying to remove the hardware in the first place.

To forestall these problems any boat with deck hardware screwed into embedded plates should have its hardware mounted on elevated bosses or plinths that shed water and so make it harder for moisture to find its way into fastener holes. Indeed, this is very desirable on any boat, but unfortunately is rarely done.

Chainplates

Chainplates are deck fittings, normally made of stainless steel, to which the standing rigging that supports a sailboat's mast (or masts) is attached. They carry much larger loads than lesser pieces of deck hardware, hence are configured differently. Plates for headstays and backstays, which support a mast fore and aft, are almost always through-bolted directly to the hull itself to ensure maximum strength. Chainplates for the shrouds, which support a mast transversely, can also be through-bolted to either side of the hull. In all cases, it is best to have substantial backing plates, rather than mere washers, inside the hull to receive the fasteners and spread loads.

In some instances chainplates are bonded to the hull as part of its laminate. These can be strong installations if properly executed. The chainplate itself should not be just a straight strip of metal, like a through-bolted chainplate, as it will pull out of a laminate relatively easily. Instead, the root of the chainplate should have some transverse element, such as a welded crossbar (or, better, crossbars) or a

Bolting shroud chainplates directly to the hull is an effective technique as long as they are secured to backing plates inside the hull. (Courtesy of SAIL Magazine; Photo by Malcolm White.)

split Y-shape that resists extraction under load. The chainplate should also be installed as the hull is laid up so that all laminate layers surrounding it form primary chemical bonds with each other. Furthermore, the laminate in the area should be engineered to carry the extra load. For example, this is an excellent place to lay in some unidirectional fabric carefully oriented to resist the stress created by the rig.

On most modern boats shroud chainplates are inboard of the hull somewhere on the side deck to minimize headsail sheeting angles when sailing to

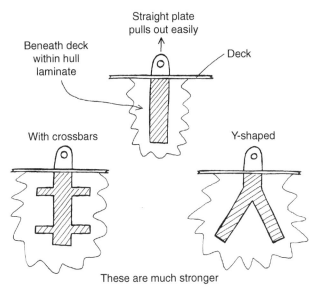

Straight plate
pulls out easily

Deck

Beneath deck
within hull
laminate

With crossbars

Y-shaped

These are much stronger

Chainplates embedded within hull laminate: the strongest installation will use a chainplate whose shape resists extraction under load.

windward. The load carried by inboard chainplates must ultimately somehow be transferred to the hull. The traditional method is to simply through-bolt the chainplate root to an interior bulkhead that in turn is bonded to the hull. The chainplate can also be bolted to a lesser structure known as a *knee*, which bridges the corner between the deck and hull (in effect acting like a partial bulkhead). Another common option is to install a tie-rod under the chainplate that is supported in turn by a block or tang that is bonded to the hull. Such assemblies must be properly engineered, and a strong primary bond is needed to carry the load.

In many inboard chainplate installations (the exception being some tie-rod installations, where

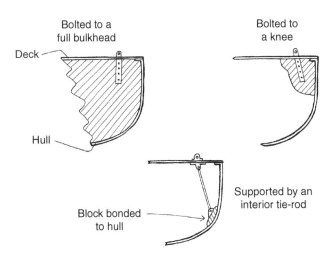

Bolted to a
full bulkhead

Bolted to
a knee

Deck

Hull

Block bonded
to hull

Supported by an
interior tie-rod

The load on an inboard chainplate installation must be transferred to the hull.

two separate fittings connected by fasteners are used on either side of the deck), the chainplate itself must pass through the deck. This can lead to saturation not only of the deck core if water intrudes, but also perhaps of a bulkhead or knee to which the chainplate is fastened. The deck core, again, should be properly sealed, and the chainplates should be capped with chainplate covers that are well bedded with sealant. But because chainplates suffer intense cyclical loading—going slack and taut as a boat tacks back and forth—they work quite a bit and sealant around them therefore fails more quickly. They are thus more likely to leak, and the consequences of this are more serious if bulkheads or knees are involved. Some conservative cruising sailors as a result have a marked prejudice against through-deck chainplates and favor outboard chainplates instead.

In a few rare cases on monohulls, and much more commonly on multihulls, you'll also find shroud chainplates through-bolted to the side of a cabinhouse. This is not like bolting a chainplate to a hull, and care must be taken to ensure that the local structure is strong enough to support the load. There should be no ports, windows, or other apertures in the area, and it may be necessary to reinforce the cabin side with a unidirectional laminate or an interior beam and/or frame.

Through-Hull Fittings

Through hulls are holes in the hull that feed raw water to onboard systems or drain water and waste away from them. These holes normally have valve fittings to secure them (though some older boats may instead have straight standpipes that reach above the waterline). Typically, cockpit drains also have through-hulls with fittings, and special through-hull fittings are used to mount speed and depth sensors.

Leaving aside plumbing, which we'll discuss in Chapter 7, it is essential that through-hulls be strong and watertight. The recommended method is to install a backing block between the hull and the body of the fitting. These blocks are normally wood and should be bonded to the hull and glassed over to guard against bilge-water saturation. The theory is to spread loads, but in reality through-hull fittings don't really carry any serious loads, so many builders simply mount them directly on the hull. This is usually strong enough, though in some cases a backing block is still needed to accommodate hull curvature.

If the hull is solid laminate a liberal bedding of sealant for a through-hull and its fasteners should make things watertight. When the sealant fails, leaks will be readily apparent. If the hull is cored below the waterline, the core must also be sealed; otherwise

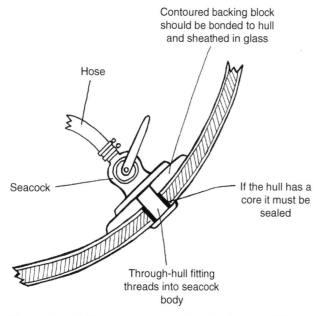

Through-hull fitting on a curved hull: a backing block is needed so the fitting seats properly.

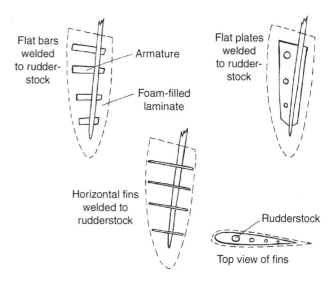

Alternate interior structures for fiberglass rudders with metal rudderstocks and lateral armatures supporting the rudderblades.

leaks may be absorbed by the hull before becoming noticeable. The techniques are similar to those used to seal deck core: the laminate should somehow be made solid in the area of the fitting, either by laying in solid laminate when the hull is manufactured, by later reaming out the core and refilling it with thickened epoxy, or by replacing the core with a solid insert. The treated area must be large enough to accommodate both the main body of the fitting plus any peripheral fasteners.

Rudders

In the early days of fiberglass boatbuilding when most sailboats had attached rudders, it was common to see rudders made of wood. These were constructed in the traditional fashion and consisted of a row of planks, often mahogany, joined end to end, usually with internal drift pins fastened to the rudderstock. A few of these rudders can still be found, but in many cases they have been glassed over or replaced entirely with new fiberglass rudders.

Ever since the late-1960s most fiberglass boats have come equipped with fiberglass rudders. Though not all glass rudders are created equal, most are built on the same basic principle. The spine of the structure is a metal rudderstock (also sometimes called a rudderpost) off of which sprouts a lateral armature that supports the rudder blade. Traditionally, this armature is welded to the rudderstock and consists of a series of lateral rods or bars, or perhaps a simple flat plate. More recently, foil-shaped fins similar to those

seen in the frames of airplane wings have become more common. This skeletal structure is embedded in a high-density closed-cell plastic foam core, which is sheathed in a thin fiberglass skin. This composite foam-core construction is relatively light with neutral buoyancy, which significantly improves the feel of the helm while sailing.

The key variable is the material from which the rudderstock and its armature are manufactured. If metal is used, the best choice is probably silicon bronze, but this is rarely seen anymore. Sometimes aluminum and even titanium are used to save weight, but the most common choice is stainless steel. We like to think of stainless steel as an "ideal" corrosion-proof metal, but this is only true in limited circumstances. It does resist corrosion well when routinely exposed to oxygen, but is subject to pitting corrosion when trapped in a deoxygenated environment, which is just what you'll find inside a fiberglass-skinned rudder when its foam core is saturated with water.

Such saturation, unfortunately, is common in any rudder with a metal stock. The joint where the stock enters the rudder blade is apt to leak sooner or later, because the three different materials involved—fiberglass, metal, and plastic foam—all contract and expand at different rates as the ambient temperature changes. No matter how well the joint is sealed when the rudder is first constructed, small gaps through which water can intrude are inevitably created. Knowledgeable boatowners take this for granted. They assume their rudder cores are constantly absorbing water and so drill holes in the bottom of their rudder blades every time they haul their boats in order to let the moisture drain out. (A better alternative, obviously, would be for builders to install drain plugs in the first place.)

Another problem with stainless steel in rudders has to do with its welding characteristics. When stainless steel is welded, the carbon and chromium in it mix to form chromium carbide. This creates two suballoys—chromium carbide and chromium-depleted steel—that are different enough in their composition to form a corrosive galvanic couple within the weld. Insert this galvanically compromised weld inside a moist oxygen-depleted foam-cored rudder, and it is much more likely the rudder's stainless-steel armature will corrode and fail. A stainless-steel rudderstock is also apt to suffer from crevice corrosion inside the shaft seal in the bearing where it exits the hull, as this is another area where water is trapped and becomes stagnant and deoxygenated.

All these problems can be ameliorated if the stainless steel inside a rudder is high-quality 316-L alloy. This variant resists pitting corrosion much more readily than its lesser 302- and 304-alloy cousins. It also has a lower carbon content (thus the L designation) and is less compromised when welded. Unfortunately, there is no easy way to distinguish between these alloys. Silicon bronze, by comparison, is virtually corrosion proof under the same circumstances, unless it is coupled directly to steel or aluminum.

Rudderstocks can also be fabricated from a composite laminate such as fiberglass or carbon fiber. The great advantage of a laminate stock is that the stock and the skin of the rudder blade can be the same material, which means the joint where the stock enters the blade can be permanently sealed. Also, the rudderstock can be bonded directly to the interior surface of the skin, thus eliminating the need for interior armature to resist twisting loads as the rudder turns back and forth.

Laminated rudderstocks generally must be wider than metal stocks in order to resist the transverse loads imposed on them. This means the rudder blade must also be wider, which tends to degrade the rudder's hydrodynamic form. One way around this is to flatten the sides of the stock into a trapezoid shape. This not only creates a narrower cross section, but also presents a larger surface area for bonding the stock to the skin of the rudder blade. Note, however, that a trapezoid stock needs bearing rounds installed where the stock passes through its rudder bearings in order for the rudder to turn properly.

In practice, unfortunately, fiberglass rudderstocks have not performed well. Some mass-production builders have embraced them, because they are cheaper and lighter than stainless-steel stocks, but there have been several incidents where fiberglass stocks have

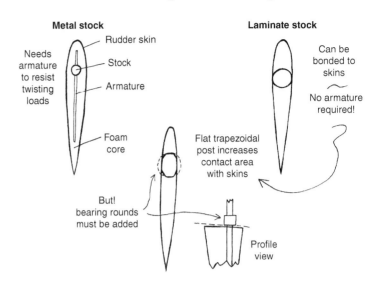

Metal vs. laminate rudderstocks.

failed in moderate sailing conditions. Builders, as a result, are now more wary of them.

Carbon fiber is another story. Carbon rudderstocks have proven much more reliable, as carbon is much stiffer and stronger. It is also much lighter. An all-carbon rudder (i.e., a carbon stock bonded to carbon skins wrapped around high-density foam) weighs less than half as much as a conventional foam-filled glass rudder with a stainless-steel stock and armature, but also costs two to three times more. Carbon rudders therefore are normally seen only on race boats and high-quality cruising boats.

Another important variable is the manner in which the rudder is attached to the hull. The more a rudder

A carbon-fiber rudderstock. Carbon stocks have performed much better than fiberglass stocks, but unfortunately are much more expensive.

Properly installed, a spade rudder in a modern cruising sailboat will withstand much abuse, but an attached rudder is inherently stronger. (See page 56 for a discussion of rudder design.)

One difference between catamaran and monohull construction is that catamaran parts can be much bigger. This is a catamaran deck mold with Divinycell foam core laid out prior to laminating. (Courtesy of DIAB Technologies)

is supported by a hull or skeg, the greater its inherent strength. Unfortunately, the weakest structure, the high-performance spade rudder, is also the most popular. Here all the transverse load, which can be large, is carried by the rudderstock where it enters the hull. The hull itself should be reinforced at this point. The top of the stock should also be well supported. On some boats the deck does this job; on others some below-deck structure, such as a transverse beam or shelf, holds the top of the rudderstock in place. Any such structure should be bonded to the hull as strongly as possible.

Issues in Multihull Construction

Building a fiberglass multihull is not fundamentally different from building a monohull. Multihulls tend to have more complex shapes—hence compound split molds are more likely to be used—but otherwise the hulls, decks, and other components are all manufactured in the same way.

What is different is the distribution of structural loads around the boat. Loads on a monohull are normally greatest in the hull below the waterline where the keel is attached. The greatest loads on a catamaran are imposed above the waterline on the structure holding the two hulls together. These torsional, or twisting, loads are created by the different motions of the hulls and can be large. I recall, for example, sitting on the cockpit floor of a fast 58-foot catamaran with my back against a settee base during an ocean passage and feeling the fiberglass floor and settee base flexing beneath and behind me. The flexing was so pronounced an icemaker installed in a nearby cockpit bulkhead was sheared off its mounting bolts during the passage.

Catamarans also experience much larger rig loads. On a monohull the heeling of the boat spills wind out of the rig and decreases its load in relative terms as wind speeds increase. Aboard a large cat that does not heel, however, there is no such safety valve, and the extra loads are all transferred from the rig to the hull. Both torsional loads and rig loads only increase as a catamaran's beam increases. They are less of a factor on trimarans, however, because tris do heel a bit and their auxiliary hulls, the amas, are smaller and less buoyant than the main hulls of a catamaran.

To carry these loads multihulls must be engineered differently than monohulls. Hulls must be more strongly reinforced around the mast step, chainplates, and crossbeams. In catamarans it is best if strong bulkheads are situated near the mast and near the sterns of the two hulls in order to resist torsional and rig loads. Crossbeams must also be meticulously engineered and well built.

As mentioned earlier, multihulls are more weight sensitive than monohulls. A heavy multihull—particularly a heavy catamaran—suffers a greater proportional loss in performance compared to an equivalently heavy monohull and also, unlike a monohull, has a less comfortable motion. On multihulls, therefore, it makes more sense to use sophisticated materials and advanced laminating techniques to increase a boat's strength-to-weight ratio. Most cat builders don't go to this trouble, however, because most cat owners don't care if their boats are slow, point poorly, and slam in a head sea. All they want is the extra space. Many trimaran builders do go to the trouble, as tri sailors are more performance oriented. If you are a multihull cruiser who places a premium on performance, you should be interested in these features.

WOOD BOATS

Humans have been building boats out of wood for more than 4,000 years. Many assume therefore it must now be obsolete. Wood certainly does not lend itself to mass production the way fiberglass does, though there were a few builders that manufactured wood boats on something like a production basis not long before the advent of glass. Wood does have some distinct virtues. It is light, even compared to modern building materials, and in terms of tensile strength is stronger per pound than common electrical-grade fiberglass. In terms of stiffness, it is stronger per pound than S-glass, E-glass, and Kevlar. In terms of its total structural efficiency, it is better than all of these, plus carbon fiber too.

One big problem with wood, however, is that certain life-forms like to eat it. Various fungi can infest and consume it, causing what is known as dry rot. Marine borers like the Teredo worm, or boring insects like carpenter ants and termites, can chew their way through a boat very quickly. Wood also rots when it gets too wet, is easily ignited, and is soft, with poor abrasion resistance. Structurally, in one important sense, it is deficient in that it is much less dense than other materials and takes up a lot of space. A wood hull must normally be much thicker than an equivalent glass hull, and its interior structural parts must also be larger. Indeed, wood cannot be used at all to make certain small parts that carry great loads (such as bolts, tie-rods, and rigging wire) simply because it is too soft and too fat to fit.

Perhaps the biggest advantage wood has over any other material, especially when it comes to boats, is that it is inherently romantic. For this reason alone, it is likely someone somewhere will always be building wooden boats, and that other people will always be sailing them.

Plank-on-Frame Construction

This is the most traditional method of building a wood boat. The principle is simple, though the details are complex. The fundamental structure of a plank-on-frame vessel is defined by a keel, which is the horizontal backbone of the hull; a more vertical stem, which forms the bow; and a vertical sternpost (plus, in the case of many yachts with long overhangs, a much less vertical horn timber that terminates in the transom), which forms the back of the boat. On deep-keel vessels, especially on sailboats, there is also often what is called deadwood fastened beneath the keel. This forms much of the lateral plane below the waterline that sailors normally call the "keel," particularly its aft section. The forward section is normally inhabited by a solid casting of metal ballast, preferably lead, that is fastened to the bottom of the boat.

Fastened to the spine created by these parts is a series of parallel transverse frames that describe the vessel's hull form. To help support the hull, lateral stringers are installed inside the frames. The skin of the hull consists of a series of planks fastened to the outside of the frames. These planks may be laid on the frame with their edges slightly overlapping, which is known as clinker, or lapstrake, construction. This is often done with smaller boats, but hardly ever with larger boats, as the many ridges formed where the planks overlap greatly increases wetted surface area. Alternatively, planks can be laid on the frame edge to edge, creating a fair, smooth surface, which is known as carvel construction. To make the hull watertight, the seams between carvel planks must be caulked with long strands of cotton and/or oakum.

The deck of the boat, meanwhile, is supported by a series of transverse deck beams, the ends of which are fastened to lateral shelves installed along the inside of the hull at the top of the frames. Traditionally, the deck consists of planking fastened to the deck beams with all seams, again, carefully caulked. Another common way to seal decks, often used on yachts, is to cover the planking with painted canvas. These days, however, many wood decks are simply good-quality marine plywood sealed with epoxy.

Even from this abbreviated, oversimplified description it should be clear this is a labor-intensive way to build a boat. Much skill is also required. Just selecting wood to build with is an art, as there are numerous criteria to meet. The best wood should be cut only in winter to minimize the retention of moisture and microorganisms. It should then be air-dried in a climate-controlled environment for as long as possible—many months at a minimum. The lumber should also be carefully milled to produce planks and pieces with the wood grain properly aligned to carry anticipated loads in the boat. Finally, if you're truly

A wooden sailboat frame with carvel planks being laid on the frames. Note the lead ballast fastened in place at the bottom. (Courtesy of Rockport Marine)

fanatic, all pieces should be hewn to size by hand, rather than ripped with power tools, as traditional hand tools do less damage to the fiber of the wood and make it much less prone to fungal attacks.

The biggest issue is embraced in that single verb "to fasten." A plank-on-frame boat consists of hundreds of pieces of wood, all of which must be carefully shaped and then bound together by thousands of small metal fasteners. Even if you use the best fasteners (silicon bronze screws and bolts are preferred, though Monel is technically superior), what ultimately limits the strength of a plank-on-frame boat is not the wood it is made from but the fasteners holding it together.

This weakness manifests itself in various ways. First, because they are made from many different pieces, and in particular because so many plank seams are permanently submerged, plank-on-frame boats are apt to leak. Many are continually taking on water when afloat, and normally the only variable is the rate at which water is coming aboard. Invariably this increases when conditions get worse. I once sailed across the North Atlantic aboard a plank-on-frame schooner—one time we almost sank; the other time we did (though, fortunately, this was in a river on the other side). Prior to the voyage, a friend warned me: "A wood boat is nothing but a collection of leaks loosely organized as a hull." Nothing in my experience proved him wrong.

Plank-on-frame boats also often have deck leaks. The problem here is that wood in the deck is constantly swelling and shrinking as it gets wet and dries out. If the deck has open seams, all this expanding and contracting is apt to create gaps somewhere. Even with painted canvas covering the seams, or with a solid plywood deck sealed in epoxy, there are again many fasteners securing hardware, each offering a potential route for water intrusion. Other structures sprouting from the deck—deckhouses, hatches, raised gunwales, etc.—also present seams

Open seams on a carvel-plank hull awaiting caulking. Note the tufts of cotton hanging out where caulking is underway. (Courtesy of Rockport Marine)

and cracks where they join the deck that water can eventually seep through.

Finally, plank-on-frame boats are a bear to maintain. All that wood, above the water and below, needs to be either painted or varnished on a regular basis. Leaks must be policed and stanched if possible. Moist areas in the structure must be sought out, constantly monitored for rot, and replaced if the rot gets out of hand. As Bernard Moitessier once put it: "The maintenance of my wooden boats had always confronted me with delicate problems and required real qualifications, for I had to be 'Doctor of Rot,' 'Doctor of Teredos' and 'Doctor of Leaks.'" Some people enjoy this sort of work and anxiety. Most, however, like Moitessier, would much rather just go sailing.

Wood-Epoxy Construction

Plank-on-frame boats still have a strong cult following, and a relatively large number of older wooden

yachts are sailed and maintained by devoted owners. Some new plank-on-frame yachts are also built from time to time, and a few boatyards—the most prominent are probably Gannon & Benjamin on Martha's Vineyard and Rockport Marine in Maine—even specialize in this sort of work. But the most exciting wooden boatbuilding these days is done with composite wood-epoxy construction.

The key ingredient is modern epoxy, which is not only a tenacious adhesive, but also highly elastic and nearly impermeable to water. By sealing and coating every piece of wood in a boat with epoxy, and by using epoxy to help glue these parts together (aided, too, by the judicious use of metal fasteners), it is possible to take full advantage of wood's structural properties while negating its tendencies to rot and swell and contract when exposed to water. Epoxy also protects the wood from hungry creatures that want to eat it. Furthermore, a wood-epoxy hull forms a one-piece monocoque structure that cannot leak unless punctured. In most cases, to improve abrasion and impact resistance, the hull and deck are also sheathed in one or more layers of fiberglass cloth. The result is a boat with many of the virtues of fiberglass, with the added benefits of built-in insulation, plus all the fuzzy romantic feelings inspired by a genuine wood finish.

There are many ways to construct a wood-epoxy boat. One could, for example, build a wood-epoxy plank-on-frame vessel, but this would be labor intensive and the boat would be needlessly heavy and thick. In practice, there are three basic approaches—strip-plank construction, sheet plywood construction, and so-called cold-molded construction. Each has many variations, and to some extent different techniques can be combined in a single hull.

In a simple strip-plank hull the frame is an important part of the structure, and the strip planks, which are narrow with a square section shape, are both attached to the frame and edge-nailed to each other. Boats were often built like this in the traditional manner (and are still built) without being encapsulated in epoxy. In more modern variations, there is more reliance on epoxy, fiberglass sheathing, and internal accommodations structures (including bulkheads) to support the hull, with framing reduced to a minimum. Some of these vessels are essentially fiberglass boats with solid wood cores. Strip-planked wood-epoxy hulls are probably the most common type built today, as they are generally the most cost effective.

Sheet plywood construction is the least common type, at least as far as larger sailboats go. Mostly this technique is used for smaller boats like dinghies, skiffs, and daysailers. The one major exception are Wharram catamarans, which are usually built of

Larry Pardey watering Taleisin's *deck to keep the planks swollen tight. Larry is a master boatwright (he built* Taleisin *himself) and maintains his boats scrupulously.*

plywood, and may or may not be coated in epoxy. In a plywood boat of any size, a substantial amount of framing is needed, but construction otherwise is relatively simple and fast, as large sheets of plywood can be set in place more easily and quickly than many narrow planks. Plywood construction does limit design options. Normally plywood hulls are hard-chined, although lapstrake construction—as seen, for example, in some very interesting Dutch Waarschip designs—can also be employed.

The third major variation, cold-molded construction, is more properly described as diagonal-veneer construction. Here the hull is composed of several layers of thin wood veneers that are laid up on a diagonal bias over light framing or a jig. The layers of veneer are oriented at right angles to each other and are glued together and stapled in place until the epoxy sets up. Often there are one or more layers also oriented laterally at a 45-degree angle to the diagonal layers. By laminating thin sheets of unidirectional veneer atop one another like this, a light monocoque structure that is strong in multiple directions can be created. These cold-molded boats

are, generally speaking, the lightest of wood boats, but this method of wood construction is also by far the most labor intensive. The technique is shunned by some, but is favored by those for whom weight reduction is critical. It is also sometimes used in conjunction with strip-planking, with layers of diagonal veneer laminated over a planked hull in place of fiberglass sheathing.

The term *cold-molded* is something of an historical anomaly. The first laminated wood hulls were composed of veneers laid up in female molds and glued together with adhesives that could only cure in an oven. The expression "cold-molded" was born later when it became possible to use adhesives that cure at room temperature. The term is still used to describe diagonal-veneer hulls, but not other types. Technically speaking, any wood-epoxy hull laid up at room temperature can be said to have been cold-molded.

Whatever they are called, wood-epoxy vessels in fact make superb cruising boats. The only problem is that wood-epoxy construction does not lend itself to series production. If you want a new wood-epoxy

Wood-epoxy construction, with diagonal veneers, of an Islander 65 catamaran (designed by James Wharram) in Asia. (Courtesy of James Wharram)

boat, you must commission its creation as a one-off, and many people with money to burn have done just that. Many modern wood-epoxy boats are based on traditional designs but take full advantage of modern design and construction techniques to minimize weight and maximize performance. Others are full-out modern superyachts measuring over 100 feet in length and a few are flat-out race boats. For example, Bruce Schwab's radical Open 60 *OceanPlanet* was a wood-epoxy boat. So, too, was *Holger Danske*, an early BOC boat designed by Dave Gerr that had a phenomenally low displacement/length ratio of 40. As far as I know, this is the lowest D/L ratio ever achieved in an ocean-racing monohull, which gives some idea of just how cutting-edge wood-epoxy can be.

Wood-epoxy boats can also be found on the used-boat market. Recently built boats are relatively rare and command a significant premium, but older boats, some dating back to the early 1970s, are often quite affordable. Be sure to have them carefully surveyed, however, as construction techniques have improved considerably in recent years. As with any older boat, there will likely be problems that need addressing.

METAL BOATS

Metal has been used in shipbuilding for about 150 years, and very large yachts were built in steel as early as the late 19th century. In 1895, for example, Nat Herreshoff designed and constructed a radical 123-foot composite metal sloop, *Defender*, to defend the America's Cup. She was built of aluminum, bronze, and steel and within six years was so debilitated by galvanic corrosion she had to be broken up. It wasn't until the 1960s (with the exception of some boats built in Holland, where steel has long been a favored material) that metal was used to build sailboats of moderate size. Bernard Moitessier, an early pioneer, commissioned the construction of his 40-foot steel ketch *Joshua* in 1961. By the middle of the decade, aluminum was also being used to build both racing and cruising boats. By the mid-1970s, aluminum was the favored construction material in America's Cup boats (the first was *Courageous*, built in 1974) and remained so until the mid-1980s.

These days race boats are rarely built of metal, though it is still popular with certain cruisers. For those tired of chasing down deck leaks on wood or fiberglass boats, one big attraction of an all-metal boat is that it is very tight. The hull-deck joint is welded, and all hardware such as cleats, genoa tracks, stanchion bases, etc., can be welded in place, with no fasteners penetrating the structure. Instead of leaks, however, one must worry about corrosion.

Pound for pound metal is far stronger than wood or fiberglass. Unlike wood and glass, which have most of their strength oriented along the lay of their grain or fibers, metal is also entirely isotropic and is equally strong in all directions. Metal is so tough one needn't worry about wasting strength because of this, and much trouble is saved because the material can be laid down any which way. In a wood or glass boat, by comparison, designers and builders must always take care to ensure that material is aligned along anticipated load paths.

The skin of a metal boat must be kept quite thin or the boat will be too heavy. The thin skin, in turn,

Look Ma, no deck leaks! One huge advantage of metal boats is that deck hardware can be welded rather than fastened in place. This cleat is strong enough to lift the 39-foot aluminum boat it is installed on.

must be completely supported by a frame or it will flex too much. The traditional approach is transverse framing similar to that found in plank-on-frame boats. There is a backbone keel with a large number of transverse frames attached to it, plus thin lateral stringers to hold them together. The alternative is longitudinal framing, where fewer but much larger ring frames are joined together by a large number of stringers. The advantage of transverse framing is that smaller, more closely spaced frames intrude less on the boat's interior than do bulkier ring frames. A transverse frame, however, takes more work to put together, as there are more frames that need to be cut to shape. Whatever type of framing is used, it is always much easier (and less expensive) to build a hard-chined hull. It certainly is not impossible to create a true round-bilged metal hull, but it does take more effort. A compromise shape is seen in radius-bilge hulls where the corners are knocked off a hard-chine hull and replaced with large radiused angles.

A metal boat must also be well insulated. Metal conducts both sound and heat very well, and living inside an uninsulated hull would be nothing less than an ordeal. The boat's interior would be much too cold when it's cold out, much too hot when it's warm out, you'd be up to your eyeballs in condensation, and every little sound on deck or in the water around you would be greatly amplified, as though you had your head inside a vast tin drum. The most common types of insulation are foam, cork, and fiberglass, which are available in sheets that can be cut and laid in place between the frames. Alternatively, urethane foam can be sprayed onto a hull's interior surface. Fiberglass is the most fire-resistant insulation; urethane foam is the least fire-resistant and also absorbs odors easily. Whatever type is used, insulation should never be laid down in a metal boat's bilges where it will inevitably get wet.

To avoid the awful fate of *Defender* different metals on a metal boat must be carefully isolated from each other. This is always the case, of course, but on a metal boat it is particularly important as one of the metal parts that need protecting is the hull itself. In theory this is simple; in practice it can be difficult and requires constant vigilance. Any bronze seacocks, winches, or other hardware—not to mention the vast universe of stainless-steel hardware and fasteners found on all modern boats, or the intricate web of copper wiring that comprises an electrical system—must all be isolated from the hull by nonmetallic spacers and inserts, insulating grease, plastic sheathing, etc., in order to ensure that no galvanic couples are created. Zinc anodes must be scrupulously maintained. Electrical wiring must be carefully organized—with a galvanic isolator or,

Transverse framing for a metal boat under construction. Note the thin lateral stringers holding the transverse frames together. Longitudinal framing, with larger ring frames, is easier, but bulkier. (Courtesy of Billy Black)

A hard-chined aluminum cruising boat. It looks a bit clunkier, but a hard-chined metal hull is easier to construct than a round-bilged metal hull.

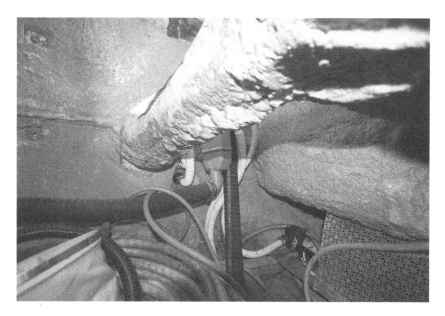

Sprayed-on urethane foam insulation in an aluminum boat. Foam is easy to install, but is not fire-resistant and it also absorbs odors.

better, an isolation transformer on the shore-power side—to protect the boat from stray electrical currents. A strong dose of stray current can chew up a metal boat in just a few days.

A handful of European builders construct metal boats on a series production basis; otherwise, like wood boats, they are built as one-offs. Metal is usually the cheapest material to work with when building just one boat. This, plus the fact that metal boats are so strong, means there will always be a cult of metal-boat cruisers. As mentioned, most acolytes are found in Europe. There are a few metal boat builders in North America (mostly in Canada), and there is always a small selection of metal boats available on the North American brokerage market, but the heart of the market will always lie on the eastern shores of the North Atlantic.

Steel

Steel is heavy and strong, but is also hard, and working it requires heavy-duty grinding and cutting tools. Cutting and welding steel is laborious, but the welding is not sophisticated and is a relatively easy skill to acquire. Most of all, steel is subject to rusting. Put it in contact with water and oxygen—two things that are never hard to find in the marine environment—and it starts corroding at an alarming rate. Add a little salt, and things only get worse.

Paint, paint, and more paint is the only answer. Bernard Moitessier liked to boast that a well-trained monkey could do this, but to maintain a steel boat properly you need a busy monkey. Modern paint systems are durable and reliable, and if a steel boat is properly prepped and painted as it is built, and

if it is designed so that all parts of its interior are accessible to a paintbrush, it is possible to keep the rust at bay indefinitely. But the bottom line is you will always be painting a steel boat, both inside and out, or will be worrying about painting it.

Because steel is so heavy, it is not possible to build a small- to moderate-size steel sailboat that performs very well. To sail fast, relatively speaking, you need a steel boat at least 100 feet long. Any steel vessel shorter than 60 feet should have its deck and superstructure built of another lighter material to keep it from getting too top-heavy. In older steel yachts this was common. The problem, however, is that you then don't have the leakproof deck that makes a metal boat seem so attractive in the first place. And all those deck leaks, of course, only help things inside start rusting more quickly.

Most contemporary steel boats, whatever their size, have steel decks. Because steel is hard and stiff and difficult to work, they often have simple shapes and hard-chine hulls. Such boats are cheap and easy to build, and home-built examples aren't hard to find on the used-boat market. If you don't care about performance, are willing to do a lot of painting, and want a boat that is incredibly tough, an all-steel boat is an excellent choice. Otherwise, particularly if you are a coastal cruiser, you'd do well to stay away from these.

Aluminum

Aluminum is weaker than steel by a factor of about 1.5 (i.e., to be as strong as steel, aluminum plate must be 1.5 times thicker), but it is also lighter by a factor of almost 3 (i.e., it weighs $\frac{1}{3}$ as much). So the bottom line is simple: an aluminum object that is as strong as an equivalent steel object weighs only half as much. On a purely structural basis, aluminum therefore makes an excellent boatbuilding material.

Aluminum is also much softer than steel, so is easier to work with. It can be cut, drilled, and shaped with common woodworking tools and can be more easily tortured into complex forms. Best of all, it doesn't rust (but is prone to corrosion, see below). Put it in contact with water and oxygen and it forms a thin oxide layer on its surface that makes it even stronger and more corrosion-resistant. No painting is required except below the waterline, where antifouling is still needed to keep life-forms from latching on. (Generally, though, it is also wise to paint an aluminum boat's decks some light color to reflect solar radiation and help keep the interior cool.)

Aluminum is considerably more expensive than steel. Commodity prices of course fluctuate, but on a strict per-pound basis, steel is usually about five times cheaper. Though you need only half as many pounds to make an equivalent aluminum boat, you'll still be spending two-and-a-half times as much on materials. This is offset to a large extent by the fact that it takes about half as many man-hours to weld an aluminum hull and deck. Still an aluminum boat, all told, costs roughly 5% to 15% more to build than a steel one.

Though it takes less time, it also takes more skill to build an aluminum boat. Welding aluminum is a sophisticated process requiring special gas-shielded equipment. Ideally, all work should be performed indoors in a well-protected environment. As a result, you almost never see home-built aluminum boats. Also, appropriate marine-grade aluminum (5054, 5083, and 5086 are the best alloys for a hull) is hard to find outside the United States and Europe, as are qualified welders, so making permanent repairs in remote locations is difficult, if not impossible. A steel boat, by comparison, can be repaired almost anywhere in the world.

The biggest drawback to aluminum is that it is highly susceptible to both galvanic and stray-current corrosion. It is low on the galvanic scale and wastes away quickly when placed in contact with salt water and more noble metals like stainless steel, bronze, and copper. Different metals must be carefully isolated, and bilges must be kept clean and dry to prevent the inadvertent creation of galvanic couples. Something like a lost coin or camera battery might literally sink the boat someday. Zincs must also be scrupulously maintained, and stringent precautions must be taken to ensure no stray electrical current comes aboard.

Otherwise, a properly designed aluminum boat is fast, strong, easy to maintain, and thus a good choice for cruising. Again, unfortunately, they are relatively hard to come by in North America.

Welding aluminum requires special equipment and should be performed indoors. Most aluminum boats are professionally constructed and cost 5% to 15% more to build than steel boats. (Courtesy of Kanter Yachts)

A few used examples can usually be found on the brokerage market, and one French builder, Alubat, recently began marketing series-built aluminum cruising boats in the United States. These, however, are quite expensive compared to mass-produced fiberglass boats. Alubat's bilge-centerboard designs, though comfortable and well thought out, are also quite idiosyncratic by American standards, and are apt to appeal only to more open-minded sailors.

FERROCEMENT BOATS

Ferrocement construction dates back to the mid-19th century and is still occasionally used today, but is largely discredited. It involves yet another composite building material, except here the binding substance is cement and the matrix supporting it is a metal frame and armature made of steel pipes and/or rods and several layers of wire mesh. For a brief period, during the 1960s and '70s, ferrocement construction was hailed as a panacea for amateur builders who wanted to head off on long cruises. Because no special skills are required to build a ferrocement hull, and because wire mesh, steel rods, and cement are all readily available, there was a great boom in cement boat building. Many of these backyard projects were abandoned. Many others were completed, but the boats they produced quickly disintegrated due to poor construction techniques. A few better-built boats survived and are still afloat today. Several different cement boats have also been professionally built over the years. As far as I know, however, cement boats have never been manufactured on a series production basis.

The process of building a ferrocement hull seems almost fantastic. First a keel and transverse frames are built out of pipe or rod. Rod is much better, as condensation can corrode the interior of hollow piping. If pipes are used, they should be filled with grout or something similar to prevent this. This frame is then covered inside and out with multiple layers (eight is the recommended number) of wire mesh. These layers must all be tightly bound together with thousands of little wire ties so that they form a single unitary surface.

Once all the wire work is complete, the structure is then plastered with cement. The cement must be packed all the way through the entwined layers of wire mesh so there are no voids. The plastering should be performed all in one go, ideally in a day or less. The entire plastered structure then should be kept wet for about a month so the cement can cure properly and achieve maximum strength and impermeability. This is accomplished by draping the curing hull with perforated water hoses. After the hull has been fully cured and has dried out, a wood deck and interior can then be installed.

Ferrocement boats are quite heavy. If not built properly they also quickly start falling apart. For example, if the steel frame and armature are not strong enough, the hull will be much too brittle and may crack open under its own weight. Also, a strong barrier coating of some kind is needed, for if the frame and armature ever get wet and start corroding, they will expand and cause *spalling*, wherein chunks of cement start flaking off the hull. One must also guard against galvanic corrosion and ensure that the steel frame and armature never come in contact with other metals.

Ferrocement boats, if properly constructed, are strong. Used boats can also be incredibly cheap. It is not unusual to see completely equipped sailboats over 50 feet long selling for well under $100,000; boats under 40 feet sometimes go for as little as $10,000. For cruisers on small budgets, they can seem tempting. A few well-built ferrocement boats have lasted many years, and the best ones are flawlessly finished. Any prospects should be carefully surveyed by someone well versed in the details of cement construction (though such persons are not be easy to find). You should also not expect much in the way of resale value. If it comes to that, you might do better if you strip off the rig, hardware, and mechanical equipment, sell them separately, and throw the hull away.

FOUR

SAILS AND RIGGING

One of the most important differences between racing and cruising sailors is that cruisers can afford to be much more ambivalent about the business of actually sailing their boats. Racing sailors must be acutely interested in how well a boat sails and must always be attuned to its sails and rigging. Cruisers are often mere slackers in comparison. In extreme cases, they are oblivious to the process of sailing and rely instead on their engines to get them everywhere. I've met cruisers like this and have wondered why they own sailboats in the first place. Indeed, one friend of mine who rarely raises his sails—a successful author and cruising columnist—once confessed to me he longed to trade in his ketch for a trawler yacht. The only problem was his editor wouldn't permit it.

In less extreme cases, a cruiser may sail his or her boat quite a bit, yet still know relatively little about the science and art of sailing. You see people like this fairly often, dawdling along the coast with old, shapeless sails that are way out of trim. They may be enjoying themselves immensely, but they would enjoy themselves all the more if they learned to sail their boats more efficiently. At the other extreme there are cruisers who are just as attuned to their sails and rigging as any serious racing sailor. People like this range from anachronistic types who cruise without engines to hardcore racing sailors who like to take off and anchor out from time to time.

Most contemporary cruisers are more intermediate types. They are very interested in sailing and take pleasure in doing it well, but also want to balance the demands of performance and convenience. One reason racing sailors spend so much time tweaking

sails is that usually there are many more sailors onboard ready, willing, and able to do the tweaking. Most cruising crews, by comparison, are small. They must weigh the effort required to constantly optimize sail shape and trim against the actual reward achieved. Crossing a finish line five minutes earlier means everything to a racer; dropping anchor in a cove somewhere five minutes earlier is normally meaningless to a cruiser. Small performance advantages are therefore willingly sacrificed for ease of sail handling. Larger advantages are another issue. Some cruisers will seriously compromise a boat's performance to save themselves from having to touch their sails. Others will not. Each cruiser, in the end, arrives at a unique compromise and develops unique prejudices as to the best way to rig and sail his or her cruising sailboat.

BASIC RIG TYPES

Almost all sailing rigs on modern yachts are variations of the Marconi, or Bermudan, rig. This is a fore-and-aft rig (as opposed to a transversely mounted square rig) with triangular sails and a relatively light mast held tightly in column by its standing rigging. The term Marconi, as mentioned in Chapter 1, refers to the structure of the mast and its standing rig, which were borrowed from the tall, light, wire-stayed Marconi radio towers that first appeared during the 1920s. The term Bermudan refers to the first commonly used triangular "leg-of-mutton" sails that appeared on some West Indian vessels, but primarily on Bermudan vessels, in the 19th century.

This cruiser may have his sails up, but it's clear he decided a while back he doesn't care too much about performance. Removing the mizzenmast from a heavy ketch is a sure way to slow the boat down, though it does open up a lot of space on the aft deck.

In most cases the foot of the mainsail in a modern Marconi rig is supported by a boom, the forward end of which is attached to the mast with a fitting called a gooseneck. The entire length of the sail's leading edge, called its luff, is held firmly to the mast via a track of some sort; the length of its foot may also be held to its boom by a track, or may instead be left "loose-footed," in which case it is attached only at the sail's forward lower corner, called the tack, and at the aft lower corner, called the clew. The entire back edge of the sail, called the leech, flies free, though it is often supported by lightweight battens that are sewn into the sail itself.

The Marconi rig is configured to present its sails to the wind as properly formed airfoils (just as a modern fin keel is presented to the water as an efficient hydrofoil) and thus is capable of generating lots of lift to improve windward performance. In the days of long keels and gaff rigs it seemed impossible to sail to windward at anything better than a 50-degree angle. These days, however, with their Marconi rigs and high-aspect fin keels, high-performance race boats can achieve angles as tight as 20 degrees. And even the pokiest cruising boat is considered something of a dog if it can't point as high as 45 degrees.

Sloops and Cutters

By far the most popular rig on modern yachts is the simple sloop rig. This has a single mast supporting a single Marconi mainsail with a single headsail supported by a single headstay flying forward of it. There are only two sails for the crew to handle, each of which can be hoisted with a single halyard and trimmed with a single sheet. Thus, while sailing, there are normally only two lines—the jibsheet and mainsheet—that need to be controlled at any given moment. Because there is but one headsail flying forward of the main, tacking a sloop is easy since the headsail, even if it is a large overlapping genoa, can pass easily through the open foretriangle.

Sloop rigs are quite efficient to windward, thanks to the so-called slot effect created by the interaction of the mainsail and headsail. How this actually works is

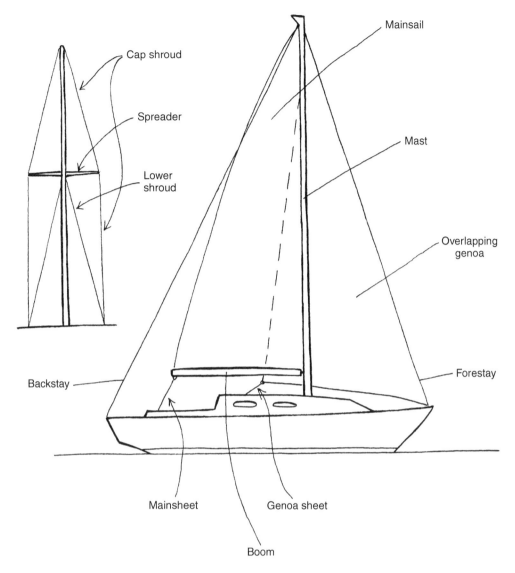

Cap shroud

Spreader

Lower shroud

Backstay

Mainsail

Mast

Overlapping genoa

Forestay

Mainsheet

Genoa sheet

Boom

A modern sloop rig and its standing rigging. This is the most common rig seen on today's cruising sailboats.

a matter of some debate. The traditional theory is that airflow in the narrow slot between the sails is accelerated, which decreases air pressure on the leeward side of the mainsail, thus increasing the lift the sail generates. The revisionist theory is that air deflected from the headsail actually works to decrease airflow in the slot, increasing pressure on the windward side of the headsail, thus increasing the lift it generates. Since increasing the lift generated by one sail seems to necessarily decrease that generated by the other, others believe a single Marconi sail must be just as aerodynamic, if not more so, than two sails. This last proposition, however, is contradicted by real-world experience, as no one has yet created a single-sail rig that is as fast and close-winded as a double-sail sloop rig.

The primary disadvantage of a sloop rig is that the sails must be relatively large. They are therefore harder to handle in that they are heavier (making

them harder to hoist) and generate larger loads when flying. Much of this difficulty, however, is obviated by modern winches and roller-furling gear, which is why sloop rigs are now so popular, and deservedly so. In light to moderate sailing conditions, which is what most sailors normally encounter, a sloop is by far the fastest, most easily handled rig currently available.

In heavier conditions sloops present some challenges. To reduce sail area forward of the mast, if the headsail is hanked onto the headstay, which was the traditional practice, you must change the sail for a smaller one. This requires crew to work for extended periods on the bow of the boat, where conditions can get wild and wet. If the headsail is on a modern roller-furler, the sail can be easily roller-reefed from the cockpit, but past a certain point a roller-reefed headsail's shape becomes inefficient. You must either

A modern sloop with an overlapping genoa beating to weather. Note the slot between the genoa and mainsail. For reasons we don't quite understand, two sails always work better than one.

live with this or unroll the sail and change it for another smaller one. The stronger the wind gets, the more distorted the roller-reefed sail becomes, and the more important it is to change it. Changing a sail on a furler in a strong wind, however, is an awful chore. The very first thing you must do (unroll the sail) greatly increases sail area right when you most want to decrease it. Then you must somehow control a large headsail as it comes off a furling rod in high winds, as the luff of the sail is unrestrained.

Coastal cruisers are never likely to sail in strong conditions for very long. On the few brief occasions their boats are pressed hard they are normally willing to limp along on an ugly scrap of roller-reefed genoa. They are also more likely to have to short-tack their boats in confined areas, thus the ease of tacking a sloop makes it the rig of choice on coastal boats. Bluewater cruisers, on the other hand, may sail in strong weather for days on end, so there are advantages to cutting up the sail area in the foretriangle into smaller, more manageable pieces. Bluewater cruisers

therefore often prefer a cutter rig, which has a single mast and a headstay like a sloop, but also an inner forestay behind the headstay from which a smaller intermediate staysail can be flown.

The big advantage of a cutter rig is that in a big blow the jib on the headstay can come right off (or be rolled up) and the smaller staysail can carry on alone, more inboard and lower in the rig, where it balances better against the reduced area of a deeply reefed mainsail. Cutters are also efficient to windward, though some claim they are less so than sloops. I've found cutters are sometimes more close-winded than sloops, at least in moderate to strong winds, as the sheeting angles on a pair of smaller, flatter headsails can be narrower than the angle on one larger, more full-bodied sail. In very heavy conditions, with just a staysail and reefed mainsail deployed, I believe a cutter is almost always more efficient to windward than a sloop.

A cutter is also good on a beam reach, as both headsails can fly unobstructed. Sailing on a broad

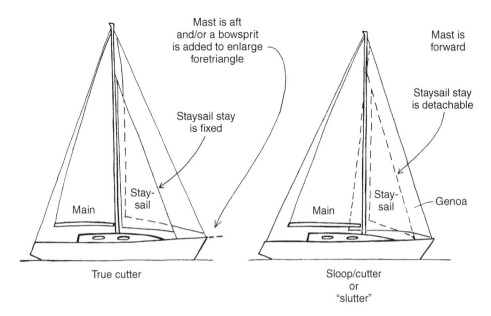

A true cutter rig (left) with a large foretriangle and a fixed staysail and a sloop/cutter or "slutter" rig (right) with a smaller foretriangle and a detachable inner forestay.

reach, however, the staysail blocks air from reaching the jib, reducing the rig's effective sail area just when the decrease in apparent wind speed caused by the wind blowing from behind the boat demands that sail area instead be increased. Another problem is that a cutter requires extra standing rigging—not only the inner forestay, but also, very often, either an extra set of swept-back aft shrouds or a pair of running backstays to help support the inner forestay from behind. This adds complexity and increases rig weight well above the deck.

The biggest disadvantage of a cutter rig is that there are two headsails to tack (or jibe) across the boat instead of just one. There is an extra set of sheets to handle, plus the jib quarrels with the inner forestay every time it comes across the foretriangle. This is less of a problem if the jib is small and high-cut (these are called yankee jibs) so that it slips more easily through the narrow gap between the inner forestay and headstay. When flying a large genoa, however, crew must often go forward to help horse the sail around the inner forestay. If you don't have enough crew for this, you may have to roll up part of the genoa (assuming it's on a roller-furler) before tacking or jibing and unroll it again afterward, which is a bother. Also, if the wind grows strong again, but not so strong that you can sail on the staysail alone, you have to either change your genoa for a smaller sail or roller-reef it into an inefficient shape, which is (theoretically) precisely the conundrum that drove you to favor a cutter rig in the first place.

On a true cutter specifically designed to accommodate a staysail, the mast is usually farther aft than it would be on a sloop and/or there is a bowsprit to enlarge the foretriangle. This allows for a larger, more useful staysail and should enlarge the gap between the headstay and inner forestay so a jib can tack through more easily. A larger foretriangle also allows the jib to be larger without overlapping the mainsail, but a big overlapping genoa will still present problems when tacking or jibing.

The staysail can also be made club-footed with its own boom. Such a spar, known as a jibboom, can be controlled by a single sheet that need not be adjusted when tacking. When short-tacking in enough breeze for the boat to sail under main and staysail alone this is the height of convenience. You can shift the helm back and forth without ever touching a line. A jibboom, however, unless sheeted tight, will flail about the foredeck whenever its sail is luffing while being hoisted, doused, or reefed. It may harm crew on the foredeck during an accidental jibe, as it can sweep suddenly across the boat with some force unless restrained by a preventer.

Bear in mind, too, that enlarging the foretriangle, particularly on a boat without a bowsprit, usually means mainsail area must be reduced commensurately. In many cases the mainsail is then too small and/or too far aft for the boat to sail and maneuver under main alone. When attempting to dock, anchor, or moor under sail this can be a significant disadvantage. (Note, however, that many sloops are also often unable to maneuver under mainsail alone.)

The author's cutter Sophie *flying a large genoa and staysail. It was difficult getting the genoa around the staysail when tacking so normally a high-cut yankee jib was flown on the headstay instead.*

Another variation increasingly popular with bluewater cruisers is a sloop/cutter hybrid, sometimes called a slutter rig, where a removable inner forestay is installed on what would otherwise be a straight sloop rig. The removable stay normally has some sort of quick-release mechanism at deck level that makes it easy to set up and tension the stay and to loosen and remove it. When stowed, the removable stay is brought aft to the mast and secured.

To a large extent, the slutter rig does offer the best of both worlds. In light to moderate winds you can stow the inner forestay and sail the boat as a straight sloop with one large genoa passing through an open foretriangle. In heavy conditions, you can set up the inner forestay, hank on a staysail, roll up or douse the large genoa, and sail the boat under main and staysail alone. Since setting up an inner forestay and hanking on a staysail is normally less taxing than stripping a large genoa off a furling rod and hoisting a smaller working jib and/or storm sail in its place, this is a viable practice.

Sometimes you see true cutters that have been converted to slutters. Here the foretriangle is normally large enough to fly two headsails simultaneously if desired, which is often not possible on a converted sloop. The downside to this arrangement is that making the inner forestay removable makes it impossible to install either a roller-furling staysail (currently a popular arrangement on cutter rigs) or a club-footed staysail.

A staysail has just been hanked onto the removable inner forestay and is ready to hoist. The genoa forward can be furled if necessary.

Converting a Sloop to a Slutter

Adding an inner forestay on a sloop is a popular upgrade, particularly on bluewater boats. Being able to hoist a staysail can also be handy on a coastal boat. I once owned a sloop that I converted to a cutter rig with a removable inner forestay (it became a true cutter, as I also increased the height of the mast and added a bowsprit to enlarge the foretriangle), and this enabled me to fly two different sets of headsails during different parts of the sailing season. In the early spring and late fall when the wind was boisterous I set up the inner forestay, hoisted a yankee on the roller-furling headstay, and so was always prepared to sail, even when the breeze was blowing dogs off their chains. During the heart of the season, when the wind was light to moderate, I put away the inner forestay, bent a large 130% genoa onto the headstay, and sailed the boat as a straight sloop.

If you'd like to convert your sloop to a slutter (or even a true cutter), or if you are pondering buying an already converted boat, there are a few key points to consider.

Structural issues. The point where the inner forestay is attached to the deck must be supported from inside the boat so the deck can resist the load on the stay when you hoist the sail. Often there is an appropriately positioned bulkhead under the deck to which you can fasten a deck-piercing chainplate or tang. Any such bulkhead should be properly tabbed and bonded to the hull. The deck core must also be sealed against moisture intrusion where it is penetrated by any hardware.

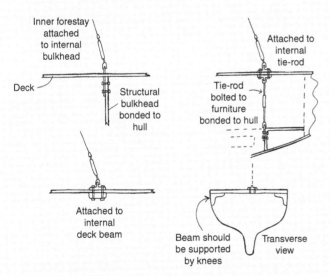

Examples of inner forestay installations. Loads on the stay must ultimately be transferred to the hull.

If no bulkhead is available, you need to create some alternative support for the new stay. The most common approach is to install a tie-rod between the underside of the deck where the stay lands and some structural component of the boat's interior, usually a bulkhead or piece of furniture that is itself securely bonded to the hull. Such tie-rods, however, often land in the middle of a double V-berth, which may interfere with conjugal relations aboard. Another option is to glass in a deck beam with generous knees at either end to help transfer the load to the hull. You can through-bolt the attachment for the stay to the beam.

Positioning and sizing the staysail. When deciding where to place an inner forestay in relation to a headstay, you should consider the distance between the two, whether they are parallel or not (purely an aesthetic concern), and the desired size of the staysail. The greater the distance between the stays, the easier it will be to tack a jib around the inner stay; the shorter the distance, the bigger the staysail can be. As a general rule, a staysail is not an effective working sail (as opposed to a mere stormsail) unless its area is equal to about 20% of the total working sail area.

This usually requires a delicate balancing of priorities, depending on the size of the foretriangle. On many sloops there isn't room for a decent-size staysail unless you accept that you won't normally be flying both headsails simultaneously. Alternatively, you can enlarge the area of the foretriangle, as I did in my conversion. In any event, it is best not to seriously compromise the size of the staysail, as it won't get used much if it is no bigger than a storm jib.

Running and standing rigging. If you enlarge the foretriangle there may be room for a staysail on a jibboom, which greatly simplifies sheeting arrangements. Furthermore, the single line needed to control the jib-boom can be rove through a block and tackle, so that no winch is required to sheet it home. As mentioned, the sail will be self-tacking, but the inner forestay in this case should be set up permanently.

If the staysail is loose-footed, without a boom, the inner forestay can be removable, but there must be sheet leads for the staysail on both sides of the deck. If you have confidence in your sailmaker's ability to predict where the leads will land, you can install single sheet blocks on either side, but it's better to install cars on short inboard tracks (these often end up somewhere on the coachroof) so that you can fine-tune the leads. If you know you will never fly a jib and staysail simultaneously, you can use one set of primary winches in the cockpit to handle both sets of sheets. Otherwise, you need a set of secondary winches for sheeting home the staysail.

As for the top of the inner forestay, if it is fastened to the mast at or near a point supported by a pair of aft lower shrouds, you need not install running backstays to help support it. Some riggers I consulted when I was

(continued)

The staysail sheet leads on my converted cutter Sophie *were fixed in place. They served well enough, but adjustable cars on tracks would have worked much better.*

converting my rig suggested running backs are unnecessary in any event. They argued that back-loading on the mast from the mainsail offsets the front-loading from a staysail. This makes sense, but if you want to be able to douse the main and run off under a staysail alone, it is best to somehow back up the inner forestay.

The alternative to running backstays, if no existing aft lowers are opportunely placed, is a new pair of permanent swept-back aft shrouds. This means installing a pair of dedicated chainplates for the shrouds at deck level, which is a project in itself. Running backs are much easier to install, but are a pain to use. They should be set up on deck farther aft than permanent shrouds and must be cast off and set up

again on the windward side of the boat each time you tack or jibe. As you reef the main, however, it should at some point be possible (usually after two reefs) to leave both running backs set up permanently, as they will then clear the head of the main. On deck the running backs can be set up on any reasonable strong point near the back of the boat—on a perforated toe rail, say, or on a pair of well-backed stern cleats.

As for a halyard for the staysail, in most cases it is easiest to install an external block just below the tang fitting for the inner forestay on the mast and reeve a new halyard through this. In some cases, however, there may already be a topping lift for a spinnaker pole on the mast that you can also use as a staysail halyard.

Split Rigs

The term split rig refers to any sail plan where sail area is divided between two masts, rather than crowded on one mast, as with a sloop or cutter. There are three basic types: ketches, yawls, and schooners. On ketches and yawls the taller mainmast is forward and the shorter mizzenmast is aft. On a yawl the mizzenmast is aft of the rudder and is rather short; on a ketch it is forward of the rudder and significantly taller.

In a classic schooner rig, the taller mainmast is aft and the shorter foremast is forward. On some schooners, however, the masts may be the same height.

For many years it was axiomatic that a split rig must be best for a cruising boat, as it divides the sail plan into smaller, more easily managed components. This was certainly true on older, more traditional boats in the days before modern winches, most particularly on gaff-rigged boats where the added

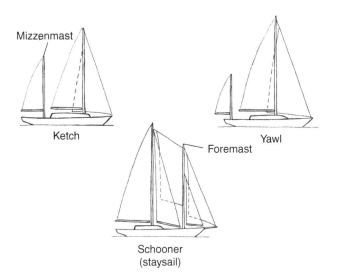

Split rig profiles. The mizzen on a ketch is forward of the rudder (not shown); the mizzen on a yawl is abaft the rudder. Staysail schooners are the best type of schooners for cruising, but there are several other variations.

A mizzen staysail flying between a mainsail (right) and mizzensail (left)—these add a lot of extra power on both ketch and yawl rigs.

weight of a heavy gaff and the extra peak halyard required made hoisting sails that much harder. For some reason, however, this conceit survived much longer than it should have. As late as the 1970s, and even into the early 1980s, many believed a ketch rig was best for cruising, and such rigs were sometimes seen on boats as small as 30 feet. As late as the early 1990s, ketch rigs were also favored on large maxi ocean racers.

These days, however, split rigs are much less popular, particularly on boats less than 50 feet in length, for a number of reasons. First, any rig with two masts is heavier, more complex, and more expensive to create and maintain. Second, split rigs are not as close-winded as sloop rigs, primarily because turbulent "dirty" air flowing off the back of the forward sail decreases the efficiency of the aft sail. Third, innovations such as self-tailing winches, power winches, and roller-furling gear have made handling large sails in a sloop rig much easier. Fourth, modern hull and deck designs tend not to favor mizzenmasts. Rudders are now usually positioned right aft, so it is not possible to put the mizzen behind the helm, as on a yawl, and many boat buyers now favor open cockpit spaces and don't like having a mizzenmast just forward of the helm, as on most ketches. Split rigs do, however, have some important advantages and still have many adherents.

The most common split rig today is the ketch. A ketch sails well on a reach, as this makes it possible to spread maximum canvas on both masts. A key tool here is the mizzen staysail, a loose-luffed midship reaching sail hoisted on the mizzenmast, tacked down somewhere just abaft the mainmast, and sheeted to the leeward rail aft or to the end of the mizzenboom. A mizzen staysail adds a lot of power to a rig and is a great cruising sail. You can launch and recover it right from the cockpit and can still fly it with the wind a bit forward of the beam. Large ketches also sometimes fly full mizzen spinnakers, which add loads of power to a sail plan. The masts in this case need some distance between them, which also improves windward performance since the mizzensail then flies in cleaner air.

Another advantage to having two masts is that if you lose one, you have another one to keep sailing with. Some conservative bluewater sailors still favor ketches for just this reason. For this to work the rig must not have a triatic stay, which is a length of standing rigging running between the tops of the masts. A triatic stay supports the mizzenmast in normal circumstances, but brings it down if the mainmast falls, and vice versa. A ketch's mizzenmast is also a fine place to mount radomes, wind generators, and other paraphernalia favored by cruisers, although a mizzenboom also hampers (though does not prohibit) the use of a self-steering wind vane installed on the stern of a boat.

Yawls, meanwhile, are increasingly rare these days. They were popular for a time under the old CCA racing rule because the rule didn't count the extra sail area in a yawl's mizzensail and mizzen staysail. Designers have pretty much ignored the rig since then, though it is still seen on some older boats.

It is a visually attractive rig and does also have some practical advantages.

Most particularly, the mainsail on a yawl is often not any smaller than it would be on a sloop of similar size. Handling the main is therefore not any easier, but there is also no real decrease in windward sailing ability. The mizzen is normally small enough that its receiving foul air from the main is not significant, and the main meanwhile is large enough to drive the boat well on its own. Indeed, you often see yawls beating smartly to weather with their mizzens furled. On most ketches, by comparison, the mizzen is much larger and the main proportionately smaller, so that power is lost driving to windward unless the masts are well separated. On any reach the yawl's mizzen and mizzen staysail again add power to the rig, though not as much proportionately as on a ketch.

One nice thing about a yawl's mizzen is that it is far enough aft to help push the stern around. The mizzen can be used, in effect, as an air rudder to balance and even steer a boat while sailing. In close quarters, you can back a yawl's mizzen at strategic moments to help turn a boat quickly or slow it down. It makes a great riding sail and can be used to keep a boat from sailing around on its anchor or mooring. It is also easy to balance against a headsail, so you can sail a boat in strong winds under "jib and jigger alone," as the expression goes, with the mainsail furled.

The third child in this family of rigs, the venerable schooner, is certainly the most neglected. During their heyday in the 19th century schooners were used primarily as cargo and fishing boats and were close-winded compared to square-rigged vessels. By today's standards, however, they are ungainly on the wind. As discussed in Chapter 1, they briefly dominated ocean racing in the early 20th century, but were soon eclipsed by more close-winded sloops and yawls and are now entirely anachronistic. Their major drawback, aside from poor windward performance, is that their mainsails are often large and can be difficult to handle.

Yet the schooner is not extinct and probably never will be. There is an active cult of schooner aficionados who maintain gaff-rigged 19th-century working schooners and early 20th-century schooner

The author's yawl Crazy Horse *at anchor in the Cape Verdes with a reefed mizzen raised as a riding sail. The mizzen can be used to help balance and even steer the boat while sailing.*

yachts as though they were holy relics. Every once in a while, too, a brand-new schooner is built. Most of these mimic traditional designs, though there are also much more contemporary examples.

The few cruisers who still favor schooners usually prefer traditional variations. Of these, the best rig is that of a staysail schooner, so named because the working sail flown between the masts is a jib-shaped staysail bent onto a diagonal stay that runs from the foot of the foremast to an elevated spot on the mainmast. Normally this is called the main staysail, assuming there is another forestaysail forward of the foremast. Staysail schooners tend to be more close-winded than straight schooners with foresails on their foremasts, as the main staysail can be trimmed to create a slot for the mainsail behind it. They are also extremely powerful on a reach, since large midship reaching sails, called fishermen and gollywobblers, can be hoisted up the foremast above the main staysail. Another nice advantage, as I discovered many years ago when crossing the Atlantic on an old staysail schooner with decrepit sails, is that it is easy to find used headsails from other boats to use as staysails.

Gaff Rigs

The gaff rig is the more traditional fore-and-aft rig from which the Marconi rig ultimately evolved. Leaving aside headsails, it consists of two parts. The major part is the lower gaff sail, so called because its head is supported by a spar called a gaff, which is essentially an airborne boom. Because of its quadrilateral shape, a gaff sail must be raised on two halyards, one

for the throat, which is the upper forward corner of the sail (nearer the mast), and one for the peak, which is the sail's more elevated aft corner. Above this can be set the lesser part, a triangular topsail. The topsail's luff can be laced to another spar, a topsail yard, which is hoisted on one halyard with its clew sheeted to the end of the gaff below it and its foot flying loose. Or all or part of the foot may be laced to its own jack yard. On larger vessels the topsail can also be set on its own separate topmast,

In some respects a gaff sail can be quite modern. This gaff "wing sail" (a foresail in this case) on a large Wharram catamaran has a sleeve that fits around its mast to minimize turbulence, is loose-footed, and has a profile similar to many modern square-headed racing sails. (Courtesy of James Wharram)

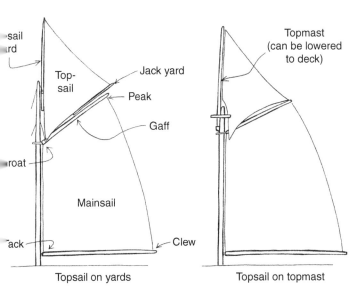

Gaff-rig variations. Topsails can be raised on yards or topmasts. Setting and striking a topsail is difficult, so modern gaff-rig cruisers often leave it off entirely.

which, with great effort, is hoisted and rigged above the main part of the mast and is taken down again when conditions warrant.

Considered together a gaff sail and topsail present to the wind a full-roached triangular form similar to that of the most modern Marconi sails. The primary difference is the unwieldy gaff, which falls off to leeward as the sails above and below it fill with air, thus spilling much wind. The rig loads are great enough that a vessel of any size still requires a lot of standing rigging to support the mast, though such rigging need not be as elaborate nor set up nearly as taut as on a Marconi-rigged boat.

Generally a gaff rig is harder to operate than a Marconi rig. Indeed, it takes some effort and skill to sail a gaff rig to its full potential. First, a rig of any size requires a pair of running backstays to support the back of the mast, as a standing backstay inevitably interferes with the gaff. The hoisting of gaffs and yards, not to mention entire topmasts, also involves a lot of work, and it takes still more work to strike these. The job is especially challenging when conditions are strong, as the solid airborne spars can slash about if the sails they are attached to start luffing much. To minimize such unpleasantness, many contemporary gaff-rig sailors don't even bother carrying topsails, much less hoisting them. The decrease in sail area, however, only causes a gaff rig to perform even more poorly compared to a Marconi rig.

Gaff rigs, if sailed to their full potential with topsails deployed, in fact perform very well on a reach or off the wind. At these angles sails need not generate lift and only need more area to create useful motive power, and gaff sails, thanks to their quadrilateral form, have a lot of extra area up high where it does the most good. To windward, however, where lift is critical, gaff sails perform poorly, since the gaff twists off to leeward. Because they lack standing backstays, the headstays on gaff-rigged boats also sag a lot going to windward, which distorts the headsail and further hurts performance. Gaff sails also have short luffs, which limits the amount of lift the sail can generate no matter how well shaped it is. Finally, gaff rigs are top-heavy due to the extra weight aloft created by the airborne spars and their running rigging.

Given that a gaff rig is more work to sail and does not perform as well as a Marconi rig, it is hard to offer compelling arguments in favor of its use as a cruising rig. Gaff rigs are more work to maintain than a Marconi rig; they are also probably nearly as expensive to create. In the end, the best reasons for favoring a gaff rig are purely emotional. Gaff-rigged vessels are evocative of the romance and tradition of sailing and seafaring, and a few traditionalists will therefore always adhere to them.

Low-Stress Rigs

For all its virtues, the Marconi rig does have certain drawbacks. Chief among these are the huge loads imposed on both the rig and hull once sails are filled with air. Because of these great loads, the hull of a Marconi-rigged boat must be overbuilt. And to maintain the rigidity that makes a Marconi rig so efficient (and that also, ironically, makes the loads so great) each of the hundreds of parts that comprise its support structure—the stays and shrouds, the terminals, the pins, the turnbuckles, the tangs, the chainplates, etc.—must all stand up to their share of the strain. If any one part fails, the whole house of cards comes tumbling down.

Most sailors, of course, are mortally afraid of losing their rigs. Only a minority, however, ever let this fear lead them to consider any of the low-stress alternatives to the Marconi rig. These alternatives, besides generating much lower loads (hence less anxiety) while sailing, are often less expensive, as they are composed of fewer parts. Most of these rigs, besides being safer and more conservative, also require much less effort to operate and maintain. Their only significant drawback is that they are not as close-winded as Marconi rigs. For cruisers who

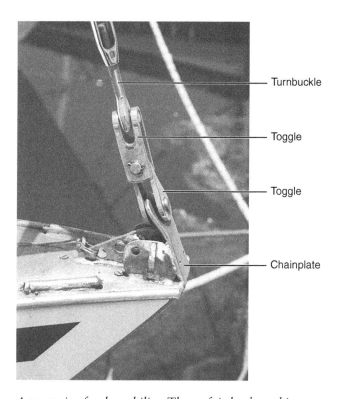

A portrait of vulnerability. The unfair lead on this headstay installation between the lower toggle and chainplate is exactly the kind of minor flaw that can lead to an unexpected failure on a Marconi rig.

avoid sailing to weather in any event and generally favor comfort and ease over speed and hard work these rigs should be considered as viable options.

Junk Rigs

The junk rig is in one sense even more archaic than the gaff rig, as it dates back well over 2,000 years, while the gaff rig is only a few hundred years old. As one early Western proponent, a British cruiser named Brian Platt, who sailed from Hong Kong to California under junk rig in the late 1950s, wrote: "Nobody could have designed the Chinese Sail, if only for fear of being laughed at. A device so elaborate and clumsy in conception, yet so simple and handy in operation could only have evolved through trial and error."

A junk rig is safer and easier to operate than either a gaff or Marconi rig, and thus deserves more attention than it currently receives. As far as we know, it was first adapted for use on a Western vessel when Joshua Slocum installed three junk sails on the 35-foot boat, *Liberdade*, that he built in Brazil in 1887 after he and his family were shipwrecked. *Liberdade* performed quite well, covering a total of 5,500 miles from Brazil to the United States in 52 sailing days, with daily runs as high as 180 miles. Afterward, Slocum pronounced the junk rig "the most convenient boat rig in the whole world."

In spite of this stamp of approval, the junk rig remained a unique creature of the Far East for another 70 years. It wasn't until 1960, when a retired British army officer, Colonel H. G. "Blondie" Hasler, took second place in the first singlehanded transatlantic race aboard a 25-foot junk-rigged Swedish folkboat named *Jester*, that Western sailors again took a serious look at this eclectic rig. Since then it has been persistently attractive to a small minority of cruisers who desire an easily handled rig above all else. At least two American yacht designers, Jay Benford and Tom Colvin, both of whom generally favor traditional craft, have specified junk rigs on a number of their designs. Of these, Colvin's 42-foot junk schooner Gazelle, designed to be built in steel or aluminum, is certainly the most popular. Junk rigs are more prevalent in Great Britain, and there have even been a small number of junk-rigged British fiberglass production boats built over the years. There is also at least one British specialty broker and builder, Sunbird Marine, that deals primarily in junk-rigged boats.

In essence, a junk rig consists of a fully battened balanced lugsail (the Chinese describe it as "an ear listening for the wind") that is hoisted on a mast that is either freestanding or only lightly supported by a few shrouds. Unlike a conventional Western sail, which has a simple unitary airfoil shape, a junk sail has a more complex scalloped shape. As such, the aerodynamics of the two sails are entirely different. Where a Western sail depends on a smooth laminar flow of air across its surface, a junk sail is believed to rely on turbulent airflow to operate effectively, although no one is exactly sure how this works. On a Western sail, battens are used only to expand the area of the roach and to help maintain a shape inherent to the sail itself. They are flat and are built into the sail so as not to disturb airflow. On a junk rig battens are integral to the rig. They are more tubular and stand proud from the sail, in effect acting as small booms that separate the panels of the sail from each other. They also disturb the airflow over the sail, creating a series of vortices across its surface. Each batten is attached separately to the mast by a rope parrel and is controlled by a separate sheet, or sheetlet. These are gathered together in series through crude friction blocks known as euphroes. In some cases, if there is not room on deck to lead a single set of sheetlets aft of the sail, two separate groups of sheetlets control the battens from either side of the sail.

This sounds complicated, but in practice the rig is simple to operate. A junk sail can be cumbersome to hoist, due to the weight of its battens and the many bits of line that can snag on something, but once up it is easy to manage. Because the sail is balanced, with area both forward and aft of the mast, there is no risk of power-jibing, since the sail brakes itself as it pivots about the mast. It never flogs in a breeze, but instead flutters quietly. Because there is no headsail to bother with, tacking is effortless. Best of all, when it comes time to reef you simply release the halyard and the sail drops neatly down into its lazyjacks, panel by panel, no matter how hard it is blowing. There's no need to luff up or ease sheets to spill air from the sail, nor is it necessary to tie down or secure the reefed portion of the sail.

A junk rig is also inexpensive to create and easy to maintain. It requires little or no standing rigging, and the sail itself is never heavily loaded, so almost any material can serve as sailcloth. The Chinese literally build sails out of rags and old canvas sacks. Some modern junk-rig cruisers like to use Sunbrella, the UV-resistant acrylic material normally used to make sail covers and dodgers, so that they never have to worry about covering their sails. Because the cloth is cut flat with no shape to it, rank amateurs can build their own sails. And if a sail ever tears, the hole can be safely ignored, as it does not decrease the sail's efficiency and the battens normally prevent it from spreading from panel to panel.

Battens for a junk sail likewise can be made from most any material. The Chinese have traditionally

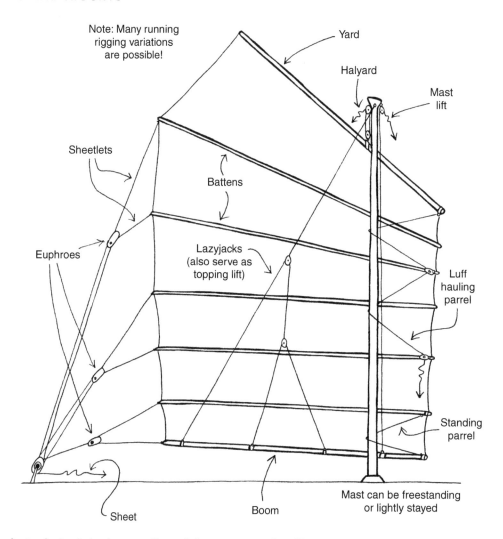

Basic parts of a junk rig. It looks complicated, but is easy to handle.

used bamboo and most modern Western rigs employ fiberglass rods, but anything with an appropriate shape and weight can be pressed into service. So it is with the whole rig. No specially made fittings are required. Just about anything found lying about that looks like it might serve most likely will.

Performance-wise it is hard to compare a junk rig to a conventional Marconi rig, as the principles involved are so different. Any sailor familiar with a Marconi rig probably won't be able to hop aboard a junk-rigged boat and sail it well without first practicing for a while. For Western sailors used to sails with a lot of draft it is hard to know when a junk sail is properly trimmed. Reportedly, even a little over-sheeting quickly stalls a junk sail and kills its drive. Those with a light touch on the helm and a strong intuitive sense of when a boat is pulling along at its best usually achieve the best results.

A junk rig generally does not sail to windward as well as a Marconi rig. Some claim, however, that though junks can't point as high, they can sail faster close-hauled. Others believe junks can point high if the panels in the sail are nicely cambered and not kept too flat. On a reach a junk sails well, since the many sheetlets allow exact control of twist; on a run, at least in a moderate to strong wind, it is nearly ideal, as the entire sail, like a square sail, can be presented to the wind at a perfect right angle. A junk rig is weak downwind in light air, however, since there is no way to increase sail area by flying spinnakers and the like. A rig with multiple masts—two-masted junk schooners are a popular Western variant, while three-masted rigs are common in Asia—can, however, be flown goose-winged with sails out on either side, which helps to some extent.

Modern Freestanding Rigs

Though junk rigs have never been widely adopted in the West, there have been several attempts to create more modern yacht rigs that are just as easy to handle. Most of these rely on unstayed masts, a concept

Junk-rig cruisers tend to think outside the box. Witness this pair of junk sails mounted side by side on a catamaran named Dragon Wings. *Similar side-by-side rigs have been tried on modern racing cats.*

that dates back at least to the 1920s, when L. Francis Herreshoff designed experimental cruising boats with freestanding masts and wishbone booms. The huge advantage of any unstayed rig is that it entirely changes the rig's relationship to the hull it is driving. The mast on a Marconi rig is under severe compression, trying its best to drive itself down through the hull while its standing rigging pulls the bow, stern, and sides of the boat upward as hard as it can. An unstayed mast, by comparison, exerts no compressive force at all and instead must be restrained from lifting out of the boat. The only strain on the hull is from the lateral loads imposed on the deck where the mast passes through it—at the mast partners, as they are called—and on the mast step below. Ultimately, most of the load on an unstayed spar is carried by the spar itself. Much of the force that can't be put to work driving the boat forward is shed by the bending of the spar. This serves as a safety valve and spills excess wind from the rig.

The most common modern freestanding rigs employ just one sail, thus are sometimes called una rigs. The most popular example is seen on the Nonsuch range of boats designed by Mark Ellis and built by Hinterhoeller Yachts in Canada. These feature a single loose-footed triangular sail bent onto a mast stepped right forward in the bow of the boat. The clew of the sail is supported by a wishbone boom that curves around the sail on either side to accommodate its draft, which is easily adjusted by easing or tightening either the clew's outhaul or a "choker" line that controls the fore-and-aft orientation of the boom. The boom slants downward, acting as a vang to keep the body of the sail from rising up and twisting off. Similar rigs have been employed on boats built by Freedom and Wyliecat.

The advantages of an una rig are similar of those of the junk rig. The sail is easy to control and can be presented square to the wind when running off, plus it can be doused or reefed by simply letting it drop

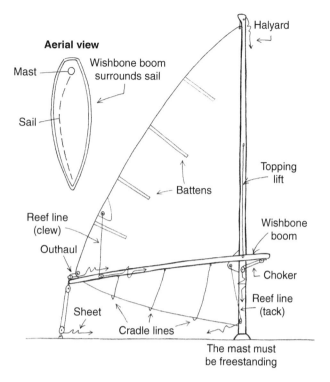

Aerial view

Mast

Wishbone boom surrounds sail

Sail

Halyard

Topping lift

Battens

Reef line (clew)

Outhaul

Wishbone boom

Choker

Reef line (tack)

Sheet

Cradle lines

The mast must be freestanding

Basic parts of an una rig with wishbone boom.

into a set of lazyjacks (cradle lines) under its wishbone boom. The primary disadvantage, again, is a lack of windward ability compared to a Marconi rig. This is partly a function of the larger than normal mast section needed to make the mast freestanding. The larger section increases turbulence at the leading edge of the sail, where it is least wanted, and interferes with the smooth flow of air across the sail's surface. (Note that, unlike a junk rig, turbulence is not a positive force here.) In some rigs this is ameliorated either by using a two-ply sail that envelops the mast, thus smoothing the transition from mast to sail, or by employing a foil-shaped "wing" mast that pivots so its leading edge is always pointing into the wind.

The other major deterrent to good windward performance is the lack of a headsail to create a slot to leeward of the mainsail. Garry Hoyt, ever the innovator, tried to solve this problem by putting a headstay on one of his Freedom designs so a jib could be bent onto it. To help maintain tension on the headstay, Hoyt devised a clever rigid full-chord batten for the jib that helps keep the stay taut. It is, however, not nearly as effective as a backstay, and the jib is necessarily quite small.

Freestanding masts are also seen on what are commonly called cat ketches. These in effect are two una rigs lined up in a row on one boat. Loose-footed sails with wishbone booms are often used,

though some variations feature full-batten sails on conventional booms. The first cat ketch was Garry Hoyt's famous Freedom 40, which was a revolutionary boat in its day, though it was not terribly successful. Other designers who have utilized the rig include Mark Ellis, Yves-Marie Tanton, and Eric Sponberg. Such rigs are fast on any sort of reach, plus they can fly their sails wing and wing on a run, but again are hampered sailing to windward. Not only do they lack headsails, but, as with a conventional ketch, the forward sail feeds dirty air to the sail behind it, thus ruining its efficiency and robbing the rig of much of its drive.

The masts on both una rigs and cat ketches were all made of aluminum when these rigs first started appearing back in the 1970s. These worked well enough and today there are many unstayed aluminum masts still standing tall and true, but there have been some spectacular failures. The first to address the problem was Garry Hoyt, who early on installed carbon-fiber spars on his Freedom boats. These days carbon fiber is pretty much standard for any serious freestanding rig. The extra expense negates the savings realized by not having standing rigging, but in all other respects carbon is ideal in this application. It is much lighter and stronger than aluminum, so the mast can have a smaller section, which helps reduce mast-induced turbulence. Carbon fiber has also played a role in the resurrection of another freestanding rig known as the swing rig. The basic concept, that of a balanced sail that pivots around its mast, is borrowed from the junk rig. Except here it is not just one sail doing the pivoting, but an entire sail plan, consisting of both a full main and jib riding together on one massive boom. The idea was first conceived in Germany during the 1920s. It was reborn on a few experimental boats built in the 1950s and again in the 1980s, but it didn't really come into its own until the 1990s, when modern carbon-fiber construction techniques made it possible to build a lightweight apparatus strong enough to support a totally mobile sail plan.

The most highly evolved example is the AeroRig, which features a freestanding carbon-fiber mast and boom assembly, with the boom extending forward to support a jib. The entire unit rotates freely on a pair of large bearings situated under the mast step and in the deck at the mast partners. There is a forestay with a furler on it for the jib, and in many cases also a backstay behind the mainsail, but both terminate at either end of the massive boom rather than on the deck of the boat. The jib is self-tending with no overlap and sheets to a short transverse track on the boom that maintains the jib at a constant close-hauled angle relative to the mainsail. Once the sails

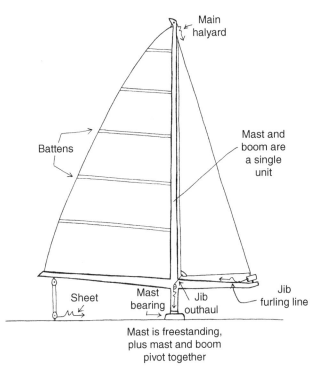

Main halyard

Battens

Mast and boom are a single unit

Sheet

Mast bearing

Jib outhaul

Jib furling line

Mast is freestanding, plus mast and boom pivot together

Swing rigs went out of production a few years ago, but are still found on a few boats.

are raised, their set is not altered and instead the entire sail plan is rotated with a single control line. The sail plan is always kept cocked at a 30-degree angle to the apparent wind direction, except on a flat run, when it is turned square to the wind. To stop the boat, the rig is let go and quietly weathercocks into the wind. To start up again, you just haul in the control line. Sailing by the lee, or with the boom well forward of the beam, is no problem. Jibing is a quiet, stress-free affair. Tacking is as simple as turning the wheel.

Though it looks rather bulky, an AeroRig is not any heavier than a conventional Marconi rig of similar size, if you count all the extra weight of a Marconi rig's hardware and deck fittings. An AeroRig is, however, many times more costly than a Marconi rig, which is probably why they were never built in great numbers. The rig's appearance is also ungainly. In terms of performance, the AeroRig is said to be faster than a Marconi rig downwind, but upwind the Marconi rig, as ever, will prevail.

SAIL CONSTRUCTION

To function as a proper airfoil a Marconi sail must present a curved surface to the wind. To the casual eye a sail may look like a flat two-dimensional piece of cloth, but in fact it has a very specific curved shape built into it. This shape is carefully engineered, depending on what sort of sail it is and how it will be used.

To turn a piece of flat fabric into a curved foil, the fabric must be cut into panels and stitched back together again. By cutting a convex curve along one edge of a panel and stitching it to a straight edge on an adjacent panel, a process is called broadseaming,

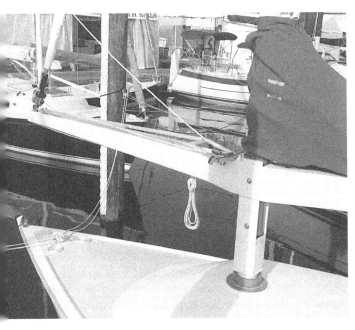

A swing rig at rest. Note the short transverse traveler for the jib just forward of the mast.

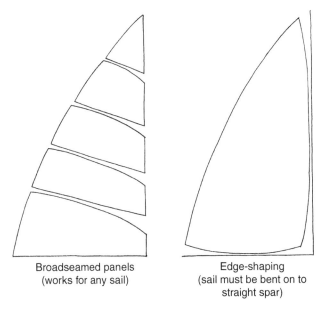

Broadseamed panels (works for any sail)

Edge-shaping (sail must be bent on to straight spar)

Shaping a sail transforms a flat piece of fabric or laminate into a foil.

a unitary curved surface is created once all the panels are joined together. Where the edge of a sail will be attached to a straight spar, as with a mainsail bent onto a mast and boom, shape can also be created by cutting a convex curve along that edge. This is called edge-shaping. In recent years there has been much publicity about shaping laminated sails by "molding" them, but this is only a marketing ploy. The so-called molds on which these sails are built are nothing more than curved workbenches, and in reality all laminated sails are built with shaped edges and broadseamed panels just like any other sail.

How the panels of a sail are laid out depends on the strength characteristics of the fabric they are made from. Like any woven cloth, common sailcloth has a warp, composed of threads running the length of the fabric, and a fill, which are those threads woven at a right angle through the warp. A cloth can be made stronger in one direction than the other, or can be equally strong in both directions, but it is always weakest when a load is imposed along its bias, at a diagonal angle to its weave. To ensure that a sail maintains its designed shape when filled with air, its panels should be oriented so that as little load as possible is carried along the bias of any given panel.

The simplest way to make a sail reasonably efficient is to use a crosscut pattern. Here the panels are laid out parallel to each other with the seams intersecting the leech of the sail at right angles. A crosscut pattern can be used on both mainsails and headsails and is still probably the most common pattern in use today. Another traditional alternative for headsails is the miter cut, where one set of parallel panels with seams bisecting the leech is joined to another set with seams bisecting the foot at a central seam that runs from the clew of the sail to the middle of its luff.

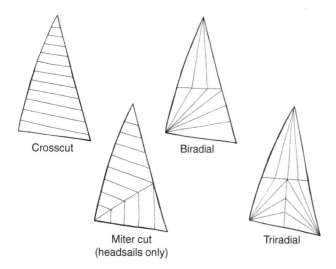

Crosscut

Biradial

Miter cut
(headsails only)

Triradial

The goal when designing a sail is to orient the weave of a woven fabric along anticipated load paths. Basic sail panel orientations are shown here.

The more sophisticated alternative to crosscut and mitered patterns are radial patterns that are designed to orient a sail's panels more precisely along its load paths. The more common patterns are the biradial cut, which has two sets of panels radiating from the head and clew that meet at a central seam that bisects the luff and leech, and the more complex triradial cut, which has panels radiating from all three corners of the sail.

Radial sails are great if you are keen on performance, for they do hold their shape better. They are also more expensive and harder to build. The other drawback is they don't like being reefed as much. They are cut to carry the specific loads generated when the full sail is deployed, but load paths on a sail inevitably shift position when its surface area is reduced. This is less of a problem for a mainsail with slab reefing, as the reefed tacks and clews can be reinforced with their own corner patches, but is more of a problem for a roller-reefed headsail. Most racing sailors rarely reef their mainsails and change their headsails rather than roller-reef them, so radial sails make a lot of sense for them. Most cruisers, however, often reef their sails, which is one reason why most still prefer to stick to the more basic, less expensive, and more versatile crosscut patterns.

Structure and Materials

Deciding what material to use when building a cruising sail used to be a simple matter. For many years, the only reasonable choice was Dacron, more generically known as polyester, which was first developed during World War II in Great Britain, where it is known as Terylene. Shortly after the war it was introduced to the recreational marine market as a sailcloth, where it quickly replaced Egyptian cotton as the material of choice for building sails for both racing and cruising yachts. For more than a generation, from the early 1950s into the 1970s, sails made from woven Dacron cloth with panels stitched together with needle and thread represented the cutting edge in sailmaking technology.

Dacron is in fact a great material for making sails, as it is strong, durable, and easy to maintain. When woven into a cloth, however, it suffers from the same weakness as any other woven material. The fibers of the cloth are slightly bent or crimped as they pass by one another, and over time the crimp in the weave, as the expression goes, is elongated. This causes the cloth to stretch, which in turn causes a sail to lose its shape. What normally happens is that the draft of the sail, the deepest part of its curved surface, which is designed to be in the sail's forward section, slowly moves aft as the sail stretches. As the after section gets baggier, the sail becomes steadily less efficient.

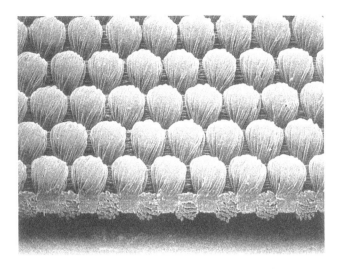

Dacron sailcoth up close and personal. Note how one line of fibers is crimped over the other. As the crimp in the weave elongates, the sail inevitably stretches and loses its shape. (Courtesy of North Sails)

It is still curved—indeed, even more curved than it was before—thus still develops a lot of power when filled with air. But because the sail's foil shape is degraded, less of this power is translated into forward motion and more of it is wasted heeling the boat and pushing it sideways.

To combat the evils of stretchy woven cloth, sailmakers first introduced laminated sails back in the 1970s. The earliest examples, which were both crude and expensive, were of interest only to racing sailors, but since then laminated sails have greatly improved. Now an enormous variety are being made from various materials, and some of these make very good cruising sails.

Where a woven sail has a unitary structure, with its cloth constituting both the body and load-bearing skeleton of the sail, a laminated sail has a composite structure. The exterior layers of the laminate, usually a strong, flexible Mylar film, form the body of the sail and are glued to an interior layer of load-bearing fibers. Additional exterior layers of light woven cloth, usually some sort of polyester, can be added to protect the inner layers from abrasion and UV radiation.

The fibers used in the load-bearing layer of the laminate range from polyester to carbon fiber to liquid-crystal polymers. In simpler sails the fibers are laid out symmetrically in a light biaxial or triaxial scrim; in the most sophisticated sails, known generically as structural sails, they are bundled into yarns or ribbons that are precisely laid out in long catenaries along the load paths of the sail. As a general rule, the stiffer, more exotic load-bearing fibers are more expensive and have shorter life spans. Carbon

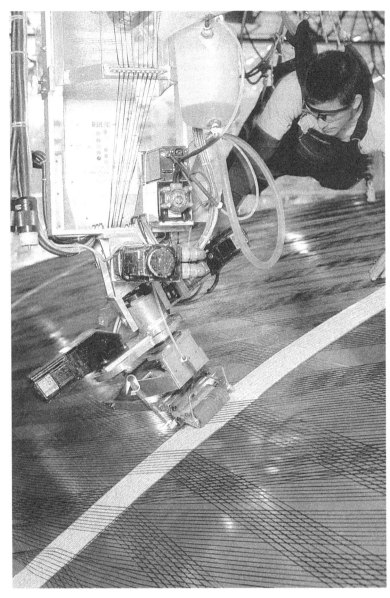

Building a laminated structural sail. This sailmaker is laying down structural fibers precisely along the sail's load paths while hanging suspended in a harness over the sail. (Courtesy of North Sails)

fiber, for example, can fail suddenly if subjected to repeated bending and folding. PBO (an acronym for polybenzoxazole) is probably the highest-performing sail fiber developed to date, but it quickly degrades in sunlight. Aramid fibers, like Kevlar, Technora, and Twaron, are brittle and don't take well to flexing and flogging. These materials are well suited to high-end race boats, where performance is critical and sails are used for only a season or two, but they are generally inappropriate on a cruising boat.

The cheapest, most durable laminated sails have polyester fibers in the load-bearing layer of the laminate. Laminated sails constructed of simple polyester are still available, but most sailmakers these days are pushing Pentex, a higher-grade polyester fiber. Pentex is twice as stiff as simple polyester, but has the same ultimate breaking strength and stands up to flexing, folding, and flogging just as well. It also stands up well to sunlight and on some laminated sails is used as an exterior UV-barrier layer. Pentex is a bit more expensive than simple polyester, but is still considerably cheaper than more exotic fibers. Of these the one that works best in a laminated cruising sail is probably Spectra, also known as Dyneema. It doesn't mind flexing and folding too much, stands up well to sunlight, doesn't weigh much, and is quite strong and stiff. It costs much more than polyester, but is still cheaper than other high-tech fibers. Vectran also has many of the characteristics of Spectra, but is not as UV-resistant and thus requires a barrier layer or coating to protect it from sunlight.

This is an oversimplified assessment of the types of laminated sails currently available (there are also many hybrid sails that blend different load-bearing fibers), but it should give some idea of how complex the subject can get. If you want to put sails like this on your boat, do your homework. If instead you are tempted to throw up your hands in confusion and cleave to woven Dacron sails, you are in good company. Dacron cloth is still the most popular sail material used by cruisers and is, indeed, a worthy substance.

The biggest downside to laminated sails is that they simply don't last long. They are much lighter than woven Dacron sails and hold their shape much better over the course of their useful life spans, but in most cases that won't be longer than five years. They need to be babied, and if you use them hard they may well last only a couple of years before they delaminate. Woven Dacron sails, by comparison, are nearly indestructible. You normally can expect them to last at least 10 years, and if you pamper them, they may go as long as 20. Unlike laminated sails, they can be repaired and recut if necessary. The only problem, however, is that for much its useful life span a woven Dacron sail will not be the shape it was designed to be. Inevitably, the shape of the sail degrades over time and becomes increasingly less efficient.

Sail Profiles

Aside from its three-dimensional shape, a sail's two-dimensional profile also affects its performance. The threshold issue is a sail's aspect ratio, which really is just a fancy way of saying how tall and skinny it is. The simplest way to find a sail's aspect ratio is to take the length of its foot and divide it into the length of its luff. For example, a sail measuring 45

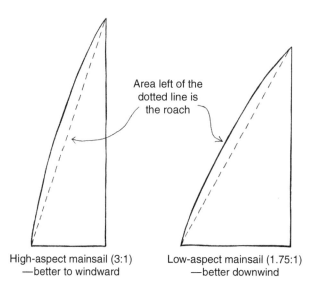

High-aspect mainsail (3:1) —better to windward

Low-aspect mainsail (1.75:1) —better downwind

Area left of the dotted line is the roach

A high-aspect sail (left) performs better upwind; a low-aspect sail is better downwind. More roach is always better in both cases.

feet along its luff and 15 feet along its foot has an aspect ratio of 3, which is relatively high. A more sophisticated and more accurate method is to square the luff length and divide it into the total area of the sail, which accounts for the roach of the sail. The distinction is really only important when discussing aspect ratio in the abstract. Otherwise, you can tell easily enough how tall and skinny a sail is just by looking at it.

As a general rule, a high-aspect sail performs better to windward. Just as a deep narrow keel generates more hydrodynamic lift as it moves through the water, a tall skinny sail generates more aerodynamic lift moving through the air, as a longer luff bends more air around the foil of the sail, while the narrower area behind the luff minimizes drag and resistance. There are limits, however. If a sail is too tall and skinny, the extra leverage exerted on the hull beneath it only increases heeling without increasing drive. Also, once a boat turns downwind everything changes. With the wind blowing from behind, lift is irrelevant and the best way to improve performance is to increase drag and total sail area. Once the wind is abaft the beam, a broader, more low-aspect profile therefore becomes steadily more efficient. It is thus necessary to strike a compromise, and in most cases a simple aspect ratio of about 3:1 for a mainsail is as high as you want to go. If you're not too worried about windward performance, don't be distressed if your mainsail in fact has a ratio much lower than this.

Headsails are another story. High-aspect blade jibs with ratios as high as 5:1 are increasingly popular because they are more efficient to windward and are easy to tack. These blades, however, provide very little drive when sailing off the wind or through a heavy seaway, so most cruising boats should also carry a more powerful lower-aspect overlapping genoa.

The other big factor affecting a sail's profile shape is how much roach it has. More roach is always good for two reasons. First, the pointy head of a Marconi sail lets the high-pressure airflow running off the windward side of the sail spill around to the leeward side. This decreases lift and sends a tip vortex of turbulence spiraling off the top of the sail. This is why you never see pointy-tipped airplane wings. Adding roach to a sail and giving its head a more rounded elliptical profile reduces its tendency to form tip vortices. Second, more roach means more sail area. Even better, it means more area high up in the sail, where the wind blows harder. This improves performance generally, particularly when sailing off the wind.

There are, however, practical limits to how much roach you can tack onto the back of a sail. You normally can't add much roach to a headsail, for example, as the extra area in the leech will tangle with the mast every time you tack or jibe. Some high-aspect blade jibs on race boats have full roaches, but on any large overlapping sail, or on a roller-furling sail, it is out of the question. You can add a great deal of roach to a mainsail, depending on how it is rigged. On most boats the backstay is the limiting feature. You can often extend a mainsail's roach out past a backstay by several inches, but if you go too far the leech will hang up on the stay when tacking, particularly in light air. Dispense with the backstay, however, and the sky is the limit. On some sorts of boats—most commonly on multihulls, which can be rigged without backstays due to their wide shroud bases, and on certain racing monohulls that rely entirely on running backstays to support their masts—you'll see mainsails with ideal profile shapes and very full roaches. On sails like this, the roach can increase sail area by as much as 20% to 30%.

However much roach a sail has, the extra area in the leech must be supported by battens. Jibs with some roach built into them must carry short battens in their leeches (which is why they can't be rolled up on furlers), and Marconi mainsails have traditionally also carried a series of partial battens in their leeches. Originally, the only mainsails (aside from junk sails) that carried full battens running all the way across the sail from luff to leech were multihull mains with fat roaches. In the past 15 years, however, full battens have become popular on all kinds of mainsails, whether they have full roaches or not.

Aside from supporting a full roach, full battens in a mainsail have many other advantages. The battens

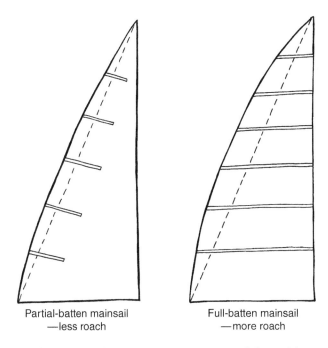

Partial-batten mainsail
—less roach

Full-batten mainsail
—more roach

Full battens (right) can support more roach but add weight and complexity. Partial battens (left) are lighter and easier to manage.

help lock in the sail's shape and prevent it from seriously distorting, particularly in strong winds when a sail's draft is apt to shift aft. They also help quiet the sail and keep it from flogging in light air or when it is doused or reefed in heavy air. Some find that full-batten mains are also easier to trim accurately, as their true shape may be easier to perceive. The weight of the battens also makes it easy to strike the sail if the boat is first brought head to wind.

Full battens also have disadvantages. The extra weight, though it helps bring the sail down faster, also makes it harder to hoist. Furthermore, full-batten mains don't perform as well in light air, because the battens make it hard to adjust the sail's shape to give it more body. The long batten pockets are also liable to chafe on shrouds when the sail is eased way out. Most important, there's a lot of extra hardware involved. A properly installed full-batten main requires a special external sail track on its mast, plus a collection of special roller-bearing cars to carry the battens up and down the track. All this is expensive, adds even more weight to the sail, and is a bother to maintain. Without this extra gear the compression loads from the sail, which push the battens in toward the mast, can make it difficult to hoist, douse, or even reef the sail without first coming head to wind.

As a compromise many who like the idea of having a little more roach in their mainsail now order sails with one or two full battens at the top of the leech and partial battens the rest of the way down.

The most advanced modern sails have full battens and square heads to reduce turbulence and tip vortices at the top of the sail.

On a full-batten mainsail of any size battens cars like these should be installed to help cope with compression loads on the mast track. (Courtesy of Seldén Mast)

This creates a little more area and allows for a more elliptical profile at the head of the sail, but is not bothersome or expensive.

SPARS AND STANDING RIGGING

In the most basic type of standing Marconi rig the headstay, backstay, and two longest shrouds (called cap shrouds in this case) all terminate at the top of the mast, or masthead. This masthead rig is preferred by most cruisers, since it is the most secure and the simplest to set up and tune.

The middle of a Marconi mast must be supported by one or more sets of spreaders. These are short transverse spars that hold the cap shrouds out away from the sides of the mast and so carry tension from the shrouds to the mast to help hold it in column. To ensure that the loads transferred to the mast are kept horizontal, spreaders should be oriented so that they bisect the angle created by the shroud as it passes over the spreader tip. To counteract spreader loads when a boat is sailing on one tack or the other—at which time the spreaders on one side of the mast

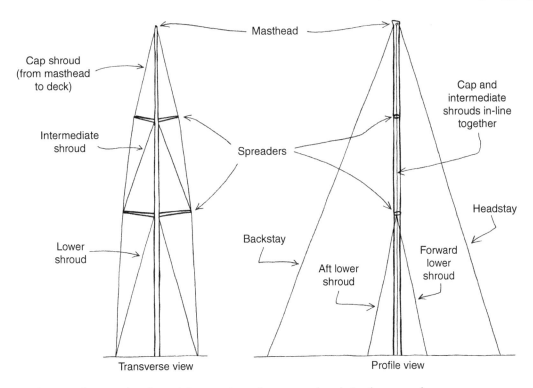

A typical double-spreader masthead rig. Most cruisers favor masthead rigs because they are more secure.

will not be under tension—the spreader bases are supported by sets of shorter shrouds. Those supporting the lowest pair of spreaders in the rig are called lower shrouds. Often there are two pairs of these, one running forward of the mast and another running aft. Shrouds supporting spreaders higher in the rig are called intermediate shrouds.

Single-spreader rigs are by far the easiest to set up and maintain. In the past they were used on boats as long as 50 feet with masts measuring 60 feet or more and are still favored by cruisers who like to keep their rigs simple. A single-spreader rig requires a heavier, thicker mast, however, and also needs a relatively wide shroud base, which creates wider sheeting angles for headsails and limits windward ability. The more sets of spreaders there are, the lighter and thinner the mast can be. This reduces weight aloft and creates less turbulence in front of the mainsail. Plus the shroud base can be narrower, which means narrower sheeting angles. For these reasons, double-spreader rigs are now very common and are found on boats as small as 32 feet. The biggest rigs on racing maxis and superyachts may have as many as six or seven sets of spreaders.

Racing sailors don't like masthead rigs because they are not very flexible. Cruisers consider this a good thing, but racers like to be able to play with the shape of their masts, as this allows them to alter the shape of their sails. They prefer fractional rigs, which are much more flexible because the only piece

of standing rigging running all the way to the masthead is the backstay. The headstay and two upper shrouds (which are not called cap shrouds, as they do not reach the masthead) instead terminate at a point somewhere below the masthead. The rig is described according to how far up the mast the headstay and shrouds run. For example, if they reach up $7/8$ the total height of the mast, the rig is called a $7/8$ fractional rig. The smaller the fraction, the more flexible the mast is.

The backstay on a fractional rig serves not so much to support the mast but as a tool to bend it. By tightening or easing the backstay while sailing, the top of the mast can be pulled back or eased forward. When backstay tension is increased and the top of the mast is bent back, the mainsail behind the mast is flattened, as the middle part of the mast bulges forward and pulls the curve out of the sail. This helps depower the sail in strong winds. When the backstay is eased, the mast straightens out and the sail's shape becomes fuller and more powerful, giving it extra drive that helps keep the boat moving in lighter winds.

Tension on the headstay, meanwhile, must be maintained by the two upper shrouds. To do this they must run aft of the mast over a pair of swept-back spreaders and must be set up very taut. Swept-back spreaders and shrouds are also found on many masthead rigs these days and are a key feature on the eccentric Bergstrom and Ridder, or B&R rig, so

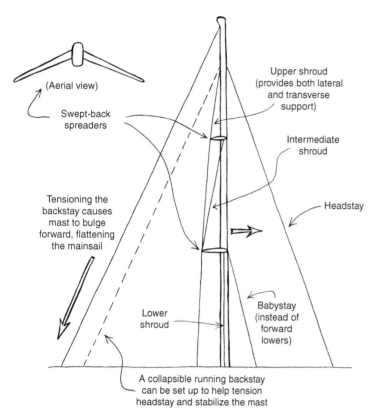

Fractional rigs are less secure, but more flexible than masthead rigs and can be used to alter the shape of the mainsail.

called after Lars Bergstrom and Sven Ridder, who invented it. In a B&R rig the spreaders are so long and are swept back so far, to an angle of about 30 degrees, that there is no need for any backstay. This makes room for a high-performance full-batten mainsail with an enormous roach, although ironically most owners of boats with B&R rigs (which are now standard on all boats built by Hunter Marine) do not take advantage of this. The drawback to dramatically swept-back spreaders is that they severely limit how far forward you can ease the mainsail. This hampers a boat's ability to sail downwind, as it isn't possible to get the mainsail anywhere near square to the wind. The theory instead is that the huge mainsail will compensate for this by making it possible to tack downwind on a series of broad reaches faster than the boat can sail on a dead run.

Similar rigs with large full-batten mainsails are also used on most multihulls, including most cruising catamarans. The wide shroud base on these boats makes it possible for a pair of swept-back cap or upper shrouds to support the mast without help from a standing backstay. Normally these shrouds are not led over spreaders, but instead run straight to the deck. Spreaders supporting the middle of the

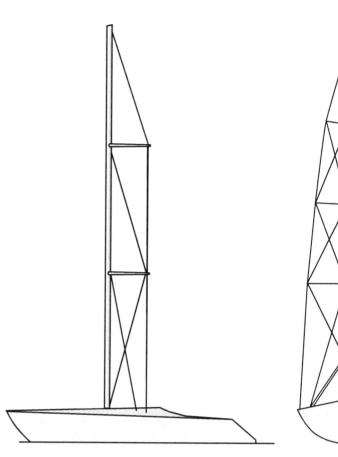

The Bergstrom and Ridder or B&R rig requires no backstay and instead relies on long swept-back spreaders to support the back of the mast. This makes it possible to fly a mainsail with a very fat roach. (Courtesy of Seldén Mast)

mast meanwhile are held in place by a pair of well-tensioned diamond stays that run from a point low on the mast, over the spreader tips, to a point much higher on the mast. In many cases, spreader bases may also be supported by a pair of aft lower shrouds.

Spar Materials

For thousands of years the only material used to fabricate spars for sailing rigs was wood. It is generally well suited to the job, as it is supple and strong for its weight. For much of the history of sailing vessels, however, spars were made of solid wood, thus were much heavier than necessary. Only in the last 100 years or so have sailors contrived to make wood spars much lighter by gluing up separate pieces of wood in a hollow box-shaped section. Wooden box masts were the spars of choice on most cruising and racing yachts through the first half of the 20th century, but after World War II aluminum quickly became the preferred material.

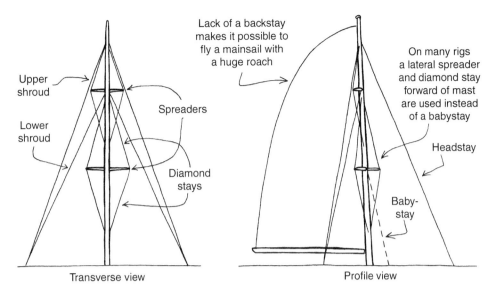

Upper shroud

Lower shroud

Spreaders

Diamond stays

Transverse view

Lack of a backstay makes it possible to fly a mainsail with a huge roach

On many rigs a lateral spreader and diamond stay forward of mast are used instead of a babystay

Headstay

Baby-stay

Profile view

The wide shroud base on a typical catamaran rig makes it possible for swept-back shrouds to support the mast without a backstay. Short spreaders and diamond stays can be used to support the middle of the mast, but are not always necessary.

A wooden box mast waiting to be stepped. The wood must be painted or varnished on a regular basis.

One huge advantage of aluminum spars is that they can be produced relatively cheaply in large numbers. They also need little maintenance.

Aluminum is in fact an excellent spar material. As discussed in Chapter 3, it is light, very strong, and does not corrode in salt water. Unlike wood spars, which must often be painted or varnished, an aluminum spar requires little maintenance. An occasional rinse with fresh water and a quick coat of wax every couple of years are normally all it wants. The only significant drawback to aluminum is that it corrodes quickly when in contact with another type of metal in the presence of salt water. This presents a problem in that the fasteners used to attach hardware to modern masts and booms are usually made of stainless steel, and the hardware itself is normally either stainless steel or bronze. To protect the aluminum such hardware should be installed with all dissimilar metals carefully insulated from the body of the spar.

A few traditionalists still cling to wood spars, but otherwise the only real alternative to aluminum is carbon fiber. Though it is arguable whether carbon fiber is the best material from which to build a boat hull (assuming factors other than weight are considered), there is no question it is a superb material from which to build a mast. In this application, where a long, thin structure must resist large compression loads, it is nearly ideal. Carbon fiber is far stiffer than aluminum, yet weighs less than half as much; its only real drawback is that it also costs more than twice as much.

A competitive racing sailor has little choice but to pony up for a carbon stick, but for cruising sailors it is a much closer question. Once a carbon mast and boom are fully dressed with hardware and rigging, the total weight saved compared to a similarly dressed aluminum rig is significantly reduced. On midsize boats around 40 feet in length a fully dressed carbon rig may weigh only 10% to 20% less than a comparable aluminum rig. This is still a substantial difference, particularly as the weight is saved high above the deck where it counts the most. More weight can also be saved if you spend even more money on exotic lightweight rigging and carbon-fiber fittings and spreaders. But unless you are truly addicted to high performance, putting a carbon rig on a small to midsize cruising boat usually isn't worth the extra expense. The calculus changes, however, as a boat grows larger. The larger the rig, the larger the relative weight difference between fully dressed carbon and aluminum spars, as hardware and rigging make up a progressively smaller percentage of the rig's total weight. The extra cost of a carbon rig also becomes progressively smaller relative to the cost of the boat as a whole. Carbon rigs therefore are increasingly common on larger, more expensive cruising boats.

The durability of the rig is another issue to consider. Aluminum spars have long, useful life spans (several decades is not unusual), but it remains to be

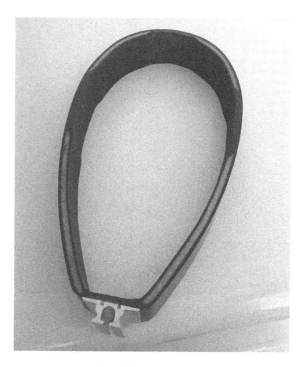

A section of a carbon-fiber mast with coring off a performance cruising catamaran built in South Africa. More and more performance cruisers are favoring carbon rigs.

A carbon mast under construction. As with any laminated structure, fibers can be oriented along load paths, thus increasing structural efficiency. (Courtesy of Seldén Mast)

seen how well carbon spars hold up over time. In some respects, we already know aluminum is more durable. An aluminum mast, for example, can easily survive a heavy impact, but one man with a hammer can knock a carbon mast to bits in a matter of minutes. Carbon masts also don't like being struck by lightning. Carbon itself conducts electricity very well, but the epoxy resin holding it together in a laminated structure does not. Resistance caused by the resin thus generates a lot of heat in a lightning strike, and this may seriously damage the laminate. This risk can perhaps be reduced by grounding the mast and installing a lightning terminal or rod at the masthead, but whether this adequately protects a carbon rig is not yet known.

Production quality may be another issue. While the basic component of any aluminum spar, a simple length of extruded metal, is mass-produced on an industrial basis, with reliable and consistent properties and quality control, carbon-fiber spars are produced on a more limited individual basis. Different grades of carbon fabric can be used in a laminate, and the laminating process itself yields varying results depending on the technique used and the skill of the manufacturer. As with fiberglass hulls care must be taken to ensure the integrity of the laminate. As the market for carbon spars grows larger and more competitive, it is increasingly likely lower-quality spars will appear on the market

Rigging Materials

Standing rigging technology has also undergone a transformation in recent years, though in this instance the progression has been more circular. The original material of choice was of course fiber, or rope, but rope made from natural fibers like manila and hemp is fairly elastic and prone to rot. After wire rope was invented in the latter half of the 19th century, wire rigging quickly became popular and, indeed, was the technological innovation that made the modern Marconi rig possible. Well over a century later wire standing rigging is still found on most sailboats.

The current standard is 1×19 stainless-steel wire rope. This has one center wire with 6 more strands of wire twisted around it in one direction to form a central core; this in turn has 12 more strands of wire twisted around it in the opposite direction. There are 19 wires in all, including the single central wire, thus the designation 1×19. The opposing lays of the two layers of wire encasing the central strand are supposed to minimize stretching, but in practice 1×19 wire rope does stretch a bit when loaded. Most 1×19 wire rope has strands of round wire, but there is one type, known as Dyform wire rope, that has triangular strands of wire that are designed to lay together

A 1×19 Dyform wire shroud in a swaged terminal. The triangular wire strands lay together tighter and reduce stretching. (Courtesy of SAIL Magazine)

more compactly. Dyform wire rope stretches less, but some believe it is also more likely to chafe lines and sails. Various stainless-steel alloys are used to make 1×19 wire rigging, including the lesser-quality 302 and 304 alloys, but again, as with any stainless-steel fitting on a boat, the higher-quality, more corrosion-resistant 316 alloy is always preferable.

Wire rigging is extremely durable and rarely fails without warning. You can reasonably expect a set of wire stays and shrouds to last at least 10 to 15 years before they need replacing; in many cases, if not used hard, they will last 20 years or more. Signs of fatigue, such as broken strands of wire or cracked terminal fittings, normally appear before anything actually breaks. If inspected carefully on a regular basis, wire rigging almost never blows apart unexpectedly.

Lighter, stronger alternatives have evolved over the years. The oldest, rod rigging, was first introduced about 25 years ago. Here, instead of constructing a wire rope composed of many small strands of wire,

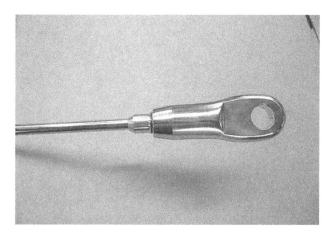

Modern rod rigging is lighter than wire rope and does not stretch, but is also more likely to fail without warning. It has grown more reliable, however, and is now favored by many performance cruisers. (Courtesy of Navtec)

one large single strand, or rod, of wire is used. It effectively cannot stretch and is much lighter than a comparable length of wire rope. A single rod of steel, however, is not as supple as multistranded wire rope, thus is more likely to fatigue and fail when subjected to flexing, as often happens at terminal fittings and spreader tips as a boat's rig is repeatedly loaded and unloaded while sailing. Racing sailors quickly embraced rod rigging when it appeared, but cruising sailors shunned it as its inflexibility at times caused it to suddenly fail without warning.

More recently the technology has been refined, and rod rigging is now much more reliable. Terminal fittings are stronger and also feature tapered sleeves that help spread dynamic loads and are designed to crack when fatigued to provide early warning of impending failure. Also, the accepted practice now is to set up rod rigging in a discontinuous configuration, with separate terminals above and below spreaders so that lengths of rod need not be bent over spreader tips. As a result of these improvements, many performance-oriented cruisers now favor rod rigging over wire rope, though it is still somewhat more expensive.

The next step in this evolution is modern fiber rigging, which in one sense takes us back to where we started. Racing sailors, at least, are once again supporting their rigs with rope, but now the rope is made of high-tech synthetic fibers instead of natural ones. The current favorite is PBO fiber rigging. It is much lighter than either wire or rod and like rod does not stretch under load, but is relatively fragile. It is easily damaged by chafe, UV radiation, and many common chemicals, so it must be sheathed in some

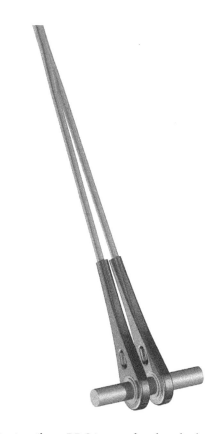

Fiber rigging (here PBO) must be sheathed to protect against UV degradation. It is lighter than both rod and wire-rope rigging, but is also expensive. (Courtesy of Navtec)

sort of protective coating. The latest development is carbon-fiber rigging. This seems to be another excellent application for the material, and carbon rigging is already usurping PBO rigging as the new gold standard on race boats.

Due to its high cost and fragility, it is unlikely fiber rigging will be widely adopted by cruising sailors in the near future. Fiber rigging has been used on some large custom one-off performance cruising boats, but for most cruisers it doesn't make much sense to spend a lot more money on exotic standing rigging that cannot last nearly as long as steel wire or rod.

The Mast Step

The heel of a sailboat's mast can be stepped either outside on the deck of the boat or inside directly over the keel. A keel-stepped mast is putatively stronger and more secure than one stepped on deck because it is supported not only by its standing rigging but also at deck level at the mast partners where the mast enters the boat.

Installing a keel-stepped mast, however, is complicated. If the mast is to be raked aft slightly, which

Wire Terminals

Stainless-steel wire usually fails at the terminal fittings that secure it in place. The most popular type of terminal, the swage fitting, is also the one most likely to cause problems.

In some cases swage fittings are improperly assembled. The fitting itself consists of a female sleeve of stainless steel into which the end of the wire is inserted. The fitting is then compressed onto the wire under great pressure. This swaging process effectively cold-welds the fitting's interior surface into the lay of the wire and is normally done by a professional rigger using special equipment. Sometimes rotary hammers are used, but these often work-harden the terminal, making the steel brittle, which can easily cause it to fail prematurely. Many boatyards use simple manual presses with twin rotary dies, but these require that the fitting be passed through the press twice, which can result in a malformed banana-shaped terminal that is also apt to fail. The best device to use is a hydraulic press that swages the fitting in one pass. If you ever order swage fittings for your rig, be sure they are swaged in this manner.

Swage fittings, even if properly assembled, are also susceptible to crevice corrosion, which occurs when moisture dribbles down a wire shroud or stay and wicks down into the body of a terminal. In this oxygen-depleted environment the trapped moisture can easily cause stainless steel to corrode, particularly if it is not 316 alloy steel. Eventually tiny cracks appear around the top of the terminal where the wire joins it, which is a sure sign the fitting will soon break apart. To prevent this, swage fittings when new should be gently heated so they expand slightly. Then wax or lanolin should be applied to the joint where the wire enters the terminal so that it flows down into the lay of the wire and hopefully seals the terminal against moisture intrusion.

The best way to avoid these problems is to instead use what are called mechanical or compression fittings. These are not as sleek as swage fittings, but they are more

(Continued)

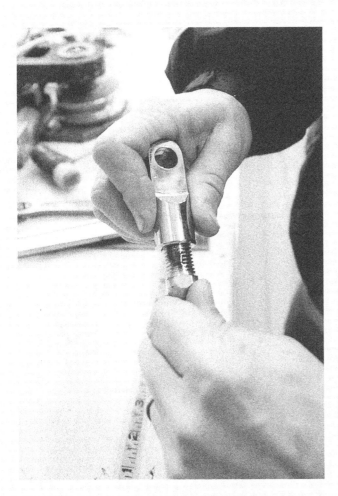 

Assembling a compression terminal. The body of the terminal is screwed together after the end of the wire is wrapped around a cone inside (left). The terminal is then tightened with a wrench (right). Note the dab of sealant to keep out moisture.

reliable and can be assembled by an amateur using simple hand tools. The body of a mechanical terminal comes in two threaded parts that screw together. Inside the body is a small compression cone. To install a terminal, you first slip the top of the body onto the wire. Then unlay the outer layer of a short section of the end of the wire, slip the cone onto the core of the wire, and relay the outer layer of wire over the cone. The bottom of the terminal is then screwed onto the top, trapping the end of the wire inside. Drop a dab of silicone sealant into the terminal body before screwing it together, and the entire assembly is rendered waterproof. The terminal can also be periodically taken apart, inspected, and reassembled, though this is easier said than done as the terminal parts can be difficult to break apart once they have been heavily loaded.

Compression fittings are strongly favored by do-it-yourself types and are increasingly popular with professional riggers. Many riggers and mast manufacturers now prefer to assemble stays and shrouds with swage fittings at the top and compression fittings at the bottom. This puts the slimmer, more aerodynamic swage fitting up high in the rig, which helps reduce windage and turbulence, but facing downward so moisture cannot wick into it. The bulkier compression fittings are installed at deck level facing upward and can be easily sealed against any moisture dribbling down the wire.

is often desirable, you must carefully adjust the position of the mast step so the mast can pass through the mast partners at just the right angle. You must also firmly wedge the mast in place with chocks at the partners and seal this joint with a mast boot to keep out water. Often the seal is not effective and some moisture trickles down the side of the mast into the cabin during heavy rains or while sailing in rough weather. If the mast has internal halyards, as is normally the case, some rain also comes in through the halyard exits at the masthead and dribbles down inside the mast into the bilge. This, combined with any water creeping down the side of the mast past the boot, plus any other water that finds its way into the bilge, is apt to pool up around the mast step itself. This in turn is likely to cause corrosion, particularly if the mast is aluminum and the step is another metal, such as steel.

The steady ingress of rainwater through the masthead to the bilge can also cause problems when a boat is stored outdoors on land for long periods of time. Unless there is a drain plug that can be opened or an automatic bilge pump that can be kept operational, a substantial amount of water can accumulate in the bilge. If the boat has shallow bilges, this water may rise above the cabin sole and damage joinery and furnishings. Even if the boat has deep bilges that can hold a lot of water, hull damage can occur if the accumulated water, freezes solid and expands. If the bilge does not have a drain, or a pump cannot be kept on, or it is not possible to bail the bilge by hand on a periodic basis, the only way to prevent water from accumulating in the bilge is to either unstep the mast or somehow cap the masthead.

A deck-stepped mast presents none of these problems. You can rake the mast by simply adjusting the

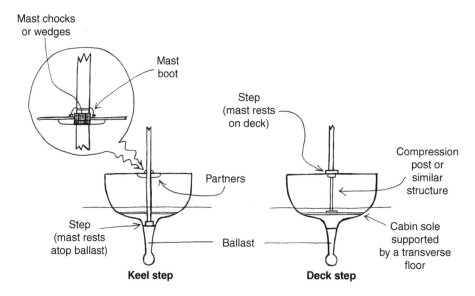

The two basic types of mast steps. A keel step (left) is more secure, but more of a bother. A well-designed deck step (right) is plenty strong enough for most cruisers.

standing rigging without shifting the position of the mast step itself. Any water coming down the mast, inside or out, drains off onto the deck. The mast step, however, must be well supported underneath the deck, as the compression loads are enormous. The rule of thumb is that a mast step must stand up to a load equal to one-and-a-half to two-and-a-half times the total displacement of the boat. In most cases a hefty compression post directly under the mast step carries this load from the deck down to the keel. Alternatively, the step may be supported by an interior transverse bulkhead, or by a partial bulkhead tied into a substantial deck beam. Note, too, that a keel-stepped mast also often needs auxiliary support in the form of a tie-rod installed right next to the mast. This keeps the huge compression load on the keel from distorting the hull by pushing the bottom of the boat away from the deck.

Though obviously the base of a keel-stepped mast must be more secure than that of a deck-stepped mast, I have never heard of any boat being dismasted solely because its mast was stepped on deck. Nor have I ever heard of a mast being saved solely by virtue of its being keel-stepped. I have heard that keel-stepped masts sometimes develop cracks where they butt up against their mast partners. I therefore have always

preferred deck-stepped masts, both because they present fewer problems and don't take up space belowdecks. More conservative cruisers still prefer keel-stepped masts. Deck-stepped masts in any case are rarely found on monohulls over 38 feet in length. They are the rule, however, on multihulls of all sizes, as these boats have no keels.

RUNNING RIGGING

The advent of modern high-modulus synthetic fibers has also complicated the business of deciding what rope to use for running rigging on a sailboat. For decades, on both racing and cruising yachts, the best material to use for most working lines was good old Dacron, or polyester. Now, however, there are materials that are much lighter, stronger, and less elastic than Dacron, so it is possible to get very particular about what rope is used for what purposes aboard a cruising sailboat.

Construction and Materials

In terms of its structure, there are two basic types of rope in use on sailboats today. The simpler, more traditional type is three-strand rope, which consists

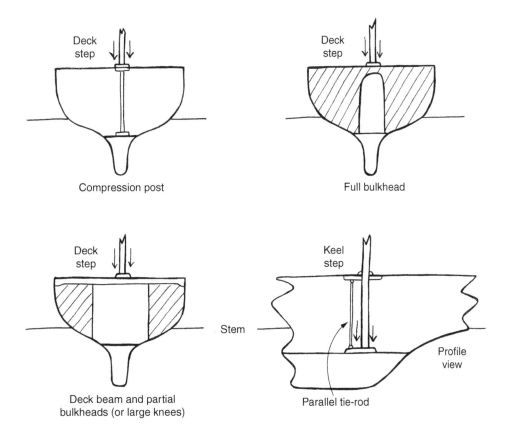

Types of mast step supports. A deck step needs a structure under it to resist compression. A keel step needs a parallel tie-rod to keep the deck and keel from being pushed apart.

of three large bundles of fibers twisted together in a spiral. Prior to the invention of synthetic fibers, this was the only type of rope found on most sailboats, and it is still favored, if only for appearance's sake, on some traditional boats. It is strong and durable, but does stretch a lot, as the three large strands of fiber have plenty of room to elongate as they come under load. Three-strand rope also tends to kink up and twist if it is turned a lot, as when looped around a winch or rove through a multipart tackle, thus can be difficult to work with. Its biggest advantage is that it's easy to splice.

The more modern alternative to three-strand rope is braided rope, which became popular after Dacron first appeared in the mid-20th century. It is by far the most common type of rope found on modern sailing vessels. There are several variations, but those most often used on yachts have a multipart double-braid structure. The rope's inner core usually consists of several smaller strands of fiber, termed plaits, that are woven together in a tight braid. In some cases the core instead has a three-strand construction, or it may consist of bundles of perfectly parallel fibers. Surrounding the core is an outer sheath of braided plaits known as the cover. In rare instances, there may also be an intermediate layer of braided sheathing between the cover and core. Another variation is single-braid rope, which is essentially a braided core with no cover.

Braided rope is often described as being either 8-plait or 16-plait, which refers to the number of plaits in the cover, not the core. Smaller ropes up to about 8 millimeters in diameter are usually 8-plait; thicker

Single-braid high-modulus (here Dyneema) rope is increasingly used for halyards on race boats and some performance cruisers.

ones are usually 16-plait. Braided rope is considerably more expensive than three-strand rope, but is generally far superior. It stretches much less, doesn't kink up as easily, and is softer and more pleasant to handle. Its one drawback is that its more complex structure makes it much more difficult to splice.

The three most common materials used to make rope for running rigging these days are polypropylene, nylon, and Dacron. Polypropylene is the lightest and least elastic, but is generally inappropriate for use on sailboats as it quickly degrades and becomes brittle when exposed to sunlight. It is also very slippery, doesn't hold knots or splices well, and is generally difficult to handle. Because it floats and is inexpensive, it is often used by fishermen. Nylon is the next cheapest material and is most often used to make three-strand rope, though single-braid nylon ropes are also widely available. Nylon is UV-resistant and extremely elastic, thus serves well in any application

This double-braid polyester rope has both a polyester core and a polyester cover. All-polyester double-braid is a great default rope for cruisers in most circumstances. There are also many different types of composite double-braids with exotic high-modulus cores and polyester covers.

Three-strand nylon rope stretches easily, making it great for docklines and anchor rode.

where large shock loads must be absorbed. Dacron, meanwhile, though the most expensive of this group, has long been the most popular rope material on boats, for the reasons described above. It is available both as three-strand and braided rope and is a great default rope as there are few jobs it does not do well.

Following Dacron is the same list of expensive high-tech synthetic fibers discussed earlier in the section on sail construction. Kevlar, Technora, Spectra, PBO, and Vectran all weigh less and stretch less than Dacron and can carry more weight, but they are also more fragile. They generally do not stand up to chafe as well, are not UV-resistant, and some are easily damaged when exposed to certain common chemicals. Worse yet, most of these exotic fibers should never be tied into knots. This greatly weakens them, as the hard fibers tend to cut each other when bent together at sharp angles. In some cases a modern high-modulus rope loses up to 50% of its breaking strength if tied into a knot. As a general rule, therefore, high-modulus rope must be spliced in place and should never be tied to anything. This doesn't present problems if all working lines on a boat are made up beforehand, but is a serious limiting factor anytime a line must be pressed into service on an impromptu basis.

Exotic double-braid ropes, like exotic sails, often have a composite structure, with high-tech fiber in the load-bearing core and Dacron in the outer cover to protect the core from sunlight and chafe. Exotic rope can often be fussy to work with. It is generally stiffer and less pliant and is usually harder to coil than simple Dacron rope. It also tends to slip in rope clutches, as the clutch will firmly grip the Dacron cover, while the stiff, slippery core inside creeps forward under load. To prevent this, you must sew the cover and core together in areas where a rope is routinely gripped by a clutch.

Uses and Applications

As with exotic sails, technophobic cruisers who dislike complexity can do worse than to simply ignore exotic rope and use nothing but Dacron. Braided Dacron serves admirably in most every application aboard a modern cruising sailboat, with just two exceptions. Lines used to secure a boat—this includes both anchor rodes and docklines—should always be nylon rather than Dacron, as these lines need some elasticity to absorb shock loads. As a general rule, three-strand nylon rope is best for anchor rodes and should also be used as a snubber line on a chain rode. Docklines should be either three-strand or braided nylon.

For those who don't mind complexity and are interested in performance, there are some applications aboard a cruising boat where the extra expense of exotic rope is easily justified. This is especially true if your boat has exotic laminated sails. Having spent extra money to buy sails that don't lose their shape, it certainly makes sense to buy some exotic rope so you can shape and trim them with more precision.

The first lines to consider are halyards, as these are the working lines that should stretch least on any sailboat. Halyard tension significantly affects sail shape (more tension makes a sail flatter and less tension makes it fuller), and fine-tuning settings is much more difficult if the line used is elastic. These days many cruising boats carry high-modulus halyards, as this is the one application where exotic rope makes the most sense. The exceptions are spinnaker halyards, as spinnaker shape is not seriously affected by halyard tension. Spinnaker halyards are also subject to shock loads caused by spinnakers collapsing and suddenly refilling with air, so here it's better to use Dacron rope instead.

The next most reasonable place to use exotic rope on a cruising boat is for headsail furling lines, as these want to be light and strong without stretching under load. Other candidates in descending order of importance are spinnaker sheets, which always work better if they are light and thin; mainsail reefing lines; and the mainsail outhaul. There is little point in using high-modulus rope for lines that run through a multipart tackle, such as a mainsheet, as these are not heavily loaded and generally work better if they are softer and more flexible. Also, as a general rule, I don't feel high-modulus headsail sheets are worth the extra expense, unless the headsail is a high-modulus laminated sail. These are the lines you usually handle most when sailing, and it is important they be pliable and pleasant to work with. They are also the lines that receive the most abuse, as they flog and whip about a great deal every time a boat is tacked and are often left exposed to the sun when the boat is not in use. Ultimately, they will last much longer if they are Dacron.

In all cases the best high-modulus fiber to use as rope aboard a cruising boat is Spectra, also known as Dyneema. As mentioned earlier, this is the one exotic fiber that stands up best to routine abuse. It is reasonably pliant and flexible, can be knotted if necessary (though splices are still preferable), and resists chafe and UV radiation much better than other exotic fibers.

If you do install a lot of high-modulus rope on your boat, it may also be necessary to upgrade your deck hardware. Because it stretches so little, high-modulus rope transfers larger shock loads to any block, sheave, clutch, or other piece of gear containing or controlling it. If the hardware in question is old and worn or undersized, there is a good chance it will eventually break under the strain.

REEFING AND FURLING

Being able to shorten sail efficiently is important on any sailboat, but it is particularly important on a cruising boat. On a race boat the deck is normally overpopulated with competent crew, and difficulties encountered when reefing sails can usually be overcome by brute force. On most round-the-buoys racers, sails are seldom reefed in any event. On a cruising boat, however, the modus operandi is to reef early and often, and the working crew is usually small. This is why many innovations pertaining to reefing and furling sails have first appeared on cruising boats.

By far the most important advance has been the development of the modern roller-furling headsail. Crude roller-furlers that wound up headsails on taut wire luffs appeared in the early 20th century, but this was strictly furling gear. Such devices could not be used to partially reef a sail and were less than perfectly reliable. It wasn't until the 1970s, when riggers hit on the notion of rolling up headsails on stiff extruded

Furling line

A contemporary headsail furling system. Pulling on the furling line rolls the sail up; setting the sail entails hauling on the active sheet to unfurl the jib. As the sail unrolls off the furling rod, the furling line is rolled up on the drum. (Courtesy of Seldén Mast)

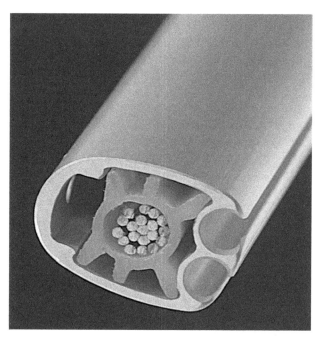

Modern headsail furling systems consist of aluminum furling rods installed around wire headstays. The luff grooves, seen on the right side of this extrusion, are used for hoisting the headsails. Twin grooves make it possible to hoist two sails (for a wing-and-wing rig, for example) or to hoist one before dropping the other during a sail change. (Courtesy of Seldén Mast)

aluminum furling rods, that roller-furlers really came into their own. Early examples, like their predecessors, were not always reliable, but after only a few years most of the bugs were worked out and these days a roller-furling headsail is considered standard equipment on most cruising boats.

This is easy to understand. For most coastal cruisers, having a roller-furler means the headsail is hoisted only once, at the beginning of the sailing season, and is doused again only when the boat is stored for the winter. The rest of the time it's a simple matter of pulling on the sheet while easing the furling line to let the sail out, and vice versa to roll it back in again. It's hard to imagine how sail handling could be made any easier.

Roller-furlers do, however, have their drawbacks. As mentioned earlier, it's not possible to reef a sail on a furler without distorting its shape. This occurs because the top and bottom sections of a sail are rolled more tightly as the sail rolls onto its furling rod, which causes the looser middle section to develop a paunch. The result is a fuller shape, whereas a flat shape is what is needed to cope with the stronger wind that prompted you to reef in the first place. To prevent this sailmakers can sew a crescent-shaped strip of foam into the luff of a furling headsail. The foam is thicker in the middle of the luff and picks up the extra material in the middle of the sail as it rolls up. This diminishes the paunch and helps keep the sail flat as it is roller-reefed.

Even with a foam luff, however, the shape of a roller-reefed headsail is less than ideal. You can only reef a sail so far, down to a bit less than two-thirds its original size, before it again develops a belly and becomes aerodynamically inefficient. Sailing off the wind this is not a problem, as sail shape is less important. Sailing to windward with an over-reefed furling headsail can be frustrating, however, as the boat is overpowered by its over-full headsail and points poorly while making too much leeway.

Another drawback to roller-furling gear is that it adds weight to the rig up high where it is least wanted.

One problem with headsail furling is that damaged sails can be hard to take down. This bluewater sailor shredded his roller-furling genoa in a gale at sea and wasn't able to cut it off until he reached port days later.

This includes the weight of the furling rod, the swivel at the top of the rod, and the weight of the sail itself. The latter, of course, can't be counted as extra weight when the sail is fully deployed, but there is excess weight aloft both when the sail is partially reefed and when it is completely furled. On a typical sloop with just one furler on its headstay, the extra weight is not too detrimental. But on a cutter with multiple furlers up forward, or worse, a boat that also has an in-mast furling mainsail, the extra weight is considerable and can undermine the boat's stability.

In-Mast Furling Mainsails

Not suprisingly, the convenience of roller-furling has planted itself behind the mast as well as forward of it, and in the past 10 years the roller-furling mainsail has passed a tipping point of sorts. Where once the furling main was decried as an unreliable abomination and an insult to sailing, it is now rapidly becoming the dominant sail-handling system on mass-production cruising boats. Some of the biggest boatbuilders are now putting furling mainsails on their boats as standard equipment, with conventional hoisting mains listed as optional equipment for which extra money is charged.

The most popular and successful systems are in-mast roller-furlers. The first iterations, which appeared in the 1980s, were aftermarket systems tacked on behind conventional masts. An aluminum furling rod fundamentally identical to those used on headsail furlers was mounted directly behind the mast, and the mainsail was rolled up on it. The furling rod, however, could not be made taut enough to prevent the mainsail's luff from sagging to leeward when the sail filled with wind. To solve this problem, the furling rod was placed inside an extruded housing that was bolted onto the back of the mast. The structure of the housing kept the mainsail's luff from sagging when the sail was deployed, but it also greatly increased windage and weight in the rig. Then at last came the final solution: the furling rod is now housed inside a specially designed mast that has a profile not much larger than that of a conventional mast. These systems are now so popular some spar manufacturers report more than half their production is devoted to masts designed to contain and support in-mast furlers.

In-mast furlers are now reasonably reliable and very convenient. To deploy the mainsail, all you do is ease a furling line while pulling on an outhaul that leads from the end of the boom to the clew of the sail. To furl or reef the sail, you simply haul on the furling line while easing the outhaul. All this can be done without leaving the cockpit.

The big problem with in-mast furlers is that they can only be used with a fundamentally inferior

Sheet Leads for Roller-Reefed Headsails

When roller-reefing a headsail the sheet lead for the sail normally must be shifted forward as the sail is reduced in size. It is possible to cut a sail so that its ideal lead remains static as it is rolled up, but headsails like this tend to be symmetrically shaped yankee jibs with a limited total area. The larger asymmetric genoas found on most sailboats need their sheet leads shifted to maintain even tension on both the foot and leech of the sail, otherwise shape is badly distorted. Either the top of the sail twists off and spills air, which means the foot is too tight and the luff is too loose (and the sheet lead is too far aft), or the bottom of the sail is too full, which means the foot is too loose and the luff is too tight (and the sheet lead is too far forward).

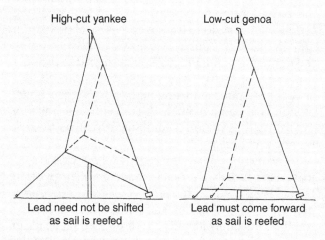

High-cut yankee   Low-cut genoa

Lead need not be shifted as sail is reefed   Lead must come forward as sail is reefed

Moving the headsail sheet lead forward as the sail is roller-reefed prevents distortion of the sail's shape and provides a means to maintain even tension on the foot and the leech. The high-cut yankee jib on the left doesn't require the sheet leads to be moved forward when reefed.

Headsail sheet leads are normally shifted on a genoa track, which is a rail running down the side deck or caprail

of a boat. In many cases fairlead cars on a genoa track must be shifted manually. Doing this when a car is loaded with a taut headsail sheet is often very difficult, however, even on smaller boats, and on large boats it quickly becomes impossible. In many cases the only way to shift the lead is to tack the boat, move the unloaded fairlead car, then tack back. As a result, cruising sailors often neglect sheet leads when roller-reefing their headsails.

The best way to avoid this problem is to rig your fairlead cars so they can be shifted easily under load. This requires a control line running from the front of the fairlead car forward to a turning block at the forward end of the genoa track and then aft to the cockpit. Pulling on this line pulls the car up the track; easing it lets it run aft. A cockpit winch or a multipart tackle forward of the car can provide the mechanical advantage needed to pull the line when the car is loaded. In either case it is best to also fit a rope clutch to secure the line once the fairlead car is shifted to the desired position.

The easiest way to tell if the lead on a headsail sheet is correct is to watch the telltales on the luff of the sail. If all the telltales start fluttering at the same time as the boat is pinched too close to the wind, then the lead is fair and the leech and foot are evenly tensioned. If the telltales at the top of the luff break first, the leech is loose and the fairlead car needs to come forward. If the telltales at the bottom break first, the foot is loose and the car needs to come aft.

Being able to easily adjust sheet leads also helps you reshape your headsail as conditions and apparent wind angles change. In light air you can make your headsail more powerful by shifting the lead forward a little to give the lower part of the sail a slightly fuller shape. Shifting the lead forward also helps maintain an ideal shape as the wind moves onto or abaft the beam. In heavy air you can spill wind out of the top of the sail by shifting the lead aft. This also helps maintain ideal shape as the wind moves forward of the beam.

mainsail. A sail rolled up on a vertical axis cannot contain solid horizontal battens, which means a furling mainsail cannot have any roach in its leech. Even worse, if a leech without battens is cut straight, it flutters in the wind when the sail is set, stressing the sail and ruining the airflow across it. So instead the leech must have a hollow cut with a slight concave curve to it. This means the total area of the sail is significantly reduced, in some instances by as much as 20%, and also that the head of the sail must be very narrow and pointed, which further decreases efficiency when sailing to windward. Because the

top of the mainsail stalls so easily, the boat is apt to develop lee helm in moderate conditions, which in turn requires a slight reduction of headsail area. The end result is poorer performance both off the wind, due to reduced sail area, and on the wind, due to the degraded aerodynamics of the mainsail.

To redress these deficiencies, sailmakers have pondered the problem of how to install battens in a sail that gets rolled up like a window shade when not in use. One interesting system features inflatable horizontal battens that are pumped full of air after the sail is deployed. Another features two opposing strips

An in-mast mainsail furler working in conjunction with a furling headsail. For many modern cruisers this is the ideal system, as both sails can be deployed, reefed, and furled without ever leaving the cockpit. (Courtesy of Seldén Mast)

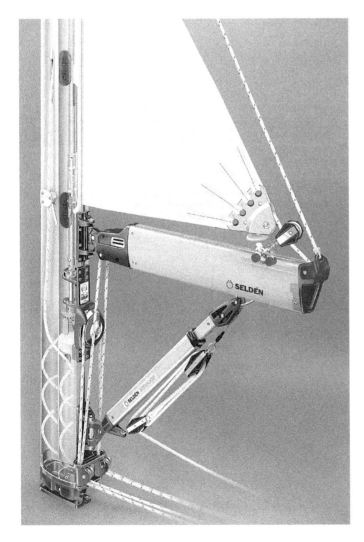

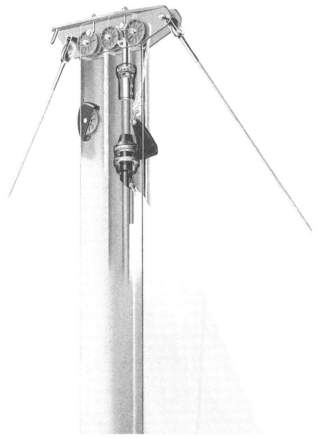

The in-mast furler in this system is turned by a bevel gear that can be driven with a pair of lines led back to the cockpit or a winch handle at the mast. (Courtesy of Seldén Mast)

of concave flexible metal, similar to a tape measure, that flex open and stiffen as the sail is unrolled and then collapse against each other as the sail is rolled up. Neither scheme, however, has proved very workable. To date the best solution has been to install vertical battens that can roll up with the sail along the length of the furling rod. Vertical battens do improve a sail's shape and can keep a straight leech from fluttering in the wind, but they cannot support a large roach. Sails with vertical battens are increasingly popular, but most in-mast mainsails still have hollow leeches and no battens at all.

In practice, whether they have vertical battens or not, in-mast mainsails are not quite as user-friendly as they appear. For one thing, because the sail track on the furling rod is located inside the mast, it can be difficult to bend on and hoist the main. Some riggers estimate that about half those who own boats with in-mast mains now hire professionals to perform this once simple job. Also, because the mainsail must feed through a relatively narrow slot in the back of the mast to reach the furling rod, some care is needed when furling or reefing it. To prevent the sail from jamming in the slot as it rolls up, it is best if there's little or no pressure on the leech or clew. This ensures the neatest furl and makes for a flatter, better-shaped sail as it is reefed, but it means the sail must be feathered into the wind a bit before turns are taken on the furler. To do this the boat must sometimes be turned to windward, at least to some extent, as the sail otherwise is pressed hard against the edge of the slot as it enters the mast, increasing friction and hampering the furl. This is more of a problem on one tack than the other, as the sail is folded hard against the leeward edge of the slot whenever it is rolled onto the leeward side of the furling rod. This is most likely to be a problem when sailing off the wind in strong conditions, which is precisely when you most want to reef the main without rounding up.

Before taking the plunge on an in-mast furler, intelligent cruisers should first ask themselves what price they are willing to pay for sail handling convenience. The reason we put up with all the highly tensioned rigging and assorted hardware of a modern

The vertical battens on this in-mast furling mainsail can be rolled up with the sail but are not nearly as effective as horizontal battens. (Courtesy of Seldén Mast)

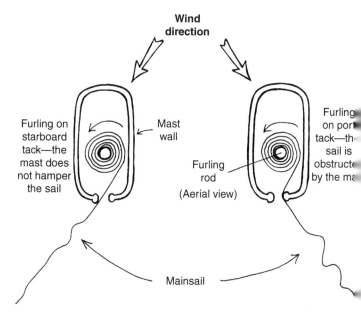

Furling the main on an in-mast system is always more difficult on one tack than the other.

Marconi rig is so we can fly aerodynamic sails that improve performance, most particularly to windward. To take this already complicated performance-oriented rig and further complicate it by installing furling gear with many moving parts inside a mast, just so we can fly a sail that degrades its performance, is only self-defeating. If sail-handling convenience rather than sailing performance is the ultimate goal, it might be better to choose a simpler rig explicitly designed to achieve this goal. Unfortunately it never occurs to most people that there are alternatives to the Marconi rig, such as those discussed earlier in this chapter, that may suit them better.

For larger boats, starting at about 45 feet, I'd say an in-mast mainsail does make some sense. Indeed, the larger the boat the more sense it makes. A large boat with a long waterline and more speed potential to begin with can better suffer some degradation in performance than can a small one. On a large boat with a proportionately larger rig, the ability to handle sail more easily is also proportionately more valuable. Also, having to round to weather a bit in strong conditions to reef or furl a sail is safer and less intimidating on a large boat than it is on a smaller one. On smaller boats—certainly on any boat where a conventional mainsail can otherwise be hoisted, handed, and reefed by a single person—I believe it is best to stay away from in-mast mainsails. Here the increase in convenience is relatively slight compared to the loss of performance.

In-Boom Furling Mainsails

These systems are descended from more primitive mainsail roller-reefing systems that were seen on some boats during the first half of the 20th century. The older systems featured booms that were rotated via a gear at the gooseneck so that mainsails could be rolled up onto them. In practice such gear is awkward to use, as it can be difficult to get the sail to roll evenly onto the boom. Even if one succeeds in doing this, there is still no way to maintain tension on the clew of the reefed sail. Under load the foot of the rolled-up sail tends to creep forward on the boom, creating an unwanted belly in the portion of the sail still flying. Another problem is how to fasten a mainsheet, boom vang, or preventer onto a boom that has a sail rolled up around it. Most solutions to this riddle left much to be desired.

The basic concept of roller-furling a mainsail horizontally along its foot was revived during the 1990s as the mania for in-mast furling systems developed momentum. Those repelled by in-mast mainsails with hollow leeches hoped boom furling might provide the best of both worlds: the convenience of roller furling plus a mainsail with horizontal battens

and a proper roach. Rolling the sail up on a furling rod inside the boom rather than around it solved the problem of how to fasten working lines to the boom. Also, putting full battens on the sail neatly resolved the question of how to maintain tension on the clew when making the sail smaller. By rolling the sail down to one of its battens when reefing, the foot of the sail is prevented from creeping forward under load, as the full batten holds it in place on the boom. Another nice thing about in-boom mainsails is that all the extra weight of the furling system—the furling rod, the furled sail itself, and the extra-large boom needed to accommodate it—is kept low in the rig where it least affects stability.

Unfortunately, the biggest problem with boom furling remains unresolved. Whether the sail is rolled up around the boom or inside it, it is still hard to do neatly. Partly this is because there is so much more material to roll up when a sail is furled along its foot rather than its luff. Partly it is because the sail's luff, which has a luff tape and bead on it that slots into the sail track on the mast, is much bulkier than its leech. Also, the luff is straight, so that it all rolls up on top of itself, while the leech runs at an angle, so that it rolls up in a spiral along the length of the boom. To further complicate matters, the sail track the luff feeds out of is normally forward of the furling rod onto which it is being rolled. To have any chance at a neat furl, the boom must be precisely maintained at a certain

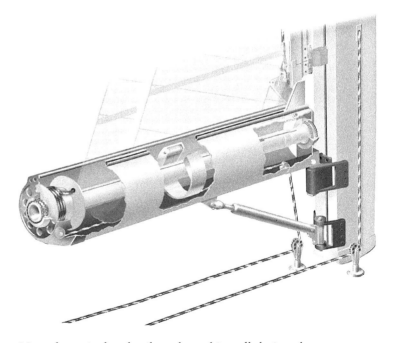

Note the articulated sail track on this well-designed in-boom furling system. It both allows the sail to be furled at wider angles and puts the luff right over the front of the boom to help the sail furl down neatly. (Courtesy of Schaefer Marine)

angle to the sail track. This requires a reliable rigid boom vang that can hold the boom at a fixed angle regardless of the motion of the boat. Lastly, it is hard to furl the sail into the boom without jamming unless it is unloaded. To keep from having to come directly head to wind when furling or reefing the sail, it helps to have an articulated sail track on the mast.

Hoisting an in-boom mainsail also presents problems. On any boat much longer than about 38 feet you may have to use a powered halyard winch to raise the sail, as there is a lot of friction to overcome as the sail is unrolled and pulled up the sail track. Unlike a vertically furled sail, where the wind catches the sail and helps unroll it once things gets started, here the wind only creates resistance and makes hoisting the sail harder.

Many cruisers I've met with in-boom furling mains have concluded they are more trouble than they are worth. Others swear by them, but do note that an in-boom system must be well designed and carefully installed to work properly.

Slab Reefing

This is the traditional way to reef a Marconi mainsail and to my mind is still the best. Unlike the mainsail furling systems described above, slab reefing allows you to maintain maximum control over the shape and trim of the sail as it is reduced in size. It is simple and reliable, with no complicated mechanical parts, plus you can normally reef or douse the sail while sailing downwind. There are a few different variations, but all work on the same basic principle. The sail is divided into sections by different sets of reef points; usually there are two of these, though mainsails on bluewater cruising boats often have three. At either end of each set of reef points is a pair of cringles, which are large reinforced grommets in the sail, one for the tack and one for the clew. To shorten sail, you first ease the mainsheet to reduce the load on the sail. Then you release the halyard, pull down the sail to the desired set of reef points, secure the two cringles, tension the halyard, and finally trim the sheet as desired. For a really neat job, you can also tie in all the intermediate reef points (they should be tied only loosely, so that they don't carry any load), but this is strictly optional.

Compared to roller reefing this is certainly a bit of work, but if the reefing gear is laid out properly one person can do it quickly and efficiently. The variations have to do with how the cringles are secured to the boom. In most cases a single reef line runs to the clew, and the tack is secured to a hook or reefing horn on the gooseneck. Alternatively, there may be a second separate reef line for the tack. On many boats such a line can also serve as a cunningham, which is a

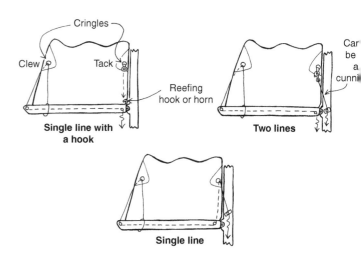

Three slab-reefing variations. Slab reefing is still preferred by many cruisers.

line used to tension the luff of a mainsail after it is hoisted. In some cases there may be a single reef line rove through both the clew and tack cringles.

Whichever method is used, all relevant controls, including the main halyard, should be at the same location—either at the mast or in the cockpit—so that one crewmember can do the job easily without having to shift positions. Normally it is best to stay away from single-line systems. These are invariably led to the cockpit, which sounds good in theory, but in practice the line often sticks somewhere, as there is a great deal of friction in the run, and you have to go forward to the boom to free things up. The system found on many production boats these days, annoyingly, has the halyard and reef line for the clew led to the cockpit, with the tack going on a reefing horn at the mast. This often leads to a frustrating scenario wherein you ease the halyard in the cockpit to let the sail down, go forward and hook on the tack, return to the cockpit, dog down the reef line, and prepare to retension the halyard, but then find the ring on the tack has shaken off its hook in the interim, thus provoking much cursing and another trip to the mast. The better solution is to reorganize things a bit: rig a reef line for the tack and lead it aft to the cockpit, or rerig the halyard and the reef line for the clew so they can be controlled at the mast.

The big drawback to slab reefing is that it limits your options as to how much sail you can take in at once. Roller-reefing systems are infinitely variable, and the amount of sail deployed can be fine-tuned so as to keep the sail plan precisely balanced. With slab reefing there are normally only three different settings (full sail, first reef, and second reef) or at most four (third reef). Given this limitation, you should think carefully about where to position reef points on a slab-reefed mainsail, taking into account both the boat's sailing characteristics and your own habits and preferences.

As a general rule, modern production boats with their shallow bilges and broad sterns tend to develop excessive weather helm and start griping off to leeward once heeled to an angle of more than 10 to 15 degrees. For boats like this, a rather shallow first reef, a moderately deep second reef, and then even a third reef will help keep the hull more level and sailing well as the wind grows stronger. Meanwhile, older designs with narrow hulls with more deadrise and fuller keels can often heel up to 30 degrees before they complain too much. Boats like this can usually get away with just two deep reefs. Other factors to consider are local sailing conditions. If it is often windy where you sail, for example, deeper reefs are called for. Or the wind may normally be light, except in the afternoon when the sea breeze suddenly comes up (a common scenario in many parts of the northeastern United States), in which case the depth of the first reef should be fine-tuned to the strength of the sea breeze. Likewise, if you sail with crew who get nervous on a steeply heeled deck, you can accommodate them by putting deeper reefs in your mainsail. If they don't mind heeling, you can make the reefs shallower, as long as the boat doesn't mind, too. In the end, however, the best you can achieve here are compromises, and in some instances you must accept you may be flying slightly more or less mainsail than you would like to.

Sail-Taming Devices

Another big drawback to a slab-reefed mainsail is that it must be stowed manually when doused. This certainly is one reason why many cruisers now prefer in-mast or in-boom mainsails. With these systems the sail is neatly rolled up inside one spar or another and needn't be touched by human hands. A slab-reefed mainsail, by comparison, usually ends up in a great unruly heap atop the coachroof after its halyard is let go. It must then be gathered up, secured neatly atop its boom with sail ties, and covered with a sail cover to protect it from the sun. On smaller boats this is not burdensome, but on boats 40 feet and longer the mainsail is often too large and heavy for one person to stow easily.

The traditional weapons of choice for wrangling mainsails are lazyjacks, a twin series of light lines running from a pair of points up the mast down to several points along either side of the boom. When lowered the mainsail is cradled by the lazyjacks and held in place atop the boom. With the sail thus contained it takes only a few tugs on the leech to get it snugged down neatly. To work properly lazyjacks should have at least three legs on each side, or the sail may slip out of their grasp. They should also be adjustable, so you can vary the tension in the lines and also bring them all the way forward to the mast, clear of the sail, and secure them out of the way when they are not needed. This makes it easier to hoist the sail, as its battens otherwise tend to catch on the lazyjacks as the sail is raised. It also simplifies covering the sail, as otherwise the cover must be cut with several slits in it to accommodate the lazyjacks.

A more elaborate alternative to lazyjacks is known generically as the stack-pack, so called after the Doyle Stack-Pack from Doyle Sailmakers, which was the

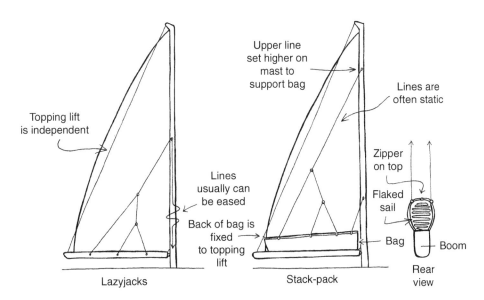

Restraining the mainsail with lazyjacks or a stack-pack. Both systems do a good job of catching the main as it comes down. Lazyjacks are more versatile, because they can be easily stowed away if designed properly. The stack-pack is more convenient, since it covers the sail, too.

When dropping a mainsail into a stack-pack (or a set of lazyjacks) a crewmember is often needed forward to pull the sail down. (Courtesy of SAIL Magazine; Photo by Malcolm White.)

brought forward and stowed away at the mast. This sometimes makes raising the sail more difficult, particularly if the wind is blowing hard, in which case you may have to bring the boat head to wind before beginning the hoist.

A third option is the Dutchman system. This consists of a single series of fine monofilament lines that are suspended from a dedicated topping lift and are led down through a series of small grommets in the body of the sail to the boom. As you drop the sail, the monofilament lines keep it from falling off the boom; ideally, once the sail has been properly "trained," it will neatly flake itself onto the boom as it comes down. Many sailors are appalled at the notion of poking a lot of small holes in their mainsail, but in fact they don't interfere with the flow of air across the sail. I've found that Dutchman systems tend to be fiddly and are apt to get snarled unless rigged very carefully. Also, even when the system does work perfectly, the vertical monofilament lines make it harder to cover the sail after it is lowered. Again, as with fixed lazyjacks, the sail cover must be cut to accommodate the lines and must be worked in place around them when placed over the sail.

DOWNWIND RIGS

One of the great ironies of modern sailing is that the Marconi rig, which is so efficient when sailed upwind, becomes rather inefficient when sailed downwind. For many cruising sailors this irony is only compounded by the fact that they would rather be sailing downwind in any event. The old saw has it that gentlemen never sail to weather. But the fact is if you want to be a gentleman and point your bow downwind and still get where you're going reasonably quickly aboard a Marconi-rigged boat, you not only need to carry some extra gear and sails, you also need to do a bit of extra work.

The problem in a nutshell is that the Marconi rig is oriented fore and aft, with a great premium placed on the reduction of drag and the promotion of aerodynamic lift. Once a boat turns downwind, however, drag and resistance become virtues, and the rig instead wants to be oriented athwartships and as square to the wind as possible. As it strives to do this, a Marconi rig can't help but get in its own way. As it turns downwind the mainsail and boom are eased out, but they can only go so far before they start chafing against the rig's shrouds and spreaders. Meanwhile the headsail is also let out, but its inboard sheet lead, which did such a fine job of holding the sail at a tight angle to the wind when sailing to weather, now prevents it from being held out square to the wind. Even worse, as the rig is turned farther downwind,

first rig of this sort introduced back in the 1980s. Here a permanent sail cover with a zipper on top is suspended from a set of lazyjacks and fixed to the boom. When the sail is dropped, it falls neatly into the bag, the zipper can be drawn closed, and the sail is at once both stowed and covered. When the sail is flying, however, the loose halves of the bag hang uselessly about its foot, which interferes with the airflow across the lower portion of the sail and also causes some chafing. The lazyjacks supporting the bag must also be rigged permanently and cannot be the headsail falls into the lee of the mainsail, starts flopping about uselessly, and ceases to function as a sail at all. Meanwhile, because the boat is now moving in the same direction as the wind, apparent wind speed has decreased. To compensate for this we need to increase sail area, but what has happened instead is that the front half of the sail plan has been knocked out of action.

In the old days, of course, sailors had the opposite problem. Square-rigged vessels had most of their sail plan oriented athwartships and were downwind speed machines. On turning to windward, however, they struggled to brace their square sails up to weather and became slow ungainly hulks. Long after the first primitive fore-and-aft gaff-rigged sailing vessels appeared on the scene, some cruising sailors remembered just how useful a square sail could be when sailing downwind. It was not unheard of in the late 19th and early 20th centuries for cruisers to carry one or more yardarms on deck, which they would hoist aloft and fly square sails from when the wind came right aft. One of these was Bill Robinson, who often flew square sails on his Alden-designed ketch *Svaap* while cruising around the world from 1928 to 1931. Another was the young Bill Crealock, who later designed several popular cruising boats manufactured by Westsail and Pacific Seacraft. In *Vagabonding Under Sail*, an account of an extended transatlantic cruise he undertook in 1948, Crealock sang the virtues of a square rig:

> At last, after seventeen days we had found our trades and we stowed our fore and aft canvas and jubilantly set the square. After an hour's work we sat back and looked up at the triangular raffee pulling above each yard, and at the squaresails and bonnets beneath. There seemed a welter of ropes festooned over the boat . . . but in practice the squaresails could easily be hoisted and lowered by one person. A few days later we lowered every sail to examine it for signs of chafe, and also examined every foot of rope. Neither then, nor at the end of our crossing, did we find any chafe. . . . [W]e discovered to our delight that *Content* would steer herself with the tiller free, the wind fine on the starboard quarter, and the starboard yard swung slightly forward. For ten days the helm was not touched. We were hundred of miles from any steamer track, and we stood no watches by day or by night. With the bit between her teeth, the old boat took charge and cantered through the night, while we slept soundly below.

More recently there has been some renewed interest in the square rig, as billionaire Tom Perkins in 2006 elected to put a modern high-tech square rig, termed a DynaRig, on his 289-foot superyacht *Maltese Falcon*. *Falcon* boasts three enormous unstayed rotating carbon-fiber masts from which sprout a series of

This thoroughly modern square-rigger, the Dyna-rigged Maltese Falcon *launched in 2006, sails well both upwind and down. The curved yardarms are fixed in place and rotate with the carbon-fiber masts. (Billy Black)*

fixed curved carbon yardarms. The sails are stowed inside the masts and are deployed along the yards via an automated computer-controlled furling system. Because the masts can pivot the square sails to windward, *Falcon* reportedly sails well to weather and also does well downwind, thanks to her athwartship rig. It seems unlikely, however, that DynaRigs will be seen on more modest vessels anytime soon. Meanwhile, there are a few other tricks we can use to prod our boats in the direction we would like to go.

Spinnakers and Such

The primary sail designed to overcome the downwind foibles of the modern Marconi rig by both increasing total sail area and deploying it at a transverse angle to the wind is the conventional symmetric spinnaker. These typically are made of lightweight nylon, have a very powerful bulbous shape, and are flown forward of the mast in place of a jib or genoa. A long pole supported at its inboard end by a fitting on a track at the front of the mast is used to hold the sail out square to the wind. By pulling the pole back nearly to the shrouds or easing it forward nearly to the headstay, you can fly the sail at angles ranging from a deep run to a beam reach.

Flying a symmetric spinnaker is complex and challenging. You can control a mainsail with just one sheet and a jib or genoa with two, but a symmetric spinnaker on any decent-size boat needs four control lines—i.e., two sheets and two guys (the latter hold the sail to the pole; the former, as with other sails, are used to trim it). This is not to mention the other lines—a downhaul, a topping lift, and (in some cases) an afterguy—you need to control the pole. Because of its large size and powerful shape, handling a symmetric spinnaker is often fraught with suspense. Even large well-trained racing crews sometimes slip up and lose control of these monsters. And even when the sail is set and pulling, you can still embarrass yourself. One slip of the wheel or an unexpected push from a wave on the quarter at the wrong moment can provoke a broach to windward, where the sail collapses and suddenly refills with a walloping thunderclap that shakes the boat to its keel. Or worse, you could broach to leeward, where

either the main is backwinded and slashes across the deck like a lethal weapon or (if the main is restrained by a preventer, as it should be) the boat is knocked down flat with its rig pinned to the water.

Serious racing sailors never flinch in the face of these perils and often launch spinnakers in conditions

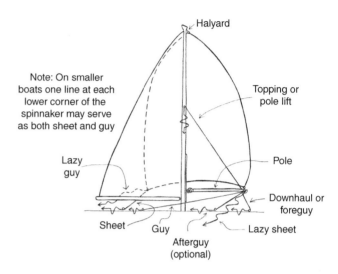

Four lines are needed to control a symmetric spinnaker (not counting the halyard), and two or three are needed to control the pole. That's a lot of rope for just one sail!

A symmetric spinnaker flown from a pole is only an accident waiting to happen. Even large racing crews sometimes have trouble handling them.

that send cruisers scuttling for their reefing lines. But there are many casual racers who want nothing to do with them, which is why non-spinnaker divisions are proliferating at big regattas and in popular ocean-racing events. Most cruising sailors, meanwhile, avoid symmetric spinnakers like the plague. Even those who lead a dual existence and indulge in serious racing normally leave the pole on deck and the chute in the sail locker when it comes time to head out for some gunkholing.

Over the years cruisers have adopted various alternatives to symmetric spinnakers. Known generically as cruising chutes, these have included drifters, multipurpose genoas (or MPG sails), and so-called gennakers. Like spinnakers these are large lightweight nylon sails cut with a full shape so they fly well and generate lots of power in light apparent winds. Unlike spinnakers, however, they have asymmetric profiles with a distinct luff and leech, are designed to be flown without poles, and are controlled with just one pair of sheets. In most cases they are tacked down at the bow of the boat with their luffs flying free. In some cases they are also flown like ordinary headsails, with their luffs bent onto a stay or furling rod.

Racing sailors derided cruising chutes for many years, then stole the idea for themselves. More modern variations, known as asymmetric spinnakers, or A-sails, first appeared on small race boats and fast racer-cruisers well over a decade ago. They are now just as common as symmetric spinnakers and have earned a place in the regular sail inventories of even the largest, most advanced race boats. They are also increasingly popular with cruisers.

The limiting factor with cruising chutes and asymmetric spinnakers is that they are still fore-and-aft sails; past a certain point as a boat turns downwind they inevitably fall into the shadow of the mainsail. A cruising chute or A-sail tacked down to the bow of a boat normally stops working at an apparent wind angle of about 140 to 150 degrees, but you can extend its range by moving its tack forward of the bow so that more of the sail is held clear of the mainsail. Small racing sport boats, some racer-cruisers, and a few high-end performance cruising boats now often carry retractable bowsprits specifically designed to accommodate asymmetric spinnakers. Some large race boats also often have small fixed sprits for flying A-sails. A few boats even have articulated sprits that pivot from side to side so the tack of the sail can be held out to windward. A poor man's way of achieving the same effect, which I've seen employed by a few canny cruisers, is to use a spinnaker pole, set low on the mast, to hold the tack of an A-sail or cruising chute a short distance out to windward. You can also use a pole, obviously, to hold an A-sail

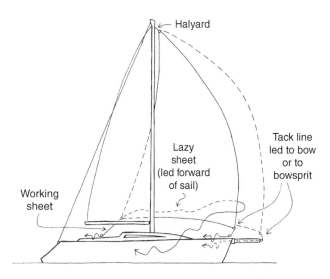

On an asymmetric spinnaker, if you include the line that controls the tack, there is only one more control line than is needed to control a genoa or jib. A-sails are often jibed forward of the foretriangle to avoid tangling with the headstay.

square to the wind when sailing at deep downwind angles. In this case, however, you may as well fly a symmetric spinnaker, as it will be just as much work, and the symmetric sail will perform better, as it is cut to be flown square to the wind.

Because they normally can't be carried at deep angles, the tactic of choice when flying a cruising chute or A-sail is to tack downwind on a series of broad reaches. The theory is that the extra speed the boat picks up sailing at a "hotter" angle with more apparent wind will more than compensate for the extra distance sailed. This is certainly true on lighter performance-oriented boats, particularly light multi-hulls. It is less effective on heavier boats that are incapable of planing or only do so when pressed hard. Even on a light boat, whether tacking downwind is faster than sailing dead downwind depends on existing conditions. Racers will switch to a symmetric spinnaker and run off when it behooves them; most cruisers, meanwhile, are happy to keep tacking downwind with an easier-to-handle sail.

The widespread use of A-sails and cruising chutes by cruisers has been facilitated by a useful tool known as the spinnaker sock or snuffer. These can also be used with symmetric spinnakers. The body of a snuffer consists of a long tube of light fabric that fits over the spinnaker like a giant condom. The bottom of the snuffer has a plastic skirt or mouth affixed to it, and there is a continuous control line running from a bridle on the bottom of the skirt to the head of the snuffer and down again to the skirt

Getting an A-sail's tack out forward of the bow increases its range and makes it easier to handle. This homemade A-frame folding sprit (left) is heavy but takes the tack well forward when deployed. The removable carbon-fiber sprit (right) is lighter and much easier to handle, but doesn't reach out very far. (Photo on right courtesy of Seldén Mast)

itself. The sail is raised ensconced inside the snuffer, where it can't catch any air and cause trouble. After the hoist is complete, the skirt of the snuffer is then pulled up the sail by pulling on the proper side of the control line, and the sail is thus unleashed and exposed to the wind. A quick trim on its sheet is usually then all that is needed to get it pulling its best. To recover the sail, you simply release the sheet and then pull the snuffer back over the luffing sail with the downhaul side of the control line. Then let the halyard go, and the contained sail drops to the deck in a controlled manner.

This sounds great in principle, but snuffers don't always work perfectly in practice. If the snuffer gets twisted up with the sail, or if the control line gets tangled with itself or the sail, the skirt of the snuffer can get locked partway up the sail, which can be a mess to sort out. A snuffer has to be carefully designed to avoid these problems. The control line should run in a segregated sleeve inside the body of the snuffer so that it is kept clear of both its other half and the sail itself. The control line's block at the head of the snuffer should have roller bearings and run as smoothly as possible. The control line itself should be a rope of reasonable diameter with a soft finish so that it doesn't cut hands too easily. The snuffer, meanwhile, should not be made of nylon, or it will adhere to the nylon sail when wet. The fabric used should be light with a soft finish to reduce friction as it slides over the sail and should have a porous open weave so that air can't get trapped inside. The head of the snuffer should have a short pendant and swivel on it so there is room for the bunched-up snuffer to ride over the head of the sail without chafing it and so the sail can pivot easily while flying without twisting the snuffer.

Another sort of large lightweight asymmetric headsail now popular with racing sailors, and with some cruisers, is the Code Zero sail, as it is known to monohull racers, or screecher, as it is known to

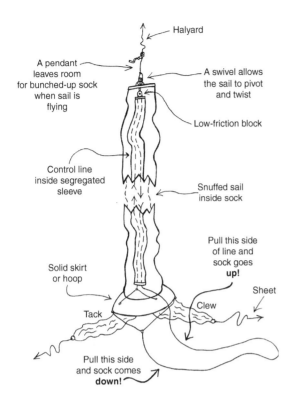

A snuffer (spinnaker sock) works great if it is properly designed. They can be used with symmetric or asymmetric spinnakers.

A poorly designed snuffer is nothing but a pain. After struggling with this beast several times during a transatlantic passage, we finally removed it and flew our spinnaker without it.

multihull sailors. These are heavier than asymmetric spinnakers and have a flatter shape, thus can be carried closer to the wind. To make handling these sails easier, they often have a pair of high-modulus Kevlar lines built into their luffs which run parallel to each other a couple of inches apart. Atop the twin luff lines there is a swivel, at the bottom a lightweight continuous-line furler, so you can furl the sail on its luff. The sail is hoisted rolled up on itself with the luff taut and then is unrolled. You can then ease the halyard to throw more shape into the sail if desired. To recover the sail, retighten the luff, furl the sail, and you can drop the entire apparatus on deck and stow it away.

Code Zero sails in effect take the place of large lightweight genoas that might be flown in light or moderate air at apparent wind angles ranging from about 50 to 140 degrees. On some cruising boats you'll see genoas like this installed on permanently mounted furlers directly ahead of the working headsail furler. This saves having to change out the working headsail for a bigger, lighter sail when the wind goes soft or shifts abaft the beam. The extra permanent furler, however, adds a lot of weight and windage to the rig and interferes with the flow of air across the luff of the working headsail right behind it. The huge advantage of using a Code Zero sail instead is that it is hoisted aloft only when needed. It is also much more versatile, as its luff is more malleable, which means you can give the sail a more productive shape when sailing with the wind on or abaft the beam.

Wing-and-Wing Rigs

Though snuffers and asymmetric sails have made flying spinnakers more palatable, many cruisers would rather not deal with them under any circumstances. These spinnaker-phobic souls prefer instead to travel downwind sailing wing-and-wing with the mainsail out as far as it can go on one side of the boat and a genoa or jib out on the other side, clear of the main. Sailing like this in flat water before a moderate to strong breeze the headsail is normally stable enough to stay open to the wind without assistance. In lumpy water, however, where both the boat and its sails are tossed about, or in light air, where there is less pressure on the sails, the headsail often collapses and flaps around. In these cases, or in any situation where a self-steering apparatus is engaged, it is best to use a pole to hold the headsail in position.

Poling out a headsail is not as challenging as flying a spinnaker with a pole, but it is more involved than sailing on the wind. In light air aboard smaller boats it is possible to use a light pole, but on larger boats, or in strong weather, a stronger pole should

TACK

Flying a screecher on a performance cruising cat (left). Note the curved luff, which can be controlled with the halyard. When the luff is taut the sail can be flown on a close reach. At the bottom of the sail is a continuous-line furler (right). There are twin high-modulus lines inside the luff so the sail can furl up on itself.

be used. It should also be rigged with its own support lines—a topping lift, a downhaul, and perhaps an afterguy—so that it remains stationary while the headsail is flying and cannot be blown back against the shrouds if the sail is backwinded. The length of the pole is an important consideration. A typical 130% genoa normally needs a pole that reaches from the mast to a point somewhere a little forward of the headstay. If a roller-furling genoa is used, the size of the sail can be easily reduced up to a point, and the pole can be eased forward a bit as the sail is rolled up. If the sail gets too small, however, the pole will be too long to work properly.

One way to cope with this problem is to use a telescoping whisker pole. The lightest, cheapest ones have sliding friction sleeves that twist and lock in place, like those on telescoping boathooks, but these eventually fail if they are used much. The best telescoping poles are the heavier, more expensive ones that have control lines instead of friction sleeves holding the sliding part of the pole in place. You can also use the control lines to shorten or lengthen the pole while it is deployed. If your boat is much longer than about 38 feet, or if you cruise offshore, you should pole out headsails on full-size fixed-length spinnaker poles. If more than one length is required, you'll unfortunately have to carry more than one pole. Larger poles are much easier to handle if they are made of carbon fiber rather than aluminum. Even if you are otherwise averse to using modern materials on your boats, you will greatly appreciate having a lightweight carbon pole on your foredeck.

Chutes for Cats

One big advantage of cruising in a catamaran is that it is far easier to fly a symmetric spinnaker and make good progress sailing dead downwind. Most cats are wide enough that a symmetric chute can be easily flown without a pole with the two lower corners of the sail attached to each of the boat's bows. Half the sail—or more, if you sail at a slightly shallower angle—is clear of the lee of the mainsail, so keeping it full is not a problem. Because the sail is held firm at all three corners by the two bows and the mast, it is much more stable than a symmetric spinnaker flown from a pole and is less likely to cause trouble. Throw a reliable snuffer into the equation and it becomes a veritable house pet, easily managed by the most laid-back of sailors.

Some catamaran rigs, however, are not designed to be sailed this way. If a mast has no inner forestay, babystay, diamond stays, or lower forward shrouds to support its forward midsection, it will have a tendency to invert—i.e., its midsection will bow backward—if the only load on it is from a headsail pulling at its top section. For such a mast to stay in column, it also needs its mainsail pushing at it from behind. Such rigs may not be compromised if a headsail is flown alone in a light to moderate breeze, but the mast may well be damaged if this is done in strong conditions. Note, too, this is true not only of catamarans, but of any rig with little or no support for the mast's forward midsection.

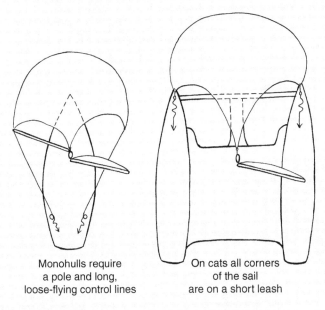

Monohulls require a pole and long, loose-flying control lines

On cats all corners of the sail are on a short leash

Symmetric kites on cats (right) are much easier to control than on monohulls (left).

With both main and chute flying, loads on the middle of mast offset one another

With more lightly stayed rigs, the middle of mast may invert under spinnaker alone

Many multihull rigs and some monohull rigs have little or no support for the forward midsection of the mast. On boats like this, large headsails (e.g., spinnakers) should not be flown with the main down!

Some cat cruisers, eager to further simplify their lives, go so far as to fly only a spinnaker and no mainsail when sailing downwind. This reduces boat speed, as the area of the mainsail is lost, but is a more balanced sail plan, as all the sail is far forward pulling the boat along by its nose. The boat consequently is easier to steer and perhaps can be handled by an autopilot or windvane where otherwise it might be necessary to handsteer to keep from rounding up.

Many cats carry a bowsprit from which an asymmetric spinnaker or screecher can be flown. A light cat will often get where it is going faster by tacking downwind on a series of broad reaches under such a sail. Because these boats accelerate so quickly once the wind is anywhere near the beam, apparent wind speeds are normally much higher than they would be with the wind right aft. Trimarans, too, are normally configured to fly A-sails on a centerline sprit when sailing off the wind because they are faster on a broad reach than a run, and because their amas, or outer hulls, are not capable of carrying rig loads.

Another way to sail wing and wing is to leave the mainsail down and pole out two headsails instead. This puts all the sail area forward and makes the boat more balanced and easier to steer. Before the advent of reliable self-steering gear, flying twin headsails was standard operating procedure on long downwind passages, as it is a simple matter to get a boat to steer itself when it is rigged like this. By leading the two working jibsheets through blocks in the cockpit to either side of the tiller, the pressure on the sails

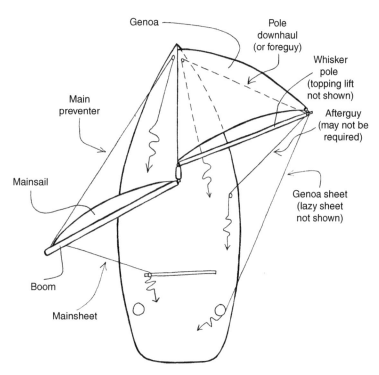

A typical wing-and-wing rig—this is the way most cruisers sail downwind.

can be used to steer the boat and keep it on a downwind course. In the days before roller furling you needed twin headstays to fly a pair of headsails, but this is no longer necessary as most headsail roller-furling rods come equipped with two luff grooves. One big advantage to flying the sails together on the same furling rod is that you can reef and furl them simultaneously.

Poling out two headsails obviously requires two poles. Back when twin-headsail rigs were common, the trick was to rig twin poles and leave them stored on the pole track against the mast so that they could be quickly deployed when needed. Some modern cruisers still rig twin poles this way to save having to shift a single pole back and forth across the boat when jibing. Storing two poles up against the mast, however, adds a fair amount of weight well above deck level. An alternative to using twin poles is to use the main boom in place of one of the poles. You can do this easily by leading one of the working jibsheets through a block fastened to the end of the boom. The boom can then be brought forward to the shrouds and secured with the mainsheet and a preventer.

Sailing wing and wing on the author's cutter Lunacy. *Note the forward position of the preventer on the mainsail. This is not as secure, but is more versatile, as the preventer can also act as a vang when sailing on a reach.*

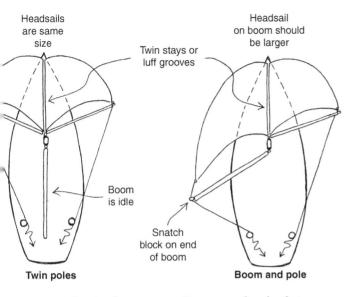

Twin headsail variations. Using two headsails in a wing-and-wing set puts the center of effort forward and makes the boat easier to handle.

Headsails are same size

Twin stays or luff grooves

Boom is idle

Twin poles

Headsail on boom should be larger

Snatch block on end of boom

Boom and pole

Twin-headsail rigs are no longer very popular, but there is no good reason for this. Some argue it is burdensome to carry two identically sized headsails, but if you aren't planning to run the two sheets to the tiller to steer the boat there is no reason why the sails have to be the same size. Flying a 130% genoa on one side of the boat poled out on the main boom and a 90% or 100% working jib on the other side poled out on a spinnaker or whisker pole is a per- fectly viable downwind rig. It does not present as much sail area as a full main and genoa flying wing and wing, but the boat will still be more balanced and easier to steer, hence more easily handled by an autopilot or a wind vane. There will also be much less chafe, as the mainsail will be saved from scrap- ing against the shrouds.

The only cruisers who should not fly twin headsails are those with rigs that do not have lower forward shrouds, a babystay, diamond stays, or a staysail stay to support the forward side of the mast's midsection. As mentioned earlier, the mast on a rig like this will invert if only headsails are flown from it.

STORMSAILS

This subject normally is only of interest to bluewater cruisers. Coastal cruisers, however, should also give some thought to what sails they can fly in extremely strong winds. Though they are less likely to sail in such winds, if they are caught out they are more likely to have some shoreline to leeward, thus should be prepared to beat away from it if necessary. This requires appropriate sails.

According to conventional wisdom a proper suit of stormsails should include both a storm trysail to fly on the mast and a storm jib to fly forward of it. To rig a trysail appropriately, a dedicated trysail track should be installed on the mast. It is unrealistic to think anyone is going to unbend a mainsail in high winds and bend on a trysail in its place. Conventional wisdom also holds that a trysail should sit bagged at the base of the mast ready to hoist at a moment's notice. In the real world, however, few people go to this trouble. The more realistic option is put a third reef in your mainsail. If the sailcloth is not too light, and if the third reef reduces the size of the sail down to about 30% of its total area, a triple-reefed main should work just as well in extremis as a trysail. The only drawback is if the sail gets damaged, you'll have to repair a large, expensive mainsail rather than a much smaller, much cheaper trysail.

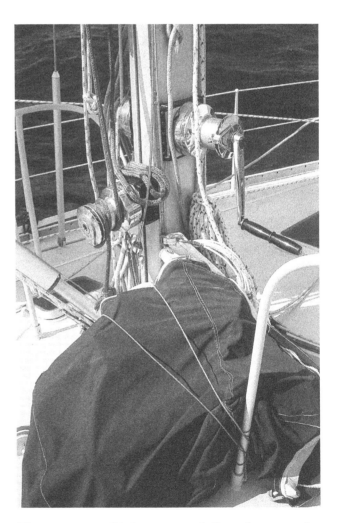

This storm trysail is bent onto a dedicated mast track and is kept bagged at the bottom of the mast ready to fly when conditions get extreme. Most cruisers don't bother with storm trysails anymore and rely on a tripled-reefed mainsail instead.

Even if you decide not to carry a trysail, you should still carry a dedicated storm jib. Don't think for a moment you can reef your roller-furling genoa to handkerchief size in a 40-knot blow and sail anywhere near the wind with it. Its shape will be far too full and the sailcloth will likely be too light. You can sail off the wind in very strong conditions with a deeply roller-reefed genoa, but it is preferable to do so under a storm jib in any event. All it takes is one broken furling line, and all of a sudden you have way too much headsail out and no easy way to get it down. If you do carry a storm jib, don't delude yourself into thinking you can hoist it in place of your regular headsail in strong conditions. This may be possible if your headsail is hanked on, but if it's on a furling rod, there's no way you'll want to strip it off the rod in a big blow.

The best way to fly a storm jib is on a separate inner forestay behind the working headstay. As mentioned earlier, you can then just roll up or douse your regular headsail and hoist the storm jib behind it. The storm jib also balances much better against a triple-reefed mainsail or trysail if it is closer to the mast. Many bluewater cruisers already have either a fixed or collapsible inner forestay on their boat, so this presents no problem for them. Most coastal cruisers, however, sail simple sloops with roller-furling genoas and no inner forestay. In this case the best answer may be to carry an ATN Gale Sail, which is a storm jib with a large luff sleeve designed to bend on around a rolled-up headsail on a furling rod. Once bent on, you can hoist the Gale Sail with a spare halyard up over the rolled-up sail. In practice it is not very easy to get a Gale Sail bent on around a rolled-up headsail, but it is easier than stripping a large headsail off a furling rod in high winds. Unlike earlier storm jibs that worked on this same principle, the Gale Sail slides nicely up the rolled-up sail when you hoist it thus it is a workable option.

FIVE

DECK GEAR AND LAYOUTS

The deck of any sailboat is the vessel's interface, the arena in which the crew struggle to maintain control of their fate. On a serious race boat this struggle is mostly focused on handling sails, with little thought given to anchoring or mooring, stowing and deploying a tender, or even where the crew might deploy themselves when idle or otherwise enjoying themselves.

The deck of a cruising boat is more complicated, for cruising crew not only must handle sails reasonably efficiently, they perform many other tasks as well. The deck of a casual weekend cruiser normally does not seem intimidating, but the deck of a bluewater cruising boat or a serious coastal cruiser is usually the product of a long series of careful compromises. Even if you don't live on your boat, the more time you spend on it, the more questions you must answer about the use of deck space.

In the end, if you own your boat long enough, you will devise a unique formula for how your deck ought to function. In many cases the details of the formula can be discovered only through trial and error. In other cases, you can make intelligent choices before gaining much experience. Your preferences, however, will certainly mature over time. For it is here on deck where many of the most important lessons pertaining to sailing and cruising are learned. The best sailors and cruisers never stop learning these lessons. They never stop asking questions, and they never stop looking for better ways to do things.

THE ALL-IMPORTANT COCKPIT

Though it takes up relatively little space on deck, the cockpit is where the cruising crew spend most of their time when not below. A cockpit functions both as the deck's working nerve center and as its social center and may sometimes need to do both simultaneously. As a general rule, serious conflicts between the two functions should be resolved in favor of working demands, but social concerns should never be ignored entirely, as this may cripple your enjoyment of the boat.

The threshold issues are cockpit size and location. As to the latter, there are three options. Aft cockpits, which are situated behind the superstructure of the cabin (if there is one) at the back of the boat, are traditional. Center cockpits are increasingly popular, however, particularly on larger boats. Here the cockpit is situated in effect on top of the cabin, in the middle of the boat behind the mast and right under the boom. Split cockpits, meanwhile, are the least common type. Here there are effectively two cockpits, one all the way aft and another smaller one in the middle of the boat.

On most boats 40 feet and shorter the cockpit is aft. There have been a few small center-cockpit boats built over the years, but these are often ugly, as they have too much freeboard, which is needed to fit in cabin space under the cockpit and tends to make a small boat look slab-sided. If the boat instead has no cabin space under the cockpit, with entirely separate cabins forward and aft, the result can be a

167

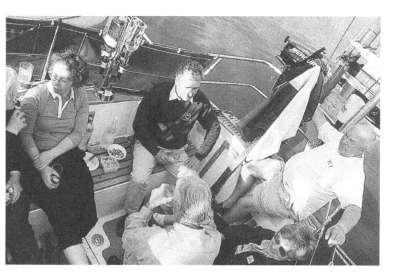

This cruiser has devised a clever liquor-dispensing winch handle to help lubricate social activity in his cockpit. It is doubtful, however, that it works well as a winch handle.

choppy deck profile. Center cockpits on small boats are also apt to be cramped. Realistically, they only make sense on boats 45 feet or longer.

One big advantage of an aft cockpit is its distance from the bow, especially when the spray starts flying

in rough conditions. Aft cockpits also normally have the largest, most accessible storage areas, with one or more lockers under the seats and also perhaps an aft lazarette in or directly behind the cockpit. Center cockpits, by comparison, have little storage, just a couple of small cubbies in the coamings, and even these are often lacking. Though center-cockpit boats often have one or two good-size lazarettes all the way aft, these are not convenient for stowing items you want accessible from the cockpit.

Center cockpits are normally superior social spaces, as you can often hang out near a center cockpit, on the side decks or on the deck immediately behind it, and still participate in cockpit society. This effectively enlarges the cockpit and makes it easier for active crew to work without displacing idlers. Even on large boats, the side decks around aft cockpits are often too narrow to lounge on; there is little or no space behind the cockpit, and the cockpit itself is usually walled off from the middle of the boat by a spray dodger. As a result, you are either in the cockpit or not, and if you're not, you are cut off from whatever is happening there.

Split cockpits are more complicated. Either both cockpits are working areas, or the aft cockpit is a dedicated working space and the center cockpit is

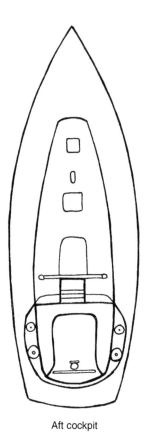

Aft cockpit

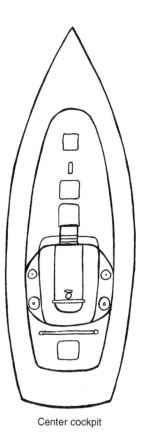

Center cockpit

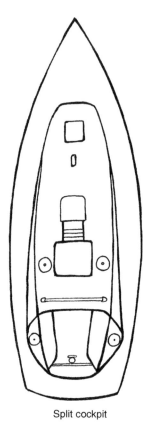

Split cockpit

Cockpit layout variations. Aft cockpits are the most traditional; center cockpits are popular on larger boats.

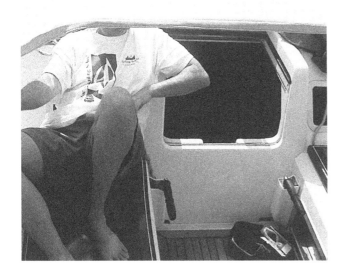

used solely for social purposes. The latter arrangement is common on large luxury yachts where professional crew are discouraged from fraternizing with the owner and guests. To that end each cockpit has its own companionway, and the center cockpit has spray protection so people can congregate there in a wide range of conditions. The former option is more common and is found on large to midsize racer-cruisers. Here the point is to spread out working stations so a large crew can race the boat more efficiently. Effectively, the entire deck aft of the mast becomes one vast working cockpit with two nerve centers. Because there is so much space, it is easy for some to work while others hang out. Usually though there is little spray protection for the more forward cockpit, at most a pramhood over a companionway. When the spray starts flying, everyone has to cram behind the dodger in the aft cockpit to stay dry.

A larger cockpit is obviously easier to both work and socialize in. Conventional wisdom has long held, however, that small cockpits are safer, as they trap less water if filled by a boarding wave and so are less likely to help a boat founder. In the past many cruisers favored tiny cockpits; some even eliminated the footwells in their cockpits, making them perfectly flush instead so they couldn't trap any water. A better solution is to make sure a cockpit has adequate drains. The larger the cockpit's footwell, the larger these should be. The best solution, at least with an aft cockpit, is to have an open transom, as this, like a flush cockpit, can't trap any water at all.

In some split cockpits both areas are for working crew and the forward area will likely have little or no shelter (top). In other split cockpits the forward area is only for socializing and is well protected (bottom).

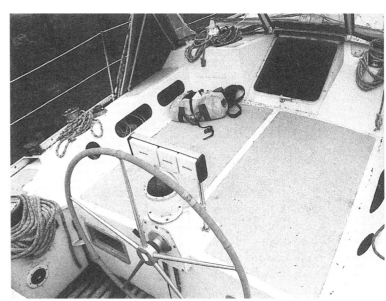

This French cruising boat has a flush cockpit with just a small footwell aft for the helmsman. It is both functional and comfortable.

An unusually deep and narrow center cockpit on an Outbound 52. This is the best-designed center cockpit I've ever seen—functional and comfortable while sailing, with a cutout in the hard dodger so you needn't stoop when going down the companionway. The seats are close enough so you can brace to windward when heeled.

A comfortable cockpit footwell is at least 15 inches deep, and the seat backs at least 15 inches high—20 inches works much better for both. Unfortunately, many modern boats have overly shallow cockpits. This has always been an issue with center cockpits, because of the need to fit accommodation space underneath the cockpit. It is increasingly true of aft cockpits for the same reason, since modern builders insist on inserting cabins under aft cockpits, even on boats as small as 30 feet.

The width of the footwell is also important. If it's too wide, you can't brace your feet against the edge of the leeward seat while sitting to windward when the boat is heeled. Depending on how wide the seats are, the footwell should not be more than 30 inches across; 24 to 26 inches works much better. Again, unfortunately, modern cockpits are generally getting wider as boats are much beamier in their after sections so builders

can fit in aft cabins. On some boats, however, there are permanently mounted tables with folding leaves running down the center of the cockpit, and these make fabulous bracing points. They also, however, make it harder to cross the cockpit when tacking.

Cockpit seats should be about 6 feet long and at least 20 inches across so people can sleep on them. On most modern boats this isn't an issue, though some boats do have curved cockpit seats, which is not helpful. If the tops of the cockpit coamings are at least 8 inches across they too can serve as seats, provided there is room to sit between any winches and/or cleats installed in the area.

Control Lines

Just as all roads once led to Rome, many cruising sailors now believe that all working lines should lead to the cockpit. The result, unfortunately, is often a pile of multicolored spaghetti. On aft-cockpit boats the most common scenario is that almost every line coming off the mast or deck forward of the cockpit is led back through blocks and organizers to a battery of rope clutches arrayed around two winches on either side of the companionway under the cockpit dodger. The more active lines are usually the mainsheet, two control lines for a main traveler situated just forward of the dodger, the main halyard, and one or more mainsail reefing lines (for either a slab-reefed main or an in-mast furling main). Less active lines led to this same location may include one or more headsail halyards, perhaps a dedicated spinnaker halyard and a spinnaker pole downhaul, perhaps one or more topping lifts (one for the main boom, plus one for the spinnaker pole), plus maybe a mainsail outhaul.

On race boats this is not too troublesome. The dodger is normally removed, so the companionway winches are easy to access and grind. The tails of all the active lines are simply flung down the companionway into the main cabin, where there is plenty of room for them to splay about without getting too tangled up with each other. Plus there is plenty of crew aboard. Each companionway winch has a grinder on it, so it easy to work the winches simultaneously if necessary, and there are people at the mast to jump halyards and clear any snags in any line running back to the cockpit.

On a cruising boat, however, the all-lines-to-Rome strategy is very much a two-edged sword. Theoretically, it enables a small crew to handle a boat without leaving the cockpit, but it can also make it harder for a small crew to work a boat. One big problem is winch access. With the cockpit dodger raised, as it normally is on a cruising boat, companionway winches are harder to use. The dodger frame may block winch handles from swinging all the way around their winches. The dodger also sometimes makes it impossible for crew to get directly over a winch, which is the preferred position for loading and unloading lines and grinding the winch. Instead the winch must be loaded and unloaded at an awkward side angle; the grinding also must be done from the side, with the grinder sawing the handle back and forth over a short throw distance, thus squandering a large part of the mechanical advantage the winch was designed to create.

Line storage and organization is another problem. Unless you dump lines down the companionway, it is hard to keep the many lines at the forward end of the cockpit neatly sorted and ready for use. Many sailors install line bags around the companionway, but inevitably several lines get stuffed in the same

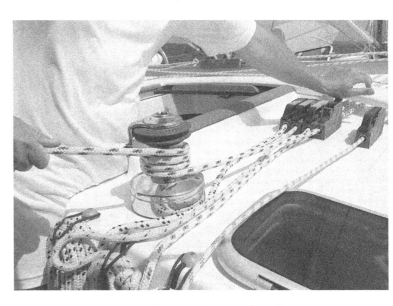

This one coachroof winch serves five lines led aft from the mast. Here the dodger has been removed, which makes line handling much easier. When the dodger is up the line handler can't see the mainsail and must stoop while working. (Courtesy of SAIL Magazine; Photo by Malcolm White.)

bag and get tangled with each other, which leads to annoying situations where much untangling must precede even the simplest bit of line handling. The alternative is to make up separate coils of line and hang them neatly on hooks or line ties, but coiling a line while crouching under a cockpit dodger can be awkward and uncomfortable.

Also, lines that must be handled more or less simultaneously are sometimes led to the same winch. A classic example is a slab-reefed mainsail, with both the main halyard and a reef line coming to one winch. This means you must first put the halyard on the winch to ease it in a controlled manner (note, too, you'll be under the dodger and won't be able to see the sail, so you won't be sure exactly how much to ease the halyard unless you have marked it), then you must clutch the halyard, unload the winch, reload it with the reefing line, take up on the reefing line, clutch the reefing line, unload the winch, reload it with the halyard, then take up on the halyard. All of which can be done much faster if the lines are on separate winches.

Yet another issue is friction in the line runs. Leading everything aft to the cockpit means lines must be longer, with one or more extra turns around blocks to create fair leads to the winches, all of which makes the lines harder to pull. This is particularly true of halyards. When a halyard is led aft to the cockpit, it is impossible for one crewmember to hoist it very

One crewmember alone can efficiently execute a hoist when halyards are on the mast (left). When halyards are led aft it takes two to do it well (right)—one at the mast to jump the line and one aft to tail the winch. (Photo on right courtesy of SAIL *Magazine; Photo by Malcolm White.)*

far by hand, so most of the hoist must be done on a winch, which takes much longer. Extra friction also makes it noticeably harder to control reefing lines on slab-reefed mainsails.

Not that leading lines aft to the forward end of a cockpit is always a bad idea. Often it makes a lot of sense, but it should not be done on a wholesale basis. Instead each line run should be evaluated independently.

First consider the mainsheet, as this is normally the most important and most frequently handled control line on board. On any cruising boat sailed by a small crew, where it is likely one person will want to handle the main and the helm simultaneously, it is critical for the mainsheet to be within reach of the helmsman. Unfortunately, the mainsheet on most modern aft-cockpit cruising boats is led to the coachroof where it can't be reached from the helm, unless the cockpit is small and the boat is steered with a tiller. Another problem with this is that if the dodger is up you often can't see the main while trimming it. The arrangement found on most center-cockpit boats, where the mainsheet is led to a full traveler directly behind the cockpit, is far superior. This takes three frequently used lines (the sheet and the two traveler control lines) out of the spaghetti mix around the companionway and puts them right where the helmsman can get to them. This way a sole watch-stander can easily cast off the mainsheet or drop the traveler if a big puff hits the boat. Another big advantage is that the mainsail is in plain view, and accurate adjustments can be made without having to duck in and out from under a dodger to check sail trim. Finally,

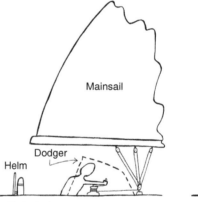

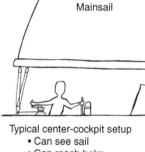

Typical aft-cockpit setup
- Can't see sail
- Can't reach helm
- Mid-boom sheeting is harder

Typical center-cockpit setup
- Can see sail
- Can reach helm
- End-of-boom sheeting is

There are various advantages to having the mainsheet traveler aft of the helm, where the helmsman can reach it, rather than forward on the coachroof under a dodger.

leading the sheet from the end of the boom rather than the middle, as is required when the traveler is forward of the cockpit, puts less stress on the boom and reduces the effort required to trim the sail.

The only problem with leading a mainsheet to a traveler behind the cockpit is that the sheet must be carefully positioned so it doesn't catch the helmsman unawares. If the traveler is close to the cockpit with the sheet angling forward over the helm position, the helmsman may be caught by the sheet in an accidental jibe. This is sometimes an issue on undersized center-cockpit boats, where the cockpit is just a bit

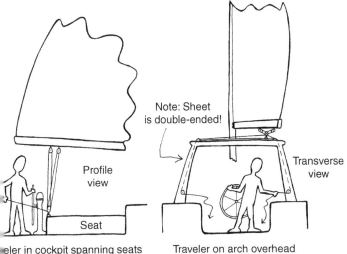

Two options for handling the mainsheet: in the cockpit (left) or over the cockpit (right).

too cramped to work well, and also on some older aft-cockpit boats with travelers behind the cockpit.

Modern aft-cockpit boats almost never have space for mounting the traveler aft of the helm, and to make the mainsheet accessible from the helm the sheet and traveler must instead go right in the cockpit, usually mounted on a rail spanning the cockpit seats just forward of the helm. Alternatively, it can be situated on a bridgedeck right behind the companionway. Cockpit-mounted travelers are often seen on race boats, but are much less popular on cruising boats. Most cruisers believe the sheet gets in the way when led to the middle of the cockpit and poses a danger to the crew if there is an accidental jibe or if the traveler is accidentally released and suddenly crashes to leeward. These are valid concerns, but the danger should be minimal if the traveler and sheet leads are properly designed and the crew is reasonably wary.

Another way to make the mainsheet more accessible on an aft-cockpit boat is to lead it to a traveler

This forward traveler arch gets the mainsheet out of the cockpit and provides solid support for the back end of a dodger with a solid windshield and canvas roof. Unfortunately the traveler here is too short to be effective.

mounted on an arch over the cockpit. In many ways, this is ideal. A double-ended mainsheet can be led down either side of the arch and can be easily reached by the helmsman on either side of the cockpit. Both the sheet and traveler are also removed from the cockpit, so there is no chance of their tangling with the crew. In some cases these arches span the aft section of the cockpit, but this only works on boats at least 42 feet long, as there must be room under the arch for crew to stand. In others the arch spans the forward end of the cockpit, where it can also serve as a base for the back end of a dodger. This works well on smaller boats, as the arch can be lower here. The one drawback to cockpit arches is that they often look a bit ungainly. Only a handful of builders now put them on boats, but I suspect they will become more popular over time. What looks good to the subjective eye, after all, is often dictated by what works best in the long run.

Halyards and reefing lines for a slab-reefed mainsail should not normally be led to the forward end of a cruising boat's cockpit. Halyards are always much easier for a single crewmember to hoist if they are left at the mast. This way you can quickly haul the line hand over hand for most of the hoist, and only use a winch at the tail end to haul the sail up the last few feet. On boats under 35 feet you really only need the winch to tension the halyard after the hoist is complete. If the mainsail's reef lines are also at the mast, you can quickly reef the sail from a single location with a clear view of the sail. In layouts like this, the reef lines are normally led to a dedicated winch on the back of the mast right under the boom, though on older boats the reefing winch or winches may be on the boom itself, which is not as convenient. The halyard, meanwhile, runs to another winch on the side of the mast nearby, so it is easy to handle the lines in rapid succession. I've found I can nearly always tuck in a reef working at the mast at least twice as fast as I can in a cockpit; it is also much easier to coil the lines and stow them afterward. The drawback, of course, is that you must go to the mast to do all this, but, as previously discussed, this is still often necessary even when lines are led to the cockpit.

The lines that should be led aft to the cockpit are those used less frequently and those requiring small infrequent adjustments. These include topping lifts, vang lines, spinnaker downhauls, and mainsail outhauls. Also, there is no harm in leading rarely used halyards for roller-furling sails back to the cockpit. Note, however, that any halyard for a headsail that is likely to be changed for another sail while underway should always stay at the mast, as all work concerning the dousing and hoisting of the sail can then take place at the mast and forward of

it. Finally, if you have an in-mast furling main, it of course makes sense to have all its control lines led aft to the cockpit. Indeed, there is little point in having an in-mast main if you routinely have to leave the cockpit to cope with it.

As to split cockpits, in most cases the purpose of such a layout, as mentioned, is to avoid concentrating too many working lines in in a single area. This is a good arrangement if there is a large crew working the boat. In most cases, the mainsheet and traveler are located on a bridgedeck between the two cockpits. All ancillary lines, such as the vang, downhaul, outhaul, and so on, as well as the halyards, are normally led to the forward cockpit. Sometimes all headsail sheets are led to the forward cockpit, sometimes to the aft cockpit, and sometimes they are split between the two, with the primary sheets led to the forward cockpit and the spinnaker and/or staysail sheets led to the aft cockpit, or vice versa. A small cruising crew will not appreciate such a layout unless they are very active and like moving around a lot when sailing the boat.

Shelter

The minimal cockpit shelter found on most cruising boats is a canvas cockpit dodger or sprayhood. These are designed to shield the forward end of the cockpit and the companionway from spray flying down the deck, thus are practically mandatory when a boat is beating to weather in vigorous conditions. They are also handy when it's raining, as they allow the companionway to stay open and dry and can shelter one or two crewmembers sitting forward in the cockpit. Dodgers are normally mounted on frames of stainless-steel or aluminum tubing and have plastic transparent windows sewn into their forward and side panels so lines of sight, particularly from the helm, can be maintained in these directions. Most frames have articulated joints so the dodger can be folded down out of the way. In practice, however, most canvas dodgers are left up permanently as their plastic windows quickly become scarred and nearly opaque if they are folded and creased very often. Some European cruising boats have folding canvas dodger roofs installed atop fixed windshields, which is a neat solution to this problem. As discussed above, a dodger can limit a crew's ability to handle lines in the forward part of the cockpit, but if a cockpit is laid out well such interference can be minimized.

The next step up is a canvas bimini top, which effectively puts a roof over the cockpit. These again are mounted on frames of metal tubing that are usually hinged so they can be folded back out of the way, though in many cases the frame may be permanently

This bimini frame makes it difficult to use this winch efficiently. This is a common problem and is a good reason not to sail with a bimini up.

Why cruisers love dodgers: without some shelter at the forward end of the cockpit beating to windward in strong conditions can be a wet and miserable experience.

installed. A bimini's primary purpose is to shade the cockpit from the sun, and in tropical or subtropical climates they are often considered essential. They also provide some protection when it rains. The big problem with biminis, however, is that their frames often interfere with cockpit sheet winches. The frame legs not only may block the rotation of winch handles, they also often make it impossible for crew to put their bodies over winches when grinding them.

Biminis also block the cockpit crew's view of the mainsail. Some biminis have small plastic windows sewn in to give a view of the sail, but these are never of any use to anyone but the helmsman and are often too small or scratched up to be helpful. The crew as a result is forever having to contort their bodies to stick their heads out from under the bimini to check the sail while trimming. Also, biminis usually make it

impossible for helmsmen 6 feet or taller to stand up straight at the wheel. For all these reasons, I won't sail a boat with the bimini raised if I can possibly avoid it. If you truly must have a bimini, I urge you never to have one permanently installed. You should also be sure its frame doesn't interfere with any sheet winches when it is folded away, as a surprising number of installations fail this critical test.

The most devoted bimini freaks not only have their biminis permanently installed, they also add side curtains. These Florida rooms, as some call them, provide perfect shelter from both rain and sun, but they also make it much harder to sail and work the boat, as they restrict access not only to winches, but to the deck itself. Reasonable cruisers deploy side curtains only when their boat is at rest and when it is actually raining; less hardy souls who fear any contact with the elements keep them on all the time, even when underway. I find side curtains often make me seasick, as there's something about looking at the

With a dodger, extended bimini top, and full side curtains these cruisers are so well protected they may as well have stayed home. The bimini is permanently mounted (note the solar panels on top) and must make it hard to trim sails.

world through sheets of smeary transparent plastic with a strong vinyl odor that makes me nauseous even when conditions are calm.

Another option is some form of solid shelter. A hard dodger, for example, is an excellent item to have on any cruising sailboat, most particularly a blue-water boat. The primary advantage of a hard dodger is that crew can climb on top of it when stowing and flaking a mainsail, whereas a more flimsy canvas dodger presents nothing but an obstacle when this chore is performed. A hard dodger is also a fine place to mount solar panels, although this may prevent you from climbing on top of it. On larger boats a hard dodger can be expanded into a doghouse that can accommodate an on-deck navigation station and/or a watch berth or two. Having once crossed the Atlantic on a large schooner with a doghouse that had two watch berths in it, I can attest this is an extremely useful arrangement.

The ultimate solid on-deck shelter is a pilothouse with an enclosed steering and navigation station. On larger traditional boats these are usually high-profile stand-alone structures situated on deck. In some cases such structures are mimicked on smaller motorsailers. On more modern boats an inside steering station may be integrated into the below-deck accommodations as a feature in a "raised saloon." On most of these there is also an outside steering station in a conventional cockpit with full access to sail-control lines. This clearly represents the best of both worlds, as you can either sail the boat from the cockpit on deck whenever conditions are fine or hunker down indoors when they are not. In either case, you must be outdoors to handle lines and sails, but for routine watchkeeping while underway, being able to steer from inside in poor conditions is a real luxury.

Miscellaneous Features

Engine controls and instrument displays. On many sailboats with steering wheels the engine's throttle and transmission controls are located on the steering pedestal directly behind the wheel. To use the controls the helmsman must reach through the spokes

The homemade hard dodger on this small cruising boat is foam sheathed with fiberglass, tough enough to stand on if necessary. The handholds on the side make it easy to move between the cockpit and deck.

The pilothouse on this Bruckmann motorsailer might also be considered a raised saloon. Whatever you want to call it, being able to steer from inside is a great convenience. Note that this boat also has an open cockpit and wheel aft.

of the wheel, which is at best awkward and in certain situations may be dangerous. On smaller boats with tillers, the controls are often low in the cockpit footwell, along with the engine's ignition and instrument panel. This means the helmsman must crouch to use the controls and/or read the instruments. Also, the panel is likely to be drowned if a wave comes aboard and fills the cockpit, and the engine control levers can easily get tangled in stray working lines or get kicked by working crew.

The best location for engine controls is someplace where the helmsman can easily reach them while steering and conning the boat. Usually this is a more elevated spot on the side of the cockpit where they are at least out of range of the crew's feet, though in most cases there will still be some concern about stray lines. On some modern steering pedestals it is possible to put the controls within easy reach, either atop a wide dashboard-type pedestal with a small wheel behind it, or on a pedestal with the wheel mounted in front. In the latter case, the wheel has wraparound spokes so you can steer from behind the pedestal with unobstructed access to the controls.

The helmsman on this cruising boat will have no problem reaching pedestal controls thanks to this forward-mounted steering wheel with wraparound spokes.

The ignition and instrument panel, meanwhile, should be mounted where it is most likely to stay dry. If mounted in the cockpit, it should be weather-proofed and elevated well above the cockpit sole. Easy access is less important, as the ignition is normally turned on and off at discrete moments when the crew is not otherwise very busy. If the panel has audible "idiot" alarms that sound when the engine operates outside normal parameters, it also need not be very visible. The best place for the panel is inside the cabin within easy reach of the companionway. This way you can reach it from the cockpit without too much fuss, but it is also much less likely to get drenched.

Sailing and navigation instruments obviously should be mounted in a visible location. On many modern cruising boats with wheel steering, they are atop the pedestal on a panel over the binnacle where the helmsman can easily see them. The problem then, however, is that they cannot be seen by anyone forward of the binnacle. If an autopilot is engaged and there is no need for anyone to stand behind the wheel, this will likely include all the cockpit crew, including any designated watch-standers. It is best

therefore to situate these displays at the forward end of the cockpit. They are often mounted on an aft-facing cabinhouse bulkhead, but here they are easily blocked by cockpit crew or by control lines dangling over the aft edge of the coachroof. The very best location is on a panel directly over the companionway, where the instruments will be blocked only by crew using (or standing in) the companionway. The ideal setup is to have one set of displays over the binnacle for the helmsman and another set of repeaters over the companionway for everyone else to see. On many race boats and racer-cruisers there are also repeaters mounted on the mast below the boom. This way everyone on deck aft of the boom can see what's going on, which is fantastic, except when the cockpit dodger is raised, in which case the cockpit crew forward of the binnacle has to read the displays through the dodger's plastic windows.

Navigation instruments mounted on pivoting arms in the companionway are plainly visible when needed and can be quickly pushed out of the way when they are not.

Tables. Having some kind of table available for use in the cockpit is a high priority for many cruisers. The most basic rig is a collapsible table mounted on the forward side of a steering pedestal. These often are only lightly supported when deployed and may not be robust enough to be used while sailing, but they are handy when the boat is at rest. Collapsible tables can usually be installed on most any size boat with a steering pedestal. They are normally unobtrusive when stowed away and do not hamper work performed in the cockpit.

The more substantial option, normally found only on larger boats, is a table with folding leaves mounted permanently in the middle of the cockpit between the seats. These are quite strong and can be used while underway. As mentioned earlier, permanently mounted tables are great bracing points but do restrict movement across the cockpit. I believe the advantage of the bracing points outweighs the disadvantage of restricted maneuverability, though I may feel differently when I am older and less adept at hopping over tables in a hurry. Another advantage is that fixed tables often have useful storage wells buried in their central bases. These are great for stowing the small bits of gear that tend to gather in a cockpit. In some cases these wells are insulated and can be packed with ice and cold beverages.

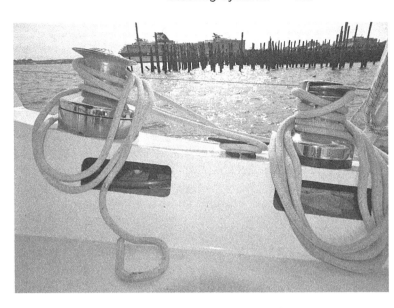

The coaming boxes on this aft-cockpit cruising boat are handy for stowing cockpit gear; such boxes unfortunately are increasingly rare.

Coaming boxes. Another useful cockpit amenity is the coaming box or cubbyhole. These were once nearly ubiquitous, and everyone took them for granted. Now they are increasingly rare, as the space inside cockpit coamings tends to get filled with interior accommodations and/or boat systems. It is absurd, of course, to say you should not have a boat without them, but you will never be sorry if you do have them. If you can't stuff stray cockpit gear into a coaming box, it tends instead to pile up on the coachroof under the dodger. Here it inevitably interferes with critical control lines.

STEERING SYSTEMS

The simplest way to control a boat's rudder from its deck is with a tiller. This is merely a lever that is attached either to the top of a transom-mounted rudder or to the top of a rudderstock if the rudder is mounted under the hull inboard of the stern. The great advantage of a tiller is that the helmsman is directly connected to the rudder and can instantly feel everything that is happening to it. The subtlest changes in helm pressure are immediately apparent, and even visual feedback is perfect and instantaneous, as the angle of the tiller constantly reflects the exact angle of the rudder under the boat, making it virtually impossible to misunderstand its relationship to the boat.

This fixed centerline cockpit table with folding leaves makes outdoor dining easy. When sailing, however, you have to hop over the table to cross the cockpit quickly. The recommended procedure is to drop your butt on top of the center structure and swing your legs over. (Courtesy of SAIL *Magazine; Photo by Malcolm White.)*

If both the tiller itself and the fasteners affixing it to the rudder or rudderstock are strong enough, there is almost nothing that can go wrong with it. Tillers therefore have long been favored by cruisers who crave simplicity.

Catamaran Cockpits

On most cruising cats what is called the cockpit is more like a vast back porch with one or more steering wheels and a few control lines sprinkled about. The companionway, instead of being a small hatch at the top of a steep ladder, is an enormous sliding glass door that opens directly into an equally spacious saloon with windows all around. Because catamaran cockpits are so enormous, there is normally no conflict between their social and working functions. There is plenty of room for folks to hang out, often at large fixed tables and/or on commodious bench seats, while the working crew flits about attending to the handling of the boat. The downside is that it is hard to centralize controls. In most cases one crewmember cannot handle the boat without relying on an autopilot; in some cases it may be difficult for two or three crew to do this.

A cruising cat's steering station is most often situated on an aft-facing cabinhouse bulkhead, offset to one side with a small raised platform and seat for the helmsman so he can see over the coachroof. The helmsman is centrally located and can easily interact with everyone around, and it is possible to lead both headsail sheets to this same location. In many cases, however, the helmsman cannot reach the mainsheet or main traveler, which are usually

situated well aft. Also, bulkhead helms in my experience often feel awkward to steer from. Usually there is a fixed bimini or hard cockpit roof overhead, which limits visibility and headroom. Plus, it is more difficult to "feel" the boat, both because of the odd location and the necessarily long steering cable runs. In some cases steering is hydraulic, and there is no feel at all.

The most common alternative is to have separate steering stations at the aft end of each hull. Cable runs can be much shorter, and the steering position feels much more open and natural, thus it is easier to sense what the boat is doing beneath you as you steer. There is also reasonable access to some control lines. Usually you can reach a double-ended mainsheet from either steering station, plus one side of the traveler controls and one headsail sheet. On larger, wider cats, however, the helmsman may be isolated from social activity taking place in the center of the cockpit. He is also more exposed to the elements.

With either type of layout take note of how critical control lines like halyards and reef lines are routed off the mast. On some boats they are led around or over the cabinhouse, in which case there will be extra friction in the runs.

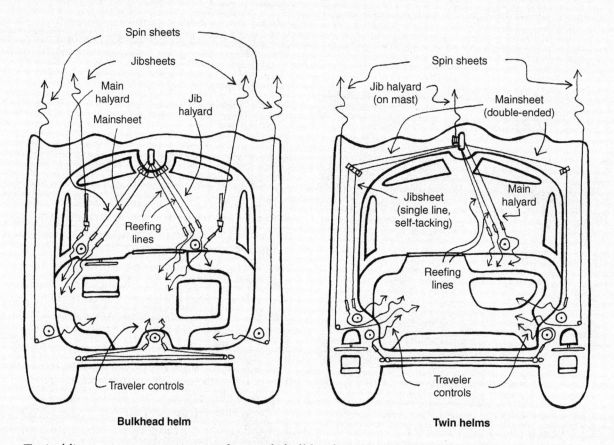

Bulkhead helm   **Twin helms**

Typical line runs on catamarans with a single bulkhead steering station (left) and twin outboard steering stations (right). Many other variations are possible.

but in reality can be troublesome, as access to the line tunnel is normally poor and reloading and clearing any lines that break or get tangled can be difficult. Also, the long line runs create a lot of friction, and most boats set up this way need power winches to cope with this. The best alternative, as on a monohull, may be to leave these lines on the mast, but few cats are set up this way.

Larger cats now often have a central forward steering station on a flying bridge atop the cabin coachroof. These afford fantastic visibility in all directions, and lines from the mast can be brought straight to the helm, with the mainsheet and main traveler controls at the back of the flying bridge. Having never sailed a cat with a flying bridge, I can't say how sensitive the steering is or how well the line handling works. However, it is clear these boats have large superstructures creating a lot of windage, and may be difficult to maneuver in close quarters in a crosswind. Also, the main boom must be raised a great deal to make room for the flying bridge, which is bound to hurt performance and may affect stability.

Central steering stations are also found on a few performance cruising catamarans. On some smaller open-bridgedeck boats with no interior accommodations outside the hulls, central helms are placed either right in the middle of the bridgedeck or slightly aft. Helm feel is normally good, and there is usually easy access to several important control lines. Some larger performance cats with interior accommodations on partial bridgedecks have central helms forward of the cabin in cockpits directly behind the mast. These have excellent forward visibility, and there is easy access to all lines coming off the mast. Such steering stations are, however, exposed to spray from the bows when the boat is driving to windward. In most cases there is also an auxiliary inside steering station in the cabin directly behind the cockpit so the helmsman can stay dry.

With bulkhead steering (top) the helmsman is closer to the cockpit and better protected; with twin outboard helms (bottom) the helmsman is more isolated and has no shelter, but can feel the boat better.

You'll need two crew on a halyard—one at the mast jumping the line and another at the winch tailing it—to execute an efficient hoist. On other catamarans all these lines may be routed through an enclosed tunnel under the bridgedeck to a central location aft within reach of the mainsheet and main traveler controls. This centralizes many control lines,

A cruising catamaran with a flybridge steering station. Note how high the boom must be raised to accommodate it. These really only make sense on large cats.

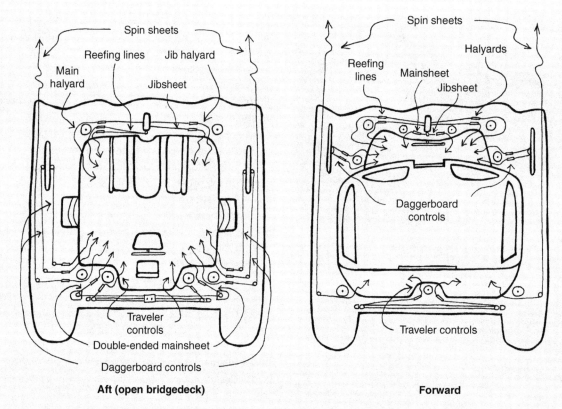

Typical line runs on catamarans with an aft central steering station (left) and a forward central bridgedeck steering station (right). Again, many variations are possible.

A forward central steering station on an Atlantic 42 catamaran showing easy access to all lines coming off the mast. Note the double-ended mainsheet (on the aft winches) must be brought forward from the stern.

Some people complain that tillers take up too much space in a cockpit, which is sometimes true, but not always. If a cockpit is small, as on some traditional boats, and especially if the tiller is long and fixed, meaning it cannot swing up and down on a vertical axis, the helmsman may indeed need most of the available space to steer. But if the cockpit is large and the tiller can pivot up and down, there is both more space available and much more flexibility. The best arrangement is to have the tiller protruding only a short distance into a cockpit with most of its length sweeping back and forth across the deck just abaft the cockpit. A tiller board with peg holes can then be installed under the tiller, and the helmsman can quickly fix the tiller in place with some tiller pegs, which is a handy feature.

Once a boat gets past a certain size and weight, steering with a tiller becomes hard work. Even on

A simple way to cope with a heavy helm on a boat with a tiller is to take a line around the tiller. On large boats a line and tackle can be set up. On smaller ones, as seen here, no tackle is necessary.

relatively small boats, helm loads in strong conditions can get quite heavy. The traditional belt-and-suspenders way to cope with this is to set up a tiller line with a tackle to steer. Even taking a straight length of line once around a tiller generates some advantage and makes it noticeably easier to steer. Or you can change the configuration of the rudder. The more balanced a rudder is—that is, the more surface area there is forward of its pivot axis—the easier it is to steer. A light hull with a deep balanced spade rudder can be steered with a tiller without too much effort, even on a large boat. Some modern interpretations of traditional designs, as discussed earlier, have semi-balanced keel-hung rudders that are easily controlled with a tiller.

Ultimately, however, the best way to cope with heavy helm loads is to chuck the tiller and put a steering wheel in its place. No matter how it is linked to the rudder, a wheel generates all sorts of mechanical advantage and can make the worst hardmouthed bull of a boat much easier to steer. Some sailboats, however, are too small to have wheels (32 feet is about the minimum length), plus a wheel is more complicated to maintain and is necessarily less responsive than a tiller.

A steering wheel does not necessarily take up less cockpit space than a tiller, but the amount of space it does take up is finite and well defined. A helmsman on a tiller always needs more room to make a bigger turn, but a helmsman on a wheel takes up the same space no matter how hard he is turning the boat. This always makes a helmsman on a wheel easier to work around, though the size of a steering wheel is sometimes problematic. There is a trend these days to make wheels large, and there are in fact two good reasons for this: a larger wheel takes less effort to turn; it also makes it possible for the helmsman to sit out and steer on the rail. Racing helmsmen love nothing better than to sit far down in the lee corner of the cockpit with eyes glued to the telltales on the jib luff, which is why big wheels are now very popular on race boats. This is indeed a fine perch for anyone steering a sailboat, but the trouble is boats have become so beamy aft a wheel must be enormous if one is to reach it from the rail. On many boats wheels are now so large a deep wheel well must be cut into the cockpit sole to accommodate them. Even with a well, the tops of some wheels can reach as high as 5 feet above the cockpit sole.

Supersized steering wheels are now so trendy many people want them just because they think they look cool. Such wheels may make sense on a race boat, but for the most part they are only a nuisance on a cruising boat. First, it can be difficult or impossible to move around these wheels without leaving the cockpit. Second, a wheel well is a magnet for stray

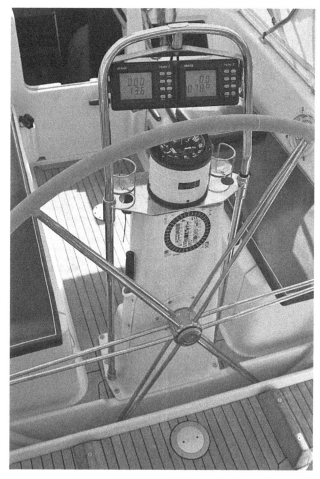

A large wheel often needs a wheel well in the cockpit sole (top); these wells can be magnets for stray lines and the wheel may restrict movement in the cockpit. Twin wheels are smaller and more convenient and make it easier to move around the cockpit (bottom).

working lines lying on the cockpit sole. Inevitably they fall into the well and may jam the wheel at inopportune moments. Third, many wheels are so tall you cannot comfortably steer while standing directly behind them. On cruising boats with wide

aft cockpits it is better to have smaller twin wheels on either side of the cockpit. This way you can still steer easily from the rail, but can also easily pass between the wheels. You can also steer while standing directly behind the wheels without imitating a brachiating ape.

Types of Wheel Steering

Steering wheels can be connected to rudders in several different ways. The most common system is open-cable steering, where the wheel's driveshaft turns a sprocket with a short length of chain running over it. The ends of the chain have cables attached to them that lead down the steering pedestal to a pair of sheaves that in turn lead the cables to either a quadrant or a radial-drive disc fastened to the top of the rudderstock. (Note that if the drive unit on the stock is a quadrant, another pair of sheaves may be needed aft of the pedestal either side of the quadrant to lead the cables onto it.) If the steering pedestal is only a short distance from the rudderstock, as on most aft-cockpit boats, this sort of system is very effective and is generally very responsive with good helm feedback. Cable tension is important, as the cables do have a tendency to jump off their sheaves when they get a little loose. The sheaves themselves must also be properly aligned and well lubricated so they turn freely. The sheaves must be well supported and firmly mounted with through-bolts rather than screws, as the loads they carry are sometimes quite large.

If much longer, more convoluted cable runs are required (as on many center-cockpit monohulls or catamarans with bulkhead helm stations), open-cable steering is often not feasible, but a closed conduit system can be used instead. Here the cables run through flexible plastic conduits that are led from the pedestal base to a special pull-pull drive unit mounted in front of a steering quadrant on the rudderstock. Conduit cable systems offer a lot of flexibility with respect to installation, but are generally not as responsive as straight open-cable systems, because the cable runs are normally so much longer. A major concern is making sure the cables do not bind in the conduits. It is best to pull the cables out of their conduits on a regular basis and regrease them, but this onerous chore is often neglected. If a cable does get too sticky, the only cure in most cases is to replace both cable and conduit. Some systems have in-line greasing studs, and these are helpful, but they are the exception rather than the rule.

A rack-and-pinion system is the best alternative to open-cable steering when connecting a wheel to a rudder over a short distance in an aft-cockpit boat. Here there is a beveled gear, or pinion, at the end of the wheel's driveshaft that engages a small geared tiller arm on the top of the rudderstock. A properly installed rack-and-pinion system is extremely reliable and has good helm sensitivity. There is little that can go wrong as long as the system's parts are kept lubricated and the gears of the rack and pinion are properly aligned so they mesh well. Unfortunately any installation involving a long run from the steering pedestal to the rudderstock, particularly if it has any turns in it, is very problematic. Also, the rudderstock must be vertical or nearly so.

Another option on aft-cockpit boats where the wheel is close to the rudderstock is a worm-gear system. These were once very common on large traditional boats, but are rarely seen these days. Here the wheel's driveshaft is quite long and has a large set of screw threads, known as a worm gear, at the end of it. A large traversing nut rides up and down the worm gear as the wheel turns and is connected via a very short lever and linkage to the top of the rudderstock. As with rack-and-pinion steering, such systems are very reliable as long as they are properly aligned and lubricated. They are also very powerful, though steering response is not as sensitive as with a cable or rack-and-pinion system.

The most high-tech way to steer a sailboat with a wheel is with a hydraulic system. Here the driveshaft on the wheel turns a pump, either directly or indirectly via a chain drive, and the pump in turn pushes hydraulic fluid through a high-pressure plumbing run connected to a piston drive that is linked to the rudderstock via a short tiller arm. Hydraulic steering is extremely powerful and works well in any situation where a steering wheel is far removed from the rudder it is turning. Also, different steering stations can be easily teed into the same hydraulic system. Hydraulic steering has poor sensitivity, however, and many sailors who like to "feel" their boats when sailing dislike it. These systems are also relatively complex compared to simple mechanical systems. The most common maintenance issues involve leaks and/ or air pockets in the plumbing system, but these usually can be fixed by knowledgeable laypeople. More serious problems involving malfunctioning hydraulic pumps or pistons or check valves in the system normally require professional attention and so cannot be resolved underway. In spite of all this, hydraulic steering systems are increasingly common on large cruising boats, particularly those set up as motorsailers or with multiple remote steering stations.

With all these systems, any fittings attached to the head of a rudderstock, such as quadrants and tiller arms, must be extremely secure. Such fittings are generally clamped to the stock and are locked in place with through-bolts, set screws or pins, or shaft keys. Through-bolts, which unfortunately are generally used only on hollow rudderstocks, are the most secure.

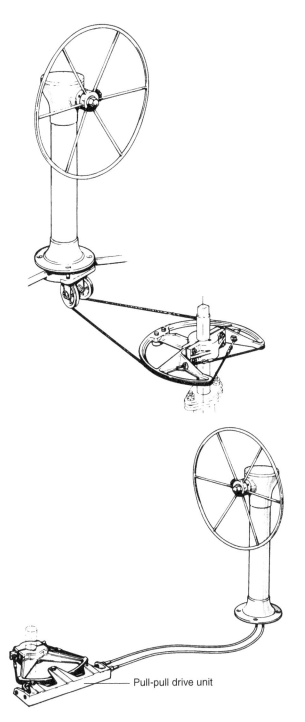

Basic cable steering systems. Open-cable steering can be used on boats where the wheel is near the rudderhead (top). Pull-pull conduit cable steering is needed on boats where the wheel and rudder are far apart (bottom). (Courtesy of Whitlock)

Pull-pull drive unit

quadrant, or rack, that is mounted either directly atop the rudderstock (in which case the wheel must be mounted almost directly over the stock) or to a solid shaft that runs down inside a remote steering pedestal. In the latter case there is a short tiller arm attached to the bottom of the pedestal shaft, and a length of solid rod connects that arm to a similar

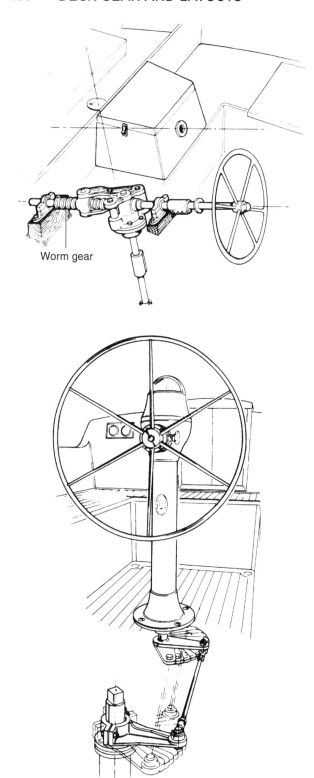

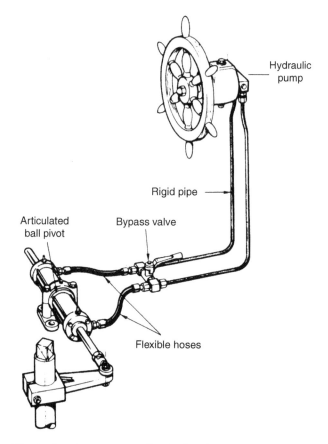

The hydraulic pump on this hydraulic steering system is directly behind the wheel. Opening the bypass valve effectively disconnects the steering so you can use an emergency tiller if necessary. Hydraulic steering has poor sensitivity but works well when a wheel is situated at a distance from the rudder and can easily accommodate multiple steering stations. (Courtesy of Whitlock)

Worm-gear steering is powerful and is often found on older traditional boats (top); it is not very responsive, but you can leave the wheel unattended without the rudder turning. Rack-and-pinion steering is reliable and is more popular on modern boats, particularly those from Europe (bottom). With both systems the wheel and rudder must be close to each other. (Courtesy of Edson International)

Keys work well on solid stocks and are probably the most common method, but they may slip out of the keyway on the stock if the clamp itself works loose. Set screws or pins are the least satisfactory method, as the point load on what is necessarily a small piece of hardware is very large. A screw threaded directly into the stock is better than a pin in any event, as it is less likely to slip out of place or work loose.

Note too that each of these steering systems must be protected by some sort of rudder stop that limits the rudder's turning radius to an arc well within the system's working range. The stop ideally should be entirely independent of the steering system. On boats with rudderstocks it often takes the form of a separate stop arm that is fixed to the stock immediately under the deck and swings between two solidly mounted blocks that limit its turning radius. On boats with transom-mounted rudders, the stops can be a couple of short lengths of light chain mounted to the rudder from the stern.

Vertical Steering Options

The first vertical steering systems were not steering wheels, but whipstaffs, which first appeared on sailing vessels in the mid-15th century. By this time vessels were getting too large to steer easily with tillers; also their aft ends were sprouting large superstructures called sterncastles, and helmsmen needed to be elevated so they could see where they were going. The whipstaff was a vertical lever attached via a gooseneck fitting to the end of a horizontal ship's tiller. This lever was led up through slots in the lower decks to the helmsman's position on an upper deck, and by pushing it to one side or the other the tiller below could be shifted left or right as needed. A whipstaff's fulcrum was normally placed to create a mechanical advantage of about 4:1, and for roughly 250 years, until the steering wheel was finally invented in the early 18th century, this was sufficient to keep most vessels on course.

Since then whipstaffs have sometimes appeared on modern sailboats. Blondie Hasler, who was always willing to plunder tradition in the name of innovation, installed one on his junk-rigged Folkboat *Jester* so that he could steer the boat from inside the cabin. Dr. David Lewis, another singlehanded ocean-racing pioneer, later rigged one on his boat *Ice Bird*, which he sailed to Antarctica in 1972. More recently, traditional whipstaffs have also appeared on a 30-foot Jim Antrim–designed trimaran and on a 33-foot catamaran designed by Tim Clissold. On Clissold's boat, the staff is positioned in the center of the bridgedeck and is connected to the cat's twin rudders by lines and blocks.

A more modern interpretation of the whipstaff is also available on a line of production fiberglass cruising boats manufactured in Belgium by Etap Yachting, whose boats are also unsinkable due to the large amounts of foam that are injected between the hull and hull liner. The Etap Vertical Steering (EVS) system is not a classic whipstaff, but is more aptly described as a vertical tiller connected directly to a rudderstock via a bevel gear. Its action, however, like that of a whipstaff, is opposite that of a conventional horizontal tiller. Also, the EVS tiller has a circular yoke at its end, so that when you are seated behind it you feel like you're behind a conventional steering wheel. Like a wheel, you turn it in the direction you want the boat to move; unlike a wheel, however, it pivots to one side as you do so.

Like a conventional tiller, an EVS tiller provides a positive feel for the helm, and the rudder angle is immediately apparent. Like a wheel, it takes up less cockpit space. Best of all, you can operate it from almost anywhere in or around the cockpit. You can sit or stand directly behind it like a wheel, or sit on the cockpit seats to either side of it. With a hiking stick you can easily control it from the forward end of the cockpit, or from the comfort of the coamings, or even from a pulpit seat on one of the aft corners of the boat. As with whipstaffs of old you can also build some mechanical advantage into an EVS tiller. The two bevel gears on most current EVS systems are the same size, so the drive ratio is 1:1; the only advantage, as with a tiller, is conveyed by the length of the lever itself. But by increasing the size of the gear on the rudderstock, you can make the system more powerful, though you'll need to move the tiller proportionately farther to achieve the same rudder angle. Etap does this on its 32-foot boat, which has a 1:1.4 gear ratio and is currently the largest boat available with EVS steering.

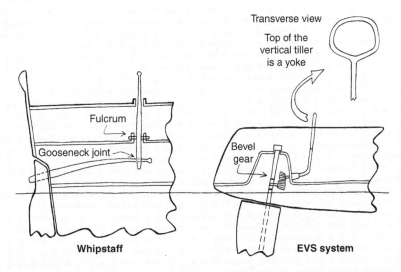

Vertical steering levers. A traditional whipstaff (left) is essentially a vertical tiller attached to a horizontal tiller. These have appeared on some modern boats. The Etap Vertical Steering (EVS) system (right) employs a bevel gear.

Emergency Steering

Any boat with wheel steering needs an effective emergency steering system in case the primary system fails. Usually this is an emergency tiller that fits onto the head of the rudderstock. In most cases the rudderhead is accessed via a small circular plate that screws into the deck or cockpit sole. On some boats, however, the rudderhead is brought all the way up through the deck, so that it is plainly visible and immediately accessible.

Even if you don't plan on taking your boat offshore, you should take the trouble to install your emergency tiller and see how it works before you actually need it. Invariably you'll find it is awkward to use. One thing you'll probably learn is that the tiller would work much better if it could be pinned or through-bolted to the rudderhead. This is rarely possible with the standard gear provided by most builders, but usually with a little drilling and tapping the gear can be appropriately modified. On most aft-cockpit boats you'll also find the steering pedestal gets in the way of the tiller. Usually this is circumvented by making the tiller short and pointing it toward the stern or side of the boat rather than the bow if necessary. The short lever arm often makes it impossible to work the tiller by hand, and in most cases you'll need a tiller line and tackle to control it. Again, you have to make up this rig yourself, as it is never provided by the builder.

On center-cockpit boats the rudderhead is normally far removed from the steering pedestal, and there is lots of room for a long emergency tiller. The only problem is the rudderhead is often buried underneath a double berth in the aft cabin. In an emergency you must rip up the berth and station one person below to work the tiller with another on deck to call down steering instructions. If you do much shorthanded cruising aboard center-cockpit boats, particularly if you want to go offshore, you should therefore favor those designs where the rudderhead is brought up to the deck.

Finally, for any emergency steering system to work properly, you must be certain the primary system does not interfere with it. With a cable or rack-and-pinion system this should not be an issue, but with a hydraulic or worm-gear system it isn't possible to use an emergency tiller unless the primary steering system is entirely disconnected. With a hydraulic system you can do this by opening a bypass valve between the two plumbing runs or by physically disconnecting the hydraulic piston drive from the tiller arm on the rudderstock. With a worm gear you must remove the entire primary steering assembly before installing the emergency tiller.

Self-Steering

Most cruising sailors these days have self-steering systems on their boats, but different types of cruisers have different requirements. Coastal cruisers who enjoy steering while sailing often want to leave the helm for only a few minutes at a time. Only when the wind dies and the motoring begins do they want the boat to steer itself for long periods of time. Bluewater cruisers, on the other hand, normally want to spend as little time on the helm as possible, no matter what the conditions are, and often keep their self-steering systems operating 24 hours a day while underway. In between these two extremes there are any number of intermediate use patterns.

No matter what sort of self-steering system you have, the regular working crew should be able to handle the boat if necessary without relying on it. If this isn't possible, you should rethink your boat's deck layout. Often changing the location of a few key control lines will enable you to handle your boat without "artificial" assistance. Ultimately, you want your self-steering system to be a valued convenience, not a necessity.

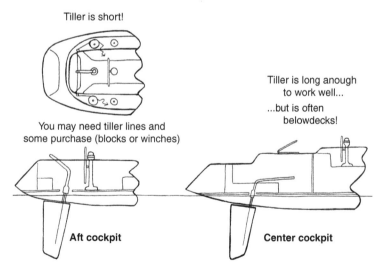

Emergency tiller configurations. On an aft-cockpit boat the steering pedestal gets in the way, and the tiller must be kept short and/or point aft or to the side; a line and tackle is often needed to control it. On center-cockpit boats the tiller must often be installed belowdeck.

Autopilots

Electronic autopilots are by far the most popular self-steering systems on cruising boats today. The simplest, least expensive units are small tiller pilots. These are mechanical linear rams normally mounted on a cockpit seat or coaming that connect directly to a boat's tiller. The ram's electric motor receives input from a microprocessor connected to an electronic compass and pushes or pulls the tiller back and forth as required to keep the boat on a user-selected compass heading. The smallest, most basic units are unitary and have their control pad, processor, and steering compass incorporated in the same housing as the motor and drive. With slightly larger, more complex units the controls, processor, and compass are housed in a separate unit that is connected to the drive unit by a remote length of wiring.

The simplest type of unit capable of steering a boat with a wheel is a pedestal pilot. Here a rotary-drive motor is mounted on a steering pedestal (or sometimes on a cockpit coaming or footwell bulkhead) and turns the wheel via a rubber belt or drive gear connected to a special drum clamped to the spokes of the wheel. The motor is controlled via a remotely mounted compass and processor.

Tiller and pedestal pilots can be easily installed by amateurs and work well on small and midsize coastal cruising boats. They are generally not powerful enough, however, to steer a boat under sail for more than short periods of time when conditions are strong. Tiller pilots are often quickly overwhelmed when helm loads get heavy, and pedestal pilots are often limited by their installation. Common problems when hard steering is required include slipping drive belts and insecure motor mounts.

By far the most robust and reliable autopilots are those mounted under the deck with fully remote

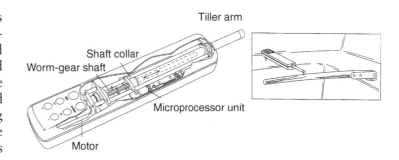

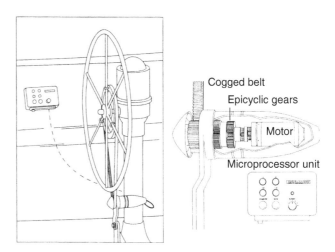

Cockpit-mounted autopilots. A tiller pilot is a simple ram connected directly to a tiller (top), while a pedestal pilot has a rotary drive that turns a drum clamped to a steering wheel via a rubber belt or drive gear (bottom). These systems are simple to install but are not very powerful. (Drawings by Jim Sollers)

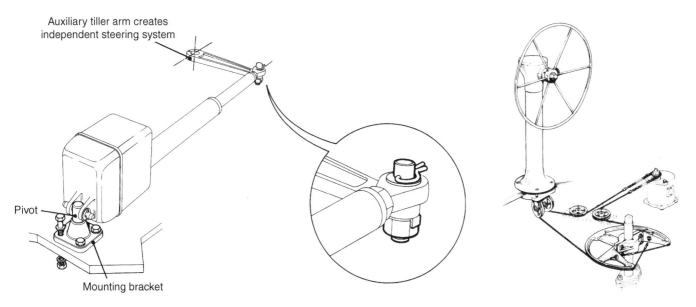

Below-deck autopilots. A linear ram can be attached to an auxiliary tiller arm mounted on the rudderstock, as seen here (left), which is better than attaching it to the main quadrant (not shown). Rotary drives can also be used (right) and work well on boats with little space around the rudderhead. Below-deck autopilots are stronger and more reliable then cockpit-mounted units. (Courtesy of Autohelm and Whitlock)

processors, compasses, and control heads and powerful drive units that are connected directly to a boat's rudderstock or steering quadrant. These below-deck units, as with cockpit units, have either linear rams or rotary drives. Linear rams are more prevalent and work well, but they require a fair amount of installation space and good access to the boat's steering gear. Rotary drives are more compact and often work better on older boats with narrow aft sections that have a limited amount of space around their rudderstocks. Hydraulic systems are also available; these normally have linear rams and work well on boats with hydraulic steering.

Below-deck autopilots have become increasingly sophisticated and can now be interfaced with other onboard electronics. Instead of just steering a simple compass course, they can also steer to a GPS waypoint (thus automatically compensating for leeway and crosscurrents) or to an apparent-wind angle (thus compensating for wind shifts). Other innovations include software-dampened compasses that compensate for the boat's motion more efficiently in rough conditions and fuzzy-logic circuits that "learn" how the boat behaves and recognize patterns in compass and wind data so they can steer a straighter course while consuming less power. Many manufacturers now offer multiple station controls, including handheld wireless controls, so that the autopilot can be operated from anywhere aboard the boat, including from up the mast. Some pilots even have automatic man-overboard features. Here a small wireless remote-control unit carried in a crewmember's pocket constantly sends a short-range radio signal to the autopilot's main control center. If the crew falls overboard, the connection is severed as soon as the boat sails a certain distance away, whereupon an audible alarm sounds and the autopilot automatically heads the boat into the wind.

Any below-deck autopilot must be robustly mounted to withstand large steering loads; otherwise its power is wasted. Bases for drive units should not be tacked or lightly tabbed in place, but should be fully integrated into the boat's below-deck structure. Units should be through-bolted to these bases with large heavy-duty fasteners. Ideally the connection from the drive to the rudderstock should be independent of the boat's primary steering system, with either a separate tiller arm on the stock for a linear ram or a separate radial fixture for a rotary drive. This way if the connection to the primary steering system fails, the autopilot can act as a backup. In many installations, however, an autopilot's linear ram drive is connected to the main steering quadrant, usually via a pin or bolt inserted into a hole drilled in the body of the quadrant. This subjects the quadrant to an intense point load that it is not normally designed to handle. In any such installation, the quadrant should be reinforced in the area of the hole to spread the load more widely.

Wind Vanes

An electronic autopilot consumes much electricity. The stronger and more reliable it is, the more power it needs. Current demand can range from less than 1 amp on average with peak draws to 3 amps for a small cockpit-mounted pilot to up to 6 amps on average with peak draws to 30 amps for a large below-deck unit. To meet this sort of demand, particularly if the autopilot is used for extended periods while sailing, a boat's battery bank must be considerably larger than it would be otherwise. Feeding the bank also requires a concomitant increase in charging capacity (see Chapter 7). To avoid complicating their onboard systems, some cruisers instead rely on mechanical wind vanes to steer their boats. In the days before electronic autopilots, these vanes were the cutting edge in self-steering technology and were considered mandatory equipment on bluewater cruising boats. Vanes are now less common, but they are still the sole self-steering system on some cruising boats and are often used as backup systems on many others.

The most basic type is a trim-tab vane. These first appeared during the 1950s and work only on boats with transom-hung outboard rudders. A narrow trim tab is mounted on the aft edge of the rudder and acts like an aileron on an airplane wing. It is linked directly to the wind vane itself, which is normally mounted over the rudder and pivots so that it is constantly aligned with the wind. The vane is adjustable, so it can be oriented at any angle in relation to the boat. The boat is brought onto the desired course, the vane is aligned with the wind, and when the boat deviates from the course, the vane pivots, turning the trim tab, which in turn shifts the angle of the rudder so that the boat comes back on course. Trim-tab vanes are perfectly reliable, but they are not particularly powerful or responsive, as the leverage exerted by the vane on the tab is necessarily limited.

Servo-pendulum wind vanes are much more refined and more powerful. These work on a principle devised by Blondie Hasler in 1960 and are still the most efficient method for steering a boat by wind power alone. The key part is an independent steering oar mounted on the boat's transom. The oar swings from side to side like a pendulum and also pivots along its vertical axis like a rudder. It is connected via a linkage known as a servo-gear to an adjustable wind vane that is aligned with the wind when the boat is on course. It is also connected via a pair of control lines to the

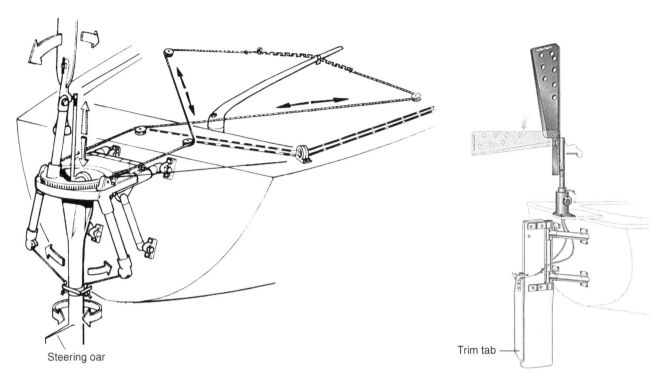

Steering oar

Trim tab —

Wind vane steering systems. A servo-pendulum system relies on a steering oar that both pivots and swings back and forth and is connected to the boat's wheel or tiller (left). A trim tab works like a wing's aileron and must be mounted on an outboard rudder (right); as seen here an auxiliary rudder can be mounted on the transom if necessary. (Courtesy of Scanmar and Marine Vane Gears Ltd.)

boat's tiller or wheel. When the boat goes off course the wind vane pivots, causing the steering oar to pivot on its vertical axis. The deflection of water rushing past the oar then pushes the oar to one side or the other, and this motion is transmitted via the control lines to the tiller or wheel, which in turn brings the boat back on course. The faster the boat is moving, the more powerful the sweep of the oar, and the more force there is available to steer the boat.

One big issue with servo-pendulum vanes is the routing of control lines. On most aft-cockpit boats the runs are fairly short, and usually it's possible to lead the lines via one pair of turning blocks from the vane assembly on the transom to the boat's wheel or tiller. With a tiller these line runs are normally unobtrusive, but with a wheel the lines are led from one side of the cockpit or the other to a drum mounted on the wheel's spokes, and this often obstructs access to half the cockpit. On center-cockpit boats, meanwhile, it is usually impossible or impractical to route the lines all the way from the transom to the cockpit. To avoid these problems an independent auxiliary rudder can also be mounted on the boat's transom. This can be connected directly to the steering vane, eliminating the need for control lines. You can also use the auxiliary rudder to steer the boat if the primary

rudder fails. (Note that one vane manufacturer, Scanmar International, also sells a kit that transforms the steering oar on its Monitor servo-pendulum vane into an emergency rudder.)

Steering a boat with a wind vane is not nearly as simple as steering with an autopilot and does require some sailorly expertise. Even a powerful servo-pendulum gear won't work well if a boat's sails are not well balanced against its helm. Also, a wind vane won't work without wind, and if the wind is shifty and unreliable, as is often the case when sailing close to shore, it requires constant tweaking to stay on course.

One clever way to solve these problems and make a wind vane more versatile is to integrate it with a small electronic tiller pilot. This is most commonly done with servo-pendulum systems. The vane itself is removed and replaced with a small tab to which a tiller pilot is connected. This allows the steering oar to steer a simple compass course, even when the sails are down and the boat is motoring. Best of all, the tiller pilot uses only a fraction of the power it normally consumes, as the steering oar is still doing all the heavy work of turning the boat's rudder. This also works with trim-tab vanes, in which case the tiller pilot either is rigged to turn the gear in place

of the wind vane or is connected directly to the trim tab. Power consumption, however, is not as low as it is with a servo-pendulum gear.

WINCHES AND FURLERS

Winches play an important role in line handling on all but the smallest of Marconi-rigged sailboats. They should be appropriately sized so they can easily handle any anticipated load, but in fact they are often egregiously undersized. This is particularly true of primary sheet winches on modern production boats. As a general rule, one of the first things you should do with a new mass-production cruising boat is strip off the primaries and replace them with winches one or two sizes bigger. When you see how much money these larger winches cost you'll understand why the builder was reluctant to put them on in the first place.

Most modern winches are self-tailing. The feeder arm and self-tailing mechanism at the top of the winch do not prevent you from using the winch in the traditional way—i.e., with one crew tailing the line while another grinds the winch—but they do give you more flexibility. With a self-tailer one crewmember can grind a winch as hard as he can with both hands unassisted. The winch itself can also secure the line, which has led many builders to eliminate cockpit cleats for running rigging. It is relatively easy, however, to accidentally knock a line out of the jaws of a self-tailer, so I prefer to see at least one cleat on each cockpit coaming so that heavily loaded lines like headsail sheets can be tied off and made absolutely secure if necessary.

Modern winches are also usually top-action winches, meaning the handle for grinding the winch is inserted at the top of the winch drum. If you position your body directly over the winch you can forcefully rotate the handle through a full 360 degrees, thus maximizing the winch's speed and power. The disadvantage is you must remove the handle every time line is loaded on or off the drum and then replace it in order to grind the winch. This inconvenience is only aggravated on many cruising boats where bimini legs, side curtains, or other cockpit impedimenta restrict both the motion of the handle and the crew's ability to get above the winch, thus making it necessary to work the winch from the side and to saw the handle back and forth to turn the drum. In these situations it is better to have a bottom-action winch, where the handle is inserted at the bottom of the winch drum and does not interfere with line handling. Such winches, which are in fact designed to be worked from the side, were relatively common 30 or more years ago, but are now unfortunately quite rare.

The Aries servo-pendulum gear on the author's
Tanton 39 Lunacy is seen here connected both to a
wind vane (top) and to a small tiller pilot (bottom).
The vane steers to the wind and cannot work while
motoring. The pilot steers to a compass course and
works while both sailing and motoring.

Bottom-action winches, with the handle at the bottom, are easier to use in many circumstances but are rarely seen on modern sailboats. Note the cleat on top for fastening a line on the winch, as on a self-tailing winch.

Another way to solve the problem of undersized winches with handles that can't be fully rotated is to motorize them so crew can grind them just by pressing buttons. Not surprisingly, equipment like this is increasingly popular. Most often electric motors are installed under the primary cockpit winches and/or under a main halyard winch located on the coachroof or on deck by the mast. On large boats hydraulic systems are often used instead and may incorporate not only every winch on the boat, but also the headsail furler(s) and a mainsail furler. Even on midsize boats with in-mast mainsails, it is now common for the mainsail furler to be motorized rather than line driven.

The abilities of a small working crew can be greatly augmented by this sort of technology. Power winches and furlers make it possible for a crew of two—or even just one person—to efficiently operate

a large sailing vessel. When standing watch alone on the deck of a 60-foot boat, being able to shorten sail by just touching some buttons is a fine feature. A boat's working crew, however, should always be able to operate their vessel, even in extreme conditions, without any hydraulic or electrical power. Wealthy wannabe cruisers often let the convenience of these systems lure them into buying boats that are otherwise bigger than they can really handle. Unfortunately, they may not realize this until they are in some highly unpleasant, potentially dangerous situation.

Power-driven sail-handling systems are much more reliable than they used to be, but they are not absolutely reliable and never will be. The systems are complex and require much more maintenance than manual winches and furlers. Electric motors and switches are especially vulnerable to moisture intrusion and can short out at inopportune moments.

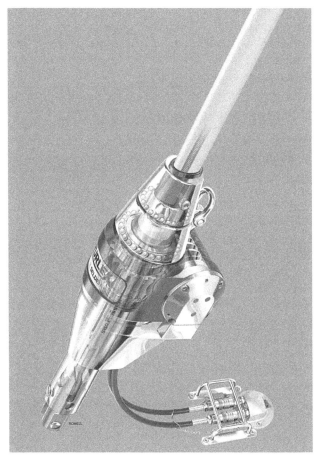

Machinery like this modern hydraulic headsail furler makes it easy for small crews to handle big boats. There is a socket on the other side of the rotary gear on this unit so it can be turned with a winch handle if necessary. Make sure any power winch or furler can be operated manually. (Courtesy of Seldén Mast)

These systems also require large amounts of electrical power, and any hobbling of the boat's power-generation capacity directly impacts their use. Hydraulic equipment is somewhat more energy efficient (the pumps for a hydraulic winch or furler will likely be electric), but is also susceptible to problems with leaks in the hydraulic lines, corrosion caused by condensation in fluid reservoirs, and faulty solenoid switches.

Any power winch or furler should therefore also be fully functional in manual mode. With winches this means making sure they are large enough that the crew can grind them when they are carrying their heaviest anticipated loads. Most power furlers, meanwhile, have manual backup systems where a winch handle can be used to rotate the furling rod, but few are reasonably efficient. Indeed, many motorized mainsail furlers are installed in such a way that the manual backup system is effectively inoperable, as the boom or some other fixture on the mast blocks the rotation of a winch handle. The best way to automate a furler is to install a conventional line-driven manual furler, then lead the line to an appropriately sized power winch. This is not quite as convenient as a straight power furler, but if you lose power or the winch motor fails, you can still operate the manual furler at maximum efficiency.

GROUND TACKLE

Except on a pure race boat, anchoring should never be an improvised catch-as-catch-can enterprise. Any cruising boat should be well equipped to drop or hoist anchor on short notice, and the foredeck should be laid out to facilitate this.

No matter how small a cruising boat is, it should be possible to store one slightly oversize anchor on the bow in a secure, properly designed anchor roller so that the anchor is always ready to be quickly deployed. On any boat large enough that a second anchor cannot be easily brought to the foredeck from a remote storage location—usually this means a boat longer than about 35 feet, depending on the physical abilities of the crew—there should also be a second roller on the bow for carrying a secondary anchor.

Anchor rollers should have cheek plates close enough to the roller wheel that the rode, be it chain or rope, cannot fall between the two and get jammed in place. The roller wheel itself should have a concave V-shape to help control and channel the rode. If rope rode is used, the roller's cheek plates should not have any sharp corners or edges that the rope can chafe against no matter how severe the angle of deployment. In all cases the roller must be far enough outboard that the anchor cannot beat against the

This large modern racer-cruiser has a retractable anchor roller that folds down and stows under the deck when not needed. A washdown pump and hose for rinsing the anchor and rode as they come aboard is also handy.

bow of the boat as it is coming aboard or if it is left dangling by its stock for a time while the crew hunts for a place to park. On any boat with a plumb or nearly plumb stem, this usually means there should be a bow platform on which to mount the roller. Finally, the roller should have a strong retaining pin or some other mechanism for fixing the anchor in place when it is stowed in the roller.

Windlasses

On many boats it is possible to haul an anchor and its rode aboard hand over hand, but even young robust cruisers will soon learn to dislike it. And even on small boats, a cruiser in top physical condition will eventually encounter a situation where he or she cannot break out an anchor by hand and bring it aboard unassisted. Then it is necessary either to get

---

more crew to haul on the rode or to lead it to a large winch elsewhere on deck. The best solution, however, is to have a dedicated anchor windlass mounted on the foredeck to help with the job.

A windlass can be either manual or power-assisted and is oriented either vertically or horizontally. On a vertical windlass the rope drum and wildcat (chain gypsy) for handling chain are stacked one on top of the other (with the drum on top and the wildcat below), and the handle for cranking the windlass manually is inserted at the top of the drum and

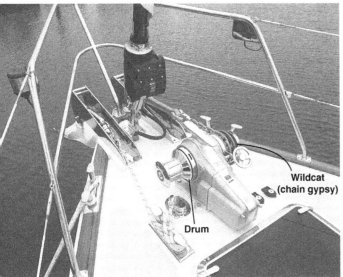

This vertical windlass has a low profile showing only a chain gypsy and no rope drum (top). Note the buttons on either side, indicating a power-driven system, and also the socket for inserting a winch handle to turn the windlass by hand when necessary. The horizontal windlass (bottom) has both a drum and wildcat (chain gypsy). It serves an impressive pair of anchor rollers!

rotates horizontally through 360 degrees, just like it would on a standard deck winch. On a horizontal windlass the drum and wildcat are side by side (with the drum normally to the left and the wildcat to the right), and the handle is a long vertical lever you crank back and forth to make the drum and wildcat turn. A horizontal windlass is mechanically more complex, due to the gearing needed to translate the back-and-forth motion of the handle into a constant rotation of the drum and wildcat. But ergonomically it is much easier to operate, provided the handle is long enough to crank while standing. A manual vertical windlass, by comparison, must be operated while crouching or kneeling.

Ergonomics are less important if you can operate the windlass by pressing a button. Power windlasses are both more convenient and safer than manual windlasses, because they allow you to hoist anchor much faster. In an emergency where you must move the boat quickly, as when dragging onto a lee shore in a strong wind, this can be critical and may save you from having to slip your rode and dump it overboard in order to save the boat. As with deck winches, however, you should not be absolutely dependent on a power windlass. If you are not capable of recovering your rode and anchor hand over hand, your power windlass should also work in manual mode. It is possible to operate most power windlasses manually, but unfortunately you often cannot keep the gears engaged while doing so. The windlass instead operates in direct-drive mode and provides only a limited advantage.

As with winches, power windlasses can be either electric or hydraulic. The electric ones, which are more common, draw enormous amounts of current. Typical working loads range from 50 to 100 amps, with peak loads as high as 400 amps. No reasonably sized battery bank can sustain such a load for very long, and the universal practice is to keep the engine running to charge the batteries when the windlass is used. Windlasses are normally installed some distance from the batteries, so cables are often undersized. It isn't practical in many situations to install appropriately sized cables for a 300 to 400 amp 12-volt draw over a distance of 40 feet or more. Also, the motors on many electric windlasses are simply modified starting motors, which are not designed to run for extended periods or under heavy loads.

You therefore should be circumspect when operating an electric windlass and should not treat it as a piece of make-or-break heavy-lifting equipment. It is best to run the windlass in a series of relatively short bursts when it carries a load, and it should not be used to drag the boat to the anchor in anything other than slack conditions. Nor should you use it to break out a stubborn anchor or to kedge a boat off a shoal. To reduce working loads, it is best to motor up to an anchor before picking up rode and to snub the rode to a cleat or post and use the main engine to break out the anchor if it offers much resistance.

As for hydraulic units, these rely on either electric or engine-driven pumps for their power. As with hydraulic winches, common problems involve leaks in the hydraulic plumbing, corrosion from condensation in the hydraulic fluid, and faulty solenoid switches. Though hydraulic windlasses are more robust than electric ones, you should still treat them with respect and use the engine when possible to bring the boat to the anchor, and so on. Also, no matter what sort of windlass is on a boat, it should not be used to secure the anchor rode once the anchor is set. Rather you should tie off the rode, or an independent snubber line (if the rode is chain), to a strong bow cleat or samson post. Inevitably, however, a windlass occasionally has to cope with full snubbing loads so should be installed with this in mind. At a minimum it should be through-bolted to a substantial backing plate or block under the deck; in some cases it may also be wise to reinforce the deck in the area around the windlass.

Anchor Rode Storage

Anchor rodes on cruising boats are traditionally stored in a rode locker in the forepeak directly under the foredeck. The rode is fed down into the locker through a small hole in the deck called a hawsehole, and the only way crew can access the locker is via the interior of the boat. Often there is a short length of pipe under the deck, called a navel pipe, that helps route rode from the hawsehole to a specific area in the locker. On larger boats there are often two hawseholes, and the locker is partitioned so that two rodes can be stored side by side.

In many respects, a traditional below-deck rode locker is a pain to deal with. Stowing a rope rode, for example, requires crew belowdeck to pull the rope down through the hawsehole. Chain rode will fall through a hawsehole and navel pipe unassisted, but tends to stack up quickly in a tall pile. If the locker is not designed properly the chain pile chokes the hawsehole; this in turn jams the windlass on deck. To prevent this, the locker must be deep enough to accommodate the length of chain coming aboard; the chain must also have a fair lead into the deepest part of the locker. Otherwise, crew belowdeck must flake the chain as it comes down so the chain pile doesn't grow too high. Either type of rode may jam when running out the hawsehole as the anchor is dropped, in which case—once again—someone must go below to sort it out. In all these situations, if you are dropping or hoisting an anchor singlehanded you may need to shuttle back and forth between the foredeck and the rode locker below, which is definitely not fun. If you use chain rode, however, and have a well-designed rode locker that the chain can stow itself into, this doesn't happen too often.

Another problem with below-deck rode lockers is that a good percentage of the water and mud coming aboard with the rode ends up inside the boat. When

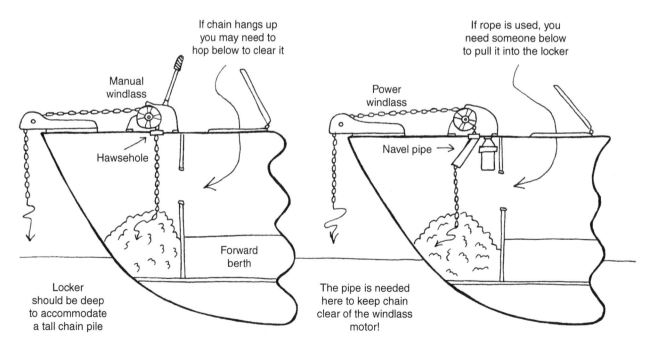

Traditional forepeak rode lockers should be deep and accessible from inside the boat. With power windlass installations (right), the windlass motor should be in a secure location clear of the chain fall.

it rains, or when the bow of the boat is awash while underway, even more water finds its way down the hawsehole. All this water should be routed via limber holes into the bilge of the boat where bilge pumps can deal with it. Inevitably, however, the extra moisture belowdeck helps raise humidity levels in the boat's living accommodations. Also, if much mud comes aboard there may be some unpleasant odors, depending on the quality of the mud. To prevent this it is a good idea to install a raw-water washdown pump with a hose on the foredeck so you can easily rinse off your anchor rode as it comes aboard.

Below-deck rode lockers are not nearly as common as they used to be. On most modern production boats anchor rodes are instead stored on deck in a recessed foredeck locker called an anchor well. Normally this is a much better arrangement, as the rode is entirely segregated from the living accommodations. The well itself serves as a collision compartment, no one has to go belowdeck to handle rode as it comes aboard, and all moisture and odors are kept out of the boat's interior. A well-designed anchor well should be deep enough to accommodate a generous amount of rode, but not so deep that it is impossible to reach the bottom of the well from the deck. The well must also have

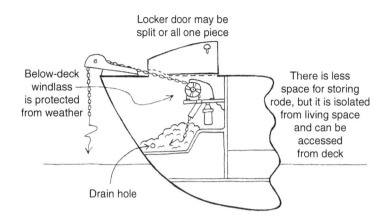

A typical anchor well should be shallow enough to allow you to reach the rode from the deck. In some cases the windlass is kept on deck.

drain holes so that any water coming in can quickly get out again. The holes should be big enough that they are not easily clogged with mud or debris, but if they are close to the boat's waterline, as is often the case, they must also be small enough that they do not ship too much water while sailing.

As a general rule, anchor wells work best on large boats, where there is room to both split the well for

This modern anchor well allows one crewmember to easily launch and retrieve the anchor from on deck without ever venturing below. (Courtesy of SAIL *Magazine; Photo by Malcolm White.)*

The Rode Warriors: Chain vs. Rope

Many cruisers believe an all-chain anchor rode is always superior to rope rode. Chain is stronger and much more chafe resistant than rope, but you can still do some serious anchoring on rope alone. With rope you do need to be more security conscious and must always check for chafe. If there is coral on the bottom, this means diving on the rode on a regular basis. You should also be quicker to set a second anchor, not only as insurance when conditions get strong, but also to keep your boat from swinging too much. One advantage of chain is that its weight keeps a boat from shifting around much in a light to moderate breeze or current. A disadvantage, of course, is that this same weight hurts a boat's performance when sailing, an effect that is only magnified when the chain is carried forward in the bow. If there's a lot of chain aboard, the best arrangement is to store it as low as possible in the middle of the boat. Few boats are set up this way, but it can be done.

Because of its weight, having a chain rode normally means you must have a windlass, too. On boats less than 35 feet long you can haul chain by hand if you are strong and resilient. But if you don't want a windlass on your boat, you're much better off with rope, as it is much easier to handle without mechanical assistance. Note too you must be careful when fitting a chain rode to a windlass. Chain sizes are not standardized, and the link sockets on a windlass wildcat must fit the chain links perfectly for the chain to run smoothly aboard.

Carrying a great deal of rope rode forward doesn't really hurt a boat's performance. Indeed, 200 feet of $\frac{5}{8}$-inch nylon rope only weighs about 30 pounds, compared to about 350 pounds for a similar length of equally strong $\frac{3}{8}$-inch chain. This means rope is actually light enough that it can be stored right on deck if you like, which does have certain advantages. Some bluewater cruisers carry their anchor line on large permanently mounted spools on deck, as this makes it easy to both deploy and recover the line quickly and neatly. When coastal cruising in a boat with a below-deck rode locker, I have often stored rope rode in open coils on the foredeck to save the trouble of pulling it through the hawsehole. When using a rope rode, there should always be a chain leader between the anchor and the rope to help the anchor set properly and to reduce the chance of the rope rode chafing on the bottom or on the anchor itself. A chain lead should be at least 30 to 50 feet long, depending on the size of the boat. An excellent compromise, particularly on smaller boats, is to put a long

When anchoring on a rope rode it is often necessary to deploy two anchors to keep from swinging too much in crowded anchorages. The two rodes can cross and get tangled as the wind or current shifts, as seen on this boat. (Courtesy of SAIL *Magazine; Photo by Malcolm White.)*

Anchoring on chain is always more secure, but you must deploy a snubber line to prevent shock loads from damaging deck hardware.

chain lead, say 60 to 100 feet, on a rope rode, as this offers much of the security of anchoring on chain, but is not so heavy as to unduly affect performance. Many modern windlasses now have special chain gypsies that can transition smoothly from chain to rope when hauling rode aboard. Rope rodes, as discussed in Chapter 4, should always be nylon, as it stretches easily and absorbs shock loads. The standard rule is that the diameter of the rope should be about 1/8 inch for each 10 feet of overall boat length. For example, a 30-foot boat requires a rope rode with a diameter of at least 3/8ths of an inch (or half an inch, as you should round up when necessary).

When anchoring on chain you should always secure the rode to the deck with a nylon snubbing line, as chain is not at all elastic and efficiently transmits shock loads to any hardware it is fastened to. The longer and heavier the snubbing line, the better. Most anchor chain is galvanized steel, though fancy boats sometimes carry stainless-steel chain instead. There are various types of galvanized chain available. High-test chain is the strongest for its weight. BBB chain is both weaker and heavier than high-test, and proof-coil chain is a little lighter than high-test and slightly weaker than BBB. The rough rule of thumb when sizing chain to a boat is that the chain's minimum breaking strength should be at least half the boat's displacement. For example, a boat displacing 12,000 pounds requires a chain rode with a minimum breaking strength of 6,000 pounds or more.

tandem rodes and fit in a windlass properly oriented to feed chain into the well. Boats below 32 feet are small enough that fitting a windlass into an anchor well is difficult, in which case the windlass must stay on deck. The well's deck door in all cases must be heavy and strong with a latch that can be positively secured. This is especially true if you carry chain, as you want to be certain the chain stays in the well if the boat is knocked down or capsized. Unfortunately, the anchor wells on many modern production boats have rather light doors with undersized latches and hinges and may well fail such a test. At a minimum the door and latch should be secure enough to withstand a good thrashing from a head sea. On a few boats there are both rode lockers belowdeck for storing chain and shallow wells on deck for storing rope, which is a worthy compromise favored by some experienced cruisers.

Types of Anchors

This is a large and potentially controversial subject, as there are many different anchors now on the market and anchoring involves many variables. Cruisers tend also to develop strong personal views as to what anchor works best, and these opinions are often based on little more than anecdotal evidence. Every once in a while attempts are made to test different anchors in an objective and quantitative manner. The most recent comprehensive anchor test I'm aware of was conducted jointly by West Marine and three boating magazines—*SAIL*, *Power & Motoryacht*, and *Yachting Monthly*—the results of which were published in the October 2006 issue of *SAIL* ("Holding Power," by Bill Springer). The test compared 14 different anchors in four different anchoring environments, including an open beach, where it was possible to observe each anchor's orientation and behavior as it set. If you are interested in studying this subject in more detail, I suggest you to start by reading Springer's article.

Many new yacht anchors have been introduced in the past 15 years, but they still fall into three basic categories. The most traditional type, the fisherman anchor, relies more on its weight to hold a boat in place. It has two long, narrow, curved flukes with diamond-shaped points at the end of a long shank at the top of which is a stock that is perpendicular to the flukes. The fisherman is said to be the best anchor

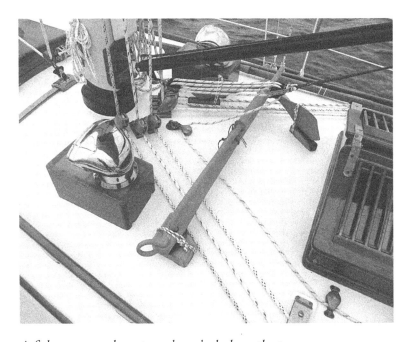

A fisherman anchor stowed on deck: here the perpendicular stock is folded against the shank for deck storage. Even when folded flat like this, however, a fisherman takes up a lot of space, and is heavy, two reasons why few cruisers carry them anymore.

to set in a rocky or coral-strewn bottom, but few cruisers carry them anymore because they are hard to stow on board and are heavy compared to other types. For example, a 70- to 90-pound fisherman suitable for use on a 40-foot boat is comparable to other anchors weighing just 25 to 45 pounds.

The next most traditional type is usually referred to generically as a Danforth anchor, although this technically is a trade name. It is also sometimes referred to as a fluke anchor, which is not particularly descriptive, as all anchors have flukes. It has two large, flat, triangular flukes set directly on top of a long stock, and the bottom of the shank pivots on the stock such that the entire length of the shank swings back and forth between the two flukes. Danforths rely primarily on their shape for their holding power and are the lightest of the three types—a 25- to 35-pound Danforth, for example, should have no problem holding a 40-foot boat. They work well in sand and soft mud, but do poorly on hard grassy or clay bottoms where more weight is needed to get the flukes to penetrate the bottom and dig in. They also are basically unidirectional anchors in that they usually break out of the bottom when the angle of the anchor rode changes dramatically due to a wind or current shift and do not easily reset themselves.

The last, most popular type is the plow or "uni-fluke" anchor, as I like to call it, of which there are now many variations. The common characteristics are a large single central fluke with a heavy curved shank sprouting out of it. The shape of the fluke is highly variable; most are classic convex triangular plows, but some are concave multipronged claws. In some cases the connection between the fluke and shank is hinged so the shank can pivot, but usually the connection is fixed and the anchor has no moving parts. Uni-fluke anchors are very versatile, thus are used by most cruisers as primary anchors. They are heavier than Danforth anchors—35 to 45 pounds is

normally sufficient to hold a 40-foot boat—but not nearly as heavy as a fisherman, and they hold reasonably well in a wide range of environments. They also normally reset themselves if the angle of pull on the anchor rode changes significantly.

Because they do not have stocks, older uni-fluke designs, such as the once ubiquitous CQR anchor, tend to fall on their sides when they land on the bottom, so they often drag a bit before digging in. Much of the tinkering with anchor design in the last 10 to 20 years has focused on this problem. Some modern uni-flukes set upright by virtue of their shape and weight distribution; others depend on semicircular roll bars built onto the back of the fluke. Judging from the results of the 2006 West Marine/magazine tests, these modern designs are in fact more reliable than the older ones. The more successful designs incorporate roll bars.

No one type of anchor holds well in all environments therefore many cruisers carry different types. For decades the conventional wisdom was you should carry one of each type, but these days coastal cruisers normally carry one uni-fluke as

Uni-fluke anchors have one big fluke with a shank coming straight off it. This more modern variation has a roll bar to keep the anchor from lying on its side as it sets. (Courtesy of Rocna)

A Danforth-type anchor has large triangular flukes with a shank that pivots between them. These are popular secondary anchors, but have trouble resetting themselves if they break out after a wind or current shift. This model can be completely disassembled and stowed in a small bag. (Courtesy of Fortress)

a primary anchor and a Danforth as an auxiliary anchor. Ideally you should store these side by side on the bow, but in fact this isn't possible on many boats. Because of its wide flukes and long protruding stock a Danforth anchor is often difficult to stow in a bow roller. Usually Danforth types are stored in other locations—normally in a lazarette or cockpit locker or flat on the coachroof—and are deployed as needed. Bluewater cruisers, meanwhile, normally carry at least three anchors, if not more, as they are easy to lose and can be hard to replace when traveling in remote areas.

There are many different technical recommendations as to what size anchor to carry, but there is also one universal aphorism almost everyone agrees on: carry the heaviest anchor you can reasonably handle. My rule of thumb is that the weight of a boat's unifluke anchor in pounds should equal or exceed the overall length of the boat in feet. If you can wrangle something significantly bigger than this, and there is room to store it on your boat, you should never hesitate to upgrade. If you are ever caught out at anchor in a big blow, you will be very happy you did.

Ground Tackle on Multihulls

Because multihulls are lighter than monohulls, it is commonly believed they require lighter anchors and rodes. Multihulls also, however, have a lot more windage than monohulls relative to the amount of hull they have in the water. The wind imposes a larger relative load on ground tackle, but this is offset by the reduction in load imposed by the weight of the boat itself. In the end the best practice is to use an anchor and rode just as heavy as you would use on a monohull of similar length, with one caveat. Because multihulls are so weight sensitive, you should think seriously about carrying rope rode rather than chain.

The big advantages of anchoring out in a multihull are its shoal draft, which makes it possible to anchor in much shallower water, and its wide beam, which greatly reduces rolling. These attributes allow multihull cruisers to anchor in spots that are off-limits to most monohull cruisers. Because of their windage and light weight, however, multihulls do tend to sail around a lot on their anchors, tacking back and forth through arcs as wide as 50 degrees. The best way to control this is to rig a bridle between the outermost hulls so that the load on the anchor rode is spread across the entire width of the boat, rather than focused on one point in the middle. Just as a bridle on a dinghy keeps it from slewing around while being towed, an anchor bridle on a multihull greatly reduces the arc through which it swings at anchor.

On a trimaran the anchor and rode are stored and deployed from the bow of the main hull, just as

they are on a monohull. The only difference is you need to rig an anchor bridle, which requires running lines out to the amas. On a catamaran the anchor and rode can be handled in several different ways. On most cats the rode is stored near the mast on the main center crossbeam. Simple boats often have an open rode box on deck; most modern production cats have below-deck rode lockers incorporated into the crossbeam. These lockers normally cannot be very deep, so they must be accessible so that the rode can be flaked down neatly if necessary. On cats that do not have lateral centerline spars or beams running between the center and forward crossbeams, the anchor roller normally must also be mounted on the center crossbeam. This means you need an anchor bridle not only to keep the boat from swinging, but also to bring the rode's attachment point forward of the bows. The advantage of this arrangement is that all the weight of the rode and anchor when stowed is

A shallow anchor well in the center crossbeam of a modern cruising cat—even with this relatively small amount of chain, the pile is already almost high enough to foul the hawsehole under the windlass. Crew must tend the chain to prevent this.

Anchor well

This cruising cat has its anchor roller all the way forward on its forward crossbeam with the chain running in a channel up the lateral centerline walkway from the anchor well in the center crossbeam. Having the weight of the anchor forward is not great, but it is easier to rig a bridle.

kept in the middle of the boat where it has the least effect on performance under sail. The disadvantage is that rigging the bridle to the bows from under the forward trampoline net can be difficult.

If a cat has some lateral centerline structure forward of the center crossbeam, an anchor roller can be positioned anywhere along it. If the roller is all the way forward it may not be necessary to rig a bridle in slack conditions, and when it is necessary it is relatively easy, as it doesn't involve handling lines under the trampoline. On the other hand the anchor roller will be a long way from the windlass and rode locker, and shuttling between the center and forward crossbeams to monitor the progress of a hoist or drop can get annoying in itself. A remote control for the windlass is a great help here. Also, having the weight of the rode and anchor so far forward, particularly if the rode is chain, hurts the boat's performance. On many boats, therefore, the anchor roller is instead positioned at an intermediate point between the two crossbeams. This brings weight aft a bit and shortens the chain run, but makes it harder to deploy a bridle.

MOVING AROUND ON DECK

Even if you aren't a hard-core bluewater sailor grappling with large seas and lumpy conditions, you should always feel comfortable and secure when moving about the deck of your boat. Even in calm conditions, you'll enjoy your boat much more if it is easy to get around. There are numerous factors

that contribute to security on deck; these are a few of the more important ones.

The cockpit-to-deck transition. Particularly on smaller aft-cockpit boats, my experience is you often feel most vulnerable when first stepping up out of the cockpit onto the deck. This is especially true on many modern production boats with low cabin profiles and rounded cockpit coamings and on some older boats with narrow side decks. It tends to be less true of large center-cockpit boats. The key factor is having something solid and somewhat elevated to grab onto as you shift your weight up and out of the cockpit.

On many boats the only elevated handhold at the forward end of the cockpit is the cockpit dodger. If this is merely canvas over a light aluminum frame, it often does not feel solid or secure. A stouter, heavier stainless-steel dodger frame with dedicated handholds on the sides and along the back edge makes a big difference. Even better is a solid hard dodger with fixed handrails along the edge of its roof. These provide excellent support both as you pull yourself from the cockpit up to the deck and as you start moving forward along the deck. They are also great for leaning on if you just want to stand in the forward end of the cockpit while conning the boat. Other solid structures that may be appropriately positioned are a boom gallows (found normally only on older, more traditional boats), a traveler arch, or a fixed post for supporting an awning or a bimini.

Side decks and rails. Moving along a side deck is normally easier if it is wide (24 inches or more is good) with a reasonably high coachroof with a solid handrail on one side and a raised bulwark or toe rail on the other. Many modern production boats are deficient in this regard. Coachroofs are often so low you must crouch or kneel to grasp the handrail. Solid bulwarks are rare these days, and most boats instead have low perforated aluminum toe rails. There's nothing wrong with a toe rail per se, as long as it is nearly as high as a human foot is wide (3 inches or more is best) so you can firmly brace a foot against it when the deck is well heeled. This is particularly important whenever you transit the lee side of a deck.

Pulpits, stanchions, and lifelines. Once upon a time yachts didn't carry these. Take a sail in rough conditions on a boat with no pulpits at the bow and stern and no lifelines ringing the deck, and you'll soon develop a strong appreciation for the physical courage of early ocean-racing crews. Unfortunately, on many modern production boats lifelines are more a psychological than physical barrier. Often they are only 20 to 24 inches high—below knee height for most male crew of average height—which makes them little more than trip lines designed to help crew fall overboard. To work effectively, lifelines should be at least 30 inches high (34 to 36 inches is much better) so they reach above the knees, preferably at least as high as the mid-thigh region, so that crew can lean into them a bit without their weight immediately shifting outboard.

On U.S.-manufactured boats lifelines are often sheathed in plastic, which is nice if you must lean against them for long, as race crews must often do when perched on the windward rail. The sheathing, however, traps moisture against the stainless-steel wire inside and hides corrosion until it is well advanced. In most cases, too, the steel used in the wire is the more corrosion-prone 304 alloy, so it is important to monitor what is going on. The best practice is to leave lifelines unsheathed, as is often done on European boats, and to use the more corrosion-proof 317 alloy.

The vertical stanchions that support lifelines also deserve close attention. On many modern boats stanchion bases are mounted flat on the horizontal edge

Stanchion bases are much stronger if they are fastened both to the deck below them and to a gunwale running beside them.

of the deck and are secured only by machine screws threaded into aluminum plates bedded in the deck laminate. If subjected to a large shock load, there's a good chance these may rip out of the deck. The most secure installation is to mount stanchion bases both to the deck and to the adjacent vertical surface of a strong gunwale or deep toe rail so they are supported in two directions. All fasteners should be through-bolts, with substantial backing plates behind them. Also, sockets in stanchion bases should have drain holes at the bottom so that water doesn't pool up and get trapped between the stanchion and the base, thus accelerating corrosion. Sockets should also be fitted with strong setscrews so that stanchions can't pull out of their bases.

Another common defect on both stanchions and pulpits are the attachment points for the lifelines. These are often little more than thin, frail hoops of stainless steel spot-welded to the tops of stanchions or pulpit frames. The welds are prone to crack open over time, and the fixture is usually too light in the first place. Strong attachment points are important, but are rarely seen on modern production boats.

Pulpit frames, meanwhile, like stanchion bases, should be firmly through-bolted in place with generous backing plates behind every fastener. Instead, they are again often just screwed into plates set up inside the deck laminate. Because the structure of the frame itself is large and multidimensional, pulpits are much less likely to give way and fail than stanchions, but the fasteners do often work loose after a while and then are prone to leak. With through-bolts this is less likely to happen. As a general rule, pulpits must be strong enough for crew to sit and lean on for extended periods. On a few boats you'll find

The ultimate in pulpit security. The bow pulpit on this aluminum cutter is welded in place and is thus very strong. Note, too, the solid welded tab for the lifeline attachment.

extended stern pulpits that wrap all the way around an aft cockpit, which is an excellent idea. This makes moving around the cockpit and climbing in and out of it much easier in all conditions.

Deck texture. Deck surfaces should be treated so they are not too slippery. This is particularly important with a fiberglass deck, as it otherwise is very slick indeed. There are several different types of nonskid surfaces to choose from. The most aesthetic option is a teak deck, where a veneer of teak decking is applied over a fiberglass deck. Teak does provide decent footing when wet and looks traditional and organic, but it also requires some care. It needs to be cleaned on a regular basis to maintain its appearance, and older planked teak decks that are screwed down eventually create big problems, as each of the hundreds of screw holes is a potential route for leaks into the core of the fiberglass deck beneath. Modern modular teak decks are glued down, thus are much tidier and leakproof, but still the veneer wears away over time and must be replaced. Teak also adds more weight to the deck than necessary, although modern modular veneers can be thin (which in turn, of course, means they must be replaced more frequently).

Another once popular alternative is molded nonskid, where a fiberglass deck has a textured surface pattern molded into it. This is reasonably effective, but like teak veneer wears away over time. As the nonskid pattern is worn smooth, it gets progressively more slippery and eventually must be renewed somehow. Since remolding the deck is not an option, this normally involves grinding away the pattern, an ugly and onerous job, and replacing it with another nonskid surface.

Which brings us to nonskid paint. This is increasingly popular, as it is the easiest surface to create and the easiest to renew once it wears away. The surface is created simply by adding some grit, such as sand, polymer beads, or even ground-up walnut shells, to deck paint. Renewing the texture is as simple as repainting the deck, and its aggressiveness can be controlled by changing the amount of grit added to the paint. Assuming enough grit is used, a painted nonskid deck provides better traction than either a teak or molded nonskid deck.

The last type of surface is probably the most effective, but is rarely seen on U.S.-built yachts. This is a British product, Treadmaster, which comes in sheets of thin nitrile rubber with an aggressive diamond matrix pattern embossed on one side. To treat a deck you cut loose sheets of Treadmaster into appropriately shaped modular sections and then glue them down with epoxy. The rubber is extremely firm and durable and takes decades to wear away. When it

does finally give up the ghost, however, replacing it is a big job, as removing old Treadmaster is always difficult. Treadmaster's nonskid surface provides much better traction than any of the alternatives, though some find it too aggressive, as it can be uncomfortable to sit or lie on.

Obviously, you want to find nonskid anyplace on deck where you routinely place your feet. It is best, therefore, to apply it liberally. Builders were once stingy with nonskid, but most decks are now well treated. The one exception may be catamaran decks, where some builders still assume that because the deck is level it must be harder to slip and fall down on. This is decidedly not the case. Catamarans do move around a bit, their motion is often unpredictable, and their decks are so wide you are often out of reach of a handhold. If anything, they need more not less nonskid than monohulls.

Granny bars. I am a huge fan of these, as they make it much easier to move around a deck while always holding on tight to something. The most logical locations for them are either side of the mast, where they should be at least butt-high so crew can lean on them while standing at the mast and handling lines, and over dorade vents, where they provide convenient handholds and also keep lines from getting hooked on the vents. Unfortunately, granny bars are not often seen on modern production boats, both because most boats have all lines led aft from the mast to

Granny bars at the mast make it easier to move around on deck and also provide fantastic support when working at the mast. This boat could also use a granny bar over its forward dorade vent, but the pair of deck-mounted handrails nearby are useful.

A scoop transom or swim platform is a tremendous amenity on any cruising boat (top). Some boats have fold-down transoms that combine the security of a full transom with the convenience of a scoop (bottom). (Top photo courtesy of SAIL *Magazine; Photo by Malcolm White.)*

the cockpit and because many don't have dorade vents. When granny bars are installed, they should be treated like stanchion bases or pulpit frames—all fasteners should be through-bolted with strong backing plates behind them.

Sugar-scoop transoms. These are a great innovation, first because they effectively increase the usable area on deck, serving as a "back porch" to the main part of the deck, and also because they make it much easier to move between the water's surface and the deck. Once you've boarded a boat from a swim ladder or dinghy over a scoop transom, you'll never want to clamber over a rail again. Last but not least, a scoop provides a fantastic venue for a deck shower. The only potential downside to a scoop is that it may complicate the installation of a wind vane. In most instances, however, it isn't too hard to make a vane fit somehow.

On boats with aft cockpits a scoop transom is even more accessible if the transom is open, with little or no barrier between the cockpit and the scoop. An open transom also guarantees that a cockpit will drain very quickly if invaded by a large wave. An open transom also, however, makes it easier for waves to get into the cockpit in the first place. Any cockpit with an open transom at one end should therefore have a bridgedeck at the other so water flooding the stern of the boat can't run straight across the cockpit sole and down the companionway. Some open transoms have a door or a removable seat so you can close off the transom when desired. Such installations must be strong enough to stand up to punishment from breaking waves. I've seen transom doors on some production boats suffer serious damage after being hit by relatively small following seas.

TENDERS

For casual weekend cruisers a tender or dinghy is often an afterthought, some scrap of a spare skiff that is towed behind the mothership just in case someone wants to go ashore. Those who like to flit from marina to marina may not even bother with a tender at all. But the more time you spend aboard your cruising boat, and the more time you spend anchored out or on a mooring, the more important a tender becomes. If you're a serious cruiser and spend a lot of time aboard, a tender is in effect your family car and needs to perform reasonably well as a general mode of transportation and as a load carrier.

The simplest, most basic sort of tender is a hard dinghy. These are normally fiberglass, wood, or rotomolded plastic; I have also seen some impressive custom-built welded aluminum tenders. Hard dinghies are easy to row, and if you don't want to bother with an outboard engine they are really your only option. They are also tough and durable. They can be dragged up beaches and across rocks with impunity, and even if you do knock a hole in one, it is relatively easy (at least with a fiberglass, wood, or

If you can't or don't want to carry an outboard engine, a hard dinghy that is easy to row is your only reasonable option. This nesting dinghy can be broken down to fit on the deck of this couple's 28-foot cruising boat.

RIB tenders like this one are popular because they jump up on a plane easily and thus are fast under power. But they are heavier than inflatables with flexible bottoms and are also harder to stow on deck. (Courtesy of SAIL *Magazine; Photo by Malcolm White.)*

aluminum vessel) to make a permanent repair. With even a minimal amount of care, a hard dinghy should last almost indefinitely. The disadvantages are that hard dinghies tend to be heavy and are relatively unstable. The latter characteristic makes them less useful as load carriers. It is possible to improve their stability by increasing their beam and/or adding flotation sponsons around their gunwales.

Most cruising sailors now use inflatable dinghies because they are faster under power (because they are much lighter and plane more easily than hard dinghies) and are remarkably stable. The simplest, least expensive inflatables, which have tubular fabric hulls and fabric floors partially reinforced with a few wooden or plastic slats, do not share these virtues and make rather poor tenders. They are a bit too amorphous and flexible to stand up to the thrust of an outboard engine and also do not row well. More sophisticated inflatables, however, have solid transoms and removable solid floors to stiffen them up and inflatable keels to help improve their tracking ability. The most sophisticated boats, referred to as rigid inflatable boats, or RIBs, have fully contoured fiberglass V-hull bottoms and inflatable topsides. These combine some of the virtues of an inflatable and a hard dinghy in that they are fast, stable, and have a durable underbody that can withstand some abuse.

All inflatables are hard to row because of their windage. If you carry an inflatable, you must also carry an outboard engine. Oars are generally used only as a last resort. A proper inflatable with a good-

sized engine, however, has tremendous range. Even a small inflatable with a removable floor and a modest 4- or 5-horsepower engine can efficiently carry you 2 to 3 miles away from the mothership, while a large RIB with a 15- to 20-horsepower engine can wander many more miles quite comfortably. Being able to travel like this in a tender greatly increases your options whenever you are anchoring or mooring your boat. Rowing a hard dinghy, on the other hand, you are unlikely to travel more than half a mile from the mothership on a routine basis.

The big drawback to any inflatable is that it is ineluctably mortal. Even a RIB won't last indefinitely, as the fabric of the inflatable tubing must wear out eventually. Cheaper inflatables are made with polyvinylchloride (PVC) fabric, which generally lasts about 5 years before it gives out. In tropical environments it may only last a year or two. Boats made of Hypalon fabric are far superior and should last about 10 years, if not longer, but are also twice as expensive. It is possible to extend an inflatable's life span by making custom canvas covers to protect the fabric of its hull sponsons, but such covers can be a pain to deal with and only forestall the inevitable. Over the course of its lifetime, any inflatable will also inevitably be punctured, but if the holes are not too large and are patched with scrupulous care this is normally not fatal. It is important, however, that an inflatable's hull have at least two separate inflation chambers so that one hole cannot deflate the entire vessel at once.

Except on large yachts, one of the biggest problems with any tender is figuring out how to take it along with you. Coastal cruisers can just tow them along behind the mothership, which is by far the most convenient option in calm conditions. In rough weather, however, this may not be possible, and you should therefore also have some way to carry the tender aboard the mothership. The most convenient method is to carry the tender in stern davits. This gets the boat out of the water, where it can't immediately be swamped by breaking waves, but it is not absolutely secure, as any wave large enough to poop the mothership may also carry away the tender and damage whatever portion of the stern the davits are attached to. For most coastal cruisers, this is a small risk, but any bluewater cruiser, or any coastal cruiser who routinely transits large open bodies of water in unsettled conditions, should always be prepared to carry their tender on deck.

Stowing a tender on deck is often problematic. On many boats less than 38 feet long, there is no room to lash down a full-size hard dinghy or a fully inflated inflatable. On boats where there is room, the tender is likely to obstruct hatches, control lines, and other equipment and will also increase windage on deck. Inflatables with removable floors can be deflated and rolled up into much smaller packages; you can also buy (or build) hard "nesting" dinghies that break down into two (or even three) components that all fit inside each other. RIBs normally can be made only a little smaller by deflating their topsides, though there are some models with bottom sections that fold in half. Remember, too, you must also have enough room on deck to reconstruct the tender when you need it. Reconstruction, of course, also takes some effort. The best compromise, in my experience, are inflatables that can be deflated and rolled up with their removable floors still installed, as these can be unrolled and pumped up again in just 5 to 10 minutes.

LIFE RAFTS

Usually only bluewater cruisers carry life rafts on their boats, but serious coastal cruisers who routinely wander in areas with minimal traffic should also give serious thought to how they might abandon ship. Many sailors expect they will board their tender if necessary, but if a tender is towed it may not be there when needed. And if it is stowed on deck in a deconstructed state, it may not be possible to launch it in a timely manner. Only those who stow their tenders completely assembled on deck—or have an inflatable with appropriately sized CO_2 cylinders so that it can be automatically inflated in

an instant—should think of their tender as an escape pod. Otherwise, it is prudent to also carry a dedicated inflatable life raft.

Most coastal or inshore rafts have a single tube construction, thus are lighter and more compact than offshore rafts, which have two tubes and are nearly twice as expensive. Single-tube coastal rafts offer less flotation and freeboard and are not designed to be inhabited for extended periods. The least expensive models don't even have canopies for shelter. Double-tube offshore rafts are more robust and comfortable and come equipped with canopies and survival kits that include food, water, medical supplies, and other gear. Clearly, these are preferable in any emergency situation, no matter what sort of cruising you do. If you do select a single-tube raft, be sure that the tube is compartmentalized and has at least two inflation chambers. That way you are at least left with half a floating raft if one chamber is punctured.

Rafts are made of rubber, polyurethane, or PVC. Rubber rafts are usually the longest lived and if maintained can last up to 20 years. Synthetic rubbers, such as neoprene and butyl, stand up especially well against environmental degradation and fungal contamination. Polyurethane rafts last on average 10 to 15 years, but are more puncture and abrasion resistant. PVC, the least robust material, is also the least expensive, and normally lasts only about 10 years or less in service. When packed, all polyurethane and PVC rafts should be vacuum-sealed to maximize their life spans.

The best way to stow a raft is on deck in a hard canister. Preferably it should be located somewhere near the cockpit, where it can be quickly deployed when needed and is less likely to get tangled in the rig if the boat is actually sinking. On many boats now there are dedicated storage compartments for life raft canisters in the aft end of the cockpit or right in the transom itself. On many other boats, the only realistic option is to mount the canister in a cradle on the coachroof, either just forward or aft of the mast. The canister is more exposed here, thus runs some risk of being swept overboard in severe conditions. It may also get tangled in the rig if the rig is in the water, but otherwise is reasonably easy to deploy from this location. Wherever it is located, a canister's cradle should be robust and through-bolted to the deck with appropriate backing plates. Many experts now also recommend that deck-mounted rafts have hydrostatic release mechanisms that automatically cut the raft canister free from its cradle when it is submerged for a set period of time.

The alternative to a deck-mounted hard canister is a soft fabric valise. These are much cheaper and

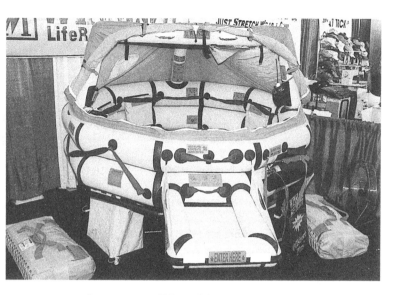

This serious offshore life raft has double-tube construction, a full canopy, a boarding platform, and ballast bags underneath.

The best way to stow an inflatable raft is in a hard canister on deck in the vicinity of the cockpit, but on many boats the only viable option, as here, is on the coachroof.

much lighter than canisters, but are not very durable. If a valise is stored on deck, the life expectancy of the raft inside is dramatically diminished. If a valise is stored below, the raft will last much longer, but will also be much harder to deploy in an emergency.

There are other important features to look for in a life raft, starting with good stability. Square or rectangular rafts capsize more easily, as their corners may dig into the water and allow the raft to trip over itself in breaking seas. Round rafts are less vulnerable, but are also less comfortable, as everyone's legs tend to end up in a tangle in the middle. A good raft has water-ballast bags on its underside to prevent capsize. These bags are weighted so they open and fill with water easily when the raft is deployed. The raft's deployment painter, meanwhile, should attach to the raft at its entryway to assist with boarding after the raft is deployed. There should be a drogue attached to the side of the raft opposite the entry so the entry always faces away from any breaking seas. Righting lines under the raft are also critical, since rafts deploy upside down about 30% of the time and sometimes need to be pulled upright by the boarding crew. A well-designed boarding ramp or bolster in front of the entry makes it easier to climb into the raft from the water. If you sail in cold water the floor should also be insulated. Canopy flaps should have zippers instead of tie strings, as zippers are much easier to secure when manual dexterity is impaired by cold and exposure.

LIVING ACCOMMODATIONS

What defines a cruising boat in the largest sense is that it may be resided upon. Your stay aboard may be long or short, but you must be able to sleep, eat, and pass waste aboard in order to embark upon a proper cruise. Depending on how spartan an existence you can endure, or how much luxury you can afford, this definition can embrace a broad range of vessels, from an open skiff or launch with a bucket for a head, a cooler for storing drinks and sandwiches, and a cockpit seat long enough to stretch out a sleeping bag on, to an enormous megayacht with an onboard Jacuzzi and home theater. Most cruisers will at least want their boat to have an enclosed cabin with some space for berths, a galley, and a proper toilet.

Installing living accommodations on a sailboat always involves compromises, because the use of space is inevitably constrained by functional aspects of a vessel's design. Creature comforts enjoyed while stationary must be balanced against the more exacting demands of sailing the boat and sustaining the crew while underway. In many cases, features that make a boat safer and more comfortable in a seaway make it less comfortable and attractive when it is anchored or tied to a dock, and vice versa. Exactly how these contradictions are resolved varies a great deal from vessel to vessel.

On older, more traditional cruising boats interior accommodations are generally conservative and strongly favor the more functional seagoing side of the equation. These boats are narrow with long overhangs, so interior space is normally restricted, and, as a result, layouts on these boats don't vary

much. Indeed, for many years the majority of midsize cruising boats had very predictable interiors. These featured a galley to port and starboard of the companionway with a stove and sink on one side and an icebox that doubled as a nav desk on the other, a pair of settee berths forward on either side of the saloon, followed by a head, and then the forepeak, which had either a V-berth or perhaps just bins for storing sails and gear with pipe berths over them. The overall effect was decidedly cramped and confining, and to get a much different interior you had to get a much larger boat.

Over the past 30 years, even modest cruising boats have grown much larger inside. Boats are beamier with shorter overhangs, and interior footprints are thus bigger. A modern 35-foot cruising boat may easily have as much room inside as a 40- to 42-foot boat had 30 or 40 years ago. Accommodations plans are now more varied, with a broader spectrum of layouts to choose from. Many of these are comfortable when a boat is at rest, but are less so when it is sailing. If anything, the pendulum has swung back, and living accommodations on boats now favor the less functional side of the equation.

What interior best suits you depends on how you use your boat. Coastal cruisers who sail only a few hours at a time and are otherwise anchored out or tied to docks can, if they like, trick out their boats like miniature land-bound vacation homes. Bluewater cruisers who live on their boats and often sleep and eat aboard while sailing must weigh their choices more carefully. The other major factor, of course, is money. A larger boat, however you use it,

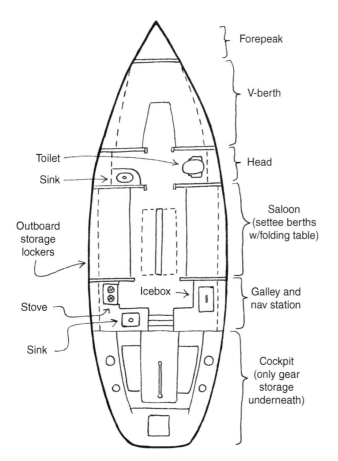

Forepeak

V-berth

Toilet

Sink

Head

Saloon
(settee berths
w/folding table)

Outboard
storage
lockers

Icebox →

Galley and
nav station

Stove

Sink

Cockpit
(only gear
storage
underneath)

An example of a typical accommodations plan for a traditional cruising boat.

Many boatbuilders today resolve compromises with respect to living space early in the construction process by building a mock interior first. This allows flaws in an accommodations plan to be corrected before they are set in stone.

will always have a roomier, more comfortable interior, whether you are sailing or lying on a dock or the hook. Small may be beautiful when it comes to paying for, maintaining, and handling a sailboat, but when it comes to living space there's no escaping the fact that living large is much easier when you have more boat to do it on.

STATEROOMS AND BERTHS

Just as they do when looking for a house to live in, the first item many consider when looking for a boat to cruise on is the number of people it can sleep. More than any other factor, this single criteria is most likely to be determinative in purchasing decisions involving both new and used cruising sailboats. To keep berth-counting buyers from dismissing their boats, builders have therefore always inserted as many berths as possible into their accommodations plans. Even back in the days of the CCA rule when boats were more likely to be both cruised and raced, extra beds were often crammed into common space in the form of pilot berths, pipe berths, and collapsible dinette tables that convert to double berths. In practice many of these were probably more useful to racing crews than they ever were to most cruising families.

Where once the market favored simply more berths, it now favors more private berths, preferably situated behind closed doors. Staterooms, so called, have thus proliferated in modern accommodations plans. A modest 36-foot aft-cockpit monohull may now carry as many as three segregated sleeping cabins, as Europeans more accurately describe them—one in the forepeak, plus two aft cabins under either side of the cockpit. A similarly sized catamaran can carry as many as four—two in each hull, forward and aft. The rise of the modern bareboat charter fleet, where a double berth behind a closed door is effectively sold as a floating hotel room, has accelerated this trend. The large demand generated by charter fleets, coupled with modern production boatbuilding capacity, has led to an enormous increase in the number of boats built with multiple double staterooms.

Meanwhile on larger cruising boats, increased expectations of privacy and exclusivity have led to the rise of the modern master aft stateroom. Most often these are found on center-cockpit boats, where a large aft cabin can be easily segregated from the rest of the interior, but they are increasingly common on large aft-cockpit boats as well. These cabins span the entire width of the boat's hindquarters, are normally equipped with an en suite head with a separate shower, and can seem almost sinfully posh and commodious.

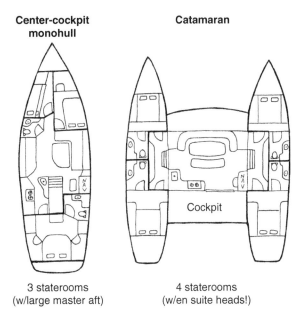

ockpit nohull	Center-cockpit monohull	Catamaran

Cockpit

aterooms doubles!)	3 staterooms (w/large master aft)	4 staterooms (w/en suite heads!)

The modern trend is to maximize stateroom space and create as many private sleeping areas as possible.

The Forepeak

Before the advent of the modern master aft stateroom, the forepeak, or forward cabin, was traditionally the most private, most exclusive area in any sailboat's accommodations scheme. It is removed from the cockpit, galley, and saloon, thus is usually the quietest spot aboard a boat at rest. It is also the closest to a boat's ground tackle, which makes it a great place for a skipper to lay his head at night, as the only thing likely to disturb his slumber is the rumble of rode when an anchor starts dragging. Thanks to the ubiquity of forward hatches, the forepeak is also always the most well-ventilated part of any boat lying on an anchor or mooring, thus is comfortable even in warm weather.

One obvious disadvantage of the forepeak is that it is in the narrowest part of the boat and has an unusual shape. On boats smaller than 32 feet this can create problems, as the peak may not be quite large enough to comfortably sleep two people. The berth may be short, and its narrow pointy end is often too cramped for two pairs of feet. On any boat smaller than 36 feet, there normally isn't room in the forepeak for doing anything other than sleeping, plus it can be hard to climb in and out of the berth.

The biggest problem with a forepeak is that it is uncomfortable underway. Because motion in a seaway is most exaggerated in the forwardmost part of any boat, sleeping in a forepeak while sailing can be difficult. In most cases, crew assigned to the forepeak reassign themselves to settee berths in the main saloon when a boat is on passage. For couples cruising on their own, this is fine, but on boats with large crews it can be problematic, as the saloon may be needed as a social center, particularly during meals and when conditions are wet on deck.

Forepeak berths come in three basic configurations, the most common of which is the traditional V-berth. It is supposedly two single berths arranged in a V, but in practice it is normally used as a double. This requires filling in the space between the arms of the V, which is usually done with a removable fill board and cushion so the berth can convert back and forth between twin singles and a full double. This is useful, but storage drawers under the separate single berths usually are inaccessible when the filler section is installed. The filler section also can be uncomfortable to lie on, in which case all but the most amorous couples end up sleeping on either side in the singles in any event. To prevent this and to make the storage areas under the berth more accessible, some layouts have dedicated double V-berths with the interior of the V permanently filled in.

Pullman doubles are shaped like parallelograms and are offset to one side of the hull. These make better use of the space in the forepeak, as two people can comfortably share the berth and there is more open floor space. When used as a double, however, one occupant of a Pullman berth always gets trapped between the hull and the other occupant. This leads to grumbling when the inside party wants to get out in the middle of the night.

A typical Pullman double berth in the forward cabin of a 39-foot cruising boat. There is an anchor-rode locker just forward of the curtain.

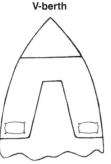
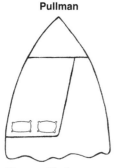
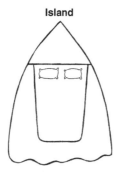

V-berth
- Sleeps two singles or a couple if filled in
- Good access
- Filler insert may be uncomfortable

Pullman
- More usable floor space
- Solid double berth is more comfortable
- Only accessible from one side

Island
- Great access
- Solid double berth
- Nothing solid to lean against in a seaway

Typical forepeak layouts.

The head of this traditional quarter berth doubles as a seat for the navigator, and the rest of it tends to get used for storage.

An island double berth doesn't have this problem. This is oriented along a boat's centerline like a V-berth, but has its wings chopped off to both open up floor space and allow equal access from both sides. An island-double layout is comfortable when a boat is idle, but does not fit on smaller boats; 40 to 42 feet is probably the shortest boat it works on, while 36 to 38 feet is probably the minimum LOA for a Pullman double. An island double is also useless when a boat is sailing. Because there is nothing solid to lean into on either side, they are hard for one person to use when a boat is heeled, never mind two.

Aft Cabins

In the past a small or midsize cruising boat never had anything like an aft cabin. The best you could hope for was a narrow open quarter berth slung under one side of the cockpit, and in most cases the head of the berth doubled as a seat for a navigation desk. Such quarter berths are in fact extremely comfortable, particularly in a seaway, but they offer no privacy and are little more than a grotto for sleeping in. The navigator may also accidentally sit on your head from time to time. Quarter berths on many boats are inevitably used as storage caves for large pieces of gear that don't fit anywhere else.

In recent years, egged on mostly by charter companies, builders have turned all the area under a monohull's aft cockpit, even on quite small boats, into enclosed cabin space. This requires boats that are much broader in the stern and also higher, with more freeboard. On aft-cockpit boats as small as 28 feet you can now find full-width aft staterooms with transverse double berths that look enormous in a layout drawing. In reality these are little more than horizontal slit trenches with almost no vertical

clearance over the berth and are not very comfortable. On boats as short as 36 feet, two separate cabins can be wedged in under either side of a cockpit. These have more headroom, but otherwise are not very large. Thanks to the charter companies, they almost always have double berths, though many cruisers with children might prefer two single over-and-under berths instead. This makes more efficient use of the space, as it opens up more of the floor. Some builders do allow buyers to specify aft bunk berths instead of aft doubles, but this is unusual.

On boats as large as 43 to 45 feet, it is possible to fit a full-width cabin under an aft cockpit with full standing headroom under the coamings on either side of a centerline double berth that has good vertical clearance under the cockpit footwell. This can be a very comfortable configuration, particularly if the berth has solid furniture around the sides to provide support when the boat is heeled. Staterooms like this are noisy, however, when things are going on in the cockpit.

To maximize privacy in such a stateroom there should be access only through the interior of the boat. But this usually must lead through the galley and/or directly past the engine compartment, which are the two areas where a fire is most likely to break out. To circumvent the risk of being trapped inside the stateroom in a fire there should be a companionway from the cockpit straight down into the stateroom, but then privacy is destroyed. Many large aft-cockpit boats with full-width aft cabins in fact have two companionways—a smaller one leading into the aft cabin from the aft cockpit, and another larger one leading into the center of the interior from a small midship cockpit. This allows for excellent traffic flow between the deck and the interior, and aft stateroom occupants can close the aft companionway when they want privacy. Sailing in strong weather, however, the midship companionway must often be closed to keep it from shipping water into the boat, in which case all the traffic between the deck and the interior must go through the aft stateroom, and there is again no privacy at all.

On a center-cockpit boat, these problems are neatly solved. First, because the aft stateroom is not under the cockpit there is much more headroom through out the cabin. There is no cockpit noise. There is also usually space on the aft deck overhead for a large hatch that can be used as an escape route in the event of a midship fire, so access to the stateroom can otherwise be restricted to the boat's interior. Really the only drawback to aft staterooms on large center-cockpit boats is that they are often equipped with island double berths. As mentioned, such berths are easier to get in and out of (they are also much easier to make up with sheets), but they can be hard to sleep in when the boat is heeled.

This island double berth in the aft stateroom on a large center-cockpit boat has furniture around the head of the bed that will provide some support when the boat is heeled. (Courtesy of SAIL *Magazine)*

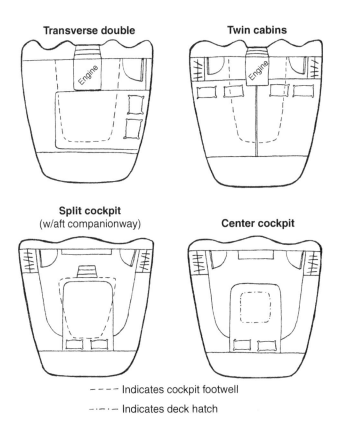

Typical aft cabin layouts.

Another point to consider is whether a large aft stateroom on a center-cockpit boat is really just a waste of space. Space is a valuable commodity on a sailboat, particularly space aft, where heavy gear and systems can be located without killing sailing performance, and where there is much less motion compared to the forward part of the boat. In one sense it is highly inefficient to devote such a large part of a boat's back end to a cabin used only by one or two people for sleeping. If the boat has a small crew, an aft master stateroom is easy to justify. But on a boat with a large crew, some crewmembers will be substantially less comfortable than others, and the master stateroom may seem a waste of space.

The biggest problem with any aft cabin is that it tends to be stuffy. This is especially true of cabins under cockpits. On some boats such cabins have a small opening port in the side of the hull and/or the cockpit footwell; if you're lucky there may be a small deck hatch (usually located under the cockpit dodger, where there is little air circulating). But none of these deliver enough air below to really cool things down. On many small boats there is no ventilation at all other than through the cabin door, which is why such doors (ironically) are almost always kept open. An aft master stateroom on a center-cockpit boat usually has a large deck hatch over the berth, and this is helpful. But when lying to an anchor or mooring, airflow to this hatch is obstructed and cannot compare to the superb airflow in a forepeak. For this reason alone, I generally prefer to use the forepeak as a master cabin when cruising in warm weather.

Midship Cabins

These are normally found only on boats larger than 46 feet and are not truly "midship," as they are almost always forward of both the main saloon and the mast. They experience less motion in a seaway than forepeak cabins, but are still much bouncier than aft cabins. I have spent many days and nights at sea in midship cabins and can attest they are habitable in rough conditions; others, however, may not agree and may sometimes be forced to move aft.

Most midship cabins have over-and-under single berths, which are useful for housing children and single crewmembers. Two such cabins side by side provide four dedicated berths, which is an extremely efficient use of space. The alternative is a Pullman double berth, which makes the space a comfortable guest stateroom for a couple, except in rough conditions.

Because they are forward of the mast, midship cabins should theoretically pull in as much air as the peak when a boat lies to an anchor or mooring, but to do so they need good deck hatches. Midship hatches are rarely as large as foredeck hatches, but should be as large as possible. Many hatches on production boats, unfortunately, are too small to keep midship staterooms comfortable when temperatures are high.

Characteristics of a Comfortable Sea Berth

Narrow sea berths are the most comfortable, as they prevent the body from flopping around too much as the boat moves. Too narrow, of course, can be a problem. The ideal width in most cases is between 1 foot 8 inches and 2 feet and the ideal length is between 6 feet 2 inches and 7 feet.

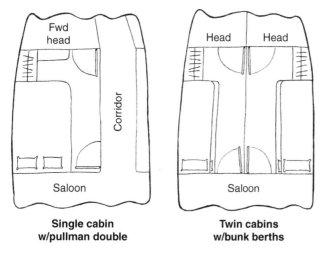

Midship cabins are often forward of the mast, where motion underway is a bit livelier than it is farther aft.

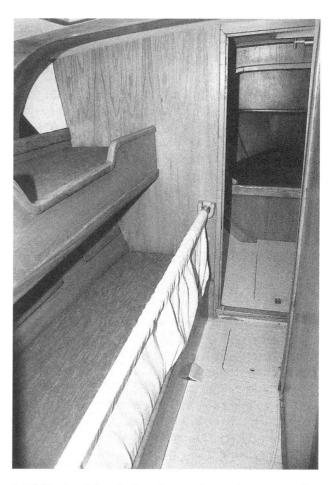

Midship bunk berths in a forward corridor on a mid-size monohull are handy for children. Note the rugged leecloth on the lower bunk.

A sea berth should always be lateral, parallel to the boat's centerline, and never athwartships. On a heeling monohull the occupant of a lateral berth can lean on one side of his or her body while trying to sleep. Leaning on your head, however, is impossible, and leaning on your feet is somewhat possible, but hardly optimal. It should also be impossible to fall out of a sea berth. Vertical support alongside the berth can take the form of solid furniture and joinery, a solid lee board, or a less-than-solid lee cloth. The best support is both solid and upholstered. It also helps if the corner between the vertical support face and the horizontal berth is somewhat curved or at least opens at an angle of something greater than 90 degrees. Some furniture or joinery with a cushion offers ideal support, as it is always in place ready for use. A lee board with a cushion, which can be deployed as needed, is next best, but these are rarely seen anymore. The most common expedient, the lee cloth, is the least satisfactory. They feel wobbly and insecure when you lean into them and can be difficult to climb in and out of. They are

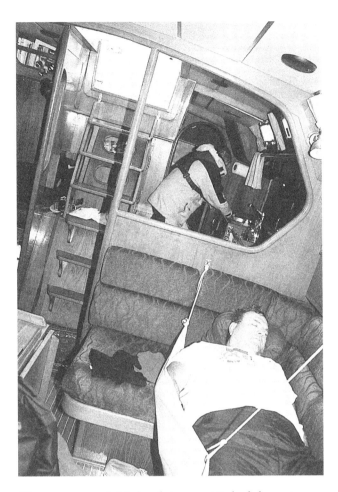

The occupant of this berth is now pitched down to leeward. When he's up on the windward side he won't feel very secure leaning into that lee cloth.

very convenient to stow, however, because they are light, take up no room, and can be easily stuffed out of the way under a berth or seat cushion when not needed.

Single berths are the easiest to convert to sea berths, as they are already narrow and normally have solid support on one side to begin with. Double berths should first be physically bifurcated if possible to maintain capacity, for it is not possible for two people to sleep together in a well-heeled berth if they are not somehow separated from each other. This requires a split mattress with either a lee board or lee cloth that can be set up between the two halves. Boards or cloths will also be needed for either side of an island double. The optimal arrangement is a double berth with solid joinery and cushions on either side that can be separated into two single berths by inserting a strong lee board down the middle. The least optimal arrangement is an island berth that cannot be divided and has only lee cloths on either side of it.

Airflow, as ever, is also important. Because deck hatches and opening ports must often remain shut when conditions are rough, each sea berth on a boat should ideally have a small 12-volt fan at its foot or head.

Berths on Multihulls

Because heeling is not a factor, sea berths on multihulls can be either lateral or athwartships. Likewise, a couple can comfortably share a double berth without its being split in two. Lee cloths or lee boards aren't really necessary, which is normally a moot question in any event, as berths on multihulls are generally well enclosed by the narrow hulls around them. The more important question on cruising catamarans is whether the bridgedeck is high enough to appreciably reduce the tendency of waves to pound at its underside. Noise from waves slapping at a low bridgedeck is the number-one enemy of sound sleep on most modern catamarans.

As on monohulls, the forwardmost part of a multihull is least habitable while sailing. Multihulls can pitch and hobbyhorse quite a bit, and such motion is amplified forward of the mast. Some modern catamarans have single berths in the very peak of their bows, but these compartments are not at all comfortable in a strong seaway and are rarely tricked out as proper staterooms in any event.

As mentioned, the most common layout on modern cruising cats has four staterooms—two right aft and two forward behind the forepeaks in each hull. As on a monohull, aft staterooms are generally more comfortable in terms of motion, but are not as well ventilated when the boat is lying to an anchor or mooring. On most modern production cats there is also an optional "owner's" layout, where all of one hull is made into an enormous master stateroom. Usually there is a double berth all the way aft, with a private en suite head and shower stall, plus a dressing

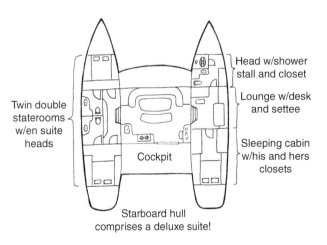

Typical three-cabin "owner's" layout on a modern cruising catamaran.

and/or office area, ranged forward of it. For those who want the largest, most lavish master stateroom possible, this is the way to go.

SALOONS

The saloon is almost always in the middle of the boat and can be organized in various ways. On small to midsize monohulls, the simplest layout consists of two straight settees facing each other across a centerline table that is either fixed and has folding leaves or folds up entirely against a bulkhead. Alternatives revolve around dinettes, which are offset fixed tables with one or more seats or long settees arranged around them. In some cases a dinette is opposite a midship galley; in others it is opposite a single long settee or some furniture with other sorts of built-in seating.

In the distant past, when saloon tables were often gimballed and cockpits were more cramped and uncomfortable, the saloon was where crew gathered to socialize and share meals while underway. I have twice crewed on ocean passages aboard traditional wooden boats with gimballed tables, and on both occasions their virtues were glaringly apparent. It is a shame they are now extinct. A fixed saloon table on a monohull, even if it has deep fiddles on its edges to theoretically contain things, is almost useless by comparison.

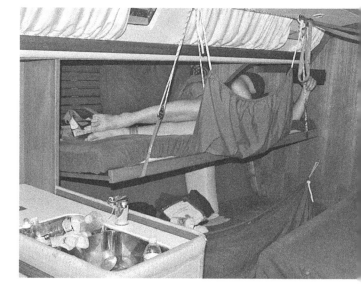

Another way to increase sleeping space in a saloon is to install settee seatbacks that swing up to form extra berths, as shown on this racer-cruiser. Note in this case, however, that the large knee for supporting chainplates cuts into the berths and makes it impossible to lean against the hull when the berths are heeled to leeward.

Modern bluewater crews usually prefer to eat and socialize outside in the cockpit whenever weather permits. The saloon, meanwhile, is often used for sleeping while underway. On small boats the saloon may be the only comfortable place to sleep while sailing; on large boats it is a refuge of last resort for crew trying to sleep forward of the mast. A saloon should therefore have as many long straight settees as possible, oriented laterally so they can easily be used as sea berths. Even quite small boats can normally accommodate at least two settees like this. Large boats can fit up to three, with straight settees either side of a dinette opposite a single settee. Plus, even midsize boats can fit in two extra dedicated sleeping spaces higher up in the saloon in the form of pilot berths or temporary pipe berths. These experience a little more motion than berths closer to the cabin sole, but are still reasonably comfortable. These were once relatively common, but are now rarely installed, except on some long-distance ocean racers.

Unfortunately, many modern saloons contain lots of swooping, sexy-looking curves. These are aesthetically pleasing when a boat is at rest, but at sea they can be a problem. Circular, oval, or otherwise curved settees encircling a round or kidney-shaped dinette table often cannot accommodate a sleeping human body if they are curved too deeply. In many cases you can sleep in them on one tack but not the other. Many of these dinettes have tables that

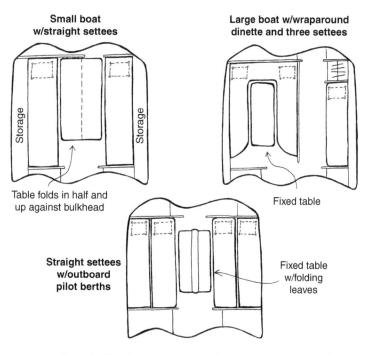

Monohull saloon layouts with maximum sea-berth potential—these are preferred on bluewater boats.

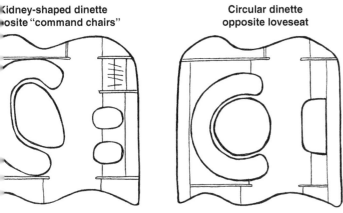

Kidney-shaped dinette
osite "command chairs"

Circular dinette
opposite loveseat

There are no good places to sleep!
(symptomatic of "CSLS" disease)

Monohull saloon layouts with minimal sea-berth potential—these are only appropriate on coastal boats.

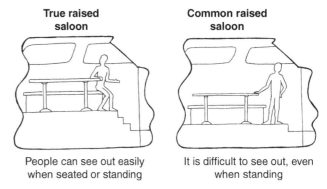

True raised
saloon

Common raised
saloon

People can see out easily
when seated or standing

It is difficult to see out, even
when standing

When not designed well, raised saloon sight lines afford only views of the sky.

collapse flush with their settees to form round double berths when filler cushions are added, but these rarely make effective sea berths. Even worse, when a stylized dinette is set opposite a foreshortened loveseat, an oversize nav station, or, worst of all, a pair of built-in "command" chairs, even more valuable sea-berth space is lost. Saloons suffering from this CSLS (curved settee and loveseat) disease, as I like to call it, are not at all appropriate on bluewater boats, but are fine on coastal boats.

Another increasingly popular variation is the so-called raised or deck saloon, where the saloon is in a raised deckhouse with oversize windows all around so that occupants can enjoy a panoramic view. It is a superb effect when done properly and really does help turn a cruising boat into a mobile waterfront vacation home. On many monohulls, however, it is hard to establish horizontal sight lines from within the boat. The windows often end up a bit too high and serve only as vertical panes in a sunroof that lets in lots of natural light while affording superb views of the sky overhead. On one large raised-saloon cruising boat I once toured, the windows in fact were so high you needed a stepladder to look out them.

Lines of sight aside, there's no reason why a raised saloon can't work on a bluewater boat. If a saloon contains a nav station with good horizontal sight lines and the station has either a remote wheel or some drive-by-wire device like a joystick or autopilot control, the saloon can operate as a useful seagoing pilothouse. Such a saloon will still hopefully have one or two sea-berth/settees, in which case it should be possible to shutter or curtain the windows to reduce ambient lighting so people can sleep. Also, the saloon windows absolutely must be strong enough to resist

blows from large breaking ocean waves. Appropriate materials for such windows are Lexan and laminated tempered glass about half an inch thick, depending on the size of the window. Any raised-saloon monohull sailboat with windows that do not meet bluewater specs should venture offshore only in settled conditions within reliably short weather windows, as the breaching of large saloon windows can easily lead to the loss of a vessel.

On cruising catamarans almost all saloons are raised-deck saloons in that they are normally on the bridgedeck over the two hulls. Indeed, the combination of sweeping "vacation home" views in a saloon with direct access to the cockpit and aft deck has helped attract thousands of cruisers

Inside a true raised-deck saloon the seats are high enough so you can see out the windows; on this one there is a nav station directly opposite.

A small bridgedeck "pod" saloon on a performance cruising catamaran—here the table collapses to form a wide double berth.

The picture of luxury—you can't beat a large conventional bridgedeck saloon for wide open spaces. (Courtesy of Catana)

to catamaran designs. On certain modern performance cruising cats and on some older designs there is no enclosed saloon, and the bridgedeck is used as a common open-air social space. This makes for a decidedly more primitive cruising experience, though the views are just as good. Some open-bridgedeck designs do have small enclosed bridgedeck shelters, referred to as pods, but they are not nearly as comfortable and pleasant as large bridgedeck saloons.

Unfortunately, the catamarans with the most expansive saloons are also usually the least sea-friendly when the boat is actually sailing. To gain headroom inside the saloon, the bridgedeck it rests upon must be lowered closer to the water,

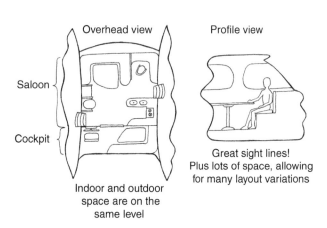

Overhead view   Profile view

Saloon

Cockpit

Indoor and outdoor
space are on the
same level

Great sight lines!
Plus lots of space, allowing
for many layout variations

A typical bridgedeck saloon layout on a modern cruising catamaran.

thereby increasing resistance, motion, and noise as more waves slap against its underbelly, and/or the superstructure must be raised, increasing windage. Window strength is less of an issue, as the breach of one or more saloon windows in extreme weather on a catamaran carrying no ballast is less likely to lead to a sinking. On true seagoing cruising cats it should be possible to seal off the hulls from the bridgedeck saloon, so if any windows are breached water will not gather in the hulls and swamp the vessel. Unfortunately, relatively few production catamarans have this feature.

One last issue to consider is handholds. Any bluewater boat should have good handholds throughout, but it is particularly important in a saloon, as it is usually the most open area on any boat. Particularly on modern beamy monohulls, there is risk of serious injury if someone falls clear across a wide saloon. This is not likely to happen on a catamaran, as they do not heel to leeward, but still a cat's motion can get quirky enough that crew will feel more secure if they have something secure to grab or while moving about. Ideally, you should be able to traverse every part of a saloon while holding onto something strong enough to support all of your weight. The most useful handholds are at waist level, as you can reach these no matter how tall or short you are; it is also easy to integrate unobtrusive handholds into waist-level furniture. Where this isn't possible, handholds should be no more than shoulder height. Handholds on overheads, though they look reassuring, often can't be reached by shorter crew.

Aft Saloons

Nowhere is it written in stone that all monohull saloons must be midships forward of the companionway. On a few cruising boats the saloon is instead behind the compan-ionway—either directly below an aft cockpit (as on some contemporary French centerboard cruisers) or behind a center cockpit (as was seen on a few early center-cockpit cruisers in the 1970s). Under-cockpit aft saloons are usu-ally large U-shaped dinette "party pits" with no standing headroom. None is required, however, as people are either seated at the enormous table or are stretched out sleep-ing on the super-long settees. Center-cockpit aft saloons do have standing headroom and are often configured as traditional great cabins with archaically charming stern windows to let in light.

An aft-saloon layout involves an interesting trade-off. A midship social space that can double as sleeping space is

This under-cockpit aft saloon on a midsize French centerboard cruiser is a great social space, with easy access to the engine (under the table). The companionway, however, is hard to use when the boat is heeled.

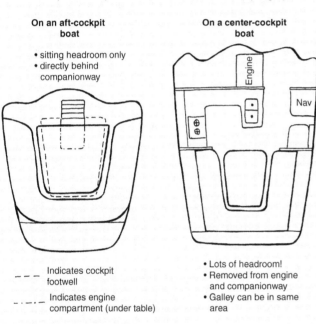

On an aft-cockpit boat

- sitting headroom only
- directly behind companionway

On a center-cockpit boat

Engine

Nav

- Lots of headroom!
- Removed from engine and companionway
- Galley can be in same area

– – –   Indicates cockpit footwell

–·–·–   Indicates engine compartment (under table)

Typical aft saloons.

moved aft and exchanged for dedicated midship sleeping space that was previously situated aft. In many respects this is an excellent idea. Midship staterooms are generally farther from the clatter and clamor of the cockpit and are also usually easier to ventilate. Cockpit noise is generally less intrusive in a social space. Poor ventilation, likewise, is more easily forgiven.

Ultimately, as with midship saloons, an aft saloon works best if people can sleep in it when a boat goes to sea. If an aft saloon can temporarily sleep two or more persons when the boat is underway, there is no good reason to dismiss it in favor of a midship saloon.

GALLEYS

Any cruise lasting more than 12 hours inevitably involves storing and preparing food; once out more than a day or two preparation and storage both become more complicated. Even a primitive cruis-ing cook will want to have immediate access to fresh water, a stove that can boil water in a reasonable amount of time, and an insulated cold box of some description. As such the galley is normally the most systems-intensive area on any cruising boat, with major plumbing, heating, and refrigeration instal-lations all within a few feet of each other. It is also

usually the busiest area on any serious cruising boat, where the hardest work is performed.

On yachts built a century or more ago the galley was often in the forepeak, where motion underway is most exaggerated, as it was out of the way there and only hired help were expected to venture into it. Having once crewed and cooked aboard a 100-year-old boat with a forepeak galley on a multiday ocean passage, I can attest it is one of the crueler punish-ments known to seafaring humans. Unless you do have hired help to cook on your boat—and are not particularly interested in their welfare—you defi-nitely do not want your galley anywhere but in the middle of the boat if you ever expect to eat cooked food while sailing.

Smaller, more traditional monohull yachts from the early 20th century onward most often had galleys arranged right around the companionway. The stove was invariably on the port side so you could heave-to on starboard tack when cooking, keep the stove down to leeward where it is easier to tend, and maintain right-of-way over other sailing vessels. An icebox loaded with pounds of block ice was to starboard of the ladder, and its top doubled as a navigation desk when the cook wasn't working. The sink was normally crammed under the bridgedeck as close to the centerline as possible so that it wouldn't flood when pitched to leeward.

Such companionway galley layouts have important advantages and can still be found on a few small modern boats and on many more older boats on the used-boat market. The galley is near the middle of the boat, and its proximity to the companionway makes it easy for the cook to hand food out to the cockpit and keeps the galley well ventilated. A working cook can feel harried here, however, what with the navigator sprawled over the icebox and crew climbing up and down the companionway all the time.

In more modern arrangements the galley is still close to the companionway, but offset to one side to keep clear of deck traffic. The navigation station is often directly opposite in its own dedicated space, which is easier on both the cook and the navigator. These modern companionway galleys are normally

In this U-shaped companionway galley the cook can lean into furniture on either tack and need not stand in front of the stove to tend it. Note the two deep sinks right on the boat's centerline. (Courtesy of Chuck Paine/Mark Fitzgerald)

configured as angles, with either an L- or U-shaped layout. The goal in both cases is to get the sink out from under the bridgedeck so it is more accessible while keeping it close to the centerline so that it drains well on either tack. On a bluewater boat, a U-shaped layout is preferable, as the cook can brace against solid furniture no matter which way the boat is heeled. On coastal boats, where the galley is normally used only when the boat is stationary, this is less important.

On large center-cockpit boats the galley is usually in a long straight alley under one side of the cockpit. The sink is on the inboard side near the centerline (albeit under the cockpit well, where vertical clearance may be somewhat limited), and the cook has solid support to port and starboard. The big advantage of such a layout is that there is lots of open counter space to work on. Access to the cockpit, however, is not as direct, so serving food to crew on deck may be slightly more difficult. Also, ventilation is not quite as good, so things get stuffy sometimes. These walk-through galleys are also sometimes found on large split-cockpit boats with full-size aft staterooms. On these boats, however, crew sometimes need to pass through the galley on their way to the aft cockpit and may interfere with the cook at times.

Another increasingly popular variation is the full-length offset saloon galley. Here the galley is oriented in a straight line all on one side of the boat, as with a walk-through galley, but is directly opposite a midship saloon dinette well forward of the companionway,

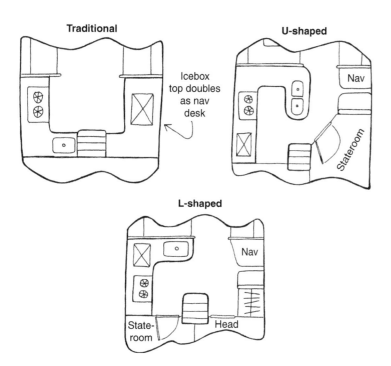

Typical monohull companionway galley layouts.

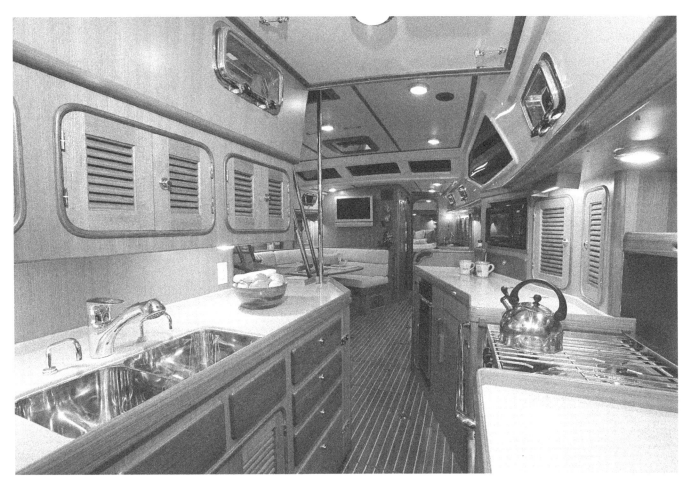

A walk-through galley on a large center-cockpit monohull showing ample counter space. (Courtesy of SAIL Magazine)

usually with a loveseat settee between the galley and the dinette table. This makes it very easy to serve food to the dinette table while interacting with those being served. The elongated configuration opens up counter space, and ventilation is normally good, as there is usually a deck hatch right overhead. Also, a cook can brace between the galley counter and loveseat when the boat is heeled on either tack. The disadvantage is the sink is outboard on one side of the boat and can't be used when heeled down to leeward. The galley is also some distance from the companionway, which makes it harder to serve crew on deck, and is right in the main traffic lane leading to the forward part of the boat, thus can get crowded at times. Finally, it robs the saloon of space that could otherwise be used for a good settee/sea-berth.

Some modern boats with raised saloons have a galley forward of the saloon and a step or two below it in what is commonly termed a "galley down" configuration. This, in my opinion, is the least satisfactory layout for a monohull sailboat. Some of these galleys are far enough forward to be markedly less comfortable than they should be in a seaway; they

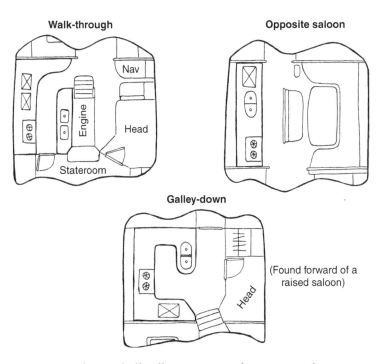

Some typical monohull galley variations for center and aft cockpit boats.

Galleys on Catamarans

Galleys on catamarans are located either down in the interior of one of the hulls (a variation of the galley-down configuration seen on some raised-saloon monohulls) or up in a bridgedeck saloon. A bridgedeck galley is far superior, primarily because it enjoys the same expansive views as the rest of the saloon and thus is a pleasant place to work. Ventilation and ambient lighting are excellent, plus the cook can easily interact with guests and/or crew in both the saloon and cockpit. A cook working in a hull-bound galley, meanwhile, is isolated in a dark, stuffy space with poor ventilation.

Bridgedeck galley configurations vary widely. Layouts can be straight-line, angled in an L- or U- shape, or can be curved. For the most part they are significantly more spacious than on monohulls. Because a catamaran does

An ideal scenario—this bridgedeck galley opens directly into the cockpit: ventilation is superb, and it's easy to hand food out to the crew.

A small galley down in the starboard hull of a performance cruising cat—this is a stuffy, cramped place to prepare a meal.

not heel, there are few peculiar constraints on design, and personal preferences can have more priority, much as they would in a proper kitchen on shore. The best bridgedeck galleys, in my opinion, are at the backside of the saloon facing the cockpit with an open countertop between the galley and an adjacent cockpit table. This way food can be instantly handed out and laid on the table outside. There should be a sliding window or some similar barrier to close off the galley in bad weather, but in most weather it should also be possible to leave the galley open. This makes the galley the most well-ventilated place inside the boat, as it should be.

The boat's motion is much less likely to interfere with cooking on a catamaran, but still it is wise to make a few concessions to environmental reality if you plan to cook while underway. Though catamarans do not heel, they can jerk about in a disconcerting manner. Objects placed on counters and tables do not perpetually get sucked down to the leeward side of the boat as they do on monohulls, but they do hop about from time to time. It is best to keep counters fiddled, though the fiddles need not be as high as on a monohull. The stove should also be gimballed, in both directions if possible. Most stoves on cats are not gimballed in any direction, but most bluewater cat cooks I know wish they were.

are also far from the companionway, and in some cases, because of the steps up and down, are not even very convenient to the saloon. Ambient lighting and ventilation also are poor in many cases.

Regardless of where it is situated, there are certain additional points to consider when evaluating any galley:

Counter space is always at a premium. In many galleys all available counter space either serves another purpose (e.g., it is also an icebox lid or a removable cover for a stove or sink) or cannot be used when certain storage compartments are opened. A well-planned galley should have at least one dedicated section of working countertop that can be used at all times. On bluewater boats all countertops should have deep fiddles on their edges to keep objects from flying off the counter when the boat is heeled. Fiddles should have scalloped exits at the corners so that counters can be easily wiped clean.

Stoves and ovens on any bluewater boat must be gimballed with proper clearances above and below the unit so that it can swing freely in both directions. There should be enough clearance over the stove top to accommodate the largest pot onboard when the stove is pitched at its maximum heel angle. The stove top should have side rails and dedicated potholders to hold things in place. The cook should also be able to comfortably tend the stove, well braced on either tack, without standing directly in front of it. This minimizes the odds of the cook being injured if hot and/or heavy objects and substances suddenly go flying off the stove.

A secure trash bin of reasonable size should be immediately accessible to the cook. Many otherwise well-appointed galleys, particularly on small and midsize boats, lack this critical feature.

Sinks on any bluewater boat, in addition to being as close to the centerline as possible, should also be deep to minimize spills, and ideally large enough to contain the largest pot and/or pan onboard. It is best to have two deep sinks side by side so one can be used for washing and the other for rinsing.

HEADS

In addition to preparing and consuming food, you must also be able to comfortably pass waste on your boat after your food is digested. Historically speaking, many vessels didn't have dedicated space and systems for this sort of activity. Indeed, the term head originally referred simply to the bow of a vessel, where crews were expected to hang their butts out over the rail. As late as the early 20th century many sailing yachts carried only buckets that were emptied overboard.

These days proper marine toilets are not only ubiquitous, they are often automated and electrified, so that waste can be instantly sucked out of sight and mind at the press of a button. Many cruising boats now also have multiple toilets, thanks again to the charter industry, which likes to see each double stateroom on a boat equipped with its own head. Space, however, is limited on sailboats, and people in reality spend little time on the toilet; thus on most boats it makes little sense to have more than one head. Nevertheless, twin heads are now often found on production sailboats as small as 36 feet.

If you spend a week or more aboard at a time, it does make sense for the head to have a dedicated shower stall. These can be fit aboard boats as small as 37 feet and are useful for more than just bathing. Being able to toss a wet mass of clothing, bedding, sails, or what-have-you into an enclosed waterproof area with a sump and a drain is an immense convenience on any sailboat. If properly designed with a raised sill several inches high, the base of a dedicated shower stall can be stopped up to create a shallow tub for soaking laundry. Most heads don't have separate

A separate shower stall in the head of a large catamaran—the opening port inside the stall is a nice touch. (Courtesy of Catana)

shower stalls, and instead you normally bathe sitting on the toilet while hosing yourself down with a combination faucet-showerhead attached to the end of a retractable hose. This works best if the area around the toilet is one-piece fiberglass pan that can be easily wiped down afterward. In warm weather it is more pleasant (and less work) to shower outside—either on a scoop transom equipped with a swim shower or on deck with a showerhead passed out through a hatch or opening port from the head below.

Even on short coastal cruises it is likely the head will be used while underway. To facilitate this, the head compartment should be aft or amidships where motion in a seaway is more subdued. This is particularly important if there is only one head aboard, as a head forward of the mast can be hard to use in rough conditions.

On monohulls a heeled toilet is easiest to sit on if it faces fore or aft and has solid bulkheads or furniture on either side to brace against. In reality toilets on monohulls are usually outboard and are oriented athwartships. At a minimum an athwartships toilet should have solid support behind it so you can lean back comfortably when the toilet is heeled to leeward; there should also be something firm to grasp on either side so you can hold yourself in place when the toilet is canted up to windward. One big problem with any outboard toilet, however it is oriented, is that its water intake may be raised out of the water when canted to windward, thus rendering the toilet inoperable. To prevent this, the intake should always be inboard of the toilet. Likewise, any outboard vanity sink will be prone to flooding when canted to leeward. As with galley sinks, these should be near the centerline whenever possible. If a sink must be outboard there should be an easily accessible valve for closing off the drain when necessary. This can be the drain's seacock, if it is in fact easily accessed and does not also service other systems. Otherwise a dedicated shutoff valve can be installed between the seacock and sink.

Ideally the head compartment should not be too large, both so that interior accommodations space is

not wasted and so people using the head while sailing don't get thrown around too much when things get rough. The compartment should be compact enough that you can lean a short distance in any direction and find something solid to brace against. Most particularly, you should be able to brace yourself in place when bending over the sink to wash your face and hands. Also, the head door, its fasteners, and its catch mechanism should all be strong enough to take the full weight of a heavy adult leaning hard against them. If there is a separate shower stall, it too should be compact and should have a seat so you can sit and brace yourself while bathing.

On the other hand, a head compartment should also not be too small. Ideally it should be just large enough that you can get undressed or dressed (in foul-weather gear or regular clothing) without too much of a struggle. In most cases the ideal compromise is a head with an open area measuring about 30 by 30 inches.

Finally, as with a galley, a head needs good ventilation. An overhead deck hatch that can be opened to let in outside air makes a head much more pleasant, keeping the compartment cool in warm climates and clearing it of odors.

NAVIGATION STATIONS

When cruising boats were smaller and simpler, it was considered a great luxury to have a dedicated navigation station with a desktop large enough to lay out a folded chart. There is nothing like sitting down in your own special seat to study a chart at your own special desk to make you feel like you are master and commander of your own sailing vessel. Besides providing an ego boost, having a secure dedicated area in which to ponder a boat's whereabouts and projected course can only improve situational awareness, and thus makes for safer sailing.

This was particularly true when navigation required a lot of precise mathematical and graphic plotting work. Even aboard coastal cruisers it once was necessary to plot multiple compass bearings on a paper chart to get a good idea of a boat's position, especially when sailing at night or in the fog. On bluewater cruisers room was needed to plan, calculate, and lay out celestial plots on paper. On most boats now none of these jobs is performed routinely, if at all, thanks to modern electronics and global satellite position-fixing systems. Navigation now is conducted by simply pressing buttons on devices with display screens that can be mounted most anywhere. Fully integrated electronic chartplotters can be mounted on cockpit steering pedestals, thus allowing all vital navigation to take place right at the wheel in open

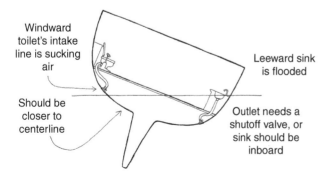

Windward toilet's intake line is sucking air

Should be closer to centerline

Leeward sink is flooded

Outlet needs a shutoff valve, or sink should be inboard

Problems with outboard sinks and toilets.

A modern vestigial nav station: the seat is the end of a settee, the desk can't accommodate large charts, and the navigation electronics are out on the steering pedestal, so you may as well install the microwave here!

and for dealing with routine personal and ship's business will be both enjoyed and appreciated.

As a general rule a nav station should be aft or amidships, where motion is more subdued and it is easy to communicate with cockpit crew. In most cases nav desks are oriented athwartships, which works well as long as you can brace yourself behind the desk on either tack. A concave seat, or one with solid vertical support on its open side, is best for this, though a flat open seat (or the head of a settee or quarter berth, as found on many smaller boats) serves well enough if you can firmly plant a foot to leeward when the seat is heeled to windward. On a few boats nav desks are oriented laterally, parallel to the boat's centerline. In some cases there is a small stool on an arm that swings out from under the nav desk. In others the navigator stands at the desk, which is elevated, often with large drawers underneath for storing charts flat. The latter is preferable both because the storage space is valuable (stowing large numbers of paper charts on boats is always a problem) and because it is usually easier to get braced in place at a lateral desk if you are standing.

The desk itself, however it is oriented, should be large enough to somehow accommodate a paper chart. Ideally it should fit the largest commonly published paper charts, which measure about 3 by 4 feet. Only boats longer than about 42 feet can easily accommodate so large a desk, and in most cases designers and builders won't surrender the space. The best compromise on a coastal boat is a desktop at least large enough to hold a wire-bound

air. All of which has caused the modern nav station to atrophy a bit. Nav desks for laying out paper charts have grown continually smaller over the years, while vertical surfaces around the desk for mounting electronic displays and controls have generally grown larger. The overall trend has favored nav stations with smaller footprints.

In determining your own preferences, remember that modern electronics can never be perfectly reliable. They may malfunction, they may be damaged, they may lose power, or the government-controlled satellites they rely upon may be turned off, temporarily or otherwise, for geopolitical reasons entirely beyond your control. It is best, therefore, to carry paper charts and practice the skills needed to work with them without electronic assistance. This is much easier in a good-size nav station with a good-size desk that it is comfortable to use. This is less important on a coastal cruiser, where simple eyeball navigation can usually get the job done if the electronics go down, and more important on a bluewater boat, where extra space for conducting emergency navigation, for operating long-range communications equipment,

In a proper nav station there's a dedicated seat and plenty of room for laying out charts and other reading material. This desk is tilted, which makes chartwork easier.

ChartKit booklet (approximately 18 by 23 inches); on a bluewater boat it is nice if the desk can hold a large paper chart folded once (approximately 2 by 3 feet). In all cases the desktop should be well fiddled, so that charts, pencils, and other tools don't slide off when the boat is heeled. Also, a desk slanted at an angle like a drafting board makes chartwork a bit easier.

STORAGE AND SYSTEMS SPACE

While modern yachts often have lots of living space, they usually have relatively little storage space. One reason for this, as discussed in Chapter 2, is that modern boats, though much wider than older boats on average, also tend to have shallow bilges. Narrow boats with full keels and deep bilges usually have lots of room under the cabin sole for large storage features like water and fuel tanks. On newer, wider boats with little space under the sole, fuel and water tanks must instead be placed under settees, thus robbing the inhabitable interior of several large storage spaces. The modern tendency to maximize the number of staterooms and heads on board also results in a loss of useful storage space. Other factors include the need to install holding tanks to comply with modern sanitation regulations and the growing number of other systems that are inserted into modern boats.

For most coastal cruisers a lack of storage space is not troublesome, as you needn't carry large amounts of food and gear on short cruises. On long cruises, however, storage space is very important. Many

long-term cruisers prefer older designs for just this reason—not only because these designs have more storage space to begin with, but also because they are heavier in general and are less affected performance-wise when carrying heavy loads. Long-term cruisers who sail modern lightweight shallow-bilged boats often end up converting some of the accommodation space into storage and/or systems space. They also must be more vigilant about policing weight generally, as the performance of their boats suffers more in relative terms when they are overloaded. This is especially true of unballasted catamarans. Indeed, this is the unique curse of the modern cat cruiser: there's lots and lots of storage space, but if you fill it up, the cat sails like a dog.

Storage space on sailboats comes in three basic varieties. There are large undifferentiated horizontal spaces, most often found under settees and berths; smaller spaces that are divided into drawers and cupboards, most often found inside furniture of various

Instead of a proper wet locker, this boat has an open grate at the foot of the companionway and some hooks for hanging wet gear.

Shallow bilge

Water and fuel tanks are above the sole

Deep bilge

Tanks are below the sole

Total storage area is decreased

More stuff can be stowed above the sole!

Storage tank locations—keeping the weight low is always preferable.

descriptions, particularly around the galley, nav station, and outboard of saloon settees; and large vertical hanging spaces, most often found these days in staterooms. On older boats there is also often a quaint, very useful hanging space close to the companionway known as a wet locker. It is used for hanging up wet foul-weather gear and has an open grate for a floor that drains directly to the bilge. Anyone who has ever come down a companionway looking to shed wet gear must appreciate such an arrangement, so it is hard to understand why wet lockers are now rarely seen. Some modern boats instead have open grates at the base of the companionway and some hooks on a bulkhead to hang foulies on. Otherwise you must rush to the nearest head to strip off wet clothing. On boats without a wet locker it is therefore wise to have a head close to the companionway. Ideally this will have a dedicated shower stall (with a sump drain, of course) that can serve as an ad hoc wet locker.

On monohulls you should pay special attention to the closing mechanisms on drawers and cupboard doors. The worst arrangement, which unfortunately is very common because it is easy to build, is to have large sliding panels covering large amounts of outboard cupboard space. These are often found in galleys and heads. Unless the shelving behind the sliding panel has deep fiddles, everything comes tumbling out all at once if the boat is heeling the wrong way when the panel is opened. The best arrangement is to have smaller, more

discrete storage spaces with doors or drawers that can be securely fastened and locked shut so they don't pop open when their contents are suddenly thrust against them. In large horizontal spaces under settees and berths there is also a tendency for smaller items to bounce around and get mixed up with each other as the boat tacks back and forth. Again, it is best to break up the space into smaller sections. You can do this by simply storing small items in larger bins and boxes that fit through the storage area's access hatch.

Finally, on some mass-production fiberglass monohulls you must beware of storage spaces that are not properly segregated from the bilge. Spaces like this are normally found on cheaper boats with large inner liners and pans that incorporate much of the interior furniture. The space surrounding drawers and shelving installed in and behind such pans may lead all the way down to the bottom of the hull, in which case that's where you'll find much of the gear that slips out of said drawers and shelving when the boat is heeled. Having to constantly look for lost stuff in the bilge is inconvenient at best; at worst it is dangerous, as paper goods and other items can clog bilge-pump intakes. To prevent this, all interior storage spaces, particularly those containing drawers or shelving, should be installed in discrete areas that are separated from the rest of the boat's interior.

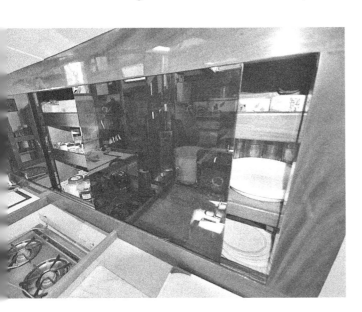

Large sliding panels covering storage areas are easy to install, but are often not too secure. In this example at least there are deep fiddles on the shelves behind the panels to keep items from falling out if a panel is opened while the boat is heeled.

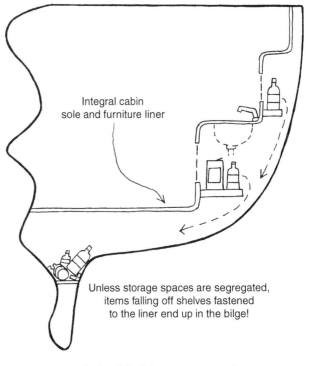

Integral cabin
sole and furniture liner

Unless storage spaces are segregated,
items falling off shelves fastened
to the liner end up in the bilge!

Storage areas behind hull liners may not be secure.

Making Space for Systems

On older sailboats originally built with few systems on board there is usually no escaping the fact that retrofitted systems must often be installed in storage spaces. If only a few discrete systems are added—a hot-water heater and some kind of refrigeration are usually the first additions—this normally isn't too much of a problem. If many systems are added, however, particularly if they include bulky items like generators, watermakers, and forced-air heating systems, the boat will lose a lot of storage capacity. Anytime you see an older boat listed for sale with lots of systems upgrades and improvements, you can be sure many of its lockers will have some machinery or device and a rat's nest of loose wiring stuffed into them. In some cases there may be little empty storage space left over.

The big problem with many retrofitted systems is they are installed in spaces that were not designed to receive them. The system therefore often occupies more space than is needed due to irregularities in the shape of the space and/or the system itself. In some cases this is exacerbated, as you then may have to restrict your use of the leftover space for fear stowed items may interfere with or damage adjacent equipment. Also, access to the system after installation is usually poor, which makes maintaining and repairing the equipment that much harder. In a proper retrofit, the new systems space should be modified to fit the equipment and to maximize leftover storage space. The area should be reshaped (or remodeled entirely), it should be separated from adjacent storage areas, new access panels or doors may be required, plus the space may need to be vented to prevent the equipment from overheating.

Many new production boats, even small ones, now have dedicated systems spaces designed and built into them. On large bluewater boats, these spaces may be quite large, more like an engine or machine compartment found on a ship, thus allowing onboard systems to be entirely segregated from living spaces. Such compartments are convenient and can greatly ease systems maintenance. No matter how well thought out a systems space is, however, it necessarily steals space that could otherwise be used for storage. If you sail a small to midsize boat and need to maximize storage space, it is best therefore to keep your boat simple and carry as few systems as possible.

A well-designed systems space on the author's 39-foot cutter Lunacy. *There's room here for the battery bank (in the box to the left), the fuel tank, plus several pumps (not visible), with lots of storage space for tools and gear left over.*

INSULATION AND VENTILATION

No matter how a boat's living space is configured, and no matter how many hulls it has, it is always more habitable if it is dry inside and the temperature is moderate. Hull insulation is an essential ingredient in achieving both these goals. Wood is a good insulating material, which is one big advantage to cruising in a wooden boat. Metal and solid fiberglass hulls, however, are not self-insulated and become uncomfortable when outside temperatures start getting dramatic. The interior of an uninsulated hull heats up and cools off quickly when it gets too hot or cold outside, and whenever it is warmer in the boat than it is outside, condensation forms rapidly. The effect is most dramatic on metal boats, which is why all metal hulls are usually fully insulated. Many solid fiberglass hulls, however, have no insulation at all. On these boats it is not unusual to wake up on a chilly autumn morning in a soggy berth with rivers of condensation pouring off ports, hatches, and other metal surfaces. Besides being unpleasant, excess condensation greatly accelerates the growth of mold and mildew aboard.

The most discrete way to insulate a fiberglass boat is to build it with cored laminate. The core, usually balsa or foam, is a good insulator and makes the hull lighter and stronger. In almost all cases decks on fiberglass boats are cored, which helps reduce condensation somewhat, but it is much better if the entire hull is cored (though this, as discussed in Chapter 3, raises other issues). When cruising in cold weather in a solid fiberglass hull, it is relatively easy to cut out panels of flexible closed-cell foam (they should be $^1/_2$ inch thick or more) and install them on exposed parts of the hull inside the boat above the waterline. This will take up a small amount of interior space and may look odd where it is plainly visible, but it will keep your boat warmer—and cooler, when you go to warm places—and drier in all respects.

The other essential ingredient when it comes to onboard comfort is good ventilation. This helps keep a boat cool when it is hot outside and dry all the time. To get a large volume of air flowing through a boat's interior you need both inlets and outlets so air can enter and exit the boat easily. When a boat is lying to an anchor or mooring and is constantly head to wind this isn't hard. Most deck hatches have aft hinges and open facing forward into the oncoming breeze, thus sucking air into the boat. An open companionway at the back of the boat makes a good exhaust port and sucks air out of the boat. Even in hot tropical climates, this keeps everything forward of the companionway reasonably cool as long as a moderate breeze is blowing. When the wind is light, you can augment airflow by installing fabric wind scoops over the largest hatches. Cabins aft of the companionway are always more difficult to ventilate. Less air flows through aft deck hatches, both because they are stuck behind dodgers and other obstructions and because air entering the back of the boat must swim upstream, so to speak, to reach the companionway. Airflow can be improved, however, by installing wind scoops over the hatches in question.

A boat parked in a marina slip is harder to ventilate, as the wind is often striking the boat from behind or from the side. The wind in a marina is also generally much weaker than in an open anchorage or mooring field. A companionway, especially one with a dodger over it, makes a good air inlet when air is coming from behind a boat, but deck hatches don't work as well as exhaust outlets. When the airflow is abeam, opening ports on either side of a boat are usually too small to create much cross ventilation. Wind scoops can be deployed over hatches at offset angles, and some deck hatches can open facing aft rather than forward. Still, it is always difficult to keep a boat cool while lying at a dock in hot weather. Technology can alleviate the problem—12-volt fans are easy to install and maintain, though air-conditioning is much more complicated. If you are a true cruiser,

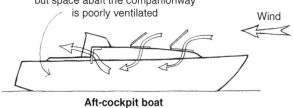

Companionway and dodger create lots of suction, but space abaft the companionway is poorly ventilated

Wind

Aft-cockpit boat

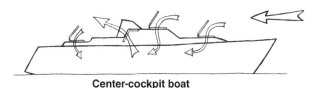

Center-cockpit boat

Less air reaches aft hatch, and has a less direct path to the exhaust outlet

Typical airflow scenarios.

however, I recommend you leave the dock and head out to a nice anchorage instead.

It is also hard, of course, to ventilate a boat when its hatches must be kept closed, as happens when it is raining, or when the boat is under sail in wet conditions, or when the boat is left unoccupied for a period of time. The answer here is to have lots of dorade vents. These were first installed on the yacht *Dorade* in 1929 (hence the name) and are still the last word on water-resistant onboard ventilation. The principle is simple: a large horn-shaped air vent protruding well above the deck is installed atop a baffled box with drain holes at the bottom. Water and air mixed together can enter the vent, but the water is trapped by the baffle in the box and drains away, while the air continues into the interior of the boat. Though dorade vents are effective and versatile (the vent can be pivoted and pointed in any direction, thus can act either as an inlet or outlet), they are deficient on many modern boats. Either the vents are too small and/or low to be of any use, or the baffled boxes are too shallow to work properly, or the vents are left off entirely. Only a few modern designers and builders with a utilitarian bent (most notably Steve Dashew) really understand how important these vents can be. Everyone else, it seems, is happy to leave crews sweltering belowdeck when rain or spray is flying outside.

If you are lucky enough to find a boat with proper dorade vents there are a couple of things to look for. First, you should be able to remove the vents from their boxes and seal them with plugs from the outside. This is sometimes necessary because even deep dorade boxes can be flooded and overwhelmed in extreme conditions. Tall dorade vents in certain areas of the

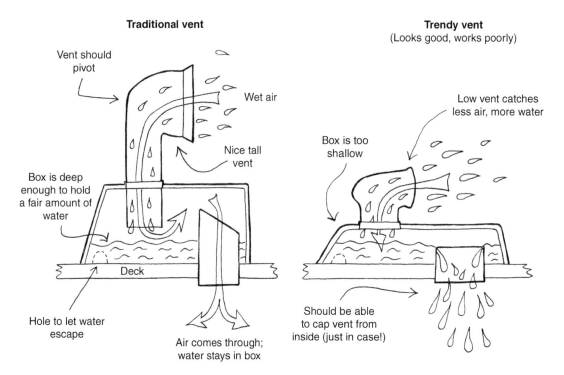

Traditional vent

Vent should pivot

Wet air

Nice tall vent

Box is deep enough to hold a fair amount of water

Deck

Hole to let water escape

Air comes through; water stays in box

Trendy vent
(Looks good, works poorly)

Low vent catches less air, more water

Box is too shallow

Should be able to cap vent from inside (just in case!)

Dorade vent anatomy: the taller and more obtrusive the vent is, the better it works. Good vents unfortunately are increasingly rare. Some modern boats don't carry any vents at all.

The real McCoy—a dorade vent on Olin Stephens's Dorade. *Note how very tall it is!*

deck can also catch headsail sheets and other running rigging and are best removed in some circumstances. Ideally, it should also be possible to seal off all vents from belowdeck so that you can weather-proof the boat's interior without venturing outside.

However outside air is brought aboard a boat, it will sometimes be polluted with insects. All exterior orifices should therefore have screens. Vertical opening ports can be easily fitted with permanent screens, but hatches or companionways normally require temporary fixtures that can be put in and taken out quickly. A hinged screen beneath an overhead deck hatch works well, as the screen can be stored in place and quickly swung up and down from inside as needed when the hatch is opened or shut. Some fancy hatches now have integral flexible screens you can pull back and forth like a window shade. On many cruising boats, unfortunately, bug screens are poorly conceived afterthoughts that are hard to deploy and harder to stow, so many cruisers end up either sorely bitten or hot and stuffy as a result of trying to avoid using them.

One final point to bear in mind when it comes to onboard ventilation is airflow through storage spaces. If locker doors are somehow perforated, with either louvered sections, woven cane faces, or simple cutouts, then air can move more easily into the lockers hidden behind them. This goes a long way to reducing the growth of mold and mildew aboard and helps keep clothing and other items from smelling skanky and stale if they are left aboard for long periods of time.

ONBOARD SYSTEMS

So far we've mostly discussed only gear and equipment used when sailing (or anchoring) a modern cruising boat. These days, however, most boats have a lot more ancillary equipment aboard, much of it devoted to providing once unimaginable creature comforts. There was a time when cruisers prided themselves on the simplicity of their craft and took pleasure in the austerity they experienced when living on them. There are some who still think this way, but most are eager to take advantage of modern technology and many try to install as much of it as possible on their boats.

Though modern boat systems are much more reliable than they were even a decade ago, they are still much less reliable than comparable shore-based systems. The marine environment has never been kind to anything mechanical or electrical, and never will be. The more systems you have on your boat, the more time (and money) you'll likely spend maintaining and repairing them, and the less time you'll have to actually use your boat. This is why the most popular book on cruisers' bookshelves today is Nigel Calder's *Boatowner's Mechanical and Electrical Manual*, which is the most comprehensible and comprehensive guide to onboard systems maintenance in print today. Even for cruisers who have nothing on their boat more complicated than a toilet, a stove, and some manual water pumps, it is an indispensable reference.

I cannot pretend to treat this subject as completely as Calder has. Rather my purpose is to acquaint you with what is available and give you a general idea of its function and complexity so you can make some simple threshold decisions about what equipment you

might like to have on your boat. As a general rule, I suggest you start with a simple boat and make it more complex as you gain experience and develop your own ideas as to which systems are really worth the trouble. By today's standards, I would define a simple boat as having the following systems: a diesel engine, two small 12-volt DC batteries (approximately 100 amp-hours each), manual freshwater pumps, an electric bilge pump (with manual backups), electric lights (with oil lamp backups), a nonpressurized alcohol galley stove, a manually operated toilet, basic navigation sensors, a small GPS chartplotter, and a VHF radio.

One advantage of making a simple boat progressively more complicated is that it should then contain only those systems you truly value. Doing it the other way around—installing everything available and then figuring out what is really useful after the fact—is far more likely to result in frustration and squandered money. The other advantage is that you will then know how to use your boat without the systems in question and can do without them when they fail. Ideally, most systems on your boat should be conveniences rather than necessities. Otherwise your cruising experience will be more focused on repair and maintenance than it should be.

PROPULSION

Auxiliary engines are now considered mandatory equipment by almost all cruising sailors. There are a few iconoclasts who still cruise under sail alone, and they do a good job of seeming both rational and evangelistic when holding forth on the sanctity of their practices. If you really enjoy sailing, there is something inherently attractive in relying only on the wind to get where you're going, but in reality you need a lot of spare time to operate this way. Often it may take hours (or even days if conditions are truly uncooperative) to sail into a specific harbor, as opposed to mere minutes (or hours instead of days) once you decide to start your engine. Since most cruisers today sail on some kind of schedule, this is an advantage few can ignore. Also, there are many locations within modern harbors and marinas that a boat maneuvering under sail alone simply cannot access without assistance. Plus, on certain canals and waterways vessels may in fact be required to operate under power.

Gasoline and Diesel Engines

The first auxiliary sailboat engines were gasoline-powered, and by the mid-20th century production of these in North America was monopolized by the Universal Motor Company. Over a period from 1947 to 1985 Universal's famous Atomic 4 engine, a.k.a. the Atomic Bomb, was installed in over 40,000 sailboats ranging in size from 25 to just over 40 feet. At its peak in the 1960s and 1970s, Universal controlled about 85% of the sailboat-engine market. One reason for the Bomb's great success was that it was not merely a marinized car or truck engine, but was instead designed and conceived from its mounting bolts up as a marine engine, hence was considerably more reliable than its competitors.

The Atomic 4 was a tenacious beast—indeed, some 20,000 engines are reportedly still in service—but it did have certain weaknesses. Most, for example, had raw-water cooling systems (sometimes referred to as "open" systems) where "raw" seawater is circulated directly through the engine block to keep it cool. The buildup of scale and corrosion inside the block over time ultimately leads to blockages that can cause serious overheating problems. Also, raw-water-cooled engines tend to run at lower temperatures. This leads to condensation in the engine and less efficient fuel combustion, which causes carbon to build up on valves and piston rings. Almost all marine engines today instead have freshwater closed systems, where fresh cooling water circulates in a closed loop between the engine and a heat exchanger, through which raw water from outside the boat also circulates, drawing away heat from the fresh water. These allow for more efficient fuel combustion and have fewer corrosion issues.

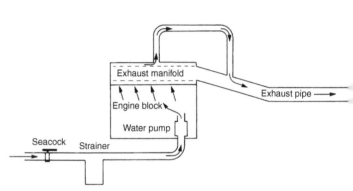

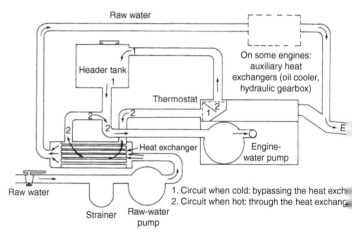

A raw-water-cooled engine (top) and a freshwater cooled engine (bottom). The raw-water system is clearly simpler, but corrosion and scale create problems over time. Most engines today are freshwater cooled. (Courtesy Boatowner's Mechanical and Electrical Systems, by Nigel Calder)

Over 40,000 Atomic 4 engines were installed in sailboats during the 20th century. Many are still in service and parts are still available. (Courtesy of Moyer Marine)

As a gasoline engine, the Atomic 4 also needs an electric ignition system with spark plugs, and these often suffer in the damp and corrosive marine environment. Finally, gasoline is a volatile substance, and over time sailors have developed a strong bias against carrying quantities of it aboard their boats. Gasoline is also considerably less efficient than diesel fuel, which effectively doubles a boat's range under power without any increase in fuel-carrying capacity. As a result, the current conventional wisdom is that only diesel engines should be installed on sailboats. Gasoline marine auxiliaries are in fact no longer produced by any manufacturer, and those who own older boats with Atomic Bombs aboard are often urged to repower with diesel engines. Indeed, for the past 20 years replacing old Atomic 4s with new diesels has been a cottage industry of sorts, and at least two manufacturers (Westerbeke, which bought Universal, and Beta Marine) currently offer drop-in replacements that fit easily into engine spaces originally configured for the Atomic 4.

For the most part surviving Atomic 4s are found on older, smaller boats with market values generally ranging between $8,000 and $30,000. Given that installing a new diesel engine costs roughly $7,000 to $10,000, you should not necessarily leap to the conclusion that this is the only option. Installing a diesel does increase a boat's value (in fact this is one of the very few systems upgrades of which this is true), but even if you sell your boat when the new engine is young, you're unlikely to recoup more than half your investment. For casual coastal cruisers who don't need extra range when powering, sticking with an old Atomic 4 may well make the most sense. There is a strong, mutually supportive subculture of Bomb owners, parts are still available, and the old engines can be tweaked and improved. For example, a fresh-water cooling system can be installed, a more reliable electronic ignition system can be added, oil filters and water pumps can be upgraded, and so on.

As for the old bugaboo about storing gasoline aboard, most cruisers carry more than enough gas for their dinghy's outboard to blow up their boats in any event. As with so many things, safe operating procedures are the key. An Atomic 4's engine compartment should always be well ventilated with a blower fan prior to starting the engine so as to evacuate lingering fumes. Follow this simple precaution and there's little chance an Atomic Bomb will detonate. Indeed, as far as I am aware, there are no known instances of a Bomb ever exploding.

Bluewater cruisers, however, should favor diesel engines in nearly all circumstances, if only because of the extra range they provide. The only bluewater

A new Beta Marine diesel is lowered down a companionway during a repowering job. This engine is probably replacing an old Atomic 4. (Courtesy of SAIL Magazine)

An outboard auxiliary on a small cruising catamaran. This is much simpler than having an inboard engine, and engine access, as seen here, is spectacular!

sailors with gas engines I've ever encountered were minimalists on smaller boats (or simple multihulls) who carried only outboard engines for auxiliary power.

Diesels are generally more reliable than gas engines and are easier to maintain. It is commonly said that a diesel engine will never stop running as long it is fed clean fuel, and under ideal circumstances this is nearly true. In reality, however, diesels on many cruising sailboats often run either for only short periods of time—to get in and out of a marina berth, for example—or for extended periods under light loads, turning just an alternator and/or compressor to charge batteries or refrigeration systems. This is less than ideal, as diesels prefer to run a bit hot under heavy loads. If a diesel runs briefly and does not get properly warmed up, or is not running under a full load, operating temperatures stay low, which creates condensation in the engine and can lead to carbon deposits, as mentioned above. Also the condensation can combine with the trace amounts of sulfur found in diesel oil to create sulfuric acid, which can damage some engine parts over time.

Because fuel purity is so important to a diesel engine (primarily because its fuel injection pumps can be crippled by even microscopic bits of dirt or water), frequent fuel-filter changes are a critical part of any diesel's maintenance regime. The common practice is to have two in-line fuel filters. The primary filter, located between the fuel tank and engine, has a sediment bowl and a replaceable filter cartridge and is designed to separate water and large contaminant particles from fuel as it flows to the engine. The secondary filter, installed on the engine itself, has a much finer cartridge to capture smaller particles before they reach the fuel injector pump. Changing these filters necessarily involves breaking open fuel lines, which introduces air into the system, and on many engines these air bubbles halt the flow of fuel altogether and prevent the engine from running. This can be remedied only by bleeding the fuel system, which is a tedious, often messy chore. To avoid this, and to encourage frequent filter changes, you should look for engines with fuel systems that bleed themselves when the engine is cranked with an open throttle.

The other most routine maintenance chore is changing engine oil. Scrupulous owners do this after every 100 hours of engine-running time, which translates to about once a year for most casual coastal cruisers, or once every few months for active bluewater cruisers. The hard part is removing the old oil from the crankcase, as normally it's not possible to access a sump plug under the engine as you can on automobile and truck engines. There are numerous pumps and vacuum devices you can buy to suck oil out of an engine, but the most convenient arrangement is to have a dedicated oil-extraction pump right on the engine itself. Unfortunately, relatively few engines include this feature, though sometimes they can be retrofitted.

Another common problem with engines on cruising boats is there sometimes is not enough electric power available to get them started. With gasoline engines, because of their spark plugs, this is critical, but with a diesel engine it needn't be. Diesels need electricity only to turn the engine to get it going, not to keep it going. If the engine is not too large and has a decompression lever and a hand crank, it may be possible to start the engine turning it by hand. Not many engines can do this, but it is, needless to say, a very useful feature. Even if an engine is too large to be started manually, a decompression lever and hand crank often prove useful in any event. Spinning a cold engine first with the starter motor or by hand with the decompression lever off often helps loosen things up a bit. Also, hand cranking while engaging the starter motor can sometimes bring a seemingly dead engine to life. Furthermore, being able to turn an engine by hand is useful in various maintenance and repair situations.

Two other important issues are access and parts availability. Engine installations vary greatly, but on small to midsize sailboats most engine spaces are cramped and awkwardly placed. Only rarely are all parts of an engine easy to reach. The most important places to get to are the oil fill and dipstick, the oil and fuel filters, the belts (which need tightening occasionally), any bleed points on a fuel system that cannot bleed itself, and the raw-water pump housing (so that its impeller can be checked and replaced on a regular basis). As to parts availability, this can vary greatly depending on your cruising ground. If you cruise in one specific area, you can easily find parts for and maintain any engine with a supplier or distributor within a reasonable distance. If you wander far and wide, you'll want an engine with distributors and suppliers situated all around a particular region, continent, or even the globe.

Propellers

Though they seem like simple devices, propellers are in fact quite complicated. More often than you'd expect, problems with a boat's performance under power can be traced to poor propeller selection. To drive a boat well a prop must be properly matched to whatever engine and transmission is turning it, and numerous variables—the engine's horsepower, its operating and maximum potential rpm and shaft speed, the boat's speed potential, and the dimensions

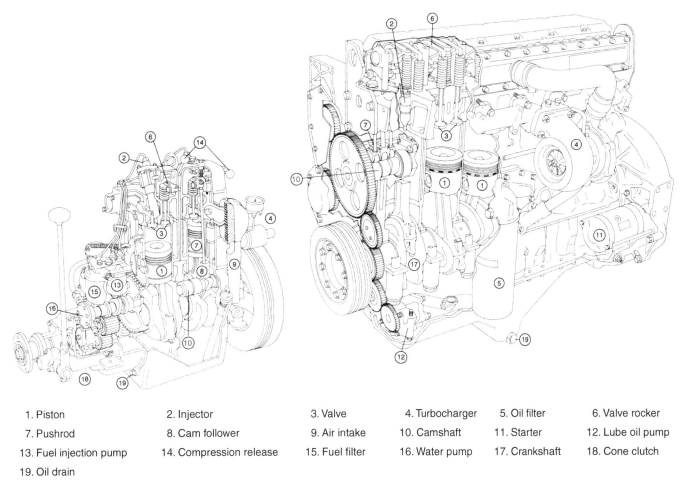

1. Piston	2. Injector	3. Valve	4. Turbocharger	5. Oil filter	6. Valve rocker
7. Pushrod	8. Cam follower	9. Air intake	10. Camshaft	11. Starter	12. Lube oil pump
13. Fuel injection pump	14. Compression release	15. Fuel filter	16. Water pump	17. Crankshaft	18. Cone clutch
19. Oil drain					

Basic diesel engine components. Diesels are more rugged and reliable than gasoline engines and are now prevalent on cruising boats. (Drawing by Jim Sollers)

and specifications of the prop itself—must be balanced against each other to achieve good performance over the broadest range of circumstances. Even professionals sometimes get this wrong. The best resource on the subject is Dave Gerr's helpful and comprehensive tome *The Propeller Handbook*.

Selecting a propeller for a sailboat is complicated by the fact that when a boat is actually sailing you very much want the propeller to go away. Don Street, who has removed three different engines from his old yawl *Iolaire*, estimates that a propeller increases total drag by 5% to 10% when a boat is sailing at hull speed and by as much as 30% to 40% when sailing in light air. Unfortunately, the features that most improve a propeller's efficiency under power—primarily greater wheel diameter and more blade area—serve only to increase drag when sailing. For racing sailors this conflict is easily resolved, as they will happily accept a large decrease in powering ability to sail faster. For cruisers who spend a lot of time motoring but also want to sail well, it is a much harder call.

In terms of maintenance, it is best to have a fixed prop. This is merely a single solid piece of bronze, and beyond wrapping a line around it or hitting and mangling it somehow, there is nothing that can go wrong with it. All you need do is keep it smooth and clean and make sure it's protected against galvanic corrosion with an appropriately placed zinc. The downside is that it cannot change shape to minimize drag when the boat is not motoring. To maximize sailing performance you can install a narrow two-bladed fixed prop with a reasonably small profile. On old full-keel CCA race boats the trick was to mark the propeller shaft inside the boat so the shaft could be locked in place with its fixed two-blade prop lined up with the keel immediately in front of it, thus reducing drag to a minimum. But a two-blade prop, particularly a narrow one, performs poorly under power and creates lots of vibration. A much bigger, more efficient three-bladed fixed prop provides a much smoother ride and drives a boat much faster under power, but it also greatly increases drag.

The best way to reduce drag with a fixed prop is to install a two-bladed prop and line it up in a locked position behind a full keel or skeg while sailing. This requires marking the shaft inside the boat so you know when the prop is in the proper position.

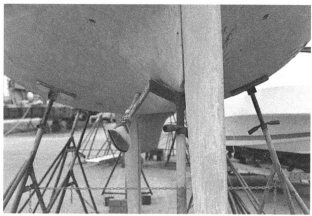

Folding props create the least drag under sail, but do not perform so well when motoring. This prop shaft is offset to one side, which is unusual. Offset installations are most often seen on boats originally designed to carry no engine.

There are propellers that can change shape and streamline their profiles when a boat is sailing, but these are more complicated and have several moving parts that must be greased on a periodic basis, are more vulnerable to corrosion, and are subject to wear over time. The two major variations are folding propellers, where the blades collapse backward and fold together to minimize their profile, and feathering props, where the blades twist and align themselves with the water flow.

Folding props are sleekest and fastest when closed, thus are favored by racing sailors. Older designs have two narrow independently hinged blades that fold straight back flat when closed and spin open when the prop shaft starts turning. When closed their profile is small, but under power performance is generally miserable, particularly in reverse. The hinges are also easily fouled with marine growth. When this happens

the prop may not open at all, or only one blade may open, which causes severe vibration. Newer folding props can incorporate three blades, which greatly improves performance under power; they also have bevel gears rather than simple hinges in the hub, so that all blades open and close together.

Feathering props have more complicated gearing in that each individual blade engages a universal bevel gear mounted directly on the propeller shaft inside the propeller hub. When the shaft turns one way, the gear flips the blades open in one direction; when it turns the other way, the blades open in the opposite direction. As a result, these propellers perform just as well in reverse as they do going forward, which is not true of fixed or folding props and is a big advantage when maneuvering in close quarters. When the shaft is not turning the blades pivot freely and align with the water flow, thus minimizing their profile and reducing drag. Props with flat blades present cleaner profiles when feathered, but are not as efficient under power; the reverse is true of those with cambered blades.

One useful feature on any feathering propeller is that its pitch can be altered. *Pitch* is technically defined as the distance a propeller is driven forward with each revolution it makes, which in turn is a function of the angle at which a propeller's blades are canted. On most props this angle is fixed, but on feathering props it can be changed by adjusting the stops that limit the pivoting of the blades in either direction. This makes the propeller much more versatile, as its pitch can be adjusted to fine-tune the prop's efficiency at different average running speeds or even to accommodate different engines and/or transmissions. On many older feathering props you

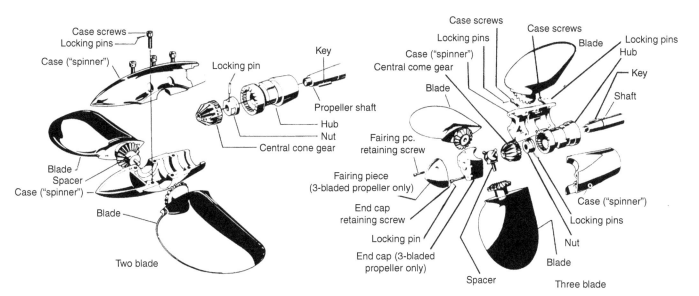

Exploded view of typical two-bladed and three-bladed feathering propellers. These are much more complex than fixed props, but are worth the bother if you value performance under sail and also want respectable performance under power. (Courtesy of Max-Prop)

must dismantle the hub to change the stop positions, but on some newer ones adjustments can be made externally without taking anything apart. In some cases you can even set different pitches for forward and reverse, which is useful, as you normally maneuver backward only at slow speeds. There are also a few propellers whose pitch can be altered while they are turning. When used properly these controllable-pitch props are maximally efficient, because the blade angles can always be matched to the shaft rpm when motoring, or feathered flat when sailing. There is also one product—the Brunton Autoprop—that automatically adjusts its pitch to variations in shaft speed without any input from the user.

Drivetrains

The most common way to transmit power from a sailboat's engine to its propeller is via a straight propeller shaft coupled directly to the engine's transmission. Though reasonably reliable, these classic drivetrain systems do have drawbacks.

First and foremost the propeller shaft must penetrate the hull underwater, and this inevitably creates some potential for major leaks. The traditional way to seal a shaft is with a stuffing box or packing gland. These consist of a rigid or flexible tube that surrounds the shaft where it enters the boat and is stuffed with rings of some fibrous packing material. Traditionally, greased flax is used, but this is often supplemented now or replaced with Teflon, which is purportedly drip free. An adjustable cap or packing nut compresses the packing around the shaft,

forming a seal that keeps water outside the boat even when the shaft is turning. These work well for the most part, but require regular maintenance. The packing nut occasionally requires a turn or two to keep the seal tight, some units require greasing from time to time (via either external grease cups or nipples), and eventually the packing itself must be replaced. Because stuffing boxes are often hard to access, this last chore in particular is often neglected. This can damage the shaft where it contacts the old, hardened packing material and increases the likelihood of leaks.

On many modern boats stuffing boxes have been replaced with mechanical face seals. These are also a popular upgrade on older boats. Here the seal around the prop shaft is formed by two flanges with flat machined surfaces that mate perfectly so that no water can intrude between them. One flange is mounted on the prop shaft itself; the other is fixed to the end of a flexible rubber bellows or some other spring-loaded apparatus that lightly compresses the face of the fixed flange against the face of the spinning flange on the propeller. When properly installed, face seals are virtually leak-free and require no maintenance beyond periodically checking the condition of the rubber bellows, clamps, and seal surfaces. Also, because the seal does not come in contact with the shaft, there is no chance of damaging the shaft through overheating or scoring. The one big drawback is that if a face seal does fail—due to a breach in the bellows or a loose shaft flange, for example—a great deal of water may enter the boat quickly, which is much less likely with a stuffing box.

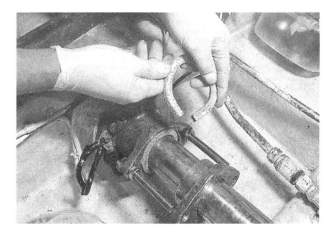

Replacing the stuffing (here flax) in a traditional stuffing box is a critical but onerous chore. This stuffing box is unusually accessible. (Courtesy of SAIL Magazine)

A modern mechanical face seal. The white hose coming in from the top carries water to the flange on the bellows to keep the flange face cool where it contacts the flange on the propeller shaft. These cooling hoses are common, but are not always required.

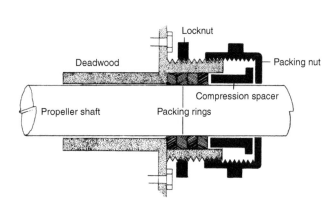

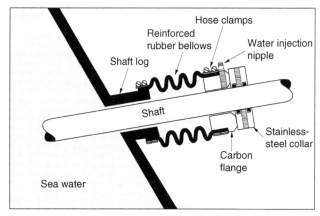

A typical traditional stuffing box (left) and a typical mechanical face seal (right). Face seals are preferred, but many boats still have perfectly reliable stuffing boxes.

A propeller shaft must also be supported at its back end by what is known as a Cutless bearing. This is a hard metal or fiberglass bearing tube with a rubber sleeve that contacts the spinning shaft and circulates water around it via a series of grooves in the sleeve's surface. On more modern boats where a length of exposed prop shaft protrudes from the bottom of a shallow-bilge hull, the Cutless bearing is in a freestanding strut that holds the end of the shaft in place. On boats where the shaft is not exposed and the propeller is in a full skeg, or directly behind an integral strut or keel, the bearing is installed in the boat itself. In either case the bearing must be replaced when the rubber sleeve wears away, which is often a challenging job. In many cases it is necessary to remove the prop shaft, which in turn may require removing the rudder if the shaft cannot be pulled back past it.

Another issue with straight-drive shaft installations is that they take up a lot of space inside a boat, and the shaft and engine must be perfectly aligned. Even a small misalignment can significantly shorten the life span of the transmission bearings and seals and the Cutless bearing; it can also play havoc with the shaft's stuffing box or face seals. Engine alignment should be checked on a regular basis (about every two years) and corrected as needed, both of which can be onerous chores if access to the transmission coupling and the engine mounts is poor. You can avoid the problem by installing a constant-velocity (CV) joint at the coupling between the transmission and shaft. These are similar to universal joints and allow for some articulation in the drivetrain. A CV joint cannot, however, carry any thrust so the prop shaft's half of the couple must be mounted on

A worn Cutless bearing (right) compared to a new replacement bearing (left). The slots in the rubber sleeve allow water to flow up between the propeller shaft and bearing to keep the shaft from overheating. Replacing a Cutless bearing can be a big job. (Courtesy of SAIL *Magazine)*

a bulkhead strong enough to bear all propulsion loads. In many cases it is difficult to interpose such a structure between the engine and the shaft, so CV joints are not very common.

As to the problem of space, one way to solve this is by fitting an engine with a V-drive transmission. Here the transmission incorporates large bevel and helical gears that reverse the direction of the drivetrain so that the prop shaft can be coupled to the

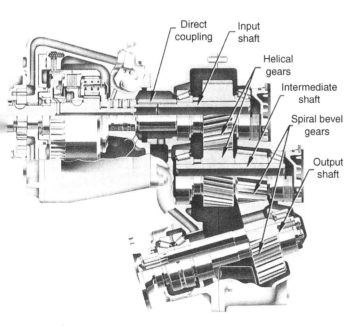

A typical V-drive transmission. These allow an engine to be installed directly over its propeller shaft, thus saving space inside the boat. Access to the shaft, however, is usually poor. (Courtesy of BorgWarner)

transmission directly under the engine rather than behind it. This allows for a much more compact installation and usually a much shorter shaft run. Access, however, is seriously degraded. The engine is installed backward, which usually makes its front end hard to get to, which in turn makes it hard to service basic items like belts and water pumps. The stuffing box or face seals, not to mention the transmission coupling, also end up underneath the engine and may be impossible to reach.

Finally, one problem common to all V-drive and most straight-drive systems is that the propeller shaft exits the boat at an angle. This degrades powering performance as some of the propeller's thrust is directed downward rather than straight backward. The amount of wasted thrust varies depending on the angle of the shaft, but in some cases it can be as high as 20%.

Aside from powering your cruising sailboat with an outboard engine instead of an inboard engine (an option normally available only on small monohulls or certain multihulls), the only way to get around having a prop shaft in your boat is to have a saildrive instead. This is similar to an inboard/outboard drivetrain, where a transom-mounted articulated outboard drive leg that can be raised out of the water is married to an inboard engine. With a saildrive, however, the drive leg is fixed in place and is permanently submerged directly under the engine.

Such an installation requires a hole in the hull much larger than that needed to accommodate a propeller shaft, but the protective seal need not accommodate moving parts, as these are all inside the drive leg. Saildrives resolve several other shaft-related problems and are easier and cheaper to install. No precise engine alignment is needed, no Cutless bearing is required, the installation is compact yet the engine can be easily accessed, and it can be fixed in place on flexible mounts, which greatly reduces vibration. There probably is some decrease in the drivetrain's efficiency due to the two right-angle turns made en route from engine to propeller, but this is more than made up for by the increased efficiency of the propeller's perfectly horizontal thrust vector. Manufacturers claim saildrives are in fact about 10% more efficient than most shaft drives and also create less drag under sail.

Because of these virtues—most particularly the ease of installation—saildrives are already popular in Europe and are increasingly more common in North America. It seems likely they will someday displace prop shafts as the drivetrain of choice on most sailboats. They do, however, have issues of their own. Number one is corrosion. As on outboards, a saildrive's drive leg is made of aluminum

A modern auxiliary engine equipped with a saildrive is easy to install and is also efficient, thanks to the prop's horizontal thrust vector. (Courtesy of SAIL Magazine and Yanmar Marine)

and is galvanically vulnerable. Zinc anodes must be replaced promptly, and the drive leg must be electrically isolated from other metals aboard. If the boat is routinely plugged into shore power, there should also be a galvanic isolator to protect the leg from stray-current corrosion generated by other boats plugged into the same system.

Another big drawback is that dealing with any mechanical problem inside the drive leg requires hauling the boat. Such problems are not common, but something as simple as winding some fishing line up into the shaft seal in front of the propeller can lead to a big yard bill. Finally, there is the matter of that large hole in the bottom of the boat. The big diaphragm seals that secure the base of the drive leg where it penetrates the hull are generally very reliable. If they fail, however, an enormous amount of water may come aboard and could quickly sink the boat. Manufacturers recommend replacing the seals every few years, but it is a big job and most owners neglect it.

Bow Thrusters

These are a huge convenience for sailors who routinely maneuver under power in close quarters, thus have become increasingly popular. Once it was unusual to

see a bow thruster on any boat smaller than 60 feet; now they're often installed on cruising boats as small as 40 feet, and I've seen a few on boats even smaller than that. The principle is relatively simple. A transverse tunnel is built into the bow of a boat below its waterline, and a propeller is installed in the tunnel. Spinning the propeller creates transverse thrust, and pushes the bow sideways. With a thruster, even a poor boat handler can look like a genius when parking in tight spots. They also (arguably) can be described as useful emergency gear; I've heard at least one (possibly apocryphal) tale in which a cruiser who lost his rudder managed to carry on by using his bow thruster to steer the boat.

In practice putting a bow thruster on a boat is complicated. First, having a tunnel in the bow of a boat must be hydrodynamically offensive. The two mouths of the tunnel must be carefully shaped, with raised deflectors on their leading edges and/ or recessed dimples on their trailing edges, or they create a great deal of drag and turbulence when the

A typical bow thruster: when installed the center of the tunnel should be at least one tunnel diameter below the water's surface. The deeper the better. (Courtesy of Vetus)

This cruiser caught a line in his bow thruster and had to haul his boat to cut it loose. Note the raised deflector on the leading edge of the tunnel mouth—this reduces turbulence when underway. A dimple on the back edge is also sometimes used.

boat moves forward. In many installations this is neglected, and a significant amount of boat speed, under both power and sail, is squandered. Even with proper fairings, a thruster tunnel decreases performance to some extent, which is why you will never find one on a race boat.

For a thruster to work well, its tunnel must be a certain distance underwater. The rule of thumb is that the center of the tunnel should be at least one tunnel diameter below the water's surface. The deeper the tunnel, the more thrust the propeller can generate, due to the increase in water pressure. Because many modern boats have shallow forefoots, it may be hard in some cases to get the tunnel deep enough for the thruster to be effective.

These problems can be resolved by making a thruster retractable, so that it descends from the bottom of the hull when deployed and pulls up into it when not in use. This way the thruster creates no drag when it's not running, but is buried deeper in the water when it is. Retractable thrusters are, however, much more expensive than tunnel thrusters, are much heavier, and are considerably more complicated, thus are normally found only on large performance cruisers.

Powering a thruster is another challenge. On most midsize boats an electric motor makes the most sense, but even a small one draws a huge amount of current. A 4 hp thruster motor, for example, pulls around 300 amps at 12 volts; an 8 hp motor pulls twice as much. If you need a motor stronger than that, you'll probably have to go to 24-volt power, which adds yet another layer of complexity. The largest electric thruster motors put out about 15 hp, but pull a whopping 650 amps at 24 volts, or 1,300 amps at 12 volts! Though thrusters are rarely run for more than a few seconds at a time, enormous cables are required to carry loads of this size over any sort of distance. Depending on the length of the boat and the capacity of the motor, it may not be practical to install the cabling necessary to power the motor off the main battery bank, which is usually located at the back of the boat, as far from the bow as possible. In this case a dedicated thruster battery can be installed near the bow, but this too will need large cables for charging purposes and also adds extra weight at the bow, where it is least appreciated.

Depending on the size of the boat and the other systems aboard, a hydraulic motor may be the best choice for powering a thruster. If a boat, for example, has no 24-volt power but already has a hydraulic system, hydraulic power makes sense even for a thruster rated at 8 hp or less. You can also run a hydraulic thruster continuously, rather than just in short bursts, as with an electric thruster. Note, however, that more powerful hydraulic thruster motors cannot be supported by electric hydraulic pumps. Instead most hydraulic thrusters need to be fed by a pump run straight off the main engine or an auxiliary generator. Using a generator as the pump's power supply is generally not a good idea, except where the main engine cannot deliver enough power at idling speeds, which may be the case with some modern turbocharged diesels. If an engine is used, you can run a hydraulic windlass off the same pump, thus saving the battery bank from having to feed two power-hungry devices and reducing the amount of heavy cable runs required.

Future Trends: Diesel-Electric Propulsion

Just as an electric motor can be used to run a bow thruster, one can also be used to turn a boat's main propeller. Theoretically, an electric motor can turn a propeller much more efficiently than an internal-combustion engine, because electric motors develop full torque at low rpm and can turn more slowly than engines, which can't run at less than idle speed. Because an engine's power curve is very different from a propeller's, marrying the two always involves a tortured compromise. Usually the engine produces more power—in some cases much more power—than the propeller can absorb. With an electric motor, the two power curves can be matched more precisely.

Early attempts to use electric motors for auxiliary power on sailboats focused primarily on using large battery banks to power the propulsion motor and did not prove practical. More recently attention has focused on coupling electric propulsion motors to diesel-powered electric generators. These hybrid diesel-electric systems have already proven themselves on large vessels such as cruise ships, warships, and ferries, and there is a good chance they may become viable on smaller recreational vessels in the near future. They have now been installed on a prototype basis on a few different production sailboats, and results are reportedly positive.

The attractions of a diesel-electric system are plain. On smaller, simpler sailboats instead of having one large propulsion engine, you can have a smaller, quieter generator in a more accessible location, and in most cases the smaller generator engine and the electric motor won't be any heavier than the large engine they replace. On larger, more complex boats that normally run both a propulsion engine plus a generator to charge batteries, there will be one less engine to operate and maintain, plus much weight is saved. On simple catamarans the one generator can drive two electric motors, thus replacing two propulsion engines and reducing the number of engines aboard by one. Even better, on large energy-intensive cats that would normally run two propulsion engines plus a generator to charge batteries, two engines can be eliminated.

The key to creating an efficient hybrid propulsion system is making sure the generator powering the motor is not running faster than necessary. On large diesel-electric vessels the electric propulsion motors are connected to several small conventional AC generators, and generator output is controlled by increasing or reducing the number of generators running at one time. On smaller vessels where one generator must do all the work, that generator's running speed must be regulated, which is more complicated. Solutions have focused on using either sophisticated variable-frequency AC generators to drive AC motors or newly available DC generators to drive DC motors. Both approaches rely on cutting-edge generator technology utilizing smart electronic controllers that are still evolving and have not yet proven themselves in long-term service aboard active cruising boats. One prototype system installed in a 49-foot production sailboat has, however, reportedly realized fuel savings of nearly 80% over a conventional propulsion engine, while maintaining equivalent cruising speeds under power. This sounds too good to be true . . . and it may be. Whether such performance can be achieved in the real world on average boats operated by average cruisers remains to be seen.

CREATING AND STORING ELECTRICAL POWER

In terms of systems, the heart of any modern cruising boat is its electrical system, as this is the teat off which most other systems feed. If you are a coastal cruiser who spends a great deal of time plugged into shore power, you can afford to be cavalier about the capacities of your electrical system, as long as you are never off the grid for long. Casual cruisers who keep their boats on moorings and rarely bring them to docks, or serious cruisers who rarely plug in yet spend lots of time aboard running electrically powered gear, need to be very aware of the limitations of their systems.

Keep in mind that what comes out must somehow go back in. If you are not feeding juice to your boat from the grid on a routine basis, you need to create enough of your own energy to satisfy your

This pocket cruiser has a small electric motor instead of a fossil-fueled auxiliary. This motor is intended primarily for docking and mooring. In the future, hybrid diesel-electric power plants capable of motoring long distances may become common on larger boats.

own demands. As demand increases, the capacity of your electrical system, and your ability to feed it, must also increase. It is common, however, for cruisers to add power-hungry equipment to their boats without thought to where the extra power is coming from. Usually this is an incremental process. You add one piece of gear, then another a couple of years later, and then another, and then suddenly in the middle of a weeklong cruise your batteries are flat for no apparent reason. Another common scenario involves the wannabe bluewater cruiser who buys a clean, well-maintained boat that has spent most of its life tied up in a marina and is packed full of gizmos and gadgets. These worked fine when the boat was never off the grid for more than a few days, but in a bluewater liveaboard situation they will quickly overwhelm an undersized electrical system.

The simplest way to deal with electricity on a boat is to keep demand low. With only a few electric lights, a VHF radio, a GPS, some simple instruments, some ice to keep food and drinks cool, a manual toilet, some manual freshwater pumps, and a oil lamp to hang as an anchor light at night you can be very comfortable on a boat and never draw more than 30 amps from your batteries in a day. If you do decide to add equipment to your boat, you need to understand how much current the new equipment will consume, figure out how much you will be using it, and upgrade your electrical system accordingly.

Alternators

The most common way to create electricity on a sailboat is with an alternator mounted on the main propulsion engine. As with automobile engines, these generate power any time the engine is running and feed it to a battery bank. Almost all marine diesel engines come equipped with standard automotive alternators with rated outputs of 50 to 60 amps. On many coastal boats these standard alternators are the only onboard source of electricity and in many cases are more than adequate for the job. If a boat is not inhabited for long periods of time, if electrical demand is not excessive, and if the engine is run routinely and/or the boat is plugged into shore power on a regular basis, a standard alternator should be all that is needed.

As a cruising boat's electrical demands increase, however, most particularly when it is lived aboard and the engine is not often used for propulsion, it is imperative to maximize an alternator's productivity. Otherwise a cruising crew may be reduced to running their engine in neutral for hours at time while lying at anchor simply to keep their batteries charged. This is not good for the engine, is never relaxing for the crew, and is an inefficient way to generate electricity.

The answer is a high-output marine alternator, which greatly reduces the amount of engine-running time needed to charge batteries. A high-output alternator produces two to four times the output of a standard alternator and comes in two basic types: small-frame

Measuring Electrical Demands

Amps are units that measure the quantity of electricity consumed by a device; watts measure the amount of work performed by that electricity. You can always find watts by multiplying voltage (on a boat this will always be 12 or 24 volts) by amps ($V \times A = W$); conversely, you can find amps by dividing watts by voltage ($W \div V = A$). Electrically powered gear for a sailboat is always rated as to its electrical demand, usually in amps (though some items, like lightbulbs, are rated in watts). That rating can be found in the installation manual that came with the gear or is printed on a label affixed to the gear. If your boat has an accurate ammeter on its distribution panel, another easy way to determine how much power a device consumes is to activate only that device and read the meter. (Note that only a digital ammeter is likely to be accurate enough to produce useful readings.)

To calculate the total daily load on a boat, first figure all loads in terms of amps per the formula above. Then multiply the amperage of each device by the number of hours each day it is operated. For example, an anchor light typically draws about 1 amp and is left on all night, or about 8 hours. The light's total daily demand therefore is 8 amp-hours. To find the total daily load, simply add all the amp-hour figures for all devices together.

Calculating loads on a coastal cruising boat is usually fairly straightforward, as coastal boats are routinely sailed a bit, then are moored or anchored each night. Bluewater boats are more complicated, in that they usually spend many days at anchor, then go into passage mode and spend many days underway. Different equipment is used in each case, and the daily loads are likely to be different. Another variable is the number of crew aboard. More people invariably consume more power, and if a boat's crew size changes a lot—e.g., a singlehander or a couple aboard one week, then an entire family the next—daily loads will vary considerably. In all cases, it is best to use the highest routine daily load as the basis for evaluating and sizing any boat's electrical system.

A standard automotive alternator (top) and a high-output alternator (bottom). The standard alternator is driven by a light V-belt, while the high-output unit needs a stronger poly-V belt because loads are higher. (Courtesy of SAIL *Magazine)*

units that fit on standard mounting brackets and have rated outputs up to 130 amps, and large-frame units that require special brackets and have rated outputs up to 200 amps or more. Unlike standard alternators that have internal regulators to control the outbound flow of charging current, high-output alternators usually need more sophisticated external regulators to ensure they do not overcharge the batteries they are feeding. On many serious bluewater boats with lots of onboard systems there are often two alternators on an engine—the original standard one, used for charging a dedicated engine-cranking battery, and a high-output one, which charges the larger, more heavily used house batteries.

Sizing an alternator to a given boat's electrical system is a relatively complex exercise. First, an alternator's output should be matched to the capacity of the battery bank it is feeding, as batteries have limits to how much power they can accept over a fixed period of time. An alternator's actual output, however, is quite variable and is normally much lower than its rated output. Relevant factors are heat (all alternators are less efficient when hot) and turning speeds (different alternators achieve maximum efficiency at different rpm). Electrical loads imposed while an alternator is running also decrease its charging efficiency. As a general rule, however, the alternator's output when hot and while running at routine charging rpm should be somewhere between 25% and 30% of the total amp-hour capacity of the batteries it is charging.

If properly installed, alternators on the whole are very reliable and require little maintenance. If you keep their belts properly tensioned and make sure they don't get too dirty or corroded, they are normally trouble free. Broken mounting brackets are sometimes a problem with large-frame high-output alternators, as they impose heavy running loads on an engine. When other issues arise—i.e., the electrical system is being over- or undercharged while the engine is running—the first challenge is always diagnosis. This requires spending time crawling about the electrical system with a multimeter to figure out where the problem is. If the alternator is the culprit (which isn't too likely), experts in most cases should handle the repairs. Usually the best DIY fix is to simply replace the entire unit with a spare.

Wind and Solar Power

Cruising sailors have been using solar panels and wind generators to create electricity on boats for well over 20 years now. The notion of extracting power from the environment is inherently attractive to sailors, and many novice cruisers nurture fantasies of living on wind and sun power alone. For this to work, however, the demand for power must be very moderate. Most cruisers instead rely on solar and wind power only to supplement other sources of electricity.

The most important limiting factor is nature itself. Sometimes the wind doesn't blow and the sun doesn't shine, in which case no power can be generated. Other factors minimize productivity even when conditions are propitious. For example, many places cruisers like to sail are reasonably windy, but when anchoring they almost always try to get out of the wind as much as possible to reduce their chances of dragging. Likewise, many popular cruising grounds are quite sunny, but sailboats, with their masts, sails, awnings, and other impedimenta, have many shaded areas on their decks where solar panels don't work well.

Wind generators, which are merely small windmills driving alternators or DC motors, are on the whole more productive than solar panels, if only because the wind blows both day and night. In ideal conditions, a big 150-watt wind generator can create 3,600 watts of power, or 300 amp-hours at 12 volts, over the course of 24 hours. This potentially can satisfy all energy demands on a systems-intensive boat. But wind generators are more expensive, require more maintenance, and have shorter life spans than solar panels, plus the spinning propeller or turbine blades that drive them tend to be noisy. Over the years manufacturers have worked hard to reduce windmill noise, but it cannot be eliminated. Unfortunately, because output is largely a function of blade area, and more blade area generally means more noise, the most productive generators tend also to be the noisiest.

Powerful wind generators with large blades also run some risk of self-destructing in high winds. Some sort of governing device to regulate blade speed is needed to prevent this, otherwise you must be aboard to physically restrain and tie off the blades when the wind is too strong. Corralling big windmill blades in strong conditions, especially while sailing, is a potentially dangerous chore; also, it obviously is preferable to be able to leave the generator running while you're away from the boat. On some generators blade speed is governed physically, with either a centrifugal air brake or pivoting blades that flutter and stall at high speed, but this increases noise levels, sometimes dramatically. The most sophisticated machines are governed electronically and short themselves out to stall the generator's blades in high winds, but such installations must be carefully done to ensure neither the generator nor the batteries it is feeding are damaged in the process.

In practice even a powerful wind generator doesn't run at maximum output much of the time. Most generators don't produce any power at all until the wind is blowing at least 5 knots and don't produce anything significant until it reaches at least 10 knots. Maximum output may not be achieved until wind speeds reach 15 knots or more, and in many anchorages and mooring fields this much breeze is the exception and not the rule. Wind speeds on average are even lower in marinas.

Solar panels are much cheaper, are virtually maintenance free, are perfectly silent, and generally last longer than wind generators. To achieve anything near maximum output, however, they require direct sunlight striking them at near perpendicular angles. Some manufacturers claim solar panels are productive for 6 to 7 hours a day, but in reality it is more like 4 to 5. Even with a large 120-watt panel operating in ideal conditions this translates at most to 600 watts of power, or 50 amp-hours at 12 volts, being created over the course of a day.

The location of panels is extremely important. Ideally, the panels should never be shaded and should have articulated mounts so they can be oriented square to the sun throughout the day. In reality this is virtually impossible on a sailboat. Most cruisers aren't willing to spend their day constantly adjusting panel angles so most panels are mounted flat in fixed positions. Panels cannot, however, be mounted flush on a surface, but rather should to be blocked up about an inch so air can circulate behind them and keep them from overheating. Many locations on deck are apt to be shaded for part of the day and panels are also more likely to be damaged if placed in areas where crew need to work. Often the best compromise is to install panels flat on dinghy davits or a stern arch at the back of the boat. Here they are out of the way of working crew, can have air circulating freely around them, and are normally shaded only by the mast (or the sails, when they are hoisted).

A serious wind and solar array on a modern cruising boat. The solar panels are mounted aft of the mainsail and are slightly raised so air can circulate under them. Though it is idle now, the wind generator will produce more electricity than the panels over the long term. The generator pictured here, an AirBreeze unit, is both efficient and relatively quiet. (Courtesy of SAIL Magazine)

The importance of a shade-free location depends on the type of panels you are using. Monocrystalline panels, where each cell in the panel is composed of one silicon crystal, are the most efficient (about 12% of received light becomes electricity), but are most affected by shade. If only a small portion of the panel is shaded, its output is almost nil. Polycrystalline panels, where each cell is composed of many smaller silicon crystals, are slightly less efficient (10% of received light is converted to power), but are less affected when part of the panel is shaded. Amorphous silicon panels, where a substrate material is coated with vaporized silicon, are the least expensive and least efficient (only 6% of received light is converted to power) but are also much more productive proportionally when they are partially shaded. Amorphous panels can also be flexible, which makes them less susceptible to damage, but they take up more space—about 26 square inches per watt of output, versus 14 square inches for mono- and polycrystalline panels—and lose about 10% of their capability over time.

As with alternators, the output of wind generators and solar panels must be regulated to avoid overcharging batteries. Voltage regulators aren't necessary if you carefully monitor charge levels while aboard and disconnect any generators and panels while away. This, however, greatly reduces productivity (unless you are always aboard) and means these auxiliary power sources can't be used to keep batteries topped up when the boat is idle. Small solar panels, which are often used by coastal cruisers merely to trickle-charge batteries, don't require regulation as they don't put out enough power to cook batteries even when conditions are optimal. Nor do they put out enough power to recharge a deeply discharged battery.

Wind generators and solar panels in particular may also require blocking diodes. These prevent the units from draining power from the batteries when they are not producing power themselves. In all cases diodes reduce output to some extent, but in some cases that reduction is greater than the amount of power lost when the units are idle. Whether diodes actually make sense must therefore be determined on a case-by-case basis, depending on the equipment and how it is installed and used. Note also that some more sophisticated voltage regulators for solar panels now have dropout features that automatically disconnect panels whenever negative current flow is detected, making diodes unnecessary.

Generators

On energy-intensive cruising boats where the daily electrical load often exceeds 200 amp-hours you normally can't generate enough power onboard to satisfy demand—even with a high-output alternator and supplemental wind and solar power—without excessive running of the main propulsion engine. Such boats also often need AC power, as opposed to the DC power supplied by batteries, to feed devices like microwave ovens, televisions and VCR or DVD players, air conditioners, toasters, hair dryers, and the like. In order to enjoy these conveniences away from a shore-power connection, many cruisers rely on diesel-powered AC generators to meet their energy needs. These are independent engine-driven power plants that can directly feed household AC devices and can also feed power to a boat's DC battery banks via a separate alternator or an onboard battery charger (such a charger can also feed batteries from an AC shore-power connection). Generators were once found only on boats over 50 feet, but these days are increasingly common on smaller boats. Some builders now provide dedicated installation spaces for generators and offer them as factory-installed options on boats less than 40 feet long.

With a generator—or genset as they are often called—you can feed a very power-hungry boat and crew without ever running the main engine just to charge batteries. Generators are smaller, quieter, and more fuel efficient than propulsion engines, but still represent a major systems complication. First and foremost, there is another engine to maintain and, if anything, generator engines are fussier than propulsion engines. They also take up space, consume fuel, and may need their own dedicated cranking batteries. It is much better, therefore, to reduce energy demands and not have a generator aboard if possible. If profligacy however cannot be averted, you should study the marine generator market closely, as it is now evolving rapidly.

The main drawback of traditional AC generators is that they are inherently inefficient and oversized. AC loads typically come online in great surges, and an AC generator's output must be rated to accommodate the surge rather than the much lower working load. AC generators must also run at a constant speed that is normally higher than that needed to meet routine demands. As a result, they are terminally underloaded, which, as discussed, is bad for diesel engines. It also wastes fuel and creates unnecessary pollutants. New DC generators, which need not confront AC surge loads and can run at variable speeds to meet the actual load imposed, can be sized and operated more efficiently. Also they can feed DC batteries directly, eliminating the need for a battery charger (if a shore-power connection is not wanted).

Even better, DC generators can be automated. Governors that automatically regulate engine

Modern DC diesel generators (here a Panda AGT4) are more expensive than AC generators but are considerably more efficient, as they need not be oversized to handle surge loads and can run at variable speeds. (Courtesy of Fischer Panda)

speed to match imposed loads, plus AGS (automatic generator start) features that monitor battery voltage and fire up the generator as needed (these are also available on some AC generators), make it possible for cruisers to use power aboard without consciously

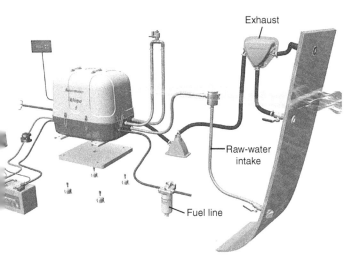

In a typical genset installation the engine (located inside the soundproof housing) has its own cranking battery, fuel line, raw-water intake, and exhaust line. (Courtesy of Mastervolt)

monitoring supply and demand, much as they do at home ashore. You can also leave power-hungry systems like refrigeration and air-conditioning running while away from the boat for extended periods (at least until the generator's fuel supply is exhausted). As seductive as this sounds, there are unique risks to consider. An AGS system cannot feed batteries intelligently and may over- or under-charge them in some circumstances, automatic governors thus far have often proven ineffective on the smaller gensets most often installed on cruising sailboats, plus simple malfunctions (a loose hose, for example) can cause serious problems on an unattended running engine.

One last option more modest cruisers should keep in mind are portable gasoline-powered AC generators that can be used on an ad hoc basis. These are compact, quiet, and powerful and can easily be stored aboard a small boat. Fed with gasoline from a supply carried for a tender's outboard, they may be the perfect answer for those who need large amounts of AC power infrequently (to run power tools while making certain repairs, for example) and would like also to have some last-resort method for charging batteries in an emergency.

AC Shore Power

On many coastal cruising boats, as mentioned, much of the power fed into the DC battery bank comes from shore. The common usage pattern here involves a boat that normally lies idle at a dock plugged into the grid and is cruised only on weekends, plus perhaps once a year for as long as a week or two. When the boat is active its DC batteries may be deeply discharged, but this is soon remedied once the shore-power cord is reconnected back at the dock. More actively cruised boats traveling from marina to marina also tend to rely primarily on shore power, and, of course, the ability to "plug in" from time to time is always valued by more itinerant cruisers.

As such, an AC shore-power connection is a standard feature on nearly all modern sailboats. Even on much older boats some sort of AC shore system often has been tacked on at some point. Such installations are often a bit creative. Some are downright dangerous, and it is not uncommon to find comments in survey reports on older boats warning prospective buyers never to plug the boat in question into shore power. If you already own or are contemplating acquiring such a boat, you should either install a new AC system or treat the boat as though it has no shore-power connection at all. Because AC current voltage is so high and thus potentially lethal, and because the marine environment is so moist and corrosive, safety must always be your primary concern.

DC-to-AC Inverters

Running an AC generator is not the only way to meet AC power demands when a cruising boat is unplugged from shore power. Inverters make it possible to change 12- or 24-volt DC power from a boat's battery banks into 110- or 220-volt AC power, and thus are increasingly popular with cruisers who like to run AC devices on their boats. Small 150-watt pocket inverters that plug into 12-volt cigarette lighter sockets and can power light AC loads have been popular even on simple boats for many years. Much larger, more sophisticated units that can service quite large loads have meanwhile become common on more systems-intensive boats. In some cases, large inverters have replaced generators altogether as the central element in extensive onboard AC systems.

Not all inverters generate the same sort of power. Some units produce electricity with a pure sine wave. This is virtually identical to what comes out of the socket in your home (or out of a generator), thus can be used to power any AC device. Others produce power with a modified sine wave, which causes some devices—like TVs, microwaves, and some cordless drill chargers—to run poorly and others—

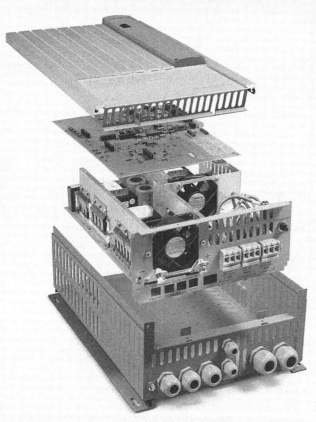

Modern line-frequency inverters like this can also function as battery chargers, thus are popular with sophisticated cruisers. High-load electrical systems designed around inverters are increasingly common. (Courtesy of Mastervolt)

like laser printers—to not run at all. Modified-wave units are more popular on the whole because they are cheaper and consume less power when idle, but may not be the best choice in all cases. There is another important distinction to be made between high-frequency and line-frequency inverters. High-frequency units are smaller, but can create excessive interference that degrades the performance of some electronics. Line-frequency units, though larger, can be easily configured as dual-purpose inverter-chargers with sophisticated multistep battery charging capabilities. Because this eliminates the need for a separate battery charger, such units are much in demand.

Any inverter must be evaluated both in terms of its capacity to satisfy AC loads imposed on it and the load it in turn imposes on a DC battery bank. On the AC side this is straightforward—find the rated power demand of the AC devices you want to run, add together any loads imposed simultaneously, and find an inverter rated to meet your total maximum running load. Unlike generators, inverters have a great deal of inherent surge capacity and need not be oversized to accommodate the big spikes created when AC devices are first activated.

The DC loads created by an inverter are more of a problem. These are quite high relative to the amount of work performed on the AC side, both because power is lost as the inverter switches current from DC to AC (typically about 20%) and the voltage differential magnifies the demand. For example, an AC television typically has a rated demand of about 100 watts at 110 volts, or 0.9 amp (100 ÷ 110 = 0.9). To find the load in amp-hours imposed on a 12-volt DC battery bank, we first divide 100 by 12, which is 8.33 amps. Multiply that by the number of hours the TV is used in a day (say 3), which is 25 amp-hours, and then add another 20% to that, which brings the total to 30 amp-hours for just a day's worth of TV entertainment while cruising. You'll recall this is equal to the approximate total daily demand on a simple boat running only some 12-volt lights and instruments. Add on just 12 minutes of microwave use (assuming a common microwave with a rated demand of about 1,200 watts) and the daily AC load increases by another 24 amp-hours (1,200 watts ÷ 12 volts = 100 amps; 100 amps x .2 hours = 20 amp-hours; 20 amp-hours + 20% = 24 amp-hours).

To cope with these loads and replace the power borrowed from the boat's batteries, you usually have to adopt one of three strategies: (1) use only a small inverter to feed light AC loads on an infrequent basis and recharge batteries as necessary with the main engine's alternator and perhaps wind and/or solar power; (2) use an appropriately sized inverter to handle light regular AC loads and run a generator for a certain period each day (usually during meal preparation) to power large AC loads and recharge batteries; or (3) use a large inverter to power all light and heavy AC loads throughout the day and run a generator as needed to recharge batteries. Option 2 has traditionally been favored by most cruisers with large energy-intensive boats, but option 3 is becoming more popular. This last strategy, an inverter-centric high-load system, as referenced above, has certain advantages in that the smallest possible internal-combustion engine can be used to meet large off-grid demands, because all surge loads are absorbed by the inverter rather than the generator. For maximum efficiency, a variable-speed DC generator can be used. In all cases, however, the DC battery bank and its charging system must be sized to properly accommodate the inverter load (for more on this see the section on batteries below). Even if only a couple of AC devices are used routinely, this load will likely be the largest on the boat, and if not accounted for the DC system will quickly crash.

An exploded view of a modern shore-power connection. Prongs and plugs are not absolutely standardized and you may need adapters to connect at marinas. (Courtesy of Mastervolt)

Shore connections are normally made via 30- or 50-amp receptacles. Except on boats with air-conditioning, a 30-amp connection is usually more than adequate. A proper installation should have a circuit breaker as close to the shore-power inlet on the boat as possible and a reverse-polarity alarm or indicator that immediately alerts you when the hot and neutral sides of the AC circuit have been inadvertently switched due to a wiring fault. All connections should be absolutely clean and corrosion free. All terminals should be protected with junction boxes with covers that are positively fastened in place.

The most important and controversial issue is grounding. Should any AC devices on board develop a fault or short, the boat's AC system must be connected to the shoreside ground; otherwise the fault current will roam the boat's circuits and connections looking for a route to the water surrounding the boat. This is potentially lethal for anyone in the boat or in the water around it. There should also be a connection between the AC and DC ground in case there is ever an AC short into DC circuits, which is particularly likely in a faulty battery charger, where AC and DC wiring coexist in the same device. There should also be a ground-continuity indicator on the AC distribution panel so that any broken ground connections are immediately apparent, and all AC plugs on board should have the "third prong," which provides ground redundancy.

Many boatowners, however, resist grounding their AC systems, and most particularly fail to interconnect the AC and DC grounds, due to concerns about galvanic corrosion. This is a problem because any properly grounded boat plugged into shore power shares a ground with every other properly grounded boat plugged into the same dock, in effect wiring them all together. Any underwater metal connected to a DC circuit or device on one boat—the primary offenders are propellers, prop shafts, radio ground plates, and bonded metal through-hull fittings—can therefore form a galvanic couple with submerged metal on other boats, thus corroding the least noble metals. Particularly on boats left plugged in at docks for long periods of time, this can be very destructive.

The best way to solve the problem is to not plug in to shore power at all, or to plug in only for brief periods of time. Many cruisers, however, cannot exercise this sort of discipline. The next best solution is to install an isolation device that blocks low-level corrosive electrical current without interfering with ground connections. The most commonly used devices are galvanic isolators, which are relatively small and inexpensive. They are not always effective, however, and better protection is provided by isolation transformers. These are larger and more expensive, but are more useful since they eliminate the need for a polarity alarm and can be configured to allow a boat to plug into both 110- and 220-volt shore-power systems.

Batteries

DC batteries are normally the key element in a cruising boat's electrical system. Except on boats that are constantly hooked up to shore power or have constantly running generators, it is the size and nature of the battery bank that defines the capacity of the system overall. If the battery bank is undersized, it will be chronically overloaded, thus chronically undercharged, and will quickly die. If properly sized, it will be subject to moderate loads, can be kept well charged, and will have a long and fruitful life.

When sizing a battery bank you must consider its effective range of operation. You cannot, for example, install a 100 amp-hour battery to service a routine 100 amp-hour demand. Even deep-cycle batteries, which should be used on any cruising boat to service house loads, cannot be fully discharged without suffering harm. Instead, to stay healthy, they should not be regularly discharged to much below 50% of their total capacity. Conversely, because it takes a long time to recharge a battery back to 100% of capacity, on active cruising boats that don't spend much time plugged into shore power batteries are often not recharged to more than 80% of capacity. This effectively means approximately only 30% of the battery's total rated capacity is available to service working loads. Thus, as a general rule, battery capacity should exceed routine demand by a factor of 3, though 4 is preferable, to allow a comfortable margin for undercharging. A boat with a routine daily demand of 100 amp-hours,

for example, should have at least 300 amp-hours of battery capacity. On boats that are often hooked up to shore power, so that their batteries are routinely pumped up to a full charge, battery capacity can be safely kept at just double the routine demand. But should the usage pattern change—when the owners, for example, decide to take a long cruise—things will need reconfiguring. Either battery capacity or onboard charging capabilities should be increased, or demand should somehow be decreased.

On small and midsize boats the physical size and weight of batteries can be a limiting factor. A large battery bank can weigh hundreds of pounds and take up many cubic feet of space. It may not be possible to significantly enlarge battery capacity on some boats without remodeling some portion of the interior. In some cases it may be impossible to fit in the desired battery bank. Note, too, batteries should be mounted in a cool location (heat can seriously degrade battery performance), but close to the engine, and low in the boat (for the sake of stability and performance), though preferably not so low that they can be easily flooded should the boat take on water.

Types of Batteries

Reduced to their basic components, lead-acid batteries consist of lead plates immersed in a sulfuric acid solution, referred to as the electrolyte. Automotive cranking batteries, which are rarely deeply discharged and can be quickly recharged, have quite thin plates. Heavy-duty deep-cycle batteries, used on boats to service house loads, have thicker plates, thus have more total capacity and can recover more easily from deep discharges, but also take longer to recharge. In all cases, the quality and quantity of lead in the battery determines its performance.

Otherwise, distinctions between lead-acid batteries have to do with the nature of the electrolyte. In a flooded wet-cell battery, the electrolyte is a liquid solution of acid and distilled water. These batteries require ongoing maintenance, yet also provide excellent potential performance in that they can run through thousands of discharge-recharge cycles. The battery cells must be topped off with distilled water on a regular basis, as this tends to gas off when batteries are fully recharged. Also, you need to equalize the batteries from time to time, so as to reclaim sulfated portions of lead plate that have become electrically inactive through chronic undercharging. Equalization is a carefully controlled overcharging of the battery, takes a great deal of time, and requires special equipment. It is therefore rarely performed by most boatowners; as a result many wet-cell batteries lose capacity over time and never fulfill their performance potential.

This large center-cockpit boat carries a huge wet-cell battery bank under its cockpit sole. The crew here is topping up the electrolyte in each cell with distilled water, a regular chore that need not be performed with sealed batteries.

Over the last 20 years, sealed maintenance-free gel-cell and absorbed glass-mat (AGM) batteries have become increasingly popular. In a gel-cell battery, the electrolyte is a soft, paste-like gelatin substance that is slathered over the battery plates. In AGM batteries the electrolyte is liquid, but is absorbed in spongy sheets of glass fibers that are pressed against the battery plates. Because the plates in both cases are not entirely immersed in electrolyte, they must be somewhat thinner than in wet-cell batteries. As a result, sealed batteries theoretically have shorter life spans than well-maintained wet-cell batteries, but they also can be recharged more quickly. Sealed batteries have other important advantages: they hold a charge much better over time, as they do not self-discharge as quickly as wet-cell batteries when left idle; they can sit idle for long periods without suffering damage; plus they can be submerged and flipped upside-down without suffering ill effects. The most important disadvantages are that sealed batteries are more expensive than wet-cells and are more easily damaged by overcharging, as there is no way to replace electrolyte once it gasses off.

In practice sealed batteries are often better suited to power-usage patterns on cruising boats that are not hooked up to shore power on a routine basis. Because they recharge more quickly, suffer neglect more easily, and are much less susceptible to environmental damage, they in many cases have a longer useful service life than poorly maintained wet-cell batteries.

In addition to conventional lead-acid batteries, there are other more advanced technologies now emerging in the market. Thin Plate Pure Lead (TPPL) lead-acid batteries, as well as nickel-cadmium and lithium-ion batteries, can all suffer deeper discharges and also recharge much faster than conventional batteries. Cutting-edge lithium-ion batteries, for example, are reputedly 70% lighter, have three times the life span, and have 20% more charge efficiency than wet-cell batteries. They are also amazingly expensive.

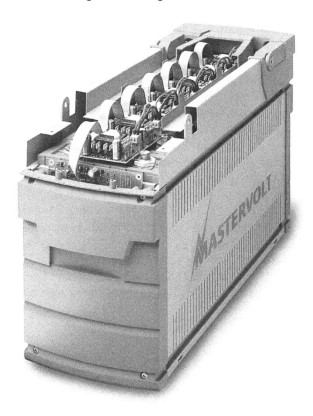

Marine lithium-ion batteries (shown here with top removed) are much lighter and more efficient than conventional batteries, but are expensive. High-tech batteries like this are clearly the wave of the future, but it may take a while for the technology to become affordable. (Courtesy of Mastervolt)

At this writing a single 160 amp-hour lithium-ion marine battery costs over $5,000.

At prices like this, high-tech batteries won't be appearing on most cruising boats anytime soon. A few well-financed race boats and performance cruisers are utilizing them, however, and as superior battery technology evolves and trickles down from the automotive industry it seems likely they will become more common and hopefully more affordable.

Battery Bank Configuration

Battery banks can be configured in numerous ways. On most older and many contemporary small and midsize boats, the most common practice is to split the bank in two, with two equally sized deep-cycle batteries connected to a single selector switch that permits either battery, or both together, to satisfy all power requirements on board, including engine-cranking and house loads. Both batteries in such cases are typically fed power by the same alternator. The traditional recommended operating procedure has been to use only one battery at a time, alternating

An absorbed glass-mat battery (rear) and a deep-cycle gel-cell battery—both types are sealed and maintenance free. (Courtesy Mastervolt)

between the two on a daily basis so both get exercised. The theory being it is safest to have one fully charged battery held in reserve at all times so that it is always possible to start the engine in an emergency. The problem with this, however, is that the effective working size of the total bank is cut in half. Each battery is more deeply discharged each time it is used than it would be if both were used together, thus curtailing the life span of both batteries.

More sophisticated arrangements have evolved as electrical loads on boats have increased. More powerful banks are often created both by using larger batteries and connecting batteries in parallel to combine their amp-hour capacity. It is also common now to install a separate automotive cranking battery for starting the engine. In many cases the cranking battery is tacked on to a dual house-bank

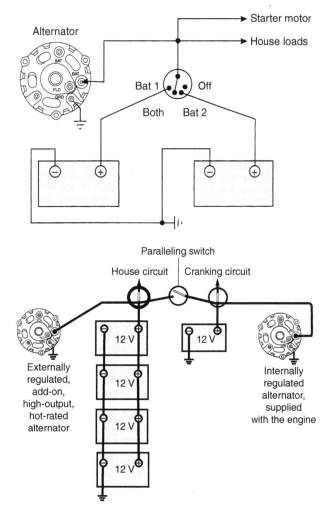

The simplest battery bank configuration normally consists of two batteries of equal size that can be paralleled or isolated from each other via a selector switch (top). More sophisticated systems (below) have both a large house bank and a dedicated cranking battery, each fed by its own alternator.

system, creating a three-bank system, and the user alternates between the two house banks as before. The best practice, however, is to hold just the cranking battery in reserve and use all house batteries simultaneously to maximize capacity and reduce discharge levels.

As far as charging goes, it is best if the cranking battery is served by the engine's standard automotive alternator and if the house bank has its own high-output alternator, though this is not always possible. Again, where both sides must share an alternator a manual selector switch is normally used to parallel all batteries while the engine is running and isolate them again after it is switched off. Alternatively, isolation diodes or paralleling relays (also known as "battery combiners") can be used to isolate batteries automatically after charging so as to reduce the possibility of the cranking battery being accidentally run down by house loads. Relays are preferable, as diodes induce voltage drops that may confuse voltage regulators. In cases where the cranking and house banks do have their own alternators, there should still be a switch connecting the two sides to preserve flexibility. Most particularly, you may want to use house batteries to crank the engine if necessary or feed output from the cranking battery's alternator to the power-hungry house batteries.

Charge Regulation

Batteries can accept only so much power over time while being charged. Wet-cell batteries have a maximum charge-acceptance rate of about 25% of their total capacity—i.e., a 100 amp-hour wet-cell battery cannot receive more than 25 amps of power at any given time. The maximum acceptance rates of gel-cell and AGM batteries are about 35% and 40% of total capacity, respectively. Thin-plate cranking batteries have much higher acceptance rates than thick-plate deep-cycle batteries. Charge-acceptance rates also vary depending on a battery's state of charge. A deeply discharged battery can be fed power at its maximum acceptance rate, but the rate steadily declines as the battery becomes more fully charged. Thus, as mentioned, it takes a long time to fully charge a battery.

To charge a battery as quickly as possible you need to feed it power right up to the limit of its acceptance rate at any given state of charge without overfeeding it. This can be accomplished through the use of a "smart" computer-controlled multistep voltage regulator. These programmable regulators pump power into a battery through three distinct phases: first a so-called bulk charge is delivered at the maximum acceptance rate until the battery's voltage rises to a certain level; next comes an absorption

Control panel for a "smart" 24-volt charge-regulation system. (Courtesy of Mastervolt)

charge, delivered at a fixed voltage for a certain amount of time or until the battery's acceptance rate declines to about 2% of total capacity; last comes a float charge, delivered at a reduced voltage level. More sophisticated regulators can also account for factors like battery temperature, have equalization programs to use with wet-cell batteries, and include fail-safe features that protect both the battery and the alternator feeding them. Such regulators are often bundled with monitoring systems that allow you to track the charging process in detail.

Multistep voltage regulators are now considered standard equipment by most cruisers who spend lots of time off the grid. They greatly increase charging efficiency by reducing charging times—sometimes by a factor of 2 or more, compared to a standard regulator—and increase battery life expectancy by ensuring batteries are not over- or undercharged on a regular basis. Note, however, that multistep regulators are

programmed to charge specific battery banks and can damage batteries with different charging requirements. Different types of batteries should not be mixed in the same bank, nor should different batteries of the same type that are different ages and/or have had markedly different service histories. If the batteries in a bank are replaced with another type, the regulator must be reprogrammed.

12 vs. 24 Volts

Ever since the 1950s when standard automotive electrical systems switched from 6 to 12 volts, standard marine electrical systems have likewise been 12 volts. In recent years, however, particularly in Europe, some builders have started installing 24-volt battery banks on their boats. At first this was done mostly on large boats, about 60 feet and longer, but now 24-volt systems can be found on boats as small as 40 feet. The great advantage of these systems is that the cabling needed to carry 24-volt current is one-quarter the size of that needed to carry 12-volt current. For low-power devices this is not terribly significant, but for power-hungry equipment like bow thrusters, electric mainsail and headsail furlers, electric winches, and windlasses it can spell the difference between cables that weigh hundreds of pounds versus cables weighing mere dozens of pounds. Because lighter 24-volt cables are much more supple, they are easier to install than 12-volt cables; they are also less expensive.

There is, however, a lot of equipment that cannot run on 24 volts, including most marine electronics. Any 24-volt boat must also therefore still be a 12-volt boat in certain respects. Often the only 24-volt equipment on a "24-volt boat" is the heavy-duty gear mentioned above; all other equipment—lights, small pumps, refrigeration, plus all navigation and communications electronics—is left at 12 volts.

The most common way to a feed a dual 12/24-volt electrical system is straight off a 24-volt battery

A small 24/12-volt converter for use on a dual 24/12-volt cruising boat. (Courtesy of Mastervolt)

bank. This usually consists of two 12-volt batteries connected in series so that the bank's voltage is doubled while amp-hour capacity remains the same. The 24-volt current coming off the bank is then stepped down to 12 volts where necessary by voltage converters. In most cases multiple converters are used and are installed close to the loads they feed. This complicates the wiring, but reduces the total amount and weight of the system's cabling. Converters also act as filters, delivering much cleaner power to the devices they serve; some come equipped with small internal batteries to smooth out sudden voltage drops caused by large loads coming online.

The alternative approach is to feed 12-volt loads from one of the 12-volt batteries in the 24-volt bank, while feeding 24-volt loads from the bank as a whole. This requires an equalizer to keep both batteries at an equal state of charge. When 12-volt loads pull down one battery, the equalizer allows the other battery to feed power to the now-weaker one to make up the difference. The battery serving 12-volt loads, however, is still cycled more often than the other, and this shortens its life expectancy. Using an equalizer is generally less expensive than using converters, but there will still be many long 12-volt cable runs.

In most dual 12/24-volt systems the starter on the engine is fed by its own dedicated 12-volt cranking battery. Ideally, there should be two alternators—one putting out 12 volts to feed the cranking battery, the other putting out 24 volts to feed the house bank. In a single-alternator system, the alternator puts out 24 volts, and that output can be converted to 12 volts to feed the cranking battery (which can be accomplished in various ways), but this should be avoided if possible.

Future Trends: Distributed Power

Though electrical devices aboard sailboats have become more numerous and complex over the past 30 years, the way electricity is distributed around a boat has remained fundamentally unchanged. Power from a DC battery bank is fed first via heavy cables to a distribution panel with a vast array of manual switches and circuit breakers (normally located at the boat's nav station) and from there via lighter cables to each individual electrical device on the boat. Each circuit is wired separately, with both a positive and negative lead serving each load. The result is a large web of wiring that leads all over the boat, yet is cleverly concealed and generally inaccessible, all terminating in a huge mass of wiring behind the distribution panel. These traditional wiring harnesses are difficult to install and service. They are also inefficient and heavy, as multiple wires must follow parallel paths

through the boat. On a modern systems-intensive midsize cruising boat, the wiring alone can weigh nearly 1,000 pounds.

Automobile and aircraft manufacturers stopped using traditional wiring harnesses several years ago and replaced them with what are called distributed-power systems. Here the central nexus is not a distribution panel, but a backbone of three major cables running the length of the vehicle. Two of the cables are positive and negative power leads, off which individual devices are wired with circuit breakers located at each junction. The breakers and switches are controlled with microprocessors via the third cable, which can serve as the spine of an entire electronic data network. It is this network that modern auto and aircraft mechanics plug into to perform computer diagnoses of vehicle systems.

Manufacturers of distributed-power systems have recently begun marketing equipment for marine use, and it is likely these systems will be adopted by most boatbuilders in years to come. Already some systems have appeared in powerboats. Besides decreasing the amount of wiring on a modern cruising boat by 50% or more, modern distributed-power systems, because of their incorporated data networks, have the potential to transform onboard systems management. In addition to simply protecting against electrical current overloads, circuit breakers can be programmed to operate as smart controllers with numerous self-operating and self-diagnostic features. Early warnings can be issued about devices drawing unusual amounts of power, bilge-pump circuits can be programmed to self-start without mechanical float switches, fuel-level sensors can be interfaced with engine and speed data to provide accurate range-under-power estimates, and so on ad infinitum. Ultimately, systems management on a complex boat can be greatly simplified, and because the total number of electrical connections is greatly reduced, overall reliability should be significantly increased. It should also be easier for laypersons to wire new equipment on their boats.

Computer-phobic sailors, however, will instantly identify the Achilles heel of any such system. A conventional wiring harness may be physically intricate, but a reasonably savvy cruiser can often troubleshoot and trace common wiring problems. That same cruiser, confronted with a distributed-power system full of software and processors, will likely be completely baffled if anything goes wrong. Even if the overall system is more reliable, most boatowners won't be able to solve problems that do arise without professional technical assistance. Different manufacturers are taking different approaches as to how to bypass and repair (or replace) faulty circuits. Almost all utilize what are called power-distribution modules,

The Evolution of Nigel Calder

I first met Nigel Calder at a boat show in the fall of 1997 after returning from an extended North Atlantic cruise aboard an old fiberglass yawl. During that cruise I often referred to the first edition of Nigel's *Boatowner's Mechanical and Electrical Manual* when struggling to repair and maintain onboard systems. Ever since I have always thought of it as "Nigel's How-to-Fix-Everything Book." One trick I learned from the book is that sticky piston pumps on manual marine toilets can be freed up with a dose of baby oil. My own toilet had become addicted to the stuff, and I was worried this might lead to bigger problems later on. On spotting Nigel

Nigel Calder at the helm of his second Nada. *How did this Trotskyist barebones cruiser morph into cruising's avatar of high technology?*

at the show, I immediately buttonholed him about this. I was relieved to find that he seemed to be, like myself, little more than a shiftless boat bum and was very friendly and personable. I was also relieved when he told me my toilet would be fine.

Later I worked with Nigel in various capacities at *SAIL* Magazine and got to know him better. A Trotskyist philosophy student and self-taught mechanic who first learned to sail in flooded gravel pits in his native England, Nigel's technological development as a cruiser in many ways mirrors that of the sport as a whole. His first cruising boat was a simple 28-footer with minimal systems that he borrowed from his brother. The boat he did much of his cruising on, primarily in the Gulf of Mexico and western Caribbean, was a traditional Ingrid 38 ketch named *Nada* that he finished from a bare hull with his American wife Terrie. In the last 15 years, however, capitalizing on the reputation he has built as a boat-systems guru since first publishing his "How-to-Fix Everything" book in 1990, he has launched three different *Nadas* in close cooperation with two different builders. In his latest *Nada*, Nigel is pushing directly at the cutting edge of cruising systems technology. There is nothing revolutionary about the boat itself—it is a stock Malö 45 built in Sweden, with a conventional cutter rig and a generous fin keel. The electrical system, however, is a modern distributed-power network, and the propulsion system incorporates both a conventional diesel engine and a state-of-the-art diesel-electric system, which Nigel intends to subject to a rigorous testing program. Noting that all claims regarding the efficiency of diesel-electric propulsion in cruising sailboats are entirely anecdotal and subjective, in spite of the fact that several prototypes have already been launched, Nigel believes his dual-propulsion system, coupled with a distributed-power network that should make it possible to efficiently analyze performance, will allow him to directly compare diesel and diesel-electric systems on the same boat under the same conditions in a thoroughly objective manner.

If Nigel's experiment is successful, systems on cruising sailboats may someday be radically different from what we are accustomed to. "I am the guinea pig," announced Nigel proudly when he described his new boat to me. His wife Terrie, meanwhile, wishes maybe he wasn't. "I liked it better when our boats were simpler," she shrugged. "All the modern conveniences take the fun out of it for me."

wherein multiple circuits are grouped together and controlled as a single group. But practices regarding the repairability of individual circuits within a module, the interchangeability and programming of modules, and software and hardware redundancies have yet to be standardized. Until standard practices do emerge and reliable idiot-proof "limp-home" features are incorporated into systems, most cruising sailors should probably refrain from embracing this technology.

PLUMBING

Even before cruisers thought to have electricity on their boats, they knew they wanted plumbing. Originally this consisted simply of a manual pump for bringing fresh water from onboard tanks to a conveniently located tap. Later it included piping fuel—first gasoline, then diesel—from tank to engine and evacuating human waste through marine toilets. More recently it has encompassed creating fresh water as well as storing human waste.

It is possible to have a cruising boat without plumbing, but in fact these are even rarer than boats without engines or electricity. I have only ever encountered one example. This was a plywood Wharram catamaran I met many years ago in the Cape Verde Islands. The owner was an eccentric Portuguese-German fellow who had two wives and prided himself on the ingenious simplicity of his craft. All fresh water was stored in dozens of separate 4-gallon jerry jugs that were tapped and drained separately as needed. The toilet, of course, was nothing more than a bucket. Auxiliary propulsion was provided by a large diesel outboard engine fueled by portable 6-gallon plastic tanks that were stored on deck. With the exception of the small fuel pump inside the outboard and its relatively short external fuel hose, no fluids onboard were conveyed by pump, pipe, or hose.

Few cruisers are willing to endure this much simplicity, and in fact there is no good reason to do so. Basic plumbing systems are relatively easy to install, require little maintenance, and are very reliable. With modern technology you can, however, greatly complicate things in the name of convenience. With watermakers, water heaters, and electric pumps and toilets, you can use water as profligately and thoughtlessly as you do ashore. As with all onboard systems, however, you should weigh the benefits of such conveniences against the concomitant costs and inconveniences.

Water and Fuel Tanks

Tanks are normally the largest component of any given plumbing system. They also create the largest headaches when they fail, as they are often buried deep in the structure of a boat and often cannot be removed without ripping out part of a boat's interior. The longevity of tanks depends largely on the material from which they are constructed. Ideally, they should be installed so that they can be removed without deconstructing the boat, but most builders consider them permanent installations and have no qualms about making them inaccessible. When buying a new boat you needn't be concerned about this, as any tank will likely last 10 to 20 years before any problems

develop. When buying an older boat, however, you should be very interested in the tanks. Unfortunately, it can be hard to evaluate their condition.

In terms of support and weight distribution, it is best if a tank is completely integral, custom shaped to fit into the space it inhabits, and positioned as low in the boat as possible. Boats with full keels or large hollow fin keels can often accommodate integral keel tanks, and in many respects this is ideal, though access is extremely limited. Such tanks work especially well on full-keel boats with wineglass sections, as the hull shape allows keel tanks to be both large and deep. Next best are shallow tanks placed in bilges below the cabin sole. Normally this is the lowest feasible location on any boat with external ballast and a bolted-on keel. The last choice are tanks installed under settees, berths, and sometimes cockpits, all of which are increasingly common as modern boats offer less and less open space beneath their cabin soles.

Custom-shaped tanks can be either metal or fiberglass. Metal is most common, because it is cheapest to work into eccentric shapes. Aluminum is popular, but is the least desirable material because of its susceptibility to galvanic corrosion. This can occur where the tank comes in contact with copper-based plumbing fittings or even bilge water containing impurities that make it electrolytic and thus corrosive. Aluminum fuel tanks are particularly vulnerable if they are bonded to other metals on the boat for purposes of lightning protection, as is recommended by the American Boat & Yacht Council.

Stainless steel is often hailed as an ideal tank material, but in fact it too can be easily corroded, particularly if the inferior 304 alloy is used, as is often the case. Stainless steel is most vulnerable wherever it is held in contact with water in a deoxygenated environment, as we discussed in the section on rudder construction in Chapter 3. The risk of corrosion is minimized if superior 316L or 317L alloys are used, but cannot be eliminated. Interestingly, mild steel tanks, if properly primed and painted with two-part epoxy paint, are not any more subject to corrosion than stainless steel or aluminum and cost much less. The best metals to use are bronze, Monel, and high-molybdenum stainless alloys, but these are expensive and are rarely seen on modern boats.

Whatever type of metal is used, any metal tank should be shaped and installed so as to minimize contact with moisture and standing water. The tank should be separated from any mounting surfaces by nonabrasive, non-absorbent materials such as high-density plastic or neoprene, should be configured to shed water when the boat is idle, and should not be located anywhere bilge water is apt to collect and stagnate. On any aluminum tank, copper-based plumbing fittings should also be carefully isolated from the tank with washers and/or sealants.

Because it never corrodes, fiberglass is a superior tank material, most particularly for tanks buried in bilges. Fiberglass, like metal, can be custom shaped, but as with any hull laminate, glass tanks must be carefully constructed to guard against moisture absorption. Fiberglass fuel tanks must comply with certain government standards. Water tanks should be laid up with epoxy or some other potable-approved resin that will not impart a styrene flavor to its contents. Epoxy is best in any event, as it also minimizes moisture absorption.

The cheapest, most commonly used tanks on modern mass-production sailboats are made of polyethylene plastic, which is durable and absolutely corrosion resistant. Such tanks are not custom shaped, but instead come in standard mass-produced sizes and shapes. Installations therefore often cannot make the best use of available space within a boat. Note too that polyethylene has two different molecular structures—linear and cross-linked. Linear plastic is only appropriate for water tanks, while cross-linked plastic should be used only for fuel tanks. In either case, the best polyethylene tanks are molded as one piece rather than welded together, as welded plastic seams may fail when the tank is filled. When first filled with fuel polyethylene tanks also swell slightly, by a factor of about 2% percent, and this permanent change in size must be accounted for during installation. Otherwise, any polyethylene tank should be firmly mounted with its total floor area fully supported and with effective chafing gear on any straps or braces. Usually, polyethylene tanks are

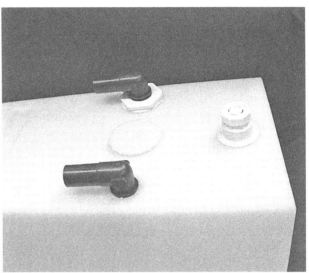

A custom-shaped fiberglass fuel tank awaiting installation (top) and a mass-produced molded plastic tank (plumbed as a holding tank) (bottom). (Courtesy of SAIL *Magazine and Trionic Corp.)*

most vulnerable where plumbing fittings are installed, as these can be knocked loose by stray pieces of gear or clumsy crew. Fittings are best installed in discrete, well-protected locations with all vent and feed lines well supported.

Whatever a tank is made of, it ideally should have inspection ports large enough to permit cleaning when necessary. There should also be an easily accessed aperture through which the tank can be sounded with a rod, as mechanical and electrical gauges are often unreliable. Large tanks should have baffles to prevent their contents from sloshing around too much, as this may threaten the tank's structural integrity, creates unwanted noise, and can affect a boat's performance in a seaway. Fuel tanks should have long fill pipes leading close to the floor of the tank to reduce foaming inside as fuel comes aboard. They should also have well-defined sumps

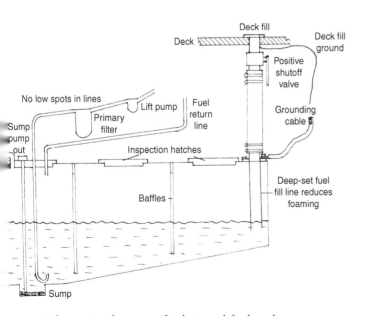

Schematic of a properly designed fuel tank.

where contaminants can settle and be extracted, either through a tap under the tank or via a sampling line led in from above.

Pipes and Hoses

What pipes and hoses are best employed in different systems depends on what sort of fluids they carry. They should not be used interchangeably. In many cases there are government regulations and/or recommendations to keep in mind. In all cases, installation is important. Runs should be fair with no kinks or hard corners, and chafing gear should be installed anywhere a pipe or hose is led through a bulkhead or compartment floor or wall. Hoses connected below the waterline to through-hull outlets should be double-clamped whenever possible. Any feed line subject to suction from a pump must be either rigid or strongly reinforced so that it does not collapse.

Fuel lines were once often made up of copper piping or tubing, but now flexible hoses are more common. These are subject to much regulation and must be both impermeable and fire resistant. The best are rated by the U.S. Coast Guard as Type A1 and are plainly marked as such. Fill and vent lines for tanks have prescribed interior diameters (38 mm and 14 mm respectively) and should not have any low spots where fuel can collect when the line is not in use.

Water lines carrying drinking water should be constructed of material approved by the U.S. Food and Drug Administration. Polyvinyl chloride (PVC) and polyethylene are now most commonly used. If PVC is used, you must distinguish between plain PVC, which can be used only for cold water plumbing, and CPVC (or chlorinated polyvinyl chloride), which must be used for hot water. In either case water lines should be perfectly opaque, as light can promote the growth of algae.

Sanitation lines must be impermeable or they will eventually stink. Appropriate sanitation hoses are normally clearly labeled as such. The two most commonly used materials are PVC and rubber. Flexible PVC hose is slightly more permeable than rigid PVC piping, but is easier to install. Heavy rubber hose is more expensive, less permeable, less susceptible to damage when married to ill-fitting hose barbs, and more flexible than PVC hose. Any sanitation hose, whatever it is made of, should have a smooth interior surface so that effluent cannot get trapped inside.

Water Pumps

Electric freshwater pumps and bilge pumps are standard equipment on most cruising boats these days. Most freshwater pumps are small diaphragm pumps; electric bilge pumps tend to be centrifugal pumps. Manual bilge pumps are most often large diaphragm pumps. Problems with electric pumps usually involve the switches that turn them on and off. Freshwater pumps have pressure switches that activate the pump when a tap somewhere in the system is opened, thus causing water pressure in the line to drop. Bilge pumps have level or float switches that activate the pump when water around it rises above a certain level. In either case it is preferable to have pumps with switches that can be easily replaced when necessary.

Electric pumps should never be relied upon exclusively. You never want to be in a situation where losing electrical power means you cannot access your freshwater supply or remove water from your bilge. In both cases, backup manual pumps should be considered mandatory. As far as I'm concerned, electric freshwater pressure pumps are completely unnecessary, as they do nothing but waste power and water. It

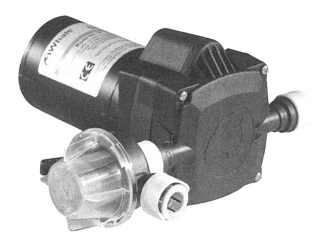

Electric freshwater pressure pumps like this are found on almost all modern cruising boats. (Courtesy of Whale Pumps)

Every boat should have a large manual bilge pump. The smaller your boat, the bigger the pump you need to keep it afloat in an emergency. (Courtesy of Edson International)

takes little physical effort to operate a small freshwater foot pump, and it is a conscious act, which means you only pump, when you want water to come out the tap. With electric pumps it is all too easy to have water flowing freely when you do not need it. On my boat I rarely run the pressure pump, except sometimes when showering or once a year when emptying water tanks at the end of the season.

Bilge pumps are another story. Most insurance companies require that covered vessels have automatic electric bilge pumps, and for good reason. Statistics show that most sinkings occur while vessels are left unattended on docks or moorings. Some local jurisdictions do prohibit the use of automatic bilge pumps, for fear they will foul harbor water with the trace amounts of oil and fuel that tend to accumulate in bilges. But if you want to have insurance, you need an electric bilge pump, whether you turn it on or not.

Both electric and manual bilge pumps should be as large and as numerous as possible. Logic dictates that smaller boats in fact need more pumping capacity than larger ones, as they fill with water and sink faster. Note that rated capacities on bilge pumps, especially electric ones, are wildly optimistic, as they do not account for the head pressure caused by resistance in the outlet line. Electric pumps also often run slower than they should due to voltage drops in their wiring runs. For maximum efficiency, outlet plumbing should be as short and straight as possible, and outlet hoses should have smooth walls to reduce friction. To minimize voltage drops, wiring to electric pumps should be oversized, should be tinned rather than plain copper to resist moisture intrusion, plus all connections should be carefully sealed with heat-shrink tubing.

Another potential problem with bilge pumps is siphoning. This can occur when the pump's hull outlet is temporarily submerged, thus allowing water to flow down the outlet line and through the pump back into the boat. The best way to prevent siphoning is to position hull outlets so they are never submerged on any point of sail. Alternatively, a one-way check valve should be installed in the outlet line. These, however, create a lot of resistance and significantly reduce a pump's capacity.

Sanitation Systems

The disposal of human waste on boats is heavily regulated, but only if it is passed through a device that is "installed" on a boat. Waste can be legally passed overboard directly from the human body, or perhaps from a loose bucket, but not necessarily from a toilet. Many cruising sailors were once happy to "bucket and chuck it," but most these days like to use toilets, so the subject of marine sanitation is fraught with legal complications.

Unfortunately, the relevant regulations are not entirely rational. Pursuant to the federal Clean Water Act, the contents of a toilet on a boat can be emptied directly overboard only when the boat is more than 3 miles offshore. Otherwise waste must pass through or into what is termed a "marine sanitation device," or MSD. Type-1 and Type-2 MSDs break up and treat sewage to certain standards (the Type-2 standards are much stricter) before discharging it overboard. A Type-3 MSD is simply a holding tank where waste is stored until it can be either legally discharged or pumped out at a special receiving facility known as a pumpout station. Under the original law, vessels 65 feet and under can use any type of MSD, while those larger than 65 feet must have either Type-2 or Type-3 MSDs.

Assuming there is a real need to regulate waste discharges from small recreational vessels (which is, in fact, arguable), it seems clear the most effective regulatory scheme should favor and encourage onboard treatment technology. Bulk loading already overloaded onshore treatment facilities with large amounts of stored effluent from holding tanks is not effective or efficient from an environmental perspective. Besides which, truly operational pumpout stations are in fact a rare commodity. Both federal and state governments, however, have chosen to favor the much cruder Type-3 MSD technology by creating numerous no-discharge zones, or NDZs. In these areas, some of which include all or most coastal waters within a state, even treated waste cannot be pumped overboard and the use of otherwise legal Type-1 and Type-2 MSDs is prohibited. In practice, therefore, it is unwise to ever install a Type-1 or Type-2 onboard treatment system, as a Type-3 holding tank must also be installed if you ever expect to enter an NDZ. In that more and more NDZs are being created each year, this is increasingly hard to avoid.

Many cruisers choose to ignore the law and pump their waste overboard on a flush-by-flush basis regardless of where they are. This probably does little harm, except in enclosed harbors and anchorages with poor tidal flushing, as the waste is emitted in very small quantities in disparate locations. Those who attempt to follow the law meanwhile are sometimes compelled to empty full holding tanks in illegal locations because they cannot find a pumpout station. This, I suspect, is much more harmful, as large amounts of waste are dumped all at once. The end result does not benefit the environment and (ironically) only encourages cruisers to disparage environmental values.

Toilets

The devices into which cruisers must actually defecate or urinate are not directly regulated and fall into four basic categories:

Manual piston-pump toilets. Here raw flushing water is pumped through the toilet bowl with a simple manually operated piston-rod pump. These are the most common marine toilets and by far the most efficient and useful. No electricity is required, the amount of flush water is controlled by the user (which is important if pumping into a holding tank), plus the user gets a little exercise. These are also the least expensive units.

Electric macerating toilets. Here an electric impeller pump flushes water (normally raw water, though some installations use fresh water) through the bowl, and an electric macerator chops up anything remotely solid into a nice manageable mush. These toilets require a lot of water to work well—about 1 gallon to clear urine, or 3 gallons to clear solids—otherwise the electric motors burn out prematurely. Holding tank capacity on a per-flush basis is thus significantly decreased, but is still variable, as the length of each flush is user-controlled. These toilets draw about 35 amps, though only for short periods of time. They are increasingly popular on systems-intensive boats and cannot be operated without electricity.

Vacuum toilets. These are efficient and simple, but strangely there are only two examples. The electric SeaLand VacuFlush uses just 1 to 3 pints of pressurized fresh water to vacuum flush waste out of the bowl, just like on commercial airliners. It makes efficient use of holding-tank space and of electricity, using just 6 amps for about 45 seconds, but cannot be operated manually. It also of course depletes a boat's freshwater supply over time. Salt water can be used instead, but this hastens the system's decline and an extra pump is needed to pressurize the water supply. The British-built Lavac toilet uses raw water in larger quantities, but can be operated with either a manual or electric pump. The pump is a simple diaphragm type installed in the outlet line and creates a vaccum in the bowl when the seat is closed. The system has no internal valves and is very reliable.

Composting toilets. This is an emerging technology that does a nifty end run around government regulations, but thus far has not proved practical on cruising sailboats. A steady, but relatively small supply of electricity is usually needed to operate a fan and evaporating plate, but no water is used and no plumbing is necessary. Composting units, however, are bulky and usually only fit on larger boats. It is questionable, too, whether they are capable of handling the bulk loading that can occur when a large crew is aboard.

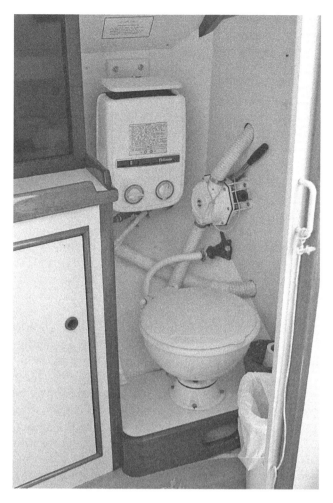

A Lavac vacuum toilet installed on the author's cutter Lunacy. *These are simple to operate and maintain. (A propane water heater is mounted on the bulkhead behind it.)*

Porta-Pottis. These are small portable toilets with integral holding tanks that are normally found only on small trailer-sailer boats. Waste in the tank is treated with chemicals to reduce odors, but the tanks are quite small (2.5 gallons is a common capacity) and must be emptied by hand on an almost daily basis. There are some larger units available that can be permanently mounted with pumpout fittings. On the whole, however, toilets like this are best used on boats that cruise for just a day or two at a time.

Treatment Systems

Because the installation of these systems is penalized under the current law, there are, unfortunately, fewer onboard-treatment options than there should be. All these systems require electrical power, sometimes in large amounts, and are relatively expensive. The oldest example is the Lectra/San, which treats waste by first macerating it, then dosing it with hypochlorous acid,

The latest generation of the Lectra/San waste treatment system. (Courtesy of Raritan Engineering)

or chlorine, which is created electrolytically from seawater. The treatment device must be activated every time a toilet is flushed and draws 45 amps for about 3 minutes each time it is used. The Lectra/San can be used in fresh water if salt is added to a special feed tank; alternatively, a freshwater version, the Pura/San, which contains an integral chlorine cartridge, can be installed instead.

Another somewhat more versatile device is the SanX, which holds waste in 10-gallon tank until it is either treated and discharged or pumped out. During treatment a chemical called TDX, a supply of which must be carried aboard, is injected into the waste, which is then macerated. TDX is expensive—about $15 a gallon—and itself poses an environmental hazard, thus may be banned is some areas. Production of the SanX has been discontinued, but many units are still in service and SanX parts and TDX are still available.

A third option is the Thermopure, which treats waste by simply heating it. It has an integral 10- or 20-gallon holding tank the contents of which are heated to 167° Fahrenheit before being discharged. Heat is provided by either AC electrical power (the heater pulls about 15 amps at 110 volts) or a heat exchanger plumbed into the main propulsion engine's cooling system. Unless you're willing to run the engine just to flush the toilet, these systems only make sense on boats with AC generators. These units also don't like cold weather. Once temperatures approach freezing, you must pump in antifreeze each time you use the unit.

Holding Tanks

Though the law effectively requires every boat with a toilet to have a holding tank, the size, construction, and installation of tanks is not regulated. Cruisers who choose to disobey the law and never use their

holding tanks often install small tanks made of inappropriate materials so they can be displayed to Coast Guard officers during inspections. Those who actually use their holding tanks should be much more circumspect.

The bigger the holding tank the better, as you often must keep waste aboard as long as possible to comply with the law. This is especially true in coastal areas where pumpout stations are few and far between and it is not possible to get offshore quickly. The other big factor is how much water it takes to flush the toilet feeding the tank. If a toilet uses little water, its holding tank obviously can hold many more flushes. Unfortunately, toilets are always cleaner and less likely to stink if lots of water is pumped through them.

As to materials, metal holding tanks should always be avoided. Urine is highly corrosive and eventually eats up both stainless steel and aluminum, never

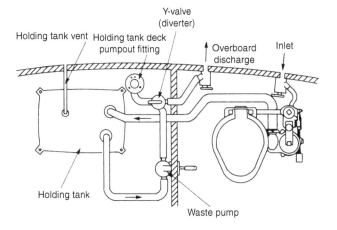

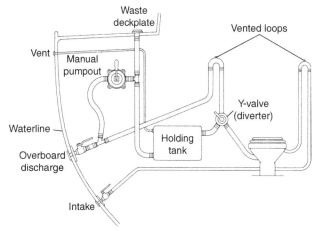

Typical holding-tank installations. New boats must have systems where all waste is routed first to a holding tank before being discharged and pumped out (top). Retrofitted systems may still direct waste either to the holding tank or directly overboard (bottom). (Drawing at bottom by Jim Sollers)

mind mild steel. Flexible plastic bladder tanks, commonly seen on older boats in make-do retrofits, are also a bad idea. They are very permeable and do not ventilate well, thus are apt to stink when full of waste; they also chafe easily and are more likely to leak. The best material for a holding tank is rotomolded linear polyethylene, with tank walls at least ¼ inch thick to resist permeation of odors. The walls should be proportionally thicker as tank size increases to ensure the tank's structural integrity when it is full.

Plumbing-wise there are two basic installations. Waste from the toilet can be routed only to the tank, or it can be routed either to the tank or directly overboard via a Y-valve. The latter arrangement is legal for retrofitted tanks, but all new boats must now adhere to the former scheme. The tank in either case can be emptied either overboard through an underwater through-hull fitting or at a pumpout station through a deck fitting. To minimize odors no plumbing run should have any low spots where waste can collect; most particularly, the line feeding waste into the tank should enter at the top of the tank so waste doesn't back down into it as the tank fills up. Also, the tank's vent line should be wide and short so that the tank's interior is ventilated with fresh air. This promotes the growth of aerobic bacteria, which break down sewage without creating odors. Ideally, there should be two generous vent lines so the tank is cross-ventilated.

Tank-type calorifier water heaters like this one are found on most U.S.-manufactured cruising boats. (Courtesy of Raritan Engineering)

Water Heaters

By modern standards, an onboard water heater is a relatively simple device; thus they've been popular on cruising sailboats for at least 30 years. Installing a water heater is certainly one of the more common DIY retrofits, and on most new boats they now come as standard equipment. As with pressure pumps, however, having a water heater aboard makes it much easier to waste fresh water. Hot showers always last longer than cold ones, plus much water is wasted simply waiting for hot water to reach a tap, whether you are showering, washing dishes, or simply washing your face and hands.

U.S.-manufactured boats commonly use tanktype heaters, often referred to as calorifiers, which heat water two different ways. The heater's integral insulated tank, which can keep its contents hot for about 36 hours, contains both an AC electric heating coil and a passive coil plumbed to the propulsion engine's cooling system. Hot cooling water from the engine circulates through the passive coil every time the engine runs, thus heating the water in the tank. On some units extra plumbing is required to divert

some part of the engine cooling flow, lest it make the water in the heater's tank dangerously hot. Capacity in most cases is 5 or 6 gallons, though much larger tanks are available.

Calorifiers are usually teed into freshwater-cooled engines, with runs leading to and from the heater before the cooling water reaches the engine's heat exchanger. They can also be plumbed to raw-watercooled engines, and in this case the heater's coil should be flushed annually with fresh water to prevent salt buildup inside. In most cases, only 30 minutes of engine running time is needed to heat the water in the heater's tank. As to the electric side of the system, the AC coil in a tank-type heater in fact draws a tremendous amount of power. Unless a boat has large battery banks, it rarely makes sense to heat water off an AC inverter. Usually the AC heater is used only when plugged into shore power, or when a generator is running. On many older boats with retrofitted water heaters the AC coil is never connected and only the calorifier is used.

Another type of water heater normally seen only on European boats are on-demand gas heaters. Often used in European homes, these small bulkhead-mounted devices have electric ignitions that fire a gas jet that instantly heats water passing through the unit whenever a connected hot-water tap is opened. Gas heaters take up less room than calorifiers, as no tank is needed, and are easier to install, assuming a boat already has a gas system aboard. An extra gas line and hot and cold connections to the boat's fresh-water system are all that are required. It is also easier to fine-tune a gas heater's output water temperature, as you need only turn a knob to adjust the amount of gas feeding the ignited jet.

Gas water heaters are shunned in the United States because they do not have sealed combustion chambers with separate air intakes and exhausts leading outside the boat. The fear is prolonged use inside a poorly ventilated boat cabin may lead to a buildup of deadly carbon monoxide fumes. Gas cooking stoves and ovens also have open combustion chambers, but Americans never seem too concerned about using these on their boats. It is assumed that stoves and ovens are used in a properly ventilated cabin and are monitored by their users. There is in fact no reason why an on-demand water heater cannot be used the same way. As long as it does not run for extended periods (which is unlikely) in a sealed space, a gas on-demand water heater poses little danger.

Watermakers

For centuries one of the primary factors limiting any vessel's cruising range has been its water storage capacity. In recent years the advent of compact desalinators, or watermakers, that turn salt water into potable fresh water has eliminated this constraint. Watermakers have transformed ocean sailing, for both racers and cruisers, as they make it possible to embark on long voyages in boats with small water tanks. Racing sailors like to exploit this to reduce weight on their boats. Prudent cruisers should still favor boats with larger water tanks, just in case the watermaker ever breaks down. Meanwhile they can enjoy the luxury of taking long showers in the middle of nowhere.

Tech-savvy sailors like to say watermakers are simple machines, but this is true only in an abstract sense. The principle is easy to understand: salt water is driven through a membrane so fine it can pass water, but not salt or other impurities (such as bacteria, minerals, or viruses). In practice there are many complications, the most important being that water must be pumped through the membrane at high pressure, on the order of 600 to 900 pounds per square inch (compared to just 40 psi for a common pressure pump). Pumps capable of doing this need lots of power and are finicky. Small interruptions in their feed-water supply can cause cavitation that quickly disables them. To assure a steady feed-water flow, a watermaker should have

its own dedicated through-hull inlet. Alternatively, competing raw-water-consuming systems sharing the inlet must be shut down while the watermaker is running to ensure no back pressure is created. Most systems also have a booster pump to help push the feed water through various prefilters up to the high-pressure pump. All fittings and plumbing runs leading to and from the high-pressure pump must also be exceptionally strong, as any serious breach under this much pressure can be dangerous.

Prefiltering is necessary to remove particles and contaminants that might foul or damage the sensitive membrane. There may be as many as four or five of these, including a special plankton filter and an oil-water separator. If you scrupulously avoid running a watermaker anywhere the feed water may be impure, such as in a harbor or silty anchorage, the number of prefilters can be decreased. Many cautious cruisers, as a rule, only run their watermakers while sailing on the open ocean. At a minimum, any system should have at least a raw-water strainer and a 20-micron filter between the raw-water inlet and the membrane. The membrane must be flushed clean even as the watermaker is running so as to remove the salt and minerals that build up as feed water runs through it. This flushing water, called brine water, constitutes the vast majority of the feed water brought up to pressure by the pump. In many systems, about 90% of the feed water is discharged overboard as brine, and only 10% becomes fresh product water that can be stored for use by the crew.

A watermaker should be carefully monitored while running. You need to keep an eye on operating pressure, as increasing pressure usually indicates fouling in prefilters or the membrane itself. This must be cleared to prevent damage to the system. To achieve maximum efficiency, pressure should be modulated depending on the salinity and temperature of the feed water. The salinity of the product water should also be monitored to prevent salty water from accidentally being pumped into a vessel's freshwater tanks. In a simple system you can do all this manually, but obviously you must be alert and attentive. More sophisticated systems have automated devices that can divert salty product water away from storage tanks, adjust operating pressure to suit feed-water salinity and temperature, and shut everything down when the operating pressure gets too high or low. Such features make a watermaker easier to operate, but they are expensive, require additional plumbing, and add extra potential failure points to what is already a fairly complex machine.

Watermakers also need ongoing maintenance. Membranes should be back-flushed with fresh water on a periodic basis (again, some machines will do this

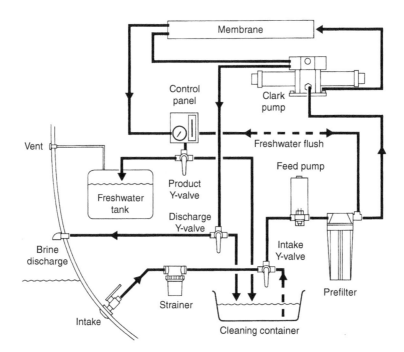

This is an example of a relatively simple watermaker installation involving a system manually back-flushed by changing valve positions. More complex systems have more prefilters, automatic backflushing, salinity probes, etc. (Drawing by Jim Sollers)

automatically), and if a watermaker is idle for more than a week its membrane must be "pickled" in biocide to prevent the growth of nasty organisms. The membrane should also be cleaned periodically with both an acid solution, to dissolve mineral deposits, and an alkali solution, to kill any festering bio-organisms.

In terms of power consumption, you generally must run either an AC generator or a propulsion engine to support a watermaker while it is operating. Units can be driven directly off an engine, but the side pull on a belt-driven high-pressure pump can create vibrations that will make the pump unhappy.

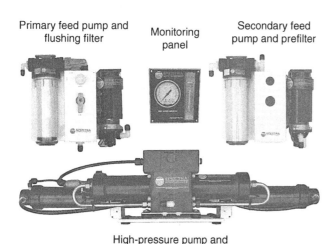

Primary feed pump and flushing filter   Monitoring panel   Secondary feed pump and prefilter

High-pressure pump and membrane housing

Components of a modern high-capacity marine water-maker system. (Courtesy of Spectra Watermachines)

Most manufacturers therefore recommend only electric pumps be used. High-output units capable of producing 15 gallons or more of fresh water in an hour normally run on AC power. Typical 12-volt DC units range from low-output machines producing just 1.5 gallons an hour on a 4-amp power draw (these conceivably could run for short periods off a battery bank alone) to relatively high-output machines producing up to 15 gallons an hour on an 18- to 20-amp draw. Some more sophisticated machines have energy-recovery systems that dramatically improve efficiency, but these as a rule are single-pump units that cannot support multiple prefilters, thus can run only in clean water. They are also quite complicated and are, on average, about half again as expensive as conventional units.

The bottom line is fairly clear: for sophisticated long-term or liveaboard cruisers who sail energy-intensive boats and are willing to operate and maintain complex machinery, a watermaker may make sense and can dramatically improve onboard living standards. For other more casual cruisers, or for bare-bones long-term cruisers, watermakers are usually more trouble than they're worth.

COOKING STOVES AND OVENS

Cooking is a fundamental requirement that fortunately can be accomplished with relatively basic equipment. Compared to many other modern boat systems, even the fanciest cooking stoves and ovens are simple to operate and troubleshoot. They are usually described in terms of the fuel they burn, but fuel type is probably less important than the physical disposition of the stove itself.

The most important distinction is between stoves used only when a boat is at rest and those used while underway. If you want to cook anything while sailing, you need a properly mounted gimballed stove. Ideally, it should be gimballed in all four directions, but this is very rare. At a minimum, on a monohull it should be mounted and gimballed athwartships to compensate for heeling and rolling. There should also be enough swinging room so that the stove, when loaded with pots and pans, can pivot freely without being brought up short. To swing properly, the stove should be counterweighted at the bottom so that its motion is smooth and even. As mentioned in Chapter 6 in the discussion on galleys, the stove should have rails and potholders, and it is best if the cook can tend it without standing directly in front of it.

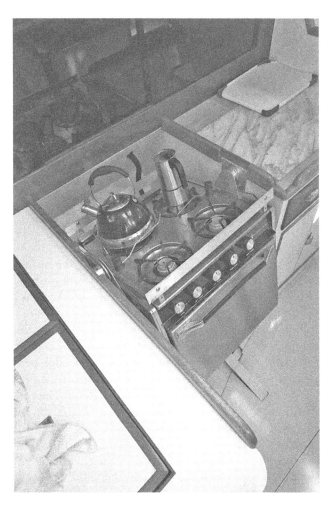

A gimballed propane stove and oven in action. There is enough clearance here so pots and kettles aren't knocked over when the stove swings back and forth. Note also the rails and potholders to keep items on the stove top in place.

If you never intend to cook while sailing, a fixed stove is perfectly acceptable. These are often found on small trailer-sailers and pocket cruisers and also on catamarans of all types and sizes. If you cook a lot at sea on a cat, however, you will definitely appreciate a gimballed stove, but these unfortunately are also very rare. Again, as on a monohull, a stove gimballed in four directions would be best, perhaps even more so, given the quirkiness of a cat's motion. If a cat's stove is gimballed on only one axis, fore and aft is probably preferable, as cats tend to pitch more than they roll and heel.

Gas

There are two different types of cooking gas used on board modern cruising boats. The first, known as liquefied petroleum gas (LPG), is currently the most popular of all marine stove fuels and includes both propane, which is widely available in the United States and other parts of the world, and butane, which is available throughout Europe. Propane and butane can be used interchangeably to fuel the same stoves, but they do come in different containers with different sorts of fittings. Bluewater cruisers sailing abroad therefore sometimes need to use adapters to get butane into propane bottles (or vice versa), but normally have no trouble finding some type of LPG fuel to burn aboard their boats.

The other type of cooking gas is compressed natural gas (CNG). Unlike LPG, CNG is lighter than air and rises rather than sinks when venting into the atmosphere. This makes it safer to use, as leaking fuel will not gather in bilges and other low spots on a boat. CNG, however, can be hard to find. It is available in the northeastern United States, thus CNG stoves are sometimes found on boats that cruise exclusively in that part of the country. Outside the Northeast, however, resupplying is a problem, as CNG and LPG fuel cannot be used interchangeably.

Because LPG fuel is heavier than air and does not dissipate upward, any marine LPG installation must be very safe. A gas explosion can wreak terrible damage on a boat and will cause serious injuries, if not fatalities, if crew are aboard at the time. Different safety standards are promulgated in the United States and Europe, but they agree as to general principles. First, gas bottles should never be stored near machinery or inside any living space. On most boats they are stored in either deck lockers or cockpit lockers that are sealed off from the rest of the boat and have large vents at the bottom so leaking gas can easily escape. Vent lines should lead straight overboard (with no traps or low points) to an outlet that is well above the waterline at all angles of heel and is not near any engine exhaust, ventilator,

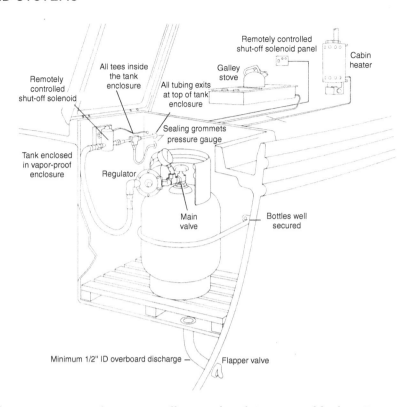

A properly installed propane system showing a well-secured tank in a vented locker. (Drawing by Jim Sollers)

or air intake. On some boats gas bottles are stored on deck in the open air, which is fine as long as the bottles are well secured. In the galley there should be a safety shutoff switch or valve that can be operated without reaching over the stove top. On American boats there is usually an electric solenoid valve inside the gas-bottle compartment that is operated remotely via a switch in the galley. European boats commonly have a manual valve directly under the stove.

If you burn LPG fuel on your boat, it is wise to install an LPG sniffer. This sensor automatically sounds an alarm and/or trips a solenoid switch if it detects LPG in the ambient air. On the stove itself, there should be a flame-failure device that automatically shuts down the flow of gas to any burner where a flame is not present. This prevents gas from flowing into the boat if a burner's flame blows out, as happens when a stove is under an open deck hatch.

The gas line running between the gas bottles and stove should be either copper tubing or special gas-resistant flexible hose. The lines should be well supported with no kinks, sharp corners, or chafe points, and all holes where lines pierce decks, bulkheads, or compartment walls should be well sealed.

Kerosene and Alcohol

Before gas became popular about 25 years ago, the most commonly used cooking fuels on cruising boats

were kerosene and alcohol. They are now discredited as being fussy and inconvenient to deal with, as well as slow and inefficient in terms of the heat they produce, but there are still many cruisers using kerosene and alcohol stoves and ovens. They do have their quirks, but once you are used to them they provide reliable service.

In traditional kerosene and alcohol stoves the liquid fuel is first pressurized inside its storage tank so that it flows smoothly to the burner when the burner is opened. The tanks are relatively small, mounted either remotely or as an integral part of the stove itself. Little pressure is required, about 20 to 30 psi, which is created with a small manual piston pump. Some cruisers retrofit Schrader tire valves on their tanks and use small bicycle pumps instead. Before it is lit a burner must be preheated so that the liquid fuel vaporizes as it flows out the burner's jets. The preheating process is a bit fiddly, but is easily mastered. First you fill a small cup under the burner with a little pool of alcohol, which you then ignite. After the alcohol burns off, the burner can then be lit. If too little alcohol is used the fuel coming out the burner doesn't vaporize completely and spits and flares up after the burner is lit; if too much is used, it overflows or slops out of the preheating cup and makes a smelly, potentially volatile mess. With kerosene stoves it is necessary to carry a small separate supply of alcohol just for preheating burners. With alcohol stoves, you need only open the burner briefly and let some liquid alcohol flow out into the cup.

Once lit, a pressure kerosene stove works almost as well as an LPG stove, producing nearly 20,000 British thermal units (Btu) of heat per pound of fuel burned compared to just over 21,500 Btu for LPG. Kerosene is also less expensive, costing two-thirds as much on a per-Btu basis. Alcohol, meanwhile, is nearly five times more costly than LPG on a per-Btu basis, producing only about 12,000 Btu per pound of fuel. In practice, unless you do a lot of cooking, these differences are not terribly significant. Certainly they are more important to liveaboard sailors than they are to casual coastal cruisers.

Pressure alcohol and kerosene stoves are still available, but they are increasingly rare, and most cruisers using them have inherited older examples from previous boatowners. They are relatively easy to maintain. Most problems stem from using poor quality fuel, which causes the burners to foul and plug up, in which case they must be disassembled and cleaned.

Another type of cooking device now popular on small boats are non-pressurized alcohol stoves and ovens, which are very simple and require almost no maintenance. The burners on these units consist of small fuel canisters filled with absorbent asbestos

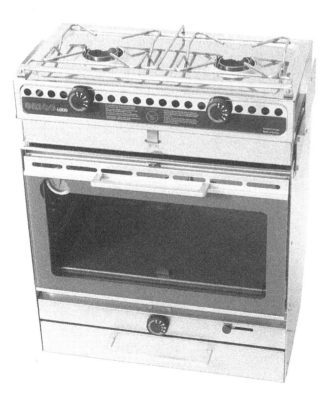

Non-pressurized alcohol stove and ovens are increasingly the most popular alternative to propane cooking systems onboard. (Courtesy of Dometic Corp.)

batting. To work the stove you need only pour alcohol into a canister, then set a match to the asbestos batting inside. The flame is controlled with a simple pivoting hatch that slides back and forth across the top of the canister. As long as you don't pour too much alcohol into the canister, there is nothing that can go wrong. Eventually the batting in the canister becomes partly saturated with water moisture, which reduces a burner's capacity, but this is easy to remedy. Pour a little gasoline in the canister and light it off (very carefully, of course) in an open area off the boat, and the moisture quickly evaporates. Alternatively, you just buy new canisters.

Kerosene is easy to find anywhere in the world. Stove alcohol is reputedly difficult to obtain in many places, but I have never had any trouble finding it. Good quality denatured alcohol that burns well in stoves can be obtained in any hardware store anywhere in the United States. During a two-year cruise of the North Atlantic on a boat with a pressure alcohol stove, I was always able to buy stove-quality alcohol when I needed it, including in the Cape Verde Islands off the coast of West Africa.

Diesel

Cooking with diesel fuel makes a lot of sense, as most cruisers carry a large supply anyway to feed their propulsion engines. Not having to carry another type of fuel just to cook with greatly simplifies provisioning. Diesel is also very efficient, delivering nearly as much heat per pound of fuel consumed as LPG, but costing only a third as much on a per-Btu basis.

Still, diesel stoves and ovens on recreational sailboats are comparatively rare. There are pressure stoves that operate in the same manner as pressure kerosene stoves, but these are hard to find. The more common type are non-pressurized drip-pot stoves that have a metering valve to deliver fuel, via either gravity or a small fuel pump, to a simple drip-pot burner. Drip-pot stoves must have fixed chimneys and/or flues to vent exhaust fumes outside the cabin, thus must be fixed in place and cannot be gimballed. These stoves are also quite heavy and are normally made of cast iron. They're slow to warm up and cool down and throw off a great deal of heat once they're going. They are usually found on large boats that cruise in colder climates, as they serve well as both cabin heaters and cooking stoves. In temperate or tropical climates, however, a diesel drip-pot can make a boat's interior too warm for comfort. Many cruisers with drip-pot stoves therefore carry portable alcohol or kerosene stoves to cook with when sailing in warmer waters.

As with kerosene and alcohol, fuel quality is important. If poor quality diesel is burned in a stove,

Most diesel-fueled stoves and ovens must be fixed in place to accommodate vents leading outside the boat; they also throw off tremendous amounts of heat and hence are found mostly on cold-weather cruising boats. (Courtesy of Dickinson Marine)

or if the draft on the stove is not properly adjusted, a great deal of soot is created, which can make quite a mess on deck around the chimney. The stove itself will also need frequent cleaning. Kerosene can also be burned in drip-pot stoves and is cleaner than diesel, but it too makes soot if fuel quality is poor and/or the stove is poorly adjusted.

REFRIGERATION

Many cruisers now believe refrigeration is essential on a cruising boat, but you can in fact live comfortably on a boat with no refrigeration whatsoever. Cruisers once of course relied solely on block ice to keep food cool. Even if you can't lay hands on ice, it still isn't hard to eat well relying solely on foods that need not be kept cold. This is important to bear in mind, as refrigerators are by far the largest energy consumers on most cruising boats. Though they are more reliable than they used to be, they also do break down from time to time, often in ways that few laypeople can comprehend. If you can cruise without refrigeration, you can run your boat much more cheaply and simply than would otherwise be the case.

Cold-Box Insulation and Construction

If you decide you must have refrigeration—or even if you decide just to use block ice instead—you want your cold box to be well insulated. An expensive high-powered refrigeration unit installed in a poorly insulated box won't work nearly as well as an inexpensive weaker unit installed in a well-insulated box. As far as ice goes, it means the difference between ice lasting a day or two compared to a week or more.

Normally some type of foam is used to insulate cold boxes; at least 4 to 6 inches is needed to be effective. Foam conducts heat more easily as it absorbs moisture, and on older boats you'll often find cold boxes with foam insulation that has become soggy over time. On much older boats you may even find boxes insulated with cork, which is very absorbent. On boats like this, before you install or upgrade a refrigeration system, you should first rip out the old box and put in a new one with proper insulation. When selecting foam insulation, you should favor more moisture-resistant foams over more heat-resistant ones, as the former normally perform better over the long-term. Two-part poured foams, for example, are very heat-resistant (*if* they are carefully poured with no voids) and were once often used to insulate cold boxes. But they readily absorb moisture, and once they get wet are not very effective. Currently the best foams to use are urethane board and Blueboard polystyrene. Blueboard is slightly less heat-resistant than urethane board, but is considerably more moisture-resistant and also less expensive.

Vacuum insulation panels are the fancy high-tech option and are both highly effective and expensive. These special structural panels have no air inside, thus conduct heat very poorly, just like a vacuum flask or Thermos bottle. With vacuum panels you can build a cold box with much thinner insulation walls, so the box can be much bigger inside. Six

Modern vacuum insulation panels provide maximum cold-box insulation while taking up minimum space. This thin panel insulates as well as 6 inches of foam. (Courtesy of Refrigeration Parts Solution)

inches of foam is nearly as effective, however, so unless space is critical vacuum panels may not be worth the extra expense.

To minimize condensation and help keep the insulation dry, there should be a ventilated air space between a box's insulation and any surrounding structures or joinery. The outer face of the insulation should also have some sort of radiant barrier (such as aluminum foil) applied to it. Any drain line leading from the bottom of the box should have a valve or U-trap in it to prevent cold air from escaping. (Unless you're using ice to keep the box cold, a drain shouldn't really be necessary in the first place.) Finally, any access door or hatch should have an effective double seal. Poor door seals are by far the most common way for heat to invade a refrigerated space.

Types of Marine Refrigeration

The marine refrigeration market is competitive and evolving rapidly. Systems can cost anywhere from under $1,000 to over $10,000, and power requirements likewise vary a great deal. Refrigeration normally represents from 50% to 75% of the total energy load on an active cruising boat, so systems must be carefully matched to a boat's total energy capacity. Improperly supported refrigeration is the number one battery-killer on all types of cruising boats. It is prudent, therefore, to research the market carefully before selecting a new system. If you've inherited an old system, educate yourself as to its capabilities and power requirements before running it a great deal.

The threshold distinction between systems is whether the cooling unit in the cold box is a holding plate or an evaporator plate. With a holding-plate system the refrigerator runs infrequently, usually just once a day. The holding plate contains a special eutectic solution that is frozen solid at a temperature well below freezing, absorbing heat from the box as it slowly thaws. Once it defrosts, the refrigerator runs again and the holding plate is refrozen. With an evaporator plate the refrigerator constantly cycles on and off to maintain a steady cool temperature inside the box. These constant-cycling systems, as they are often called, are similar to common household refrigerators.

Holding-plate systems are attractive in that they only consume power for discrete periods of time. During that time, however, energy demand is very high. Also, no matter how powerful a refrigerator's compressor is, there are limits to how quickly a holding plate can be frozen. Realistically, a holding-plate fridge must run hard for at least an hour every day; in warmer climates it is more like two. Temperature variations within the box are also quite high, and this

may interfere with the preservation of certain sorts of food. A constant-cycling system, by comparison, requires a much less powerful compressor, thus consumes much less power at any given moment, but must receive power on an ongoing basis. They are also less expensive than holding-plate systems, and there is little temperature variation within the cold box as long as the system keeps running.

The power source is another important distinction. Engine-driven systems, where a refrigerator's compressor is belted straight off a propulsion engine, are normally only mated to holding plates. These place no demand on the electrical system and make a lot of sense on cruising boats where the engine is running one or two hours a day in any event. If you have to run the engine just to drive the fridge compressor, however, they may not be very efficient. Also, having to run an engine to power a fridge while tied to a dock bristling with shore-power outlets seems silly. Engine-driven fridges are therefore not popular with cruisers who spend a lot of time in marinas. They are also quite expensive. But if you rarely spend time at a dock, and running an electrical fridge requires a major upgrade of your entire electrical system, an engine-driven system may be cost-effective after all.

Electric fridges run on either 12-volt DC or 110-volt AC power and can be mated with either holding plates or evaporator plates. The cheapest alternative, in terms of acquisition costs, are common domestic constant-cycling AC systems. But once away from a shore-power connection these require a constantly running AC generator, thus are normally found only on large superyachts. An AC holding-plate system is a more realistic alternative, particularly on boats that run an AC generator for a couple of hours every day to service other loads. Again, however, if it's necessary to run a generator just to run the fridge, these units may not be very efficient. Because of their large power demands, it is not possible to run any AC fridge off an inverter thus these systems are only suitable on boats with AC generators.

Electric DC fridges are generally the most popular option because they allow the most flexibility. As long as a boat has a battery charger, a DC system can run off shore power or off an AC generator. It can also be fed by a propulsion engine via an alternator, or it can be fed with wind and/or solar power. The key ingredient, however, is a suitably sized DC battery bank. Precise requirements will vary, but generally speaking you need a house bank with a capacity of at least 400 amp-hours to feed a DC fridge as well as other common DC loads. This can be adjusted downward on boats with constant-cycling DC fridges that stay in cool or temperate climates and are often plugged into shore power or have a lot of

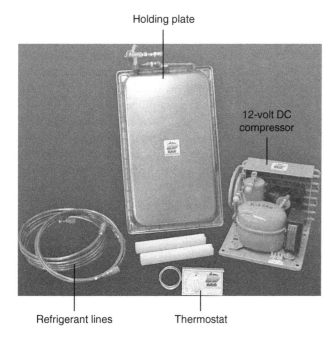

Holding plate

12-volt DC
compressor

Refrigerant lines   Thermostat

*DC constant-cycling refrigeration systems offer the
most flexibility but must be supported by appropriately
sized battery banks. (Courtesy of Technautics Inc.)*

wind and/or solar support. Boats with DC holding
plates where the fridge's intermittent load is usually
only imposed when an engine or generator is running can also survive with less battery capacity. But
on any boat that stays off the grid for long periods
and cruises in warmer climates, and particularly
on boats where DC holding plates are often fed off
unsupported batteries, the required battery capacity
may escalate as high as 600 amp-hours or more.

It is possible to blend all these different systems
together in various ways. Two entirely different systems can be installed side by side, cooling the same
cold box, or different ones; different electric and
engine driven compressors can be mated to the same
holding plate; different AC and DC compressors can
be mated to the same evaporator plate; and so on.
Such hybrid variations are obviously expensive, but
they also allow for much customization depending
on individual use patterns and requirements.

One last factor to consider with any fridge system is whether its condenser, the critical component
that dissipates heat extracted from the cold box, is
air-cooled or water-cooled. Air-cooled condensers
are both simpler and more common, but in tropical
climates, where ambient air temperatures in closed
compartments in a boat can rise over 100°F, they may
become dysfunctional. One solution to this problem is to improve ventilation around the condenser.
Another is to use a water-cooled condenser instead.
These usually require small pumps to circulate cooling

water, in which case the pump increases the system's
total power consumption. More recently, however,
passive through-hull and keel-cooler condensers have
become available. Through-hull condensers require
that a boat stay in motion, either moving through
the water or at least rocking a bit on a mooring, in
order that heated water inside the through-hull fitting is continually exchanged for cooler water. Keel-
cooler condensers, meanwhile, must be scrubbed
clean from time to time and also don't work well
in cold water.

CLIMATE CONTROL

In an ideal universe all cruisers would sail in perfectly temperate climates, padding about in sandals
and T-shirts, worrying only about the wind and
occasional bouts of precipitation. Seasonal coastal
cruisers based in temperate zones and bluewater voyagers who never stray too far south or north at the
wrong times of year can indeed spend little time fretting about whether they are too hot or cold aboard
their boats. Many others, however, are either not so
lucky, or may willingly cruise in less clement locales.
Depending on their circumstances and preferences,
such sailors may conclude that having some sort of
climate-control system aboard their boat is worth
the bother.

Cabin Heaters

For some cruisers cabin heaters are mandatory equipment and are much more useful than many other trivial
conveniences. With a small heater aboard, a seasonal
coastal sailor who might otherwise stop cruising at
summer's end can keep sailing a month or two longer.
He or she can also launch earlier and try cruising in
the spring. Over the course of a lifetime, this can add
up to several extra years of cruising. Bluewater cruisers, meanwhile, if they have effective, reliable heaters
aboard, may feel emboldened to visit unique destina-
tions in chilly high-latitude cruising grounds.

The simplest heaters are stand-alone units that
burn solid fuels such as wood and/or coal. For traditional sailors there is something inherently attractive
about this, but in fact solid fuels are not too practical.
They are bulky and messy to store, plus they leave
behind lots of ash that must be disposed of after they
are burned. Those cruising on a shoestring may be
attracted by the fact that wood at least can be scav-
enged for free, but to regularly create large amounts
of heat you need a large supply. For the most part,
solid-fuel heaters make sense only on boats heated
intermittently for brief periods of time.

Stand-alone heaters burning diesel or gas are far
more popular. Diesel heaters have drip-pot burners

with metering valves identical to those in the drip-pot diesel cooking stoves discussed earlier. Such heaters are fed via gravity or a small electric pump from either a small day-tank (in which case kerosene can be burned instead) or the main engine's fuel tank. Smaller units are bulkhead mounted; larger ones are floor mounted. Gas heaters (which usually burn propane gas) are normally all bulkhead mounted. All these stand-alone units are fixed in place and are vented via chimneys or flues to the boat's exterior. This is particularly important for heaters, because they are often left burning for extended periods, perhaps even when crew are sleeping. An exhaust vent greatly reduces the amount of condensation created inside the boat due to fuel combustion and obviates the risk of carbon monoxide poisoning. Most units, however, draw their combustion air from inside the boat thus there is still some risk of oxygen depletion unless the cabin has sufficient ventilation to replace air consumed by the heater. There are a few so-called balanced-draft units available, where all combustion air is drawn from outside the boat. These are more expensive and more complicated to install, but perform better because they are less likely to suffer from downdrafts or backdrafts and you need not vent cold air into the cabin to keep them burning.

The primary disadvantage of any stand-alone heater, whatever type of fuel it burns, is that it only heats the area of the boat where it is installed, which is normally the main saloon. To circulate heated air around the boat, you can run small electric fans. The larger the boat, however, the harder this becomes, and even on small boats it's never really possible to get warm air everywhere.

You can solve this problem by installing central heating, where one central furnace circulates heat to a number of heating elements situated around the boat. Central heating, however, is much more expensive (costing thousands instead of hundreds of dollars) and is more complex. The furnaces on most of these units burn diesel drawn from the main fuel tank, are controlled with thermostats, have vents to

A bulkhead-mounted propane cabin heater with a cabin fan mounted above it to help move heated air around the boat.

inhale combustion air and exhale exhaust fumes, and now usually have some sort of digital processing capability that shuts them down automatically if malfunctions occur. They move heat around the boat in two different ways. Forced-air heaters simply blow hot air through large 4-inch ducts that snake around the boat feeding registers in each cabin. Most

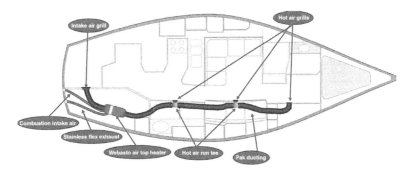

In this typical forced-air central heating system, warm air is delivered to all parts of the boat, but the ducting takes up a great deal of space. (Courtesy of Sure Marine)

draw their "make-up air" (i.e., the air they are heating, as opposed to combustion air) from inside and outside the boat so as to increase the temperature of the make-up air while reducing recirculation of interior moisture and odors. Coolant heaters, also called hydronic heaters, circulate heated water around the boat through a dedicated plumbing system to a series of radiators or fan heaters.

Coolant heaters are more expensive and more complicated than forced-air heaters, but are also much more sophisticated. The flexible coolant hoses are easier to install than the bulky ducting required for forced-air heat. The plumbing can also be segregated into zones so that different areas of the boat can run on different thermostats and thus can be kept at different temperatures. Even better, coolant heaters can be used to heat domestic water if desired and can be plumbed into the propulsion engine's cooling system. This allows water from the central heating system to preheat the engine so it starts more easily in cold weather; it also allows the engine to heat the boat while it is running without help from the central heater's burner.

The primary drawback of any central heating system compared to a stand-alone heater, aside from the added expense and complexity, is that they require electricity to operate (anywhere from an amp or two to over 15 amps, depending on the system) and take up a lot more interior space. On the whole, therefore, they are best suited to large energy-intensive boats. I have seen boats as small as 35 feet with retrofitted forced-air systems, but the benefits of more evenly distributed heat are negligible on a boat this size and a lot of valuable storage space is lost to the installation, particularly the ducting.

Air-Conditioning

An air conditioner is little more than a refrigeration system applied to an entire boat's interior. They are extraordinarily power hungry, much more so than refrigerators. Unless you are hooked up to shore power or are running an AC generator, you normally can't run an air conditioner without devastating your battery bank. On most cruising boats, fortunately, it is entirely unnecessary. No matter how hot the climate, as long as you are anchored out or lying on a mooring in open water, you can usually get enough air flowing through your boat to stay comfortable. You may have to run a few small fans from time to time, and you may not actually be cool, but you will not be suffering.

Still, air-conditioning has become ever more popular. The simplest, least expensive machines are stand-alone portable units that are installed in an open deck hatch much like a household air conditioner is slotted into an open window. Just like

Portable marine air conditioners can be temporarily installed in deck hatches when needed and stored away when they are not. (Courtesy of Dometic Corp.)

portable household units, these are air cooled and require no modifications to the boat. All you need do is drop one in a hatch and plug it into an AC power supply. These machines are perfect for those cruisers who want to air-condition their boats only on an occasional basis when tied to a dock in some hot and stuffy marina. Really the only drawback to these units is that they must be removed and stored somewhere when the boat is underway.

The next most complex machines are so-called self-contained marine air conditioners. These are also stand-alone units in that they operate in discrete locations, but unlike portable units must be permanently installed with raw-water cooled condensers. This requires substantial modifications to a boat, but not so much that a retrofit is impossible. All the machinery is mounted together on a single chassis that can be installed in a locker or cabinet with a short duct leading to a nearby register. The more complicated bit is the water cooling, as this requires an underwater intake through-hull fitting for the cooling water with a strainer to filter out debris, a dedicated electric pump, plumbing runs to and from the air conditioner, plus an overboard outlet fitting at least 3 to 5 inches above the boat's waterline. To fully air-condition a large boat it may be necessary to install more than one unit, in which case multiple units can run off the same cooling circuit.

Central air-conditioning systems are considerably more complex and expensive and are normally installed only on new boats, as retrofits are rarely feasible. The most basic systems have a central water-cooled condenser and evaporator mounted together in the same location with large air ducts pumping cold air to several different outlet registers around the boat. There are also distributed-refrigerant systems, where a single central water-cooled condenser feeds refrigerant to several small evaporators around the boat, each equipped with its own fan and outlet register.

These systems take up less space, as the multiple refrigerant lines are much smaller than a network of air ducts. Unfortunately, the great extent of the refrigerant plumbing also complicates installation and maintenance, as the system cannot be precharged with refrigerant and has a much greater potential for developing leaks. The most sophisticated machines are coolant or hydronic systems similar in principle to the coolant heaters described above. Here a central water-cooled condenser cools water instead of air, and the cold water is piped around the boat to different radiators, each with a fan. Plumbing runs for the water take up little space; plus it is possible to have different zone controls allowing different temperatures to be maintained in different parts of the boat.

All these systems, both stand-alone and central, require large amounts of AC power to operate. There are also some small DC systems with small evaporators tied into DC holding-plate refrigerators that can provide a modest amount of air-conditioning capacity when the DC battery bank is being charged via shore power, an engine alternator, or a generator, but these are not yet common. Note, too, that many water-cooled systems can be configured with a reverse-cycle feature where the refrigerant flow is reversed and heat is extracted from the raw water and is used to heat rather than cool the boat. For any cruiser seeking to both heat and air-condition a boat, this obviously is very attractive, though heating capacity is limited to some extent by ambient raw-water temperatures. The most effective reverse-cycle systems are those coupled to hydronic central air conditioners, as it is a relatively simple matter to add

a supplemental diesel heater to heat the circulating water when raw-water temperatures are too low.

ELECTRONICS

Of all systems now found onboard cruising boats none are evolving more dynamically than marine electronics. Advances in digital data-processing technology, as well as in communications media, have transformed what was once a relatively discrete category of onboard equipment into what promises to be an interconnected category embracing nearly all other systems. The best I can do in the context of a book like this is provide a quick snapshot of the current state of affairs. Things will have changed by the time you read this book, and any electronics you install will be outdated by the time you have learned to use them to their fullest potential.

My advice is to study the electronics market closely before acquiring equipment and err on the side of simplicity. One big advantage of waiting to buy is that the gear is constantly improving and getting cheaper. As to resources to consult, the best electronics writer I know is Ben Ellison. Ben follows developments in the industry on a day-to-day basis and is constantly evaluating new gear in his lab and on his boat. He has written no books, but writes regularly for several magazines and maintains a very current marine electronics blog at www.panbo.com.

In general terms, the most significant trend in marine electronics is networking. Where once each piece of electronics equipment was isolated, delivering discrete data for a skipper to process and relate to other pieces of data as he or she saw fit, now different pieces of equipment communicate with each other and share data. The first universal networking

Twelve-volt DC central air-conditioning systems are not yet as common as AC-powered systems, but work well on boats with modest air-conditioning demands. (Courtesy of Dometic Corp.)

A modern multifunction control unit presenting 3-D electronic cartography plus radar and sonar data all on the same screen. The networking and integration of multiple systems is only just beginning. (Courtesy of SAIL Magazine and Furuno)

protocol, promulgated by the National Marine Electronics Association (NMEA) was NMEA 0180, released in 1980. It was soon supplanted by NMEA 0183, which remains the most common standard, though this is rapidly changing. By modern standards NMEA 0183 is quite crude, allowing just one piece of equipment to transmit data at a time to a limited number of receivers. It is now being supplanted by NMEA 2000, a "multi-talker, multi-listener" protocol, where all equipment on a network can send and receive data simultaneously. Meanwhile, various manufacturers have developed different proprietary networking systems of their own.

One important aspect of NMEA 2000 is that it has been developed as a "plug-and-play" system, where all equipment in the network tees off one central power-and-data cable through universal interchangeable connectors. This greatly simplifies network creation, as it is no longer necessary to individually wire every piece of equipment in a network to every other piece. Nor is it necessary to individually wire each piece of equipment back to a power distribution panel. At some point in the future, once the distributed-power systems described earlier in this chapter come into their own, it will be possible to create a data network that encompasses every piece of electrically powered equipment on a cruising boat. Such a network can act as a central nervous system, enabling manufacturers to incorporate any number of automatic operating and diagnostic features into systems they create.

Navigation

In the past all aspects of navigating a sailing vessel involved simple tools—a leadline for measuring water depth, a compass for keeping courses and taking bearings, parallel rulers and dividers for marking off courses and positions on paper charts, and perhaps a taffrail log for measuring speed and distance traveled. Even the mysterious sextant is in fact a relatively facile device that does nothing more than measure angles. Today all these tools have been supplanted by complex electronic devices that make navigating a modern cruising boat as easy as playing a video game. Even dedicated traditional cruisers cannot ignore the convenience they offer.

Basic Sensors

The most important navigation sensor is the depth-sounder, which has been around for several decades. These are sonar devices that send pulses of acoustic energy down into the water from a transducer mounted in a boat's hull. By timing how long it takes each pulse to bounce off the bottom back to the transducer, the sounder can "sense" how deep the water is.

Most sailboats carry only simple numeric sounders, but more sophisticated sounders, called fish-finders, offer much more nuanced information. Fish-finders present a graphic display of the bottom under and behind the boat, which makes it possible to easily track contour trends. They also analyze reflected signals to give some sense of whether the bottom is hard or soft and whether certain reflections are instead from thermoclines in the water or intermediate obstacles, such as kelp, submerged debris, or fish. Though marketed primarily to fishermen, these devices are reasonably priced and can be useful to cruising sailors in evaluating anchorages and potential diving and snorkeling spots. The most advanced depth-sounders have forward-looking sonar, which scans down and forward at an angle of about 180 degrees. Some units can even paint a picture of the entire water column ahead of a boat, including floating objects. Such information is valuable, but forward-looking sounders thus far are prohibitively expensive and are normally found only on high-end cruising boats.

The next most useful sensor is probably a wind sensor, which is normally mounted at the top of a mast. These have two components—a small anemometer,

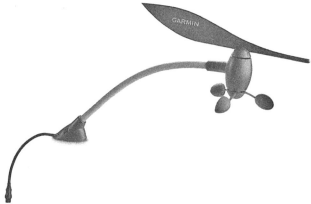

A pair of boat speed and depth transducers (top) and a masthead wind sensor incorporating a small vane and anemometer (bottom). (Courtesy of Airmar and Garmin)

which measures wind speed, and a small vane, which gauges wind direction. Though this information obviously can be perceived sensually by any discerning sailor, digital processing makes it possible to manipulate it in useful ways. By cross-referencing wind data with boat speed data, most wind displays can present values for both apparent and true wind, plus can calculate true tacking angles, all of which makes it easier to plan ahead when sailing is tactically complex, as when beating into a crowded harbor entrance. More important, wind data can now be sent to electronic autopilots that steer to apparent wind angles rather than simple compass courses, thus allowing the autopilot to follow wind shifts without human supervision.

The last standard nav sensor is the speed log. The most common units have little paddle wheels mounted in through-hull fittings that measure the speed at which water moves past a boat. Using this data they can also calculate the distance a boat has traveled. Because the sensor only measures water flow it cannot, however, account for speed variations caused by currents in the water. Most modern speed logs also incorporate thermometers that measure water temperature, which is useful when navigating along or across warm ocean currents such as the Gulf Stream, also when trying to find a nice place for a swim. One big drawback of conventional paddle-wheel logs is that they are easily fouled with marine growth and frequently must be cleared by hand in order to function properly. More sophisticated log sensors that measure boat speed sonically by pinging passing particles in the water are also now available and have no moving parts, thus cannot be fouled by growth. These transducers, however, are considerably more expensive, and according to some users do not yet provide entirely reliable data.

Position Finding and Charting

Starting in the 1970s land-based radio navigation systems such as Loran-C (in the U.S.) and Decca (in Europe) made it possible for recreational mariners to obtain reasonably accurate electronic position fixes within a few hundred miles from shore. In the 1980s the first satellite navigation systems became available. These were capable of obtaining fixes far from shore, but only sporadically, and were for the most part prohibitively expensive and were not widely adopted by cruising sailors. The first commercial Global Positioning System (GPS) receivers triangulating signals from a permanent constellation of geostationary satellites, which made it possible to continually obtain highly accurate fixes anywhere in the world, appeared in the early 1990s. Since then GPS receivers have become less expensive and more

accurate, with margins of error now of only a few feet, and this has inexorably transformed all aspects of modern navigation.

The impact of GPS on cruising has been enormous. Prior to 1990, any aspiring bluewater cruiser had little choice but to buy a sextant and learn to use it. After 1992, when the price of small GPS receivers dropped below $1,000, any sailor of relatively modest means capable of transferring latitude and longitude coordinates to a paper chart could navigate offshore all over the world with perfect confidence. This led many coastal cruisers who were intimidated by celestial navigation to embark on their first ocean voyages. Nowadays, with the advent of GPS chartplotters, which continually display a vessel's position on an accurate digital chart on a real-time basis, many aspiring coastal cruisers intimidated by maintaining plots on paper charts are now embarking on expeditions they once thought beyond them. On the one hand, any advocate of cruising as a sport must hail and embrace such enabling technology.

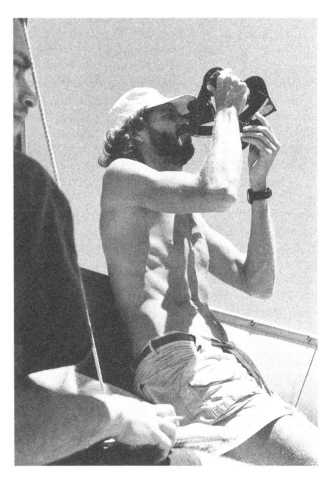

The author taking a noon sight with a sextant en route to the West Indies from Africa. Thanks to GPS you don't need to do this anymore, but you should still learn and practice traditional navigation techniques.

On the other hand, it is important to understand that the technology is not 100% reliable. Responsible cruisers should school themselves in traditional navigation techniques, should always carry traditional tools, and should be able to navigate their vessels even when their GPS receiver and/or chartplotter fails them.

Besides telling you where you are, accurate real-time position data can be used in any number of ways. For example, even a basic GPS receiver can calculate and display values for a vessel's actual speed and course over ground, as opposed to its relative speed and course through the water as revealed by a compass and speed log. By comparing the actual and relative values, the direction and speed of water currents can also be calculated. If a destination waypoint is created, a GPS unit can easily calculate the relative bearing to your destination on an ongoing basis, the time it will take to get there, and how fast you are moving toward it in absolute terms—a concept usually referred to as velocity made good, or VMG. This is particularly useful for sailors, who often must sail oblique routes to get where they are going. By comparing VMG values, it is easy to determine what route is most productive. GPS data can also be sent to autopilots, which can use it to steer directly to a destination waypoint, automatically compensating for any offsetting currents. If a series of GPS waypoints is linked together in a route, many autopilots can now follow the route without supervision, automatically making course changes where necessary. Finally, position data can be sent to communications devices, as discussed below.

Electronic cartography has magnified the impact of this technology. Once upon a time the fact that a chart could not be perfectly accurate (indeed, many "modern" charts are based on old inaccurate surveys) was not troublesome, as position-finding techniques were not accurate enough to expose a chart's deficiencies. With the advent of GPS this is no longer true. Charts based on old surveys (this includes both paper charts and early generations of electronic charts derived from them) are now the weak link in the navigation equation. But now anyone with an accurate depth-sounder and a GPS receiver also has the means to correct and perfect a chart. Since all government charts have been digitized and can now be downloaded online for free, private chart publishers have a great incentive to improve on those charts to justify charging money for their own products. As a result, privately published electronic charts of popular cruising grounds are increasingly more accurate and contain an astounding amount of detail, down to the exact location of marina toilets and garbage dumpsters. Publishers are not only conducting their own private surveys to improve chart accuracy, some

also accept cartographic data and corrections from customers using their products, who can collect and store the information automatically by interfacing their depth-sounders with their chartplotters. Indeed, some of the most advanced chart programs now available not only can present charts in a three-dimensional bathymetric format that makes it much easier to visualize bottom contours and features, they also can automatically correct themselves using real-time data collected from an interfaced depth-sounder (that data in turn having been automatically corrected for tidal variations).

And, of course, you can interface an electronic chart with more than just a depth-sounder. Connections to radar sets and weather data sources, for example, make it possible to create overlays displaying radar images or weather charts on top of a chart. The manipulation of weather data, in particular, is now quite advanced and several different weather-routing programs projecting optimum courses to sail given a current forecast are widely available. Chartplotters can also play a more active role in conning a vessel. Some autopilots, for example, can now read chart data and utilize it to automatically steer along a specific depth contour or to automatically change course to avert collisions with charted obstacles.

Communications

Advances in marine communications have been just as enormous as those in marine navigation, but are somewhat less significant, I would argue, because communications are more optional. You have no choice but to navigate your vessel while cruising. You may or may not choose to communicate while cruising, however, and a strong argument can be made that too much communication destroys the essence of the experience. The fact is, however, humans are instinctively social and love to exchange information, one way or another. Most cruisers therefore are always interested in improving communications capability on their vessels, and in recent years there have been several ways to do this. The two aspects of communications that are truly critical are distress calling and collision avoidance, so you should always give these priority when upgrading equipment.

VHF Radio

VHF (very high frequency) radio is the most basic form of electronic marine communication, is still the primary form of ship-to-ship communication, and has long been considered mandatory equipment by most cruisers. On most modest coastal cruising boats, a VHF radio is likely to be the only piece of dedicated marine communications equipment aboard.

VHF radios have only a limited line-of-sight range, from about 5 miles to something over 25 miles at most, and are available both as portable handheld or fixed-mount units. Recreational vessels are not legally required to carry VHF radios (though commercial vessels are), but if you have a radio you are obliged to monitor the main distress and hailing frequency (usually Channel 16) whenever you're underway.

All new fixed-mount VHF radios now have at least minimal DSC (Digital Selective Calling) capability. The most basic DSC units have an automatic digital distress call feature (allowing you to send out a mayday just by pressing a button) and otherwise operate just like conventional VHF radios. The distress call contains a vessel's unique Maritime Mobile Service Identity (MMSI) number and, if the radio is interfaced to a GPS receiver, its precise current location. The call is broadcast on Channel 70, which is reserved for digital distress and hailing calls, until another station receives and acknowledges it. Unfortunately, only other DSC radios can hear the call, and until recently there were relatively few of these around. Now that the Coast Guard, after many delays, has at last started developing its own system for receiving and responding to emergency digital VHF calls (called Rescue 21), DSC distress calls should be increasingly effective in the future.

Advanced DSC radios, which are much more expensive and still relatively rare in the United States, have many more features. To take full advantage of DSC technology these radios have twin receivers so they can receive and respond to emergency and routine calls even when the radio is in use. You can also privately hail one or more stations via Channel 70 by referencing their MMSI numbers. The receiving radio rings, much like a telephone, to notify its user of an incoming call and displays the caller's MMSI number (or actual identity, if the number is already in the radio's memory) and location (assuming the caller's radio is connected to a GPS receiver). If the receiving radio is interfaced with a chartplotter, the caller's location can also be displayed on screen. If the receiving radio's user is present and chooses to take the call, it is automatically transferred to an open working channel preselected by the caller, whereupon a normal VHF conversation can then take place. If the call is not taken, the receiving radio logs the hail so it can be answered later.

Cellular Phones

Many coastal cruisers who never venture far from civilization increasingly rely on cell phones for routine onboard communications. Many bluewater cruisers also rely on them for local communications when in port. Ironically, however, as cell phones designed for shoreside use have become more sophisticated, they have become less effective on boats. Older analog phones had more powerful transmitters and more effective antennas, thus were better equipped to function on the fringe of a cell tower's range. Today's lighter, less powerful digital phones, many of which don't even have any sort of protruding external antennas, often won't work more than a couple of miles from shore.

Fortunately, improving onboard cell-phone performance is relatively simple. Specialized marine cell-phone amplifiers that boost a phone's receptivity and transmitting power have been available for several

This DSC-VHF radio has only limited DSC capabilities, but more sophisticated DSC radios have long been available in Europe and are becoming increasingly common in the United States.

This well-conceived marine cell-phone system includes an amplifier and a large antenna to boost the reception of the portable cell phone (center, mounted in a socket), which in turns outputs to a waterproof cordless phone (right) that can be used on deck. (Courtesy of Ben Ellison)

years. These generate enough power that a phone can be connected to a dedicated external antenna mounted on a mast's spreaders or perhaps even at the masthead, depending on the antenna used. With an amp and a good external antenna mounted as high as possible, a cell phone's range can be increased to as much as 50 miles offshore.

Cell phones are great for casual conversation and also for contacting shoreside facilities and services, but they are not capable of making general distress calls. VHF radio distress calls, because they are made *en plein air* and can be heard by all other stations within range simultaneously, are far more effective. The Coast Guard much prefers to receive calls for help via radio and therefore urges all recreational mariners to carry VHF radios in addition to cell phones whenever possible. Cell phones are also useless in collision-avoidance situations, unless you happen to know the phone number of someone on the vessel you want to avoid hitting.

So-called "smart" cell phones, which are in effect handheld computers, can however be used for more than just voice communications. With a smart phone, as long as you are in range of a cell tower, you can send and receive e-mail and access weather and navigation data via the Internet. With the proper software installed, the phones can display electronic charts and can also, if equipped with a GPS receiver (an increasingly common feature), act as a chartplotter. Although they cannot be interfaced with autopilots, radar sets, DSC radios, and onboard sensors like a full-size hardwired plotter, a GPS-enabled smart phone can be a useful backup nav system and can certainly take the place of a common handheld chartplotter.

HF Radio

HF (high frequency) radio includes both marine SSB (single-sideband) and amateur ham radio, which together were once generically referred to as shortwave radio. For many decades these were the only viable options for bluewater cruisers seeking truly long-range communications capability. Though other options are now available, SSB and ham radio are still popular. The distinction between the two is one of licensing: an SSB license can be obtained by filling out some forms and paying a fee; a ham license is free, but there is a written exam and minimal proficiency in Morse code is required. Also, by law no business or commercial activity, except for ship's business related to the operation and maintenance of a vessel, may be conducted on ham frequencies.

HF radio transmitters are much more powerful than VHF transmitters (signal strength is 100 to 150 watts compared to just 25 watts maximum for VHF) and also more complicated. HF signals travel long

distances by skipping off the earth's upper atmosphere, and some expertise is required in selecting broadcast times and frequencies. An effective ground plane is also needed, as well as a large antenna (usually on sailboats this is a special insulated backstay) that must be specifically tuned to each frequency used. Frequency propagation software and automatic antenna tuners make all this easier than it used to be, but still you do need a certain amount of specialized knowledge to use an HF radio effectively.

Bluewater cruisers have long used HF radio to create far-flung "cruiser nets" on both ham and SSB frequencies. These consist of roll-call voice broadcasts in which active stations participate at fixed times each day on predetermined frequencies. Net members exchange detailed weather and technical information, keep track of each other's locations, engage in much idle banter, and normally form strong friendships with each other. Many long-distance cruisers are very dependent on these nets, particularly while on passage, thus consider an HF radio to be essential equipment. Others find the nets time consuming and a bit tedious and prefer not to get involved.

In spite of advances in satellite communications, many cruisers still depend on SSB and/or ham radio systems like the one shown here.

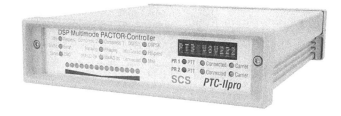

This unassuming little PACTOR HF radio modem makes it possible for an SSB or a ham radio to send or receive e-mail. Many bluewater cruisers now consider these modems essential equipment. (Courtesy of SCS)

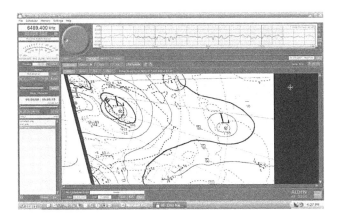

This weatherfax image came aboard via a digital HF receiver and is displayed here on a laptop computer. (Courtesy of Ben Ellison)

HF radios can also be used to send and receive data. The crudest technology, the weather facsimile, or weatherfax, has been around for years. These are black-and-white weather charts that are sent out on a regular schedule on different SSB frequencies by national meteorological offices all around the world. With an SSB radio and a special computer program or printer, or just a dedicated weatherfax receiver, you can receive images of small-scale surface analysis or forecast charts. Though many sailors now access weather charts via e-mail services (through a radio or satellite receiver, as discussed below), weatherfaxes are still a primary source of weather information for some bluewater cruisers.

More recently, special modems have been developed that enable HF radios to send and receive e-mail via the shore-based Internet. This is a capability many bluewater sailors want to have, and HF e-mail has done much to keep HF radio popular on long-distance cruising boats. In most cases, in addition to sending and receiving text e-mail messages, users can also access a broad range of text and graphic weather-forecasting products. These include gridded binary (GRIB) files, which contain raw weather data that can be loaded into sophisticated weather-routing programs that run in conjunction with GPS chartplotters. By far the most popular and sophisticated HF e-mail service is Winlink, which operates on ham frequencies, is run entirely by volunteers, and costs nothing to use. Another popular nonprofit system, SailMail, operates on SSB frequencies and charges a low flat annual fee to handle limited amounts of traffic. There are also several other less popular commercial services, all on SSB frequencies, that charge for data transmission on a per minute or per kilobit basis, thus are considerably more expensive.

Satellite Communications

Marine satellite communications have been a reality since 1979 when the International Marine Satellite Organization (Inmarsat) was created, but it is only fairly recently that satcom has become affordable enough to be of interest to the average recreational sailor. This is the most rapidly developing area of marine communications, and though it seems inevitable satcom will one day eclipse HF radio as the cruising sailor's medium of choice for long-range voice and data communication, it is unclear how long this transition will take. Already there is a large selection of satcom products and services available, ranging from simple handheld transceivers capable of sending and receiving brief text e-mail messages to sophisticated systems that can handle voice and broadband data transmissions. But the high end of this market is still very exclusive. The fastest, most reliable satcom services involve hardware costing tens of thousands of dollars, the installation of large sat-dome antennas that can fit comfortably only on large vessels, and ongoing service fees that can quickly gobble up the better part of a middle-class salary. The lower end of the market, meanwhile, is somewhat unstable, as the costs of launching and maintaining satellites in orbit are quite high, and the number of potential users is still relatively low. As a result, service providers appear and disappear and occasionally reappear at irregular intervals.

The two more affordable services currently making the biggest inroads into the mainstream bluewater cruising market are the sat-phone companies Globalstar and Iridium. Iridium's satellites offer truly global coverage, but its portable phones cost more than Globalstar's and its per-minute service charges are generally higher (about $1 per minute and up, depending on the service plan). Both companies have data-transmission packages that enable their phones to send and receive e-mail and gather weather information, including GRIB files. Transmission speeds are superior to HF radio, but still are nowhere near fast enough to do anything like surf the Internet. Globalstar, as of this writing, is about twice as fast as Iridium, but offers only limited coverage—up to about 200 miles offshore in North and South America, Europe, the Caribbean, and Australia and New Zealand. Both companies are less than perfectly stable. Iridium nearly folded and was saved by the U.S. Defense Department. Globalstar, meanwhile, has suffered service outages due to problems with its satellites.

Another interesting low-cost satcom option is satellite radio. Two services—Sirius and XM—currently broadcast live marine weather forecasts that can be received throughout most of North America

Large well-financed boats can afford to carry large sat domes that don't fit on small boats. More modest folk can use handheld sat phones.

and the Caribbean basin as well as several hundred miles offshore, and some cruisers have found this to be an effective low-cost way of gathering weather information in relatively remote locations. A wide variety of satellite radio music and news channels are also available, but all communication is strictly one-way. The two companies have recently merged, and it seems likely the resulting single entity will be able to survive for some time.

Distress Beacons

The first Emergency Position-Indicating Radio Beacons (EPIRBs), designed to help search-and-rescue (SAR) authorities locate mariners in distress, were relatively crude devices. These transmitted an anonymous analog radio distress signal on frequencies of 121.5 and 243 MHz that could be picked up either by passing airplanes or by certain itinerant low-earth-orbiting satellites. Satellites receiving the distress calls could pass them on to authorities on shore only if they happened to be simultaneously in view of a shore station and the source of the distress signal at the time the

signal was received. Plus, the initial location of the signal source could be fixed only within a radius of about 12 to 15 miles, thus creating a potential search area as large as 500 square miles. For cruising sailors operating relatively close to shore, where aircraft pass overhead on a frequent basis and SAR assets are nearby, this sort of capability did provide some security, but for long-distance sailors far out at sea it only marginally increased the likelihood they would ever be located and rescued in an emergency.

This all changed in the early 1990s when the first 406 MHz EPIRBs became widely available. These send a digital signal on a frequency of 406 MHz to a dedicated constellation of geostationary satellites providing full-time global coverage between the latitudes of 70 degrees north and south. The initial location of the signal can be fixed within a radius of about 3 miles, which translates to a search area of just 25 square miles, and if the user has properly registered the EPIRB, the signal also identifies the subject vessel, the vessel's owner, plus his or her home address and phone number. This allows SAR authorities to quickly check whether any received signal is a false alarm and alerts them as to exactly who and what they are looking for. In the past 10 years this technology has been further refined and improved with the advent of the GPS Position-Indicating Radio Beacon, or GPIRB. These contain an integral GPS receiver and broadcast signals with precise rescue location coordinates accurate to within a few hundred feet.

The bottom line is that cruising sailors with modern EPIRBs can always summon help wherever they are. This has changed the zeitgeist of bluewater cruising in particular. Previously the presumption was that bluewater sailors must be self-reliant and capable of coping with emergencies themselves. If they failed to keep their vessels afloat, they faced the prospect of a long survival drift in a life raft. Nowadays, however, a castaway with a 406 EPIRB is unlikely to spend more than a day in a raft before being recovered. Furthermore, the ease of summoning help has lowered in many sailors' minds the threshold of what constitutes a real emergency. Unfortunately, some sailors now panic, light off their EPIRBs, and seek rescue from their vessels only because they are scared and uncertain of how to cope with a threatening situation.

Modern distress beacon technology has also made it much easier to locate and recover crew who have fallen overboard. Pocket-size 406 EPIRBs, commonly referred to as Personal Locator Beacons (PLBs), are now widely available and are small enough to be easily carried by individual crewmembers. Many of these, like the larger GPIRBs, also have integral GPS receivers, hence can provide the pinpoint accuracy needed to find a person in the water. A 406 MHz distress signal, however, can only alert distant SAR authorities as to the location of a man overboard (MOB) and cannot help the crew on board immediately find and recover their lost shipmate. Many 406 beacons do also transmit a 121.5 MHz locator signal that a short-range radio direction finder can home in on, and several such direction finders can now be purchased by recreational mariners. Using such a device to find a person in the water takes some practice, however. Note, too, that some devices marketed as PLBs don't transmit on 406 MHz at all. Those that transmit on 121.5 MHz alone may alert passing aircraft to an MOB's predicament (satellite reception of 121.5 MHz distress signals was phased out as of 2009) and may aid onboard crew in locating and recovering an MOB, *if* they have a direction finder aboard and know how to use it, but it cannot provide the ultimate security offered by a personal 406 EPIRB.

Finally, there are also an increasing number of man-overboard alarm systems available. These are not designed to locate overboard crew, but rather

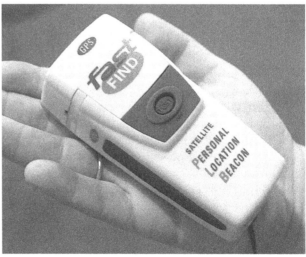

A top-of-the-line modern 406 MHz GPIRB beacon with an integral GPS receiver (top) and a personal locator beacon (bottom). (Courtesy of ACR Electronics, McMurdo, and Ben Ellison)

This modern man-overboard alarm system includes a small transmitter fob (left) that continuously transmits over a short range to a small receiver (right). If the crew falls overboard the connection is broken and the alarm (center) is activated. (Courtesy of Ben Ellison and Raymarine)

to alert those on board when someone falls off the boat in the first place. Typically these systems involve equipping deck crew with small short-range transmitters that continuously send a radio signal to a base unit aboard the boat. If anyone carrying a transmitter falls overboard, thus causing the transmitter to travel outside its broadcast range (usually 40 to 50 feet) and break its connection to the base unit, a loud alarm sounds. The most sophisticated MOB alarms can be interfaced with GPS units, allowing an MOB waypoint to be plotted automatically as soon as the alarm sounds; or with engine controls, allowing for an automatic engine shutdown when motoring; or even with an autopilot steering to a wind sensor, which can then automatically bring the boat head to wind to stop it.

Collision Avoidance

All cruising sailors are apt to find themselves in situations where they must evaluate the speed, course, capabilities, and intentions of other vessels in their vicinity and take action (or not) to avoid collision. When cruising in coastal waters, the complexity of the task is compounded by proximity to land or shoal water and the need to sometimes travel in narrow channels where large commercial vessels cannot maneuver freely. In near-offshore waters fishing vessels that move in erratic patterns are commonly encountered. Far out at sea traffic is typically much lighter, but is far more likely to consist of large autopiloted freighters and tankers traveling at top speed with little human supervision. In situations where visibility is severely restricted the job only becomes that much harder.

The nonelectronic tools for avoiding collisions are fundamental. The importance of having crew on deck, a modicum of judgment, and perhaps a hand-bearing compass for tracking the relative position of potentially threatening vessels should never be discounted. Otherwise, modern technology offers useful tools that cruisers are ever more willing to rely on.

Radar

The technology known as **ra**dio **d**etecting **a**nd **r**anging, or radar, has been around since the 1940s, and radar sets have been small and cheap enough to fit on recreational vessels since at least the 1960s. The basic operating principle is well known: a revolving antenna (often situated inside a circular radome) emits strong pulses of microwave radiation, then receives the reflections of those pulses and displays them on a screen. As such, radar is effectively a real-time sensor, similar to a depth-sounder, except it perceives objects in a two-dimensional plane all around the boat.

Since the 1960s radar sets have grown ever smaller and less expensive. Radomes and display screens are now compact and efficient thus radar sets are found on increasingly smaller and more modest boats. Radar sets have also become easier to operate. Early sets were not particularly user friendly, as tuning up a raw image of amorphous, incoherent microwave echoes to achieve maximum resolution and consistency in fact requires some expertise. Most radar sets now, however, boast auto-tuning features that work very well, although some experience and informed intuition is still required to accurately interpret most radar images.

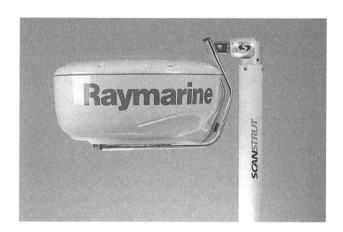

Compact radar sets have made it possible for even small boats to carry radar. This radome has a nifty gimballed mount that improves performance by keeping the antenna inside the dome parallel to the horizon. (Courtesy of Ben Ellison and Raymarine)

The automatic display of radar information on an electronic chart makes it much easier to interpret radar reflections. (Courtesy of Ben Ellison and Nobeltec)

For decades radar has been an extremely useful navigational tool, most particularly aboard vessels operating in low-visibility conditions. A major part of any radar operator's job once consisted of constantly relating radar images to paper charts in an effort to figure out which images represented charted navigational aids and geographic features. Since the advent of GPS chartplotters, however, this is no longer necessary, as it is easy to track a vessel's position in poor visibility on an electronic chart. Furthermore, the task of correlating charts to radar screens can now be performed automatically, with live radar images now directly overlaid onto same-scale electronic charts.

Radar is also an important collision-avoidance tool, and this is now the primary rationale for installing the technology on any cruising sailboat. Radar is especially adept at locating and tracking large metal vessels, and many cruisers who routinely cross paths with such beasts therefore consider radar a must-have bit of gear. The traditional features used to keep track of potentially threatening radar contacts are electronic bearing lines (EBLs) and variable range markers (VRMs), which measure relative bearings and distances to contacts right on the radar screen. By making these measurements every few minutes and plotting the results on a separate maneuvering sheet (or directly on the radar screen with a grease pencil, given a large enough screen), you can calculate a contact's true speed and course and evaluate whether there is a risk of collision. To do this, however, your vessel must maintain a steady course and speed; also, the process is labor intensive, especially when there are multiple contacts to track.

Fortunately, again, the latest electronic wizardry makes all this much easier. When interfaced with a GPS receiver a modern radar set can "know" the true course and speed of its own vessel, thus can itself calculate the true courses and speeds of up to 10 contacts selected by a radar operator, regardless of any course and speed variations, and will automatically identify any contact that becomes a collision threat. This useful feature, known generically as automatic radar plotting, is most often described by manufacturers as MARPA, for Mini (or Manual) Automatic Radar Plotting Aid. For MARPA to work properly, however, radar contacts must be strong and discrete. It cannot be counted upon to track weak or intermittent radar reflections, as are typically returned by wooden or fiberglass vessels, thus should never be relied on exclusively. Even with the latest radar plotting technology aboard, cruisers should always be prepared to track contacts themselves and must also always keep their eyes and ears open and maintain an effective deck watch, as not all collision threats necessarily appear on a radar screen.

Two other collision-avoidance features found on many modern radar sets are guard zones and sleep mode. These are especially useful to singlehanders or small crews sailing in open waters who have trouble maintaining a truly vigilant deck watch on a 24-hour basis. A *guard zone* is simply a user-defined area around a boat—it can be defined either as a radius or as a vector out to a specific distance—within which the appearance of any radar contact activates an audible alarm. Sleep mode, meanwhile, is an energy-saving feature. The radar set is left activated in standby mode, but is programmed to become active at set intervals, whereupon it takes a few sweeps of the horizon within a set range, and then reverts to standby mode. If any contact is detected within the predetermined guard zone during a sweep an audible alarm is sounded, thus alerting the crew to the presence of a potential threat.

The flip side to detecting collision threats with radar is being detected yourself. Fiberglass, as mentioned, does not reflect radar signals very well, and in many cases a fiberglass boat will never appear on the radar screens of other vessels around them. To ameliorate this problem you must install a radar reflector in your rig. Many different types of passive reflectors are available, but few are effective. In laboratory conditions the two best passive radar reflectors have proven to be simple corner reflectors, which are crude octahedral spheres composed of intersecting aluminum plates, and Tri-Lens reflectors, which are composed of an array of three spherical Luneberg lenses. Otherwise, the best way to be sure of showing up on radar is to install an active radar reflector, sometimes referred to

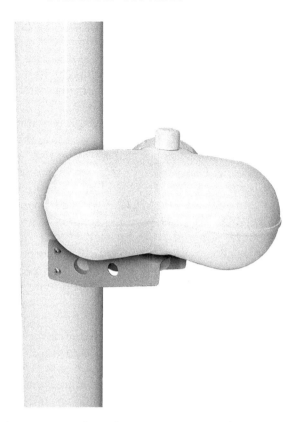

The TriLens radar reflector incorporates three Luneberg lenses mounted back to back. These are currently the most effective passive reflectors.

as radar target enhancers. These units are connected to a vessel's power supply and go active whenever they are painted by another vessel's radar beam. By amplifying and retransmitting the signal they receive, they greatly improve the chances of detection. They also can be set to sound an alarm whenever they go active, thus alerting the crew to the presence of another radar-bearing vessel in the area. Because they consume power, however, and are expensive, active target enhancers are not often found on cruising sailboats. Some cruisers do install simple radar detectors. Like units used by speeding motorists to thwart police radar guns, these devices merely sound an alarm when painted by incoming radar signals. Because they are relatively inexpensive and consume very little power, they are somewhat more popular among cruisers than active reflectors.

Automatic Identification System

This technology was previously employed only on large commercial vessels, but is now trickling down into the recreational market. The critical piece of equipment involved is an Automatic Identification System (AIS) transponder/transceiver, which is interfaced to a vessel's GPS receiver and continually broadcasts

the vessel's identity (including its name, description, MMSI number, registry, and reported destination), position, true speed, and true course on dedicated VHF radio channels. All other AIS transceivers on other vessels within VHF range (typically about 20 miles) automatically receive all this information and can display it either on a dedicated text or graphic display screen or on a compatible chartplotter. As with a MARPA-equipped radar set, the closest point of approach for each AIS contact is automatically calculated, and those presenting potential collision threats are at once identified. Because of the great accuracy of GPS, because VHF radio transmissions are much more reliable and consistent than reflected microwave radar beams, and because AIS transponder transmissions (at least on the most sophisticated units) are made more frequently than radar sweeps (a maximum of 30 every minute versus 24 a minute), AIS is a much more precise collision-avoidance tool than radar. Unlike radar, however, it cannot detect vessels that are not equipped with AIS transponders, thus is not an ultimate panacea.

Large commercial vessels are now required to carry Class-A AIS equipment, so AIS does provide a reliable way of tracking the largest, most potentially dangerous collision threats. Tech-savvy cruisers on well-equipped boats have thus been carrying simple AIS receivers that can only monitor AIS transmissions from other vessels for the past few years. Though large vessels are also likely to return large, consistent radar echoes, AIS is far more energy efficient, as a VHF receiver draws considerably less power than an active radar array. AIS, because it

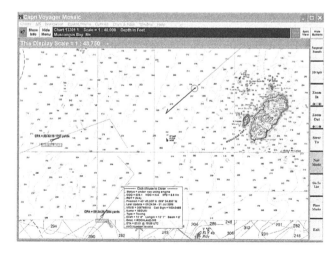

There is a great deal of information on this AIS display concerning the vessel at the bottom of the screen, including its name, destination, course, speed, heading, dimensions, and disposition (towing). (Courtesy of Ben Ellison)

explicitly identifies the subject vessel, also allows for more precise voice communication, as you can call a threatening vessel by name on a VHF radio, or even dial its specific MMSI number if you have a DSC unit.

The next step in the development of the system is for smaller vessels to transmit as well as receive AIS data so they, too, can be detected by vessels around them. Class-B AIS transponder/transceivers for recreational use have been available in Europe for some time and have recently been authorized for use in U.S. waters. Class-B units, however, do not transmit data nearly as frequently as Class-A units (just twice a minute), and vessels required to carry Class-A equipment are currently allowed to filter out Class-B contacts if they wish. As the technology evolves, however, and as more types of vessels are required by law to carry AIS equipment, this will likely become the primary collision-avoidance tool on cruising vessels in the not-too-distant future.

GALLERY OF CRUISING SAILBOATS

This is a collection of profiles of 40 cruising sailboats I hope you'll find worthy of your attention, either as boats you might like to acquire, or as concepts to inform your thinking about what sort of boat might be best for you. In deciding what boats to write about I have used various criteria. First, I have tried to present a wide variety of cruising boats. Rather than focus on the most popular types of boats, I've included as many different types as possible and have refrained from listing multiple examples of the same type. Second, I've included only boats I can truly recommend as examples of their type. I see little point in wasting ink telling you about boats I don't think you should be interested in. This does not mean, however, that only those boats presented are worthy of notice. Unfortunately, there are many fine designs and very good boatbuilders not represented here. Third, I have favored boats I have some direct experience with so as to provide you with more nuanced information. This does not mean that every boat I've ever sailed is on the list; it does mean that when forced to choose between a boat I've sailed and one I haven't, all other things being equal, I have selected the former.

I have limited myself to boats between 27 and 66 feet, not because there are no interesting cruising boats smaller or bigger than this, but because I had to draw the line somewhere. Boats smaller than 27 feet are more micro-cruisers than compact cruisers, and boats 70 feet and up, as far as I'm concerned, start to smell like superyachts. To a limited extent I have favored boats in the middle of the range (35 to 45 feet), because I assume these are the size boats most people are interested in. For the same reason I have favored production boats no longer being built that are available only on the brokerage market. I have included, however, several boats still in production, plus a few limited-production and custom one-off designs of particular interest.

I am sure I will hear from readers and others in the sailboat industry who feel strongly that I have committed egregious errors in not including certain boats. Such passions, of course, are what make lists like this so much fun. There are indeed many boats not here I would have liked to have included, but I would also point out: a) this is not intended to be a list of "best boats" so please don't read it that way; and b) if you buy lots of copies

of this book, I can include even more boats in the next edition.

Finally, a word about the specifications. Where possible I have discovered and have listed both light and heavy published displacement figures and have made separate calculations of performance ratios based on these. Likewise, if separate 100 percent foretriangle and "downwind" sail areas have been published, I have included them and have made separate ratio calculations. In many cases, however, the published figures are unqualified and are presented as such here. As mentioned in Chapter 2, it is best to presume such figures are optimistic—i.e., displacement is understated and sail area is overstated—although unfortunately there's no way of knowing for sure. As to the nominal hull-speed calculations, I have relied on Dave Gerr's generally more accurate formula (see page 44 in Chapter 2) rather than the classic formula, except with respect to a few heavy boats that actually rate faster under the classic formula, in which case I have offered the higher number. As for prices, those given here were current as of September 2009. Though price ranges will have changed since then, these will give you a good idea of the relative costs of the boats.

Corsair F-27

First introduced in 1985, this trailerable trimaran proved to be a seminal boat in the world of multihull sailing. Designed by Ian Farrier, a New Zealander who emigrated to California (by way of Australia) with the specific goal of perfecting his concept of a series of production trimarans with folding amas, the F-27 is both an excellent high-performance coastal cruiser and a competitive one-design racing machine. During a 12-year production run that ended in 1997, a total of 453 hulls were launched, making this by far the most successful boat of its type to date. Indeed, it can be argued that the F-27 is effectively still in production, as Corsair's successor design, the F-28, though it has a rotating wing mast and is generally more sophisticated, is quite similar and is built with much of the same tooling.

Certainly the F-27 is not a boat for anyone interested in roomy accommodations. Though the body of the main hull flares out a great deal above the waterline to maximize interior space, the layout and furnishings are cramped and strictly minimal. There is only sitting headroom, except under the pop-top roof near the companionway where the simple galley is located. Berthing is limited: in the tiny aft cabin there is a narrow double berth, there are two narrow settee berths in the saloon (separated by a small removable table), plus there's a tiny berth suitable for a small child in the forepeak. Even a couple sailing alone will want to spend much of their time, weather permitting, hanging out in the cockpit or on the wide nets between the amas and the hull. As such, the F-27 serves best as a weekend cruiser with perhaps occasional stints aboard as long as a week or two. Though several of these boats have made ocean passages, they are not suitable for long-range bluewater cruising unless you are a masochist.

What the F-27 lacks in amenities and comfort it makes up for in cruising range. Because it can be trailered, the boat can get to all sorts of places—inland lakes and distant shorelines, for example—that would otherwise be out of reach. And because it is so fast, it can cover a lot more ground than most boats once it is in the water. In a little speedster like this you can potentially travel over 100 miles during a long daysail. If you don't really care about sailing fast and aren't interested in taking advantage of this sort of capability, this is definitely not the boat for you.

As originally conceived the F-27 carries no bowsprit and flies a conventional triangular (or "pinhead") mainsail hoisted on a fixed aluminum mast. In 1996 a "formula" version of the boat was introduced with both a square-headed main that carries a lot more roach and a fixed bowsprit for flying a big screecher or asymmetric spinnaker. Many of the earlier boats have since been updated with formula rigs, as they are both faster and easier to manage. On the whole, the boat is not hard to sail shorthanded. The self-draining cockpit is quite small with the mainsheet within immediate reach of the tiller, which extends from the transom over the top of the short aft coachroof and under the raised main traveler. Other controls, likewise, are right nearby. If anything, unless you can convince idlers to stay clear of the cockpit, the boat is harder to sail with a big crew.

There is a large central daggerboard to hold the boat to weather, and unlike many multihulls the F-27 is rather close-winded and makes excellent progress to windward in light air. I once spent a delightful hour beating up a very narrow channel in an F-27 in a mere whisper of breeze and had no trouble maintaining apparent wind angles of 40 degrees. In a moderate breeze the boat points as high as 35 degrees apparent and chugs along at 8 knots no problem. With the wind on the beam, if you press hard with a spinnaker up, you can get up to 20 knots, which is a thrill and a half in a vessel this size. If there are kids aboard and you don't want to terrify them, just douse the headsail and the boat still sails well under main alone. Or stash them all in the aft cabin where you can keep an eye on them while steering and let it rip anyway.

The F-27's construction is structurally impeccable and thoroughly modern. The S-glass laminate is set in epoxy resin with a PVC foam core to reduce weight and increase stiffness. Kevlar and carbon fiber are used to reinforce high-load areas, and all components are vacuum-bagged when

laid up so as to minimize voids and achieve uniform resin saturation. The patented folding ama arms are well engineered, with few if any reports of failures or problems. The amas can be folded up while motoring through the water, which is a great convenience when pulling into a marina berth. When launching the boat from a trailer it takes about 30 minutes for an experienced owner to step the mast and set up the rig without assistance. Because they are so well built these boats are not cheap given their size, but if you factor in the savings realized from being able to store the boat on a trailer, they are in fact quite affordable over the long run.

Systems are primitive and therefore are easy and inexpensive to maintain. Auxiliary power consists of an 8 or 9 hp outboard engine hanging in an offset engine well at the stern. The stove is usually a simple two-burner non-pressurized alcohol rig; the icebox (never mind any kind of refrigeration) is a loose cooler dragged aboard and stowed in a convenient nook or cranny. The boat has a 12-volt electrical system powering a few lights and instruments and probably requires some extracurricular charging from a solar panel or two if used very much. The toilet is often nothing more than a Porta-Potti stashed under the forward berth. To those who value comfort and convenience all this no doubt sounds unpleasant, but to those who enjoy sailing fast and cherish simplicity it should seem like heaven afloat.

LOA		27'1"
LWL		26'3"
Beam		
	Amas extended	19'1"
	Amas folded	8'5"
Draft		
	Board up	1'2"
	Board down	4'11"
Displacement		
	Light ship	2,600 lbs.
	Maximum payload	3,800 lbs.
Sail area		
	Original rig	446 sq. ft.
	Formula rig	502 sq. ft.
Fuel		6 gal.
Water		14 gal.
D/L ratio		
	Light ship	64
	Maximum payload	94
SA/D ratio		
	Original rig/Light ship	37.69
	Original rig/Max load	29.26
	Formula rig/Light ship	42.42
	Formula rig/Max load	32.93
Nominal hull speed		
	Light ship	11.6 knots
	Maximum payload	10.3 knots
Typical asking prices		$25K-$60K

Nor'Sea 27

Legend has it the idea for this unique pocket cruiser was born round a campfire in Baja California in the early 1970s as two brothers, Dean and Stan Wixom, speculated on alternative modes of exploring Baja and the Sea of Cortez. They were on motorcycles, had tired of the dusty ride, and thought a small, but truly ocean-worthy cruising sailboat on a trailer might be a better way to travel. Dean later queried several yacht designers, but the only one who thought such a craft feasible was Lyle Hess, who allegedly took only a few minutes to sketch out the basic concept of what became the Nor'Sea 27. Wixom built hull number one in a makeshift plant in Southern California in 1977, then three years later built himself a boat, hull number 77, and sailed off over the horizon in it. His new business, Heritage Marine, he sold to Bob Eeg, who renamed the company Nor'Sea Marine and has continued building Nor'Sea 27s ever since. To date over 450 have been launched, and many believe it to be the most seaworthy cruising sailboat in its size range.

The Nor'Sea is certainly not the only robust pocket cruiser that can be hauled on a trailer. Several others fit the same basic criteria: shoal draft (under 4 feet to slip on and off a trailer on a ramp), narrow beam (not more than 8 feet to transit highways without permits), and moderate displacement (not much more than 8,000 lbs). But the Nor'Sea may well be the deepest, heaviest sailboat ever explicitly designed to be trailerable. Indeed, its proponents readily admit it is not a true trailer-sailer, but is instead "transportable" by trailer. A large tow vehicle and preferably a triple-axle trailer are needed to move it, and many owners who do tow Nor'Seas to distant cruising grounds don't launch on ramps but instead hire Travelifts to insert them in the water. Though the mast is deck-stepped in a hinged tabernacle, rigging the boat is said to take a minimum of 3 hours.

What is most unusual about the Nor'Sea 27 is its standard layout. Defying all dicta stating that an attractive, functional center-cockpit sailboat must be large, the little Nor'Sea features a center cockpit in front of a tiny aft cuddy cabin that houses a pair of quarter berths and, amazingly, the arrangement works very well. The boat's lines, which incorporate a broad canoe stern, are clean and pleasing to the eye without exhibiting excessive freeboard, and the cockpit, though small, is very serviceable. The helm, most notably, consists of a long tiller that reaches over the top of the aft cabin from a large transom-hung rudder. Though there is also a much more conventional aft-cockpit version of the boat, the quirky center-cockpit version is far more popular.

Down below in the main cabin in the standard layout there is a decent galley to starboard, an enclosed head and small nav station to port, plus two settee berths either side of a saloon table that collapses to form a full double berth. (The aft-cockpit layout is similar, with twin quarter berths aft in the main cabin.) There is also a great deal of storage, with over 30 lockers to stash gear and supplies in. The end result is a functional small-boat interior that comfortably accommodates two couples or a couple with two children and also offers a remarkable amount of privacy.

The boat's construction is extremely strong. The hull is solid handlaid laminate, composed of up to 22 layers of mat and woven roving, with faux lapstrakes molded in. The lapstrakes, which require some care during layup, enhance the boat's traditional appearance and also stiffen the hull, which is further supported by interior bulkheads and a partial molded

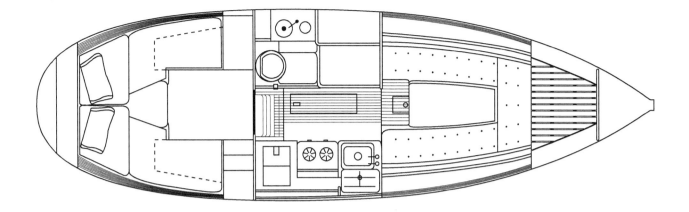

liner. The plywood-cored deck is fixed to an inward flange with adhesive sealant and though-bolts on 6-inch centers. Deck fittings and hardware are through-bolted to stainless-steel backing plates. The ballast is encapsulated lead. The boat's rig and many critical pieces of hardware, including the rudder pintle and gudgeons, are also significantly oversize. The interior joinerwork on factory-finished boats meanwhile is good, though there are also many owner-finished interiors of much more variable quality.

Given the Nor'Sea's long production run, remarkably few chronic flaws have appeared. Early boats were fitted with raw-water-cooled Farymann diesels that inevitably suffer from internal corrosion over time. These eventually must be rebuilt or replaced. Engine access is tight, but the engine (located under the cockpit) is reportedly relatively easy to remove. The biggest potential problem is the aluminum fuel tank, buried in the keel directly under the engine. On early boats these have often been corroded by seawater dripping off the propeller's packing gland and must be either glassed over entirely to preserve their integrity or excavated and replaced, which reportedly is an onerous job.

As to performance, the Nor'Sea by all accounts sails very well. It's not hard to find Nor'Sea owners who boast of overtaking longer, lighter boats while cruising, though presumably this is much easier with a tall rig, as opposed to the once optional short rig. The boat's interesting hull form features a long waterline and what is effectively a full keel with all of its forward end cut away. This facilitates launching and recovering the boat on a trailer ramp, and also reduces wetted surface area while still imparting good directional stability. The boat reportedly tracks well to weather given its draft, and its helm is relatively light, though some complain it is not very well balanced. Most important, the boat has a reputation for handling well in a seaway. This is reflected in both its

motion comfort ratio, which is exceedingly high for a boat this size and weight, and its capsize screening value, which is reassuringly low. Note, however, that Nor'Seas built prior to 1980 carry less ballast (either 2,500 or 3,000 pounds, depending on which ballast package the original owner specified), thus are likely to feel at least somewhat less stable than newer boats carrying the now-standard 3,100 pounds.

The Nor'Sea 27 is a cult boat and used examples rarely stay on the market for long. Less than half are normally sold with trailers, and trailers large enough to haul a boat this heavy are expensive, so be sure to take this into account when considering prices. New boats can be built to various stages of completion.

LOA	27'0"
LWL	25'0"
Beam	8'0"
Draft	3'10"
Ballast	3,100 lbs.
Displacement	8,100 lbs.
Sail area	
Tall rig	376 sq. ft.
Short rig	335 sq. ft.
Fuel	25 gal.
Water	50 gal.
D/L ratio	231
SA/D ratio	
Tall rig	14.89
Short rig	13.26
Comfort ratio	30.44
Capsize screening	1.59
Nominal hull speed	7.6 knots
Typical asking prices	$32K–$90K
Base price new (without trailer)	$149K

Tartan 27

The Tartan 27 is sometimes hailed as the first fiberglass boat ever designed by Sparkman & Stephens. This is not accurate, however, as a few years prior to its creation S&S designed a similar, but slightly smaller glass boat, the 25-foot New Horizons, for Ray Greene. The introduction of the Tartan 27 in 1961 is said to have ruined the market for the earlier boat, a fact that Greene always resented. The 27 was the first Tartan ever built, though its builder was originally known as Douglass & McLeod Plastic Corp. and did not reorganize as Tartan Yachts until 1971, after its first plant in Ohio was destroyed in a fire. All told 712 Tartan 27s (including 24 built under license by W. D. Schock in California in the mid-1960s) were launched over the course of an 18-year production run, making it one of the more successful fiberglass auxiliary sailboats born during the CCA era.

Unlike larger CCA boats, the Tartan 27 has short overhangs, but also sports a shoal-draft full keel and centerboard as popularized by Carleton Mitchell's *Finisterre*. In typical CCA fashion, the 27 was also sold as both a sloop and a yawl, though few of the latter were ever built. It was a successful racing boat in its prime, both on a one-design and handicap basis, but ultimately has endured as a great low-budget pocket cruiser. Most every hull built is still afloat, but a relatively small percentage are ever for sale at one time, as owners tend to cling to them.

Construction is typical for an early fiberglass sailboat. The hull is solid laminate composed of mat and woven roving set in polyester resin and built to heavy scantlings—³⁄₄" thick at the keel—with tabbed bulkheads and glass-reinforced stringers helping to stiffen the structure. The deck is balsa-cored with plywood substituted

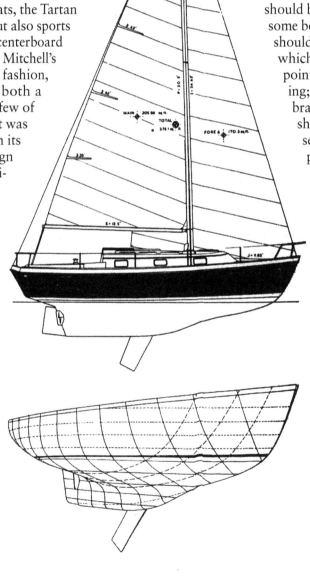

under deck hardware. As with many old balsa decks there is a good chance areas will have delaminated over time as moisture invades the core, particularly around the chainplates. The original deck joint, which is "mechanically and chemically bonded," according to old brochures, is quite secure and reports of leaks are rare. The lead ballast in the first 200 or so boats was external, but in 1966 was increased by 350 pounds and encapsulated in the keel. Likewise, the centerboards on the first dozen boats built in 1961 were bronze, but on subsequent boats were steel sheathed in fiberglass.

Like any older boat, the Tartan 27 has weak points that sooner or later must be addressed. These include the wood mast step over the keel, which eventually rots and needs replacing; the rudderstock, which lacks a bearing that should be retrofitted; the fuel tank (on some boats), which may leak and if so should be replaced; the centerboard, which is prone to wear at its pivot point and eventually wants replacing; the gate valves threaded onto brass through-hull fittings, which should be replaced with proper seacocks; and a lack of backing plates under deck hardware, which also should be retrofitted. The boat is worthy of the attention, however, particularly as its overall finish quality is superior to that of most production boats of similar vintage. Many Tartan 27s are extremely well cared for in spite of their age, thanks in part to the builder, which still sells critical replacement parts like centerboards, tanks, hatches, and rudders.

By modern standards the Tartan 27's original accommodations plan is cramped and awkward. This features a small dinette to port in the saloon opposite a small midship galley, aft of which is a somewhat exposed quarter

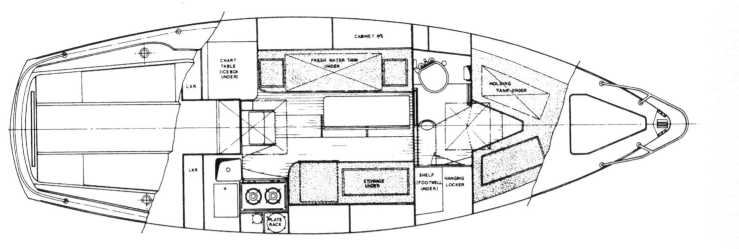

berth. Because the stove is fixed and the outboard sink floods when the boat heels to starboard, the galley is not too useful while underway. The icebox is also unusual: it is to port, overhanging the aft end of the dinette settee, with access hatches both inside the cabin and out in the cockpit. Up forward there is a good-size V-berth, but the head compartment behind it is tiny. In 1977 the boat was redesigned, with a raised sheerline and a longer, rounder cabin-house to increase interior living space. Drawings of the 27-2, as it was designated, are shown here. The revised accommodations plan on the remodeled boat is more conventional and liveable, with an aft galley opposite an icebox/nav desk, two long settees between a fold-down table, plus a larger athwartship head. The great drawback to the 27-2, 63 of which were built before production finally stopped in 1979, is that it is not nearly as attractive and shippy look-ing as the original. Also, raising the sheer without changing the hull mold required a more vulnerable outward-facing deck joint.

Because of its relatively long waterline, the Tartan 27 does sail faster than one might expect, especially on a reach, but compared to much lighter, more contemporary boats it inevitably seems slow. It is well balanced, however, and you can report-edly steer it by letting go the tiller and shifting the centerboard up and down. Like many CCA boats with slack bilges it does heel easily, leaning to an angle of about 20 degrees before stiffening up. Usually, though, it sails best when kept more upright, so it is wise to reef early. When overpow-ered the boat also develops quite a bit of weather helm, but otherwise is moderate in its habits and is easy to sail singlehanded. The later version, it should be noted, does not sail much differently than the first, as Tartan was careful to preserve parity for the sake of what was then a lively one-design racing class.

The original standard power plant was the ven-erable 30 hp gas-driven Atomic 4, which reportedly drives the Tartan 27 at hull speed with the throttle just half open. In the mid-1970s a smaller 12 hp two-cylinder Farymann diesel engine was offered and evi-dently became standard in 1977 when the boat was redesigned. The Farymann by all accounts is too weak to drive the boat well, causes excessive vibration, and requires expensive replacement parts. Some Tartan 27s have been repowered, but many are still equipped with their original engines, presumably because the boat is so inexpensive it is hard to justify splurging on a new one. If you do want a boat with a diesel it probably makes more sense to buy an older one with an Atomic 4 at a discount and invest the difference toward an appropriately sized new diesel than it does to pay extra for a funky undersized Farymann.

Tartan 27

LOA		27'0"
LWL		21'5"
Beam		8'7"
Draft		
	Board up	3'2"
	Board down	6'4"
Ballast		2,400 lbs.
Displacement		7,400 lbs.
Sail area (100% foretriangle)		
	Sloop	376 sq. ft.
	Yawl	394 sq. ft.
Fuel		20 gal.
Water		30 gal.
D/L ratio		336
SA/D ratio		
	Sloop	15.82
	Yawl	16.57
Comfort ratio		28.07
Capsize screening		1.76
Nominal hull speed		6.2 knots
Typical asking prices		$6K-$19K

Bristol Channel Cutter 28

This is a salty-looking traditional cruising boat that evokes a strong emotional response from most sailors, but is also surprisingly functional and performance-oriented for a vessel of its size and type. Conceived by Lyle Hess, the BCC (as it is often referred to) is based on earlier Hess designs built in wood—specifically *Renegade*, a small gaff-rigged cutter that won the Newport-Ensenada Race two years running back in the 1950s, and *Seraffyn*, the famous 24-foot Marconi-rigged cutter that took Lin and Larry Pardey on an 11-year circumnavigation that began in 1969. Built in fiberglass by Sam L. Morse Co. of Costa Mesa, California, the BCC first appeared in 1976. The company went through three changes of control before finally closing its doors in 2007, at which time Cape George Cutter Marine Works, based in Port Townshend, Washington, acquired the molds for both the BCC and its smaller sibling, the 22-foot Falmouth Cutter, and announced it would continue building both boats. In all, over 125 Bristol Channel Cutters have been built to date.

With its long bowsprit, long keel with a full forefoot, and nearly vertical stem and stern, the BCC evokes classic pilot cutters and working boats that plied British waters in the 19th century. Unlike those old British boats, however, the BCC is much beamier relative to her length, with relatively hard bilges and a flat run aft. This makes her stable (her AVS is 133 degrees) and allows her to stand up well to a large press of sail. The sail plan, though relatively low aspect, is large enough to take full advantage of this, thanks to the bowsprit forward and boomkin aft, which together add nearly 10 feet of length to the base of the rig. By modern standards you cannot call the BCC a fast boat, but for a 28-foot boat with a full keel its performance is exceptional. Owners have reported maintaining average speeds of nearly 6 knots during long ocean passages. Daily runs as high as 180 miles have been logged on transpacific cruises; plus at least one owner, aided by a strong current to be sure, has reported a 24-hour run in excess of 200 miles. The boat, thanks to its long keel, also tracks well and has a good motion in a seaway.

None of the boat's speed can be attributed to a lack of weight, as its construction is heavy and nearly bombproof. The hull is solid handlaid laminate composed of up to 10 layers of mat, woven roving, and cloth. Laminate thickness varies from $3/8$ inch at the sheerline, $1/2$ inch at the waterline, to nearly $1 1/2$ inches at the bottom of the hull. Exterior layers are set in vinylester resin to retard osmosis, and many hulls also received an optional epoxy barrier coat at the factory. The deck likewise is a heavy glass laminate with a $1/2$-inch plywood core throughout, joined to the hull on a generous inward flange that is bedded with 3M 5200 adhesive sealant and through-bolted every 5 inches with fastener holes staggered to spread the load. Inside there are no less than four full-height bulkheads tabbed to both the hull and deck with fat 6-inch margins. The main bulkhead is drilled out every 18 inches all around its perimeter with the tabbing on either side bonded together through the holes to lock everything in place. There are also three-quarter bulkheads to further stiffen the structure; all interior furniture is likewise tabbed in place with 4-inch margins. The lead ballast is internal, carefully encapsulated in resin and glassed over in the bottom of the keel.

Thanks in part to all those bulkheads the BCC's interior feels neither open nor spacious. This is aggravated by the short, narrow cabinhouse, which terminates just aft of the keel-stepped mast. Inside the house there is a full 6'1" of headroom (on some boats there is even 6'6", as this is offered as an option), but moving forward you need to stoop to get to the small forward cabin, which again has headroom, but only under the raised scuttle hatch. Though the interior feels chopped up and segmented, it has volume and is cleverly designed to make smart use of what space there is. The furniture is riddled with useful storage compartments,

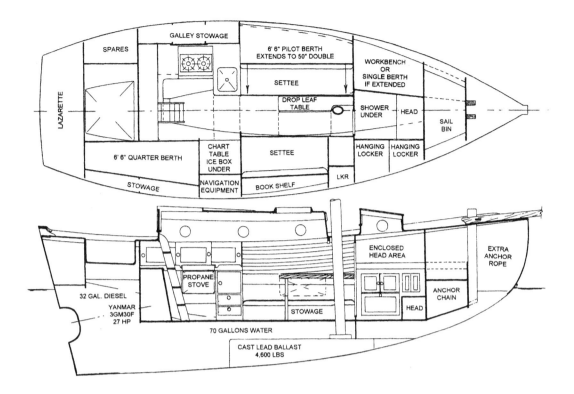

and the berthing is well conceived. In addition to the quarter berth aft to starboard, there is a pilot berth in the saloon to port that pulls out to form a full double. Another optional berth can be inserted in the forward cabin in place of the standard workbench; there is also an option wherein the entire saloon can be transformed into a giant queen-size berth. Though compact, the interior is well lit and ventilated, thanks to the traditional butterfly hatch over the saloon, numerous opening ports, that lofty scuttle forward, and a pair of full-size dorade vents.

The BCC's systems are simple and should be kept that way. Many boats don't even have pressure water, though most do have a bulkhead heater to keep things cozy down below. The earliest boats had undersize 13 hp Volvo diesel engines; later ones have 27 hp Yanmar engines, which work much better.

By far the most daunting thing about the BCC is its price. It is an exceptionally well-crafted vessel, with superb joinerwork below and scads of quality hardware on deck, all of which costs good money. Early on (up to hull number 26), Sam L. Morse Co. sold bare hulls for owners to finish, and these should sell at a significant discount. But a factory-finished BCC is built like a piece of furniture (so goes the cliché), and though these cost a lot they do hold much of their value over time. They are so carefully built there are few, if any, chronic flaws to repair or worry about. The biggest bother is keeping up with all the brightwork on deck. On later boats all the

exterior wood is mahogany, so it does need minding. Among other minor improvements the new builder, Cape George, is again making all the exterior wood teak, so if you really want to neglect your brightwork you can pony up for one of these. Cape George is also again offering bare hulls for owners to finish, so if you feel inclined to fit out your own piece of furniture to cruise the world in, you are welcome to try that, too.

LOA (with bowsprit and boomkin)	37'9"
LOD	28'1"
LWL	26'3"
Beam	10'1"
Draft	4'10"
Ballast	4,600 lbs.
Displacement	14,000 lbs.
Sail area	
100% foretriangle	556 sq. ft.
Full working sail	637 sq. ft.
Fuel	32 gal.
Water	64 gal.
D/L ratio	347
SA/D ratio	
100% foretriangle	15.28
Full working sail	17.51
Comfort ratio	36.92
Capsize screening	1.67
Nominal hull speed	6.8 knots
Typical asking prices	$74K–$200K
Base price new	$295K

Sabre 28

This solid little pocket yacht is both the first and smallest boat ever produced by Sabre Yachts, a quality production builder based in southern Maine. Designed by the company's founder, Roger Hewson, and introduced in 1971, the Sabre 28 was the only boat produced by Sabre until 1977. Production did not cease until 1986, by which time 588 hulls had been launched. The boat has a generous rig, is not at all slow for its size, and early in its career was often raced as a Half-Tonner under the old IOR rule. Today many Sabre 28s still sail in club races with PHRF ratings below 200, but they are primarily used as cruising vessels. Though most suitable for coastal work due to their small size and low-capacity tanks, they are certainly strong enough to take offshore if desired.

The boat's construction is straightforward and well executed. The hull is solid fiberglass laminate set in polyester resin with eight layers of mat and woven roving down low tapering up to four layers at the sheerline. The exterior gelcoat is excellent. The deck is balsa-cored with plywood substituted in high-load areas where hardware is mounted; the hardware is also supported by heavy aluminum backing plates. Secondary bonds between the hull and bulkheads and other structural members are superb, as is the finish quality of the glass work generally. The ballast is lead, mounted externally on stainless-steel keel bolts that are easily accessed in the bilge. The deck joint consists of an inward-facing flange bedded in nonadhesive butyl sealant and fastened every 6 inches with stainless-steel bolts. One significant flaw in earlier boats is that the through-deck chainplates were sometimes poorly sealed. This can cause the main bulkhead, to which the chainplates are fastened, to delaminate and eventually rot if it is not corrected.

Several modifications were made to the Sabre 28 over time. In 1976 a new deck mold was created. This incorporated an anchor well up forward, a reconfigured T-shaped cockpit that more easily accommodates a pedestal and wheel (only about 10% of the boats have the standard tiller steering), plus a more attractive split aft window on the cabin side. The deck-stepped rig was also improved about this time. Forward lower shrouds were added to keep the mast from pumping too much, and the chainplate seals were improved. In 1982 the height of the mast was slightly increased from 41 feet to 43 feet (increasing sail area by 12 square feet), the standard keel's draft was increased 4 inches, ballast was increased by 200 pounds, and the mainsheet traveler was moved from the transom (where it sometimes caused the mainsheet to quarrel with the helmsman's head) to the coachroof forward of the companionway.

There were four different auxiliary engines installed in the Sabre 28 over the course of its production run. The old gasoline-powered Atomic 4 was available until 1978, plus a 10 hp (later a 13 hp) Volvo diesel. Finally, after 1981, a 13 hp Westerbeke diesel was installed. On many of the early boats the prop shaft is slightly offset to one side or the other, depending on which way the propeller turns. It is critical when repowering one of these boats to make sure the new engine turns the prop the same direction as before or handling under power will be severely degraded.

As mentioned, the Sabre 28 sails well for a boat its size, thanks both to its large sail plan and its well-formed fin keel and skeg-supported spade rudder. For a boat that is not terribly light it is particularly handy in light air; it is a bit tender and heels quickly when the wind gets up unless sails are promptly reefed. Because the chainplates are well inboard, headsail sheeting angles are potentially quite narrow. Boats equipped with the optional inboard genoa track (there is also a standard toe rail track) and a standard deep keel (as opposed to the optional shoal-draft keel) are therefore reasonably close-winded. Note, however, that boats with offset prop shafts sail a bit better on one tack than they do on the other.

The one drawback to the Sabre 28 from a cruiser's perspective is that its interior can feel cramped. It does have good standing headroom for a small boat (about 6 feet throughout), but the cockpit is also large (7 feet long) and this inevitably shrinks the space available

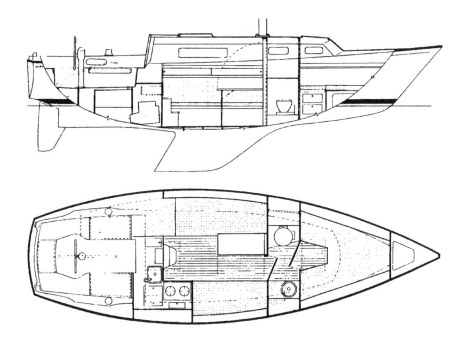

belowdeck. Also, the standard sleeping layout on most boats is overambitious, theoretically accommodating six people (two in the V-berth forward, two on the port settee extended to form a double, one on the starboard settee, and one in a quarter berth). The six-berth layout reduces galley space, which is unfortunate. The sink, though it is close to the centerline and drains well on both tacks, is also right beside the companionway so that you can easily put a foot in it when coming below. The fixed countertop stove is hard to cook on while sailing, and the tight space makes it hard to install a gimballed stove in its place. There is also a much more realistic four-berth layout with a somewhat larger galley, but this appeared in only a few of the earlier boats.

The interior in other respects is very pleasant. The quality teak joinery, rare on a boat this small, makes it warm and attractive, the fold-down bulkhead table works well, and the athwartship private head compartment is as functional as you can expect on an older boat less than 30 feet long.

Due to the quality of its construction, the Sabre 28 is more expensive than other used boats in this size range. The extra money spent, however, is not wasted. Because they are nicer boats to begin with, most owners maintain their Sabre 28s in good to excellent condition. Sabre still provides lots of technical support for their out-of-production boats, so it isn't hard to get parts or good advice when planning upgrades and structural repairs. The boats also hold their value well compared to similar vessels.

In the end, the Sabre 28 is a very safe compromise boat. It has relatively modern lines, yet is attractive to traditionalists, is very well built, sails well, and has a great ambiance below, if not an ideal layout.

Unfortunately, these boats rarely appear on the brokerage market on the West Coast, but if you live on the East Coast they are readily available.

Sabre 28

LOA	28'5"
LWL	22'10"
Beam	9'2"
Draft	
Standard (before 82/after 82)	4'4"/4'8"
Shoal	3'10"
Ballast	
1971–81	2,900 lbs.
1982–86	3,100 lbs.
Displacement	
1971–81	7,400 lbs.
1982–86	7,900 lbs.
Sail area (100% foretriangle)	
1971–81	391 sq. ft.
1982–86	403 sq. ft.
Fuel	20 gal.
Water	20/30 gal.
D/L ratio	
1971–81	277
1982–86	296
SA/D ratio	
1971–81	16.45
1982–86	16.23
Comfort ratio	
1971–81	24.24
1982–86	25.88
Capsize screening	
1971–81	1.88
1982–86	1.84
Nominal hull speed	
1971–81	6.8 knots
1982–86	6.7 knots
Typical asking prices	$10K–$22K

Cornish Crabber Pilot Cutter 30

No matter how seductive the performance and convenience of modern sailboats may seem to most cruisers, there will always be a passionate minority willing to a pay a premium, both in terms of effort and money, to cruise aboard a traditional gaff-rigged boat. The cult of the gaffer, though not unknown in the United States, is particularly strong in Great Britain, where many people still maintain ancient wooden examples of the breed. More pragmatic cultists prefer fiberglass boats that are much easier to care for, and a number of builders have sought to fill this niche over the years. One of the more successful is Cornish Crabbers, based in Cornwall, England, which a builds a number of "modern" gaffers, including a 19-foot weekender, the Shrimper (its most successful boat, with over 1,000 launched), and this flagship of their fleet, the 30-foot Pilot Cutter, of which more than 85 have been built since its introduction in 1985.

In spite of its name and traditional appearance, the lines of the Pilot Cutter 30, drawn by Roger Dongray, are a bit different from those of the classic British cutters of the 19th century. The Crabber 30 mimics its ancestors with its plumb stem, short stern overhang, rakish extra-long bowsprit, and low deck profile, but is also proportionally beamier with harder bilges and a flatter run aft. This increases interior volume and makes the boat stiffer than its forbears. The Crabber is also a shoal-draft centerboard boat, thus is much more versatile when it comes to poking into coastal nooks and crannies. I believe it is also more attractive than classic antique cutters, thanks primarily to its springy sheerline and faux-lapstrake planks, which parallel the sheer and give the hull an elegant appearance.

The Crabber 30 can be ordered with a full ballast keel and modern Marconi rig if desired, but according to Frank Colam, managing director of Cornish Crabbers, only one has ever been built this way. Anyone who buys a boat like this is obviously not obsessed about performance, but a gaff-rigged Crabber sails better than you might expect. During a test I conducted on Chesapeake Bay I had the boat cranking along at just over 4 knots on a close reach in a light 10-knot breeze. With a topsail up I guessed she might do 5 knots, but as Colam notes most owners only hoist their topsails on the Queen's birthday. Since the stated sail area for the gaff-rigged boat does not include the topsail and is still slightly greater than that for the Marconi-rigged boat, I expect the gaffer can outsail its sister on a reach or off the wind and really only suffers when close-hauled. Sailing a gaffer does take more work, however. Even on a fairly simple boat like the Crabber there are two halyards to set and tension when hoisting the main, running backstays to handle when jibing or tacking, two roller-furling headsails to handle, plus, of course, the dreaded topsail if you are serious about sailing at top speed.

By modern standards the boat's interior is definitely cramped for a 30-footer, particularly for tall people, who will not quite find standing headroom. Still, there are enough amenities and space inside for a couple or even a small family to enjoy an extended cruise. There are two standard layouts. The six-berth interior features a large V-shaped double in the forepeak, which is comfortable for two, although hard to climb in and out of. There are also four single berths—two straight settees in the saloon (one is shortened and suitable only for a child), plus two large quarter berths aft. There is also a nav station and a small galley with a refrigerator, pressure water, and propane stove behind the saloon, plus a small head forward of it. In the

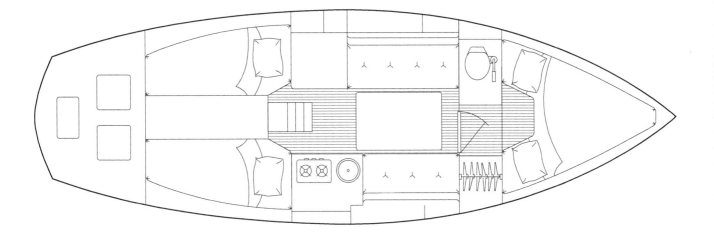

four-berth interior the forward double berth is left out, and the galley, head, and nav station are all much larger. Many aspects of the interior can be customized if ordering new construction, and the finish quality is excellent. With white Herreshoff-style bulkheads and lots of mahogany trim, the interior has a clean, slightly modern look that is plenty warm enough to appeal to traditionalists.

The boat's construction, though conservative, is also modern. The hull is solid handlaid fiberglass, while the deck has a balsa core with plywood substituted in most areas where hardware is installed. Most hardware is through-bolted to the deck, except for winches and clutches, which are screwed into stainless-steel plates that are laid up in the deck laminate. The deck joint, meanwhile, constructed on an inward flange, is first glued together, then fastened with screws, and finally is glassed over. The more popular centerboard version of the boat is ballasted with steel punchings encapsulated with resin in the bilges around the centerboard trunk; the rare ballast-keel version has internal lead ballast.

The deck layout, like the interior, has both traditional and modern elements. The spars, for instance, are spruce. The mast is hollow, but all other spars are solid, including the formidable 9-foot bowsprit, which is slightly offset in the traditional style, passing to one side of the stem but with its working end right on the centerline. The bobstay is on a multipart tackle, and the sprit can be canted upward, which reduces overall length and saves on berthing fees when pulling into pricey marinas. It also allows the sprit to be used as a gin pole to raise the mast, which is deck-stepped in a hinged tabernacle. All the deck fittings, meanwhile, are glittering stainless

steel, and most of the working hardware is modern high-end gear from Harken. This may be a mistake aesthetically, as bronze fittings and gear would look much more authentic, but the stainless steel is easier to keep bright. The modern blocks also greatly reduce friction when handling the many working lines on board. Similar thinking has been applied to the deck—most Crabber 30s have simple glass decks, which need only be rinsed from time to time, while a few have teak, which looks nicer and more traditional but is more trouble to keep up.

LOA (with bowsprit deployed)		39'0"
LOD		30'0"
LWL		25'9"
Beam		9'6"
Draft		
	Board up	3'6"
	Board down	5'3"
	Ballast keel	4'6"
Ballast		5,500 lbs.
Displacement		14,000 lbs.
Sail area		
	Gaff rig (working sails)	600 sq. ft.
	Marconi rig (working sails)	566 sq. ft.
Fuel		23 gal.
Water		52 gal.
D/L ratio		367
SA/D ratio		
	Gaff rig	16.49
	Marconi rig	15.56
Comfort ratio		39.64
Capsize screening		1.57
Nominal hull speed		6.8 knots
Typical asking prices		$80K–$140K
Base price new		Approx. $200K

299

Gemini 3000

The Gemini, the first production cruising catamaran ever built in the United States, was born from the ashes of a terrible fire that in 1981 destroyed the molds for the successful Telstar 26 folding trimaran that English multihull enthusiast Tony Smith had just brought over from Great Britain. Eager to save his new Maryland-based business, Performance Cruising, Smith immediately started building catamarans instead, using molds for an old British cruiser, the Aristocat, designed by Ken Shaw back in 1970. The original Gemini 31, appropriately named the Phoenix, was rebranded with minor changes as the Gemini 3000 after the first 28 hulls were launched. In all, 153 of these boats (including the first 28) were built from 1981 to 1990, when the 3000 was discontinued and replaced by the Gemini 3200. All subsequent Gemini models, including the 3200, the 3400, and two 105 models, though they have grown slightly, have the same basic hull and deck form and interior layout as the first. A total of nearly 1,000 Geminis have been launched over the past quarter century, making them the most popular American-built cruising cats to date.

Though the Gemini design concept is archaic by today's standards, it still works well for contemporary cruisers who want a great deal of living space in a small, inexpensive sailboat. As catamarans go, all Geminis are quite narrow, just 14 feet across, which fortunately means they can fit into most standard marina berths. In spite of the narrow beam, there is still enough room inside for a queen-size double berth forward in the master stateroom between the hulls, plus two small doubles in separate guest staterooms at the back of each hull, as well as a small but serviceable raised saloon with two settees and a table that can collapse to form yet another double berth. What it adds up to, in the case of the Gemini 3000, is a 30-foot boat with standing headroom that can honestly sleep four couples in a pinch, or three couples quite comfortably in private cabins, or a couple with several small

children (or two older children who demand some space of their own). Throw in a good-size galley, a roomy head with a shower, a nice long nav desk, plus a large, comfortable cockpit, and you have a veritable poor man's cruising palace.

When it comes to performance Geminis are a mixed bag. They have a solid bridgedeck stretching the entire length of the boat from the stern to the bow, plus the bridgedeck is fairly close to the water, and this inevitably hampers a catamaran's performance to some degree. The boats will pound and hobbyhorse a bit sailing into a chop, especially when overloaded. On the other hand, Geminis have relatively deep pivoting centerboards to provide directional stability and lift underwater, rather than the inefficient shoal keels found on most dedicated cruising cats. In flat water a Gemini with its lee centerboard down could be rather close-winded for a boat of its type. On the Gemini 3000s, unfortunately, the genoa track is outboard, and the wide sheeting angle makes it hard to take advantage of this potential. (On later models the track was moved inboard to the coachroof.) Because their centerboards can be raised and wetted surface area thus reduced when desired, all Geminis are reasonably fast off the wind compared to others of their ilk, particularly if you hoist a spinnaker. Unlike most modern cats, however, they have conventional rigs with backstays, and cannot fly a large main with a fat roach. Still, as long as they are not overloaded (an important proviso aboard any multihull), Geminis do surprisingly well in light air and can generally outsail most monohulls in their size range. They also have retractable rudders housed in stainless-steel cassettes, which allows them to take full advantage of their boards-up shoal draft when venturing into thin water.

Construction quality is mediocre at best, and though a few bold souls have taken Geminis offshore, the boats are best suited to coastal cruising. The entire hull (that is, both hulls plus the underside of the full-length bridgedeck) is

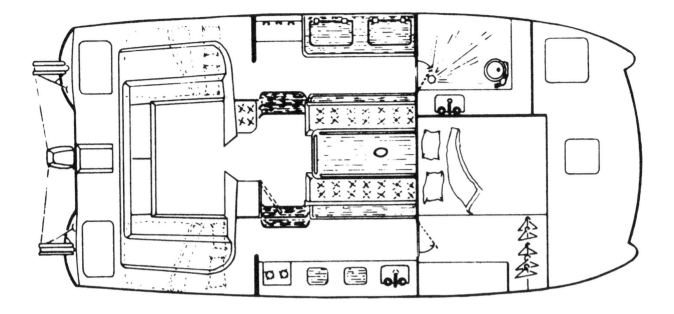

formed in a single mold and is laid up as a solid fiberglass laminate of mat and woven roving. In the Gemini 3000 hulls polyester resin was used, and according to one consumer survey conducted back in the 1980s about 20% of owners reported some blistering. All subsequent models were built with an exterior layer of vinylester to prevent this. The deck, also formed in a single mold, is cored with balsa in all horizontal areas and is through-bolted to the hull on a flange. To save weight neither the deck nor hull laminate is terribly thick, and this, combined with the free-floating bulkheads inside the hull, makes for a somewhat flexible structure. Flexing in older Gemini 3000s often leads to some crazing and spider cracking in the exterior gelcoat. This problem is usually only cosmetic, but more severe stress cracking may indicate delamination in some areas and should be carefully checked. Older Gemini 3000s may also have problems with leaky Plexiglas windows. These were later changed to Lexan, which works better in windows of this size. Other problems to look for include corroding steering cables and undersized deck hardware.

Though optional inboard diesel engines were available, almost all Gemini 3000s are powered instead by a single long-shaft outboard engine mounted in the middle of the transom. The outboard turns with the rudder cassettes, which greatly improves close-quarters handling under power, and it can be raised when sailing to reduce drag. When the boat was in production outboard-powered 3000s were delivered with either 35 or 40 hp motors, but many boats currently are driven by 25 hp motors. Reportedly even a 10 hp motor can drive the hull along at 5 knots or better.

Because alternators on outboard engines cannot generate much electricity, most Gemini 3000s have propane-fueled water heaters and refrigerators. The refrigerators can also run on 110-volt AC power when plugged in at a dock. All other DC electrical loads for lights, pumps, electronics, etc., must be kept at a minimum, or generation capacity must be augmented with solar panels and/or a wind generator. In most cases owners prefer to cope with the undersized DC system by keeping other systems as simple as possible.

LOA		30'6"
LWL		27'7"
Beam		14'0"
Draft		
	Boards down	4'9"
	Boards up	1'9"
Displacement		7,000 lbs.
Sail area		
	100% foretriangle	425 sq. ft.
	With spinnaker	675 sq. ft.
Fuel		20-40 gal.
Water		60 gal.
D/L ratio		.149
SA/D ratio		
	100% foretriangle	18.55
	With spinnaker	29.46
Nominal hull speed		9.1 knots
Typical asking prices		$35K-$65K

Nonsuch 30

The Nonsuch 30 was the first and most successful of the Nonsuch line of una-rigged cruising catboats built by Hinterhoeller Yachts of Ontario, Canada, from 1978 to 1994. Designed by Mark Ellis at the instigation of Gordon Fisher, a famous Canadian racing sailor who wanted a fast, easy-to-handle cruising boat for his retirement, this boat in particular and its four siblings (the Nonsuch 22, 26, 33, and 36) are among the most popular alternative-rigged production boats ever built. In all a total of 975 Nonsuchs were launched over the years; of these 522 were 30-footers. The Nonsuch remains a popular cult boat, and its active owners' organization, the International Nonsuch Association (INA), has over 700 current Nonsuch owners enrolled on its lists.

The most distinctive feature of any Nonsuch is its sail plan, which resembles that of a windsurfer. A freestanding tapered aluminum mast, situated all the way forward in the bow of the boat, supports a loose-footed mainsail that is hoisted inside a wishbone boom, the end of which is sheeted to the boat's transom. The boom, because it is canted downward, acts as a vang and keeps the clew of the sail from riding up as it is eased. Sail shape otherwise is controlled with a single line called the "choker," which when tightened pulls the boom aft in relation to the mast, thus flattening the sail. When eased the choker allows the boom to shift forward, thus increasing draft. The only other controls (aside from the one halyard) are slab-reefing lines for the tack and clew. The reefed portion of the sail (or the entire sail when doused) falls unassisted into a set of permanently rigged lazyjacks hanging under the boom.

The great advantage of this rig is its simplicity. Tacking the boat involves no line-handling whatsoever (just turn the wheel), though jibing is more challenging, as the sail is very large and like a conventional main is unbalanced, with no area forward of the mast to dampen momentum as it swings across the boat. The rig automatically spills air when pressed, as the head of the unstayed mast is flexible, reportedly falling off as much as a foot in just 10 knots of wind. The crew therefore need not work a sheet or traveler to keep the boat on its feet when gusts come barreling through. The lack of shrouds also makes it possible to set the sail square to wind when running off. Not having any standing rigging to worry about is also a big maintenance bonus.

The downside to the rig is there is no headsail slot to improve windward performance. Nor is there any way to increase sail area when running off in light air, though more zealous owners do sometimes try to fly bloopers to help things along. There may be questions, too, as to the aluminum mast's structural integrity when sailing in rough conditions. For example, one Nonsuch 36 I was familiar with was twice dismasted during different offshore passages. It is worth noting that more contemporary unstayed wishbone rigs, like those seen on the much sleeker Wyliecat, have stiffer carbon-fiber masts. Indeed, there was also a carbon-rigged version of the Nonsuch 30, known as the Nonsuch 324, but only a handful were built before Hinterhoeller folded in 1996.

The other distinctive feature of any Nonsuch is its hull form. Like a classic Cape Cod catboat, which it deliberately mimics, a Nonsuch hull is very beamy and carries a lot of extra volume into its ends. The underbody, however, is modern, with a fin keel and semi-balanced spade rudder right aft. This keeps the boat from developing a heavy helm like a classic catboat and helps windward performance. The boats reportedly can sail just under 45 degrees off the wind when close-hauled. All that beam also creates a lot of initial stability and allows for an enormous interior. The Nonsuch 30 certainly has about the roomiest accommodations plan of any boat its size.

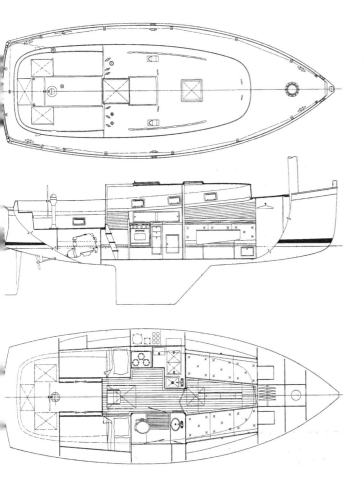

is external lead hanging on stainless-steel keel bolts. All structural bulkheads are right up forward, running both laterally and transversely, to support the area around the base of the unstayed mast and are well bonded to the hull. The quality of construction generally on any Nonsuch is very high, as is reflected in the superb interior joinery. The most commonly reported problems—such as poorly designed propane locker drains, slipping rudder quadrants, and gate valves on through-hulls—are relatively minor and easily remedied. There have also been some bigger problems with corroding aluminum water tanks, but it is now possible to buy custom replacement plastic tanks through the INA.

Though Nonsuchs are strong and well built, I hesitate to recommend them as bluewater cruisers. Aside from the mast concerns mentioned above, the cockpits have no bridgedeck and open onto a large companionway with a low sill. If the companionway is not closed, there is little to stop boarding waves from jumping below. I wonder, too, about the motion of a Nonsuch in a seaway, as they are light and beamy with flat bottoms, a combination likely to be uncomfortable in a steep chop. Nonsuchs do, however, make excellent coastal cruisers, as they are fast, easy to sail, and have extremely comfortable interiors. They are expensive compared to other used boats in their size range, but this reflects both the quality of construction and the fact that interior space is comparable to that seen on much larger vessels. (Note, too, if you are determined to have a brand-new Nonsuch, the Nonsuch 33 is still being built to order by Wiggers Custom Yachts for a base price of $222,000.)

The so-called classic layout, with single and double quarter berths aft and a saloon with two full-length settees all the way forward, can honestly sleep five people if necessary. The more conventional "ultra" layout, offered as an option beginning in 1983, with a Pullman double forward and a large saloon aft, makes a comfortable long-term liveaboard space for a couple and even includes a head with a separate shower. The great sense of space aboard is accentuated in both layouts by the generous headroom (well over 6 feet) afforded by the crowned coachroof and, in the classic layout, by the lack of bulkheads aft of the forepeak.

To save weight the fiberglass decks and hulls on all Nonsuchs, including much of the area below the waterline, have balsa cores. Both Hinterhoeller and its near-sister firm C&C Yachts were well practiced in this sort of construction—solid laminate, for example, is used around all through-hull fittings—but still the structure of any Nonsuch should be carefully examined for moisture intrusion. The deck joint is an inward flange bedded with non-adhesive butyl sealant and through-bolted at regular intervals; the ballast

LOA	30'4"
LWL	28'9"
Beam	11'10"
Draft	
Standard keel	5'0"
Shoal keel	3'11"
Ballast	4,500 lbs.
Displacement	11,500 lbs.
Sail area	540 sq. ft.
Fuel	28 gal.
Water	80 gal.
D/L ratio	216
SA/D ratio	16.93
Comfort ratio	22.47
Capsize screening	2.09
Nominal hull speed	8.3 knots
Typical asking prices	$45K–$80K

Golden Hind 31

Though not well known in the United States, the Golden Hind 31 is an iconic boat in Great Britain, where it is still built today. Conceived as a shoal-draft bilge-keel cruiser for gunkholing the tidal creeks and swatchways of East Anglia, it is also a proven bluewater boat. For many years it was said to hold the record for most transatlantic crossings by a production sailboat, and at least one has been around Cape Horn. Though it does have its quirks, the Golden Hind is extremely versatile. With less than four feet of draft it can sail into all kinds of nooks and crannies where other boats dare not venture. Thanks to its bilge keels, it stands up straight when aground and can be anchored with impunity in areas that dry out at low tide. Add to this the ability to cross oceans, and you have a unique package, particularly for a small boat exhibiting a great deal of traditional charm and character.

The original design, drawn up by Maurice Griffiths, was commissioned in 1965 by a British coffin manufacturer, Hartwell's, that decided to try its hand at boatbuilding. They built 120 Golden Hinds in plywood over six years, whereupon their yard manager, Terry Erskine, took over in 1971 and began building the boat with a fiberglass hull and a wood deck and cabinhouse. Erskine closed up shop in the early 1980s, but in 1995 production was resumed by Golden Hind Marine. Using Erskine's molds they built only a few fancier, more modern "Mark II" versions of the boat before selling out to Newson Boatbuilders in 2006, which is building the boat to all stages of completion (see www.goldenhindyachts.com for details). In all, over 250 Golden Hinds have been launched. Most surviving examples were built by Erskine, who filled several orders for Americans thus the boat can be found on both sides of the Atlantic.

Most Golden Hinds were built with the "standard" sloop rig, which is very short, reaching just 32 feet from deck to masthead. These boats tend to be slow and rarely sail anywhere near their hull speed, except when conditions are boisterous. The more modern Mark

II boats have much taller cutter rigs (over 39 feet from deck to masthead), plus over 1,000 pounds more ballast, and though they have a lower hull speed due to the increased weight, they routinely sail much closer to it. A few of the older boats have also been converted to taller rigs. I did this myself with a 1977 Erskine boat I owned for several years and was very pleased with the results.

With both a long full keel and two small bilge plates in the water, the Golden Hind's underbody presents a lot of lateral surface area in three different planes. The boat tracks well as a result and does not like to change direction. This makes it easy to sail singlehanded, even without self-steering gear. It also sails to windward better than you'd expect, and the bilge plates help to dampen the boat's motion in a seaway. The plates also increase wetted surface area, which hurts light-air performance, most noticeably on boats with shorter rigs. The heavy steel plates can be removed if you like, and I know at least one owner who tried this before embarking on a transatlantic passage. He reported his boat rolled much more than it had before and was more tender and that he did not consider the relatively small increase in boat speed to be worth the bother and discomfort.

Many of the original all-plywood boats have deteriorated over time, but the fiberglass boats are strong and durable. The double-chined hull is solid laminate, while the cabinhouse sides are solid mahogany. The deck and coachroof beams are hardwood covered with marine plywood, which is sheathed with 6-ounce cloth and epoxy resin. The cast-iron ballast is encapsulated within the center full keel, while the bilge plates are through-bolted into a heavy steel support frame installed inside the hull. This allows the plates to carry the weight of the boat when aground without unduly stressing the hull. Structural maintenance revolves mostly around keeping moisture out of the

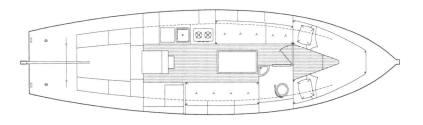

There is also a small removable table that can be set up in the center of the saloon. The V-berth forward can honestly function as two separate single berths, or as a roomy double if the midsection is filled in. An optional dinette layout also allows for the creation of a double berth in the saloon if desired. The galley is a bit undersized with inadequate counter space and can be difficult to use while underway.

The author's Golden Hind Sophie.

wooden parts of the boat, as any leaks lead to water wicking quickly along the plywood's horizontal sections. Fortunately, the structure of the wood deck and house is not complex. All deck sections are easily accessed from inside the boat, and cutting out and replacing saturated areas is relatively easy. The later Mark II boats are built to a finer standard than the Erskine boats, with a more modern hull-laminate schedule and superior interior joinery. The Mark II models also have a redesigned rudder, with some surface area forward of the pivot point in the oversize prop aperture, and this helps relieve the boat's sometimes heavy weather helm.

For a small traditional boat with a narrow beam, the Golden Hind has a remarkably roomy interior. There is over 6 feet of standing headroom throughout the main cabin, which has both a dedicated nav station and a proper wet locker for hanging up foul-weather gear right by the companionway. The traditional layout has a full-size settee berth to starboard, plus a love-seat to port that can be converted to a full-length berth by opening a small hatch in the forward bulkhead, which allows prostrate crew to insert their feet into the bottom of the adjacent hanging locker.

Golden Hind 31

LOA		31'6"
LWL		26'9"
Beam		9'0"
Draft		3'8"
Ballast		
	Original	4,100 lbs.
	Mark II	5,196 lbs.
Displacement		
	Original	11,600 lbs.
	Mark II	13,500 lbs.
Sail area (100% foretriangle)		
	Original	370 sq. ft.
	Mark II	510 sq. ft.
Fuel		20 gal.
Water		40 gal.
D/L ratio		
	Original	271
	Mark II	315
SA/D ratio		
	Original	11.53
	Mark II	14.37
Comfort ratio		
	Original	33.86
	Mark II	39.40
Capsize screening		
	Original	1.59
	Mark II	1.51
Nominal hull speed		
	Original	7.5 knots
	Mark II	7.13 knots
Typical asking prices		
	Original	$12K-$50K
	Mark II	$90K plus
Base price new		$149K

Seaward Eagle 32 RK

Lifting keels have become increasingly common on small high-performance skiffs and sport boats and also on large custom performance cruisers, but are practically unheard of on small or midsize production cruisers. As far as I know, the Seaward Eagle 32 and 26, designed by Nick Hake and built by Hake Yachts in Stuart, Florida, are the only boats of this type available. The 32 was originally introduced as a shoal-draft fixed-keel boat in 1998, and over a two-year period a total of 60 hulls were built. Subsequently the boat was reengineered with a retracting keel, as Hake terms it (thus the "RK" designation), and was reintroduced in 2000. Since that time an additional 75 hulls have been built.

One of the greatest advantages of having a lifting keel on a cruising sailboat this size is that it makes the vessel much more portable. With its keel up the SE 32 draws just 20 inches and can easily slide on to a large triple-axle trailer. You'll need a large truck to tow the load (figure about 10,000 pounds all up), and you obviously won't be launching and recovering the boat on a whim, but trailerability does afford a much greater range of potential cruising grounds and also simplifies long-term and/or seasonal storage. Reportedly it takes an experienced hand about an hour to launch and rig the boat solo, or about 40 minutes if you have an able assistant.

Of course, the other big advantage of the lifting keel is that it allows the SE 32 to sail well as either a deep-draft or shoal-draft vessel. The boat's stated design brief is to be able to cruise shoal water in southern Florida, cross the boisterous Gulf Stream as a deep-water boat, then revert to shoal mode in the Bahamas, and for this application it is, indeed, just about ideal. The keel itself is a high-aspect fiberglass foil with lead ballast fully encapsulated in the keel's lower section and in a large bulb. The foil retracts vertically into a fiberglass trunk that is molded into the hull and glassed to the deck overhead. The heavy lifting is done by a dedicated 12-volt electric wire-reel winch mounted in a special housing on deck; the keel can also be raised manually with the mainsheet block and tackle if the winch fails. Protruding from the top of the keel is an upper keel arm that pierces the deck and is perforated to allow the keel to be pinned in a fully raised, half-raised, or fully lowered position. The pin prevents the keel from dropping, but not from riding up in the trunk if, for example, it grounds out. Intermediate settings are also possible, but in this case the weight of the keel must be carried by the winch and its lifting cable.

Complementing the keel, there is also a retractable transom-hung rudder. Originally the rudder simply kicked up, but in 2005 this was replaced by a one-piece foil housed in a strong stainless-steel cassette that can be fixed in several different positions. This allows for a deeper, more effective steering foil when the rudder is fully lowered and also for more effective steering at intermediate depths. With rudder and keel all the way up, the boat can ground out on the tide or be driven up on to a beach, as both the rudder and exposed propeller and shaft are higher than the retracted keel's minimum draft.

In terms of its construction, the SE 32 is an odd blend of high-end glass work and mass-production expediency. The hull layup features vinylester resin and triaxial cloth with carbon-fiber reinforcements around the keel trunk and in the rudder and keel itself. The hull is cored with Coremat, with Coremat stringers. The deck is mostly solid with some PVC foam core in horizontal areas, and the joint, on an inward flange, is secured with screws and putty. To

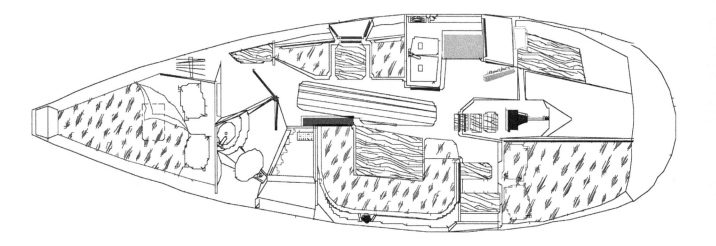

simplify the finishing of the interior, in contrast, there is both an overhead liner and an all-encompassing furniture pan that together make the living accommodations seem somewhat plastic and cheap.

The accommodations plan is also idiosyncratic. The galley and especially the nav station are quite small and cramped, but the head features a separate shower stall, which is practically miraculous on a boat this size. The massive keel trunk intrudes less than you would expect, thanks in large part to the generous headroom (nearly 6½ feet!). Dedicated berthing is limited to the V forward, which though long has an extremely narrow foot, and the double quarter berth, which is cave-like even for a quarter berth. The port-side dinette table can also be collapsed to form yet another double berth, plus a filler can be added between the two small jump seats to starboard to create a single berth. Behind the galley there is also an odd low-slung pantry tucked under the starboard cockpit seat, and this makes an excellent storage area, unless it is filled with a genset, which is offered as a factory option to help power the optional air-conditioning system.

Where the SE 32 really shines is under sail. I got to spend time aboard one of the first RK models after the Annapolis show in 2000 and was most impressed with the boat's performance. The plumb stem and extended reverse transom (replete with a scoop and walk-through stern for easy access to the water) allow for a nice long waterline. There's a good bit of sail area and a very efficient square-headed mainsail. Add in the light, stiff hull and deep high-aspect fin keel, and the result is a boat that is quick and close-winded and also quite fast downwind, particularly when you hoist an asymmetric spinnaker from the nifty bowsprit/anchor platform and pull up the keel a bit to reduce wetted surface area.

Compared to other large trailer-sailing cruisers that rely on centerboards and static water ballast to stay on their feet and resist leeway, the SE 32 sails like the proverbial witch. With its keel all the way down it is reasonably stiff, and though obviously it becomes less so as the keel is raised, it still tracks and steers well, as the lateral position of the foil and ballast remain unchanged.

The SE 32 may seem expensive for a boat its size, but it does hold its value well, as used examples rarely come on the market. It makes an excellent coastal cruiser for a couple or small family. It should also be strong enough for occasional short offshore passages, though the ride may be a bit wild and uncomfortable. With its keel all the way down, I suspect the boat is a bit more stable than its capsize screening value suggests.

LOA		34'7"
LOD		32'2"
LWL		30'7"
Beam		10'6"
Draft		
	Keel up	20"
	Keel down	6'6"
Ballast		2,500 lbs.
Displacement		8,300 lbs.
Sail area (100% foretriangle)		460 sq. ft.
Fuel		20 gal.
Water		65 gal.
D/L ratio		129
SA/D ratio		17.92
Comfort ratio		17.89
Capsize screening		2.07
Nominal hull speed		10 knots
Typical asking prices		$80K–$110K
Base price new		$126K

Seaward Eagle 32 RK

Pearson Alberg 35

Designed by the Swedish emigrant Carl Alberg, who also conceived such iconic fiberglass production boats as the Pearson Triton and all of Cape Dory's product line (including the Cape Dory 36, 40, and 45, which are still built today by Robinhood Marine), the Alberg 35 is a prime example of a CCA-era cruiser-racer that is still a viable low-budget coastal and bluewater cruising boat. Over 250 were built during a 6-year period starting in 1961, and the majority are still in service. The original Alberg 35 could be ordered as either a sloop or yawl, with either tiller or wheel steering, and had two optional interior arrangements. The first features a traditional saloon with twin settee berths (plus two roll-away pipe berths over these) and a fold-down table with a small galley aft. The second is a dinette plan with two quarter berths aft and a larger galley in the saloon opposite the dinette. The forward cabin in both versions is rather commodious for vessels of this type and vintage, with a generous V-berth, a hanging locker, and a small bureau. There is standing headroom of 6 feet or better through most of the interior.

Performance under sail is typical for a classic CCA design. Thanks to its long overhangs and cutaway keel the Alberg 35 does sail a good bit faster than its abysmal D/L ratio suggests, but its narrow beam and slack bilges also make it a tender boat, in spite of all the ballast it carries. In a moderate breeze to windward it quickly heels to an angle of about 30 degrees, with its lee rail just awash, and then sticks there. Having spent two years roaming the North Atlantic aboard one of these boats, I can attest they have a very seakindly motion and make excellent ocean boats, but they are a bit wet in strong conditions, thanks to their low freeboard. The mainsail is quite large relative to the foretriangle, and with its rudder so far forward an Alberg 35 can develop some strong weather helm, particularly when reaching. Some owners cure this by putting on short bowsprits to enlarge the foretriangle; others choose to shorten the rather long boom and shrink the main a bit. The downside to making the mainsail smaller, however, is that you may lose the ability to sail the boat under main alone, which often comes in handy. Note, too, the long overhangs and forward rudder position make it hard to back down under power.

Construction is very simple and robust. The hull is solid fiberglass with more than an inch of laminate below the waterline. The lead ballast is fully encapsulated, so there are no keel bolts to worry over, though some boats have voids under the ballast that may need filling with epoxy. The deck is balsa-cored, and with boats this old there is a good chance some part of it will have become saturated over the years. Depending on how much of the core is wet, this is potentially the largest structural repair an owner will have to confront. In some cases, too, the core under the deck-stepped mast gets crushed and needs to be replaced with a stiffer core material or solid laminate. The original exterior gelcoat on both the deck and topsides was laid on thick and is likely to have crazed over time. This is solely a cosmetic issue, unless the underlying laminate is exposed, in which case the hull's exterior should be faired and refinished. On earlier models, the deck joint is also a bit suspect and is prone to leak if buried in the water for prolonged periods.

The Alberg 35 is a great project boat, and most contemporary examples have been significantly modified by their owners. The original standard power plant was the gasoline-powered Atomic 4, and most of these have been replaced with more modern diesel engines. Those still equipped with original engines should sell for a significant discount. The original rudder was mahogany, and many of these have been replaced with custom-fabricated fiberglass rudders. The original roller-reefing boom was spruce, and though a suprisingly large

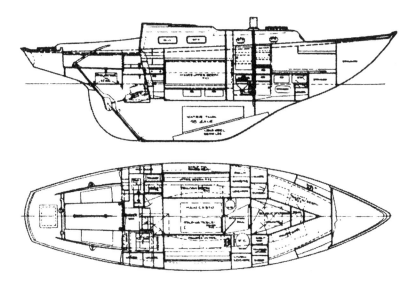

number have survived, most have been converted to slab reefing. Originally there was no traveler for the mainsheet, which was led aft to a pair of blocks either side of the cockpit behind the helmsman. On many boats travelers have been installed, either behind the cockpit, which is not optimal as there is not enough beam aft for a traveler to work well, or just forward of the cockpit on the bridgedeck, which works much better. Other typical upgrades include installation of a bow roller (and perhaps a small manual windlass) for ground tackle, replacement of the undersized sheet winches, fabrication and installation of a seahood over the companionway slide, refinishing of the boat's hideous faux wood-grain Formica interior, replacement of the original hot-and-cold pressure water system (the Alberg 35 was one of the first production sailboats to offer these as standard equipment), installation

of refrigeration, plus rewiring and replacing the minimal electrical panel, to name only a few.

This seems like a lot of work, but the fact is there are few boats you can buy for so little money that are truly capable of extensive offshore work. I purchased a structurally sound Alberg 35 for about $28,000 in the mid-1990s, put another $15,000 into repairs and upgrades, and had myself a very serviceable liveaboard bluewater cruiser. If you are willing to spend more upfront, it is not hard to find an Alberg 35 whose previous owners have already made extensive improvements. If you have little to spend and like to work on boats, you can buy one dirt cheap and fix it up as you go along. By today's standards the boat is somewhat slow and its living space is cramped and primitive, but it is a solid, safe vessel offering lots of value for the money.

The author's Pearson Alberg 35 yawl Crazy Horse.

LOA			34'9"
LWL			24'0"
Beam			9'8"
Draft			5'2"
Ballast			5,300 lbs.
Displacement			13,300 lbs.
Sail area (100% foretriangle)			
		Sloop	545 sq. ft.
		Yawl	583 sq. ft.
Fuel			30 gal.
Water			50 gal.
D/L ratio			430
SA/D ratio			
		Sloop	15.52
		Yawl	16.60
Comfort ratio			36.53
Capsize screening			1.63
Nominal hull speed			6.55 knots
Typical asking prices			$10K–$35K

Wauquiez Pretorien 35

This well-built French cruiser-racer, designed by Holman & Pye, a British firm, first appeared on the market in 1979, just as the IOR rule was peaking in popularity. The Pretorien 35 thus exhibits features common to many boats of this era: it is beamy amidships with somewhat pinched ends and has a smallish high-aspect mainsail and a large foretriangle. It is not, however, an extreme example of its type. Nearly half the boat's design weight is contained in its lead ballast keel, which makes it rather stiff and stable (its AVS is a very respectable 124 degrees), it does not have pronounced tumblehome along its flanks, and its rakish "wedge-deck" profile, similar to that seen on Swans and Baltics built around the same time, give it a distinctive look many sailors find highly attractive. The Pretorien as a result is valued as both a bluewater and coastal cruiser and is considered by many to be an excellent value despite its relatively high price. A total of 212 hulls were built before production ended in 1986, and many of these were exported to the United States, so good examples are not too hard to find on this side of the Atlantic.

Construction quality generally is very good. The Pretorien's solid fiberglass hull is laid up with multiple layers of 18-ounce biaxial cloth and is stiffened by six lateral stringers that run the length of the boat and intersect a series of athwartship beams that are also glassed to the hull. Bulkheads, meanwhile, are tabbed to both the hull and deck in the conventional manner, plus are firmly anchored in place by lateral tabs that pass through holes in lower portions of the bulkheads and are bonded to the hull on either side. The deck is cored with balsa, except under hardware and fittings, where solid laminate is substituted. The coring is laid up in strips segregated by barriers of resin so that any moisture that does intrude cannot migrate easily. The deck joint, on an inward flange, is both through-bolted and glassed over. The external ballast keel is mounted

on a deep keel stub with ¾" stainless-steel bolts. The rudder is mounted on a full skeg.

There are a couple of flies in this ointment. The Pretorien's hull laminate is set in polyester resin, and as is often the case with boats built during the early 1980s there have been some reports of osmotic blisters. Also, on many boats the headstay fitting as originally installed is supported under the deck with mere washers rather than a proper backing plate, and this should be checked and remedied if necessary. Some owners have been less than thrilled with the engine installation. Most Pretoriens were sold with Volvo diesel saildrives (these were unusual in the U.S. at the time), and over the years a number of the aluminum drive legs have developed corrosion problems. Meanwhile, on those boats with conventional shaft drives, the shaft reportedly is too steeply angled to be very efficient. Access to the engine compartment is marginal, making some maintenance jobs difficult. The original 23 hp engine found on some boats may be a bit small; the optional 28 hp engine is preferable.

For those used to the cramped accommodations of older CCA boats the Pretorien's interior will seem spacious, particularly in its beamy middle section. It also compares well to interiors found on more modern boats. The layout itself is straightforward, with a roomy V-berth forward, followed next by a head to starboard with hanging lockers to port, then a large saloon with two straight settees and a dinette, then a spacious galley to starboard with a less spacious nav station to port. Aft to port is another small separate stateroom with a modest double berth. There is a great deal of useful storage space throughout, and the joinery work and general finish quality is excellent. Interior ventilation, however, is inadequate, and some owners have felt compelled to install opening ports and/or cabin fans. Also the twin galley sinks, which

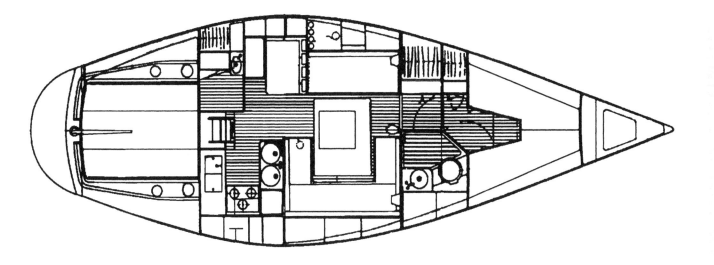

are reasonably close to the centerline, are a bit shallow to work well when the boat is well heeled.

On deck the Pretorien's sleek profile translates to low-slung handholds that are awkwardly placed for the crew as they move forward to the bow. The standing rig features single-point shroud attachments abreast the mast, which means both a babystay and running backs are needed to stabilize the mast when conditions get rowdy. Back in the cockpit there is an effective bridgedeck traveler to help control the mainsail. It may sometimes interfere with a cockpit dodger, however, as will the forward location of the primary winches on the cockpit coaming. The best solution is to move the winches aft about 12 inches so winch handles clear the dodger and are also easier to reach from the helm. Teak decks were optional on these boats and help to enhance their high-end Euro look. Now more than 20 years later, however, any original teak decks will need removing or replacing. If you like the look of teak you should be willing to pay a premium for a boat with a newly laid deck; if you prefer the low maintenance of a glass deck you should also have no problem finding a Pretorien that suits you.

The boat by all accounts is reasonably fast in any breeze blowing harder than 8 to 10 knots. In the light stuff, however, you must be willing to bend on a 150% genoa to keep it sailing nicely. If like many cruisers you are unlikely to change out your working genoa for anything bigger, you need to be ready to use your engine when the wind falters. Beating to windward you can count on sailing relatively narrow angles of 40 degrees or better. Where the Pretorien really shines is in heavy conditions. Owners report they can carry spinnakers in high winds without any tendency to spin out or broach, as was common with so many other IOR designs. And in spite of its relatively high capsize screening number and relatively low comfort ratio, the Pretorien has a strong reputation as a stable, dry boat with a seakindly motion. For a boat with a fin keel, it also balances well and is easy to steer. For many cruisers looking for affordable older boats with a turn of speed, a comfortable motion, solid build quality, and a touch of Euro class, the Pretorien should therefore be a strong candidate.

LOA	35'1"
LWL	30'4"
Beam	11'7"
Draft	6'0"
Ballast	6,400 lbs.
Displacement	13,600 lbs.
Sail area	538 sq. ft.
Fuel	25 gal.
Water	66 gal.
D/L ratio	217
SA/D ratio	14.79
Comfort ratio	25.15
Capsize screening	1.94
Nominal hull speed	8.5 knots
Typical asking prices	$65K–$90K

Allied Princess 36

The Princess 36, built by the long defunct Allied Boat Company up the Hudson River in Catskill, New York, is a robust character ketch that does not pretend to be anything other than a simple, comfortable cruising boat. Designed by Arthur Edmunds and first introduced in 1972, the Princess enjoyed a 10-year production run during which about 140 hulls were built, which likely makes it the most successful boat produced by Allied during its 22 years of existence (1962–84). Of all the boats Allied built—including the Luders 33, sailed by the famous boy-cruiser Robin Lee Graham; the Seawind 30, first fiberglass boat to circumnavigate the globe; and the Seabreeze 35, a very handy CCA cruiser-racer—the Princess is the one that still commands the most loyal following among modern cruising sailors.

Though the Princess is undeniably a chunky craft, it is not unattractive. Its somewhat exaggerated sheerline leads up to a high bow, but blends nicely with its moderate overhangs and shoal-draft cutaway full keel. The boat's performance under sail, though unspectacular, is smooth and steady. The Princess is a bit beamy for a vessel of its vintage, and this, combined with the shallow keel and modestly sized ketch rig, makes it slow to windward. Reportedly a dozen boats were built with deeper keels (5'1" instead of 4'6"), as were a few sloop- and cutter-rigged boats, and all these should be faster and/or more close-winded than the standard boats. A ketch-rigged Princess sails best on a reach, particularly if a mizzen staysail is set between the masts. The long keel tracks well, the ketch rig is easy to balance, and many owners report that this, together with the nonreversing worm-gear steering found on most Princesses, makes it easy to leave the helm unattended for long periods. The boat is said to be a bit tender initially, though it rarely buries its rail, and otherwise has a comfortable motion in a seaway.

As with all boats built by Allied, construction is strong and simple. The Princess hull is solid hand-laid fiberglass—24-ounce woven roving and mat with a surface layer of cloth under the gelcoat—with thicker laminate at the turn of the bilge and down low around the keel. The ballast is lead, glassed over and encapsulated within the keel. The deck is balsa-cored. All bulkheads are tabbed directly to the hull. The rudderstock, impressively, is bronze. The deck joint, fastened on an outward-turned flange, may be susceptible to damage in relatively minor collisions. The joint itself is durable enough—bedded in sealant, through-bolted on 5-inch centers, and then glassed over—and is covered by an extruded aluminum rubrail, but still its exposed position may be a cause for concern when maneuvering around docks and other hard objects. The upside is the joint is easy to access for repairs, though replacing any part of the rubrail with an identical extrusion will be difficult if not impossible.

Though well built, early Princesses were minimally equipped. The heart of the original electrical system consisted of one woefully inadequate 60 amp-hour battery, which later was increased to 90 amp-hours. Battery capacity on most boats will likely have been upgraded by owners over the years; installation quality will inevitably vary. On the very best boats all wiring and panels will have been professionally replaced. Similarly, the original engine, a 25 hp Westerbeke diesel, was not strong enough to power the Princess effectively through head seas and was later replaced with a 40 hp engine. Look for at least 40 horses on any repowered boats. The fuel tank, located under the cockpit, was originally fabricated of black iron and often corroded over time; later tanks were built in Corten steel. In most cases the large stainless-steel water tanks, buried in the bilge of the boat, have lasted much longer.

For a boat of its size and era, the Princess has a roomy interior with standing headroom well over 6 feet. There are at least four different accommodations plans, each with a good-size V-berth up forward, with a head behind it to port and drawers and a hanging locker to starboard. Aft of the main saloon bulkhead there were variations. Some boats have collapsible dinette tables (always to port), some have fold-down centerline bulkhead tables, some

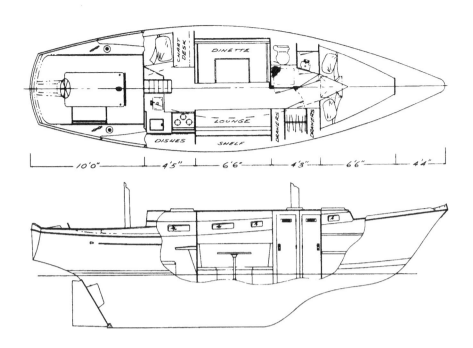

interior finish featured lots of faux-wood Formica veneer. Later, natural wood was used, which looks much better but requires more maintenance.

The Princess, thanks to its shoal-draft keel, is a near-perfect low-budget family cruising boat for skinny-water cruising grounds like Chesapeake Bay, the Florida Keys, or the Bahamas. It will serve admirably, too, as a coastal cruiser in any deep-water locale as long as you aren't in too much of a hurry. With its stout construction and easy motion it could also make a good bluewater cruiser. It would be wise, however, to increase fuel capacity, as the boat sails poorly in light air, and to enlarge the cockpit drains, as these are too small on some boats, and the cockpit is quite large.

have smaller or larger galleys (always aft to starboard), some have single quarter berths aft to port, and some have small enclosed quarter cabins with double berths.

The quarter cabins, though quite cramped, usually have cut-outs in their forward bulkheads to create a sense of space and improve ventilation. The quarter berth arrangement to my mind is superior, however, as it allows space for a modest nav desk. The larger galleys, meanwhile, force a truncation of the starboard-side settee that renders it too short to be used as a berth. Earlier boats have no deck hatch in the main saloon, though later boats do. Which variation works best for you will depend on how many people you want to cruise with and how they are related to each other. Most cruising couples, I suspect, will likely find all the variations work well enough and should probably be more concerned about what systems upgrades have been made. As for aesthetics, the quality of the interior joinery is no better than average. Allied apparently preferred to focus resources on basic construction quality, which is not a bad thing. Before 1979 the

LOA			.36'0"
LWL			.27'6"
Beam			.11'0"
Draft			
		Standard keel	.4'6"
		Deep keel	.5'1"
Ballast			6,000 lbs.
Displacement			15,400 lbs.
Sail area			
		Standard ketch	604 sq. ft.
		Sloop	595 sq. ft.
Fuel			40 gal.
Water			80 gal.
D/L ratio			330
SA/D ratio			
		Standard ketch	15.58
		Sloop	15.35
Comfort ratio			32.25
Capsize screening			1.76
Nominal hull speed			7 knots
Typical asking prices			$30K-$50K

Pacific Seacraft 37

Originally dubbed the Crealock 37 after its designer, "Gentleman Bill" Crealock, this boat is now deemed a conservative cruiser, though when first conceived it was considered a more cutting-edge performance cruiser, thanks to its long fin keel and skeg-hung rudder. Molds to produce the boat were originally created by Clipper Marine, which went bankrupt before building could begin. The molds were acquired by a firm called Cruising Consultants, which launched 16 hulls in 1978 and 1979 before selling out in turn to Pacific Seacraft. Pacific Seacraft produced the boat in Fullerton, California, for 27 years before closing its doors in 2007, whereupon a marine archaeologist, Stephen Brodie, acquired the company name and tooling for several boats, including the 37, and shifted production to North Carolina. As of this writing the new Carolina-based Pacific Seacraft is at work on PSC 37 hull number 274.

Pacific Seacraft has long been renowned for quality work, and this is reflected in the construction of the 37, which has been steadily upgraded over the years. Prior to 1993 hulls were solid laminate composed of mat and woven roving, and decks were cored with plywood; since then stitched biaxial fabrics have been used in the hulls, and decks have been balsa-cored with plywood interposed beneath hardware. All hardware is through-bolted on backing plates with fastener holes carefully sealed in epoxy beforehand. More recently the hull laminate has also included a layer of Kevlar fabric to increase impact resistance. Since 1988, to resolve issues with blistering, vinylester resin has been used in exterior layers. In some cases PSC 37 hulls also have layers of foam or balsa included in the laminate as insulation. The optional insulation cores are added on the interior side of the regular layup, so these boats have slightly less interior volume and are heavier and stronger than their siblings.

The hull is stiffened with a molded pan riven with apertures that allow it to be securely glassed in place. The pan incorporates major furniture components, the engine beds, and

the sides and bottoms of the water tanks, which are covered with Formica-faced plywood lids. The main bulkhead is tabbed to both the hull and the deck and is also through-bolted to a teak deck beam. All partial bulkheads, cabinets, and shelving are glassed to the hull. The ballast is external lead, which is epoxied and bolted to a solid keel stub with stainless-steel keel bolts supported by stainless-steel backing plates that are also bedded in epoxy. The rudder skeg has a stainless-steel plate molded into its leading edge for extra strength. The deck joint, on an inward flange atop a 4-inch-high bulwark, is bedded in adhesive sealant, secured by stainless-steel bolts and backing plates, and topped by a heavy teak caprail.

The PSC 37 is relatively heavy and narrow with long overhangs and consequently has an easy motion and is not inclined to pound in head seas. It tracks well and has great ultimate stability. Reportedly it doesn't bury its rail until heeled to 35 degrees and achieves maximum righting moment at 75 degrees, with only a small decrease at 90 degrees, when its mast is parallel to the water. Its AVS is an impressive 140 degrees. It is also a very attractive boat, with well-balanced lines that appeal to a broad spectrum of sailors.

Like many boats with short waterlines, the PSC 37 sails faster than its D/L ratio suggests. Thanks to its split underbody and somewhat lighter displacement, it is certainly faster than older CCA designs of similar size. In spite of its stern overhang and narrow canoe transom, many owners report hitting 10 knots or better surfing down big waves. The boat's shrouds are secured to outboard chainplates through-bolted to the hull (a very strong installation), but its narrow beam still allows for decent sheeting angles, so apparent wind angles when close-hauled can usually be kept within 40 degrees sailing in flat water. Boats equipped with the optional (and quite popular) shoal-draft Scheel keel, which features a flared ballast bulb, are slightly less close-winded. Most boats have cutter rigs, though a few were also built as sloops and yawls. Most also have wheel steering, though the original design called for a tiller.

Thanks to its narrow beam and pinched hindquarters, the PSC 37 has limited interior space and a

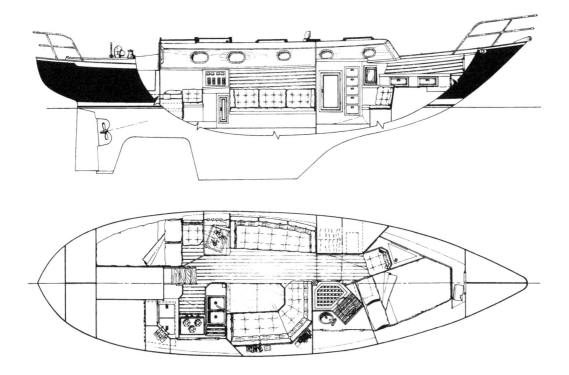

straightforward layout. The forward stateroom seems large and boasts a comfortable offset Pullman double. The only other berths are settees in the saloon (the dinette table on the starboard side can be converted to form a double berth) and a roomy single quarter berth. The nav table just forward of the quarter berth has its own dedicated seat, so the navigator need not sit on anyone's head while working. Headroom throughout is well in excess of 6 feet, courtesy of the tall cabinhouse. Ventilation is very good. The interior finish is neat and traditional with lots of teak trim. Joinerwork is high quality, but not flashy.

Over the years the PSC 37 has been equipped with various engines, all of them diesels. The smallest was a 24 hp Volvo, which probably isn't strong enough in some situations; the largest, standard since the late 1980s, is a 50 hp Yanmar, which is probably more powerful than necessary, particularly given the boat's rather small fuel tank. The tank is aluminum and is situated in the bilge, where it reportedly suffers corrosion over time. Fortunately, it is relatively easy to access and can be removed without dismantling or destroying any joinery. Engine access is also superb; the cockpit floor can be unbolted and removed, putting all parts of the engine and the stern tube within easy reach. On early boats with wheel steering the pedestal must first be removed before lifting the cockpit floor, which is a huge hassle. Later, after wheel steering became standard, the floor was redesigned to make this unnecessary. On all boats the engine can also be accessed at the front through the companionway and via a panel on the port side.

In sum, the PSC 37 is an extraordinarily strong, well-built ocean boat and is priced accordingly. It makes an ideal bluewater cruiser for a couple and also works well as a coastal cruiser for a small family. For those interested only in a coastal boat, it may be a bit heavy and expensive, but compared to many other lighter, less expensive boats it does hold its value well.

LOA		.36'11"
LWL		.27'9"
Beam		.10'10"
Draft		
	Standard keel	5'6"
	Scheel keel	4'5"
Ballast		.6,200 lbs.
Displacement		.16,000 lbs.
Sail area		
	100% foretriangle	.573 sq. ft.
	Cutter	708 sq. ft.
	Yawl	619 sq. ft.
Fuel		40 gal.
Water		.95 gal.
D/L ratio		335
SA/D ratio		
	100% foretriangle	.14.41
	Cutter	.17.80
	Yawl	15.57
Comfort ratio		33.71
Capsize screening		1.72
Nominal hull speed		7.1 knots
Typical asking prices		.$100K–$230K
Base price new		.$370K

Tayana 37

This is the most successful of the several Taiwan-built double-ended full-keel cruisers conceived in the mid-1970s in the wake of the great success of the Westsail 32. Designed by Bob Perry and originally marketed as the CT 37 when introduced in 1976, over 600 Tayana 37s have since been built. Technically it is not still in production, but Tayana, a.k.a. the Ta Yang Yacht Building Co., has all relevant molds and tooling and still fills orders for new boats on a spot basis. The Tayana 37 is heavy by today's standards, but it sails remarkably well and can serve effectively as both a coastal and bluewater cruiser. It has a particularly strong reputation as an offshore boat and is certainly one of the most popular bluewater cruisers ever built. Reportedly there are more Tayana 37s out there wandering the globe than any other single type of sailboat.

In designing this boat Perry sought to retain the character of strictly traditional full-keel double-enders like the Westsail while injecting as much performance into the formula as possible. The forefoot of the full keel is cut away, and the rudder has a more modern, efficient profile. The hull's cross section is not a classic wineglass shape in which hull and keel are a unitary form. Instead the hull is very round, and the keel constitutes a distinct and separate foil-like appendage. The rig is large and quite tall for a boat of this type. The original sail plan called for a cutter rig with a sharply raked mast, but this resulted in a heavy helm. Perry therefore preferred the optional ketch rig, which is better balanced, but the overall sail area of this rig is smaller and few were built. As it turned out, the cutter rig balances just fine if the mast rake is eliminated, and cutter-rigged Tayana

37s have proven to be relatively fast and weatherly. One good friend of mine who made both solo and doublehanded transatlantic passages in his cutter-rigged Tayana 37 claims to have sailed as many as 186 miles in a day. Though the boat carries its fair share of ballast, it is a bit tender initially with its tall rig and heavy teak-laden topsides and deck. Its motion, however, is smooth and comfortable in a seaway.

Ta Yang is one of the better Taiwanese builders, and the Tayana 37's construction quality on the whole is very good. Still, Ta Yang had a bit to learn as it went along, and later boats are better built than earlier ones. The hull is solid handlaid glass stiffened with strong bulkheads and stout floors, the deck is balsa-cored, and the iron ballast, glassed into the hollow keel section, is internal. All deck hardware is through-bolted and supported by robust stainless-steel backing plates. Flaws on boats built before 1981 include inferior electrical wiring and the use of inferior stainless-steel alloys in some hardware and fittings. Also, deck joints on early boats are prone to leaking, as the joint forms a hollow raised bulwark that is pierced by several hawsepipes and scuppers that may not be well bedded in sealant. On later boats the bulwark's interior cavity is glassed over from the inside, thus is more watertight. Some early boats may also have spruce spars, which are heavy and prone to rot, and sloppy worm-gear steering systems, which were later replaced with more sensitive pedestal/cable systems.

Almost all Tayana 37s were built with teak decks. These look nice, but are fastened with screws, a likely source of leaks later in a boat's life. Another common problem is the bronze rudder heel, which is fastened to the

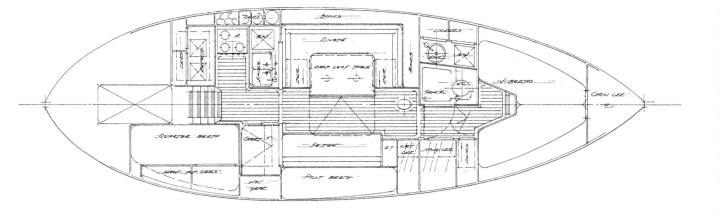

hull with stainless-steel bolts and thus prone to galvanic corrosion. Prospective buyers should also be wary of the laminated wood bowsprit, which tends to rot underneath over the years if not scrupulously maintained. Look for varnished sprits with no signs of moisture damage; a painted sprit is often a sign of trouble.

For a production builder Ta Yang has always offered a surprising number of options. The Tayana 37, for example, was offered as a cutter or ketch, with either wood or aluminum masts that could be deck- or keel-stepped. The boat is also available in a pilothouse version. Tank locations are likewise somewhat variable. The original design called for fuel tanks under the settees in the main saloon, but Ta Yang instead installed one large tank under the V-berth in the forward stateroom to create more storage space in the saloon. This, unfortunately, only hobbled the boat's performance. Later a midships keel tank was offered as an option, and this proved far superior. In most cases fuel tanks were built of black iron, thus are prone to corrosion. Fortunately, the tanks are relatively easy to access (this includes the midships keel tank) so this is not as troublesome as it might be.

One of the most variable aspects of the Tayana 37 is its accommodations plan. Ta Yang effectively customizes interiors at no extra charge, and owners ordering new boats have generally taken full advantage of this. The standard layout is straightforward with a large V-berth forward, a simple open quarter berth aft, and a conventional saloon between the two. The earliest standard layout featured a pilot berth in the saloon. Many boats have offset Pullman doubles forward, a few have separate aft-quarter staterooms, and custom-built storage/seating arrangements are common. Most boats have separate shower stalls alongside the head, a luxury in a yacht this size. The interior is finished in solid teak, and the quality of the joinery work is superb, as good as on any high-end European boat.

One of the best things about the Tayana 37 is its affordability. Older boats in need of work can be had for under $50,000; younger boats in very good condition, crammed to the gills with all kinds of off-shore equipment and systems upgrades, can often be had for less than $100,000. Usually there are many boats on the brokerage market at any given time, which makes it easy for buyers to press for bargains and hard for sellers to recover money spent on extra gear and upgrades.

LOA		36'8"
LWL		31'0"
Beam		11'6"
Draft		5'8"
Ballast		7,340 lbs.
Displacement		24,000 lbs.
Sail area		
	Cutter rig	861 sq. ft.
	Ketch rig	768 sq. ft.
Fuel		100 gal.
Water		90-100 gal.
D/L ratio		359
SA/D ratio		
	Cutter rig	16.52
	Ketch rig	14.74
Comfort ratio		43
Capsize screening		1.59
Nominal hull speed		7.5 knots
Typical asking prices		$40K-$120K
Base price new		$245K

Beneteau First 38

The French firm Beneteau was formed in 1884 as a builder of wooden fishing boats and switched to building fiberglass recreational vessels in 1964. They first started building sailboats in 1972 and today claim to be the largest boatbuilder in the world. Beneteau's First series of performance cruising sailboats was introduced in 1979 and quickly blossomed to include this boat, which was branded as the First 38 because it measures 38 feet on deck, though in fact it is 40 feet long overall.

Designed by Jean Berret and introduced in 1982 the First 38 was one of the earliest sailboats to boast the popular three-stateroom layout now found on many mass-produced monohulls. It also was one of the first production boats built with a reverse scoop transom, another widely adopted feature. (The transom on the First 38 is convertible, with solid sections that can be inserted to fill in the scoop.) It is attractive and solidly built for an inexpensive mass-produced boat, an excellent value for anyone looking for a strong, fast cruising boat that can also be successfully raced (typically its PHRF rating is about 108). Like all Beneteaus, the First 38 had a relatively short production run, from 1982 to 1985, but during that time over 200 hulls were built, several of which were exported to both coasts of North America. In 1986 much of the tooling for the First 38 was used by Beneteau to create the First 405, which has a different interior (just two staterooms instead of three), a deeper keel and more ballast, and is finished to a slightly higher standard.

Unlike many modern cruising boats that have very wide aft sections and thus have a strong tendency to round up while going to windward, the First 38 has a more balanced shape with a tapered stern and handles well on all points of sail. Owners describe the boat as being very close-winded, with less of a tendency to pound hard going to weather in a seaway compared to more modern performance boats that have flat bilges forward. The boat can do better than 7 knots sailing upwind in moderate conditions and will surf downwind when pressed, reportedly achieving top speeds in excess of 13 knots. The First 38 also tracks well, and its helm is light and balanced in most conditions. Average runs sailing offshore on extended passages are said to be between 150 to 170 miles per day.

Structurally the First 38 is significantly stronger than most mass-produced boats built today. The hull is solid fiberglass laminate stiffened with a large pan incorporating a structural grid that is firmly glassed to the hull. The pan is quite shallow, thus does not limit access to most of the hull above the bilge, and it features several access ports so most of the bilge can be reached, too. Bulkheads are glassed along their entire perimeter to both the hull and the deck and are also bolted to the floor pan. The deck joint is simple and solid—bonded with sealant and through-bolted. The deck is balsa-cored for stiffness, with solid laminate underneath hardware. There are also raised bosses under key fixtures, such as the chainplate covers amidships and the big genoa sheet turning blocks aft, to shed water that might otherwise try to wriggle its way below. The ballast is cast iron externally mounted on stainless-steel keel bolts. One thing to watch out for are osmotic blisters. Like many fiberglass boats built during the 1980s, the First 38 has had more than its fair share of these. In many cases repairs have been made at Beneteau's expense; in some cases, however, multiple repairs have been needed.

For a vessel of its size the First 38 can theoretically sleep an enormous number of people. Originally there were narrow pilot berths either side of the saloon, and these, plus the two settees, plus the double berths in the three staterooms, make it possible to cram in as many as 10 slumbering bodies. The V-berth forward, however, is quite narrow at its foot, as are the pilot berths, and the doubles in the aft staterooms are a tight fit for two. This isn't a problem during a short-distance race,

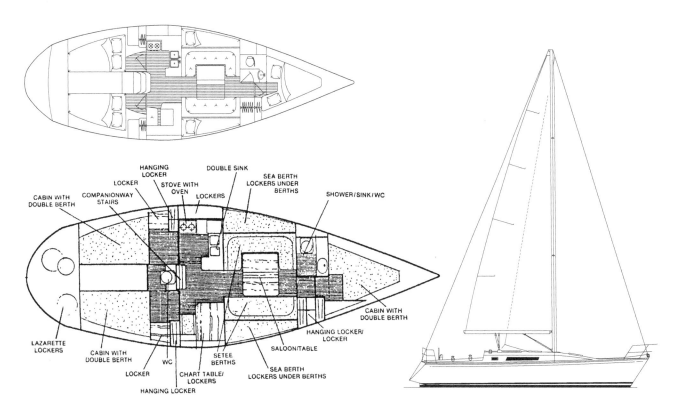

HANGING LOCKER
LOCKER
DOUBLE SINK
STOVE WITH OVEN
SEA BERTH LOCKERS UNDER BERTHS
CABIN WITH DOUBLE BERTH
COMPANIONWAY STAIRS
LOCKERS
SHOWER/SINK/WC
CABIN WITH DOUBLE BERTH
LAZARETTE LOCKERS
CABIN WITH DOUBLE BERTH
WC
LOCKER
CHART TABLE/ LOCKERS
SETEE BERTHS
SALOON/TABLE
HANGING LOCKER/ LOCKER
SEA BERTH LOCKERS UNDER BERTHS
HANGING LOCKER

but cruisers, particularly live- aboards, will probably be happier keeping the body count down to four or five. Indeed, the layout is nearly perfect for families with children who want to cruise for long periods. The emphasis on berthing limits storage space, but there is more of it than you would expect on a boat of this type. On many boats the cramped pilot berths have been converted to cupboard or shelf space. In some cases, particularly on boats used for bluewater cruising, owners have also converted the tiny aft head behind the companionway into a giant pantry or storage locker.

The finish quality down below is good for a mass-produced boat and features lots of pleasing teak veneer and trim. The headliner, however, is a problem. In the main saloon the liner consists of vinyl-covered plywood panels that are easy enough to remove and replace when accessing hardware fasteners. Throughout the rest of the boat the liner is a foam-backed vinyl fabric glued directly to the deck and hull. Eventually the foam oxidizes and crumbles, the adhesive fails, and the vinyl comes tumbling down. The lazy man's solution is to simply glue the existing fabric back in place, but with the crumbling foam still underneath this inevitably looks bumpy and ugly. The best solution is to remove it all and replace it with something stronger and more attractive, but this is a big job. It is also common for overhead hatches to suffer severe crazing over time, and these, too, often need replacing.

The standard engine on the First 38 was the extremely reliable Perkins 4108 diesel. The engine is no longer manufactured, but parts are still widely available and rebuilds are common. A well-cared-for 4108 is capable of running well over 10,000 hours, but the beast is not immortal. Be particularly wary of any boat that has been in charter service. Engines on these vessels will have idled hours in neutral to charge batteries and may be worn out. Such boats are also likely to be ragged around the edges, with dated systems, and should sell at a significant discount. Many privately owned boats, however, have been well maintained and are filled with new gear and sails. These sell at a premium and are well worth the money.

LOA	40'2"
LWL	31'9"
Beam	12'9"
Draft	
Shoal keel	5'8"
Deep keel	6'10"
Ballast	6,600 lbs.
Displacement	16,600 lbs.
Sail area (100% foretriangle)	754 sq. ft.
Fuel	35 gal.
Water	105 gal.
D/L ratio	231
SA/D ratio	18.50
Comfort ratio	25.03
Capsize screening	1.99
Nominal hull speed	8.5 knots
Typical asking prices	$40K-$80K

Beneteau First 38

319

C&C Landfall 38

The Landfall 38 is one of a series of four Landfall models designed by Rob Ball and produced by C&C Yachts in Ontario, Canada, from the late 1970s into the mid-1980s. Unlike most C&C boats, which were designed as straight racers or racer-cruisers, the Landfalls were conceived and marketed as performance cruisers. They were a bit ahead of the curve and were not as commercially successful as they should have been, as many cruising sailors at the time still favored heavier, more traditional designs. The Landfall 38 was the most successful boat in the series—about 180 were built from 1979 to 1985—and today it makes an excellent choice for both coastal and bluewater cruisers looking for an older boat that is fast, comfortable, affordable, and well built.

C&C was a dominant player in the 1970s racing scene, yet managed to resist many of the design extremes inspired by the IOR rating system. The Landfall 38's hull form, for example, is directly derived from an earlier C&C 38 racer-cruiser, and though very much a creature of the IOR—with a raked bow and fine entry, beamy midship section, and somewhat pinched stern—it is not extreme. Compared to the earlier 38, the Landfall has a longer shoal-draft keel and a much shallower spade rudder (draft is 5' versus 6'1"), plus a nearly vertical transom (as opposed to an IOR-style reverse transom). The Landfall is heavier and has slightly less sail area, but is said to sail nearly as well as its racing sister. The Landfall's tall double-spreader rig (supported by rod rigging, no less) and narrow sheeting angles make it quite close-winded, even with its shoal keel. The boat also balances easily, has a light helm and a relatively smooth motion in a seaway, and is stiff in a breeze. It is generally fast and easily driven, as evidenced by the fact that the seemingly undersized standard 30 hp Yanmar diesel reportedly has no problem pushing the boat up to hull speed.

The Landfall has a longer, fuller cabinhouse than its racing predecessor. The extra space inside is put to good use, and the accommodations are unique and well thought out. Most Landfall 38s feature a large athwartship aft cabin set off by a full bulkhead and door just forward of the companionway. In some cases there is an undersized double quarter berth to port and a single berth to starboard; in others the portside double is larger and there is a small nav station to starboard. The space forward of the aft bulkhead, in the widest part of the boat, is dedicated to the head and galley, both of which are uncommonly spacious for a boat this size. The galley to port, laid out in either a U- or L-shape, has two deep centerline sinks and scads of storage space; the head to starboard on some boats even includes a separate shower stall. Forward of the galley and head is the saloon, with a fixed centerline drop-leaf table between the straight settees (a few boats have a fold-down bulkhead table instead), followed by a separate forward stateroom with a V-berth whose foot, alas, is a bit narrow for two large adults to share.

One significant drawback to the ambitious floor plan is that engine space has been short-changed to accommodate it. The engine is mounted backward deep under the cockpit with a V-drive and is difficult, though not impossible, to get to. Access forward (to the back of the engine) is via a bureau assembly under the companionway that realistically can only be displaced after its drawers have first been emptied. Access aft (to the front of the engine) is via a small panel alongside the port quarter berth or through the starboard cockpit locker, which also must be emptied before the engine can be reached. Funnels and hoses are normally needed to add fluids. The bottom line is that routine maintenance may seem too troublesome for some lazy owners to bother with. If buying one of these boats you should check the engine carefully; if you own one,

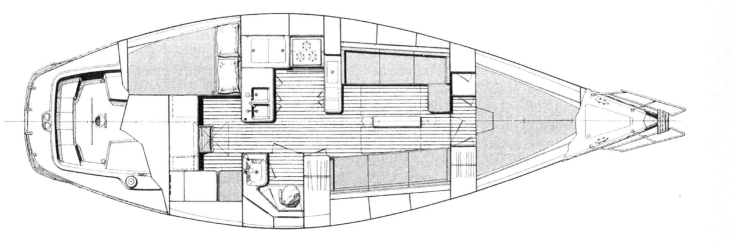

you need to stay motivated about taking care of it. The engine space lacks sound insulation, so the quarter berth (or berths) can be noisy when motoring.

Structurally the Landfall 38 is well put together and is certainly strong enough for offshore work. As on most C&Cs, the deck and most of the fiberglass hull are cored with balsa. This saves weight and stiffens the laminate, but the core is vulnerable to moisture intrusion over time. C&C pioneered balsa-sandwich construction in the mid-1960s and by the late 1970s was quite adept at it, and there have been few reports of major delamination problems on Landfall 38s. Evidently, however, fasteners for deck hardware may penetrate the core in some areas; prospective buyers should therefore make sure there is no significant core saturation on boats they are interested in. A new owner would be wise at some point to remount and rebed all hardware, making sure to seal off any exposed core with epoxy.

The deck joint, on an inward flange, is throughbolted and sealed with butyl tape, which is not adhesive and reportedly may leak eventually. The Landfall 38 rarely buries its rail while sailing so this should not be a huge problem. More bothersome are leaks around stanchion bases caused by uneven loads on backing plates that can't seat flush on the narrow deck flange. To cure these it is necessary to build up a flush surface under the plate with some fairing compound and remount and rebed the bases. The ballast is external lead bolted to a strong keel stub. The mast is keel-stepped, and though the mast step is well designed to prevent mast-heel corrosion, the partners are prone to leak.

Other complaints about the Landfall 38 are relatively minor. Both the on-deck anchor locker and the anchor roller on the stem are a bit undersized (the former is impossible to cure, while the latter is not); the nonskid surface on deck is not very aggressive and eventually needs to be renewed; plus there is a fair bit of teak on deck that takes some work to keep up. Otherwise the fit and finish on the boat is very good and generally superior to that found on most production boats built around the same time. The Landfall 38 was an expensive boat to buy new in its day, but prices on the brokerage market are reasonable and the boat now represents an excellent value. With some patience and effort it is not too hard to find one in good condition.

LOA	37'7"
LWL	29'7"
Beam	12'0"
Draft	5'0"
Ballast	6,500 lbs.
Displacement	15,000 lbs.
Sail area (100% foretriangle)	649 sq. ft.
Fuel	30 gal.
Water	103 gal.
D/L ratio	259
SA/D ratio	17.04
Comfort ratio	26.28
Capsize screening	1.94
Nominal hull speed	7.9 knots
Typical asking prices	$45K–$80K

Jeanneau Lagoon 380

The Lagoon 380 is not the smallest Lagoon catamaran ever built—both the Lagoon 37, its immediate predecessor, and the Lagoon 35CCC were smaller—but it is the smallest Lagoon currently built and one of the smallest dedicated cruising cats that succeeds in combining both reasonable performance and a "big cat" accommodations plan in a single package. It is a carefully balanced exercise in moderation. Designed by Marc Van Peteghem and Vincent Lauriot Prevost and first introduced in 2000, the Lagoon 380 is intended to serve both as a charter fleet workhorse (it is co-branded as the Moorings Lagoon 380) and as a serious entry-level cruising cat for private owners. As I write, hull number 500 is about to be launched, with a new hull launched every three days, making this boat the most successful contemporary cruising cat currently on the market.

The key to the 380's popularity, without a doubt, is its supple accommodations plan. The hulls are just wide enough to fit a good-size double berth in each "corner" of the boat. In the four-stateroom charter version of the layout (four doubles with two small midship heads) four couples can enjoy complete conjugal privacy while cruising together, which is impressive on a boat just 38 feet long. In the three-stateroom "owner's" version the entire starboard hull becomes a deluxe master suite with a small office and large forward head with a separate shower stall, just like on much bigger cats.

The main saloon, slung between the hulls on the bridgedeck, is relatively compact, but its layout makes it seem larger. The galley is just large enough to work comfortably in (though it could use a bit more counter space) and lies along a partial horizontal aft bulkhead fit with a sliding glass panel that permits generous access to the cockpit and outside breezes. The table and settees forward of the galley are large enough to be very useful and benefit from Lagoon's trademark vertical saloon windows. These both increase usable interior space and afford fabulous wraparound views of the outside world. The only area that receives short shrift is the vestigial nav station, which has minimal room for electronic installations and even less room for spreading out charts.

The cockpit and deck layout also work well. The single-station helm is to port, behind the aft cabin bulkhead on a small raised dais with good views of both bows and transoms. There is also a good view of the sails through a small hatch in the umbrella-type canvas bimini. Most sail controls (the main halyard, main sheet, and port jibsheet) are led to the helm. Though the main traveler must be controlled at the back of the cockpit and the starboard jibsheet is opposite the helm, the cockpit is compact enough that one or two crew can operate the boat efficiently. The side decks and foredeck just in front of the cabinhouse are perfectly flat and quite wide (which is not always the case on smaller cruising cats), so going forward and handling ground tackle is easy. The cockpit is just large enough to serve as a great social venue.

The 380 is not terribly light for an unballasted cat and is very much a mass-production boat. The handlaid hull is solid fiberglass below the waterline and is cored with a mix of foam and balsa above the waterline, with vinlyester resin in the outer layers of the laminate to resist blistering. The deck, also laid up by hand, is balsa cored with solid laminate interposed under the deck hardware. Hardware is backed by a mix of washers and backing plates, and the deck joint is bonded and fastened with screws instead of through-bolts. Interior bulkheads are merely bonded to the outer sides of the hulls, but are tabbed to the inner sides, where they help stiffen the hulls in the area of the crossbeams and bridgedeck.

The 380's sailing performance, as with many dedicated cruising cats, is hampered by certain aspects of its physique. Its hulls, as mentioned, are wide, though not extremely so, and are symmetrically shaped. To resist leeway there are a pair of fixed low-aspect keels, which are not as efficient as daggerboards or centerboards and are harder for the boat to pivot on when tacking. The bridgedeck is reasonably high for a cruising cat, about $2\frac{1}{2}$ feet off the water, and does not

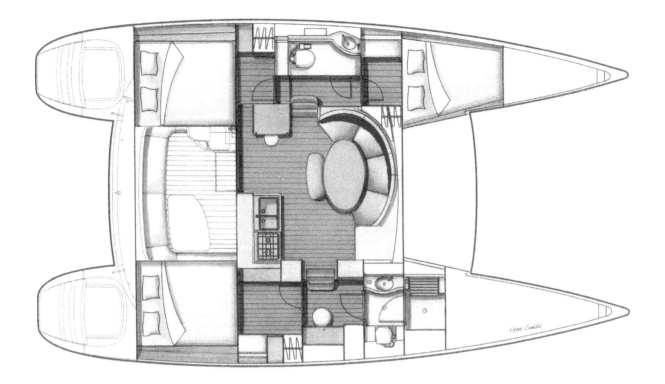

stretch too far forward. The sail plan, though it features a modern full-battened main with a full roach, is modest in size.

What this adds up to is a cat that can sail 10 knots or better with a strong wind near its beam but is not very close-winded. I test-sailed a 380 on Chesapeake Bay when they first appeared on the market and later chartered one for a week in the West Indies and found they don't maintain much speed if held closer than 50 degrees to the apparent wind. They also tend to dog it in lighter air, though this can be cured by fitting the optional sprit forward and flying a lightweight gennaker. Once the wind drops much below 10 knots, however, most cruisers will want to kick on the twin engines and get the saildrives turning. Still, the 380 sails better than most fat "condo cats." If you're willing to set a spinnaker you can keep it moving nicely when sailing off the wind. If you are careful to build momentum before putting the helm down you can also tack it cleanly through the wind without stalling. In a moderate sea there is little problem with the bridgedeck pounding, though I expect this would be more noticeable in larger waves.

All up the Lagoon 380 delivers a great deal of attractive living space for the money and makes an excellent family coastal cruiser. There are also now a number of owners who use 380s for extended bluewater cruising,

though many might prefer vessels with a bit stronger construction and larger fuel and water tanks. A few different models of the 380 have been marketed in recent years, but differences between them are not substantive and mostly involve accommodations details and standard equipment packages.

LOA		37'11"
LWL		36'1"
Beam		21'5"
Draft		3'9"
Displacement		
	Light ship	13,010 lbs.
	Loaded	15,697 lbs.
Sail area		833 sq. ft.
Fuel		53 gal.
Water		79 gal.
D/L ratio		
	Light ship	124
	Loaded	149
SA/D ratio		
	Light ship	24.05
	Loaded	21.22
Nominal hull speed		
	Light ship	11.0 knots
	Loaded	10.4 knots
Typical asking prices		$195K–$325K
Base price new		$300K

Scape 39 Sport Cruiser

As I write only one of these boats has ever been built, but I am including it here because it is perhaps the best and most attractive example I've yet encountered of a very fast open-bridgedeck catamaran with enough living space to keep two couples (or a small family) comfortable during an extended cruise, or even three couples (or a large family) during a short one. The boat is built by a small family-owned firm, Scape Yachts, outside Cape Town, South Africa, which is also where several of the most popular mass-production charter/cruising cats sold in North America now come from. The design, by Alexander Simonis and Maarten Voogd, is derived from a day-charter catamaran that Scape has sold to headboat operators in both Cape Town and Mauritius. The one Sport Cruiser created thus far was sold to an American owner in Florida.

The Scape 39's construction is light and extremely stiff. The crane operator who launched the first Sport Cruiser in Cape Town (he has also launched many cats for big South African builders) proclaimed it the stiffest boat he's ever handled. The laminate consists of stitched E-glass fabric vacuum-bagged in epoxy resin over a PVC foam core with carbon-fiber reinforcements in the crossbeams. The two hulls are quite narrow with very fine plumb bows and deep daggerboards and are connected by a high bridgedeck. The rig features plain aluminum spars, a large mainsail with a very full roach, a non-overlapping solent jib, and a fixed bowsprit for flying large reaching sails and asymmetric spinnakers.

The main feature on deck is the distinctive hardtop pod directly behind the mast. This is the only shelter outside the hulls and contains two settees with a narrow table between them. Drop the table, add a filler cushion, and you've got a super-sized on-deck double berth. Leave it up and the pod serves as a great social center where meals can be shared or deck watches maintained in sheltered comfort. Behind the pod is a central steering pedestal

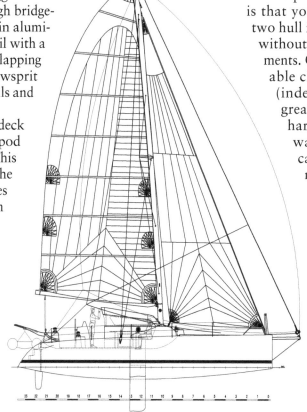

surrounded by a battery of four winches controlling the double-bridle mainsheet, headsail sheets for any sails flown from the bowsprit, and the control lines for the daggerboards. All halyards and reefing lines and the single-lead sheet for the solent jib are fed through organizers and clutches to two winches mounted on each side of the pod. This deck layout works well and makes it possible for one crewmember assisted by an autopilot, or two experienced crew working without a pilot, to sail the boat in most conditions.

The accommodations in the hulls are a bit minimal, but are still more comfortable than those I've seen on other truly high-performance cruising cats in this size range. There are good-sized double-platform berths all the way aft in each hull plus a head for each hull forward. In the middle of the port hull there is a small stand-up nav station; the starboard hull has a small galley with a fixed range and sink. Both hulls also have narrow single berths in the bows forward of collision bulkheads. These can only be accessed through bow hatches and for most mortals are not habitable while sailing in anything like a seaway. Standing headroom in the hulls is a whisker under 6 feet. Storage is limited, though there are some useful large open shelves behind the daggerboard cases.

The problem with the living space is that you cannot move between the two hull interiors and the pod on deck without exposing yourself to the elements. On a coastal cruise in an agreeable climate this not troublesome (indeed, to many it will seem a great asset), except when it rains hard. But when sailing in open water in strong conditions it can be uncomfortable, though not impossible, to deal with. I helped deliver the first Scape 39 Sport Cruiser from Cape Town as far as Brazil, and though conditions were moderate most of the way, the few hours we spent in heavy air and rough seas were pretty wild. With incessant spray flying over the deck it was impossible to move from galley to dinette table to nav station

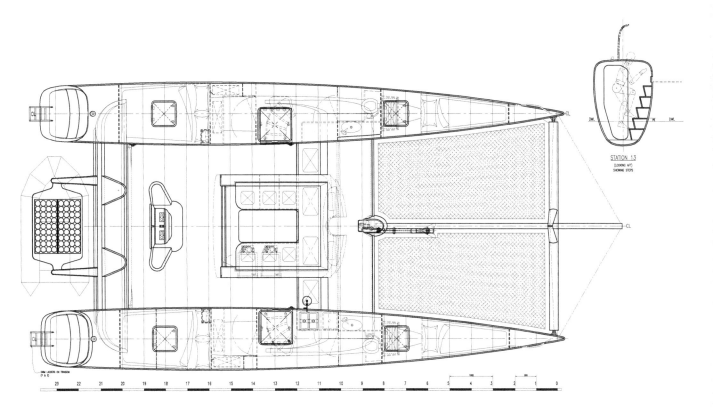

STATION 13
(LOOKING AFT)
SHOWING STEPS

without first donning foul-weather gear. Every time we opened a hatch to go anywhere we stood a good chance of shipping a wave below. Sleeping below when it was rough was something like trying to relax while going over Niagara Falls in a barrel.

Of course, the best thing about the Scape 39 is how fast it sails. Put a moderate breeze anywhere near its beam and it takes off like a banshee. It can easily sail faster than its nominal hull speed when conditions are right and has an actual top speed somewhere around 20 knots. It can and will fly a hull when pressed hard, thus is not a boat for the faint of heart. Because it does accelerate so hard, apparent wind speed and direction can be extremely variable and are often very different from the true wind. This seriously changes how you think about passage planning. We sailed over 225 miles in one day, which is remarkable for a cruising vessel of this size, and at one point were doing a steady 15 to 17 knots while staying reasonably comfortable. During most of our voyage, with light to moderate winds right aft, we made good about 160 miles a day sailing conservatively. Thanks to its deep daggerboards, which provide plenty of lift, the Scape also performs well to windward, a big plus on a catamaran.

In terms of systems, the boat can be kept very simple. Hull number 1 has twin inboard Yanmar diesels with saildrives, a very nice refrigeration system, and electric toilets. None of this is really necessary. An outboard engine on a bracket, a well insulated icebox (or even a couple of big portable coolers), and a pair of manual toilets would work just fine on the sort of cruises for which this boat is best suited.

LOA		39'5"
LWL		39'0"
Beam		21'0"
Draft		
	Boards down	6'6"
	Boards up	3'0"
Displacement		10,362 lbs.
Sail area		
	100% foretriangle	967 sq. ft.
	With gennaker	1,850 sq. ft.
Fuel		80 gal.
Water		80 gal.
D/L ratio		78
SA/D ratio		
	100% foretriangle	32.50
	With gennaker	62.17
Nominal hull speed		13.3 knots
Base price new		approx. $350K

Lunacy, ex *Star Cruiser* (Tanton 39)

This is a one-off aluminum cutter I purchased in the summer of 2006 from an active cruising couple, Bob and Carol Petterson, who commissioned the boat's construction and launched her in 1985. They cruised the boat extensively on the U.S. East Coast and in the Bahamas and also completed a circumnavigation. The bare hull was built by Kingston Aluminum Yachts in Ontario, Canada, and was finished in Rhode Island. The design is by Yves-Marie Tanton, who worked with both Bob Perry and Chuck Paine in Dick Carter's office in Boston before making a name for himself designing several successful custom IOR race boats in the mid-1970s. The boat's hull is identical to that of an earlier 37-foot Tanton design featuring a simple cat-ketch rig with freestanding masts, but has a two-foot scoop tacked onto its transom. Though a number of the cat-ketches, dubbed "ocean-going Volkswagens" by Tanton, were built by Kingston Aluminum, *Star Cruiser*, as she was originally known, was the only cutter-rigged boat built.

Lunacy, as I've chosen to call her (after daughters Lucy and Una), is typical of the many metal cruising boats that have been custom-built on the cheap to stock designs (primarily in Europe) since the 1970s. To simplify construction the boat's hull is hard-chined (it is in fact triple-chined, though it seems double-chined, as the bottom chine is quite soft) and her deck is flush, save for a small cabinhouse just in front of the cockpit. Construction is robust. The hull skin is supported by T-shaped frames on 18-inch centers and is composed of 5 mm plate down low, shifting to 4 mm plate in the topsides and deck. All of the structure above the waterline is insulated with blown foam. The topsides are unfinished, and the deck is painted white and beige. Aside from keeping the deck paint up, there is no exterior cosmetic maintenance to worry about. Already

during my tenure the boat has survived a collision, suffering only a small dent in her toe rail. A fiberglass boat, I am sure, would have been severely damaged in similar circumstances.

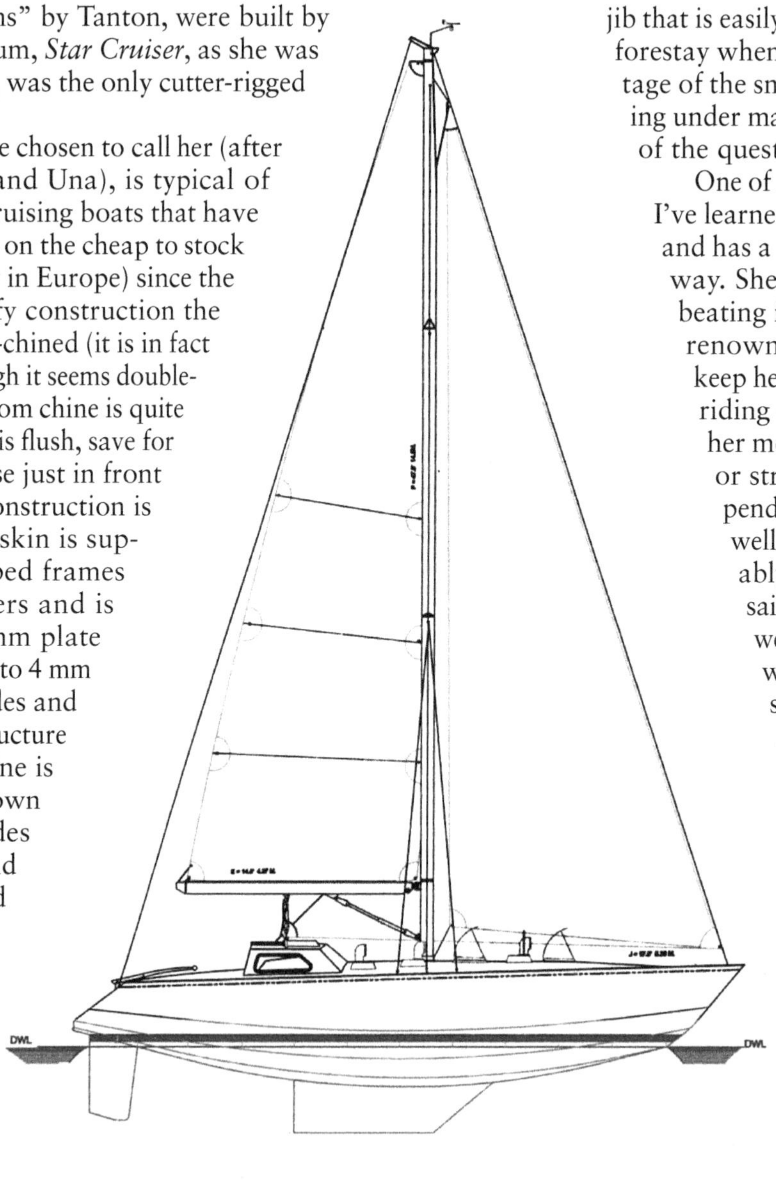

Lunacy's hull form is reminiscent of older IOR designs in that she is beamy amidships with a pinched stern. Her underwater profile features a well-shaped long fin keel and a transom-hung rudder (turned with a tiller) mounted on a full-length high-aspect skeg. Because the boat is aluminum rather than steel, her displacement is moderate. The ballast is internal lead, encapsulated and insulated within the keel. The boat's rig is quite tall (62 feet from waterline to masthead) with a rather small high-aspect mainsail and a large foretriangle. The advantage of the large foretriangle is that even in moderate conditions the boat sails well with a non-overlapping jib that is easily pulled around the inner forestay when tacking. The disadvantage of the small mainsail is that sailing under main alone is normally out of the question.

One of *Lunacy*'s greatest virtues, I've learned, is that she is very stiff and has a smooth motion in a seaway. She does not pound much beating into a steep chop and is renowned at the yard where I keep her in Portland, Maine, for riding out fall northeasters on her mooring without pitching or straining too much at her pendant. Her chainplates are well inboard so she is reasonably close-winded and can sail with the apparent wind well inside 45 degrees in flat water without scrubbing speed. She is also reasonably fast on all points of sail and is more easily driven than I expected. Her helm does load up when she is driven hard, so there's a tendency to reef sooner than would otherwise be necessary. It would be easier to sail her to her best potential if she had a wheel rather a tiller, but her cockpit is very small and

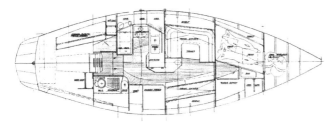

retrofitting a wheel is out of the question. Because her cockpit is so tight, *Lunacy* is easy to manage singlehanded. All sheets and control lines, with the exception of the traveler controls, which are forward of the dodger, are just a short reach from the helm. But with more than two people in it the cockpit feels overcrowded when there is serious work to be done. Fortunately, the boat's flush deck and stiff ride make it easy for idle crew and guests to hang out forward of the cabinhouse.

Auxiliary power is provided by a 40 hp Lister Petter diesel engine mounted amidships inside a centerline island housing twin galley sinks. This central location, which places the engine's drive-train right in the keel sump, allows the prop shaft to be oriented almost horizontally, thus maximizing the thrust of propeller, which is mounted directly behind the keel. Because the prop is in the middle of the boat, the effects of prop walk are minimized, and it is relatively easy to back the boat down straight. The downside to the engine installation is that the island housing the engine is small and is directly behind the keel-stepped mast. Access for routine maintenance, particularly to the front of the engine where the raw-water pump and belts are mounted, is therefore poor. For big repair jobs the island can be removed, providing superb access, but this is big job in itself, as the island is very heavy and all the plumbing to the sinks must first be disconnected.

The accommodations plan is straightforward and works very well. The center of the boat, housing the saloon, galley, and nav station, feels enormous, thanks to the beamy midship sections. In spite of the flush deck, there is standing headroom to about 6'2". There's a Pullman double berth in the owner's cabin forward, and another smaller double aft in

an open quarter cabin under the cockpit to port. The straight settees in the saloon, on each side of the fixed centerline table with folding leaves, are the best berths in a seaway, as the motion in the middle of the boat is smooth and noise from the cockpit is not intrusive, as it tends to be in the aft berth. Sailing *Lunacy* offshore I have found her to be the most comfortable boat under 40 feet I have ever slept aboard at sea. Ventilation is very good. There are seven large dorade vents to pump air below when things are wet and wild outside, plus five deck hatches that can be popped open when conditions are calm.

LOA	39'6"
LWL	33'0"
Beam	13'0"
Draft	5'10"
Ballast	8,500 lbs.
Displacement	21,000 lbs.
Sail area	850 sq. ft.
Fuel	80 gal.
Water	135 gal.
D/L ratio	261
SA/D ratio	17.83
Comfort ratio	30.26
Capsize screening	1.88
Nominal hull speed	8.4 knots
Last known asking price	$115K

Lunacy, ex *Star Cruiser* (Tanton 39)

327

Hinckley Bermuda 40

With its classic long overhangs, perfectly pitched sheerline, wide sidedecks, graceful cabin profile, and distinctive near-vertical transom, the Bermuda 40 has inspired lust in the heart of many a cruising sailor. Designed by Bill Tripp, Jr., it is without doubt one of the most attractive production sailboats ever conceived. The B-40, as it is often called, was the first fiberglass boat created by the famous Hinckley Company of Southwest Harbor, Maine, and was one of several CCA-era keel-centerboard yawls built on a production basis after the great success of Carleton Mitchell's *Finisterre*. Unlike its contemporaries, however, the B-40 endured for a very long time, surviving both the advent and the demise of the IOR regime that supplanted the CCA rule in the early 1970s. The first of these gorgeously proportioned hulls slipped down the ways in 1959. The last hull, number 203, was launched over three decades later in 1991. So far this is the longest production run enjoyed by any fiberglass auxiliary sailboat anywhere in the world.

Three distinct models of the boat were produced over the years. The original version, known as the Bermuda 40 Custom, was replaced around 1968 by the Mark II model, which boasted a bit more sail area and a reshaped foil centerboard. The longest-lived model, the Mark III, introduced in 1972 in response to the new IOR rule, incorporated more significant changes. Even more sail area was added as the mast was stretched four feet and moved aft two feet to create a higher-aspect mainsail and a larger foretriangle. More ballast was added, and a sloop rig was offered as an option.

Like other CCA production boats introduced around the same time, the B-40 is robustly constructed. Unlike its contemporaries, however, the B-40 also boasts outstanding finish quality and superb joinerwork and is fitted with many components—much of the stainless-steel hardware, all spars, the steering pedestal, etc.—that were manufactured by Hinckley

to its own exacting standards. The hull in all versions is solid fiberglass laminate, though in the most recent boats a more exotic hybrid Kevlar/E-glass knit fabric was employed. The two early models have solid glass decks; the Mark III boats were built first with balsa-cored decks and later with foam-cored decks that were vacuum-bagged. The strength of the deck joint is legendary. It consists of an inward flange half an inch thick and 6 inches wide that is both laminated and through-bolted. Hinckley crews reportedly spent two days on average making sure the fit between hull and deck was perfect before marrying the two parts together. All bulkheads are tabbed to the deck and to the hull. All deck hardware is well bedded and mounted over generous backing plates, with stainless-steel machine screws tapped through the deck and into the plates to minimize the potential for leaks. The ballast is external lead mounted on stainless-steel bolts at the front of the keel. The centerboard is cast bronze and is controlled by a reliable worm gear with an override mechanism that permits the board to kick up in a grounding.

Compared to most modern sailboats the B-40 has a small interior, though in its day it was considered quite spacious. Hinckley claimed to build custom interiors, but variations from the norm are relatively minor. Most boats have a standard CCA-era racing layout with a V-berth forward and a saloon with pilot berths outboard on each side, narrow settees that pull out to form extension berths, and a fixed centerline drop-leaf table. The galley is aft, ranged around the companionway, with the top of the icebox doubling as a nav desk. The rode locker in the forepeak, complete with shelving, is large, as are the two cockpit lockers and lazarette all the way aft. The cockpit lockers, notably, are fully gasketed and can be secured from inside the boat—a very seamanlike

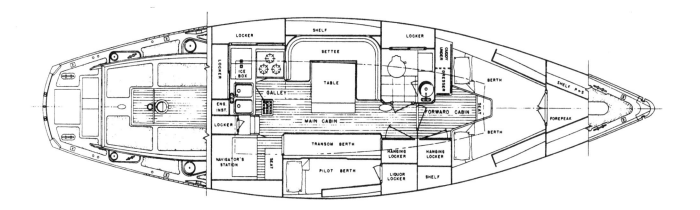

feature. Alternative layouts featuring dinette tables and dedicated nav stations are seen on several of the later Mark III boats. A few examples also have double Pullman berths forward.

The B-40 in its prime was a competitive racer but these days must be considered relatively sedate under sail. As with any CCA design it is not as slow as its exaggerated D/L ratio might suggest. The boat tracks well with its centerboard down and has a light helm but is initially tender, heeling quickly to 15–20 degrees before it firms up and builds forward momentum. Thanks to its long shoal keel the boat is reportedly a little slow to tack and needs to be babied a bit through the eye of the wind, but it is also reasonably fast once the wind is on or abaft the beam. The B-40's motion, as with most boats of this type, is regular and smooth, thanks to its heavy displacement and full keel. These features also, unfortunately, make it a difficult boat to back down under power.

Though a few of the earliest B-40s came equipped with gasoline engines, most had diesel engines installed at the factory. Hinckley in fact was one of the first builders to put diesels on its boats as standard equipment. By now the vast majority of older B-40s, whatever engine they had originally, have been repowered. It makes some sense to look for a boat where this has happened recently, as the engine space and companionway are cramped and repowering is a difficult job. Be aware that the original Monel fuel tank is directly under the engine and cannot be replaced or repaired without removing the engine first.

Compared to any other CCA-era boat, the B-40 is undeniably very expensive to buy. An appreciation of the boat's great beauty and of the quality of its construction is required to justify this, as one could easily buy a brand-new boat that sails faster and has more living space for about the same price or even less. Still, I feel the B-40 is an excellent value. It serves well as both a coastal or bluewater cruiser and is excellent in shoal-water grounds such as Chesapeake Bay or the Bahamas. Most examples that come on the market are in very good condition, as it takes a callous owner to neglect a boat like this. Equipment is usually current, and a few boats even boast such major conveniences as in-mast mainsail furling and electric winches. Because they are so beautiful and so well built B-40's hold their value much better than most comparably priced new boats.

Mark III Model

LOA		40'9"
LWL		28'10"
Beam		11'9"
Draft		
	Board up	4'1"
	Board down	8'9"
Ballast		6,500 lbs.
Displacement		20,000 lbs.
Sail area		
	Yawl	776 sq. ft.
	Sloop	725 sq. ft.
Fuel		50 gal.
Water		110 gal.
D/L ratio		415
SA/D ratio		
	Yawl	16.82
	Sloop	15.71
Comfort ratio		36.36
Capsize screening		1.73
Nominal hull speed		7.0 knots
Typical asking prices		$110K–$290K

Valiant 40

Often hailed as the first performance cruiser, the Valiant 40 was an important breakthrough boat both for its designer Bob Perry and for cruising sailors in general. The genius of the design is that it married what above the water looks like a beamy double-ended traditional cutter with a much more modern underbody featuring a fin keel and separate rudder mounted on a skeg. First introduced in 1974, the Valiant 40 was for at least a decade the definitive production-built offshore sailing vessel. Besides making successful appearances in transatlantic races in the 1970s, it was also prominent in round-the-world races in the early 1980s. In 1983 it was Mark Schrader's weapon of choice when he set a record for the fastest singlehanded circumnavigation. Originally built in Washington State, production of the Valiant 40 shifted to Texas in 1984 and ultimately ended in 1993 after a run of 200 boats (Valiant 40 hull numbers begin at 101). It was supplanted by the Valiant 42, a similar vessel that is still being built.

When it first appeared the Valiant 40 was criticized by some as being too lightly built for offshore work, an opinion that today seems laughable given the nature of its construction. The hull is solid laminate composed of mat and woven roving laid up an inch thick at the keel, decreasing to $3/8$ inch at the caprail. To stiffen the structure, a series of 12 foam-cored transverse floors are glassed to the hull, as are the bulkheads and all furniture components. The deck is cored with balsa, with high-density foam substituted under hardware. The deck joint is on an inward flange at the top of a high bulwark and is both through-bolted and bedded with a strong adhesive sealant. The rudder skeg is not part of the hull molding, but rather is a foam-filled steel component that is epoxied and through-bolted to the hull and then glassed over. The ballast is external lead through-bolted to a stout keel stub. Weak spots on some early boats were the chainplates, which originally were undersized and needed upgrading, and also the aluminum fuel and water tanks, which in some cases corroded and have needed replacing.

The most controversial aspect of the Valiant 40's construction concerned

blistering. From 1976 into 1981 a number of Valiants developed blister problems that ranged from merely bothersome to quite severe. In some cases the blisters were as large as 10 inches in diameter and affected hulls, decks, and cabinhouses both above and below the waterline. Repairs were sometimes extensive and extremely expensive, but not always effective. Eventually the cause was traced to an inferior resin used in the laminate, and a blizzard of lawsuits forced the change of control that took the company from Washington to Texas. Later hulls were laid up with isophthalic resin and were also barrier-coated with epoxy, and blisters became a non-issue. Boats built from 1976 to 1981 now often sell at a discount because of uncertainties about the efficacy of repairs and the likelihood of blisters either occurring or recurring. Some consider these boats excellent bargains, but some caution is warranted. If you buy a boat that has been repaired, you need to know exactly what was done; if you buy one that needs repairs, you need to know what you're getting into.

The accommodations plan of the Valiant 40 is very seamanlike and straightforward. A feature unique in its day was the separate aft stateroom to port, which contains a good-sized double berth. Otherwise the standard layout features an excellent U-shaped galley opposite a large nav station, a pair of straight settees between a centerline table, and one head forward just behind a large V-berth. Storage is generous and includes a large wet locker to starboard of the offset companionway. Valiant was willing to customize interiors to some extent, so there are often variations, most notably with respect to the areas outboard of the settees, which may be inhabited by pilot berths or by cupboards and shelves. Later in the production run there was also an optional layout with the head aft opposite a single quarter berth and a Pullman double in a separate forward stateroom. The original layout, obviously, is better suited to family cruising; the later one works well for a couple. There is also a pilothouse

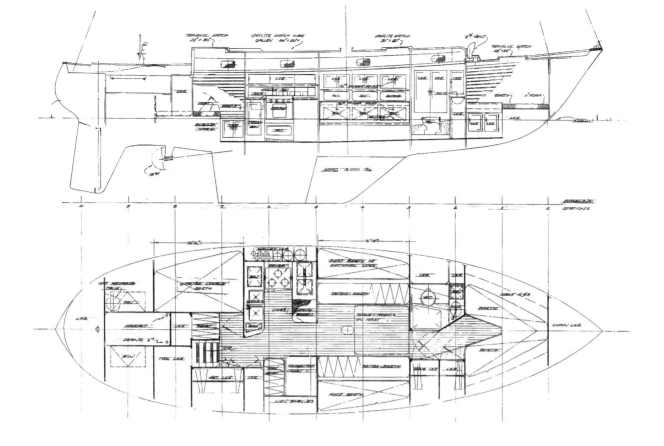

version of the boat with a raised saloon layout, but these are hard to find.

To open up space in the back of the boat the engine is mounted under the cockpit with a V-drive transmission. The engine space, however, is large and accessible, so it is not hard to get to the front of the engine to perform routine maintenance. There is room to mount a generator, and the space is sound insulated. The hull interior is also thermally insulated throughout with a layer of closed-cell foam to prevent condensation.

Bob Perry fiddled with the keel design on the Valiant 40 a few times while the boat was in production, and reportedly the later boats are a bit stiffer and faster than the earlier ones. By all accounts even the early boats were considered fast in their day, and few contemporary cruisers are likely to be disappointed with their performance. The boat tracks well to weather and according to some published reports can sail as close as 30 degrees to the apparent wind, though I find this hard to credit, given the boat's beamy hull and outboard shrouds. The broad flared bow, though it does keep the foredeck dry, is also said to pound a bit sailing close hauled into steep waves. In such conditions it is far better to ease sheets and crack off a bit. The boat is quite powerful on a reach and can be driven hard without the helm becoming heavy and unbalanced.

Though the Valiant 40 is revered as a bluewater boat, there's no reason it can't work well as a coastal cruiser, too, unless you really like to sail in shoal water. Though some shoal-draft boats were built, they are not very common. Many owners are fanatically devoted to their Valiants and are loath to sell them—according to one survey about half the original boats had never changed hands as of the late 1990s—so the brokerage market is relatively small. Valiant 40s in good condition tend to be expensive, but are still an excellent value compared to the newer Valiant 42s, which run from about $280K used to around $400K new.

LOA	39'11"
LWL	34'0"
Beam	12'4"
Draft	
Standard keel	6'0"
Shoal keel	5'3"
Ballast	7,700 lbs.
Displacement	22,500 lbs.
Sail area (100% foretriangle)	772 sq. ft.
Fuel	95 gal.
Water	120 gal.
D/L ratio	255
SA/D ratio	15.46
Comfort ratio	34.29
Capsize screening	1.74
Nominal hull speed	8.6 knots
Typical asking prices	$65K–$200K

Maine Cat 41

This midsize cruising catamaran inhabits the middle ground between performance-oriented open-bridgedeck cats with limited accommodations and little or no on-deck shelter and bulkier, more unwieldy cats with enclosed bridgedeck saloons and fantastic accommodations. Its most distinctive feature is a permanently mounted hardtop roof supported by aluminum posts that shelters all of the otherwise open bridgedeck area abaft the mast. If desired the bridgedeck can be fully enclosed by deploying flexible transparent acrylic side curtains. This concept was first introduced by designer/builder Dick Vermeulen when he launched his first boat, the smaller Maine Cat 30, back in 1996. The 30-footer has proven quite successful, with over 50 boats built, but is a bit too small and cramped for extended cruising. The 41 redresses this deficiency and has also been successful, with over 20 boats built since its introduction in 2004.

In terms of its hull form and construction, the Maine Cat 41 tilts heavily toward the performance side of the equation. The individual hulls are fairly narrow and are set well apart, the underwater foils are high-aspect daggerboards, the bridgedeck is well elevated, and the entire boat—hull, deck, hardtop, and interior components—is built of lightweight vacuum-bagged composite laminate cored with high-density Core-Cell foam. There are, however, a few telling concessions to cruising comfort and convenience. The bridgedeck is rather large, and there is a fair amount of structure forward of the mast. This includes a solid centerline plank that runs out to the forward crossbeam and supports chain runs for twin anchor rollers, plus the forward portion of the bridgedeck, which houses extra interior living space and a serious rode locker with an electric windlass and plenty of room for two segregated rode piles. There are also raised blister cabinhouses with large fixed windows on both hulls, which increase both headroom and ambient lighting below.

Whether this design works for you as a cruising platform depends largely on how you feel about the deck layout. The one steering station is located right in the middle of the covered bridgedeck. Two winches and one set of controls (for the mainsheet, traveler, and gennaker sheets) are situated just out of reach behind the helm. Another pair of winches (one of which is electric, primarily for raising the mainsail and gennaker) and another set of controls running off the mast (including mainsail reef lines and the sheet for the self-tacking solent jib) are situated just out of reach forward of the helm. The controls are well concentrated for a catamaran, but you'll still need a reliable autopilot to singlehand this boat. Sprinkled around the control stations are the boat's only common social areas—two long L-shaped settees and a pair of swivel chairs either side of the aft winches, plus a dinette table and two short settees between the forward winches.

If you crave the comfort of a proper bridgedeck saloon this glorified "Florida room" of a working cockpit, which is apt to be drafty and cool when conditions are inclement even with the side curtains down, may be a disappointment. On the other hand, if you enjoy being in the open air, but also like staying out of the sun and rain, the Maine Cat's spacious cockpit/open-air saloon may well seem like an ideal onboard environment. The warmer your cruising ground the more likely you are to fall into the latter category. In terms of sail handling, the layout works quite well, though the hardtop blocks the crew's view of the sails and makes it hard to gauge sail trim from control stations. There are three small hatches in the hardtop—one over the helm, the other two over the forward winches—that remedy this to some extent.

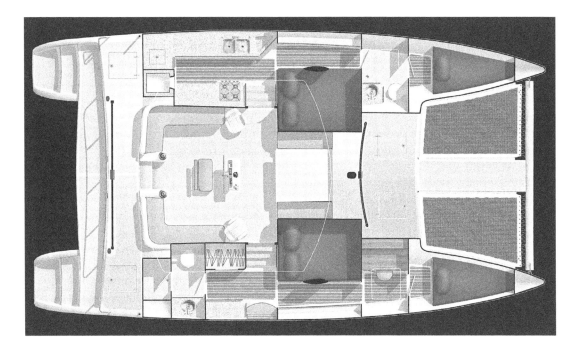

The accommodations within the hulls are more limited than what you'll find on a fat condo cat, but are considerably more comfortable than those found on other leaner open-bridgedeck boats. Several owners consider them perfectly adequate for long-term liveaboard cruising. The large, functional galley occupies all of the aft end of the port hull, with a double berth on an offset inboard shelf amidships, followed by a head, then a single berth right up in the bow. The starboard hull features a head with a separate shower stall plus a small dressing area aft, followed by another double berth amidships, then a nav desk and another single berth right forward. Storage space is limited, but savvy owners cite this as a plus, since it makes it easier to keep the boat light, which is always critical when it comes to catamaran performance.

The sail plan is efficient, with a fat-roached full-batten mainsail, but moderately sized. The mast and boom are both aluminum; the standing rigging is all stainless-steel wire. (The boom has a retractable "stinger" that is used to lift a RIB tender onto dedicated chocks on the aft deck.) A removable carbon-fiber bowsprit for flying a gennaker or asymmetric spinnaker is listed as optional equipment, but should be considered mandatory on a boat like this, as you'll need it to keep the boat sailing well on a reach or off the wind. The Maine Cat 41 reportedly has excellent helm sensitivity for a catamaran. Thanks to its daggerboards it can tack through 90 degrees in flat water, and though the claimed top speed of 18 knots may be a bit of stretch, several owners report hitting average speeds between 11 and 14 knots.

To many the Maine Cat will seem a very expensive boat. What you're paying for is the high-end composite construction, plus an amazing array of standard systems and equipment. The boat comes complete with Pentex working sails, a RIB tender and outboard, a 1,020 amp-hour battery bank, top-of-the-line electronics and refrigeration, an inverter/battery charger, a hydraulic autopilot, and an array of four 100-watt solar panels installed on the hardtop over the bridgedeck. Despite its high price, the boat is hard to come by. There's a waiting list for new construction and so far few existing boats have changed hands on the brokerage market.

LOA		41'6"
LWL		40'6"
Beam		23'0"
Draft		
	Boards up	2'6"
	Boards down	7'0"
Displacement		
	Light ship	12,200 lbs.
	With max. payload	19,200 lbs.
Sail area		
	Working sail	996 sq. ft.
	With gennaker	1,290 sq. ft.
Fuel		92 gal.
Water		120 gal.
D/L ratio		
	Light ship	82
	With max. payload	129
SA/D ratio		
Working sail		
	Light ship	30.01
	With max. payload	22.18
With gennaker		
	Light ship	38.87
	With max. payload	28.73
Nominal hull speed		
	Light ship	13.3 knots
	With max. payload	11.6 knots
Last known asking price		$399K
Base price new		$499K

Morgan Out Island 41

The story goes that designer/builder Charley Morgan conceived this boat in a fit of pique when the IOR supplanted the old CCA racing rule in 1970. If so it was an auspicious sort of tantrum. The Out Island 41 was extremely successful and ultimately helped transform the business of fiberglass sailboat production. The OI 41 was not only one of the first designs targeted at the emerging bareboat charter industry (the original "charter barge," if you will), it was also one of the first center-cockpit boats and one of the first to blatantly trade off sailing performance in favor of maximum accommodations space. The OI 41 is a boat many serious sailors love to hate—for its bulky, plastic appearance, for its less-than-mediocre performance, and for the profound change it wrought in mass-production priorities. It is also, however, still much loved and prized among more pragmatic cruisers who value comfort, space, and low prices.

Many different variations of the OI 41 were created during a 20-year production run (1971–91) that ultimately saw the launching of some 1,100 boats. The biggest change came in 1986 after Catalina Yachts acquired Morgan Yachts and fundamentally reshaped the OI 41's hull, replacing the full shoal keel and attached rudder with a somewhat deeper long fin keel and skeg-hung rudder. About 150 of these redesigned boats were built and were branded (ironically) as the Out Island 41 Classic. They definitely sail much better than their predecessors, though the interior layout and appearance of the deck and topsides is much the same. OI 41 models prior to the Classic are differentiated by three-digit numbers: the earliest was the 413; the last was the 416, which was introduced in 1981 and featured a much larger sail plan. Many of the changes made in the intermediate 414 (1973–76) and 415 (1977–80) models were relatively minor interior alterations. The most important changes were

the introduction of a walk-through interior in 1974 and the offering of a sloop rig as an alternative to the standard ketch rig in 1977.

Having spent two weeks aboard an older OI 41 ketch during a bareboat charter in the Bahamas, I can attest that full-keel OIs are not as unwieldy under sail as their detractors like to suggest. It is often said they cannot tack without a push from an engine, but this is probably only true if you are a poor sailor to begin with. Many boats unfortunately have hydraulic steering systems, which reinforces the impression that the OI sails like a pig. If helm feedback is important to you, look for early 413 and 414 models with cable steering or for later boats retrofitted with push-pull systems. Though sheeting angles are wide, I found it is possible to sail a full-keel OI at about 45 degrees off the wind without making too much leeway in flat water. In rough water, however, the boat slides off at an alarming rate so motorsailing to windward is usually the order of the day once the waves are up. Not surprisingly, the OI loves a good reach and tracks well with the wind on or near its beam. On this point of sail I found it easy to balance the boat and leave the helm unattended. The OI also sails well enough off the wind, particularly if you're willing to fly a spinnaker.

Structurally the OI 41 is fairly solid, though not as strong as it could be. The hull is solid laminate with bulkheads and all furniture securely tabbed to it. The bulkheads, however, are not tabbed to the plywood-cored deck, but instead are bonded to the molded deck liner. There are transverse deck beams that help keep the deck from lifting when the rig is loaded, but bulkheads on some boats may show some twisting and/or cracking where they join the liner. The through-bolted deck joint on boats built before 1975 is below the fat covestripe under the

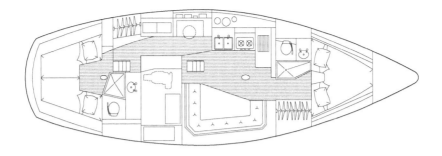

sheerline and thus is vulnerable to damage from docks and Travelift slings. Later it was moved up to deck level where it belongs. Other areas to pay attention to are the main mast step over the keel, which is iron and may cause the aluminum mast heel to corrode once the insulation between the two breaks down, and the tanks, which are polyethylene and are prone to fail over time. Because the tanks were originally installed with the deck off and are sized accordingly, it is usually necessary to replace them with smaller tanks that can fit through the companionway.

As a charter barge at heart, what's most important about the OI is its expansive interior. The OI's basic accommodations footprint, with a large private owner's stateroom aft, lots of communal living space in the middle, and another guest stateroom forward, has been mimicked by most center-cockpit boats following in its wake and has not been substantially improved upon. Theoretically on most OIs it is possible to sleep seven people, but it works best as a family boat or as a spacious home for a couple who like to have a spare cabin for visitors. Details vary quite a bit from model to model. Some forward staterooms have V-berths; some have overlapping over-and-under single berths. Most have dinette tables in the saloon, but some have fold-down bulkhead tables. Most have full-length settees in the saloon, but some have a pair of captain's chairs on one side. And so on. Finish quality on older boats is likely to seem dated and a bit rough around the edges, but some old OIs have been remarkably well cared for, with thoroughly updated interiors and lots of new equipment. Naturally, interiors on the newer Classic boats seem fresher and more attractive.

The OI 41 is one of the most comfortable, most affordable shoal-draft coastal cruisers you are likely to come across. There are those who take these boats offshore, but some might feel circumspect about this. Earl Hinz, who earned a large reputation cruising the Pacific in the 1970s and 1980s, did all his ocean sailing in an OI 41, but it is worth noting that he and his wife Betty were very conservative in picking weather windows and rarely if ever experienced very strong conditions. Hinz's own evaluation of the boat perhaps sums it up best: "It was a Tupperware charter boat, but it had shoal draft, lots of storage, and we could afford it."

LOA		41'3"
LWL		34'0"
Beam		13'10"
Draft		
	Pre-1986	4'2"
	Classic	4'10"
Ballast		
	Pre-1986	9,000 lbs.
	Classic	8,500 lbs.
Displacement		
	Pre-1986	27,000 lbs.
	Classic	23,000 lbs.
Sail area		
	Pre-1981 ketch	683 sq. ft.
	Classic sloop	780 sq. ft.
Fuel (Classic)		85 gal.
Water (Classic)		215 gal.
D/L ratio		
	Pre-1986	306
	Classic	261
SA/D ratio		
	Pre-1981 ketch	12.12
	Classic	15.40
Comfort ratio		
	Pre-1986	34.62
	Classic	29.49
Capsize screening		
	Pre-1986	1.84
	Classic	1.94
Nominal hull speed		
	Pre-1986	8.1 knots
	Classic	8.5 knots
Typical asking prices		
	Pre-1986	$40K-$80K
	Classic	$80K-$125K

Morgan Out Island 41

Catalina 42

The Catalina 42 was introduced in 1989 and was one of the first mass-produced American boats to feature both a sugar-scoop transom with a swim platform and a three-stateroom layout with two aft cabins under the cockpit. It was very much a response to similar boats that appeared in Europe in the mid-1980s, but unlike its contemporaries it is still in production. To date over 1,000 have been built, making it one of the most successful cruising sailboats of its size ever created. This type of boat now dominates the mass-production market, but what distinguishes the Catalina 42 from its current contemporaries is its moderation. Where many modern mass-production boats now have exaggerated shapes to maximize interior volume, the Catalina 42 has a much more balanced form. Its bow is well raked and has a clean entry, but its waterline is not too short. Its beam is carried well aft, but not excessively so, and tapers quite a bit at the transom, so the boat does not gripe too much sailing hard to windward. Freeboard is not too high, the coachroof lines are crisp, and the boat has a clean, handsome profile.

Performance under sail is crisp but amiable. The Catalina 42 is just fast enough and close-winded enough to win club races if appropriately handicapped (a PHRF rating of 105 is typical), but is not given to extremes. It is a relatively stiff boat—it normally doesn't heel much past 15 degrees—and can be pressed hard if you like. Loafing along in cruising mode, however, the boat trims out quite nicely and doesn't need a lot of fiddling to keep moving well. During a month spent skippering a Catalina 42 in the West Indies in moderate trade wind conditions, I found I didn't have to work hard to keep the boat sailing around 7 knots. There are two keels available—a shoal-draft (4'10") wing keel and a deeper (6'8") straight fin keel—and the deeper one, not surprisingly, helps the boat point and track better. There are also two different rudders, both installed behind shallow partial skegs. On earlier Mark I boats (477 were built between 1989 and 1995) the rudder is rather short,

and on the later Mark II boats it was replaced with a deeper, more elliptical foil that improves handling. On some Mark I boats the deeper rudder has been retrofitted.

Aside from the rudder, the only real difference between the two versions of the boat is that the Mark II has a rounder transom and more cockpit storage, plus a fixed, rather than collapsible, cockpit table. Otherwise, the cockpit on both boats is quite roomy and comfortable with 6'8" long seats that are great for stretching out on. The one drawback to the large cockpit is that the mid-boom mainsheet is led to the coachroof and cannot be reached by the helmsman. Without an effective autopilot, it is therefore not easy to singlehand this boat, though it is quite easy to sail doublehanded.

The Catalina 42 is a mass-produced boat and is constructed accordingly. The hull is solid handlaid fiberglass, and though there have been some reports of blisters, both before and after Catalina started applying vinylester barrier coats in 1995, most blistered hulls have been repaired at Catalina's expense. The hull is stiffened with a large molded fiberglass liner/pan that incorporates furniture foundations as well as the cabin sole. Frank Butler, Catalina's founder, pioneered the use of liners at Coronado Yachts in the 1960s and has relied on them ever since to reduce costs and speed production. The liner here, as on many mass-produced boats, severely limits interior access to the hull. Also some storage compartments are not segregated from the space behind the liner, so gear can get lost back there if you're not careful. The deck is balsa-cored with plywood substituted in places where deck hardware is installed; the deck joint is of the shoebox type, bonded with adhesive sealant and through-bolted with stainless-steel fasteners on 8-inch centers. Quality overall is good compared to most other mass-produced boats. Though it was designed primarily for coastal cruising, several Catalina 42s have been used for bluewater cruising in tropical and middle latitudes. On many of these bluewater boats, aside from the usual systems upgrades, the only

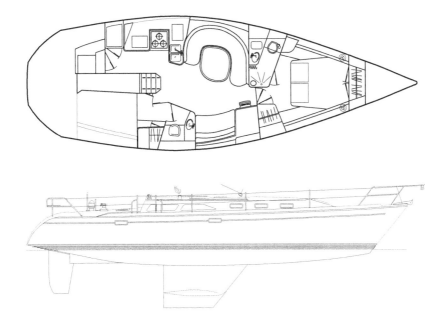

significant modifications have been the addition of extra fuel tanks and handholds below.

There are three different accommodations plans. The original three-stateroom layout, the only one installed in the first 238 hulls, can comfortably sleep three couples (or a couple and a large bunch of kids who don't mind sharing double berths) for a reasonably long period of time. During my monthlong West Indian cruise I shared this layout with five other people. We were a bit pressed for storage space, but we were definitely happy campers. Bulkier, more modern three-stateroom boats in this size range may offer the illusion of more space, but in practice it usually doesn't amount to anything terribly useful. There are two two-stateroom plans, one with a Pullman double berth forward (as in the three-stateroom layout), the other with a centerline island double. To my mind, the Pullman layout is superior. It affords more storage space and a larger forward head with a separate shower stall, plus the berth itself is a bit farther aft and can be fit more easily with a lee cloth, thus is more likely to be habitable in a seaway. The biggest advantage of the two-stateroom layout, regardless of which forward stateroom you prefer, is the super-sized galley aft with a cavernous pantry space that is great for systems installations and serious gear storage.

Gerry Douglas, Catalina's inhouse design maven, considers the Catalina 42 one of his finest creations. I'm inclined to agree with him. It is one of the best cruising sailboats of its type ever produced in North America and represents an excellent value. The new boats compare well to current competitors. Younger used boats, in large part because the design is still in production, hold their value better than most other mass-produced boats. Older used boats are attractively priced and make great project boats, both because the 42 offers a reasonably sound foundation on which to build and because Catalina, unlike many builders, works hard to support owners of older boats.

LOA		.41'10"
LWL		.36'0"
Beam		.13'10"
Draft		
	Shoal wing keel	. 4'10"
	Deep fin keel	. 6'8"
Ballast (both keels)		.8,300 lbs.
Displacement		.22,500 lbs.
Sail area (100% foretriangle)		.797 sq. ft.
Fuel		. 46 gal.
Water		
	3-cabin layout	. 131 gal.
	2-cabin layout	. 111 gal.
D/L ratio		.215
SA/D ratio		. 15.97
Comfort ratio		.27.65
Capsize screening		. 1.95
Nominal hull speed		. 9.3 knots
Typical asking prices		.$85K–$250K
Base price new		.$264K

Colvin Gazelle

American shipwright and boat designer Tom Colvin, who has long championed both metal construction and junk rigs on cruising sailboats, has designed about 300 small ships and boats over the course of a career that has now spanned almost 70 years. *Gazelle*, which he designed and built for himself and his family to cruise aboard back in 1967, has proven to be both his most successful and perhaps most interesting creation, with over 700 sisterships launched to date.

The original *Gazelle* was conceived as a no-frills light-displacement boat that could function both as a shoal-draft coastal cruiser on Chesapeake Bay, where Colvin was based at the time, and as a bluewater cruiser. She was built of 10-gauge Corten steel (i.e., about 3.4 mm thick), except for the main cabintop, which was marine plywood. The ballast consisted of lead bricks stacked in the keel and capped with cement. To save weight, *Gazelle* carried no engine and her hull form was long and lean. Her most distinctive feature was her schooner rig, which consisted of two Chinese junk sails mounted on lightly stayed aluminum masts with a Western-style triangular jib out front flying from a long bowsprit. She also carried a triangular "fisherman" sail between her masts or sometimes flew a loose-luffed reaching staysail from her main masthead.

By all accounts the first *Gazelle* sailed quite well, as is reflected in her performance ratios. She balanced well on all points of sail, her helm requiring little attention except when running dead downwind, and was reasonably fast. Colvin reported hitting top speeds of around 9 knots in his boat; a sistership built soon after the first, *Migrant*, once reported a best day's run of 202 miles and a best week's average of 163 miles per day during an extended bluewater cruise. *Gazelle*'s windward performance was, in Colvin's words, "less than breathtaking," as she usually needed to sail 50 degrees or more off the wind to maintain speed and course. With her narrow beam, shoal draft, and generous sail plan she also needed reefing early, though this is easily accomplished on a junk-rigged vessel.

Very few of *Gazelle*'s many sisterships are as simple—or as light—as the original. Almost all, for example, have engines installed in the large midships cargo area that separates the main cabin from the aft cabin. Colvin himself installed a 10 hp Sabb diesel in his *Gazelle* before selling her; most other owners have specifed much larger engines and in some cases have overpowered their boats. Most sisterships also have heavier interior joinery, and in some cases scantlings have been increased. Colvin estimates the average displacement is about 6,000 pounds heavier than that of his first boat; in one extreme case a boat was built almost 20,000 pounds overweight (this before even the rig and ballast had been installed). On the plus side, most sisterships have electrical systems (a feature lacking on the original) and many other modern amenities. Several Gazelles have been built in aluminum, which does save a bit of weight, and a small handful have also been built in wood. The vast majority are junk-rigged, though some have gaff-schooner or gaff-ketch rigs, which also reportedly work well. The least successful sail plans, according to Colvin, are single-mast Marconi sloop and cutter rigs, as the boat has trouble standing up to a taller single spar and does not balance as well.

The interior layout is similar to that seen on modern center-cockpit boats, except there is no cockpit. Instead the helmsman is stationed on a flush-decked area between the main and aft cabins, directly abaft the mainmast and directly over the engine or cargo area. The first *Gazelle* originally had a small laterally oriented double berth offset to starboard in the aft cabin. Colvin later changed this and installed separate single berths port and starboard, which he felt was more seamanlike. Many sisterships instead have large athwartship doubles all the way aft. These are comfortable in a calm harbor, but are considerably less so when the boat is underway or rolling at anchor. They also interfere with the worm-gear steering system specified by Colvin and require the installation of hydraulic steering instead, which dampens the helm's responsiveness. As originally designed, the aft cabin, which also houses the nav station, has no standing headroom, as the deck overhead is

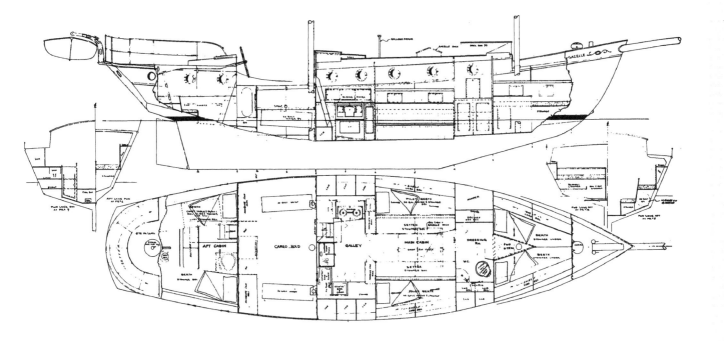

flush save for a large scuttle housing its forward-facing companionway. On several sisterships, however, an aft cabinhouse has been added.

The main cabin connects to the aft cabin below-deck via the engine or cargo area, which has only stooping headroom. The main cabin has full standing headroom and can support various different layouts. In most cases the forepeak is occupied by a narrow V-berth that is bisected by the keel-stepped foremast, which precludes installing a filler section to make the berth a double. On some boats, however, the foremast is deck-stepped and the space is configured differently. Directly behind the peak there is an athwartship head (the original design also calls for a second toilet in the aft cabin though not in an enclosed head compartment). In the first *Gazelle* the galley was originally at the aft end of the main cabin, ranged around the companionway, with two outboard pilot berths and a pair of narrow settees either side of a drop-leaf table in the saloon forward of the galley. Colvin deemed this inadequate and later changed things around, placing the galley forward, just abaft the head, with one outboard pilot berth and a dinette aft to starboard of the companionway opposite a single straight settee. In the majority of sisterships, however, the galley is aft, where the motion should be more comfortable in a seaway.

In that used Gazelles are attractively priced and construction costs keep escalating, it is ever harder these days to justify building a new one. As of 2006, there was a firm in India, Kondo Syokai, offering to sell new Gazelles for a sail-away price of 50,000 British pounds, but according to Colvin they have actually built but one boat to date. If shopping for Gazelles on the brokerage market, be warned that listed specifications are often based on the original design displacement rather than actual displacement, thus may be wildly inaccurate.

LOA		49'0"
LOD		42'2"
LWL		33'0"
Beam		11'4"
Draft		3'10"
Ballast		7,500 lbs.
Displacement		
	Original	18,000 lbs.
	Average	24,000 lbs.
Sail area		854 sq. ft.
Water		60 gal.
D/L ratio		
	Original	223
	Average	298
SA/D ratio		
	Original	19.86
	Average	16.39
Comfort ratio		
	Original	30.45
	Average	40.60
Capsize screening		1.73
Nominal hull speed		
	Original	8.8 knots
	Average	8.0 knots
Typical asking prices		$30K–$70K

Hallberg-Rassy 42

Though it dabbled briefly with more performance-oriented racing designs during the 1980s, the well-known Swedish builder Hallberg-Rassy has otherwise focused exclusively on creating moderately proportioned cruising boats with understated modern styling. The HR42E, so designated in honor of its designer, Olle Enderlein, predates its immediate successor, the HR42F (designed by German Frers), and was built from 1980 to 1991. It is one of the purest expressions of the Hallberg-Rassy ethos and features all of the firm's signature design elements—a center-cockpit layout, a flush teak deck crowning a high-freeboard hull, a distinctive fixed windshield, and a well-appointed mahogany interior. There are smaller Hallberg-Rassys that attempt to blend these same ingredients in more compact packages, but 42 feet is about the minimum length required to make it all work properly. In all, 255 hulls were launched during the boat's 11-year production run, only a few of which were sold into the North American market. Good examples are routinely found all over the world, however, including in the Caribbean and, of course, in northern Europe. Cruisers who value these boats are often willing to travel some distance to obtain one.

Hallberg-Rassy is one of the most respected builders in Europe, and this reputation is reflected in the 42E's construction. Finish quality, both structurally and cosmetically, is very good. The hull is solid fiberglass stiffened with stringers and fully tabbed bulkheads; the deck is cored with PVC foam. The joint is glassed over, so the hull and deck together form a monocoque structure; the iron ballast is encapsulated within the long fin keel. Most 42Es have integral fiberglass water tanks that are bonded to the hull (further stiffening the structure), though a few have stainless-steel tanks instead. In all cases the fuel tanks are stainless steel and come fitted with sump pumps, a detail neglected by most builders. The rudder, mounted on a full skeg, is built around a bronze stock, an impressive feature in a modern boat. The one significant long-term maintenance headache is the teak deck, which eventually must be removed or replaced. Though glass decks are far easier to care for, most owners elect to replace the teak to maintain the boat's appearance.

The interior joinerwork is excellent and features a wealth of hand-rubbed selected mahogany, both on bulkheads and in the furniture components. The accommodations plan is quite straightforward for a boat of this type, with the exception of the great cabin aft. This features a split single and double berth arrangement rather than one large island or athwartship double. The split-berth arrangement is preferable when the boat is underway, as two persons can sleep more comfortably in a seaway in separate lateral berths. The double to starboard may seem a little tight for two when the boat is in port. Also, the en suite head does not include a separate shower stall, though the forward head, just abaft the forward stateroom, does. Some owners may therefore be tempted to claim the forward V-berth for themselves, leaving children or guests to enjoy the more spacious aft cabin. The saloon, with opposing straight full-length settees separated by a fixed drop-leaf table, has not two but three potential single sea berths, as the back support for the starboard side settee can swing up to form an upper pilot berth. The boat can thus sleep a total of eight people, though it will be most comfortable for four or five on an extended cruise.

As to its sailing characteristics, the 42E has four different configurations revolving around two variables. It was available as either a ketch or a sloop with either a deep or shoal keel. Those most interested in windward performance should favor the sloop rig and deep keel, while those who cruise in shallower water and prefer sailing with the wind on the beam will prefer a ketch rig and a shoal keel. It seems the vast majority of 42Es were delivered with deep keels (a reflection of its European origin) and a somewhat smaller majority are rigged as ketches.

Under the water the boat's hull form is decidedly conservative. The

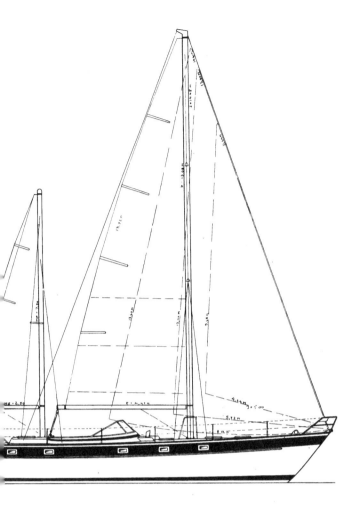

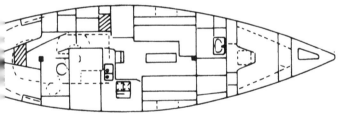

true of most Hallberg-Rassy designs) is a very efficient motorsailer. The four standard engines installed over the years (all four-cylinder Volvo diesels) range from 52 to 62 horsepower and reportedly are capable of pushing the boat at close to hull speed. Fuel capacity also is generous enough to take advantage of this in most circumstances.

In terms of its systems, the 42E is a class act. The standard battery bank, consisting of four 125 amp-hour 12-volt batteries, was considered large in its day. Some may now find it necessary to upgrade to accommodate more modern power-hungry appliances. The standard alternator, rated at 55 amps, is admittedly quite small and should definitely be replaced with a higher-output unit. The factory-installed wiring is well organized and is neatly routed through conduits, so it is easy to upgrade if desired. Many owners have spent considerable sums improving these boats, and a large number of 42Es now have such posh amenities as bow thrusters, AC generators, watermakers, air conditioning, electric winches, and in-mast furling mainsails. Asking prices are consequently rather high, especially for boats lying in European waters. Most 42Es, however, are well maintained and hold their value well over the long run. Fortunately, the best bargains are in North America. If you have your heart set on a boat like this, be prepared to act quickly if one comes on the market near you.

keel, though technically a fin, is but one step removed from a classic CCA keel with a cutaway forefoot. The boat's performance, therefore, is solid. It tracks well in a seaway, has a comfortable motion, and is exceedingly stable, thus has a great reputation as a bluewater boat. It is faster and more weatherly than most full-keel boats, but is outperformed by more contemporary designs with longer waterlines and shorter, more efficient underwater foils. Those interested in a fast modern coastal cruiser may therefore find this boat disappointing. For cruisers inclined to rely on engines as much as their sails, the 42E (as is

LOA		42'4"
LWL		35'3"
Beam		12'5"
Draft		
	Deep keel	6'9"
	Shoal keel	5'11"
Ballast		9,920 lbs.
Displacement		25,353 lbs.
Sail area (working sails)		
	Ketch	850 sq. ft.
	Sloop	813 sq. ft.
Fuel		105 gal.
Water		192 gal.
D/L ratio		258
SA/D ratio		
	Ketch	15.73
	Sloop	15.04
Comfort ratio		36.31
Capsize screening		1.69
Nominal hull speed		8.7 knots
Typical asking prices		$170K-$280K

Wharram Pahi 42

The catamaran designs that British multihull pioneer James Wharram first created for amateur boatbuilders in the mid-1960s were influenced by the boats he had built and voyaged upon during the 1950s. These "Classic" designs, as Wharram termed them, feature slab-sided, double-ended, V-bottomed plywood hulls with very flat sheerlines and simple isosceles triangular sections. The hulls are joined together by solid wood beams and crude slat-planked open bridgedecks. Wharram's second-generation "Pahi" designs, which he started developing in the mid-1970s, still feature double-ended V-bottomed hulls, but the sections are slightly rounder and the sheerlines rise at either end in dramatically upswept prows and sterns. The most successful of these in terms of number of boats built—and also probably the most successful of any of Wharram's larger designs—is the Pahi 42. It is an excellent example of a no-frills do-it-yourself cruising catamaran with enough space for a family to live aboard long term.

First introduced in 1980, the Pahi 42, a.k.a. the "Captain Cook," was the first Wharram design to include accommodations space on the bridgedeck in the form of a small low-profile pod containing a berth and/or (in some variations) a nav station. Unlike the Classic designs, which have no underwater foils other than rudders, the Pahis also have daggerboards, though these are quite shallow and are set far forward in each hull. The rudders are inboard, rather than transom-hung, set in V-shaped wells behind the aft crossbeam. As on the Classic designs the crossbeams are flexibly mounted to the hulls, but are lashed with rope rather than bolted on with large rubber bushings. Hull construction likewise is very simple, all in plywood, and explicitly conceived to facilitate home-building by amateurs. The frames consist of a series of flat bulkhead panels fastened to a long centerline backbone with longitudinal stringers running down either side to support the plywood skin panels. Through the main central

area of each hull, the bulkheads all have large cutouts in their midsections to allow room for interior accommodations space. To increase moisture and abrasion resistance the hull exteriors are sheathed in fiberglass cloth and epoxy.

As designed the Pahi 42 has a single mast and flies a loose-footed mainsail with a wishbone boom. There is also a staysail on a wishbone boom and a conventional genoa flying on a bridle over the forward beam. Many owner-builders have substituted other rigs, including Wharram's unique gaff "wingsail" rig, where the main has a luff sleeve enveloping the mast, but conventional Marconi rigs are probably the most common. The original design also calls for a single outboard engine mounted on the stern deck to serve as auxiliary power, but many owners have engineered other arrangements, including inboard diesel engines and even electric drives.

As its light-ship D/L and SA/D ratios attest, the Pahi 42 has the potential to be a very fast performance cruiser. Wharram claims top speeds in the neighborhood of 18 knots with average cruising speeds of 9 to 12 knots. In reality, however, it probably takes an unusually attentive, disciplined sailor to achieve anything like this. The Pahi seems to be more weight sensitive than most cats, and typical owners, who carry lots of stuff on their boats, report average speeds more on the order of 5 to 8 knots. The boat also does not sail well to windward, as its daggerboards are not large enough and are not positioned properly to generate much lift. Instead they act more like trim boards and help balance the helm while sailing. They also make it difficult to tack. Most owner-builders therefore consider the boards more trouble than they're worth and don't install them, preferring instead to retain the extra space below for storage and accommodations. With only its V-shaped hulls to resist leeway the Pahi reportedly sails close-hauled at a 60 degree angle to the wind, though performance-oriented owners who keep their boats light claim they can

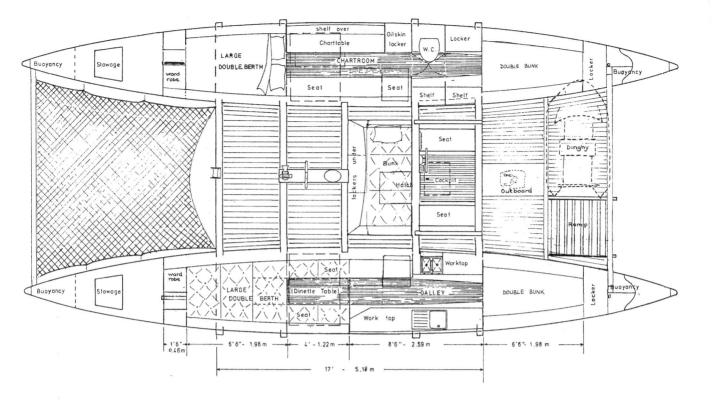

make progress upwind faster than other boats sailing tighter angles. A few builders have also put long fin keels on their boats, and these reportedly improve windward performance to some extent.

As for its accommodations plan, the Pahi 42 has much in common with other open-bridgedeck catamarans. Except for the small pod on deck all sheltered living space is contained within the narrow hulls, which have a maximum beam of just 6 feet. The standard layout puts double berths at both ends of each hull, though many may regard the aft "doubles" as wide singles. The central part of the port hull contains a small dinette table and a large galley; the center of the starboard hull is given over to a long chart table or workbench, plus a head. Naturally many owner-builders have fiddled the design a bit to suit their own tastes. The most significant changes involve the deck pod. Those who crave more living space tend to enlarge it; in at least one case it has blossomed into something approaching a full-on bridgedeck saloon, which must hurt sailing performance. In other instances, in an effort to save weight and improve performance, builders have omitted the pod entirely.

The great advantage of a Pahi 42, or any Wharram cat for that matter, is its relatively low cost compared to other cats in the same size range. To obtain one new, however, you normally must build it yourself. Wharram estimates this takes between 2,500 to 3,000 hours of effort. The alternative is to buy one used. There is an active brokerage market with boats listed for sale all over the world. The best sources for listings are Wharram himself and another Brit, Scott Brown, who operates mostly online. Because Wharrams are built of plywood, even if sheathed

with epoxy and glass, the most important defect to look for is simple rot. This, however, is not hard to detect and, because the boats are structurally so simple, is also not hard to repair.

Wharram Pahi 42

LOA		42'0"
LWL		34'0"
Beam		22'0"
Draft		
	Boards up	2'1"
	Boards down	3'6"
Displacement		
	Light ship	7,840 lbs.
	Maximum load	14,560 lbs.
Sail area		
	Working sail	640 sq. ft.
	Maximum sail	1,000 sq. ft.
Fuel		Variable
Water		Variable
D/L ratio		
	Light ship	89
	Maximum load	165
SA/D ratio		
Working sail		
	Light ship	25.91
	Maximum load	17.14
Maximum sail		
	Light ship	40.48
	Maximum load	26.78
Nominal hull speed		
	Light ship	11.9 knots
	Maximum load	9.8 knots
Build cost		$70K-$120K
Typical asking prices		$40K-$100K

J/133

The J/133 is certainly not the most cruising oriented of the many fine boats produced by J-Boats over the years. It is, however, the smallest of their so-called sprit boats with enough accommodation space to be comfortably cruised by a family or multiple couples for an extended period. It thus offers an excellent blend of modern high-end sailing performance and liveability. This boat is fast enough to contend for top honors in the most competitive regattas (as proven on many race courses in both North America and Europe), but is simple enough to sail that it can be easily handled by an experienced singlehander or by a couple of average ability. J-Boats introduced its famous J/105, one of the first production sailboats with a retractable bowsprit for flying large asymmetric spinnakers, in 1991 and since then has sold over 2,500 sprit boats in several different models. The J/133, measuring 43 feet overall (the "133" moniker is a metric designation), was first introduced in 2003. With over 55 hulls built as of this writing it is the most successful of the company's larger sprit boats.

J-Boats, which now has production facilities in both Rhode Island and France, is well known for turning out boats that are a joy to sail. The 133 does not disappoint in this regard. The hull is narrow by modern standards, with a low center of gravity, and is easily driven and tracks well given its high-aspect rudder and fin keel. I helped deliver the first 133 from New York to Annapolis, plus have tested a number of different J-Boats for magazines, and I am always thrilled by the feel of a J's helm. Steering is light, precise, and not at all twitchy. The boat slips easily into a groove and likes to stay there. Even when the boat is significantly overpowered, the rudder gives no hint of stalling out. With an impressive turn of speed (10-plus knots is not unusual), good pointing ability (within 35 degrees apparent), and excellent light-air performance, you'll have no problem keeping the engine switched off most of the time.

The rig is large, yet manageable. The standard carbon-fiber mast, stayed with two pairs of swept-back spreaders, requires no runners or checkstays. The 105% blade jib is easy to tack, and the double-ended mainsheet can be controlled by a seated helmsman. The boat sails well under main alone, and in many cases, rather than reefing, you need only roll up the jib on its furler to keep sailing comfortably at speed when the wind gets up. The boat also does well sailing under jib alone. Even handling the asymmetric spinnaker is no big deal, as long as it is fitted with a good snuffer, which reportedly can be rigged to be controlled from the cockpit.

J-Boats designs hulls to maximize sailing ability rather than living space, but their interior layouts make the most of what's available without offending common sense. On the 133 this translates to ample headroom (6'4"), lots of attractive cherry joinery, and enough room aft for twin double staterooms (the standard layout) or for one stateroom and a second head (the optional "cruising" layout, which also allows for plenty of storage space under the cockpit). The forward stateroom is particularly spacious for a performance boat of this size, and, surprisingly, the enormous tube housing the sprit pole that slices down the starboard side of the cabin doesn't really get in the way. The galley, however, is slightly undersized with minimal storage. Aside from four small drawers, everything stowed in the galley must fit in a large cupboard covered with long sliding panels. This is okay on port tack but on starboard, if the boat is heeled, everything inside comes tumbling out when you open a panel.

The boat's construction is impeccable and thoroughly modern, with a hefty price tag to match. To maximize stiffness and minimize weight the hull and deck are molded using the SCRIMP resin-infusion process, with biaxial and quadraxial fabrics set in vinylester resin vacuumed over a low-density balsa core. The hull molding includes a unitary grid (i.e., it is not bonded to the hull, but is a part of it) comprising longitudinal stringers, transverse keel floors, and the mast step. The main bulkhead is also a SCRIMPed laminate (with a cherry veneer), tabbed to both the hull and deck with

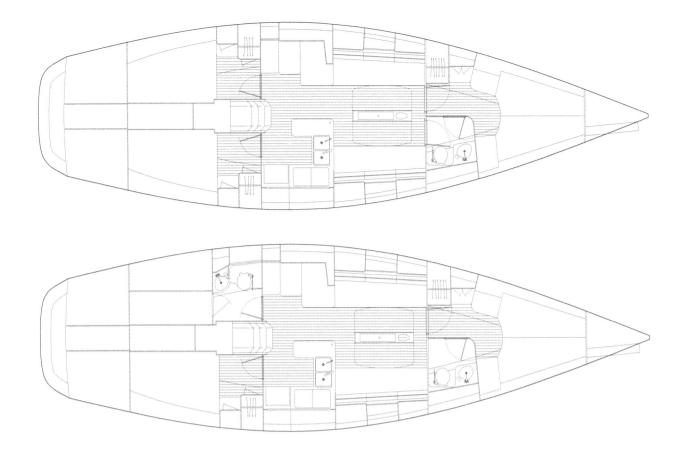

epoxy. The intermediate bulkheads are likewise fully glassed in place. The deck joint is bonded with a special structural-grade methacrylate adhesive with no mechanical fasteners. The external ballast is lead, bonded with epoxy and fastened with stainless-steel bolts to a deep molded keel sump. General finish quality and the joinerwork below are very good, though hardly ostentatious.

Most of the equipment aboard is first rate. As mentioned, the mast is carbon fiber (the boom, however, is aluminum), as is the sprit pole and the rudderstock. The standing rigging is Nitronic 50 rod, and much of the standard running rigging is high-modulus Spectra line. Most of the deck hardware is top-of-the-line Harken gear. Systems installations are also quite good. The 55 hp diesel engine comes standard with a high-output alternator, though curiously the standard battery bank is a bit undersized. Fuel and water capacity is also a little low for long-distance work.

For any coastal cruiser who wants a boat that sails extremely well and also likes to race from time to time, the J/133 is a dream come true. Likewise if you're a hardcore racer who wants to spend a few weeks cruising every year. On the whole, I'd say the 133 bridges the gap between cruising and racing as completely as any contemporary boat could ever be expected to. Whether it makes a good bluewater cruiser is a harder call. Certainly it is strong enough to go to sea, but like many boats it would need some systems upgrades. Compared to many modern performance boats it has a relatively smooth motion in a moderate seaway, but like any light-hulled boat with flat bilges it pounds furiously sailing hard to windward in steep waves. The 133 is also apt to be wet in strong conditions, since it hasn't much freeboard and waves can easily come roaring down the deck into the cockpit. Whether you are willing to put up with such things to be seen sailing the world in a sexy low-slung sports car of a boat is in the end a matter of personal style and preference.

LOA	.43'0"
LWL	.37'10"
Beam	.12'9"
Draft	
Standard keel	.7'6"
Shoal keel	.6'3"
Ballast	.7,250 lbs.
Displacement	.17,900 lbs.
Sail area (100% foretriangle)	.964 sq. ft.
Fuel	.45 gal.
Water	.90 gal.
D/L ratio	.147
SA/D ratio	.22.49
Comfort ratio	.23.43
Capsize screening	.1.94
Nominal hull speed	.10.7 knots
Typical asking prices	.$350K–$450K
Base price new	.$549K

Gusto (French & Webb 44)

This is a one-off cruiser-racer designed by Chuck Paine for a client, Jay Cushman, who was interested in building a heavy full-keel sailboat capable of showing a good turn of speed. *Gusto* demonstrates that traditional design concepts can be blended with more modern concepts and building materials to produce a unique and appealing vessel. Though he is now known for several contemporary performance cruising designs, Paine first established himself during the 1970s with much more traditional designs to which he is still strongly attracted. *Gusto* is but one of a number of "modern traditional" cruising boats he has helped create in recent years.

Central to *Gusto*'s design is a creative reinterpretation of a full-keel hull with an attached transom-hung rudder. The canoe-shaped hull form does not present a classic wineglass section with soft bilges. Rather the bilges are much harder, though not flat, and the keel joins the hull at a near 90 degree angle. The keel itself, though it has a classic cutaway profile forward, is in fact a carefully shaped NACA foil. The profile aft is distinguished by an enormous curved aperture encompassing all of the keel's trailing edge, such that the keel in effect forms a long swept-back fin, the trailing bottom tip of which happens to support the rudder heel. Besides reducing wetted surface area, this huge aperture allows a portion of the rudder to be moved forward of its pivot axis, alleviating helm loads, so the boat can be steered with a tiller instead of a wheel. To further relieve the helm, the rudder is a high-aspect carbon-fiber foil weighing just 73 pounds. With all of its leading edge exposed to water flow, it essentially functions like a semi-balanced spade rudder and is thus very efficient.

Above the waterline *Gusto* strongly reflects her commissioning owner's preferences. Cushman liked the idea of a flush deck, but was unwilling to let his boat grow too large. He also wanted plenty of headroom below for his 6'2" frame. To achieve this without raising the boat's sheerline too high, Paine drew an extremely low-profile cabinhouse just 6 inches tall. Seen in profile the boat reads as a flush-deck vessel; when working on deck it feels like one, too. Viewed from overhead, the house's forward end is pointed rather than square, elegantly echoing the shape of the bow. Cushman also wanted a fixed windshield to protect the cockpit, and Paine obliged with a traditional Down East–style fixture that blends in well with the broken sheerline, whale stripe, and elliptical portlights set in the hull.

Gusto was launched in 2002 by French & Webb, a high-end custom builder in Belfast, Maine, that specializes in cold-molded wood construction. The boat's hull, $1\frac{3}{8}$ inches thick, is composed of an exterior layer of strip-planked mahogany, three intermediate layers of diagonal red cedar veneers, and an interior layer of strip-planked Douglas fir, all vacuum-bagged and laid up in epoxy. For abrasion resistance, the hull is sheathed with two layers of 9-ounce E-glass cloth also set in epoxy. Strong floor timbers tie the keel to stringers that help distribute the load from the external lead ballast. The keel itself is of stack-laminated wood and is strengthened in its fine aft section with extra S-glass sheathing. To save weight there is no interior framing. Instead the hull skin above the keel root is entirely supported by interior bulkheads and furniture components. The interior joinery is world class and features Herreshoff-style trim and beautiful white beaded-panel bulkheads, including a gorgeous oval-framed partial bulkhead aft.

The accommodations plan is traditional, with a no-nonsense emphasis on sea berths. The seatbacks of the two straight settees in the saloon swing up to form adjustable overhead pilot berths. With a V-berth forward, plus a large double quarter berth aft, the boat can sleep eight in harbor

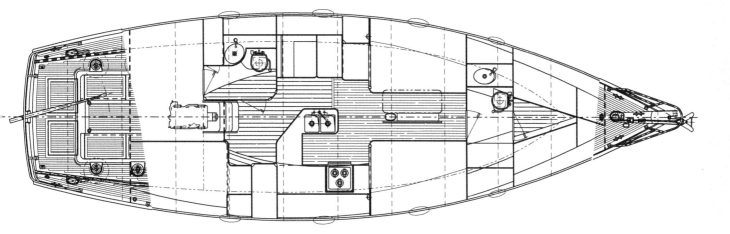

or five comfortably at sea. There are two separate heads, both fitted with showers. Both the galley and nav station, just forward of the companionway, are large and secure with lots of modern gear and conveniences. Behind the aft head to port there is a great systems space through which the 56 hp Yanmar diesel engine (mounted facing aft with a V drive) can be easily accessed and serviced.

Gusto's rig, meanwhile, is much more modern than traditional. The sail plan, a straight slutter rig with a detachable inner forestay that can support a hanked-on staysail or storm jib, is rather conventional for a bluewater cruising boat. Materials, however, are thoroughly contemporary. The spars are all carbon fiber; the standing rigging is all lightweight Navtec rod, with a hydraulic adjustable backstay. The sail inventory boasts a full suit of both cruising sails in Pentex and Dacron and racing sails in carbon fiber and Spectra. To help with the grinding when tacking there's a pair of electric primary winches in the cockpit. More recently, Cushman has added a detachable carbon-fiber bowsprit to facilitate the flying of large asymmteric spinnakers.

I was lucky enough to sail aboard *Gusto* in a fresh 20-knot breeze during the fall of her freshman year. With her somewhat beamy, hefty full-keel hull and lightweight rig she has both good form stability and a low center of gravity and is therefore quite stiff. It is difficult to put her rail underwater. She has a smooth, easy motion in a seaway and tracks nicely. Her shrouds are well inboard, so sheeting angles are narrow and the boat is close-winded, but she does not pound sailing to weather. In terms of raw speed *Gusto* can't keep up with a modern lightweight sled, but she is certainly no slouch. During our sail we surged along at well over 8 knots and occasionally topped 9. As promised, though the boat weighs as much as a modern 50-footer and boasts a large sail plan, she was easy to handle under tiller alone. Under sail she is well balanced. I cannot pretend her helm was always feather-light, for the tiller did load up a bit when gusts came barreling through, but it was never unmanageable and never required more than one hand to control.

As of this writing, *Gusto* was for sale on the brokerage market for the price given below. Though obviously she is not cheap, I have no doubt she will have sold by the time we go to press. I don't know for certain what she cost to build, but one party involved in her creation gave me an informal estimate of $800K.

Gusto (French & Webb 44)

LOA	43'8"
LWL	36'1"
Beam	13'7"
Draft	5'9"
Ballast	11,500 lbs.
Displacement	28,500 lbs.
Sail area	953 sq. ft.
Fuel	82 gal.
Water	165 gal.
D/L ratio	270
SA/D ratio	16.31
Comfort ratio	35.30
Capsize screening	1.77
Nominal hull speed	8.7 knots
Last known asking price	$475K

Aerodyne 47

First introduced to some acclaim in 2001, this modern performance cruiser was originally conceived by an experienced American bluewater cruiser, Vic DeMattia, who wanted to downsize from a Sundeer 56 he had lived aboard with his wife for several years. In collaboration with designer Rodger Martin and a South African builder, Aerodyne Marine, DeMattia helped launch production of the boat and accepted delivery of the first hull. Since then Aerodyne has changed hands and is now based in Finland. Two more AD 47s, as the current builder refers to them, have been launched and delivered, also to American owners. Hull number one, meanwhile, has twice changed hands on the brokerage market. Although its production run thus far has obviously been limited (due in part to foreign exchange rates), the AD 47 is an excellent example of a modern purpose-built cruising vessel that is fast and easy to sail.

The central tenet of DeMattia's original design brief was that the AD 47's hull must be very strong and safe, but also light enough that a) about half of its total displacement could be dedicated to ballast; and b) it could be easily driven by less than 1,000 square feet of working sail. The boat's construction consequently relies heavily on modern lightweight cored laminates. Not only all of the deck and hull, but also all interior bulkheads and furniture sections, are biaxial and unidirectional E-glass and Kevlar fabric set in wet prepreg epoxy and vacuum-bagged over balsa and PVC foam coring. The many composite bulkheads and structural panels, including a massive box grid installed around the keel root and mast step, are tabbed with epoxy directly to the hull with generous 6-inch margins. The hull and all stiffening structures are then baked together at 140 degrees Fahrenheit to ensure the epoxy resin is fully cured. The keel foil, a low-aspect fin, is molded as part of the hull and is filled with thickened epoxy. The external lead ballast bulb is bonded and cross-bolted to the solid keel tip with horizontal fasteners, so there is no chance any damage to the ballast joint can result in water entering the boat. Likewise, the carbon-fiber rudderstock, which supports a foam-cored balanced spade rudder, is encased in a tube rising 18 inches above the

waterline so that any water passing through a leaking rudder bearing is contained. To protect the hull and deck core, solid laminate is interposed under major pieces of deck hardware and around all through-hull fittings. The deck joint, meanwhile, is on a broad inward flange and is bonded with methacrylate, a tenacious structural aircraft adhesive said to be stronger than epoxy.

The sail plan driving this very stiff hull features a large full-battened mainsail with a generous roach and a relatively small 100% roller-furling working jib mounted on a pivoting carbon-fiber jibboom. The jibboom makes it possible to tack the boat without touching a line. A short stainless-steel bowsprit incorporates a serious anchor roller and can also support the tack of a roller-furling flat-cut gennaker or a fuller asymmetrical spinnaker. The standard spars are aluminum, with carbon fiber as an option, and the standing rigging is discontinuous rod. All control lines are led aft through a solid doghouse/dodger and inside the cockpit coamings to either side of the wheel. As a result, the boat is easy to sail singlehanded.

I had a chance to sail hull number one with Vic DeMattia on Narragansett Bay in Rhode Island shortly after the AD 47 was first introduced. I found the boat to be remarkably quick and close-winded, making 8 knots or more in a moderate breeze at an apparent-wind angle of less than 30 degrees. The high ballast ratio, plus the careful concentration of major systems weight (a 1,000 amp-hour battery bank and a 56 hp diesel engine) within a few feet of the boat's center of gravity, help keep it stiff. The hull form also helps, as the boat's bottom is quite rounded with a narrow waterplane that flares out quickly to a generous maximum beam. The shape provides good form stability, but the waterplane stays largely symmetrical as the boat heels, so it does not gripe going to windward. Rounded sections forward also help reduce pounding when beating into chop.

Off the wind the low wetted surface and a nice run aft keep the boat moving well. In strong winds under working sail, or in moderate air under a gennaker or an asymmetric spinnaker, it sustains double-digit speeds no problem and

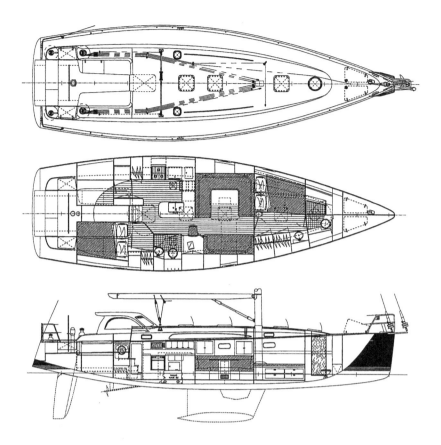

surfs quite readily. If you don't want to bother with big headsails, you can usually make good progress running wing and wing with the jib flopped out on its boom. There's a track on the boom and a well-designed outhaul, making it easy to control the jib's shape and to roller-reef or furl it. My only complaint sailing the boat was that it's hard to squeeze the main's fat roach past the backstay when jibing or tacking in light air, as there is well over a foot of overlap between the stay and the main's leech. Also, I'd worry about getting pooped running off in rough weather. The companionway sill is nearly flush with the cockpit floor, which allows tall folk to hop below without stooping too much under the hard dodger. But it also invites waves to hop below, as the cockpit floor runs aft to a partially open transom.

As far as amenities go, the AD 47 gives little away to performance; a racing version of the same boat (of which none so far have been built) purports to be over 5,000 pounds, or about 20%, lighter than this cruising version. The layout features a generous owner's stateroom forward with two large hanging lockers and an en suite head with separate shower. Behind the saloon to starboard there's another head and a large guest stateroom with a full-size double berth. The enormous galley to port features a dedicated pantry (where an

optional washer/dryer can be installed) leading aft into a systems/workshop space that has standing headroom when the cockpit hatch seat is popped open. (A three-stateroom layout without the pantry and workshop can also be specified.) The interior ambiance is light and spacious with a healthy dose of traditional warmth imparted by cherry veneer paneling installed over the composite bulkheads and furniture sections.

LOA	46'7"
LWL	42'1"
Beam	14'4"
Draft	6'0"
Ballast	10,330 lbs.
Displacement (half load)	25,370 lbs.
Sail area (100% foretriangle)	990 sq. ft.
Fuel	100 gal.
Water	200 gal.
D/L ratio	152
SA/D ratio	18.31
Comfort ratio	25.83
Capsize screening	1.95
Nominal hull speed	11.2 knots
Typical asking prices	$325K-$500K
Base price new	$800K

Garcia Passoa 47

Aluminum centerboard cruisers like this are rarely seen in North America, but they are common in Europe, particularly in France. Garcia Aluminum, a highly respected French builder, often works on a custom basis but also builds to several standard designs, including this Passoa 47, drawn by Phillipe Harle, which is very representative of its species. Unlike the keel/centerboard boats most Americans are familiar with, these French boats have integral centerboards descending directly from their bilges. They draw little water when their boards are up and make great coastal gunkholing boats. They stay upright when aground and can be driven straight on to a beach if desired. They also carry a great deal of fixed internal ballast in their bilges and are self-righting, thus are also suitable for ocean sailing.

Garcia is renowned for its workmanship and builds only in marine-grade 5086 H3 aluminum alloy. The Passoa 47 has a robust construction with 10 mm plate down low that decreases in thickness as it climbs the hull. The chainplates are supported underneath by curved I-beams girding the breadth of the hull's midsection and are strong enough to lift the boat with. The fuel and water tanks, including the tank baffles, are integral parts of the boat's bilges and form, in effect, a series of collision compartments that provide extra security when scraping over reefs and rocks. The ballast, consisting of 11,000 pounds of iron pigs (preferred over lead for galvanic security), is sheathed in glass and fixed in place in sealed bilge tanks filled with an insulating bed of tar.

The boat is reasonably light for its size but is driven by a conservative rig. A standard Passoa 47 has a relatively short deck-stepped mast (just under 60 feet from the waterline) supporting a cutter rig that yields an SA/D ratio that seems timid for a modern design. This helps the boat's stability, as does its relatively wide hull form, but its theoretical AVS, about 110 degrees, is still a bit low compared to most conventional boats. In the real world, however, a Passoa with its board up should be able to skid away from breaking waves that send conventional boats tripping over their keels. Several Passoas have circumnavigated and have cruised in high latitudes, and there is no record of any significant capsize problems.

In spite of the nonaggressive sail plan the boat can be fun to sail. In addition to the centerboard, there is a daggerboard between the skeg that supports and protects the propeller and the low-aspect spade rudder. Adjusting these two underwater foils makes it possible to precisely balance the boat against the pressure in her rig and to vary the amount of the hull's wetted surface area. On an offshore passage I made aboard a Passoa 47 from Massachusetts to Virginia, I was amazed at how much balance can be introduced into the helm by playing the boards a bit. In moderate wind with the sails and boards set right you can leave the wheel to itself with no brake on. I often found the cleanest, quickest way to steer was almost totally hands-off, with just a touch on a spoke from time to time to make small corrections. The boat can also significantly outperform its numbers sailing off the wind in a good breeze. Pull up the centerboard, leave down the daggerboard, and what you've got is a big metal surfboard with a nice fin aft to keep everything lined up straight. With 20 knots apparent wind on a dead run under the main and a poled-out jib with the board up, we maintained a steady 9 knots of boat speed during my passage and frequently hit 14 knots while surfing in moderate seas. Best of all, because all the ballast is right up in the hull, the boat has a much smoother motion than its comfort ratio suggests.

Garcia built 60 of these boats between 1983 and 2000, but no two are exactly alike. Metal construction, unlike fiberglass construction, does not depend on molds, and this allows for a great deal of customization. Most of the boats have an integral solid-aluminum stern arch abaft the cockpit, some of which are sharply raked and have lifting arms for hoisting tenders aloft as though on stern davits. These stern arches, of course, are great for mounting radomes, solar panels, and various antennas. Some boats also have smaller integral arches forward of the cockpit,

23'-2"
24'-6"
9'-7"
16'-9"
9'
GENOA TRACK

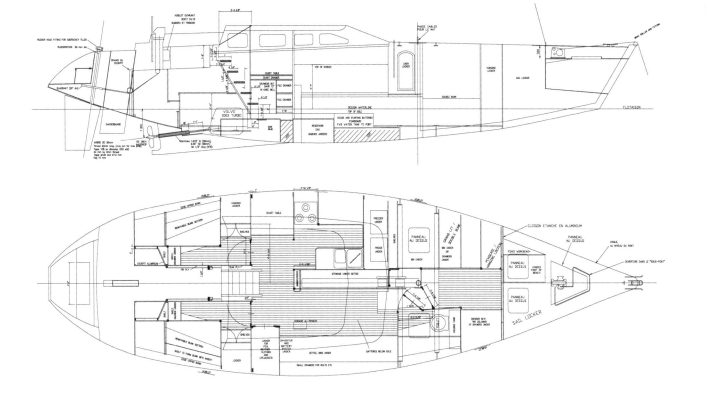

and these provide a great foundation for a dodger and can support a mainsheet traveler if desired. Having solid vertical supports to grab onto at either end of the cockpit makes it easy to move around this normally busy space in a seaway; they also make it easy to rig an awning over the cockpit when anchored out under a tropical sun. At least one boat I inspected also has a unique super-large flush bridgedeck instead of a conventional cockpit, with just one small footwell all the way aft for the helmsman behind the wheel.

The interior accommodations likewise are extremely variable. Garcia will build boats to any stage of completion, and there are a few Passoas with owner-finished interiors. Most, however, were finished for Garcia at its yard by the respected French firm Rameau. The standard layout has two small staterooms aft with a large master stateroom forward of the galley/saloon area and a large forepeak forward of a watertight collision bulkhead. The galley/saloon is situated within the short raised trunk cabin, and on all Passoas I've seen this is the only area with full (over 6 feet) standing headroom, though Garcia may have extended the trunk cabin by request on some boats. On the two boats I've been aboard (one owner-finished, the other yard-finished) the saloon table is situated all the way aft right under the cockpit and is surrounded by an enormous wraparound settee. I thought this worked extremely well, though it does cost two aft staterooms. It allows for a large galley and nav desk under the trunk cabin and turns the entire after half of the boat into an enormous social space that can serve as party central in amiable

anchorages. As a bonus, the settees also make great sea berths while sailing.

LOA		46'11"
LWL		38'0"
Beam		14'1"
Draft		
	Boards up	3'5"
	Boards down	8'1"
Ballast		11,000 lbs.
Displacement		
	Light ship	26,200 lbs.
	Loaded	32,000 lbs.
Sail area (100% foretriangle)		797 sq. ft.
Fuel		180 gal.
Water		250 gal.
D/L ratio		
	Light ship	213
	Loaded	260
SA/D ratio		
	Light ship	14.43
	Loaded	12.62
Comfort ratio		
	Light ship	29.17
	Loaded	35.63
Capsize screening		
	Light ship	1.89
	Loaded	1.77
Nominal hull speed		
	Light ship	9.0 knots
	Loaded	8.3 knots
Typical asking prices		$200K–$580K

Swan 48

Nautor Swan of Finland, founded originally by Pekka Koskenkyla, has an excellent reputation and has been building high-end production fiberglass sailboats for over 40 years. Most of its boats have been classic cruiser-racers. They have sleek, modern hull forms, according to the era in which they were built, but are also solidly constructed with teak decks and lots of heavy solid-teak interior joinery. This traditional design bias ended in 1998 when Nautor was acquired by the Italian fashion magnate Leonardo Ferragamo. Since then new

Swans have been either luxury performance cruisers 70 feet and longer or smaller (45 feet or less) racing yachts. The German Frers–designed Swan 48, first introduced in 1995 and discontinued in 2004 after a production run of 57 hulls, is one of the last of the old breed.

Unlike most (but not all) of the pre-Ferragamo Swans, the 48 was available either as a "regatta" racer or as a straight "cruiser-racer." The regatta version features a deeper high-aspect keel (9'6" as opposed to 7'11") and a taller $\frac{7}{8}$ rig (1,241 sq. ft.)

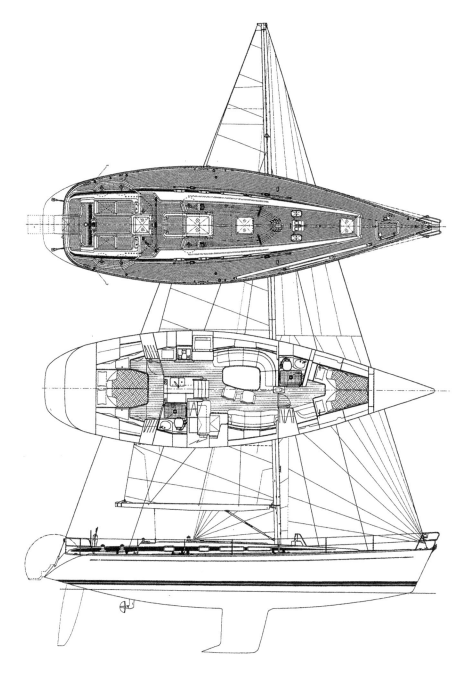

and is almost 6,000 pounds lighter, thanks mostly to a simplified interior that is still, by modern race-boat standards, a bit heavy on the teak. The cruiser-racer, with which we are concerned, was offered with two optional sail plans—a mildly fractional ($^{15}/_{16}$) rig (1,168 sq. ft.) and a straight masthead rig (1,142 sq. ft.). It also features a fold-down transom with built-in steps. Both boats have the same basic construction. The hull is solid laminate composed mostly of unidirectional hybrid glass/aramid fibers set in polyester resin. The deck is also a glass/aramid laminate set in polyester over a Divinycell foam core with high-density core inserted under deck fittings. The teak deck overlay is glued and vacuum-bagged in place with no penetrating fasteners.

As with many pre-Ferragamo Swans, the 48's deck layout is idiosyncratic and not particularly cruiser-friendly. The cockpit is split with two separate companionways and two separate working areas. The midship cockpit, little more than a shallow footwell, has all halyards, reefing lines, spinnaker-pole controls, etc.—a total of 11 lines—led through organizers and clutches to a single pair of winches on either side of the main companionway, making this a busy area. All sheets (as well as a pair of running backstays) are led to the aft cockpit. The mainsheet is double-ended and can be controlled either from the aft companionway or from the helm, which is a handy feature. Ultimately, however, because the controls are so spread out, this is not an easy boat for one or even two people to sail. Things work best when there are at least three people on deck.

The most salient feature of the interior layout—aside from the superb joinery work—is the aft stateroom. The centerline aft double berth is one of the best I've seen, for it is fully enclosed by furniture on both sides and can be easily divided into two comfortable sea berths. The aft companionway stairs, which land just forward of the double berth, consist of a light ladder with stainless, steel rails and small teak treads. This can be removed and stowed away, thus isolating the stateroom from the deck when privacy is wanted. In rough weather, however, as I learned during two fall deliveries aboard different Swan 48s, the aft ladder is the primary route to the deck, because the main companionway must be kept shut to keep out spray and boarding waves. In such conditions the aft ladder can be hard to negotiate, especially when the boat is well heeled. And, of course, any pretense of privacy for aft-cabin occupants must be abandoned. Farther forward there are two optional layouts—one featuring a single forward stateroom with a V-berth, the other featuring smaller twin staterooms, each with two single bunk berths. The latter arrangement

is perfect for families with large clumps of kids or for people who like to cruise with lots of friends. Given the deck layout, either sort of crew would be an asset on a boat like this.

The electrical system has parallel 12- and 24-volt systems in the European style, each fed by its own alternator. The 12-volt bank is dedicated solely to engine cranking, and small converters are used to step down the 24-volt current for other devices requiring a 12-volt feed. Several of these converters are located outboard down low under the nav seat. Thanks to the boat's shallow bilges, they can be quickly drowned if the boat takes on water while heeled, as I discovered on one of my deliveries. The converters can be easily moved, however, and in most other respects the systems installations are impeccable.

The best thing about any Swan 48 is sailing it. The high-aspect balanced spade rudder is extremely responsive, but not at all twitchy, and the boat balances well given its rakish underwater foils. Though not terribly light, the hull is fast, with a long waterline, a narrow waterline beam, and minimal wetted surface area. Light-air performance is quite respectable, so you need not turn on the engine every time the wind speed drops below 10 knots. In moderate to strong winds the boat is just plain exciting to sail. The first 200-mile days I ever sailed were on a Swan 48 (we had three in a row between Bermuda and the British Virgin Islands), during which we maintained a steady 9 knots of boat speed with long spikes to 13 and 14 knots when surfing.

The other best thing about owning any Swan is that they hold their value extremely well. They are not cheap to buy, but used Swans in very good condition can often be sold for just as much as they cost new.

Cruiser-Racer Version

LOA	48'8"
LWL	41'0"
Beam	14'2"
Draft	7"11"
Ballast	12,125 lbs.
Displacement	30,900 lbs.
Sail area (100% foretriangle)	
Masthead rig	1,142 sq. ft.
Fractional rig	1,168 sq. ft.
Fuel	79 gal.
Water	114 gal.
D/L ratio	200
SA/D ratio	
Masthead rig	18.52
Fractional rig	18.94
Comfort ratio	32
Capsize screening	1.80
Nominal hull speed	10.2 knots
Typical asking prices	$600K-$850K

Gulfstar 50

ulfstar was founded in 1970 by Vince Lazzara, an industry pioneer who in the early 1950s helped make a success of Aeromarine, one of the first fiberglass boat builders. In the early 1960s he did the same at Columbia Yachts, which was the biggest sailboat builder in its day. Early on Gulfstar emphasized low price and maximum interior space over build quality and sailing ability, but in the mid-1970s the company shifted gears and made a conscious effort to deliver a more high-end product. The most notable manifestation of this was the Gulfstar 50, a center-cockpit cruiser first introduced in 1975. The GS 50 proved to be perhaps the best boat Gulfstar ever built and also the most popular, with 172 hulls launched during a six-year production run that ended in 1980. Designed by Lazzara himself, the GS 50 boasts superior interior joinery, generous accommodations, robust construction, and a well-proportioned hull and rig. Currently it is one of the best values on the brokerage market among larger center-cockpit boats.

Though the GS 50 is better built than most Gulfstars, it is not without its faults. Its construction is simple and straightforward, with a solid hull laminate composed of multiple layers of mat and woven roving. (Note, however, a few hulls may be cored with balsa.) The hull is stiffened, not with liners, but with full bulkheads and furniture components that are tabbed in place. The deck is balsa-cored, with a through-bolted joint glassed over from below. The full-length rudder skeg is also bolted in place. The ballast, which consists of lead chunks embedded in concrete slurry, is encapsulated within the long fin keel. Problems over the years have included hull blisters, which normally are just cosmetic, but in some cases have involved saturated cavities surrounding the ballast. These must be drained and flushed before they are filled in. The main mast step, an iron plate in the bilge directly over the keel, is subject to corrosion, while the mizzen step on ketch-rigged boats may have crushed the deck core beneath it. Leaking deck fixtures, hatches, and port windows are other common complaints. In some boats the bronze stern tube housing the rudderstock may eventually separate from the surrounding hull laminate and must then be rebonded in place. There have also been reports of loose tabs around bulkheads and subfloor structures that also need rebonding. The good news is that many owners value their GS 50s enough that they are willing to make repairs. Well-maintained boats are not hard to find; boats in poor condition are priced accordingly and normally are worthy of reconstruction.

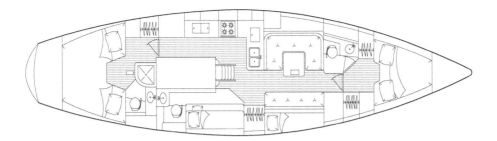

For most owners the boat's most attractive feature is its interior. The more popular layout, originally developed for the charter trade, features three staterooms and works well for families. The master stateroom aft with an en suite head and separate shower boasts an enormous U-shaped double berth with enough space for a couple to sleep together athwartship while in harbor or separately in lateral positions while at sea. The forward stateroom, which shares a head with the saloon, has a large V-berth that fills in to form a double, and the third stateroom, midship to starboard, has two single bunks with yet another small en suite head. The L-shaped galley runs down the walk-through alley under the center cockpit to port, with twin sinks close enough to the centerline to drain on either tack. The saloon has a dinette to port and a settee plus a pilot berth to starboard. In the two-stateroom layout, which is more appropriate for a cruising couple entertaining occasional guests, instead of the midship stateroom there is a fabulous wraparound nav station and expanded engine space beneath the cockpit.

In a seaway the GS 50 is very well mannered. Its forefoot has enough bite and its bilges are deep enough that it does not slam much in a chop. It is relatively narrow with a moderate hull form and does not gripe when sailing to weather. All tanks are below the floorboards, which keeps the center of gravity low, sweetens the motion, and also creates extra storage space under berths and settees. The sail plan is not particularly large, in either the ketch or sloop configurations, and I would advise against a roller-furling mainsail if you value sailing performance. A number of GS 50s were fitted with early aftermarket behind-the-mast mainsail furlers, and these in particular should be avoided or quickly replaced. Sheeting angles are not very narrow, as the mast spreaders are wide and the chainplates are set nearly all the way outboard. Most owners report the boat will not sail well to windward unless the apparent wind angle is 45 degrees or greater. Still the GS 50 is not exactly a slouch when it comes to speed, though it does like moderate to heavy weather better than the light stuff. It's not hard to keep the boat moving at 7 knots or better under working sail if the wind is blowing over 12 knots;

below that you'll need to break out spinnakers and mizzen staysails to maintain good speed.

If you like to motorsail, bear in mind the original engine on most GS 50s was a 62 hp Perkins diesel, which, though reliable, is not quite powerful enough to push the boat well into a head sea. Later on an 85 hp Perkins engine was offered as an option, and this does a much better job of driving the boat to speed. Several boats now on the market have been repowered—turbocharged Yanmar diesels seem to be a popular replacement engine—and these may command a significant premium. The standard fuel capacity, 100 gallons, is a bit low for a boat this size, so if you plan to do some long-range cruising you may want to carry some jerry jugs on deck or expand capacity a bit. The fuel tank is quite low in the boat, which forces the engine's fuel pump to work hard, so adding a day tank higher in the boat with an effective transfer link to the main tank would be an excellent upgrade. Many GS 50s were delivered new with Onan generators installed. These are notorious troublemakers (on one boat I once cruised aboard we referred to ours as Onan the Barbarian) and should probably be replaced sooner rather than later.

LOA		50'0"
LWL		39'8"
Beam		13'8"
Draft		6'0"
Ballast		10,500 lbs.
Displacement		35,000 lbs.
Sail area		
	Sloop	895 sq. ft.
	Ketch	963 sq. ft.
Fuel		100 gal.
Water		210 gal.
D/L ratio		250
SA/D ratio		
	Sloop	13.35
	Ketch	14.37
Comfort ratio		38.56
Capsize screening		1.67
Nominal hull speed		9.3 knots
Typical asking prices		$75K–$220K

Amel Super Maramu 53

Boats produced by the French builder Chantiers Amel occupy a unique niche in the cruising sailboat market. The company founder, Henri Toncet, who changed his name to Henri Amel while serving with the French resistance during World War II, became a pioneer of fiberglass boat building in Europe after studying floating pontoons built of polyester-impregnated burlap that had been deployed by Allied invasion forces. Amel emerged from the war crippled in one leg, missing one eye and nearly blind in the other, but possessed of an iron will and obsessive personality. He channeled these into the creation of a line of extremely clever yachts he described not merely as cruising boats, but as "integrated cruising systems."

The Super Maramu, the culmination of a series of six different Amels produced in Henri Amel's lifetime, was first introduced in 1989 and was discontinued in 2005, the year Amel passed away, after a production run of 497 hulls. It is very much a production boat in that most everything about it is set as firmly in stone as possible at the factory. New Amels are delivered, quite literally, ready to sail anywhere in the world with option lists that are very short. Either you buy into the Amel system or you don't. If you don't, you are well advised to buy another boat rather than try to make one of these into something it isn't.

As on all Amels, the focus aboard the Super Maramu is on comfort and convenience. The boat, consequently, is very systems intensive. Standard equipment includes a generator, dishwasher, washer/dryer, a fridge and freezer, and a microwave oven, not to mention myriad lesser bits of kit, including a vacuum cleaner, hair dryer, and a specially designed shopping cart. Most Super Maramus were also delivered with optional watermakers and air conditioners. The same comfort-and-convenience philosophy applies on deck. The boat is designed to be operated from the confines of the well-protected center cockpit by a single individual capable of lifting no more than 50 pounds. Both the headsail and in-mast mainsail are controlled with push-button electric furlers; the smaller in-mast mizzen is controlled by a direct-drive furler

turned with a winch handle. All sheet winches are electric. The power windlass, complete with chain counter, can also be operated from the cockpit, as can the integral anchor washdown system installed in the bow roller. There is a retractable bow thruster to help out when docking, but somebody may have to step out on deck to handle dock lines.

Equipment lists like this often translate into lots of maintenance and repair headaches, but Amel minimizes these as much as possible by making all original systems installations standard and identical. All gear on the Super Maramu was manufactured by Amel itself to its own standards, or was sourced from suppliers considered absolutely reliable. To ensure systems are accessible and easy to work on, all machinery is installed under the cockpit in a large engine room with close to standing headroom. Amel provides superb technical support for all owners of its boats and has dedicated service centers in both Europe and the United States that are staffed by certified technicians.

Amel is also focused on safety, and this is reflected in the Super Maramu's overzealous construction. Hulls are solid handlaid laminate composed of biaxial cloth set in polyester resin. The cloth is a special flat woven type created especially for Amel that bonds well to itself with minimal voids without intervening layers of mat. Amel also applies a proprietary blister barrier coating directly underneath the gelcoat on all its boats; this so far has reportedly prevented osmotic blisters from appearing on any Super Maramu hull. Balsa-cored decks on Amels are installed with the hull still in the mold, and the joint is laminated with six layers of cloth so hull and deck together form a monocoque structure. Inside the Super Maramu there are four full-height watertight bulkheads (two are fitted with watertight interior doors) that are also bonded in place while the hull is still in its mold. The deck is solid laminate anywhere hardware in installed; all hardware is mounted with stainless-steel fasteners tapped into stainless-steel plates buried in the laminate.

The boat's interior is designed to keep water intrusion to an absolute minimum. There are no fewer than eight

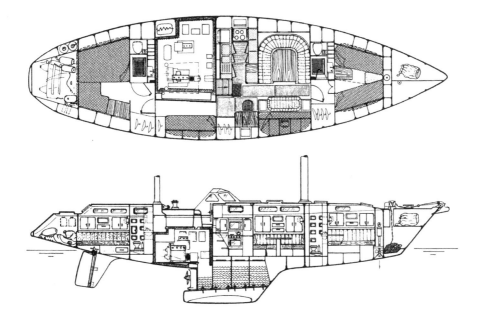

watertight compartments aboard with special valved limber pipes routing any stray moisture to a deep central sump. Originally the Super Maramu was built with just three raw-water intakes in the hull (one for each toilet, plus one for all other machinery) and later, in the so-called Millennium edition of the boat produced after 1998, this was reduced to just one intake with one master sea chest. All outlets, meanwhile, are above the waterline.

The engine installation incorporates a unique proprietary U-drive. The engine faces aft and its thrust is transmitted via two right-angle joints to a special integral drive leg mounted on the back of the keel. The propeller's thrust is perfectly horizontal and is all carried by the keel. This allows the engine to be mounted on soft mounts, thus keeping vibration to a minimum. Add on some top-notch sound insulation and what you get is a quiet ride while motoring.

Though hardly a dog (particularly on a reach with a mizzen staysail set), the Super Maramu is not terribly fast under sail. The boat has a modern underbody with a well-shaped fin keel and a separate rudder on a skeg, but its waterline is relatively short. Both the main and mizzen are handicapped by the hollow leeches required for in-mast furling, and the shrouds are outboard, so sheeting angles are wide. A spinnaker can be flown if desired, but the assumption, in keeping with the emphasis on ease of sail handling, is that headsails will be poled out instead. To facilitate this there is a unique and easy-to-use twin-pole system for booming out sails from the shrouds.

There are many other idiosyncratic details on this boat that you will either love or hate, depending on your personal biases. Many, for example, are put off by the faux-teak decking, at least until they realize that it requires no maintenance. A lot of people, too,

don't think much of the blue fiberglass cabin sole that was introduced on the Millennium edition. Almost everyone agrees that the solid rail encircling the entire deck is a fabulous idea. The Super Maramu, like all Amels, is packed with clever ideas, both large and small, and really the only way to figure out if you appreciate them is get aboard a boat and examine it in detail.

LOA		52'6"
LWL		41'4"
Beam		15'1"
Draft		6'9"
Ballast		12,320 lbs.
Displacement		
	Light ship	31,360 lbs.
	Loaded	35,840 lbs.
Sail area (100% foretriangle)		1,047 sq. ft.
Fuel		158 gal.
Water		264 gal.
D/L ratio		
	Light ship	198
	Loaded	226
SA/D ratio		
	Light ship	16.81
	Loaded	15.37
Comfort ratio		
	Light ship	29.00
	Loaded	33.14
Capsize screening		
	Light ship	1.91
	Loaded	1.83
Nominal hull speed		
	Light ship	10.2 knots
	Loaded	9.8 knots
Typical asking prices		$350K-$625K

Hylas 54

Boats carrying the brand name Hylas are built by Queen Long Marine in Taiwan and originally were sold into a bareboat fleet operated by Caribbean Yacht Charters (CYC), which was founded by Dick Jachney of Marblehead, Massachusetts. During the 1990s a strong independent market for the boats developed, particularly for the Hylas 49, a successful Sparkman & Stephens design originally branded as the Stevens 47. Shortly after introducing the German Frers–designed Hylas 54 in 1998, Jachney severed connections between Hylas and CYC and has instead focused on building up Hylas Yachts as an importer and purveyor of semicustom luxury cruising boats. A raised-saloon version of the 54, marketed as the Hylas 54 RS, was introduced in 2000. Though the RS deck is different, with a taller cabinhouse aft of the mast, its hull is identical to that of the standard 54. There is also now a keel/centerboard hull available that can be ordered with either deck. In all respects the 54 is an excellent example of a large modern center-cockpit cruiser and is currently the most successful boat in the Hylas line, with over 60 hulls launched as of this writing.

According to Jachney about 80 percent of the Hylas 54s built so far have raised saloons. To my eye the standard boat, with its sleeker, better proportioned deck profile, is more attractive. The larger windows in the raised saloon do allow in more light and make it possible for shorter people to see out while standing. It is not possible, however, to see out through the windows on a straight line of sight while seated at the saloon table. Interior finish on both versions is excellent and features lots of superb teak joinerwork, which is set off nicely on most boats by a distinctive blonde bamboo cabin sole. Though interior layouts can be customized to a great extent, most owners have not strayed far from the standard layout. This has an enormous owner's stateroom with an en suite head aft, plus two guest staterooms with double berths forward sharing one head between them. Probably

the best feature is the galley, which is to starboard in the alley under the center cockpit and boasts 12 feet of functional counter space. Because the boat was not explicitly designed for the charter trade (i.e., an extra stateroom and/or head have not been crammed into the accommodations plan), there is a great deal of useful storage space. On both versions of the boat the bilges are deep enough that all tanks fit under the cabin sole (the RS has room for 100 extra gallons of fuel and water), which leaves all the space under settees and inside furniture available for dry storage.

The Hylas 54 has a powerful modern hull with a long waterline and a great deal of beam carried aft. The boat therefore is stiff and has good form stability (maximum righting moment is at about 50 degrees) and generally sails best at lower heeling angles. The rig is quite tall (air draft is 77 feet) and yields a generous SA/D ratio for a dedicated cruising boat. Most 54s built thus far have in-mast furling mainsails (though increasingly they are being delivered with in-boom mains instead), but the boat's waterline is long enough and its sail plan large enough that this does not unduly hinder performance. I once delivered a 54 with an in-mast main from Maryland to Florida, and we easily maintained an average boat speed of about 7 knots. In winds of 15 knots or more we could usually sail at over 8 knots. Some owners report average long-term speeds of almost 8 knots and claim 200-mile days are not unusual. Sailing on the wind in 17 knots of breeze, I found our 54 carried 9 knots of boat speed at an apparent wind angle of 45 degrees. This fell off to about 7 knots at a 40 degree angle. The best speeds are normally achieved with the wind abaft the beam at an angle of about 120 degrees.

Because the boat is large and is often operated by smaller crews that are middle-aged or older, most Hylas 54s are equipped with lots of power-assisted sail handling gear. Electric furlers and winches are common and truly do make it possible for one person to sail the boat in most circumstances, as long as everything is working properly.

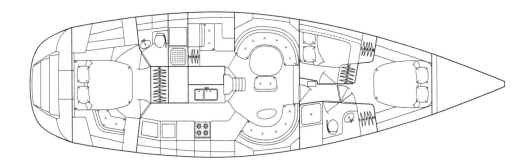

It is wise, however, to be circumspect. I found the backup manual mainsail furler on the boat I sailed was not at all functional (the winch handle driving it could not be turned through 360 degrees), and I would certainly look for and redress any such problems before cruising the boat any great distance. The boats are generally systems-intensive in other respects. Features like air conditioners, watermakers, electric heads, washing machines, trash compactors, etc., are liberally installed on most Hylas 54s, and the boats therefore require generators and large battery banks to keep everything going. The electrical wiring, it should be noted, is all first rate and properly sized and very well organized.

The boat's construction is also very strong. The hull is solid laminate composed of fiberglass interspersed with layers of Twaron, an impact-resistant aramid fiber, all set in vinylester resin inside two epoxy barrier coats. The deck, also a Twaron composite laminate, is balsa-cored with solid laminate interposed under major pieces of hardware and in other high-load areas. The joint is on a wide inward flange bonded with adhesive sealant and through-bolted on 4-inch centers. The hull is stiffened with a generous network of floors and stringers, and all interior bulkheads are properly tabbed to the hull and deck. One of these is a watertight collision bulkhead just aft of a forward segregated sail locker. The ballast keel is external lead and is bolted to the hull with 35 mm stainless-steel bolts backed by an 8 mm stainless-steel plate.

The boat's only potential weak point has proven to be its rudder, which is mounted on a short partial skeg. Some Hylas 54s have suffered serious rudder damage, including two boats (one of which was the boat I sailed to Florida seven years earlier) that had large portions of their rudders break away under load while sailing in the 2005 Caribbean 1500 rally from Virginia to the British Virgin Islands. Since then the 54's rudder skeg

has been lengthened by about 14 inches and no further problems have been reported. If considering a boat built prior to 2005, be sure therefore to ascertain what steps have been taken to strengthen the rudder.

LOA		54'1"
LWL		45'9"
Beam		15'9"
Draft		
	Draft keel	7'0"
	Keel/centerboard up	5'9"
	Keel/centerboard down	9'5"
Ballast		20,105 lbs.
Displacement		
	Light ship	47,184 lbs.
	Loaded	53,000 lbs.
Sail area		1,821 sq. ft.
Fuel		205 gal.
Water		350 gal.
D/L ratio		
	Light ship	220
	Loaded	247
SA/D ratio		
	Light ship	22.26
	Loaded	20.60
Comfort ratio		
	Light ship	38.14
	Loaded	42.84
Capsize screening		
	Light ship	1.74
	Loaded	1.67
Nominal hull speed		
	Light ship	10.4 knots
	Loaded	10.0 knots
Typical asking prices		$625K-$950K
Base price new		
	Standard deck	$795K
	Raised saloon	$835K

Hylas 54

Catana 58

This is a high-end performance cruising catamaran from France that tries to split the difference between high-speed sailing and posh liveaboard comfort. The design by Christophe Barreau includes all the important features that keep cats sailing their best—narrow hulls, high bridgedeck clearance, plus daggerboards instead of keels. Construction is also very high-tech, with an emphasis on lightweight strength. The hull and deck are fiberglass laminate set in vinylester resin vacuum-bagged over a Divinycell PVC foam core. The hull has an inner skin of Twaron aramid fabric laminated over the core to increase stiffness and impact resistance. The deck joint is bonded, then glassed over to form a monocoque structure. The only solid laminate is in areas where hardware is mounted. All furniture components and floor sections are also cored with Divinycell foam; the internal bulkheads—21 in all—are laid up with Nida-Core honeycomb coring.

To flesh out the comfort side of the equation, these boats are normally equipped with lots of heavy systems—generators, watermakers, hydraulic dinghy lifts, large engines and battery banks, washer/dryers, and the like. This is especially true of the 582 version of the boat, first introduced in 2001, as opposed to the somewhat simpler 581 version, introduced in 2000. The 582 (later marketed as the Catana 58 Ocean Class) also features a more luxurious interior finish with leather upholstery and lots of high-gloss hardwood veneer. This all adds up to extra weight, which turns out to have been controversial, as one irate owner evidently sued Catana when he found out his boat was heavier than advertised. Catana as a result stopped publicizing the boat's original light ship design displacement and from then on published very conservative figures that belie the boat's performance potential.

Another concession to comfort is seen in the hull form. The hulls are narrow at the waterline with a slightly splayed-out asymmetric shape that helps to create lift and increase form stability. Their inboard sides, however, flare out in a pronounced hard-angled box chine just above the waterline. This increases interior volume for accommodations, but the flat bottom of the chine is close enough to the water to increase resistance and underbody slamming in a seaway. On the other hand, the bow form below the waterline is also slightly bulbous—Catana terms it a "tulip bow"—which increases buoyancy forward. This limits pitching and helps prevent the bows from submarining when sailing at speed.

Having sailed transatlantic on a 582, I can attest that the boat's creature comforts have not entirely smothered its speed potential. The generous sail plan features a fat-roached mainsail and solent jib for windward work, plus a fixed bowsprit for flying a lightweight gennaker or asymmetric spinnaker. Though aluminum masts were available, all Catana 58s were ordered and delivered with carbon-fiber sticks. The 582s also feature Kevlar fiber standing rigging, plus carbon-fiber booms and bowsprits. (The 581s have aluminum booms and sprits and stainless-steel rigging.) The boat I sailed was systems heavy and carried a lot of extra gear, but still was quick and lively when pressed hard. Beating to weather early in our voyage we maintained apparent wind angles of about 40 degrees while carrying 7 to 10 knots of boat speed under a triple-reefed main and full solent jib in winds blowing 25 knots apparent with gusts to 40. Off the wind with a chute up we could easily maintain double-digit boat speeds in apparent winds over 15 knots. With 20 knots or better on our quarter, we maintained double digits under the main and gennaker with the solent belayed out to the windward bow. Reportedly the boat can hit 20 knots off the wind when the wind is blowing 35 or harder.

The most distinctive feature of the 58's deck layout is the central electric cockpit winch to which much of the running rigging is routed via a large tunnel that runs under the cockpit and bridgedeck saloon. This allows most line handling to take place in a single location, with the inevitable spaghetti kept reasonably well sorted in line lockers on either side of the winch. Unfortunately, lines lost up the tunnel (as we learned during our transatlantic passage) can only be retrieved via ports under the bridgedeck that cannot be accessed while sailing. The mainsail meanwhile is controlled with a twin-sheet bridle rather than a

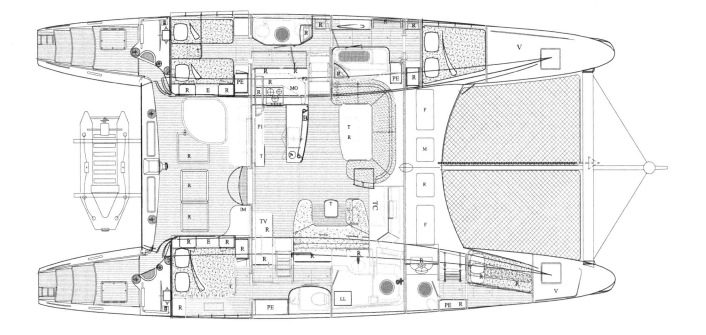

traveler. None of these controls are within reach of the two helm stations, located aft on the outboard hull corners, so the boat cannot be singlehanded without an autopilot, though it can be handled by two people fairly easily. The outboard helms are also far from the shelter of the hardtop bimini that protects the central cockpit, so you need a good hat or some foulies when it's sunny or rainy outside. The upside is you can feel the boat much better from out there and have an open view of the sails.

What really makes it possible to mix comfort and performance on a cat like this is the sheer size of the thing, as is evident in the accommodations plan. The boat is big enough that the low-profile bridgedeck saloon, which also has a relatively small horizontal footprint, is still quite spacious. Likewise, though the hulls are narrow, there's still room enough to live large inside of them. There are a few different layouts, but all put the galley at the back of the saloon, giving the cook direct access to the cockpit via a sliding window panel, which works very well. In some versions the owner's stateroom occupies the entire starboard hull; in others it gives up space to a small segregated crew cabin forward. The port hull meanwhile is given over to guests with twin singles aft and a double berth forward. In one version these two cabins are segregated, with separate entries and en suite heads. In another they share the same entry and have much smaller heads.

A total of 27 Catana 58s were built over a period of nine years, 18 of which were the fancier 582 version. The last new hull, being built as I write in spring 2009, was priced at $2.4 million. Used 58s can be had for much less, but still are very expensive. If you can afford one you'll find few boats as fast and as comfortable.

Catana 58

LOA (including bowsprit)		62'4"
LOD (including transom steps)		58'0"
LWL		57'0"
Beam		29'11"
Draft		
	Boards up	4'7"
	Boards down	10'2"
Displacement		
	Design light ship	35,840 lbs.
	Post litigation	52,910 lbs.
Sail area		
	Mainsail and solent jib	1,797 sq. ft.
	Mainsail and gennaker	2,540 sq. ft.
Fuel		416 gal.
Water		211 gal.
D/L ratio		
	Design light ship	86
	Post litigation	127
SA/D ratio		
Design light ship		
	Main and jib	26.39
	Main and gennaker	37.30
Post litigation		
	Main and jib	20.35
	Main and gennaker	28.77
Nominal hull speed		
	Design light ship	15.6 knots
	Post litigation	13.8 knots
Typical asking prices		$1.2M–$1.8M

Sundeer 60

This innovative bluewater performance cruiser was one of a series of designs developed by offshore sailing guru Steve Dashew starting in 1978. Dashew's basic concept of a long, narrow, fast boat designed to be sailed long distances by a couple first saw fruition in his Deerfoot line, which he built in fiberglass and in aluminum on a sporadic basis at several locations. The Sundeer line was more refined and focused and consisted of three boats—the Sundeer 64, 60, and 56. These were the only Dashew designs ever built on a true production basis. The ketch-rigged 64 boasts three double staterooms and is arguably quite a bit larger than a couple would ever need. The cutter-rigged 60 and 56, which are absolutely identical but for an extra four feet of lazarette space tacked on to the transom of the 60, are probably truer expressions of Dashew's original vision. In all there were 27 Sundeers built at TPI Composites from 1994 to 1999, nine of which were Sundeer 60s. I helped deliver the last one built from Rhode Island

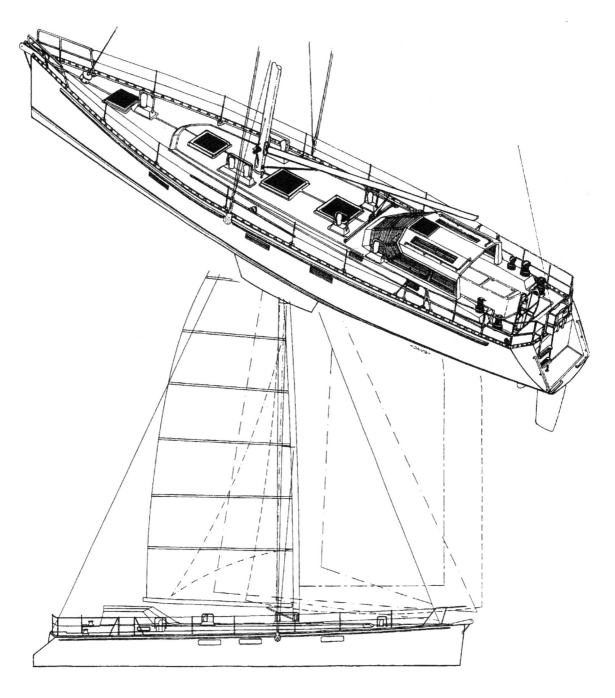

to Florida through two February gales (including one right off Cape Hatteras), and to this day I remember it as perhaps the most impressive bluewater cruiser I've ever sailed.

Glancing at this boat's numbers you should immediately note its low D/L ratio, just 80, which effectively qualifies it as an ultra-light racing boat. This is not achieved through radical lightweight construction, though the Sundeer's hull layup is thoroughly modern. Both the deck and hull, above and below the waterline, consist of quadraxial and biaxial glass cloth set in vinylester resin vacuum-bagged over a balsa core using TPI's proprietary SCRIMP resin-infusion process. Much of the weight saving, however, is simply a result of the boat's hull form, which maximizes waterline length and minimizes beam. The long, light hull is easily driven, as is reflected in its high nominal hull speed, but is powered by a short inboard sail plan (air draft is just 64 feet) that yields only a modest SA/D ratio. Because the long, narrow hull has good directional stability and doesn't need a tall rig to drive it, the keel can be kept short and shallow. This reduces wetted surface area and enhances structural integrity. For cruisers this has added benefits: the 6-foot draft allows reasonable access to shoal-water cruising grounds, and the mast just fits under most U.S. highway bridges.

Under sail the Sundeer doesn't feel like a 60-foot boat. The loads involved in hoisting, trimming, and reefing the sails are moderate enough that they can be handled without power winches; from behind the wheel the impression is of a fast, easily managed 45-footer. It also has a surprisingly comfortable motion. Though the bilges are shallow, the bottom of the hull is round, and this, combined with the narrow beam, helps cushion the blows when pounding into a head sea, reduces pitching, and allows for a smoother motion generally. The Sundeer is not as comfortable as a heavy-displacement full-keel boat, but it is considerably more comfortable than most modern shallow-bilged boats. It tracks much better than most other modern boats and like more full-keeled boats can be trimmed out to steer itself for a while. A Sundeer rarely sails up to its hull speed, thanks to the short rig, but much of the time it lopes along quite comfortably at 9 to 11 knots, which is fast enough to cover 200 miles a day.

The interior layout is a triumph of functionality. The living space is segregated from the mechanical systems, which are all situated in an enormous aft lazarette/engine space, and from the major storage area for sails and deck gear, which is a large forepeak with lots of big canvas storage bins framed by sturdy stainless-steel rails. The three areas are separated by watertight collision bulkheads. The master

stateroom is an enormous forward cabin with scads of storage and hanging space, perfect for a couple lying to a hook in a tropical anchorage. The only other stateroom is a small quarter cabin aft with two single bunk berths—perfect for a couple on passage, for a pair of children, or for putting up guests while in port. There is just one large, well-appointed head, situated aft, where it can be used comfortably at sea, plus a large, well-laid-out galley.

The deck plan likewise is superb. There are no less than 10 tall dorade vents to shovel fresh air below, each with sturdy granny bars that provide lots of handholds for working deck crew. The cockpit is laid out so that a helmsman can easily reach most of the working lines and winches. Also, most Sundeers were built with functional solid doghouses to protect crew on watch. These feature full-length settees that are great for on-deck snoozing.

The basic systems layout emphasizes simplicity over complexity. You can load up on gadgets if you want, but it's possible to live very comfortably on this boat without them. There is room for a 1,000 amp-hour DC battery bank down low in the middle of the boat where the weight helps stability, so a generator is not necessary. Also, the freshwater tanks are enormous, and the deck is configured to route all rainfall to the tank fills, so a watermaker is superfluous. The tanks are outboard on either side of the boat, with a cross-linked gravity-fed plumbing system that allows water to be transferred from one side to the other to help reduce heeling. The fuel tanks have large accessible sumps underneath, and the vents are positioned as high as possible on deck, cleverly concealed inside the tops of the aft stanchion posts. The Sundeer is literally filled with thoughtful little touches like this, all of them designed to make a bluewater cruiser's life simpler and safer. Very few bluewater boats are so carefully conceived. It is a shame so few were built and that the boat is no longer in production.

LOA	59'11"
LWL	59'0"
Beam	13'6"
Draft	6'0"
Ballast	11,500 lbs.
Displacement	36,500 lbs.
Sail area	1,205 sq. ft.
Fuel	220 gal.
Water	400 gal.
D/L ratio	80
SA/D ratio	17.5
Comfort ratio	29.49
Capsize screening	1.62
Nominal hull speed	16.2 knots
Typical asking prices	$400K-$575K

Spirit of Adventure (Owen Clarke 64)

This sophisticated one-off bluewater cruiser blends dedicated cruising systems and conveniences with some of the latest go-fast technology from the realm of singlehanded ocean racing. The commissioning owner, a fan of Ellen MacArthur and IMOCA Open 60 racing, initially sought to acquire an existing Open 60 and convert it to a cruising boat, but then turned to the UK-based firm Owen Clarke Design, which had designed MacArthur's *Kingfisher*, to create a new purpose-built vessel. Constructed by New Zealand–based Marten Yachts, which also built *Kingfisher*, some America's Cup and Whitbread boats, plus several large custom performance cruisers, *Spirit of Adventure* was launched in early 2004 and has since been actively cruised by her owner.

Spirit's hull form and underwater foils closely mimic those of an Open 60. Her long waterline, flat bottom, characteristic "aircraft-carrier" deck, and broad transom are married to a matched pair of high-aspect spade rudders and a long, thin strut of a canting fin keel from which depends a large lead ballast bulb. As with the most expensive, cutting-edge Open 60s, *Spirit*'s extremely lightweight construction is primarily carbon fiber and epoxy vacuum-bagged and oven-cured over Nomex honeycomb coring. She also carries a pair of twin 200-gallon water-ballasting tanks aft to help control fore-and-aft trim while sailing at speed. Her rig is all carbon fiber. Unlike the most modern Open 60s, however, *Spirit* carries just one centerline daggerboard to deploy when her keel is canted (as opposed to two opposing asymmetric foils to be deployed on opposite tacks). Her standing rig, likewise, is much simpler. Instead of fiber stays and shrouds that are lashed to chainplates directly with high-modulus line and tensioned with mast-jacks, she carries conventional stainless-steel rod rigging tensioned with turnbuckles. Also she carries a fixed mast with conventional mast-based spreaders rather than a rotating mast with super-wide deck spreaders.

Integrated into this detuned race package are a number of very

cruiser-friendly features. The deck plan abaft the mast, for example, is dominated by a cabinhouse that, though it mimics the blister shape of an Open 60's house, is much larger and contains a full deck saloon. The house also has a long overhang aft that shelters a dedicated lounging cockpit with a removable table for entertaining guests outdoors. Certainly the most amazing feature, which depends on a technology more sophisticated than that found on any race boat, is that the keel not only cants but also can be lifted so that the boat can access shoal-water harbors and anchorages. The operation of this versatile appendage depends on a large hydraulic system. There is one set of hydraulic rams to shift the keel up and down inside its casing, plus another set to cant both the casing and keel together from side to side. The 24-volt hydraulic power pack that does this heavy lifting also runs a retractable bow thruster, a windlass integrated with a retractable bow-roller system, the main halyard winch, and an in-boom mainsail furling system.

Spirit's accommodations plan, though much more opulent than an Open 60's, is still quite limited compared to other luxury cruisers her size. There are four watertight bulkheads, and all the area forward of the third bulkhead immediately abaft the keel, which is occupied only by a small workshop, the keel's working mechanism, and a pair of pipe berths, is left open and unfinished. The heart of the accommodations plan aft of the keel, aside from the large forward-facing nav station and the table and settees in the raised saloon area, consists of a long galley to starboard, one pilot berth and one large head with a separate shower stall and washer/dryer facility to port, plus two mirror-image staterooms with gimballed Pullman double berths right aft under the cockpit. All interior components, including the cabin sole, are cored composite structures, just like the hull and deck. The high-tech interior finish features a wealth of wood veneer and blue-lacquer trim. Other systems that help

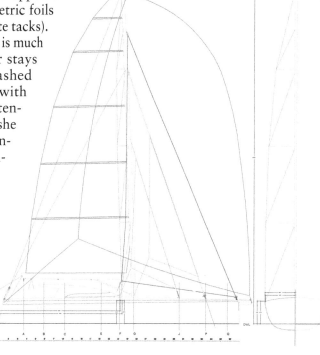

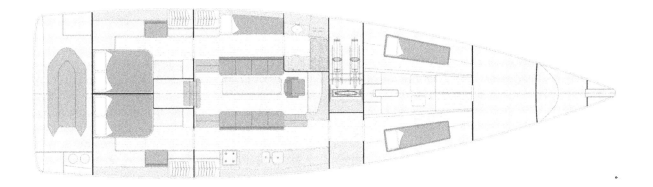

enhance life aboard include an AC generator and a watermaker.

The business of actually sailing this craft, in spite of the furling mainsail and helpful hydraulics, is more intensive than on most modern cruising boats. As on a racing Open 60 there are manually operated roller furlers for deploying the headsails (a genoa and staysail). There is also a manually driven coffee-grinder aft for trimming the various sheet winches in the working cockpit just behind the lounging pit. The steering system consists of twin wheels (as opposed to the twin tillers found on most competitive Open 60s) positioned just in front of an open transom with a clever bench seat over it that pivots out to serve as a passarelle in Medmoor situations. Under the twin helms is an enclosed transom garage big enough to house a medium-sized inflated RIB tender. There is no fixed backstay, which means the crew must carefully cast off and pick up running backstays every time the boat is tacked or jibed. The canting keel is controlled by pushing buttons in the cockpit (the lift controls are located at the nav station to minimize confusion), but its companion daggerboard must be deployed and retracted manually with a line and tackle. There is also the water ballast to manage (this is velocity- and gravity-powered via custom Venturi scoops located under each aft cabin), as well as a manually deployed retractable carbon-fiber sprit pole from which an asymmetric spinnaker can be flown.

Stay on top of all this and there's little doubt this boat can be very fast. *Spirit* reportedly will sail at wind speed in a breeze as low as 10 knots and will maintain the same speed with her keel fully canted (32 degrees) going to windward in 12 knots of wind. Her owner reported hitting top speeds of 16 knots running off under reduced sail in a gale during the boat's maiden cruise. My guess is she can be pressed up to at least 18 knots no problem, even when loaded to cruise. Whether a cruiser really wants to do this is another matter. Though the canting keel obviously reduces heeling (and, of course, increases stability when correctly deployed), the boat's motion is still apt to be quite lively when sailing at speed, particularly while going to windward in a steep chop. It is worth noting that *Spirit*'s light-ship comfort ratio is the second lowest, and her capsize screening value is the highest of all the monohulls profiled in this book.

LOA		.64'0"
LWL		61'6"
Beam		.18'1"
Draft		
	Keel down	.13'2"
	Keel up	.8'6"
Ballast		8,810 lbs.
Displacement		
	Light ship	.36,596 lbs.
	Loaded	.46,296 lbs.
Sail area		
	100% foretriangle	2,345 sq. ft.
	With spinnaker	.4,650 sq. ft.
Fuel		290 gal.
Water		66 gal.
D/L ratio		
	Light ship	70
	Loaded	88
SA/D ratio		
100% foretriangle		
	Light ship	.33.96
	Loaded	29.09
With spinnaker		
	Light ship	.67.35
	Loaded	57.57
Comfort ratio		
	Light ship	.19.13
	Loaded	24.20
Capsize screening		
	Light ship	2.17
	Loaded	2.01
Nominal hull speed		
	Light ship	.17.2 knots
	Loaded	16.1 knots
Build cost		Approx. $3.6M

Wylie 66

Tom Wylie, a well-known California-based racing sailor, has made a career of designing and building high-performance sailboats. In the latter part of his career Wylie has focused on perfecting the unstayed wishbone rig, and his line of una-rigged Wyliecats, ranging in size from 17 to 48 feet, are certainly among the fastest, most efficient alternatives to conventional Marconi-rigged monohulls ever developed. The Wylie 66, one of his few dedicated cruising designs, evolved out of a purely speculative project in which he initiated construction of a light motorsailing ocean-research/school vessel with an easily handled sail plan. Fellow Californian Randy Repass, founder of West Marine, became a partner in this project and financed completion of the vessel, *Derek M. Baylis*, which was launched in 2003 and is now active in various environmental projects on the West Coast. Repass also commissioned the design and construction of a slightly reconfigured sistership, *Convergence*, launched in 2004, for family cruising. The end result was a comfortable, spacious bluewater cruiser that is fast under both power and sail.

As with Wylie's smaller una-rigged boats, the key to the Wylie 66's performance potential is its lean, narrow hull and very modern lightweight composite construction. The hull consists of a blend of E-glass and Kevlar vacuum-bagged over Core-Cell foam, while the deck is carbon fiber cored with balsa. Epoxy resin is used throughout. Interior structural components, including three separate watertight bulkheads, are fully tabbed to the hull and deck. The deck joint is completely glassed over, so the entire structure is unitary. Interior components, including the furniture, are a mix of cored composite structures and plywood skinned with fiberglass. The high-aspect spade rudder is carbon fiber (both the stock and skins) cored with foam. The efficiently shaped fin keel is steel with a lead ballast bulb.

Unlike the smaller Wyliecats, which have low-profile coach-roofs and rather minimalist interiors, the major

feature on the Wylie 66 is a roomy high-profile pilot-house with large windows all around. This contains all of the boat's common space and effectively takes the concept of a "deck saloon" to whole new level. A spacious galley runs along the starboard side of the house. Opposite there is a settee and dinette and a large nav desk with an inside helm station with a 4-foot bench seat. There is nothing inside the house to obstruct the inhabitants' view of the outside world in any direction.

Stepping belowdecks from the house there is a master stateroom all the way forward with an en suite head and two midship guest staterooms (one with a double berth, the other with a single) sharing a head between them. Off the aft end of the house down to port is another small stateroom for guests or crew with twin single bunk berths. Directly beneath the pilothouse is a large pantry with lots of room for storage, water and fuel tanks (note there is also fuel stored in a tank inside the keel), plus a washer/dryer. Behind this, under the cockpit, there is an enormous engine room, which features a working sink, a 7-foot workbench, room for additional systems, and opening ports for ventilation.

On deck the Wylie 66 is extremely functional. Instead of stanchions and wire lifelines, a solid stainless-steel railing runs all the way from stem to stern. The open transom allows easy access from the water onto a 10-foot "dinghy deck," which has plenty of space to house auxiliary craft and gear like inflatable RIBs, kayaks, and scuba tanks. Just forward of this open stern platform is a raised cockpit (with a large cockpit table for entertaining outdoors) from which a helmsman at the outside steering station can easily see over the top of the pilothouse.

Of course the Wylie 66's most distinctive feature is its rig. Unlike the una-rigged Wyliecats the 66 is a cat-ketch, with two masts. Like its smaller brethren, however, all of the 66's sail area consists of full-batten sails flown from tapered freestanding carbon-fiber masts and carbon-fiber wishbone booms. As with other

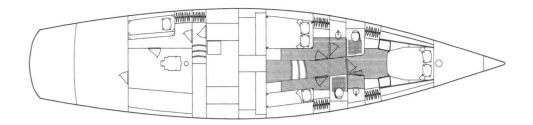

The Achilles heel for many wishbone-rigged boats is windward work, but Wyliecats reputedly are just as fast and close-winded as many conventionally rigged boats. Wylie himself reports that the Wylie 66 is not as efficient sailing to windward as the Wyliecats, both because of its ketch rig and because its keel is proportionally shallower. He claims the Wylie 66 can tack through 85 degrees and will hit speeds in excess of 8.5 knots when sailing close-hauled. Ideal conditions for the boat are with a moderate to strong wind abaft the beam. Speeds of 14 knots running off before 20 knots of wind have been documented, and Wylie believes the boat will top 20 knots in more boisterous conditions.

The boat is weakest in very light conditions, as no additional sail can be set to augment its working rig. The Wylie 66 does, however, perform exceptionally well under power, thanks to its light, narrow hull and long waterline. With its 100 hp diesel engine the boat can cruise at over 10 knots under power burning about two gallons of fuel an hour. With its generous fuel capacity this gives it a range of about 2,000 miles, which compares favorably with seagoing trawler yachts.

unstayed wishbone rigs, the amount of rigging and hardware involved is minimal. There is of course no standing rig, and each sail is controlled by only a halyard, one sheet, an outhaul, a choker, and reefing lines. Only four winches are needed to manage the sail plan, which compares favorably to the eight to ten winches minimum needed to control a conventional Marconi rig on a similarly sized boat. As with other unstayed rigs, the flexibility of the masts helps forestall the need to reduce sail area quickly, as the entire rig deforms under pressure and spills wind automatically in gusts. Tom Wylie, in his efforts to perfect this sort of rig, has also gone to some lengths to fine-tune construction of the carbon masts, which are engineered to maintain the most effective sail shape even as they are deflected by the wind.

LOA	65'6"
LWL	57'6"
Beam	14'9"
Draft	7'6"
Ballast	11,500 lbs.
Displacement (lightship)	35,000 lbs.
Sail area	2,012 sq. ft.
Fuel	400 gal.
Water	300 gal.
D/L ratio	82
SA/D ratio	30.02
Comfort ratio	24.87
Capsize screening	1.80
Nominal hull speed	15.9 knots
Estimated price in 2004	$1.8M
Estimated current base price	$2.6M

BOOKS FOR CRUISING SAILORS: A SELECT BIBLIOGRAPHY

Beiser, Arthur. *The Proper Yacht.* 2nd ed. Camden, Maine: International Marine/McGraw-Hill, 1978.

Bishop, Nathaniel. *Four Months in a Sneak-Box: A Boat Voyage of 2,600 Miles Down the Ohio and Mississippi Rivers, and Along the Gulf of Mexico.* Detroit, Michigan: Gale Research Corp., 1975. First published 1879.

Brassey, Anna. *A Voyage in the* Sunbeam: *A Family Sailing Around the World for Eleven Months.* Coventry, England: Trotamundas Press, 2007. First published 1880.

Brewer, Ted. *Understanding Boat Design.* 4th ed. Camden, Maine: International Marine/McGraw-Hill, 1994.

Calder, Nigel. *Boatowner's Mechanical and Electrical Manual: How to Maintain, Repair, and Improve Your Boat's Essential Systems.* 3rd ed. Camden, Maine: International Marine/McGraw-Hill, 2005.

Calder, Nigel. *Nigel Calder's Cruising Handbook: A Compendium for Coastal and Offshore Sailors.* Camden, Maine: International Marine/McGraw-Hill, 2001.

Carrick, Robert W., and Richard Henderson. *John G. Alden and His Yacht Designs.* Camden, Maine: International Marine/McGraw-Hill, 1983.

Colvin, Thomas E. *Coastwise and Offshore Cruising Wrinkles.* Revised ed. Alva, Florida: Colvin Press, 1996.

Crealock, W. I. B. *Vagabonding Under Sail.* New York, New York: David McKay Co., 1978. First published 1951.

Cunliffe, Tom. *Hand Reef and Steer: Traditional Sailing Skills for Classic Boats.* Dobbs Ferry, New York: Sheridan House, 1992.

Davin, Tom. *The Rudder Treasury: A Companion for Lovers of Small Craft.* Dobbs Ferry, New York: Sheridan House, 2003. First published 1953.

de Bisschop, Eric. *The Voyage of the* Kaimiloa: *From Honolulu to Cannes via Australia and the Cape of Good Hope in a Polynesian Double Canoe.* Translated by Marc Ceppi. London, England: G. Bell, 1940. First published Paris, France: Plon, 1939.

del Sol Knight, Lucia, and Daniel Bruce MacNaughton. *The Encyclopedia of Yacht Designers.* New York, New York: Norton, 2006.

Dodds, Don. *Modern Cruising Under Sail.* Guilford, Connecticut: Lyons Press, 2001.

Doherty, John Stephen. *The Boats They Sailed In.* New York, New York: Norton, 1985.

du Plessis, Hugo. *Fiberglass Boats.* 3rd ed. Camden, Maine: International Marine/McGraw-Hill, 1996.

Edmunds, Arthur. *Building a Fiberglass Boat.* Harrisburg, Pennsylvania: Bristol Fashion Publications, 1999.

Eliasson, Rolf. "STIX." *Professional Boatbuilder,* February/March 2003.

Garden, William. *Yacht Designs.* Camden, Maine: International Marine/McGraw-Hill, 1977.

Gerr, Dave. *The Nature of Boats: Insights and Esoterica for the Nautically Obsessed.* Camden, Maine: International Marine/McGraw-Hill, 1992.

Gerr, Dave. *The Propeller Handbook: The Complete Reference for Choosing, Installing, and Understanding Boat Propellers.* Camden, Maine: International Marine/McGraw-Hill, 1989.

Gerr, Dave. *Boat Strength for Builders, Designers, and Owners.* Camden, Maine: International Marine/McGraw-Hill, 2000.

Gerr, Dave. "Stable by Design." *SAIL*, September 2004.

Gerr, Dave. "Ultimate Stability." *SAIL*, October 2004.

Gerr, Dave. "Stability is the Key." *Westlawn Masthead*, June and September 2007 (available online at www.westlawn.edu).

Giorgetti, Franco. *The History and Evolution of Sailing Yachts.* Edison, New Jersey: Chartwell Books, 2000.

Greene, Danny. *The Art, Science & Magic of Cruising Boat Design.* St. Michaels, Maryland: Tiller Publishing, 1997. First published 1984.

Harvey, Derek. *Sails: The Way They Work and How to Make Them.* Dobbs Ferry, New York: Sheridan House, 1997. First published 1977.

Hasler, H. G., and J. K. McLeod. *Practical Junk Rig: Design Aerodynamics and Handling.* Camden, Maine: International Marine/McGraw-Hill, 1988.

Henderson, Richard. *Choice Yacht Designs.* Camden, Maine: International Marine/McGraw-Hill, 1979.

Herreshoff, L. Francis. *The Common Sense of Yacht Design.* New York, New York: Caravan Maritime, 1974. First published 1946.

Herreshoff, L. Francis. *The Compleat Cruiser: The Art, Practice and Enjoyment of Boating.* Dobbs Ferry, New York: Sheridan House, 1972. First published 1956.

Herreshoff, L. Francis. *Sensible Cruising Designs.* Camden, Maine: International Marine/McGraw-Hill, 1973.

Hill, Annie. *Voyaging on a Small Income.* St. Michaels, Maryland: Tiller Publishing, 1993.

Holm, Donald. *The Circumnavigators: Small Boat Voyagers of Modern Times.* New York, New York: Prentice-Hall, 1974.

Killing, Steve, and Douglas Hunter. *Yacht Design Explained: A Sailor's Guide to the Principles and Practice of Design.* New York, New York: Norton, 1998.

Knight, E. F. *The* Falcon *on the Baltic: A Coasting Voyage from Hammersmith to Copenhagen in a Three-Ton Yacht.* Crabtree, Oregon: Narrative Press, 2003. First published 1889.

Knight, E. F. *Small Boat Sailing.* New York, New York: E. P. Dutton, 1923.

Kretschmer, John. *Used Boat Notebook.* Dobbs Ferry, New York: Sheridan House, 2002.

Kunhardt, C. P. *Small Yachts: Their Design and Construction.* Brooklin, Maine: WoodenBoat Books, 1985. First published 1887.

Larsson, Lars, and Rolf E. Eliasson. *Principles of Yacht Design.* 3rd ed. Camden, Maine: International Marine/McGraw-Hill, 2007.

MacGregor, John. *A Thousand Miles in the* Rob Roy *Canoe on the River and Lakes of Europe.* Murray, Utah: Dixon-Price, 2000. First published 1867.

MacGregor, John. *The Voyage Alone in the Yawl* Rob Roy. Mineola, New York: Dover, 2001. First published 1868.

Marchaj, C.A. *Seaworthiness: The Forgotten Factor.* Camden, Maine: International Marine/McGraw-Hill, 1986.

Marshall, Roger. *The Complete Guide to Choosing a Cruising Sailboat.* Camden, Maine: International Marine/McGraw-Hill, 1999.

Mate, Ferenc. *Best Boats to Build or Buy.* New York, New York: Norton, 1983.

McMullen, Richard. *Down Channel.* London, England: Grafton Books, 1986. First published 1869.

Moitessier, Bernard. *Cape Horn: The Logical Route.* Translated by Inge Moore. London, England: Grafton Books, 1987. First published Paris, France: Arthaud, 1967.

Moitessier, Bernard. *Tamata and the Alliance.* Translated by William Rodarmor. Dobbs Ferry, New York: Sheridan House, 1995. First published Paris, France: Arthaud, 1993.

Nicolson, Ian. *Understanding Yacht Design.* Arundel, England: Fernhurst Books, 2003.

Nielsen, Peter. *Sailpower: Trim and Techniques for Cruising Sailors.* Dobbs Ferry, New York: Sheridan House, 2004.

Perry, Robert H. *Sailing Designs, Vols. 1–6.* Port Washington, Wisconsin: Port Publications, 1977–2006.

Perry, Robert H. *Yacht Design According to Perry: My Boats and What Shaped Them.* Camden, Maine: International Marine/McGraw-Hill, 2008.

Phillips-Birt, Douglas. *The History of Yachting.* New York, New York: Stein & Day, 1974.

Pidgeon, Harry. *Around the World Single-Handed: The Voyage of the 'Islander.'* London, England: Rupert Hart-Davis, 1950. First published 1933.

Piver, Arthur. *Trans-Atlantic Trimaran.* Mill Valley, California: Underwriter's Press, 1961.

Practical Sailor. Practical Boat Buying, Vols. 1 & 2. 6th ed. Greenwich, Connecticut: Belvoir Publications, 2003.

Professional Boatbuilder. "Blisters." *Professional Boatbuilder*, 1994.

Rousmaniere, John. *Desirable and Undesirable Characteristics of Offshore Yachts.* New York, New York: Norton, 1987.

Rousmaniere, John. *The Golden Pastime: A New History of Yachting.* New York, New York: Norton, 1986.

Scott, Ken. *Metal Boats: A Practical Guide for Building and Buying Small Steel and Aluminum Craft.* Dobbs Ferry, New York: Sheridan House, 1994.

Scott, Robert J. *Fiberglass Boat Design and Construction.* Tuckahoe, New York: John de Graff, 1973.

Slocum, Joshua. *Sailing Alone Around the World.* New York, New York: Dover Publications, 1956. First published 1900.

Slocum, Joshua. *Voyage of the* Liberdade. Mineola, New York: Dover Publications, 1998. First published 1890.

Spurr, Daniel. *Heart of Glass: Fiberglass Boats and the Men Who Made Them.* Camden, Maine: International Marine/McGraw-Hill, 2000.

Spurr, Daniel. *Spurr's Guide to Upgrading Your Cruising Sailboat.* 3rd ed. Camden, Maine: International Marine/McGraw-Hill, 2006.

Staton-Bevan, Tony. *Osmosis & Glassfibre Yacht Construction.* Dobbs Ferry, New York: Sheridan House, 1995.

Stephens, Olin J. *Lines: A Half-Century of Yacht Designs by Sparkman & Stephens, 1930–1980.* Boston, Massachusetts: David R. Godine, 2002.

Stephens, William P. *Traditions and Memories of American Yachting.* Camden, Maine: International Marine/McGraw-Hill, 1981. First published 1939.

Street, Donald. *The Ocean Sailing Yacht.* New York, New York: Norton, 1973.

Tarjan, Gregor. *Catamarans: Every Sailor's Guide.* Boston, Massachusetts: Chiodi Publishing, 2006.

Taylor, Roger C. *Good Boats.* Camden, Maine: International Marine/McGraw-Hill, 1977.

Van Dorn, William G. *Oceanography and Seamanship.* 2nd ed. Centreville, Maryland: Cornell Maritime Press, 1993.

Vigor, John. *Twenty Small Sailboats to Take You Anywhere.* Arcata, California: Paradise Cay, 1999.

Wharram, James. *Two Girls Two Catamarans.* Bologna, Italy: Crociera Totale, 2001. First published 1969.

Wharram, James. *The Wharram Design Book: Build Yourself a Modern Sea-going Polynesian Catamaran.* 4th ed. Cornwall, England: James Wharram Designs, 1996.

White, Chris. *The Cruising Multihull.* Camden, Maine: International Marine/McGraw-Hill, 1990.

METRIC CONVERSION TABLES

Feet − meters 1 foot = 0.3048 m							
ft.	m	ft.	m	ft.	m	ft.	m
1	0.305	**16**	**4.877**	31	9.449	**46**	**14.021**
2	**0.610**	17	5.182	**32**	**9.754**	47	14.326
3	0.914	**18**	**5.486**	33	10.058	**48**	**14.630**
4	**1.219**	19	5.791	**34**	**10.363**	49	14.935
5	1.524	**20**	**6.096**	35	10.668	**50**	**15.240**
6	**1.829**	21	6.401	**36**	**10.973**	51	15.545
7	2.134	**22**	**6.706**	37	11.278	**52**	**15.850**
8	**2.438**	23	7.010	**38**	**11.582**	53	16.154
9	2.743	**24**	**7.315**	39	11.887	**54**	**16.459**
10	**3.048**	25	7.620	**40**	**12.192**	55	16.764
11	3.353	**26**	**7.925**	41	12.497	**56**	**17.069**
12	**3.658**	27	8.230	**42**	**12.802**	57	17.374
13	3.962	**28**	**8.534**	43	13.106	**58**	**17.678**
14	**4.267**	29	8.839	**44**	**13.441**	59	17.983
15	4.572	**30**	**9.144**	45	13.716	**60**	**18.288**

Inches	Millimeters	Inches	Millimeters	Inches	Millimeters
0.001	0.0254	0.010	0.2540	0.019	0.4826
0.002	0.0508	0.011	0.2794	0.020	0.5080
0.003	0.0762	0.012	0.3048	0.021	0.5334
0.004	0.1016	0.013	0.3302	0.022	0.5588
0.005	0.1270	0.014	0.3556	0.023	0.5842
0.006	0.1524	0.015	0.3810	0.024	0.6096
0.007	0.1778	0.016	0.4064	0.025	0.6350
0.008	0.2032	0.017	0.4318		
0.009	0.2286	0.018	0.4572		

Inches – centimeters
1 inch = 2.54 cm

inches	cm
1	2.54
2	5.08
3	7.62
4	10.16
5	12.70
6	15.24
7	17.78
8	20.32
9	22.86
10	25.40
11	27.94
12	30.48

Meters – Feet
1 metre = 3.2808 feet

met.	feet
1	3.28
2	6.56
3	9.84
4	13.12
5	16.40
6	19.69
7	22.97
8	26.25
9	29.53
10	32.81
11	36.09
12	39.37
13	42.65
14	45.93
15	49.21
16	52.49
17	55.77
18	59.06
19	62.34
20	65.62

Square Measure Equivalents

1 square yard = 0.836 square meter
1 square foot = 0.0929 square meter = 929 square centimeters
1 square inch = 6.452 square centimeters = 645.2 square millimeters

1 square meter = 10.764 square feet = 1.196 square yards
1 square centimeter = 0.155 square inch
1 square millimeter = 0.00155 square inch

Cubic Measure Equivalents

1 cubic inch = 16.38706 cubic centimeters
100 cubic inches = 1.64 liters
1 Imperial gallon = 4.546 liters
1 Imperial quart = 1.136 liters
1 US gallon = 3.785 liters
1 US quart = 0.946 liter

1 cubic centimeter = 0.061 cubic inch
1 liter (cubic decimeter) = 0.0353 cubic foot = 61.023 cubic inches
1 liter = 0.2642 US gallon = 1.0567 US quarts = 0.2200 Imperial gallon

Weight Equivalents

1 Imperial ton (UK) = 2,240 pounds (long ton)
1 short ton (US) = 2,000 pounds
1 ton (of 2,000 pounds) = 0.9072 metric ton
1 ton (of 2,240 pounds) = 1.016 metric tons = 1016 kilograms
1 pound = 0.4536 kilogram = 453.6 grams

1 metric ton = 2204.6 pounds
1 kilogram = 2.2046 pounds

Miscellaneous Equivalents

1 Imperial gallon (UK) = 1.2 gallons (US)
1 hp = 2,544 Btus
1 kw = 3,413 Btus

ACKNOWLEDGMENTS

I have fooled around in boats since childhood and have worked with boat magazines in various capacities since 1986, and along the way many different people taught me many things that have wormed their way into this book. My educators are far too numerous to list here, but there are a few I should single out.

In my magazine work over the years there are two yacht designers, Dave Gerr and Jay Paris, who have always willingly and patiently tutored me in technical minutiae. Our conversations have been wide-ranging and always entertaining (for me, at least) and have helped immeasurably in my ongoing efforts to comprehend all things nautical. Other people I've worked and sailed with who have taught me a great deal include (in no particular order) Tim Slaney, Glenn Belcher, Ted Wheeler, Hank Schmitt, Nim Marsh, Jeremy McGeary, Nigel Calder, Ben Ellison, Chuck Husick, John Procter, Don Street, Scott Appleby, and Rob Benson.

There are many others who have provided me with invaluable assistance as I have struggled to pull this book together. These include (again, in no particular order and not exclusively): Karen Larson of *Good Old Boat* magazine, Mark Fitzgerald, James Wharram, Hanneke Boon, Peter McGowan, Billy Black, Yves-Marie Tanton, Tom Colvin, Stephen Moyer, Larry Cohan, Robert Hu, Maria Simpson of Rockport, Maine, Bentley Collins of Sabre Yachts, Tony Calvert, Dan Spurr, John Rousmaniere, Gerry Douglas of Catalina Yachts, Vic DeMattia, Mark Smith of North Sails, Scott Alexander of Seldén Mast, Beau LeBlanc of Navtec, Peter Nielsen and Ryan Jolley of *SAIL* Magazine, Kim Shinn of Raritan Engineering, Joel Potter, Holly Robinson of Dometic USA, Peter Burlinson of Edson International, Frank Colam of Select Yachts, Susan Lee of Volvo Penta, Michael French of Southwest Windpower, Steve Brodie of Pacific Seacraft, Chad Godwin of Fischer Panda, and Michelle Goldsmith of Mastervolt. Other firms and organizations that have provided assistance include Alubat, Catana, Owen & Clarke, Glen-L Marine, Fiber Glass Industries, Alcan Baltek, West System Inc., DIAB Technologies, Fortress, Rocna, Vetus, Trionic Corp., Whale Water Systems, Dickinson Marine, Refrigeration Parts Solutions, Technautics Inc., Sure Marine, SCS, Rozendal Associates, Kanter Yachts, Wyliecat Performance Yachts, Scape Yachts, Lagoon America, Nor'Sea Yacht Corp., Maine Cat, J/Boats, Hylas Yachts, Hake Yachts, and Cape George Marine Works.

On the publication side I have received unfailing support and encouragement from Jon Eaton, Molly Mulhern, and Bob Holtzman of International Marine. They have borne with me through several missed deadlines and have offered much valuable advice.

Be advised, however, that all errors you find buried within these pages are my own and can in no way be attributed to the flawless persons cited above.

INDEX

Numbers in **bold** indicate pages with illustrations

CPSIA information can be obtained
at www.ICGtesting.com
Printed in the USA
LVHW061309180722
723764LV00003B/19